SPANISH CATHEDRAL MUSIC
in the Golden Age

SPANISH CATHEDRAL MUSIC

in the Golden Age

by ROBERT STEVENSON

University of California Press

BERKELEY and LOS ANGELES, 1961

UNIVERSITY OF CALIFORNIA PRESS, BERKELEY AND LOS ANGELES

CAMBRIDGE UNIVERSITY PRESS, LONDON, ENGLAND

COPYRIGHT, 1961, BY

THE REGENTS OF THE UNIVERSITY OF CALIFORNIA

LIBRARY OF CONGRESS CATALOG CARD NO. 61-7518

PRINTED IN THE UNITED STATES OF AMERICA

DESIGNED BY JANE HART

PREFACE

During the eight years that *Spanish Cathedral Music in the Golden Age* has been in the writing, I have profited from the advice and aid of numerous friends in Spain, France, Italy, England, the United States, and Mexico. The tribute of an alphabetical list by no means discharges my debt of gratitude. But as a preliminary token, I have set down the names of some of my principal benefactors in the next paragraph.

Sr. Fernando Aguilar Escrich, formerly an agent of Viajes Marsans in Seville; D. Norberto Almandoz, distinguished chapelmaster of the Seville Cathedral; Dr. H. K. Andrews, organist and master of the choristers at New College, Oxford; Monsignor Higinio Anglés, world-renowned head of the Pontifical School of Sacred Music and of the Spanish Institute of Musicology; Sr. Jesús Bal y Gay, chief of the musicological section in the Palace of Fine Arts, Mexico City; Robert D. Barton, former U.S. cultural attaché at Madrid; Dr. Gilbert Chase, U.S. Cultural Affairs Officer at Brussels, author of *The Music of Spain* and of numerous other indispensable books and articles; R. Thurston Dart, fellow of Jesus College, Cambridge, author of *The Interpretation of Music* and of other penetrating studies; Exmos. Sres. Duques de Medinaceli, with whose kind permission the finest privately owned Spanish musical collection in existence was explored during the spring of 1952; Dr. Charles W. Fox, editor of the *Journal of the American Musicological Society*; P. Nicolás García of Ávila and of Rome; D. Julián García Blanco, gracious and knowing chapelmaster of the Valladolid Cathedral; D. Juan Miguel García Pérez, canon-archivist at Seville, brilliant scholar, and friend-extraordinary; D. Santiago González Álvarez, canon-archivist at Toledo and generous patron of historical studies; Sr. Francisco Guerrero of the Biblioteca Colombina at Seville; D. Ferreol Hernández, *chantre* at Ávila, author of a stimulating book on Santa Teresa and of a definitive study of Victoria's Ávila connections; Professor Macario Santiago Kastner, collaborator in the Spanish Institute, sympathetic friend, and discerning scholar; Dr. Adele Kibre, fellow at the Archivo de Indias in

Seville and renowned paleographer; Professor Edmund King of the Spanish Department at Princeton University; Srta. Luisa de Larramendi, authoress and librarian-archivist at the Spanish Embassy to the Holy See; M. François Lesure, coeditor of *Annales Musicologiques*; D. Pedro Longás Bartibás, authority on Aragonese history and librarian to the Duke of Medinaceli; Marqués de Santo Domingo of Ávila and Madrid; Marqués de Villa-Alcázar, trustee of the Del Amo Foundation; D. Juan Montejano Chico, illustrious historian and canon-archivist at the Jaén Cathedral; Sr. B. Municio Cristóbal of the Department of Manuscripts in the Biblioteca Nacional; Miss Mary Neighbour of Oxford; D. Ricardo Nuñez, *párroco* of Santiago Church at Valladolid and gracious host; Miss Clara L. Penney of The Hispanic Society in New York City; Srta. Carmen Pérez-Dávila, learned archivist at Ávila; Professor Gustave Reese of New York University; D. Francisco Ribera Recio, eminent head of the Biblioteca Capitular at Toledo; Dr. Bernard Rose of Oxford University; P. Samuel Rubio, Victoria specialist and music chief at El Escorial; Sr. Adolfo Salazar, revered musicologist residing at Mexico City; Sr. Francisco Sánchez, Sevillian paleographer; D. Manuel Sánchez Mora, Toledan organist; J. Niles Saxton, organist and choirmaster at White Plains; Sr. Alfredo Sixto Planas, tourism executive at Toledo; Robert J. Snow, instructor of music at Notre Dame University and authority on Old Roman Chant; Sr. José Subirá, stimulating author and collaborator with Monsignor Anglés; Earl O. Titus, formerly U.S. cultural attaché at Madrid; J. B. Trend, late Professor of Spanish at Cambridge University; Professor John Ward of Harvard University; Dr. Ruth Watanabe of the Eastman School of Music; Professor J. A. Westrup of Oxford University.

Lengthy as this list has grown to be, I must confess that it is but fragmentary and incomplete. During the two years that I spent in Spain (1952 and 1954), I was so constantly accorded extraordinary kindnesses that a complete list would of necessity become a catalogue of the names of the principal Spanish archivists, librarians, and paleographers. Some seasons ago I published in *Notes of the Music Library Association* (2d ser., X, i [Dec., 1952], 49-57) an account of my first Spanish trip ("Music Research in Spanish Libraries"). This article cannot be reprinted here, but for a fuller account of my indebtednesses to numerous individuals mentioned in the above list, and to others as well, I refer the reader to my *Notes* résumé.

I have received aid not only from individuals: the present project has been generously supported by the Del Amo Foundation in Los Angeles (1952), the Ford Foundation (1953-54), the American Philosophical Society (1955), the Faculty Fellowship Committee of the University of California (1955), and the Research Committee of the University of California at Los Angeles. The Carnegie Foundation made it possible for me to spend a year as Visiting Assistant Professor of Music at Columbia University (1955-56), during which time the actual writing of the present volume was completed.

Various unforeseen delays have intervened since the manuscript was finished to prevent the prompt publication that I should have preferred. When books and articles of later date have reached my hands, I have sought to interweave allusions to more recent findings that seemed important to my narrative.

There is one other challenge that I perhaps have not met successfully— that of allotting due space throughout the present volume to composers of lesser stature than Morales, Guerrero, and Victoria. Some critics may feel that I have been overcome by the temptation to see these three as isolated pinnacles rising in solitary grandeur above the plains of Spanish music during its golden age (1530-1611). Like the art historian who idolizes El Greco and Velázquez at the expense of Zurbarán and Ribera, I may be charged with having acclaimed Morales, Guerrero, and Victoria as heroes in Carlyle's sense when I should have viewed them as mere peaks in a chain of Alps.

In extenuation, I can but announce that in a later volume I hope to return to Lobo, to Navarro, to Vásquez, and to those many other excellent composers whom I have been forced to submerge in deep lakes of footnotes. To have given adequate appreciations of Navarro, Lobo, and a score of others would have so extended the present already overgrown volume that it could not have reached publication within another five years.

R.   S.

Los Angeles
March 17, 1958

CONTENTS

ABBREVIATIONS

AM   Anuario musical, 1946——.

DML   *Diccionario de la Música Labor.* Edited by
      Joaquín Pena and Higinio Anglés.
      Barcelona: Editorial Labor, 1954. 2 vols.

HSMS   Pedrell, Felipe. *Hispaniae schola musica sacra.*
      Barcelona: J. Pujol, 1894-1898. 8 vols.

MGG   *Die Musik in Geschichte und Gegenwart,* 1949——.

MME   *Monumentos de la Música Española,* 1941——.

PW   G.P. da Palestrina, *Werke.* Edited by F. X. Haberl and others.
      Leipzig: Breitkopf und Hartel,. 1862-1907.

VicO   Thomae Ludovici Victoria Abulensis, *Opera omnia.*
      Edited by Felipe Pedrell. Leipzig: Breitkopf und Hartel,
      1902-1913. 8 vols.

1 Cristóbal de Morales (ca. 1500-1553)

I Cristóbal de Morales (ca. 1500-1553)

Morales's Preëminence in Musical History   No Spanish composer of the sixteenth century was more lauded during his lifetime and for two hundred years after his death than Morales. He first began to publish in 1539. Two years later he was called "the most excellent Morales,"[1] and in the next two decades forty different publications containing his compositions appeared at such diverse centers as Antwerp, Augsburg, Lyons, Milan, Nuremberg, Rome, Salamanca, Valladolid, Venice, and Wittenberg. On the one hand he was the only Spanish composer of his century whom the Lutherans admired sufficiently to include in their own denominational collections.[2] On the other hand his music enjoyed the favor of so wise and witty a writer as Rabelais, who in the year of Morales's death published a fanciful description of a garden where in imagination he heard "Morales and other delightful musicians sweetly singing."[3]

In Spain he was honored during his lifetime as the leading national composer. As early as 1539 Cristóbal de Villalón, the Francis Meres of his time, called Morales "unique both in composition and in singing."[4] Villalón, sometime student in both Salamanca and Alcalá de Henares Universities, published his *Ingeniosa comparación entre lo antiguo y lo presente* in 1539 with the avowed purpose of proving that "modern" achievements in letters and arts equaled and often surpassed those of antiquity. His list of composers began with Francisco de Peñalosa's name, followed by Rivafrecha's. Next he extolled Josquin des Prez, who throughout the entire century was to be the foreign composer most highly esteemed in Spain. Morales, the only Spaniard among the several then enrolled in the papal choir whom Villalón singled out for praise, was in his opinion already a *maestro*—great alike as both creator and performer.

Later, when Morales returned to Spain after his ten-year sojourn in Rome, Juan Bermudo—the most knowledgeable vernacular treatise-writer of the age—called him the "light of Spain in music,"[5] and thought that no better testimonial for his own treatise could be obtained than a recommendatory letter from the "unsurpassable" Morales. Whenever mentioning him, as he did frequently in both the 1549 and the 1555 editions of his *Declaración de instrumentos* and in his smaller work *El arte tripharia* (1550), he apostrophized him as the "excellent," the "outstanding," or the "unique" Morales. Juan Vásquez, entirely free from the envy that frequently besets less-renowned composers, joined Bermudo in calling Morales the "light of music." In the dedication of his *Recopilación de sonetos y villancicos* (Seville: Juan Gutiérrez, 1560), Vásquez eulogized Morales as chief among those who knew how to lift the human heart to the contemplation of things divine. Martín de Tapia, in his *Vergel de música* (Burgo de Osma: Diego Fernández de Córdova, 1570 [folio 76ᵛ]), called him *el singular, y muy celebrado Christobal de Morales*. Diego Ortiz, the Toledan composer whose *Glose sopra le cadenze* (Rome: V. and L. Dorico, 1553) won him the protection of Pope Julius III, was another who was as outspoken in praise of Morales as were Bermudo and Vásquez. Describing Ortiz's devotion to Morales, Cerone said:[6]

Diego Ortiz, one of the best composers of his time, strove always, insofar as he was able, to imitate Morales, whose works were everywhere in Spain held in high repute; but he admitted that he lagged far behind Morales. Hoping to keep pace with Morales, he said, was a futile dream; and he added that he could no more hope to equal him than could a mere hobbler hope to stay abreast the fastest Lydian charioteer. He said that his own efforts to imitate Morales reminded him of the feeble efforts of the historian Timaeus who unsuccessfully strove to imitate the great Thucydides.

Nor was Morales's fame confined to the Eastern Hemisphere. As far afield as Peru and Mexico his music was copied, admired, and performed in the second half of the sixteenth century. His two books of masses published at Rome in 1544 were already the proudest musical possession at the ancient Inca capital, 11,440-ft.-high Cuzco, when the first inventory of Cuzco Cathedral treasure was taken on February 21, 1553.[7] In 1559 at a brilliant commemorative ceremony honoring the deceased Charles V, several of Morales's compositions were chosen for performance at Mexico City because they were thought best suited to the dignity of the occasion. The chronicler, Cervantes de Salazar, listed each composition and said that they dissolved the audience in tears and gave "great contentment to the hearers."[8] The present wide dispersal of manuscript copies of Morales's music in Mexico, Spain, and Italy proves the geographic spread of his reputation. The number of publishing centers where his music continued to be printed for two-thirds of a century after his death also proves the wide currency of his music. Between 1553, the year of his death, and 1600, more than thirty imprints containing his music appeared at Alcalá de Henares,

Antwerp, Louvain, Nuremberg, Paris, Seville, Venice, and Wittenberg. Even after 1600, despite the change in musical taste, his music was still reprinted at Venice, and as late as 1619 one Venetian publisher found his magnificats still in sufficient demand to make a profitable commercial venture out of issuing a new transcribed version for equal voices.[9]

The extent of Morales's fame in Italy during the second half of his own century is shown not only by the imposing list of Italian imprints but also by the frequent references to his music encountered in Italian bibliographies and music treatises. In the *Libraria* of 1550—a bibliography— Anton Francesco Doni listed Morales's motets with those of Willaert, Gombert, and Jachet of Mantua; and placed Morales's masses in the same category as those of Josquin des Prez.[10] In *L'arte del contraponto* (1586-1589), Artusi appealed to Morales as an authority for certain procedures that could not be justified from Palestrina's works.[11] In *Prattica di musica* (1592), Zacconi not only invoked Morales's authority but also quoted liberally from his works[12]—so eagerly indeed that on one occasion he even cited an example from a *Mente tota* Mass that recent research has shown to have been not Morales's but Willaert's.[13] In Book III of his Vesper Psalms (1594), Baccusi cited Willaert and Morales as the two principal masters of four-part writing during the century and professed them rather than any others as models because of their purity in the conduct of voices.[14] An even more convincing demonstration of his high repute in Italy can be brought forward: Palestrina parodied Morales's motet *O sacrum convivium* in his own mass of the same name—Morales being the only Spaniard whom he ever chose to parody. What is more, Palestrina added extra voice parts of the *si placet* type to six of Morales's Magnificat movements.[15] In further proof of his eminence, both Francisco Guerrero and Victoria borrowed from Morales but from no other Spanish composer: Guerrero opening his *Liber primus missarum* (1566) with a *Sancta et immaculata* Mass based on Morales's winsome motet *a 4* of the same name,[16] and Victoria borrowing from Morales's festal motet *a 6*, *Jubilate Deo omnis terra*, when he composed his *Gaudeamus* Mass *a 6* (1576).

Morales's fame having been established so securely at home and abroad during his own century, it was only natural that theorists of the seventeenth and eighteenth centuries should have mentioned him frequently. In *El melopeo y maestro* published at Naples in 1613, Cerone still commended him sixty years after his death as one of the best sacred composers for contemporaries to imitate.[17] Filippo Kesperle at Venice in 1625 listed Josquin des Prez, Morales, Arcadelt, Palestrina, and Nanino as the five best polyphonists who had written for the pontifical choir before 1600.[18] Athanasius Kircher, in his *Musurgia universalis* published at Rome in 1650, cited a dozen composers whose ecclesiastical compositions he considered still worthy of imitation. In a list headed by Josquin des Prez, Arcadelt, Orlandus Lassus, and Palestrina, Morales was the only Spaniard.[19] Portuguese as well as Italian theorists continued to hold Morales in highest esteem throughout the seventeenth century. In 1618 Pedro Thalesio, music professor at Coimbra, called Morales "Principe dos Musicos de seu Tempo" (chief of musicians in his time); Antonio Fernandez (1626), Alvares Frouvo (1662), and Nunes da Sylva (1685) all looked to Morales's work as decisive precedents when discussing moot points of contrapuntal theory.[20]

In eighteenth-century musical criticism Morales continued to be recognized as one of the twin giants of Spanish music—the other being Victoria. The three Italians of the century who treated him most fully were Adami, Fornari, and Martini. Andrea Adami in his *Osservazioni* (1711) called Morales's five-voice motet *Lamentabatur Jacob* the "most precious" composition in the Sistine Chapel archive—not even excepting any work of Palestrina—and described its performance as an annual event.[21] In his historical observations, Adami decreed that Palestrina's two most notable choir predecessors were the Fleming, Josquin, and the Spaniard, Morales.[22] After examining Morales's masses he called them "admirably polished works, learnedly contrived, and composed in a strictly ecclesiastical style." Matteo Fornari, author of the *Narrazione istorica dell'origine, progressi, e privilegi della Pontificia Cappella* (1749), commended Morales as the only predecessor who had shown Palestrina how to set words contrapuntally but at the same time intelligibly.[23] Assuming that in the Pope Marcellus Mass Palestrina had come nearest to preserving word clarity while writing independent voice parts, Fornari claimed Morales's magnificats to be the only earlier compositions that showed Palestrina how to proceed. In the *parte prima* of his *Esemplare o sia saggio fondamentale pratico di contrappunto* (1774), Martini printed excerpts from three of Morales's magnificats—those in Tones II, III, and V—submitting them as models still worthy of being respectfully studied by aspiring contrapuntists of his own generation.

Moreover, when histories began to appear in English, Morales headed the list of Spanish composers. Both Hawkins and Burney dwelt on his importance. Hawkins included a portrait; and Burney, after scoring two of Morales's three-part compositions preserved at the British Museum, tried to estimate the characteristic features of his style.[24] In 1812 John Stafford Smith—now remembered principally as the composer of the "Star-Spangled Banner"—scored and printed a Morales madrigal in *Musica antiqua*, a collection published at London. Although 113 years elapse before the results of the next research by an English scholar are published,[25] Morales continues to take rank in English historical works throughout the intervening years as one of the twin major luminaries in the sixteenth-century Spanish constellation.

In Spain itself Pedrell began his great series, the *Hispaniae schola musica sacra*, with a volume devoted to Morales (1894). Only a decade ago, the Instituto Español de Musicología chose Morales as the first composer whose complete works are to be issued under the aegis of the Institute. On the historical side, all the eminent Spanish scholars from Mitjana to Anglés have recognized Morales's unique importance, and have therefore given special attention to his career.

Sevillian Origins With such clear signs of Morales's musical importance, it may seem strange that the year of his birth—unlike that of such earlier composers as Anchieta and Encina—should still be so much a matter of conjecture. A certain specious exactitude was achieved in 1859 by Mariano Soriano Fuertes, who under the pseudonym of "Roberto" published a musical calendar at Barcelona listing Morales's birthdate as January 2, 1512.[26] This date, manufactured out of whole cloth, has in the meantime come to be accepted rather widely. The standard Spanish encyclopedia, *Espasa-Calpe*, repeats it.[27] Even the *Enciclopedia Cattolica* (1952) reaffirms it.[28] Yet it is manifestly erroneous. Morales, as will be shown a little later, became chapelmaster at Ávila in 1526. Such an appointment at the age of fourteen cannot be imagined. Even at twenty-four he would have been young for so responsible a post. In the absence of a better date, the best-informed Spanish scholars—Mitjana[29] and Anglés[30]—have propounded 1500 as a likely year.

Although the year of Morales's birth must be guessed at, there is no uncertainty about his birthplace—Seville. Several pieces of evidence can be adduced in proof. First, Morales called himself a Sevillian. Both of the sonorous Latin dedications that stand at the heads of the two volumes of masses published at Rome (1544) under his personal supervision are subscribed thus: *Christophorus Morales Hyspalensis*. That he was ordained in Seville diocese can be proved from the records of his entrance into the pontifical choir on September 1, 1535, when he was called "clericus hispalensis d[ioecesis]"[31] and of his induction into the chapelmastership of Toledo Cathedral on August 31, 1545, when he was called "clérigo dela diocesis de Sevilla."[32] In adult life, he always called Seville his home: as is known from the leave that the Plasencia cathedral chapter gave him in 1530 to "return home to Seville" for the purpose of marrying off his sister—his parents being dead by this time.[33]

The family name Morales was an extremely common one in Seville during the early years of the sixteenth century. At least three of the Sevillian Moraleses for whom documentation survives bore the Christian name of Cristóbal. The first Cristóbal de Morales served as a singer in the household of the Duke of Medina Sidonia during 1503; the second held appointment as a royal boatswain in 1505; the third continued active as a painter from 1509 until approximately 1535.[34] The first of these three Moraleses, a resident of San Miguel parish, may have been the father of the composer; but not the third (the composer's father died before 1530). Among the other possible close relatives of the composer were an Alonso de Morales who was cathedral *thesorero* (treasurer) in 1503,[35] a Francisco de Morales who was a cathedral canon in the same year (d. July, 1505),[36] and a Diego de Morales who was cathedral *notario* in 1525.[37] Somewhat later, another Francisco de Morales applied for a cathedral chaplaincy (1538).[38] A Rodrigo de Morales was appointed second organist of Seville Cathedral (por otro tañedor de organos de la dicha santa iglesia) on November 29, 1540, at a salary of 30,000 *maravedís* and 4 *cahizes* of wheat yearly.[39] Although the terms of his appointment forbid our supposing him to have been an important musician, he too may have been a member of the composer's immediate family.

The principal musicians in Seville between 1503 and 1526 (the latter being the year in which Morales became chapelmaster at Ávila) were Francisco de la Torre, Alonso de Alva, Juan de Valera, Francisco de Peñalosa, Pedro de Escobar, and Pedro Fernández de Castilleja. All these musicians contributed to the *Cancionero Musical de Palacio*. The choirboys were ruled in succession by Francisco García (1498-1502),[40] Torre (1503), Alva (1503-1504), Valera (1505-1507), Fernando de Solís (1507), Escobar (1507-1513), and Fernández (1514-1549). Peñalosa, although never cathedral chapelmaster, resided at Seville in the following years: 1510, 1513, 1515, 1517, and 1525-1528. Obviously, Morales lived in a musically refined atmosphere throughout his entire youth. Although he may not have studied formally with such leaders as Escobar and Peñalosa, at least he was in the best possible place to profit from their advice and example; never in Spanish history were more eminent musicians gathered in one cathedral than in Seville during the first quarter of the sixteenth century.

The choirboys enjoyed enviable privileges. After 1503 they occupied a large house "detras del consistorio"[41] (behind the consistory). In 1505 the chapter required them to share space with the cathedral stained-glass window makers;[42] but this arrangement can have lasted only temporarily. They assisted in cathedral ceremonies every day of the year and were meanwhile grounded in the three traditional subjects of the trivium. Morales was later to recall with pride that from earliest life he had assiduously devoted himself to the liberal arts, studying intently so that no one could despise his proficiency *in his que liberalium artium disciplinis continentur*.[43] Nor was the life of a Sevillian choirboy merely a taxing routine of cathedral ceremonies and school studies. The chapelmaster often took them about to entertain the nobility by singing *chançonetas* and acting in *farças*. In 1519 these occasions had so multiplied that the chapter admonished Fernández de Castilleja to discontinue using the *cantorçicos* in such singing of secular part-music and in the acting of plays, except when a very *grand señor* of Seville requested them.[44] By 1526, the year in which Morales gained his first known professional appointment, the *chançonetas* and *entremeses* (songs and interludes) that Fernández allowed his choirboys to sing had grown so hilarious and even offensively boisterous that Canon Cristóbal Tello was deputed by the chapter to examine the Christmas texts some two months in advance.[45]

Certain special occasions that arose from time to time also served to divert the attention of a rising musician from the regular cathedral functions. One such occasion was the marriage of Charles V to Isabella of Portugal, which took place in Seville on March 10, 1526. The preceding week was given up to festivities in which the cathedral choristers took a prominent part.[46] At the head of Charles's choir was, of course, the celebrated Fleming, Nicolas Gombert—making his first certified visit to the peninsula.[47] It is not known whether Morales met Gombert on this occasion; but he later paid him the tribute of placing a mass based on a Gombert motet in the honored position of first among his parody masses published at Rome in 1544. (Guerrero, Morales's pupil, was later to pay like tribute when he opened his first volume of masses [1566] with one parodied on Morales's *Sancta el immaculata* motet.) Certainly, Morales shows evidence of Gombert's influence in the texture of his music—this point being one to which fuller reference will be made later. Even if they did not meet at Seville, Gombert and Morales are linked inseparably in the first Venetian collections including motets by the Spaniard: the Girolamo Scotto print of 1541, *Nicolai Gomberti musici excellentissimi pentaphthongos harmonia;* and the same printer's *Gomberti excellentissimi et inventione in hac arte facile principis*, also of 1541.

Although no certain reference to Morales, the composer, has yet been found in Sevillian cathedral documents, the capitular acts do contain three references to "Morales" (without Christian name) which cannot be ignored. The first of these, dated August 27, 1522[48]—a "lycencya a Morales capellán"—vouchsafes "Morales" a two-month leave of absence from a cathedral chaplaincy during which time someone by the name of Luys Ordoñes is to act as his substitute. The second reference, dated April 18, 1524,[49] records the chapter's gift to "Morales clérigo de la veyntena" of a more lucrative cathedral chaplaincy than the one he had hitherto been holding. The phrase "de la veyntena" here means that in this year "Morales" was one of the twenty beneficed clergymen hired specially to sing early services in the cathedral.[50] The third notice, dated June 26, 1525,[51] records the chapter's pleasure that another "clérigo de la veintena" by the name of Gonzalo Pérez shall take temporary charge of the organs in the Antigua Chapel of the cathedral while "Morales"—customarily the officiant on them—is busy with the *"marqués"* (the marquis's name is not divulged). This last notice is the most interesting of the three, since it proves that the "Morales" in question was a sought-after organist as well as a beneficed singer.

These capitular notices alone may not be sufficient to identify the "Morales" as Cristóbal de Morales. However, there is still another biographical clue that has yet to be followed up as it deserves. This further hint was dropped as long ago as 1672 by the renowned Sevillian bibliographer Nicolas Antonio in his *Bibliotheca hispana nova*. In this compendium Antonio—a graduate of Salamanca University—inserted a short list of Morales's published compositions. The bibliographical heading reads thus: *Christophorus de Morales, musicae artis magister.*[52]

Early Chapelmasterships The earliest document unequivocally naming the composer was brought forward by the eminent diplomat and musicologist Rafael Mitjana in 1919.[53] Unfortunately, the book of Ávila Cathedral capitular acts in which he saw it has since disappeared from view.[54] But Mitjana's reputation for scholarly integrity sufficiently certifies a notice that he claimed to have seen at folio 99 under date of August 8, 1526: "Se nombro a Xpoval de Morales con cien ducados de salario al año." Mitjana added that after setting the chapelmaster's annual salary at 100 ducats, the cathedral chapter on the same day ordered the installation of a pair of large organs to replace the portatives used previously. This new pair cannot, however, have been available for use during Morales's stay in Ávila. As late as February 23, 1529, the cathedral chapter ordered that no other improvements in the cathedral property were to be attempted until the installation of the organs was completed.[55] In February, 1529, Morales had already transferred from Ávila to Plasencia Cathedral.

As for the number of cathedral singers at Ávila, a list of salaried personnel made up on September 14, 1529, suggests that the chapelmaster commanded enough boys and men to perform at will such large-scale works as the masses of Josquin des Prez and Noel Baudouin.[56] At this date the cathedral staff included seven singing prebendaries, two music masters (one of plainchant, the other of polyphony), and two organists, all of whom were full-time employees.[57] For trebles the chapelmaster relied on the half-dozen or so choirboys whose upbringing was part of his official duty. The seven adult singers in the 1529 list received their salaries in cash and in kind—the actual value of what they were paid varying widely. The choirboys received small cash stipends—four ducats a year being mentioned as a sufficient salary;[58] meanwhile they were lodged, boarded, and clothed at cathedral expense. In addition they were trained (free of charge) in reading, writing, *canto de órgano*, and *contrapunto*.[59] Morales's professional associates at Ávila may have included the Juan Vásquez of Badajoz who in 1551 and 1560 published two important collections of Spanish secular polyphony. "Juan Vazquez" was *maestro de canto llano* on September 14, 1530—the *maestro de canto de órgano* on that date being a contralto singer by the name of Barrionuevo temporarily substituting in the chapelmastership. Four weeks later (October 12, 1530) Francisco de Sepúlveda was appointed *maestro de capilla*, whereupon Barrionuevo resumed the status of singer—retaining it until September 17, 1551. As for his later career, he may have been the same Gerónimo de Barrionuevo who competed for the post of chapelmaster at Cordova on July 5, 1563, in succession to Rodrigo de Ceballos. As the latter's emissary, this Barrionuevo presented a book of Ceballos's compositions to the Málaga cathedral chapter on June 12, 1560. His fourth part for a Ceballos canción has recently been printed.[60]

Morales's reasons for moving from Ávila to Plasencia can be conjectured easily enough. His salary at Ávila was a mere 100 ducats (37,500 maravedís); his starting salary at Plasencia was 60,000 maravedís. The diocese of Plasencia taken as a whole was much wealthier—enjoying revenues equal to almost twice those collected in Ávila diocese.[61] From 1526 to 1528 Ávila was governed by a parsimonious deputy for an absentee bishop; whereas Plasencia from 1524 to 1559 was ruled by Gutierre Vargas de Carvajal (b. 1506), one of the highest-born and most enterprising Spanish bishops of his generation.[62] This bishop's predecessor was the distinguished dean of the college of cardinals, Bernardino López de Carvajal (born in Plasencia), whose influence at Rome enabled him to procure from Adrian VI a bull (March 23, 1523) completely reorganizing the table of canons and dignitaries in Plasencia Cathedral.[63] When Morales arrived, probably in early 1528, he therefore joined a newly reorganized *cabildo* (the governing corporation) and found himself working for a vigorous bishop only twenty-two years of age. What is more, the whole of the surrounding region was enjoying unprecedented prosperity during this period. Both Cortés and Pizarro came from towns near Plasencia, and much new wealth from the Indies was flowing into the province. In Plasencia itself, an imposing new cathedral was under construction—plans having been drawn in 1498 by Gutierre Álvarez de Toledo (this younger brother of the second Duke of Alva became bishop of Plasencia after resigning office in Salamanca University). At the same time, much other new ecclesiastical building was going forward in this thriving walled market town.

One other exceptional condition that obtained at Plasencia while Morales held his half-prebend (*media ración*) was the right to vote at sessions of the cathedral *cabildo*. In most Spanish cathedrals during the sixteenth century—including all the others served by Morales—a mere *racionero* was never a voting member of the cabildo; only canons (and above) enjoyed this privilege. As a rule, racioneros did not even attend chapter meetings as observers. At Plasencia, by a quirk of local tradition, racioneros were until 1560 expected to attend chapter meetings and to take part in discussions and chapter business.[64] In consequence, Morales's name often enters the lists of those present at cabildo meetings until May 7, 1529, after which date he stopped going:[65] probably because he considered the meetings too time-consuming. (This unusual status of Plasencia racioneros came to an end in 1560 when, on the advice of Salamanca University legal advisers, the Plasencia chapter decided to withdraw the vote from all cathedral staff-members in grades lower than that of canon.)

The capitular act first naming Morales chapelmaster at Plasencia has not been found. However, on July 8, 1522, a certain Juan de Altamirano was appointed chapelmaster at an annual salary of 35,000 maravedís (93⅓ ducats), to be paid in three equal instalments; and probably Altamirano—who still held office in January, 1525—was Morales's predecessor in the office.[66] The difference between the salaries of Altamirano and Morales may in part be ascribed to the fact that Altamirano held no *media ración*. Morales's larger salary was cut by an unspecified amount after May 5, 1529—this being the date on which the chapter granted him permission not to attend future cabildo meetings.[67] On February 4, 1530, the chapter gave him a month's leave of absence so that he might visit Seville and attend his sister's wedding. In addition the chapter made him a present of forty gold ducats to defray the costs of his sister's dowry.[68] This sister was an "orphan" (*huérfana*),[69] noted the chapter secretary. The fact that Morales was so eager to exert himself in his sister's behalf while standing on the threshold of his own promising career shows how strong were his family ties. But it also proves that his family cannot have had money.

Morales overstayed his leave, and on March 31 the chapter voted to stop payment of his salary.[70] Before another week had elapsed he had evidently sent such an acceptable explanation that the chapter decided to reverse its March 31 decision. He was certainly on hand before April 29, for on that date a statute was passed by the cabildo requiring the adult cathedral singers to appear every day of the week for a music lesson with the chapelmaster.[71] The singers named in the statute were Ortiz, Roa, and Serradilla. The first of these, a contralto, was the best singer of all and as a reward was appointed a cathedral chaplain on August 26, 1531.[72] Serradilla, on the other hand, was given to such idle pursuits as fishing; and together with another singer, Oliva, he was dismissed in 1531.[73] In order to force the singers to study, the statute of April 29, 1530, stipulated that each time a singer missed his lesson with Morales he should be fined two *reales* (68 maravedís). As for the other cathedral clergy, the chapter specified in the same statute that all below the grade of racionero should meet each Thursday for an intensive rehearsal under the chapelmaster's direction.

Whatever else the Plasencia capitular acts reveal, they do at least show that Morales took his duties seriously. Moreover, he enjoyed such favor from the chapter that: (1) he could be given permission to absent himself from chapter meetings; (2) extra rewards to cover family expenses were allowed him; (3) a statute was passed forcing his singers to study intensively under his direction. Usually in Spanish cathedral documentation the chapelmaster is the one reproved for laxity in his teaching. Morales, on the contrary, reminds us of young Bach at Arnstadt and at Mühlhausen overdoing his prescribed duties in order to attain unwonted excellence.

On December 9, 1531, the chapter appointed a commission to search for a new chapelmaster.[74] On February 9 of the following year, a Diego Bruxelas was appointed at an annual salary of 50,000 maravedís; but he did not accept. A certain Villafranca was named in his stead on June 7, 1532; he in turn was succeeded on October 3, 1534, by Hernando Díaz, a married man.[75] Morales's whereabouts during these years are uncertain. Mitjana has suggested that he went to Rome in 1531 in the entourage of Alfonso Cardinal Manrique, archbishop of Seville and grand inquisitor of Spain.[76] Fornari said that upon arriving in Rome, Morales studied with Gaudio Mell, a "Fleming,"[77] but this report, like that of Palestrina's study with the same teacher, must be discounted as the invention of an over-zealous and uninformed eighteenth-century chronicler. In 1540 the Ávila choral library possessed three masses by Morales, supposedly written before his departure from Spain.[78] At Ávila today is conserved an eighteenth-century manuscript copy of his four-voice *Officium defunctorum* (*Libro de facistol 1*, pp. 100-131);[79] and if this was a composition from the pre-Roman period he was already a competent composer, if not yet a profoundly learned contrapuntist, before he left Ávila.

Roman Decade (1535-1545) Morales joined the papal choir on September 1, 1535,[80] the same day on which Pope Paul III commissioned Michelangelo to paint the altar wall of the Sistine Chapel. Later, Morales said that Paul III personally chose him for the choir.[81] Two methods are known to have been used by sixteenth-century popes in recruiting foreign singers for their personal choir. Either they sent out scouts, as did Clement VII when he sent Jean Conseil (= Consilium) to Bourges and to Cambrai with instructions to capture the best singers for his personal choir;[82] or they sent notice of vacancies to their nuncios in France and Spain, offering to pay travel expenses to Rome for likely singers proposed to the nuncios by leading chapelmasters in the countries concerned.[83] In any event, Sistine Chapel records show that throughout most of the century the papal choir was made up of three well-defined groups of singers—the French (with a sprinkling of Flemings), the Spanish, and the Italian. Cognizance of this tripartite division along national lines was taken on all principal feast days when the singers separated to attend their respective national churches in Rome—the French going to the Church of St. Louis, and the Spanish to the Church of St. James.

Early in the century the foreign singers considerably outnumbered the Italian; and on February 19, 1512, Pope Julius II—concerned over the poor showing made by locally trained singers in competition with Spanish and French singers—issued a bull, *In altissimo militantes*, providing for the establishment of the Cappella Giulia as a training choir for a dozen talented Roman youths.[84] The efforts to nourish a generation of Roman singers who could compete successfully with the better-prepared French and Spanish did not produce immediate results, however; and at the time when Morales was admitted more than half the papal singers were still foreigners. The Spanish contingent included the elderly Escribano (dean of the choir but already in semi-retirement), Blas Nuñez, Antonio Calasanz, and Juan Sánchez. Two other Spaniards, Bartolomé de Escobedo (August 23, 1536) and Pedro Ordoñez (April 29, 1539), joined during Morales's first five-year term. Because of the clannishness of the national groups in the choir, it is among this group of six Spaniards that one should look for Morales's closest personal associates during his decade in Rome. The published Sistine Diaries show that on those infrequent occasions when Morales wished a day off he asked Escobedo or Sánchez, and not any of the Italians or French, to substitute for him. Also, he sometimes sacrificed his own regular weekday off to substitute for Escobedo or Sánchez.

Morales's ten years in Rome are documented with gratifying fullness. Two diaries, one for his first five-year term (*Liber punctorum Capelle / s.mj dnj nrj pape Incipiens / prima die Januarij anno / dnj millesimo quingentesimo trigesimo quinto*) consisting of 149 leaves, and another for his second five-year term (*Puncta Cantorū 1541 usque ad 1545 per totum*) consisting of 94 leaves, tell where the choir sang each day, who was absent and for what cause, what special or unusual ceremonies the choir participated in, what gifts were received for distribution among the choir members, and what types of official action were taken by the choir on voting matters. Because of the detailed character of the entries, all of which were written by the *punctator* (the diarist, who was a choir member elected annually to the post) and all of which were recorded on a day-by-day basis, these entries are of paramount value. They enable the student of Morales's life to reconstruct his everyday movements throughout an entire decade.

Morales's name appears 441 times in the two volumes of diary covering his time in Rome. Of these entries, 339 relate to tardiness for, or absence from, matins. Sixty-five notices record his absences on account of illness. The remaining entries are scattered under several headings, such as "ad septem ecclesias," "ad ripam," "habuit scatulam," "mutauit domum," "licentiam eundi foras," and "condenpnati in scutis duobus." Not only the entries listing his name but also those telling what the choir did when he was present are obviously useful. The best way of handling these notices will be to begin with the first and proceed chronologically.

On the day of his admission Morales received the surplice at the hands of Bartholomeo de Crota, the pope's delegate charged with governing the choir. In the presence of the whole group, which at the time consisted of twenty-four singers, he swore to uphold the traditions of the choir, not to divulge its secrets, and to respect the senior members of the choir. Immediately after having been received he paid ten ducats into the choir chest for distribution among the senior members—this amount being a set fee for his privilege of sharing the tips handed out on special occasions such as the anniversary of the pope's coronation, the creation of new cardinals, and other ceremonies not provided for in the liturgical calendar.[85] In addition, he paid two ducats for his surplice. Since his title *cantor cappellanus* meant that he was a "chaplain" as well as a singer, he was obliged to wear the cassock off as well as on duty: this obligation applying to all in the choir and not simply to members in major orders. His monthly salary was fixed at eight ducats.[86]

After Morales's entry on September 1, 1535, his name does not appear again until seven weeks later. On October 23, 1535, the *punctator* records that "Moralis advenit de Napoli" (Morales arrived from Naples). Since Naples was a part of Spanish dominions after 1504, Morales perhaps had held some official appointment at the court of Pedro de Toledo (viceroy from 1532 to 1553) immediately before he entered the papal chapel. In any event, the Neapolitan viceregal chapel some few years later did enroll such other outstanding Spanish musical celebrities as Diego Ortiz and Francisco Salinas (chapelmaster and organist respectively). It is, moreover, rather interesting that Eleonor of Toledo, the viceroy's daughter, should have become in 1539 the wife of Cosimo de' Medici, duke of Florence; and that Morales dedicated his *Missarum liber primus* to Cosimo in 1544.[87]

On November 9, 1535, Morales received his first permission to cross over the Tiber to the section ("rione") where public markets selling produce, dry goods, and hardware were situated.[88] Inasmuch as the Ripa Magna was to be his destination only seven times during his decade in Rome, he can hardly have spent much time in frivolous bargaining at any of its bazaars. On January 3, 1536, he was absent from his choir duties on a one-day pilgrimage to the "seven churches," that is, to seven designated ancient churches, including the four patriarchal ones. This one-day pilgrimage is still taken by visitors to Rome or by Romans themselves as a special act of piety; but the difficulty of covering all seven in a day was much greater in Morales's time. A little later in the diary for January, 1536, we read the first notices of Morales's illnesses. As time progresses these will become ominously frequent.

During the early spring of 1536 Pope Paul III, a devotee of spectacle, brought his court to a high pitch of readiness for the entry into Rome of the Emperor Charles V. Two printed pamphlets in the Biblioteca Angelica describe the preparations and the entry: for example, it is recorded that eleven churches fallen into disuse were torn down to make a broad highway for his approach. On Wednesday, April 5, Charles entered the city and on the same day went to St. Peter's, where the papal choir greeted him with a specially composed antiphon. He remained in the city until Easter; on the Tuesday following, April 18, he left in the evening after having distributed 100 scudi to the papal singers as a mark of special favor for the music they had sung during Holy Week and at Easter.[89] The diaries show that events of this type occurred frequently. Thus Morales could sing with a small band of the best musicians of his day and have his own music performed in the presence of kings, emperors, cardinals, and great nobility: such prestigious performance opportunities undoubtedly having much to do with the immediate spreading of his fame throughout the whole of Europe. If it cannot be proved that Morales's music was sung in the Emperor's presence in April, 1536, it is at least certain that in the same year he had already written one of his most masterful motets, the six-voice *Veni Domine et noli tardare*; for in that very year it was copied into Cappella Giulia MS XII, 4 (folios 98[v]-100). At the next meeting of pope and emperor two years later in Nice, Morales was the composer of the official welcome music.

On June 18, 1536, and again on the following July 25, the Spaniards were in their own national Church of St. James (Santiago). During Morales's epoch the strongly interknit Spanish laity in Rome gathered on every July 25—their national saint's day—in this church. When available, the entire papal choir was engaged for special music. Twice during Morales's decade in Rome the whole choir sang: both times receiving handsome honoraria. Not only did the entire choir sing at Santiago on occasion but also individual Spaniards in the choir took an honored and active part in the parish life of their church. Blas Nuñez and Juan Sánchez, for instance, frequently took such a part.[90]

On Wednesday, August 23, 1536, Morales's compatriot Bartolomé de Escobedo (a clergyman from Zamora diocese) was inducted into the choir. The French contingent, led by the stiff-necked basso Charles d'Argentilly, protested violently: refusing even to attend his inauguration. An extremely delicate balance between the French and the Spanish was maintained at this period: Escobedo's induction brought the number of Spaniards to the same figure as that of the French. For refusing to attend Escobedo's inauguration the French were each fined a month's salary.[91] But their protest was effective: the next three foreigners chosen for the choir were French. The cause of their specific complaint against Escobedo in 1536 is not known. However, he, like the other Spaniards in the choir—with the single exception of Morales—left a record of being a hot-tempered man. On one occasion, just before Mass was to begin, he called a fellow singer "a fat pig" in a loud tone of voice,[92] and once at vespers he called a singer who had missed his place "you ass" in a raised voice.[93] Juan Sánchez, first admitted in June, 1529, was the most flamboyant member of the generally hot-tempered Spanish section of the choir. In February, 1538, he was in trouble for striking someone who fled; and in January, 1540, not wishing to sing the part allotted him by the director, he hit him "in the presence of the Sacrament," thus creating a "very great scandal." He was imprisoned, but the Spaniards in the choir banded together and sent Ordoñez to plead with the pope, who indulgently reinstated him with only the proviso that Sánchez lose senior status in the choir and return in the rank of a beginner. In their negotiations the Spaniards stuck together and pleaded collectively. No better illustration of their clannishness could be given.[94] Even after reinstatement, however, Sánchez continued to behave badly—often pretending to be sick when he wanted a day off, and quarreling with other choir members. Ordoñez was another who was fined heavily for his quarrelsomeness and for pretending to be sick when he wanted a holiday.[95] Even the senior Spaniard still active in the choir during Morales's decade—Nuñez (who had entered in 1520 and who had a daughter old enough to be professed in religion during Morales's second term)[96]—quarreled with a fellow singer during a religious act, thereby scandalizing the pope. Like Sánchez and Ordoñez, Nuñez was not above pretending to be sick when it suited his convenience to work in his garden.

The individual records of the other Spaniards in the choir must be studied if Morales's own rather restrained record is to be appreciated. Morales has on occasion been called a "restless" man by modern historians. His choir record shows that he was the most pacific of the Spanish crew. Only once was he fined for quarreling; and even then the fine was later remitted, since the hard words had passed outside chapel. His record does show frequent illness, especially in his second term, but he was never found malingering. All his sicknesses must have been real: for otherwise his choir colleagues would surely have exposed him—as they did Sánchez, Ordoñez, and Nuñez when these three feigned illness. Even though Morales may have behaved with Sunday School correctness, it should be added that he was never elected to any office during his ten-year sojourn in the choir. Calasanz, Ordoñez, and even Sánchez held choir offices to which they were elected by their fellow choir members in the period 1535-1545: but not Morales. His preoccupation with composing cannot have been the sole reason for his failure to gain any elective post. Arcadelt, admitted December 30, 1540, was as prolific a composer as Morales; but within three years (1544) he built up a sufficiently large personal following to be elected treasurer (*abbas*). So far as manner is concerned, Morales—even if always a thoughtful and courteous member of the choir—was probably quite reserved. Such a retiring manner would indeed be what one would expect of a man so frequently sick as he.

Paul III, already sixty-seven when Morales joined the choir, proved to be a traveling pope. Morales accompanied him on three extended journeys: the first to a peace conference at Nice in June, 1538; the second to Loreto (on the Adriatic) in September, 1539; and the third to Busseto for a parley with Charles V in June, 1543. After Morales's six-voice *Veni Domine et noli tardare*, the next composition for which any evidence of date survives is his six-voice motet in two movements, *Jubilate Deo omnis terra*, written for the June, 1538 peace celebrations at Nice. It was at this Riviera haven that the pope finally succeeded in persuading Charles V and Francis I to conduct a peace parley. Convinced that music might somehow soothe the principals to a peace treaty, the pope brought along twenty of his own singers: all richly garbed in new velvet cassocks and silk surplices (the cost of these sumptuous garments having been paid for out of his private discretionary funds).[97] En route to the conference he added several instrumentalists—trombonists from Bologna, violinists from Milan, and trumpeters, drummers, and bombard players from Genoa.[98] Morales's motet evidently made the desired impression,[99] if its long-continuing popularity after the peace conference is accepted as sufficient evidence. In Spain it was published first in an arrangement for two vihuelas[100] (Enríquez de Valderrábano) at Valladolid in 1547, and next in an arrangement for one vihuela (Fuenllana) at Seville in 1554 (the names of Paulus, Carolus, and Franciscus were printed each time as in the order of the original cantata text, but in deference to the emperor his name in the series was raised to capitals—CAROLVS). Not only these vihuela arrangements but also the printing of the vocal parts, first at Lyons in 1542 and then at Venice in 1549[101] testify to the continuing popularity of a cantata that can have been conceived originally as no more than an occasional composition. It was still popular so late as 1576, if the fact that Victoria borrowed extensively from it when he composed his own sonorous six-voice *Gaudeamus* Mass is considered significant.

The two sections of Morales's cantata are welded together by the repetition throughout both *partes* of a short melodic ostinato confided to an inner voice (in the Venice print, the "quintus"). The six-note motto in unreduced time values reads as follows:

Gau- de- a- mus

This six-note plainsong incipit is repeated eighteen times (with rests between repetitions). Meanwhile, the other several voices discourse on the merits of pope, emperor, and king; and exhort the whole earth to sing praises to God because the two princes, Charles and Francis, have ushered in a new and happy age by concluding a most Christian peace. The constructive plan of this motet was obviously a favorite with Morales. Otherwise he would not have used the same unifying device in such important motets as his earlier six-voice *Veni Domine et noli tardare* (1536), his later six-voice *Gaude et laetare Ferrariensis civitas* (1539), and his undated five-voice motets, *Tu es Petrus* and *Emendemus in melius*. As will be shown below at page 293, his pupil Francisco Guerrero approved the device, refusing it in another *Veni Domine* (1555). Following in Guerrero's footsteps, Juan Esquivel used it in still another *Veni Domine* (1608).

This unifying device was not Morales's own invention. In Spain it had already been used with conspicuous success in such a "canonic" item of the *Cancionero Musical de Palacio* repertory as item 149, *A los baños del amor*, throughout which an inner voice incessantly repeats a four-note motto-theme (in breves): G-A-E-D = sol-la-mi-re = *Sola m'iré* ("Alone I shall go"). It had also been used with great effect by one of Morales's predecessors in the papal choir, Jean Conseil (Consilium), a Parisian priest whose choir term lasted from 1526 until his death in 1535. Conseil's six-voice motet *Tempus faciendi Domine* can be found at folios 77-82 of Toledo Cathedral Codex 13—the copying of which was completed in 1554.[102] In this motet, an inner voice incessantly repeats the interjection "O clemens!" sung to a short motto-tune while the five other voices (singing different words) weave their own contrapuntal web. The likeness in constructive plan—an inner voice incessantly repeating an ejaculation sung to a short motto-tune while the other voices weave their web singing other words—is self-evident. Not only is the formal plan the same but even the allotment of the parts is the same; since in both Conseil's motet and Morales's peace cantata a voice of tenor range sings the motto-theme. It is quite possible, of course, that other pieces in addition to Conseil's *Tempus faciendi Domine* influenced Morales in behalf of this particular unifying device. But the presence of the Conseil motet in a Toledo codex—the copying of which was commissioned after Morales returned from Rome to occupy the Toledo chapelmastership and most of the contents of which are Morales's own compositions—shows conclusively his acquaintance with Conseil's prior experiments in unification; and his approval. From whatever predecessor he learned the idea, he was to make it his own with singularly dramatic power.

In his next datable composition he returned to the same constructive principle. The tenor in *Gaude et laetare Ferrariensis civitas* incessantly repeats a short plainsong incipit with these scriptural words: "Magnificabo nomen tuum in aeternum"; in the meantime the five other voices discourse contrapuntally on the great good fortune that has come to the city of Ferrara because the wise pontiff Paul has chosen Ippolito d'Este II from among the other shining lights of Italy to be a cardinal. The pope made his appointment on December 20, 1538, but withheld the news from the public ("riservato in pectore") until March 5, 1539. The announcement reached Ferrara the following Sunday, March 9. In the intervening months Ippolito, who knew of the coming announcement, prepared an expensive celebration. Morales, though he may not have visited Ferrara at any time, was a composer whose works were already well known at the Ferrarese court. Ercole II, fourth duke of Ferrara (succeeded in 1534) and brother of Ippolito, had in the middle of 1536 received two Morales motets forwarded from Rome by his own erstwhile chapel singer, Antonio Capello[103] (after March 28, 1536, a papal choir singer): one of which was for six voices, the other for five. On November 6, 1538, Capello had sent Duke Ercole still another motet *a 5* and an unnamed five-voice mass—both by Morales.[104] The best proof that these were well liked is the commission to compose *Gaude et laetare.* On March 9 in a ceremony during which the bishop, Ottaviano Castelli, sang a *Missa de Spiritu Sancto* at the Duomo, Morales's two-movement cantata was sung.[105] He was absent, however.[106] A record of the amount paid him for this festive cantata has not been found, but the munificent sums Ippolito gave other musicians[107] (Palestrina was the most famous of the many whom he is known to have patronized)[108] suggest that Morales was well paid.

When appraising Morales's financial advantages at Rome we must take account of numerous emoluments other than his regular monthly cash salary of first eight and later nine ducats. Only a month after the Ferrara celebration, for instance, he is mentioned in the Sistine Diaries as receiving the feast box sent regularly from the pope's kitchen to choir members on a rotation basis.[109] Although this was payment in kind rather than in cash, it certainly must be considered as additional income. Each of the choir members was also provided at papal expense with a servant and (when traveling) a horse.[110] The name of Morales's servant during his first term in Rome has not been discovered, but on July 22, 1539, he received permission to be away three or four days while searching for suitable medicines for his servant, then sick. On the following September 9 he left Rome with eleven other singers to accompany the pope on a month-long trip to Loreto.[111]

Another important financial advantage enjoyed by the French and Spanish papal singers was a paid leave of ten months given after every five-year term so that they might revisit their native lands.[112] Having completed his first term in 1540, Morales sought license for a Spanish trip and received it on April 4. He stayed away more than a year; for his name is not mentioned again in the Sistine Diaries until May 25, 1541. His name continues to appear every month, however, in the papal pay vouchers—the "mandati di pagamento ai Cappellani cantori."[113] In December, 1540, Paul III raised the base pay of everyone in the choir from eight to nine ducats a month. Whatever inducements to remain at home Morales may have felt while in Spain, he found it impossible to resist returning to Rome. The financial advantages can have been no small part of the reason.

Morales's first printed compositions appeared in 1539, two of them at Lyons and one at Venice. The Lyons imprint (containing his two four-voice motets, *Jam non dicam vos servos* and *Sub tuum presidium confugimus*) was Jacques Moderne's *Motteti del fiore . . . quartus liber*. The Venetian imprint (containing his madrigal *Ditemi o si o no*) was Antonio Gardane's *Il quarto libro di madrigali d'Archadelt. . . . con alcuni madrigali d'altri autori*. Nothing can better illustrate the pronounced contrast between the publishing careers of Morales and Victoria than the circumstances surrounding their maiden publications. Morales's compositions appeared in anthologies, without patronage, and in partbooks. Victoria's 1572 *Motecta*, on the other hand, was a one-man show—the Maecenas who paid the costs having been Truchsess von Waldburg. Morales was presumably in his fortieth year, and Victoria in his twenty-fourth. Of the seventy-odd imprints containing Morales's music published before 1600, more than fifty were anthologies. Victoria, however considerable his contemporary reputation, was not anthologized. Only two anthologies printed before 1700 contained any Victoria, if we are to trust Robert Eitner's *Bibliographie der Musik-Sammelwerke des XVI. und XVII. Jahrhunderts*.[114]

Not merely Morales's short motets but even his lengthy masses were anthologized. In 1540 a beginning was made when three were published— the four-voice and five-voice *De Beata Virgine* masses, and the five-voice *L'Homme armé*. These appeared in Venetian collections alongside masses by Jachet and Gombert. In 1541 a sheaf of motets appeared in a pair of imprints devoted primarily to works of Gombert. Having once begun, Morales's compositions continued to flow from the press in increasing numbers in every year but one of the next decade. Although in only one year did he see his compositions through the press in the sort of sumptuous folio that Victoria achieved almost invariably, at least his compositions were popular enough to see print without patronage.

After his return to Rome in May, 1541, Morales delayed rejoining the choir as a regular participant in its daily exercises until the end of October. On May 25 it is recorded that he received the special feast box from the pope's kitchen ("habuit scatulam"); but his name does not recur again in the diary until October 25. When regularly present, he missed on average one matins a week—always duly recorded in the diaries. One therefore infers that he was not on the roster of duty singers during the five months from May 25 to October 25. As soon as he again started singing regularly, he reverted to his habit of missing early service once a week on average.

Morales's second term with the choir is notable because of the increasing number of days lost from duty on account of sickness. His change of residence ("mutauit domum") on July 10, 1542, may have reflected his desire to transfer to a healthier site. No one would now presume to decide the specific cause of his recurring sicknesses, but malaria would suggest itself as a possibility.[115] If malaria was in fact the disease, it was of the intermittent type which allowed him to know in advance when he would have an attack.[116] His record of days lost on account of sickness shows only 9 in 1536, and 14 and 15 in the two years following. But in his final three years (1543, 1544, 1545) he lost 35, 90, and 60 days respectively.

He took his last considerable journey as a member of the pope's retinue in the spring of 1543. Paul III, though now seventy-five, still considered a personal encounter with Charles V to be the best means of reconciling certain differences that had arisen since the meeting at Nice in 1538. On March 4, 1543, the pope therefore licensed his twenty-two able-bodied singers (Costanzo Festa and two others were left behind) to proceed to Bologna: advancing to each singer personal expense money for the trip and for servant and horse. On March 17 he made a triumphant entry into Bologna (within papal dominions) and his choir sang a Te Deum. Shortly after Easter the retinue moved to Modena, then to Parma, then to Piacenza, then back to Parma, then to Ferrara, and at the end of April back to Bologna. There on May 15 Morales obtained a special license for one month in order to visit Genoa.[117] His reason for wishing to visit this city can be conjectured: Charles V was expected there, and Morales may have hoped by means of a personal interview to secure the imperial chapelmastership, which was then vacant. If the chapelmastership was his objective, he was unsuccessful. The post went instead to Thomas Crecquillon, chapel-master from 1544 to 1557.[118] Charles V remained in Genoa from May 25 until June 2. Morales then cut short his month's leave and returned to the pope a week before his leave was to have expired. The pope's next move was toward Parma, where he arrived on June 11. Within the next few days arose the only altercation during Morales's papal decade when he became violent and in consequence was assessed a stiff fine. The angry words were exchanged with another choir member—the Catalonian bass Calasanz.[119] Both were fined equal amounts; provocation on both sides is probable. If Morales had returned from an unsuccessful suit to the emperor, a mood of pique and disappointment may account for his unique outburst. It is signifi-cant that he quarreled not with an Italian or Frenchman, but with one of his Spanish colleagues. In their personal quarrels the Spaniards time and again (as the Sistine Diaries show) fought with each other, not with other nationals.

At midday on June 21 the pope met Charles V at Busseto and there con-tinued in personal conference with him during the next four days. The assemblage was brilliant—the pope having brought thirteen cardinals to enhance the dignity of the occasion. Both emperor and pope were attended by honor guards of 500 footmen and 200 horsemen. Each day the office was sung, followed by Mass. Titian was present to paint pope and emperor.[120] The meeting was made resplendent in every other way that the aged but still astute pontiff could devise. After their successful exertions in adding splendor to the occasion, the pope rewarded his singers with a three-month vacation (beginning July 6).

Despite this vacation, Morales was an ailing man when he returned to Rome early in October. He was absent sick during most of November and during the whole of the January and February following. In 1544, the year when he published his two thick folio volumes of masses, he was ill for ninety days. That he was genuinely sick, and not simply reading proof for his masses (which were being printed by the Dorico brothers—two Brescian music printers who monopolized the Roman business at mid-century),[121] is proved by such annotations in the diary as: "Habuit licen-tiam vsque ad festum purificationis *pro sanitate recuperanda*."[122] Thus, the year that we might naturally suppose to be one in which Morales had reached his pinnacle at Rome turned out to be the worst so far as pro-tracted illness was concerned. His subsequent decision not to return to Rome after his second leave (which began on May 1, 1545) may relate, at least in part, to his serious health problem.

It is obvious from the dedication of his *Missarum liber primus* that Morales in 1544 was already seeking employment outside Rome. In his dedication to the twenty-five-year-old Cosimo de' Medici (1519-1574), Duke of

Florence, he pointedly suggested that Cosimo ("whose ancestors had always liberally patronized music") take him into service. Should Cosimo thus honor him, Morales promised that in future all his works would be dedicated solely to the duke. But that his sonorous 550-word Latin dedication failed of its intended effect is proved by Cosimo's failure to engage him. Later in the same year, Morales dedicated his second book of masses to the pope. Cosimo can have given him not the smallest encouragement if so shortly after Morales's promise to dedicate all future works to the duke he was constrained to fall back on the pope for his second dedication.

Granted that his dedication to Cosimo was a thrust in the wrong direction, it is still worth studying for the light it throws on Morales's character and personal history. In the absence of any evidence to the contrary, his dedications to Cosimo and to Paul III must be accepted as products of his own pen: especially in view of the claims made in his dedication to Cosimo. Only the fact that the Latinity of the dedications is of a rather superior order would give anyone reason to suspect that they might have been written for him. If he did himself write the dedications, he had certainly mastered the language. The elegance of Goudimel's Latin prose proves that at least one other contemporary composer had mastered the best humanist brand of the language. In his dedication to Cosimo, Morales wrote as follows:

If up to the present moment I have not made my mark in extremely weighty or distinguished affairs, nevertheless my exertions are known in those fields of study that comprise the liberal arts, for in mastering them I have continuously exercised myself from early youth. I have worked with such diligence that no professional musician can, I believe, despise my learning. How fruitful have been my studies is of course not mine to say but is for others to judge. . . .

Throughout his dedicatory epistle to Cosimo, he seems to have been bent on proving that his culture extended beyond music to at least the arts in the trivium.

If there are any false modulations in his carefully polished dedication, one such is surely to be found in his strictures against light and amorous music. Cosimo was sufficiently obsequious in church matters to have had his adolescent son made a cardinal. But in music his taste was entirely for light and wanton madrigals. Don Luis Zapata, an inveterate traveler and a distinguished musical connoisseur to boot, knew Cosimo for the most frivolous ruler in Italy; and in his miscellany of anecdotes he described Cosimo as a tireless practical joker.[123] Corteccia, the Florentine *maestro di cappella* since 1538,[124] dedicated the first book of his *Madriali a quattro voci* to the duke (Venice: 1544) with a but half-hearted apology for the grossness of the texts. Morales, who cannot have known his duke, pointedly distinguished on the other hand between "light and playful music . . . fittest for wanton love" and "grave and decorous music suitable for divine praises," bestowing all his accolades on the latter. In Morales's behalf it can only be said that Cosimo I was still in the first years of his reign and his assumed air of piety was not yet fully appreciated for the Machiavellian mask that it turned out to be. Moreover, Morales may have hoped that Eleonor of Toledo, Cosimo's young wife, could do more in his behalf than it was in her power to do.

In his second dedication, to Pope Paul, he also discoursed at length on the superiority of grave and serious music written in praise of God to all light and trifling love songs. The dedication closes as follows:

> If Your Holiness will but favor me and out of the boundless store of dignities at Your disposal but confer upon me some testimonial of Your favor, my own indigence will be relieved, and Your patronage will stimulate me to compose better works in days to come. Others also will by the example of Your generosity be encouraged to turn from vain and trifling songs to divine praises. Farewell.

Morales's dedication to the pope, a hundred words longer than that to Cosimo, should certainly have won him some tangible marks of favor. Paul III had from earliest years notably favored musicians. Also, he appreciated learned music, whereas there is no reason to believe that Cosimo did. As a youth he had for instance studied Ptolemy's *De musica* in the original Greek,[125] and, if we are to believe his master of ceremonies, Blasius de Cesena, he was sufficiently well trained in the theory of music to understand the intricacies of the art.[126] Morales appealed to Paul's love of learning by mentioning in his dedication a second-century Roman author who had written on the affective powers of music.[127] Moreover, Morales began this second collection with a mass—*Tu es vas electionis, sanctissime Paule*—the title of which closely resembles a passage of Scripture (Acts 9:15) that Paul III applied to himself. Throughout this mass the tenor constantly intones the text, "Thou art a chosen vessel, Paul":[128] these being words that were spoken by Christ to Paul the Apostle on the Damascus road.

But if Paul III was a "vas electionis" he was also, in the words of a punning pasquinade, a "vas dilationis." Always slow and deliberate of speech, he was proverbially tardy in rewarding his suitors with the lucrative benefices for which they pleaded. His previous personal attentions to Morales can be summarized thus: (1) a rescript of ennoblement had been issued in Morales's behalf early in October, 1536—this honor being identical with ennoblements conferred on Escribano, Calasanz, and Escobedo, to name only Spanish singers in the papal choir;[129] (2) in the pope's name, request for reversion of benefices in Ávila, Cartagena, and Segovia dioceses, should any be vacant or fall vacant, had been made to the respective bishops of those dioceses in 1536 and 1537;[130] (3) similar requests had been forwarded to the diocesans of Seville and Orense in 1538 and 1539;[131] (4) actual possession of a benefice in the parochial church of Pucudia, diocese of Cuenca, had been conferred sometime before April, 1545.[132] Of the favors in the above list, only the last can be said with assurance to have carried with it any financial reward; and even it reverted to Juan Sánchez in April, 1545, shortly before Morales's final departure from Rome.

After the dedication, the pope seems still to have found nothing more tangible with which to reward Morales than further promises—or at all events P. José M. Llorens, who valiantly searched in the Secret Archives of the Vatican (1952-1953),[133] could find no evidence of anything except further promises. The penury of notices concerning benefices actually conferred, and financial rewards actually obtained, contrasts strikingly with the record of Victoria, who returned from Rome possessed of benefices paying the large sum of 1,200 ducats a year.[134] The financial disparity between Morales and Victoria upon leaving Rome is confirmed by the fact that Morales on his return was so poor that he had to go into debt immediately (at Toledo, where he occupied the chapelmastership from August 31, 1545, until August 9, 1547). Victoria on the other hand was so well placed financially that he could afford to refuse two of the most lucrative chapelmasterships in Spain—those at Seville and Saragossa—both of which could have been his for the asking.[135]

It is certain that for other reasons Morales's last months in the choir cannot have been happy ones. The new episcopal intermediary between pope and choir, Ludovico de Magnasco (bishop of Assisi), though not yet formally in charge of discipline, was already heartily disliked.[136] On Morales's last Holy Saturday, while the pope and several cardinals were present, two of the oldest choir members flew at each other during the blessing of the new oils, shouting in a loud voice and scandalizing the pope, along with everyone else present.[137] On Easter day Blas Nuñez and another singer caused a scandal in the presence of the pope and cardinals by calling each other names in a loud tone of voice.[138] Recurring incidents of this kind indicate considerable tension in the choir during Morales's last weeks. A contributing factor may have been the wrangling over what provisions to include in the new *Constitutiones Capellae Pontificiae*, then in the process of being framed. On Easter Monday (April 6, 1545) a committee of six was elected to sit with the bishop of Assisi to compose the new constitutions.[139] But because the new rules touched every singer, every one wished to have a part in framing them. The old constitutions had been destroyed in the 1527 sack of Rome and during the intervening period oral tradition had prevailed as an insecure guide. Morales's part in drafting the new constitutions can have been small at best; but a place was left for his ratifying signature when they were completed some seven months later in November, 1545.[140]

The constitutions comprise fifty-nine chapters[141] and touch every phase of the singers' lives. Since they show the customs prevailing during Morales's epoch, the more important provisions are summarized briefly in the following paragraph.

A singer need not be in holy orders but must be a man of honor and of good repute. When a new member is proposed, his character shall first be examined, and then he shall be brought to a musical examination conducted by the choir members themselves. The first requisite is his voice quality; the second, his ability to keep his part in homophony; the third, his sufficiency as a singer of contrapuntal music; the fourth, his ability to sing plainsong; and the fifth his sight-reading ability. A secret vote shall be taken after his musical examination, and no singer may be admitted unless two-thirds of the singers plus one, vote for his admission. After being admitted and having attended to all the financial formalities, he must give himself solely to the daily routine in the pope's chapel and may not sing elsewhere nor carry on other business. His duties as a new singer include moving the heavy choirbooks into place; as soon as a newer singer enters he no longer moves them into place for everyday singing, but he still carries them with his junior novice in the choir during processions. Only when two singers are junior to him can he consider his chores as porter ended. Absolute silence during divine office is required. All business such as requests for leaves of absence must be directed to the most senior member of the choir present. Special requests must be approved in a secret vote by two-thirds plus one. Heavy fines are to be assessed for malingering or other false reports. Every five years an extended leave is granted—five months for Italians; ten for French and Spanish. The feast box from the pope's kitchen is to be awarded in rotation to choristers, who should divide it among their colleagues. Ceremonies for creation of new cardinals, for the exequies of a pope, and for the creation and coronation of a new pope are to follow a prescribed routine. All unusual choir business not covered by clauses in the constitutions shall be entrusted to a committee of three, six, or nine members, composed of Italians, French, and Spaniards in equal numbers. The reason for this division by nations is that "experience has shown the singers divide always into their own national groups, and speak their own language with each other."

The constitutions as adopted in 1545 did not prescribe any exact number of singers. An undated sixteenth-century memorial in the Sistine archive said, "From the time of Martin V until Clement VII there was no fixed number in the pontifical choir. . . . Clement fixed the number at 24, of whom 7 should be sopranos, 7 contraltos, 4 tenors, and 6 basses."[142] During the pontificate of Paul III, the number of singers rose from twenty (in 1535) to thirty-two (in 1545).[143] Although the 1545 constitutions do not fix the total number of singers in the choir, they do set eight singers—of whom two each must be sopranos, altos, tenors, and basses—as the minimum number necessary for any choral service.[144] When the pope wanted mass sung in summer vacations, he never called for less than eight singers, and usually for twelve.[145] Only once during Morales's decade did an occasion arise when, the choir being present, the ordinary of the mass was said instead of sung.[146] What is more, the mass was always sung polyphonically instead of being merely plainchanted. Once in 1545 it was recorded that "on account of rain there was an insufficient number of singers present, sopranos being entirely lacking; therefore mass was not sung [polyphonically] but plainchanted and those not present were fined."[147] Even at the most solemn occasions polyphonic music, and not plainsong, was the norm. For instance, the constitutions prescribe the singing of *cantus figuratus* even at a funeral.[148]

Considerable attention was paid to the distribution of parts. It is therefore likely that when a singer of a certain range quit the choir he was succeeded by another singer of corresponding range. Although Morales's exact range is not specified in the Sistine Diaries, his immediate successor was a baritone ("indutus est cotta pro baritono").[149] The next singer admitted was a tenor.[150] Morales, Escobedo, and Sánchez freely substituted for each other; but never Morales and Nuñez, who was a soprano; and never Morales and Calasanz or Ordoñez, both of whom are known to have been basses. Still further evidence, if it were needed, is found in Morales's appointment to the *Raçion de tenor* at Toledo Cathedral in September, 1545. Because many Spanish singers hired at Rome later in the sixteenth century were falsettists, Burney assumed mistakenly that all Spaniards in the choir were falsettists. But of the Spaniards contemporary with Morales, only Escribano (retired in August, 1539) and Nuñez were sopranos.[151] The evidence now available leads strongly to the conclusion that Morales's range was that of a tenor.

The Toledo Chapelmastership (1545-1547)

Morales's May journey in 1543 having netted him nothing, and his dedications of the 1544 books of masses having stimulated neither Cosimo I nor Paul III to any extraordinary exertions, his attention must have been drawn immediately to the vacancy in the chapelmastership announced by the canons of Toledo Cathedral on March 16, 1545. The chapelmasterships in Spain during this particular epoch were all publicly advertised by means of placards on the doors of the principal churches in Salamanca, Valladolid, Alcalá de Henares, and Madrid, and in other public places—it being the intent of the cathedral chapters that no chapelmastership should be filled until several competitors had offered themselves for a public trial of skill.[152] Important chapelmasterships and organistships were not infrequently held open for six to ten months until a sufficient number of acceptable competitors offered themselves. The examination set at Toledo Cathedral differed little from those at other leading cathedrals. A candidate at Toledo was required to compose trial compositions in three, four, and five parts above a given plainsong melody, to write a *fabordón* (psalm-intonation formula in homophony), to compose a motet with given words, and to write a double-choir *Asperges*. His compositions were put to the test of an actual performance, and the canons of the cathedral decided in secret vote which candidate was most suitable for the post. If a candidate enjoyed such repute that the canons knew in advance of the competition who would be the victor, the public trial might itself be waived, but the principle of a publicly announced competition open to all interested contenders was never abandoned.

Morales in this instance may have been appointed with less formality than the usual competition at Toledo entailed. But he was certainly interviewed in advance of his appointment by two of the most responsible members of the trial jury, the *abad de Sant Viçente* and Bernardino de Alcaraz. These two canons were deputed by the Toledo chapter on August 10, 1545, to speak with the "singer Morales" to find out if he wished to accept the chapelmastership. Three days later the same two canons were authorized to come to a financial agreement with him. On August 31 he was formally appointed, and the next day—exactly a decade to the day after entering the papal choir—he was seated in his prebend and became Toledo chapelmaster. In addition to the amount regularly budgeted for chapelmaster's salary, he was awarded an extra 6,000 maravedís "because of his outstanding powers as a composer demonstrated in the books of polyphony published at Rome where he lived with His Holiness, Pope Paul III."[153]

The Toledo canons thought they conferred no small favor when they bestowed a chapelmastership on a successful candidate. As Cardinal Siliceo (1486-1557), archbishop of Toledo and primate of Spain, contended in 1549:[154] "It is a well-known and verified fact that the Cathedral of Toledo is the most illustrious, the richest, the most splendid, the best staffed, and the most completely staffed, of any in all the Spanish dominions. Except St. Peter's in Rome, in fact, there is no cathedral in Christendom to surpass it." The Toledo canons therefore had every right to feel that they had done handsomely by Morales when they gave him the post and added the sum of 6,000 maravedís to the regular annual salary of 37,500 maravedís. Their feeling of self-satisfaction is more than amply brought out in the record of their later financial dealings with Morales—who unfortunately did not find it possible to live within his salary and perquisites. To understand Morales's financial difficulties it is necessary first to appreciate what his salary actually amounted to. At his first post in Ávila he had received 100 ducats a year. A ducat equalled 375 maravedís.[155] Therefore he was earning as much at Ávila as the regular chapelmaster's pay at Toledo before the bonus was added. At Plasencia he had evidently received much more; and in Plasencia he had also been more of a cathedral official—at least until he stopped going to chapter meetings. Yet the Toledo canons let it be emphasized several times in the course of their dealings with him that in their opinion he was, if not overpaid, at least very well paid.

The chapelmaster's duties at Toledo, just as everywhere else in sixteenth-century Spain, included instructing the choirboys (*seises*) in singing and in music theory, boarding them in his house, and fulfilling all the functions of a parent.[156] The number of choirboys whom Morales had to board and train was certainly larger than the antiquated number of six, which the word *seises* connotes. Records of the numbers of choirboys admitted each year were kept during the mid-years of the sixteenth century, and are now preserved in Legajo 65 at the Toledo Capitular Library. In 1549 and 1550, eight new choirboys were admitted each year.[157] In 1553 eleven were admitted. Assuming eight, however, as a fair annual average for new choirboys and two years as an average length of service, it can be computed that not less than fifteen or sixteen would have been under the chapelmaster's care at any one time. If three years is accepted as a likelier length of service for a choirboy, then their number at any one time rises to the middle twenties. Whether their number was nearer fifteen or twenty-five, Morales obviously faced major problems of household management and discipline. His immediate superior, so far as educational responsibilities were concerned, was the *maestrescuela* ("schoolmaster").[158] The latter was a canon, and he was responsible for the boys' progress in such other subjects as reading and writing the Latin language; and for their welfare in general.

Whatever hopes Morales may have entertained for success in his new Toledo post were soon to be dashed. Almost at once he found that he could not manage his finances. According to the terms of his engagement, he was obliged to "maintain the choirboys at their previously accustomed level of subsistence." But in attempting to comply he had already so grossly overspent within seven months that he was forced to apply for a loan of twenty ducats from the chief steward (*refitolero*)[159] on March 26, 1546. The cathedral chapter, although approving this loan, did so only because of the "dearness of the times"—the early months of 1546 having been a season when food prices were suddenly forced upward by crop failures.[160] Not only did Morales have to borrow on March 26 but he had to apply for another loan on October 13 of the same year. In the interim, to complicate matters, he had been seriously ill. As early as December 24, 1545, the cathedral chapter had granted him permission to wear a heavy cloak while he was on duty in the *coro* (choir).[161] That his health had not in the meantime been safeguarded is shown by the chapter's approval of a further loan of twenty-eight ducats on October 13, 1546, expressly "to help him pay the expenses of his illness."[162] Even with this loan his financial condition had so deteriorated by the end of 1546 that on the last day of the year the chapter voted to forgive him half the sum he had borrowed in October— that is, fourteen of the twenty-eight ducats.[163] This mercy of the chapter highlighted the fact that within his first thirteen months at Toledo he had spent two-thirds more than his predecessor (Andrés de Torrentes) had spent in an equivalent length of time. For a fuller evaluation of his personal finances one would have to add to this two-thirds overdraft in Toledo the further large sum of ninety ducats from the pope's treasury at Rome, granted to him during his ten-month leave from May 1, 1545, until March 1, 1546. The Toledo canons had every right to consider him either a wanton with money or an intolerably bad manager.

Nor were the sources of cash thus far enumerated Morales's only ones during his short Toledo career. Within the first month of his arrival he began adding to the choral library of the cathedral. On September 25, 1545, the chapter appointed a commission of three to investigate the monetary value of various polyphonic books that he had brought with him and presented to the cathedral.[164] How much he was paid for these choirbooks is not known. But however much he received, the sale of these added still another cash sum to the following incomes already mentioned: (1) 100 ducats base pay; (2) an additional 16 per cent (6,000 maravedís) as a bonus for his foreign reputation; (3) loans of 20 and 28 ducats "on account of the dearness of the times" and to "help defray the costs of his illness"; (4) terminal leave pay from Rome of 90 papal ducats. When therefore he threw up the chapelmastership on August 9, 1547, less than two years after his appointment, the Toledo authorities can hardly have been sorry to see him go. The *Actos Capitulares desde 1545 asta 1547*, now conserved at Toledo, contain a minute record of cathedral business during Morales's 23-month service; but no entry has yet been found to suggest that the canons pleaded with him not to resign. Instead of trying to hold him, the chapter at once set their protonotary to work with a group of canon lawyers to rescind the salary "bonus" of 6,000 maravedís annually added to the chapelmaster's salary during his term, so that the next incumbent should be hired at the old salary of a flat 100 ducats.[165]

If the Toledo chapter was glad to see Morales leave, he was probably no less happy to go. The only contemporary likeness of him—a woodcut in the 1544 second book of masses—shows a man with sunken cheeks, bags under his eyes, and thinning hair. His wan, unhealthy look—if habitual—can hardly have endeared him to adolescent choirboys. Such problems in household management as beset him at Toledo, however much the odor of them recalled his salad days at Ávila and Plasencia, were certainly not of the type to which he had grown accustomed during his Roman decade. There he had consorted with the best musicians of the age. The caliber of his musical companions in Rome may be judged by naming only those singers who shared the same day off (Wednesday) each week—Costanzo Festa and Arcadelt,[166] assuredly two of the best composers of the epoch. But at Toledo he was expected to associate on terms of near-equality with his two organists: neither of whom was a person of much distinction.[167] He did not have the right to tell either organist when to play or when not to play. The times for organ music were already rigidly prescribed by a capitular act of March 29, 1509, which said: "The organist . . . shall play during the entire office, at early Mass and at High Mass, and at vespers . . . except during Lent, Advent, and other prohibited seasons."[168] If any specific directions were needed, the first organist, whose cathedral rank was as high as that of the chapelmaster, took his instructions not from the chapelmaster but from two canons.[169] Morales's duty was not to instruct or command but to coöperate with the two organists and with the other instrumentalists hired by the cathedral chapter.

Whatever else is known of musical practice at Toledo in the 1540's, *a cappella* singing was not the norm. On the contrary, accompanied music was the rule throughout the entire year, except during penitential seasons. Six instrumentalists, in addition to the two organists, were on the regular payroll. Gaspar Maynete, the chief *ministril*, received an annual salary of 41,000 maravedís in 1547, and the two other principals only slightly lesser amounts. These *ministriles altos* were serving a twenty-year contract signed in 1531, and were allowed to play nowhere except at cathedral functions. Most of their energies went into processions and first-class festivals.[170] The polyphony heard in the cathedral at all festive occasions throughout Morales's sojourn was therefore "broken music," involving voices, wind instruments, sackbuts, and organs.[171]

That Morales's creative urge slackened at Toledo can be inferred from the compositions copied into the Toledo choirbooks. Of his thirteen masses in these *libros de coro* only one had not been published at Rome; and that one is a *Missa cortilla* ("short mass"). Several codices contain dates that tell when the copying was completed. Only a small fraction of his motets in Codices 21 (1549), 17 (1550), and 13 (1554) remained unprinted when he left Italy. The exceptions, such as the somber five-voice *Circumdederunt me*, the quietly intense five-voice *Salva nos stella*, and the dark-hued four-voice *Solemnis urgebat dies*, are conspicuously shorter than Morales's older motets. One telling proof that he felt no compulsion to create during his two years at Toledo is the absence from the choirbooks of any motets honoring Toledan saints. At Rome he had published motets honoring such unscriptural saints as Anthony, Martin, and Lucy; but at Toledo he wrote none for SS. Ildephonsus, Eugenius, or Leocadia, all of whom were first-class saints in the Toledan calendar. Andrés de Torrentes, the chapelmaster before Morales who was invited back to succeed him, wrote motets (preserved at Toledo in Codex 18) honoring all three of these. Alonso Lobo, after Morales the most distinguished sixteenth-century chapelmaster at Toledo, composed hymns honoring SS. Eugenius, Hermenegild, Isidore, Justa, and Rufina. Even Victoria, although he remained at Rome considerably longer than Morales, did not neglect such local favorites as Ildephonsus and James—composing a hymn to honor each. Victoria's *Vexilla Regis* "in the Spanish manner" made another bow to his native land. In contrast with these, Morales's repertory seems conspicuously international. Even his style must have seemed foreign: at least to his fellow townsman Cristóbal Mosquera de Figueroa, who in his preface to Guerrero's *Canciones y villanescas espirituales* (Venice: 1589) classified Morales as an Italian rather than a Spanish composer. Another Andalusian with much the same opinion was Juan Bermudo, who in his *Declaración de instrumentos* (Osuna: 1549) spoke of the "*foreign* music that today comes from the excellent Cristóbal de Morales, the profound Gombert, and other outsiders,"[172] going on to explain that he counted Morales "as a *foreign* composer, because if his music has the charm and sonorousness of Spanish music it at the same time lacks nothing of the profundity, the technical polish, and the artifice of foreign music."

Marchena Interlude (1548-1551) On August 14, 1546, Morales was granted a forty-day leave of absence by the Toledo chapter so that he might spend some time in Seville.[173] However, any aspirations he may have had to the chapelmastership in Seville with its warmer climate and more hospitable atmosphere were thwarted by the continuing good health of Fernández de Castilleja, Sevillian chapelmaster since 1514. Seville being out of the question, it had to be in the small but sunny Andalusian town of Marchena, thirty miles east of Seville, that Morales found employment during the next three years after leaving Toledo. His employer was, like Handel's Duke of Chandos, an extremely wealthy magnate who chose to live in his private palace away from the metropolis but near enough so that frequent visits could be made. The Duque de Arcos at this time was the youthful Don Luis Cristóbal Ponce de León (1518-1573). In 1539 his annual income had been reported to be 25,000 ducats.[174] That this was a respectable sum can be verified by comparing it with the incomes enjoyed by several of the richest men in Spain during the 1540's: Archbishop of Toledo, 80,000 ducats; Archbishop of Seville, 24,000 ducats; Archbishop of Burgos, 20,000 ducats; Duke of Alva, 50,000 ducats; Marqués de Tarifa, 30,000 ducats; Conde de Ureña, 20,000 ducats.[175] The largest income in the realm was, of course, that of the primate at Toledo, whose cathedral Morales was just leaving. But the duke whose chapelmaster he was to be for the next three years was, apart from royalty, one of the six or seven wealthiest laymen in Spain. Furthermore, this duke "was sincere, generous, and beloved by all; he was valorous in war, courageous in counsel, and a born leader."[176] His wealth and titles were his by inheritance from a collateral ancestor, Rodrigo Ponce de León (1443-1492), who in 1482 had captured Alhama, the richest town of its size in the kingdom of Granada. It was the taking of this Moorish stronghold which had inspired the popular romance *Ay de mi, Alhama*. This ancestor's wealth was already so great in 1480 that he could maintain his own private chapel. Just as Don Luis Cristóbal's riches were inherited, so also were his tastes for music and for poetry. His mother was María Téllez Girón and his maternal uncle was Juan Téllez Girón, fourth count of Ureña. Not only was the latter a magnate, a university founder, and a saintly man but also he was a music lover and amateur composer. Don Luis Cristóbal's sister was a distinguished poetess whose works were still printed in the next century. The duke's liberality to Morales is beyond dispute: Guerrero vouched for it in 1555 when he wrote a dedicatory epistle to Don Luis Cristóbal mentioning the duke's passion for the music of Morales, *in quem maxima tua extant beneficia* ("who received the greatest benefits from your hands").[177]

The first of several documents signed by Morales while maestro to the Duke of Arcos bears May 10, 1548, for its date; and is, interestingly enough, a receipt for fourteen ducats to purchase a *clavicordio* in Seville.[178] This instrument was destined for the duke's chamber in the palace at Marchena. Since Morales personally intervened in its purchase, he was probably to be the player. What his repertory included may be inferred from the keyboard sample of his music printed below at page 105 (*Sacris solemniis*: first published in Venegas de Henestrosa's *Libro de cifra nueva para tecla, harpa, y vihuela* [Alcalá de Henares: 1557]). Not only was Morales in Seville for the purchase of this instrument in May, 1548, but he obviously took trips to other Andalusian towns while serving the Duke of Arcos. Sometime before August 10, 1549,[179] for instance, he purchased pairs of boots at Montilla for two choirboys in his charge (a Rodrigo and a Martín). Montilla, thirty miles south of Cordova, was the seat of the celebrated convent of Santa Clara. Doña Isabel Pacheco, the mother superior in 1549, was an aunt of the Duchess of Arcos. A patroness of music in her own right, Doña Isabel it was who encouraged Fray Juan Bermudo to write his excellent instruction book *El arte tripharia* (1550). Bermudo, in his *prólogo epistolar*, claims to have preached at the convent in Montilla during Lent of 1549; he had then "received such favors from you that I am perpetually indebted."[180] Doña Isabel wished "to sing plainsong and play a keyboard instrument for spiritual recreation";[181] in all likelihood, Morales's own trip was prompted by this same noble kinswoman of the Duchess of Arcos.

It is not yet known how many other choirboys besides Rodrigo and Martín fell to Morales's charge while he served in Marchena. But he received regular allotments of wheat (August 31, 1550) and barley (February 21, 1551);[182] and also money to purchase caps, coats, cloaks, jackets, shirts, breeches, and shoes for his choirboys. His salaried adult singers included individuals named Alonso Verdugo, Nicolás de Velasco, and Juan Navarro.[183] This last-named singer was in time to become one of the famous figures in Spanish musical history. Since Navarro was already hired at a yearly salary of 10,000 maravedís in 1549, it is obvious that he came under Morales's personal supervision at least two years before Morales left Marchena for Málaga. Interestingly enough, Juan Navarro's name crops up next in 1553, when he had the courage to contend for the Málaga chapelmastership in succession to Morales.[184] Proof is therefore now at hand that both Francisco Guerrero[185] and Juan Navarro were Morales's personal disciples.

Another musical light whose talents were developed by Morales while in Marchena was the Minorite theorist from Écija—Juan Bermudo. In August, 1549, Bermudo referred to Morales as "maestro de capilla de mi señor el duque de Arcos."[186] If the Duke of Arcos was *mi señor* in 1549, it is indeed quite possible that in the same year Bermudo was a stipendary along with Morales in the duke's household. In any event, Bermudo tirelessly praised Morales as the greatest composer alive and knew his music thoroughly. In turn, Morales demonstrated his high esteem for Bermudo's powers as a theoretician. This regard becomes abundantly evident in the commendatory letter that Morales wrote on October 20, 1550, for the forthcoming second edition of Bermudo's *Declaración de instrumentos*.[187] Just as his two Latin dedications in 1544 are Morales's only extant Latin prose, so this commendatory letter is his only Spanish prose. The letter, occupying one printed page, not only commends the *Declaración* but sets forth Morales's educational ideals and is therefore worthy of review here.

Morales begins by saying he knows of no other book so useful as Bermudo's. He finds the style fluent and pleasing, and above all succinct, so that the reader is immediately taken to the heart of a matter rather than lost in circumlocutions. Bermudo's order of presentation is commendable, he says, because it leads from the known to the unknown, the imperfect to the perfect, the least complicated to the most complex. This order of presentation, thinks Morales, is to be preferred above all others in an instructional book because it is the natural order, and the natural in art is ever best. Though always going directly to the point, Bermudo has suitably amplified his instructions when the subject is vital. Moreover, Bermudo has welded practice and theory together. For the first time, Morales has found a book in which the actual procedures used by performing musicians are explained. The drift of Morales's letter is clear enough: he is using all his powers of persuasion to woo prospective buyers of Bermudo's text. But his letter also stirs present-day sympathies because while boosting the *Declaración* Morales reveals his own thoroughly progressive educational outlook.

In comparison with all Spanish music texts printed before it, the *Declaración* is the fullest and the best; it is also the most *avant-garde*. "When the times change, so does the music; avoid old-fashioned music," was Bermudo's constant theme. "A composer of genius invents new musical ideas; Vives and Erasmus improved Latin; so have composers of our time improved music,"[188] contended Bermudo. "The composers whom I recommend are Antonio de Cabezón, Cristóbal de Morales, and Gombert; . . . the best music to begin with . . . is that of Juan Vásquez; . . . then the music of Josquin, of Adrian [Willaert], of Jachet of Mantua. . . ."[189] In like vein, Morales had said in the dedication of his second book of masses: "We musicians ourselves are aware that the spirit of the times constantly demands something new from us." It was this same progressive musical outlook that Morales endorsed when he wrote his recommendatory epistle for Bermudo's second edition.

Málaga Chapelmastership (1551-1553)

Morales's last appointment took him to the Mediterranean haven with the blandest climate of any city in Spain—Málaga. Here he was formally inducted as chapelmaster on November 27, 1551. Unlike appointments at Toledo or Seville cathedrals, those at Málaga in the sixteenth century were directly within the gift of the Crown. At the time of the reconquest of the Kingdom of Granada, the right of naming all ecclesiastical officials in that realm was conceded by the papacy to Ferdinand V. For instance, when Encina wished to take up the archdeaconate at Málaga, he was obliged first to have the papal nuncio ask Ferdinand V for a writ naming him to the vacant post.

In practice, the Málaga chapter was usually permitted to send two names to the Crown when a vacancy arose in the reign of Charles V: a first choice and an alternate. But since in theory both Charles V and Philip II made direct appointments, the Málaga capitular acts always contain some phrases such as those italicized in the act of possession quoted below—this being the act in which Morales's induction into the Málaga chapelmaster's prebend is recorded.[190]

The cathedral chapter met in a regular business session under the presidency of the bishop. Cristóbal de Morales, singer, entered and presented through me, secretary of the chapter, a royal decree signed by His Highness the Prince

[Philip] and by certain of his councillors, bestowing upon him the musical prebend left vacant at the death of the former legally entitled occupant, Diego Hernández, chapelmaster, the said Cristóbal de Morales having entered his name as contender for the post when notice of its vacancy was publicly distributed and having duly competed. He presented also a writ and deed of possession of the said prebend signed by the Most Reverend and Illustrious Don Fray Bernardo Manrique, Bishop of Málaga. The royal patent properly notarized by Andrés de las Cuevas *instructing, and if necessary, commanding* the cathedral chapter to confirm the episcopal deed of possession and to bestow the prebend of chapelmaster upon Cristóbal de Morales having been seen by all the canons and read aloud by me, the secretary, the canons agreed *to accept and obey the provisions of the royal decree with all due reverence and to submit to the order therein contained;* in compliance with which they declared and decreed that possession of the said prebend should be conferred upon the said Cristóbal de Morales. To comply with the royal will the chapter entrusted the task of institution to Canon Sebastián de Çorita, Juan de la Peña, verger, and me, secretary; for which purpose we went into the choir of the cathedral with the said Cristóbal de Morales, and after placing him in the archdeacon's upper choir stall designated for such installation ceremonies, the said Morales being properly attired in surplice, I then asked and demanded that Canon Çorita proceed with the installation ceremony.

In the installation ceremony, Morales performed such ritual as scattering money among those present in the *coro.* He then returned to the assembled chapter and while kneeling before the bishop placed his hands on a missal brought for the purpose. The ceremony closed with his swearing on the gospels to uphold the statutes of Málaga diocese and especially the one in "chapter 59."

The fact that Morales ran into serious disciplinary problems immediately after induction may cause some surprise if the previous history of the Málaga chapelmastership has not been at least briefly reviewed.[191] Diego Fernández, his predecessor, had died as recently as August, 1551. But he had been moribund for more than fifteen years. Even by January 5, 1535, he was regarded by the chapter as being so "old and decrepit" that he could be justifiably excused from a major share of his duties: Francisco Ramírez—a clergyman who was a native of Málaga and who had been in cathedral service since February 15, 1528—being delegated after January 5, 1535, to fill the chapelmaster's role so far as teaching was concerned. This same Ramírez assumed the aged Fernández's obligation to compose the Christmas chanzonetas in 1545—for which service he was paid an extra six ducats on December 30 of that year. On February 11, 1550, Fernández was reported as "extremely sick." *Edictos* announcing the vacancy were not distributed until August 18, 1551. Fernández seems to have spent the entire intervening period as a helpless invalid in his brother's house.

Morales contended for the vacant post shortly after October 20, 1551, on which date the chapter met to decide upon the order of the examination. Since he was inducted on November 27 the chapter must have reached its decision with all possible speed—such posts often going unfilled for several months in even larger cathedrals. But although the chapter had acted rapidly in this instance, it had been unable to act so quickly in attending to the sorry state of discipline that had prevailed during the preceding years. Moreover, it cannot have helped matters for Ramírez, Fernández's long-entrenched deputy, to remain on hand after Morales's induction. (Ramírez, himself near retirement age, was pensioned off on January 9, 1555, and died sometime between April 27 and May 11 of 1558.) Furthermore, music at Málaga had so long been a family matter—Fernández having been chapelmaster from 1507 to 1551 and his brother the organist from August 18, 1512, until November 18, 1551—that upon arrival Morales found an heir on hand (none other than a son) ready to uphold the family tradition by occupying the organ bench. Thus, for a proper appreciation of Morales's difficulties at Málaga, it must be remembered that there were five factors to contend with from the start: (1) long-continued laxness, (2) impoverished repertory, (3) absenteeism on account of illness, (4) entrusting of duties to deputies, and (5) family possessiveness. Only then can one understand why he met with such formidable resistance that frequently the chapter had to intervene in his behalf. As early as December 4 (1551)—only a week after his installation—the chapter issued a strict order that the "singers of this cathedral must heed the correction of Cristóbal de Morales, chapelmaster; and obey him in everything touching their duties, without straying to the right or left of what he tells them or requires them to do."[192] Again, on July 22, 1552, the chapter had to reinforce his authority by officially notifying the singers that "all of them must come every Saturday properly habited in surplices to sing the *Salve Regina;* and if anyone misses he shall be fined half a real [17 maravedís] for each absence."[193] As of this same July 22 the chapter transmitted the following order to the cathedral succentor (director of plainchant): "On days when the choir sings the Agnus in plainchant, the singers are to wait until the organist has played one Agnus, and then are to reply with the next Agnus sung all the way through; and are not to do as they have heretofore been doing."[194] On August 8, Bishop Manrique expressed his personal displeasure at the slovenly way in which invitatories were being sung at matins, and he threatened fines unless more singers attended.[195]

Morales's popularity cannot have increased—at least among the deceased chapelmaster's kin—when the chapter announced on December 2, 1551, that a new organist would soon be engaged. On Wednesday afternoon, February 3, 1552, the dean consulted with him in order to determine how best to examine the candidates for the post.[196] Although Morales did not vote in the election following the trial, his opinion was no doubt extremely influential. The successful candidate was a Navarrese *presbítero* named Juan Doyz; the loser, a certain Jerónimo Nuñez.[197] In the cathedral acts Doyz is referred to as an "organista y músico de tecla" (organist and keyboard player). That he was a person of some consequence may be inferred from the courteous title of "el venerable don Juan Doyz" encountered in the acts. He was engaged "to play on all those days in the church calendar designated by cathedral statute."[198] His formal induction took place on Saturday, March 5, 1552.

Not only did the chapter express concern for musical standards in the cathedral by tightening reins on singers, by admonishing the succentor, and by adding a new and presumably more competent organist in the spring of 1552, but the canons kept even Morales under rather short leash during his twenty-odd months at Málaga. Evidence of this stringency is found first in the chapter's reaction to a request that Morales made on June 13, 1552, for a short leave of absence to visit Seville.[199] In his request he called attention to the fact that on June 30 he would be completing the statutory residence entitling him to such a leave. After hearing him out in person the chapter replied that he might have just so much time as the applicable cathedral statute allowed "and no more." Some months later his singers were especially unruly during a procession (May 6, 1553). Irked by his failure to control his singers, the chapter voted not only to fine the singers an amount equal to three days' wages but also to fine Morales. On June 14, 1553, he came forward asking for a special leave of absence;[200] one that turns out to have been his last. Concerned for the welfare of his subordinates, he coupled his own "humble request of their Worships for permission to take a short trip which of necessity he was obliged to make" with a plea that the chapter "remit the three days' fine assessed his singers [for misbehavior] during the procession of May 6, *S. Joann. ante Portam Latin.*" The chapter complied and at the same meeting went even further by quashing the fine levied against him (after someone mentioned the bishop's disapproval of the fine). As for the exact purpose of the short business trip on which Morales proposed to go, one can do no more than speculate. But later events make it fairly certain that he already regretted having settled in so provincial a place as Málaga. Significantly enough, neither Seville nor any other definite travel objective was named in his request of June 14.[201] On the contrary, he was vague—telling the canons at Málaga merely the noncommittal fact that "necessity obliged him to make a short trip." Perhaps he wished to visit Montilla. Or even Toledo.

Less than a fortnight later—on June 26 to be precise—Torrentes addressed a letter to the Toledo chapter declaring his intention of again resigning from the Toledo chapelmastership. Two days later his resignation was accepted.[202] On July 4, *edictos* announcing the vacancy were publicly distributed. Morales may well have had an inkling of just this impending change when he applied for leave on June 14; and Toledo may have been his target while on leave. In any event his was one of the first names brought in for consideration at a Toledo chapter meeting after the *edictos* were distributed.

On August 11 the Toledo chapter met to discuss, among other business items, a letter that one of the prebendaries (a certain Diego García) had received from Morales stating that he wished to be considered anew for the post that he had quit six years previously.[203] The reaction of the canons was mixed, as well it might have been when one considers the many mishaps during his earlier two years at Toledo (1545–1547). A canon by the name of Francisco de Silva was the first to find difficulties: "The chapter should carefully see whether its authority would not be exceeded by inviting Morales to come back to this worthy cathedral just now; and besides, since the announcement of a vacancy had publicly been made the competition should be held."[204] The *maestrescuela*, Bernardino de Alcaraz, took a similarly dim view: "If Morales wants to compete, well and good; let him go ahead; but the chapter here should not endorse him."[205] Rodrigo Çapata, *capellán mayor*, agreed with the maestrescuela. The Toledo chapter, if it wished, could have invited Morales back without the necessity of another formal competition. Torrentes—who like Morales, renounced the Toledo chapelmastership and then reapplied for it when it was again vacant—merely sent the chapter word that he would like to return, whereupon he received a polite invitation (dated November 19, 1547) to come back without going through the motions of a competition.[206] But Torrentes had virtues that Morales lacked. For one thing, he looked after the choirboys: the Toledo chapter could not praise him sufficiently for his attentiveness to the choirboys' physical welfare.[207] Because the *maestrescuela* liked the way he housed and boarded them, Torrentes could name his own time for a return, and could come back with only the formality of a letter of invitation. But this was not to be their procedure with Morales.

Morales's partisans sent two canons to talk the matter over with Cardinal Siliceo, who, however, merely referred the matter back to the chapter for decision; adding that as for Morales's salary, should he return, the chapter would have to consult the best interests of the cathedral. This report was given at a chapter meeting on August 14. On September 2 the matter was still pending but the scales were turning against Morales's partisans. Not finding a basis for agreement on that day, the chapter postponed the final date for formal applications until September 30.[208] Two days later—September 4—with Diego García acting as his proxy, Morales formally applied for permission to compete; his application was attested with the signatures of two Toledans—Alonso de León and Diego de Lunar. Morales was the second of five who made formal applications—the first having been Bartolomé de Quebedo, "chapelmaster to the princess of Portugal." The others who subsequently entered their names were Juan de Çepa, a clergyman from Ciudad Rodrigo diocese who was "chapelmaster to the duchess of Calabria";[209] a certain Juan Gómez de Alçaga from Segovia; and Rodrigo Ordoñez, "chapelmaster at Zamora." The trial was held during the week of December 4, 1553; but Morales had died sometime between September 4 and October 7.

On the last-named date the Málaga chapter met under the presidency of the archdeacon. Because this was a general meeting, the canons invited the cathedral dignitaries of lesser rank to attend—these including all the singers who held cathedral prebends. The archdeacon began the meeting by commending the choir for their recent excellent services,[210] but had no word of commendation for their deceased chapelmaster. Instead, the archdeacon read a formal announcement declaring the chapelmastership vacant, because Morales—not the "esteemed," or the "venerable," or the "excellent," but simply "Morales"[211]—was dead. The cathedral property that Morales had occupied, announced the archdeacon, would now be leased to the highest bidder. The first bidder was Canon Molina, who offered 5,000 maravedís and "20 live chickens annually" for the property. Three days later another cathedral official offered the same amount of money and 60 live chickens annually. On October 15 a further canon offered 6,000 maravedís and 60 live chickens annually. This last offer proved to be the highest bid and was accepted on October 25.[212]

The chapelmastership was not disposed of so quickly. On December 6, since an insufficient number of competitors had applied, the chapter obtained royal permission to extend the final entry date another two months. In the meantime, notices of the vacancy were to be distributed "in many cities and at the Universitites of Salamanca and Alcalá de Henares."[213] Finally, on February 7, 1554, the competition was declared closed, and the chapter appointed two of its own number, Canons Çorita and Çumel, to set the examination. Six days later the chapter met to vote on the five candidates who had been heard during the competition—Francisco Guerrero, singer in Seville Cathedral; Luis de Coçar, chapelmaster at Granada; another Coçar, related to the preceding; Gonzalo Cano of Jaén; and Juan Navarro. Guerrero, who received eighteen votes, was declared elected. He took possession by proxy on April 2 but renounced on April 19—the Seville cathedral authorities having decided in the meantime that he was too valuable a man to lose. When after a further delay the Málaga canons discovered that their offer had served no other purpose than to enhance

Guerrero's salary and prestige at Seville, they chose the much less con-
sequential Juan de Çepa.[214] After some delay he was inducted on December 24, 1554—fourteen months after Morales's death had been announced.

Only a few allusions to Morales have been found in the Málaga capitular
acts after the notice of his death. One such occurs at folio 198[v] of the *Actos
Capitulares*, Volume IX (1550-1554), under date of April 2, 1554: "The
chapter met [names of the eleven canons present are given] and before
them appeared Canon González Quintero, who produced a royal decree
naming Francisco Guerrero, priest of Seville diocese, to the prebend of
chapelmaster in this cathedral, the said prebend having become vacant at
the death of Cristóbal de Morales, whom God pardon." Another mention
occurs in the act dated June 9, 1563, on which day the chapter ordered
that "Tomorrow, Thursday, Corpus Christi Day, . . . after the singing of
the hours there shall be sung the shortest mass in the Morales book" (*aca-
badas las horas successivamente se diga la misa cantada lo mas breve del libro de
Morales*).

Unlike the Ávila, Cordova, Seville, Tarazona, and Toledo cathedrals,
that at Málaga today preserves no compositions by Morales, even though
he was her most distinguished *maestro de capilla*. Nor was any commemoration of his fourth centenary observed at Málaga in 1953. On the other
hand, Guerrero's magnificats, a volume of his masses, and another containing vespers music for the whole year are still extant in her cathedral
archive. Thus it would seem that Guerrero, who renounced the chapelmastership, has continued to enjoy greater honor at Málaga than Morales,
who held it.

The only sacred music by Morales still surviving which conjecturally
may be connected with his last few years is an anonymous Requiem mass
in a large choirbook (folios 127[v]-141) now conserved at Santiago parish
church in Valladolid. The copyist of this particular codex was Diego
Sánchez, who fervently admired Guerrero and served under him as *maestro
de canto llano* at the Seville Cathedral in the late 1590's.[215] Along with the
Requiem there are to be found in this Santiago codex nineteen Morales
motets. *Accepit Jesus panes*, the four-voice motet at folios 34[v]-35, does not
bear an ascription, but is known to be his because it concords with the
motet at folios 30[v]-31 in the Biblioteca Medinaceli MS 13230 ascribed to
"Morales." At folios 141[v]-149 in the Valladolid Santiago codex is copied,
without title, a four-voice mass known from concordances in the Medinaceli MS 607 and the Tarazona MS 1 to be Morales's *Caça* Mass. On purely
circumstantial grounds it could be contended that the Valladolid codex
now belonging to Santiago parish would be one of the likeliest manuscripts
in which to look for a "lost" work of Morales's later years because of the
date, the Sevillian provenience, the large number of pieces correctly as-

cribed to Morales, the fact that *Accepit Jesus* is his despite its anonymity in the Santiago codex, and the discovery that the only other mass in the codex is Morales's. That toward the end of his life Morales did write a Requiem for the fourth Count of Ureña can be learned from Juan Bermudo, who said (*Declaración* [1555], Bk. V, chap. 32):[216]

Fa against *mi* [a diminished fifth] is usually considered a prohibited interval. . . but you will often find it in Gombert's work, though in minims [unreduced]. In my opinion, another composer prepares this forbidden interval even better— namely the excellent Cristóbal de Morales. In a Requiem Mass that he wrote for the Count of Ureña [Juan Téllez Girón (1494–1558)], in the introit verse *Te decet* at the words "votum in Hierusalem" one finds the following passage:

The aforementioned interval (sounded between the tenor and bass) is here prepared in two ways: first, by the octave between bass and alto, and second, the stationary position of the tenor on B♭. Because the tenor does not change pitch when the diminished fifth is sounded the interval does not seem to have been struck and does not make a harsh effect. The octave between bass and alto comes in so gracefully and smoothly that no disturbance is created. Any singers can sound the diminished fifth—if prepared in these two ways—with the greatest ease. I hold in no slight esteem this feat [of Morales's] because it is [one of] the most delicate and beautiful that I have seen.

In the anonymous Requiem at Valladolid, a passage strikingly similar to the one quoted by Bermudo occurs, and in precisely the same place: that is to say, at the words "votum in Hierusalem" during the introit verse *Te decet*. The passage in the Santiago codex reads thus (measures 42-44):

in Hie - ru - sa - lem

It will of course be readily admitted that whereas the diminished fifth occurs at the same place, the alto, on the other hand, reads differently in the Santiago codex. A reason for its moving from *d* to *G* can be found: the melodic line in the three previous bars hovers so constantly around *f* and *e* that to have repeated *f–e* yet again in the alto would have created this tedious melodic line: *f–e, f–e, f–e*. Whether or not the dissimilarities between the two examples are more important than the similarities will be a problem that can perhaps be settled only after the whole Requiem is published in an appendix to Morales's *Opera omnia*. In the meantime, however, the statement that manuscript versions of Morales's music never differ significantly among themselves must be vigorously impugned. In *Accepit Jesus panes*—the motet that is anonymous in the Santiago source but identifiable as Morales's because of a Medinaceli concordance—the bass of the Santiago version is, for instance, quite different at mm. 73–74 from the bass of the Medinaceli version; so is the treble at mm. 74–76.

The Count of Ureña (who had succeeded to the title in 1531 when he was thirty-seven) was a principal lay benefactor of the Málaga cathedral during Morales's term as chapelmaster. The count's name appears frequently in the capitular acts, and all the entries show the extraordinarily high regard in which he was held by bishop and canons alike. A typical entry showing the esteem in which Bishop Manrique held him even in matters strictly spiritual, may be quoted: "His Reverence the Bishop ordered that since the Count of Ureña has sent notice of his particular devotion to the feast of the Immaculate Conception, special preparations for the day, which comes on December 8, must be made well in advance."[217]

[The count] had an imposing presence and a venerable face; he was a little above medium height . . . his voice was refined and agreeable. He had a keen intellect, was of prudent judgment and affectionate disposition. . . . He was carefully brought up during his youth, and studied [Latin] grammar and music extensively, in which two disciplines he was a consummate scholar, for he could read any Latin book on whatever subject and understand it immediately, translating it with ease. His musicianship was such that however difficult the part, he could sing it easily at sight with both expression and dexterity. He composed various works that sounded very agreeably.[218]

From this description, written shortly after his death, the count can be seen to have been a cultivated patron. He founded the collegiate church at Osuna in 1534. Fifteen years later he established the University of Osuna, hoping to raise it to equal rank with the University at Alcalá de Henares. From the presses of the Osuna University printer Juan de León ("impressor dela universidad del illustrissimo señor Don Juan Tellez Giron, Conde de Urueña") both first and second editions of Bermudo's magnum opus, the *Declaración de instrumentos*, were issued (1549 and 1555, respectively). Juan

Vásquez was a third Andalusian musician in addition to Morales and Bermudo who benefited from this count's largesse—his first book of *Villancicos i canciones* having been published at Osuna in the year that Morales became chapelmaster at Málaga. Rarely in Spanish musical history has one noble patron joined his name to so many distinguished musical enterprises as Juan Téllez Girón.

Masses In contrast to such immediate contemporaries as Gombert, Arcadelt, and Crecquillon, Morales eschewed the writing of secular music. Sacred compositions occupied him almost exclusively; and in the sacred field he showed his mettle when he chose so exalted an area as the mass for his favorite personal territory. No other composer of his generation approaches him in sheer number of masses. Gombert composed but ten; of which seven saw publication during his lifetime. Arcadelt apparently wrote no more than three. Festa, who with Arcadelt was the most important composer among the papal singers in Morales's decade, wrote only two. Willaert, the best-known composer of sacred music in northern Italy during Morales's time, left less than ten masses. Both Crecquillon and Jachet of Mantua [Jaquet Collebaud de Vitré (d. before 1559)] left approximately fourteen. Morales wrote at least twenty-one; of which sixteen were published under his personal supervision at Rome (Valerio and Ludovico Dorico, brothers) in 1544.

Not only did Morales take the weightiest and most demanding type of sacred music for his specialty but he also stamped his masses (rather than his magnificats or motets) as his personally preferred masterpieces by choosing them, and them only, for publication *in magno volumine*. Nothing but his sixteen masses can be shown to have been published under his personal supervision. Nothing else was sent forth with formal dedications. True, he was not the first composer whose masses were used to make up an entire volume. Petrucci had so honored Josquin in 1502, 1505, and 1514; La Rue in 1503; and Mouton in 1515. Neither were Morales's masses the first to be printed in a monumental folio volume. Andrea Antico had pioneered in that direction with his *Liber quindecim missarum* (Rome: 1516) collected from Josquin, Brumel, Févin, La Rue, Mouton, Pipelare, and Rosselli. But Morales seems to have been the first in Italy to have brought out his own works in so luxurious a format, and at his personal risk.[219]

As far as source material is concerned, his masses fall into the following categories: (1) seven parodied after motets by such Franco-Flemish masters as Gombert, Mouton, Richafort, and Verdelot;[220] (2) six founded on plainsong themes—one of these being a canonic mass (*Ave maris stella*), another a tenor mass (*Tu es vas electionis*), and the others paraphrase masses;[221] (3) three based on French secular tunes, of which two are on *L'Homme armé* and one on the superius of the Josquin chanson that was the favorite of Charles V—*Mille regretz*; (4) three built on Spanish secular songs; (5) two constructed on solmization syllables. It was the masses in these last two categories which were either not ready for publication or were held back deliberately in 1544. Classified not on the basis of source material but according to the technique of composition, one is canonic, one is a "treble" mass, three are tenor masses, seven are parodies, and nine are paraphrases. The *Ave Maria* and *Desilde al caballero*, although predominantly paraphrase masses, contain tenor movements.

Eight of Morales's published and four of his unpublished masses are for four voices; six of his published and one unpublished are for five voices; and two of the published are for six voices. Or, summarizing, 12 are *a 4*, 7 *a 5*, and 2 *a 6*. Of Gombert's ten masses, on the other hand, only 4 are *a 4*, whereas 4 are *a 5* and 2 are *a 6*. Morales holds the range of individual voices within a ninth or tenth, widening to as much as an eleventh in only rare instances. The highest written note in his published masses is g^2, and the lowest, F_1. Two of his masses *a 4*—*Vulnerasti cor meum* and *Ave Maria*— were published at Venice in 1542 and 1544 in collections for "equal voices"—the combined outer vocal limits in the latter extending to only the double octave. In his other published masses the combined vocal limits usually reach a double octave plus a fifth or sixth. By way of exception the outer limits in his five-voice *L'Homme armé* reach from F_1 to f^1—a triple octave. The particular voices used in any Morales mass, whether a high or low set, definitely tend to match the emotional tone that he was wishing to establish.

At the end of each published mass, except those *a 6*, he increases the number of voices (last Agnus). In the last Agnus of *Benedicta es celorum Regina* and *Ave Maria*, indeed, he adds not one but two extra voices. By other means as well—stiffening the texture with canon, presenting a borrowed theme with unwonted simplicity in treble or tenor, or combining an unusually large number of melodic strands from his source motet—he always reaches upward for a climax in the last Agnus. Outer movements of the five main sections of the ordinary are invariably scored full. In his published masses (1544), he scores only one movement for duo: the isolated example being the Pleni of his five-voice *Ave maris stella* Mass. Gombert on the other hand included movements for duo in no less than five of his ten masses;[222] *Da pacem* and *Je suis desheritée* (both *a 4*) contain two duos each. Although Morales seized the opportunity to lighten texture by interspersing duos in both his Tone III and Tone VI Magnificats, he only once reduces below a trio or quartet in his 1544 masses.[223] Occasionally in a four-voice mass for SATB he finds another way to vary the texture: by calling for a novel quartet in solo movements—AATB in the Benedictus of *Tu es vas electionis* and SSAA in the Benedictus of *Benedicta es celorum Regina*, for instance.[224]

In all except three of his masses, Morales uses either ₵ or C for his basic mensuration sign. Significantly, the two published masses that make much use of triple meter (signature: O) were his only two published tenor masses; were both written specifically for musical patrons who counted themselves rather learned; and are both to be found in Book II—*Tu es vas electionis* and the four-voice *L'Homme armé*. The fourteen other masses contain but a handful of movements in triple meter; and never do these movements make use of "mood perfect of the less prolation" (signature: O). On the contrary, they carry the signature ₵ $\frac{3}{2}$. Throughout the fourteen masses basically in ₵ or C, individual movements in triple meter (throughout) are indeed so scarce that only ten are to be found; and these ten are all Osannas.[225] The signature of these, moreover, is "proportional"—and rightly so, since it was always Morales's intention when using ₵ $\frac{3}{2}$ for a signature in his Osannas to indicate that three semibreves must equal in duration a breve of the preceding Pleni or Benedictus.

Although there are only ten movements in triple meter in Morales's fourteen published duple-meter masses, he weaves a considerable number of passing interludes into his duple-meter movements which involve a momentary shift into triple meter. The proportional signature in these brief interludes is not ₵ $\frac{3}{2}$ but rather the numeral, 3. The 3 signifies that three semibreves of the intruded triple-meter passage must equal in duration a breve of the surrounding duple-meter music. Instant confirmation of this rule may be found in the mass that opens his first book—the *De beata Virgine, a 4*. At bar 51 of the Credo, the proportion starts a breve later in the tenor[226] than in the other voices. As a result, the tenor must sing two semibreves ("fa - ctum") against three semibreves ("con-sub-stan-") in the other already proportioned voices.

If theoretical as well as practical confirmation of Morales's rules for proportional signatures is desired, it is readily available in Juan Bermudo's *Declaración de instrumentos* of 1555.[227] If a proportional mensuration sign is used at the beginning of a movement and applies to all voices, "two numerals must be used in the signature," declares Bermudo. "Do not imagine that this rule is the mere whim of theoreticians," he adds, "for the most learned practitioners abide by it and consider it an essential rule; observe, for instance, what the eminent Cristóbal de Morales has done in the Osanna of his *De beata Virgine* Mass and in others of his sixteen masses, and profit by his example." On the subject of the 3 as a proportional signature, Bermudo writes as follows: "The foregoing rule calling for two numerals allows of an exception when one voice shifts into proportion for but a few measures: in which case use only the single numeral [3]. . . . In the masses of the famous Cristóbal de Morales will be found such use of the single numeral, and this practice prevails generally throughout Spain.''[228]

Still a further use to which Moralas put the Ⓟ$\frac{3}{2}$ signature must next be considered—its use after a movement not in ₵ but after one in Ⓞ. A highly instructive example occurs in his phrygian *L'Homme armé*. Agnus I carries Ⓞ as its signature, but Agnus II (the last Agnus) bears Ⓟ$\frac{3}{2}$. The proportional signature can in this context be proved beyond reasonable doubt to mean that the semibreve in Agnus II must go much faster than in Agnus I. We need only observe that although both Ⓞ and Ⓟ$\frac{3}{2}$ call for three semibreves in the bar, Agnus I contains no less than eighteen quavers (unreduced values); whereas Agnus II includes no quavers, and indeed but one lone crotchet.[229]

Not only Ⓞ and Ⓟ$\frac{3}{2}$ but also ₵ and ₵ implied definite tempo distinctions in Morales's mind. Proof is at hand in the three Agnuses of his five-voice *L'Homme armé*. Agnuses I and III carry ₵ as signature; Agnus II carries ₵. The outer Agnuses are scored for five and six voices respectively. The inner Agnus is scored for three voices: SAT. Quite apart from any considerations of signature, the heavily scored movements at once suggest a more ponderous tempo, and the solo movement for light, high voices, a quicker speed. Harmonic analysis shows that the bass in the outer movements clogs the speed, its skips often producing so many as three or four chord-changes in the bar. For relief, he thins the texture in Agnus II and allows the alto and tenor to glide up and down the scale in innocuous parallel thirds. Still further evidence that Morales distinguished between ₵ and ₵ comes to light in his five-voice *De beata Virgine*. The Kyries carry ₵ as signature; the Gloria and Credo movements bear ₵. The more "soulful" Kyrie movements boast no less than ten printed accidentals (1544 copy). The much-longer Gloria (divided into Et in terra, Qui tollis, and Cum Sancto Spiritu movements) shows a total of but four.[230]

Another mensuration sign (used only once in his published masses) remains for mention—the "cut-time" signature printed in reverse: ⱷ. Morales uses the retorted signature in conjunction with the normal sign ₵ in this fashion: ⱷ₵ (the movement in which this combination occurs being the Sanctus of his *Ave Maria* Mass: tenor voice). The sense of this double signature is as follows: first sing the tenor-part through in the written values; and then at the repeat diminish the values by one-half. The repeat sign at the close of the tenor in this movement reads thus, ·:‖ :

Returning again to Bermudo for a theorist's approval of the ways in which Morales uses Ⓞ and Ⓟ, ₵ and ₵, and ₵ and ⱷ, we find the following information. "₵ in comparison with ₵ is *dupla* proportion, just as Ⓞ is in relation to Ⓟ."[231] Bermudo adds that the retorting of imperfect time signatures is another—though less commonly used—way of signifying *dupla* proportion: a statement that is echoed by numerous foreign theorists from

Zarlino to Morley. According to Bermudo, Spanish singers did not always distinguish between C and ¢ —often hurrying C movements so that they sounded as if written in ¢.[232] But this fault he attributes to their ignorance or impatience. Morales, he assures us, was always *doctissimo* in his use of proportional signatures.[233]

The next interesting aspect of Morales's metric practice is his use of opposing rhythms. These include not only threes against twos after the manner of Josquin des Prez's *Missa Hercules dux Ferrariae* (Gloria, mm. 88-93) but also threes against eights after the manner of the elder master's *De beata Virgine* Mass (Credo, mm. 184-190). In the latter instance, Josquin used three sets of three black breves each in his superius to set the words, "Who [the Holy Spirit] with the Father and the Son"—perhaps with symbolical intent. On the two occasions when Morales employs three black breves to indicate that three breves in one voice must occupy the time of two breves (eight minims) in the other voices, he uses them to set the word "Christ" in Christe eleison movements.[234] The first use is in the *Ave maris stella* Mass (mm. 35-36) and the second in *Mille regretz* (mm. 28-29). So unusual, however, did these three black breves seem to musicians of the subsequent century who were familiar with only the peninsular repertory, that Alvares Frouvo (1602-1682; librarian to the royal music savant João IV) wrote a learned treatise, *Discursos sobre a perfeiçam* (Lisbon: 1662), the purpose of which—at least in part—was to show that Morales had not erred when he wrote *os três breves negros* as a means of notating the cross-rhythm of three breves against eight minims; but on the contrary knew perfectly well what he was doing.[235]

The number of times in his masses that Morales pits three minims against two is considerably greater than the number of times that he writes three breves against eight minims—fifteen instances having been inventoried in Book I and two in Book II. This inventory is of more than academic interest, because in the first place it discloses that the cross-rhythm of three against two does not occur merely at random. On the contrary, this cross-rhythm is clustered in a few masses that for other reasons can be presumed to have been his earliest. All twos against threes thus far noted in his published masses are clustered in the *De beata Virgine* Masses (the four-voice in Book I, the five-voice in Book II), *Vulnerasti cor meum*, *Ave maris stella*, *L'Homme armé* (the five-voice in Book I), *Mille regretz*, and *Si bona suscepimus*. The highest incidence is found in *Mille regretz*—the 1544 printed version showing six instances.[236] (The version of this particular mass published in 1544 was reworked from the considerably more "Gothic" version copied in Cappella Sistina MS 17 and later published with an erroneous attribution to Crecquillon in 1568.[237]) *Ave maris stella*—after *Mille regretz* the mass with the highest incidence—is a canonic exercise written (so it would appear) in competition with the *Ave maris stella* of Josquin. However, Josquin brought forward his canons only in his three Agnuses. Both Morales's *De beata Virgine* Masses can be presumed to have been early compositions from the fact that both were published in Venetian collections as early in 1540: already before 1540 they must have circulated widely to make commercial printing a profitable venture. Of the remaining masses, the five-voice *L'Homme armé* was published also in 1540 in a Venetian commercial collection, and the *Vulnerasti cor meum* in 1542 in a similar collection. Thus, all seven of his masses with the cross-rhythm of two against three were published before 1543 (except the *Ave Maria*, which shows other archaic features). Significantly, none published for the first time in commercial collections after 1542 makes any use of this two-against-three rhythmic tag.

To the list of Morales's published masses exploiting cross-rhythms must be added one unpublished mass—the five-voice *Tristezas me matan* extant today only in the same Cappella Sistina MS 17 at the Vatican which contains the obsolete version of *Mille regretz*. If what has been deduced concerning earlier and later manners holds true, the very presence of twos-against-threes in this mass provides strong a priori argument for placing it among his earliest essays. Passages involving the rhythm

$\overset{3}{\wideparen{\rho\cdot\ \rho}}\ \rho(=\overset{3}{\wideparen{\rho\cdot\ \rho}}\ \rho$ in modern transcription) or $\overset{3}{\wideparen{\rho\ \rho}}\ \rho(=\overset{3}{\wideparen{\rho\ \rho}}\ \rho)$

in one voice while the others sing notes equaling two minims (= crotchets in transcription) begin so early as the second Kyrie (mm. 52, 58-59), and occur again in the Patrem (meas. 33), Agnus I (mm. 37, 41, 44, 46) and Agnus III (meas. 83). Two objective pieces of evidence can be added to the argument for an early date. *Tristezas*, a tenor mass written with a Spanish ditty for its *cantus firmus*, was copied into Capella Sistina MS 17 while Morales was still a member of the choir.[238] It therefore must have been in his portfolio before 1535—there being no likely reason why he should have composed so Spanish a mass while in the pope's service. Second, the Kyries are bitextual—the tenor singing in Spanish these doleful words: "Sorrows slay me—unhappy me; her whom I most desire I see with another who is enjoying himself and laughing—ah, unhappy me!"[239]

Yet another type of rhythmic opposition finds its way into Morales's masses. Quite frequently he writes short passages in which the rhythmic figures suggest a different meter from that which heads the movement. For instance, in the *Tristezas me matan* Mass he writes the following rhythmic pattern in the bass at mm. 99-103 of Agnus III:

Though this passage is not heralded by a change of signature it cannot but suggest triple meter to the ear. Two of the upper voices participate in this same contradictory rhythmic figure during these very measures. In *Mille regretz* (Et iterum trio [mm. 1234-1303]) he writes the following melodic figure in the upper of the three voice parts:

The signature, as in Agnus III of *Tristezas*, remains ₵. However, no one would contest the fact that the "natural" rhythm here goes in threes. As if isolated passages in single voice parts were not enough, Morales went still a step further in his *Si bona* and his phrygian *L'Homme armé*. In the Osannas of these two masses the written meter is again ₵. But, as reference to these two Osannas will soon show, Morales might equally well have written both movements in triple meter: the first with a signature transcribable as $\frac{3}{4}$, and the second with a signature transcribable as $\frac{3}{2}$. The syncope dissonances in both Osannas, not to mention the natural contour of individual voice parts, will as happily fit $\frac{3}{4}$ and $\frac{3}{2}$ as they do ₵. Such ambivalence cannot have been accidental. In both these exulting movements Morales has stirred further excitement by opposing the written ₵ meter to an equally plausible harmonic rhythm in threes. The effect is that of some lustrous piece of satin that when flashed in one light appears as violet-colored and when in another, as gold. In addition to passages that oppose written ₵ to felt triple meter, he also writes passages ostensibly in Φ$\frac{3}{2}$ which parse naturally in duple meter. There are fewer examples because Morales wrote fewer movements with triple-meter signatures; but the close of Agnus II in the phrygian *L'Homme armé* can be adduced. The accompanying example shows the last eleven bars of this movement.

L'Homme armé Mass (four-voice)

Liber II, fols. 124ᵛ-125.   Agnus II

Morales, 1544

It would be irresponsible historical criticism to venture any claim of novelty for passages such as these. Far too many instances of the same type of rhythmic counterpointing occur in the works of Josquin, Isaac, and Brumel to allow of any such claim. But rhythmic counterpointing is a vein that Morales obviously worked with such vehemence in his masses, both published and unpublished, that often the ore extracted from his lode seems quite bright and new.

None of Morales's masses goes beyond one flat for a "key signature."[240] Moreover, printed accidentals of any sort are rare in the 1544 books. But those that do occur force us to conclude that he occasionally desired false relations of the kind that were to become a late Tudor hallmark. To diagnose only three cases: (1) no remedy for the false relation between $B_1\flat$ in the bass and $B\natural$ in the tenor of two successive chords in Kyrie II (meas. 83) of the *Ave maris stella* Mass can be found in *musica ficta*; (2) neither can a cure be found for the $e\natural$ and $e\flat$ which succeed each other (alto 1 and tenor) in Agnus I (meas. 29) of the five-voice *L'Homme armé*; (3) nor can a palliative be found for the $E\flat$ in the bass followed by $e\natural$ in alto 1 which occurs in the Osanna (mm. 82-83) of the five-voice *De beata Virgine*. As for other printed accidentals besides $B\flat$'s, $B\sharp$'s (= $B\natural$'s), $E\flat$'s, $E\sharp$'s (= $E\natural$'s)—only $F\sharp$'s and $G\sharp$'s are to be seen in the 1544 imprints. These sharps prefix closing notes in various movements of the *Ave maris stella* (Book I) and *L'Homme armé* (Book II), respectively. Strangely enough, printed $C\sharp$'s do not appear in either book.[241] But that $F\sharp$'s, $C\sharp$'s, and $G\sharp$'s found extremely frequent usage, at least when his masses were sung in Spain, is an opinion from which no one who is familiar with other lines of historical evidence dissents.

The first type of testimony supporting this view is found in the numerous vihuela intabulations. Thirteen different movements from Morales's masses are intabulated in Enríquez de Valderrábano's *Silva de sirenas* (Valladolid: 1547) and in Miguel de Fuenllana's *Orphénica lyra* (Seville: 1554). Enríquez de Valderrábano intabulated two movements, and Fuenllana, eleven.[242] Nowhere in all eleven of Fuenllana's intabulations has he altered the letter-names of the notes from those in the 1544 imprints. But the store of accidentals that he lavishes with his numerals (and which were in no wise specified in the 1544 imprints) can be inferred from the following statistics. His eleven intabulations comprise 455 measures. In the versions of these eleven

movements printed at Rome in 1544, Morales specified no more than 8
accidentals. Fuenllana in these same movements calls for 151 accidentals.
Thus, Fuenllana adds accidentals in every third measure (on average).
As a rule, Fuenllana ciphers all the voice parts of the original for the vihuelist to play; one of these parts is to be sung while being played.[243] Of
particular interest are the accidentals implied by the red numerals (used
only in the part to be sung). The intervals thereby created include at times
so surprising a melodic interval as a diminished fourth. Fuenllana's intabulation of the Et resurrexit from Morales's four-voice *L'Homme armé* is reproduced by way of example.

Missa   L'Homme armé (four-voice)

Et resurrexit

Missarum liber secundus, fols. 118ᵛ-120.

Orphénica lyra, fol. 8ᵛ.

Morales-Fuenllana

- ras ,   se - cun-dum Scri - - - -ptu -

ras.   Et a-scen - dit in coe-

lum, et a-scen - dit in coe-lum: se-det ad dex-te-ram Pa-tris.   Et

i-te-rum ven-tu-rus est cum glo- ri- a, ju-di-ca-re vi- vos

et mor- tu- os: cu-jus re- gni,

cu- jus re-gni   non   e-   rit fi-   nis.

The 1544 imprint shows not a single accidental; whereas the 1554 intabulation boasts 23—22 of which are sharps (8 G♯'s, 7 F♯'s, 7 C♯'s). In this 48-bar intabulation we need only observe the G♯-c♮ in meas. 2, the c♯-f♮ in meas. 11, the G♯-c♮ in meas. 15, the same in meas. 35, and again in meas. 45, to appreciate the consistency with which the leap of a diminished fourth was applied in the sung *bassus* as well as in the instrumental upper melody lines.

Further evidence that sharps were added lavishly is found in Bermudo's *El arte tripharia.*[244] He claims that the penult is always to be sharped when cadencing in dorian and mixolydian modes; sharps are also to be used on many other occasions. Concerning sharps that cause a diminished fourth in a melodic line, he writes:

The interval of a fourth when composed of a tone and two semitones . . . may be used, even though contrary to diatonic principles; for it does not violate the principles of semichromaticism, which is the basis of modern music. . . . No stepwise progression is more often used than semitone, tone, and semitone, making a diminished fourth. . . . I see no reason for excluding the interval when it comes in as a leap since it so constantly appears in stepwise progressions.

Leaving in abeyance the always fascinating problems posed by *musica ficta*, and returning to the 1544 imprints, we come next to the problem of modality in Morales's masses. Apart from the three choral masses (two *De beata Virgine* and *Pro defunctis*), they each adhere to one particular mode throughout—or, to say it in another way, the last chord in every movement ending a principal division of the ordinary is always the same in any one mass. (When putting this rule to the test, we must remember that in Sanctus movements the Osanna comes last, not the Benedictus. Occasionally, as in the four-voice *De beata Virgine* and the *Vulnerasti cor*, Morales wrote a new Osanna to succeed the Benedictus. As a rule, however, he simply indicated *Osanna ut supra*.) The initial or intermediate movements in any main division of the ordinary end either on the same chord as that which closes last movements in these five main divisions; or they end on a chord plagally or authentically related to the final. To illustrate from masses without flat in the signature: (1) if the final is D, initial and intermediate movements may end on A (example: *Gaude Barbara*); (2) if the final is E, initial and intermediate movements may end on A (*Mille regretz* and four-voice *L'Homme armé*); (3) if the final is G, initial and intermediate movements may end C (*Benedicta es celorum Regina*); (4) if the final is C, initial and intermediate movements may end on G (*Quem dicunt homines*). To illustrate, next, with masses carrying B♭ in the signature: (1) with finals on F, initials and intermediates may end on C (*Quaeramus cum pastoribus*, five-voice *L'Homme armé*, and *Tu es vas electionis*); (2) with finals on G, initials and intermediates may end on D (*Aspice Domine, Vulnerasti cor,* and *Ave Maria*); (3) with finals on A, initials and intermediates may end on D (*Si bona suscepimus*).[245] The ratio of movements ending on chords plagally or authentically related to the closing chord of final movements varies from mass to mass. *Ave maris stella* (no flat in signature) contains 15 movements, or 16 if we count the *da capo* of the Osanna which comes after the Benedictus as a new movement. Of these, every movement ends uniformly on the D chord. (This mass, a canonic tour de force, is exceptional in more than one way.) *Vulnerasti cor meum* (B♭ in signature) contains 15 movements, and here the first Osanna is set to music entirely different from the second. Of these 15 movements, 14 end on G chords, and 1 ends on a D chord. Similarly in the four-voice *L'Homme armé,* every movement but one ends on an E chord—the exceptional movement ending on an A chord. Coming down the scale, the printed *Mille regretz* runs to 15 movements ending on E (Osanna counted twice) and 2 ending on A; the five-voice *L'Homme armé* shows 15 ending on F and 2 on C. Without troubling to enumerate the intermediate examples, it may be said that at the opposite end of the scale comes *Si bona suscepimus* with 16 movements (Osanna counted twice), less than half of which end on A—although this is the chord on which the last movement in each of the five major divisions of the ordinary closes. Nine movements of *Si bona suscepimus* end on the D chord.

These figures may not sound very remarkable. Yet Morales's practices (1) of concluding every major division of the ordinary with an identical chord, (2) of using no more than one other cadencing chord at the close of initial and intermediate movements, and then (3) of so disposing this alternate ending chord that it always lies a fourth or fifth away from the main final, certainly show greater consistency than is to be found in Gombert, or even for that matter in Josquin. Gombert closes the final movements of the ordinary on the following chords in *Media vita*: G–A–A–G–A. Not only does he therefore break Morales's rule by ending on different chords but he goes further and chooses chords that are distant from each other by a whole step rather than by a fourth or fifth. In his coronation mass *Sur tous regretz,* Gombert ends consistently on the G chord until the close of the last Agnus, which ends on D instead.[246] In *Je suis desheritée* he transgresses another of Morales's rules by choosing two, rather than just one, intermediate cadencing chords. The principal cadencing chord is that of D; but two movements end on an F chord (Christe and Qui tollis) and three end on an A chord (Et in terra, Patrem, and Agnus I).[247] Or to compare Josquin's masses: *La sol fa re mi* ends on E until the Agnuses, which end on A instead; and *Malheur me bat* similarly ends on E until the last two Agnuses—the final Agnus sinking into G for a closing chord instead. No one who has studied Morales's art has failed to be impressed by his consistency. The uniformity with which he adheres to his own rules of modal usage strongly confirms that impression. If his consistency does not necessarily make him the greater artist, it at least stamps him as a craftsman who was remarkably loyal to his principles.

Morales did not label his six-voice *Si bona suscepimus* "Mode IV," his four-voice *Tu es vas* "Mode VI," his *Benedicta es* "Mode VIII,"[248] his *Aspice Domine* and his *Ave Maria* "Mode II." But such will be their proper classifications if the tenor voice dictates the modes to which they belong. It is, of course, well known that he labeled his magnificats "primi toni," "secundi toni," and so forth. He classified the magnificats, which are all basically *a 4*, by tenors: not basses. The masses call for similar classification by tenors. To do otherwise would not only contravene the theorizing of Aron (1525)[249] but would also run counter to the practice of so renowned a master as Josquin. It was, of course, the latter who named a mass in which the bass ranges between F_1 and F while the tenor ranges between C and c, *L'Homme armé sexti toni*—a classification he could never have given it had he looked to the bass to determine the mode.

Peninsular theorists from Juan Gil to Bermudo agreed in teaching that each of the modes had the power of arousing quite distinct emotions. If Morales (who claimed for himself some erudition in his preface to his *Missarum liber primus*) was at all influenced by their teachings on the emotional connotations of the modes, then it must be believed (1) that not only would he have classified his published masses according to their tenors but also (2) that he would have selected modes for each that express a suitable emotion. How these two corollary facts may both be true can easily be illustrated: first from his pair of *L'Homme armé* masses. Classified by their tenors rather than basses, the five-voice (Book I) belongs to Mode V and the four-voice (Book II) to Mode III. According to Ramos, these modes respectively signify major good fortune and martial enterprise.[250] Classified by its bass, on the other hand, the four-voice *L'Homme armé* would belong to Mode IV—which, according to Ramos and Bermudo,[251] is the mode of Mercury, not Mars. If Morales had a martial rather than mercurial mood to express, this mass ought to belong to the mode of its tenor. Fortunately, he has left us an unmistakable clue to his meaning. Heading the treble of this as well as every other mass in his 1544 books is a huge ornamental "K". The woodcut at the beginning of the four-voice *L'Homme armé* shows a crowned and bearded warrior, his eyes as well as his sword being uplifted. Atop his crown is a cross, and further above one reads the motto *plus ultra*. This obviously can be no "mercurial armed man." On the evidence of the identifying motto, the warrior is none other than Charles V.[252] An entirely different warrior—beardless, helmeted rather than crowned, eyes front rather than gazing upward, and without identifying motto—

appears in the woodcut preceding the five-voice *L'Homme armé*. Morales would hardly have undergone the expense of two different woodcuts had he not conceived the Jove and Mars masses on different levels of emotion—which correspond neatly with their tenor modes.

We come next to *Quaeramus cum pastoribus*. In 1525 Aron classified Mouton's joyous Christmas motet as belonging to Mode V.[253] Obviously Morales's parody mass *a 5* ought equally to belong to Mode V—the mode that Ramos associated with *fortuna major* and which he said is always used to "denote joy." On the other hand, Mode VI—in which the mass would have to be classified if basses rather than the tenor determine mode—"provokes to pious tears." Morales again comes to our aid with a clue to his intentions. Heading the treble of *Quaeramus*, as well as all the other masses published under his personal supervision, a distinctive woodcut has been inserted. In this cut, two bearded shepherds adore the Christ-child. Between the shepherds stand kine. Above floats an angel with arms outstretched. This can be only a moment of sheer joy; not an occasion for "contrite" or "pious" tears.

Or two other examples: *Vulnerasti cor meum*, a four-voice in Book I, would belong to Mode II if classified by its bass; if by its tenor, to Mode I. Aron in 1525 attributed the source motet to Antoine de Févin,[254] Josquin's "gifted emulator," and assigned it to Mode I. The text is taken from Song of Songs 4:9-10—"Thou hast ravished my heart . . . How fair is thy love! how much better than wine! and the smell of thine ointments than all spices!" Mode I, according to Ramos in 1482, "raises all earthly exhalations and marine vapors by the rays of the sun." Mode II, on the contrary, is the mode of phlegm and humid humors. With these dicta Bermudo in 1555 agreed emphatically, adding: "All joyous, uplifted, and gracious texts may properly be set in Mode I."[255] If the mood of the source motet at all influences the mass—as the woodcut of Christ's mystical spouse heading the *Vulnerasti* mass certainly suggests—then Mode I rather than II befits the mass, just as surely as it befits the motet. On the other hand, *Aspice Domine*, which precedes *Vulnerasti cor* in Book I, belongs to Mode II if tenor rather than bass determines mode. In *pars 1* of the source, Gombert's four-voice *Aspice*[256] motet, the text is that of the antiphon sung on Saturday evening before the second Sunday in November: "Behold, Lord, how desolate has become the city which was filled with riches, how she who was mistress of nations sits in sorrow with none to console her except Thou, Our God." That Morales was bent not only on parodying the notes but also on recapturing the desolate mood of Gombert's motet in his mass can be deduced from the woodcut again adorning the intial "K." We see an old man, his head heavily swathed in rolls of sackcloth, his hands clasped. He gazes up at a crucifix from which emanate rays piercing the gloom. Mode II, which according to both Ramos and Bermudo exhales dark, moist, nocturnal humors, was obviously an appropriate choice if Morales placed any credence in such modal doctrine as his two compatriots taught.

Morales again wisely chooses his mode, if the tenor determines the classification, in *Si bona suscepimus*—one of his two six-voice masses. The source motet by Verdelot sets Job 2:10 ("If we have received good things at the hand of God, why should we not receive evil?"). In the woodcut heading this mass Job appears in all his nakedness; above him is spread the motto: "The Lord gave, the Lord taketh away." On the evidence of the woodcut Morales intends here, as in the other examples thus far adduced, to catch the exact mood of his source motet. The hypophrygian mode belongs to Mercury, declared both Ramos and Bermudo. Mercury can "turn with equal ease to evil and good, to sadness and gladness, to excitement and to sedation." The motet text states explicitly that God rains down good and evil; Job's case proves it; and the motto at the head of the mass tells the same tale. The mode could not be more aptly chosen if the mass, as its tenor implies, belongs to the hypophrygian; and if practicing composers accepted such theories as both Ramos and Bermudo taught. That such an inherent emotional quality was indeed discerned in this mode as late as 1578 can be learned from Palestrina's letter written on November 1 to Guglielmo Gonzaga, Duke of Mantua; in it he said that Mode IV lacks brightness.[257] He also declared that he would have to transpose a *canto fermo* from this mode to make it suitable for a mass the Duke wished him to work on. If Palestrina so regarded the mode, then Ramos and Bermudo were no mere pedants when they gave it so distinctive a personality.

However much one argues over the correct way to classify Morales's masses modally—or however one regards the "modal characteristics" theories propounded by Fernand Esteban of Seville in 1410, Ramos de Pareja of Baeza in 1482, and Juan Bermudo of Écija in 1555—Morales obviously intended each mass to express some one distinctive emotion; which was not exactly the same even when (as with the two *De beata Virgine* Masses and the two *L'Homme armé*) he chose identical source material and identical titles. The woodcuts heading the two *De beata Virgine* differ, just as the number of voices differ. Moreover, the musical treatment, although consistent throughout in each individual mass, differs greatly from one to the other.

As for the woodcuts which adorn the initial capitals of the other masses: the Queen of Heaven with stars surrounding her belongs appropriately with the five-voice *Ave maris stella* Mass; the apostle Paul reading from a book belongs appropriately with the four-voice *Tu es vas*; and Christ giving the keys to Peter belongs appropriately with the five-voice *Quem dicunt homines*. A woodcut of a skeleton (spade in hand) digging a fresh grave precedes the five-voice *Pro defunctis*: it was of this particular Requiem mass that Ambros wrote as follows:[258]

The *Missa pro defunctis*, though magnificent, inspires terror. One shivers in the presence of this somber, nocturnal masterpiece. One feels as if he were wandering in dark hollows beneath leaden vaults supported by heavy pillars. In it, all adornment has been stripped away, and everything is as plain as could be. Before the face of death all colors fade, and all gaiety ceases. Morales, the Spaniard, conceives death in all its terrible seriousness. . . . Coming from his Requiem immediately upon that of Palestrina, one is struck by the strange feeling that into the blackness of the graves has shot a ray of heavenly light, and that the stern messenger from an unknown land whom Morales presented to us has given way to an angel, serious but benign. One should always hear these two works in succession.

Obviously, if what Ambros wrote in any way fits the facts, then for a wood-cut symbolizing his emotional intent Morales did well to choose not an angel of reconciliation or the figure of a Judas Maccabaeus gathering 12,000 drachmas of silver "to be offered for the sins of the dead, thinking well and religiously concerning the resurrection," but a skeleton digging in the earth.

Two last woodcuts must be mentioned for what they reveal concerning the history of *Mille regretz* and of the four-voice *L'Homme armé*. The bearded and crowned "armed man" in the latter woodcut has already been identified as Charles V on the evidence of his personal motto printed above—*plus ultra*. Up to the present no commentator would seem to have observed the connection with Charles V; but it cannot be gainsaid, since this was the motto he chose upon being crowned Holy Roman Emperor. The emblem in the woodcut of *Mille regretz* is just as plainly his—a two-headed eagle with wings outstretched surmounted by a crown tipped with a cross.[259] Narváez's identification of the Josquin four-part chanson as "the emperor's song" in his intabulation (*Delphin de música*, 1538) has caught the attention of music historians on several occasions. But until this recent discovery of the iconographic evidence, it has been merely a matter of conjecture that Morales's mass based on "la canción del emperador" was intended for Charles V. Since *Mille regretz* and the four-voice *L'Homme armé* can both be said to have been composed for the emperor on the strength of this new evidence, the problem of dating is somewhat simplified. During his service in the papal choir, Morales came into the emperor's presence on three occasions: in April, 1536; May, 1538; and June, 1543. The earlier dates, 1536 and 1538, seem likelier for *Mille regretz*, at least in the obsolete version now preserved in Cappella Sistina MS 17. The facts that Morales replaced the original canonic Sanctus by an "accompanied-treble" setting, the original Pleni for only $C_{II}A_{II}B$ by a five-voice setting, an Osanna in ¢ by one in Φ³₂, a Benedictus departing from the chanson by one adhering to it, and Agnus I and Agnus III by other settings of the same, show that he was not wholly satisfied with the original version. His 1544 version is a much more homogeneous and consistent work of art. It does not show so much learning, but the new Sanctus and Agnus movements at least carry forward with the same kind of treatment that in both the Capella Sistina MS 17 version and the 1544 printed version had been given the chanson in the Kyrie, Gloria, and Credo movements: that is to say, they make of the chanson tune an accompanied treble throughout the entire mass.

Since Morales in so many other ways showed remarkable consistency, it will perhaps be worth noting that: (1) the emperor's masses, and they alone, are in E-modes; (2) A, Morales's intermediate final, is used for a closing chord in but one *L'Homme armé* movement and but two *Mille regretz* movements; (3) each occupies an analogous position in its book—coming seventh; (4) each is followed by a mass that is the most somber in its book— *Si bona* recalling Job in his nakedness and misery (Book I), and *Pro defunctis* dealing with death and the judgment (Book II).

Morales's "detail technique" in his masses cannot here be analyzed with the thoroughness it deserves. A statistical approach such as Jeppesen used in studying Palestrina's detail technique has yet to be applied, and probably should not even be attempted until the Spanish Institute of Musicology edition has more nearly reached completion. However, the following observations may prove of value until a scholarly monograph on the subject can be published. (1) Morales's detail technique was somewhat more refined than that of Gombert, if anticipating Palestrina's rules is a sign of refinement. (2) The very mass that seems to show the largest incidence of "incomplete" changing notes (eighteen instances)[260] is *Aspice Domine*, his one mass parodied after a Gombert motet. (3) Dissonance of the escaped-note or "incomplete" changing note variety does not occur in either of his Spanish masses, *Tristezas me matan* and *Desilde al caballero*, which were almost certainly composed before 1535. (4) Dissonance of these same two types is extremely rare in another mass that is manifestly one of Morales's earliest—the four-voice *De beata Virgine* (anthologized in 1540)—only a single "incomplete" changing-note, a single upper neighboring note (unreduced crotchet), and a single escaped note having been inventoried. (5) No matter how the bass moves, Morales takes pains to see that the tenor and soprano make satisfactory two-part counterpoint when extracted: for this reason he never writes parallel fourths between them, although he often does so between tenor and alto, or alto and soprano.

In support of the contention that Morales's detail technique much more frequently anticipates Palestrina's than does Gombert's (although Gombert outlived Morales), a brief comparison of the Fleming's four-voice *Aspice Domine* with the Spaniard's parody mass must be attempted. In 193 bars, Gombert introduces 8 incomplete changing-notes—more than Morales usually allows himself in an entire mass.[261] Though he has fallen under Gombert's influence to the extent that he uses them more freely in his *Aspice Domine* Mass, Morales has used only 18 in 701 bars. Gombert has used an escaped note 6 times; Morales in his mass, 9 times.[262] But what is more significant is the fact that Morales, like Palestrina, has always leaped upward from the escaped note. Twice, however, Gombert jumps downward.[263] The dissonance in Gombert is much more protuberant—especially when the escaped note is in the treble (meas. 60). Gombert does some other interesting things: he writes a skip of a seventh in crotchet-motion (unreduced values), and, moreover, above one syllable (meas. 46); he fails to resolve a suspended seventh (meas. 153); and he leaps to an unprepared dissonance (mm. 23 and 71). Morales allows himself none of these three liberties anywhere in his *Aspice Domine*, nor for that matter are such freedoms to be encountered elsewhere in his masses. True, he does once resolve a dissonant suspension upward in stepwise motion—in his canonic *Ave maris stella* Mass (Kyrie I, mm. 24-25); and once, and it would seem once only, he writes a skip of a seventh in crotchet-motion—in his five-voice *L'Homme armé* (Agnus III, meas. 112). Having cited the exceptions to be found elsewhere in Morales's masses, we can return to our first contention: namely, that he is on the whole more restrained than Gombert so far as detail technique is concerned.[264]

Morales also differs from Gombert in other respects. Among these is the large amount of canon to be found in his masses, unpublished as well as published. Gombert only by way of exception concluded with a canon in the last Agnus of his *Quam pulchra es* Mass (even then devising an entirely new type). Moreover, Morales employs the ostinato-principle more rigorously than Gombert did. In such a movement as, for instance, the Benedictus from his *Quem dicunt homines* Mass, Morales treats the following melodic fragment from the Richafort source motet as an ostinato—requiring his bass to repeat it eight times (the first four singing "Benedictus qui venit" and the last four times, "In nomine Domini").

Gombert, although he often repeated a melodic idea or sequenced it, never gave way in his masses, even in the earliest, to so rigorously contrived an ostinato. For a third matter, Morales is often bitextual, whereas Gombert in his masses is only once so.[265] Both Morales's four-voice *Ave Maria* and five-voice *De beata Virgine* are bitextual, for instance. In the Sanctus of the first, the tenor twice repeats *Ave Maria gratia plena Dominus tecum Benedicta tu in mulieribus Alleluia*—the second time going through the 32-note plainsong theme with the note values diminished by one-half. In the Osanna that follows, the tenor again repeats the same Gregorian melody (upon which, indeed, this whole mass is based). Here again, however, as in the Sanctus, the words are those of the angelical salutation, rather than those that rightly belong to this movement of the mass. In the five-voice *De beata Virgine*, Morales requires his tenor to sing the angelical salutation rather than liturgical text in the following three Credo movements: Patrem omnipotentem, Crucifixus, and Et in Spiritum Sanctum.

As if different sacred texts sung in Latin were insufficient, he went even further in his two unpublished Spanish masses by writing movements during which the tenor has a popular Spanish song for a cantus firmus. The two accompanying examples will show what is meant. The first excerpt was printed by Trend in 1925, having been transcribed for him from Cappella Sistina MS 17.[266] The second is based on the same popular tune of which Gombert availed himself in his only preserved Spanish villancico. In Gombert's villancico, true to his own characteristic methods, he made of each phrase in the original tune the head of a closely worked imitation. Regardless of how they may have regarded the problem of mixing sacred and secular elements in a mass, it is highly instructive to compare Morales's cantus firmus treatment of the tune with Gombert's madrigalesque treatment of the same popular melody. Gombert's preference in vocal texture was always for homogeneity; and in all but his two earliest masses he therefore avoided rigorous canon, cantus firmus, and extended ostinato. In all but his two six-voice masses—these being apparently his earliest—Gombert plays the role of an Orpheus who has promised Pluto never to gaze backward upon the Eurydice represented by the constructivist methods that were most highly beloved of Gombert's Flemish predecessors.

Missa Tristezas me matan

Cappella Sistina MS 17, fols. 79ᵛ-80. Kyrie I Morales

When time values have been quartered and rests between phrases have been eliminated, the tenor melody in the Kyries reads as follows:

Tris- te- zas me ma- tan, tris- te de mi [Ky- ri- e

e- le- i- son.] La que yo mas quie- ro, con o- tro la ve- o:

Hol- gan- do y rien- do, tris- te de mi [Ky- ri- e

e- le- i- son Ky- ri- e e- le- i- son.]

Missa Desilde al caballero

Sanctus

Milan: Biblioteca Ambrosiana, MS Mus. E46, fols. 47v-48.

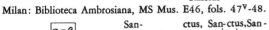
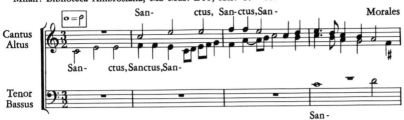

Before quitting the comparison of Gombert's technique with Morales's, we must balance the ledger somewhat by alluding to certain traits that link them as Palestrina later is linked with Victoria. (1) Both Gombert and Morales eschewed long rests in any single voice part during the course of a movement. (2) They were both fond of repeating or sequencing a melodic idea in voice I after that idea had already been bandied about in imitation through voices II, III, and IV. (3) They were at one in working their imitations at close time intervals. (4) They both kept the texture recognizably polyphonic throughout—lapsing into chords only on rare occasions. (Morales's five-voice Requiem falls outside this generalization—it being homophonic like his lamentations.) (5) Both showed a strong harmonic sense in various ways: such as by refusing to let any one voice drop out on a chord of resolution, writing many leaps of fourths and fifths in their basses, and ending sections and movements with plagal or authentic cadences rather than leading-tone cadences.

The next area into which a foray will be attempted is the notoriously treacherous and difficult one of bibliography. It must at once be confessed that it is still too early to attempt any "final" bibliography. Indeed, one editor of the masses has publicly declared that the difficult task of assembling a "complete" bibliography is not worthwhile because the editions thus far observed do not offer significantly different readings.[267] This is, of course, not true.[268] But even if it were, there are other reasons for thinking such a bibliography would be of paramount value.

In studying even a provisional bibliography, for instance, we are immediately struck by this fact: although the Book I *L'Homme armé* Mass was anthologized no less than four times in Venetian collections (1540, 1543, 1547, 1563), the Book II of the same title was not once anthologized in such a commercial collection. But on looking further, we discover that three movements of the Book II were intabulated, by Fuenllana, whereas nothing from the Book I *L'Homme armé* was intabulated in *Orphénica lyra* or in any other collection. A likely explanation would be that during his service at court Fuenllana intabulated movements from the Book II because this was the *L'Homme armé* written specifically for Charles V. The transcriptions from *Mille regretz* can be similarly explained. Although never anthologized in a Venetian collection, *Mille regretz* was excerpted for intabulation by Enríquez de Valderrábano as early as 1547, and again by Fuenllana in 1554. Moreover, there are an unusually large number of manuscript copies of *Mille regretz* in Spain[269]—it being the only mass from Book I copied into any of the polyphonic manuscripts preserved at the Real Monasterio de El Escorial, for instance.

Even a provisional bibliography will disclose such other interesting information as the fact that the two masses reprinted most frequently in vocal anthologies—the four-voice *De beata Virgine* and *Vulnerasti cor meum* (anthologized five times each at Venice)—aroused neither Enríquez de Valderrábano, Fuenllana, nor Matelart to any efforts at intabulation. On the other hand, *Benedicta es* was never anthologized in any Venetian commercial collection; yet it is the only mass copied from Book II into an El Escorial manuscript, and the one mass of the sixteen excerpted for intabulation not only in Spain (1554) but also in Italy (1559). The evidence now available therefore suggests that the masses oftenest excerpted for intabulation were liked by specific employers for personal reasons and were not necessarily the masses esteemed most highly by performing choirs in general. A bibliography of the masses, if it were really complete, could serve still other useful purposes. Certain masses, for instance, would seem to have enjoyed popularity neither with anthologists nor intabulators. Such a mass was the canonic five-voice *Ave maris stella*, a work that though great stands aloof in the same sense of Bach's *Vom Himmel hoch* set. Similarly "unsuccessful" were Morales's two distinctly papal masses, *Tu es vas* and *Quem dicunt homines*.

One final bibliographic observation must be added: Morales's two books of masses are the oldest polyphony either (1) inventoried in the New World or (2) still preserved in a Western Hemisphere archive which can be shown to have been brought over by colonists. They were inventoried as early as 1553 in the ancient Inca capital of Cuzco (see above, page 4). Extant copies are to be found in a city off the musicologist's beaten track—Puebla, Mexico. The first scholar to direct attention to the Puebla copies was the eminent Steven Barwick, who in his Harvard Ph.D. dissertation "Sacred Vocal Polyphony in Colonial Mexico" (1949) told of the treasures of Puebla Cathedral that had until then gone unnoticed.

List of Masses

Manuscript sources are mentioned only when no known sixteenth-century imprint exists. The following sixteen imprints contain masses varying anywhere in number from one to eight. In the alphabetical list below, the numerals enclosed in parentheses refer to the imprints mentioned in this paragraph.
(1) *Quinque missae Moralis Hispani, ac Jacheti musici excellentissimi: Liber primus, cum quinque vocibus* (Venice: Girolamo Scotto, 1540); (2) *Excellentissimi musici Moralis Hispani, Gomberti, ac Jacheti, cum quatuor vocibus missae . . . Liber primus* (Venice: G. Scotto, 1540); (3) *Missae cum quatuor vocibus paribus decantandae, Moralis Hispani, ac aliorum authorum* (Venice: G. Scotto, 1542); (4) *Quinque missarum harmonia diapente* [Morales and Lupus] (Venice: G. Scotto, 1543); (5) *Christophori Moralis Hyspalensis missarum: liber primus* (Rome: Valerio and Luigi Dorico, 1544); (6) *Christophori Moralis Hyspalensis missarum liber secundus* (Rome: V. and L. Dorico, 1544); (7) *Christophori Moralis Hyspalensis missarum quinque cum quatuor vocibus secundus liber* (Venice: Antonio Gardane, 1544); (8) *Liber quartus*

missarum quinque cum quatuor vocibus paribus canendarum (Venice: Ant. Gardane, 1544); (9) *Christophori Moralis Hyspalensis, missarum liber primus* (Lyons: Jacques Moderne, 1545); (10) *Quinque missarum harmonia diapente* [Morales, Jachet Berchem, and Lupus] (Venice: Ant. Gardane, 1547); (11) *Christophori Moralis Hyspalensis missarum liber secundus* (Lyons: J. Moderne, 1551); (12) *Missarum quinque cum quatuor vocibus* (Venice: Ant. Gardano, 1557); (13) *Missae quinque cum quatuor vocibus* (Venice: Rampazetto, 1563); (14) *Quinque missarum harmonia cum quinque vocibus quarum nomina* (Venice: G. Scotto, 1565); (15) *Praestantissimorum artificum lectissimae missae cum quinque tum sex vocum*, edited by Michael Voctus (Wittenberg: Johannes Schwertelius, 1568); (16) *Christophori Moralis Hyspalensis missarum quatuor cum quatuor vocibus* (Venice: Alessandro Gardano, 1580).

Aspice Domine, four-voice. (5, 7, 9, 12, 13, 16)
> In the manuscript version at the Biblioteca Medinaceli (MS 607), an intermediate Agnus II not in any of the printed versions is added.

Ave Maria, four-voice. (3, 6, 8, 11, 16)
> Et resurrexit, Osanna, and Agnus Dei intabulated by Fuenllana, *Orphénica lyra* (Seville: 1554).

Ave maris stella, five-voice. (5, 9)

Benedicta es celorum Regina,[270] four-voice. (6, 11)
> Et ascendit and Benedictus intabulated by Fuenllana. Benedictus and Osanna intabulated by Jean Matelart in *Intavolatura de leuto* (Rome: Val. Dorico, 1559).[271]

Caça, four-voice. Three handwritten copies survive: Biblioteca Medinaceli MS 607, pp. 248-259; Santiago Codex (Valladolid), folios 141ᵛ-149; Tarazona Cathedral MS 1, folios 18ᵛ-30. The single Agnus in Medinaceli MS 607 is a different piece from that in the Santiago Codex. For his parody source, Morales presumably used Mateo Flecha the Elder's ensalada *a 4*, *La Caça* (Barcelona: Biblioteca Central MS 588/2, folio 48ᵛ). Although already used as early as 1503 or 1512 in the *Cancionero Musical de Palacio* (item 447) to describe Peñalosa's *Tú, que vienes de camino*, the term *ensalada* in Mateo Flecha's usage had come to mean a through-composed piece, incorporating traditional fragments of popular verse and song, and closing with a Latin rubric. Flecha, the most vigorous and forthright secular Spanish composer of his generation, inspired Morales to write a forceful collection of F-Major movements, none of which incorporates any learned devices. Chains of melodic sequences give such movements as the Medinaceli Agnus an extremely popular flavor.

Missa Caça

Kyrie [I]

Valladolid: Santiago Codex, fol. 141ᵛ-142.

Morales

-ctus,

[two alternate settings survive]   Agnus Dei
Valladolid: Santiago codex, fol. 148ᵛ

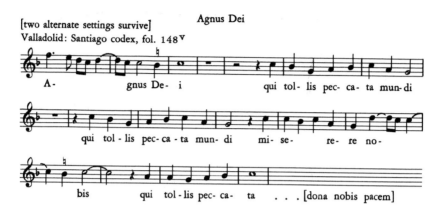

A-   gnus De- i   qui tol- lis pec- ca- ta mun-di

qui tol - lis pec- ca- ta mun- di   mi- se-   re- re no-

bis   qui tol - lis pec- ca-   ta   . . . [dona nobis pacem]

Madrid: Biblioteca Medinaceli MS 607,p.258.

A- gnus De- i   A-gnus De-   i   A-gnus De- i   A-

gnus De- i   A- gnus De-   i   . . .

Cortilla (= Fa re ut fa sol la), four-voice.

Toledo Codex 28, folios 57ᵛ-69. Biblioteca Medinaceli MS 607, pp. 750-759. Kyries, Gloria, and Sanctus-Osanna-Benedictus are each continuous movements. The head motive had been used previously at the outset of a polyphonic piece—Sebastian Virdung's four-voice *O haylige onbeflecte zart iunckfrawschaffe marie*, a Marian motet printed at pages 64-65 in mensural notation and at pages 66-67 as a solo with intabulated accompaniment in his *Musica getutscht* (Basel: 1511). Perhaps, then, the *Missa Cortilla* head motive (used at the beginning of every major section) tags it as a Marian mass. Juan de Lienas, a highly accomplished composer whose works are preserved in the Convento del Carmen Codex (Mexico), used the same head motive in every movement, soloistic and full, of his *Missa a 5*, subtitled JHS MARIA. See Jesús Bal y Gay's transcription (*Tesoro de la Música Polifónica en México*, I [México: Instituto Nacional de Bellas Artes, 1952], 86-113). Still another five-voice *Fa re ut fa sol la* Mass was composed by Melchor de Aragon (=Robledo?) and copied into a large choirbook once owned by the Toledo chapter, although apparently now in German hands. See G. A. Trumpff, "Die Messen des Cristobal de Morales," *Anuario musical*, Vol. VIII, p. 121, n. 150.

Robledo's untitled Mass in Cappella Sistina Codex 22 is described on pages 325-326 below (note 26).

Missa Cortilla (=Fa re ut fa sol la)

Kyrie I

Toledo Cathedral: Codex 28, fols. 57ᵛ-58.

De beata Virgine, four-voice. (2, 5, 7, 9, 12, 13, 16)

De beata Virgine, five-voice. (1, 4, 6, 10, 11, 14)

  Cum Sancto Spiritu intabulated for two vihuelas by Enríquez de Valderrábano in *Silva de Sirenas* (Valladolid: 1547).

Desilde al cavallero, four-voice. A handwritten copy, apparently unique, survives at Milan in Biblioteca Ambrosiana MS Mus. E 46, folios 41ᵛ-50. The eight other masses in the manuscript are by Josquin (six) and La Rue (two). This very fact in itself would strongly suggest an early date for Morales's mass.

In addition, seven movements of *Desilde* (Kyries I and II, Patrem, Et in Spiritum, Sanctus, Osanna, and Agnus I) are in triple meter: O being their mensuration sign. Kyrie, Sanctus, and Agnus movements treat the popular tune as a tenor *cantus firmus*. With the exception of the Crucifixus *(a 3)*, which ends on G, the sixteen other movements end on C. The tenor in the Osanna is answered by a canon at the octave and the bass of the Benedictus by a canon at the fourth.

Gaude Barbara, four-voice.[272] (6, 11)

Benedictus intabulated by Fuenllana.

L'Homme armé, five-voice. (1, 4, 5, 9, 10, 14)

L'Homme armé, four-voice. (6, 11)

Et resurrexit, Benedictus, and Agnus Dei intabulated by Fuenllana.

Mille regretz, six-voice. Two versions exist: one that of Cappella Sistina MS 17, folios 97ᵛ-119, in which the Sanctus movements and Agnuses I and III differ completely from the 1544 printed version. The Cappella Sistina MS 17 version must have circulated, however, since it was printed in Germany as late as 1568. Indeed, this would be the only version of any Morales mass which was printed in Germany in the sixteenth century (see item 15 in list of imprints). The other imprints (items 5 and 9) replace the "Gothic" canons of the Cappella Sistina MS 17 version with free-flowing accompanied-treble movements. Benedictus intabulated for one vihuela by Fuenllana. Et in Spiritum Sanctum intabulated for two vihuelas by Enríquez de Valderrábano in *Silva de Sirenas*. The antiquated canonic movements in the Cappella Sistina MS 17 version carry such titles as *Intercessoribus* (fol. 111ᵛ) and *Duplicatam vestem fecit sibi* (fol. 113ᵛ). The Pleni at folio 112ᵛ does not allude anywhere to the Josquin chanson melody, and ends plagally. The Sanctus and Osanna sections do refer to the Josquin source melody, but in inner voices.

Pro defunctis, five-voice. (6, 11) The movements run in the following order (asterisks indicate that the movement is preceded in the 1544 imprint by a printed plainsong intonation): *Dona eis, *Et tibi reddetur votum, Kyrie eleison, *Dona eis—In memoria eterna—Non timebit, Pie Jesu, *Libera animas—Hostias et preces—Quam olim Abrahe, *Sanctus—Pleni—*Qui venit, *Qui tollis peccata mundi, *Luceat eis—*Et lux perpetua.

Quaeramus cum pastoribus, five-voice. (4, 5, 9, 14)

Quem dicunt homines, five-voice. (6, 11)

Si bona suscepimus, six-voice. (5, 9)

Tristezas me matan, five-voice. The unique surviving copy is found in Cappella Sistina MS 17, folios 79ᵛ-96. The only movement in triple meter is the Osanna, with ₵ 3/2 mensuration (C and A_II) instead of the ◯ 3/2 found in his printed masses.[273] Modally this is a rather impure mass by Morales's standards for these two reasons: (1) Christe ends on A, ten other movements on F, and four on C; (2) the final chord at the ends of four of the five major divisions of the ordinary is F, but the Osanna ends on C—thus violating a rule of modal unity elsewhere observed in Morales's masses. This is also the only mass except his *Ave maris stella* to contain a duo (Agnus II).

Tu es vas electionis, four-voice. (6, 11)

Ut re mi fa sol la, four-voice. Mentioned by Cerone in *El melopeo y maestro* (Bk. XII, chap. 13),[274] this mass was presumed lost until rediscovered in Biblioteca Medinaceli MS 607, pages 608-625. Trumpff, in his "Die Messen des Cristobal de Morales," mentioned another copy originally belonging to Toledo Cathedral, which in addition to Morales's Hexachord Mass contained those of the same title by Boluda (five-voice) and Palestrina (six-voice).[275] Presumably the large Toledo choirbook containing these and six other masses was taken to Germany toward the turn of the present century. Morales's Hexachord is a much more elaborately wrought work than the *Caça* Mass. Like Palestrina's, it ends with an Agnus II exhibiting a canon at the fifth, although in Morales's mass the canon involves his lowest voice and an added part, rather than cantus 11 and altus 111. The *Missa super voces* a 4 in the Capilla Real archive at Granada, reported by José López Calo in "El Archivo de Música de la Capilla Real de Granada" (*AM*, XIII) is probably this same Mass.

Vulnerasti cor meum, four-voice. (3, 5, 7, 9, 12, 13, 16)

Morales's Use of Borrowed Material

Borrowed material enters not only Morales's masses but also his motets. In *Missus est Gabriel*, for instance, the tenor quotes in recognizable if somewhat embellished form the first two incises of the Hail Mary plainsong. In *Quanti mercenarii* (= *Pater peccavi*), tenor 1 sings the Lord's Prayer. Both Morales's Salves draw on plainsong. The magnificats similarly requisition traditional plainsong tones. However, it is in his masses that he goes beyond the plainsong repertory for borrowed material; and it is therefore the masses that we should principally study. Not one of his published masses is a *sine nomine*; not one is freely invented.

In discussing the masses above at pages 45-63, we drew a number of contrasts with Gombert. Throughout the present analysis of source material, we can again compare Gombert's procedures in his ten masses with Morales's in his twenty-one masses. Only two of Gombert's masses are based on plainsongs,[276] as opposed to six of Morales's. Of Gombert's parody masses, *Media vita* and *Beati omnes* are founded on his own motets of those names, but Morales parodied none of his own motets. In the same two masses, Gombert reduced his number of parts, using one less than in the original source motet; Morales never reduced parts in a parody mass: rather, on three occasions (*Quaeramus cum pastoribus*, *Quem dicunt homines*, and *Si bona suscepimus*) he added a part. Another distinction between Gombert's and Morales's masses is found in the uses to which they put plainsong in their parodies. Gombert ends his six-voice *Quam pulchra es* with an Agnus II during which the added seventh voice intones the plainsong antiphon, *Ecce sacerdos magnus*. But as soon as the antiphon begins he abandons any further attempt at quoting in his outer voices melodic motifs taken from the Noel Baudouin source motet. In the Credos from his two parody masses, *Vulnerasti cor meum* and *Si bona suscepimus* (a 4 and a 6 respectively), Morales contrives not only to quote a mensuralized version of the eleventh-century Credo now printed first in the *Kyriale Romanum*; he also manages to keep his parody of the source motets alive in the outer voices. For a predecessor in this kind of "juggling," Morales could have looked to Peñalosa, who combined plainsong in one voice with a melody by Urrede in another throughout the Credo of his *Nunca fue pena mayor* Mass. However, Morales went far beyond Peñalosa in literal fidelity to the plainsong—exact literalness in quoting a plainsong being always a cachet of Morales's style. Reese quite aptly summarizes when he writes that "Morales treats Gregorian melodies with an almost severe regard for the preservation of their essential contours: he embellishes sparingly and applies his ingenuity instead to providing the melodies with a setting that his rather grave artistic personality considers suitable."[277]

In the excerpt from the *Ave Maria* Mass printed in *Music in the Renaissance* (p. 589), or for that matter in most movements from his paraphrase masses, Morales invents a short characteristic motive of his own to accompany the borrowed plainsong. In the *Ave Maria* excerpt it was a scale

motive in the following rhythm:

This scale motive was bandied about from voice to voice while the plainsong (canon at the unison) wended its way in notes of longer value. In this particular excerpt he usually contrived for the newly invented motive to run up to the "tied note" and then down; although sometimes he varied by continuing in stepwise ascent after the "tie". Occasionally his figure started on the second "beat" of the measure, rather than the first. However introduced, it gave textural unity to a movement already welded by canonic treatment of the plainsong cantus firmus.

Morales is nowhere more adroit in finding ways to unify a *missa choralis* than in the first mass published in Book I, the four-voice *De beata Virgine*. The problem that he then took in hand, and that neither Josquin nor Brumel before him had attempted to solve in the same way,[278] finds especially able solution in Kyrie, Sanctus, and Agnus movements. His problem was, of course, not made easier by the different modality of the source chants. Moreover, if one accepts the grouping in the present *Kyriale Romanum*, the chants chosen by Morales do not even belong to the same plainsong mass (Kyrie and Gloria belonging to Mass IX, Sanctus and Agnus to Mass XVII). His unifying device in this mass is an invented countersubject to the plainsong which he can repeat not only in one movement but in several. This newly invented subject—which is found at least thirty-four times in Kyrie, Sanctus, and Agnus movements—assumes from the outset a dominant role in counterpointing the borrowed plainsong. In Kyrie I it is heard in the alto (mm. 1-3), then tenor (mm. 3-4); in the

Christe it appears in the alto (mm. 15-16); in Kyrie II successively in tenor (mm. 31-32), alto (mm. 34-35), bass (mm. 38-39), and soprano (mm. 41-43). In the Sanctus it migrates from bass (mm. 11-12) to tenor (mm. 14-16) to alto (mm. 16-18), and thereafter at sporadic intervals to soprano (mm. 38-39), alto (mm. 33-34), and bass (mm. 34-35). In Osanna I it

Missa De beata Virgine (four-voice)

invades successively the bass, alto, and tenor (first seven measures). In the Benedictus, the alto commences with it and is immediately answered by the tenor. Agnus I shows it at mm. 4-5 (B), 12-13 (B), 26-27 (B), 27-28 (A); Agnus II has it at mm. 44-45 (S), 50-51 (T); Agnus III repeats a variant of it at mm. 1-2 (Q), 3-4 (C), 5-6 (T), 9-10 (Q), 11-12 (S), 21-22 (Q), 25-26 (Q), 37-38 (Q). The accompanying illustration shows several of the guises assumed in Kyrie and Sanctus movements by the motive with which we are now dealing. The reader who would pursue the motive further may turn to the mass in either Peter Wagner's transposed version,[279] to the *Monumentos de la Música Española* [= *MME*] edition (1952), or to the separate issue of this mass published by the Spanish Institute of Musicology as a fourth centenary tribute to Morales in 1953.[280]

An attempt at imposing a still tighter unity upon a mass of plainsong derivation is made in Morales's *Ave maris stella*. When Josquin wrote his mass of the same title (*Liber secundus*, 1505), he ended with Agnuses, each of which boasts a canon—Agnus I between bass and tenor at the fifth, Agnus II between alto and soprano at a fourth, and Agnus III between tenor and soprano at an octave. This was insufficient for Morales, who insisted on going further: with a canon in every full movement, always at the interval of a lower fourth, and always between alto and tenor II. In the earlier movements, his canonic voices recall the plainsong rather fragmentarily, the outer voices carrying it instead. But in the Sanctus he even has the two canonic voices sing the hymn, and—as usual when he quotes plainsong—with the utmost fidelity to the Gregorian original. During the climactic final Agnus *a 6*, Morales elevates the original hymn to cantus firmus status in cantus I. Each incise is separated by a rest of several breves, and each ends with a clearly defined cadence. The cadences resolve thus: seven on D, four on A, and one on C. He spaces these symmetrically, with the longest rest in the plainsong succeeding the exceptional cadence on C. Symbolically the plainsong—like the star hailed in the hymn text—shines above a turbulent sea of churning voices. In the nether surge, the three "accompanying" voices continually pick up for imitation melodic fragments thrown out by the two canonic voices. The whole mass is one of surpassing grandeur, comparable in peninsular art only with such achievements as the fifteenth-century Gothic nave of Seville Cathedral. What can be called peculiarly Spanish in Morales's accomplishment are (1) the subordination of science to an expressive purpose, and (2) the application of the most rigorous devices, by preference, to a plainsong. In Josquin's *Missa ad fugam* (*Liber tertius*, 1514), each full movement embodied a canon between superius and tenor at the interval of an under-fifth. But neither Josquin nor Palestrina in his like-named work attempted canon simultaneously with plainsong paraphrase. It remained Morales's special prerogative to rise highest in the display of his contrapuntal powers while yoking himself most securely with a plainsong.

Coming now from the masses based on plainsong to those founded on Franco-Flemish motets, we search for a single term that will characterize Morales's parody technique and find it in the word compression. The first Morales mass transcribed into modern notation was the resplendent Christmas mass, *Quaeramus cum pastoribus*. Charles Bordes conducted the Singers of Saint-Gervais in the first modern performance on December 25, 1894, but without knowing that Morales's source motet was the same as Willaert's for his mass of identical name. It remained for Michel Brenet to announce discovery of the Jean Mouton source motet in the December, 1899, issue of *La Tribune de Saint-Gervais*.[281] In this and in the next issue of the journal, Bordes analyzed Morales's parody technique, entitling his critique an *Étude Palestrinienne*.[282] The most remarkable characteristic of Morales's parody technique, in Bordes's opinion, was his dexterity in fashioning his themes in every movement entirely from Mouton's motives; always presenting them in new combinations that would not, perhaps, have even occurred to Mouton (d. 1522). From the first Kyrie—at the outset of which two basses, symbolizing the "two bearded shepherds" of tradition,[283] combine with the head motive of the motet another motive that in the motet is used only in the *noe, noe* refrain—Morales shows on every hand his ability to devise new and effective combinations of themes not previously brought together. Not only does he make them fit: he also uses them to generate numberless imitations.

Bordes, while admiring this skill, was constrained somewhat to apologize for Morales: because the identification of the source motet left practically no "new" melodic ideas in a mass that had added greatly to Morales's fame in 1894 when it was first performed.[284] Bordes feared that the "admiration of the hearers for the exalted beauty of the work and for the thrilling joy and majesty expressed in the mass" might decline when they learned that all the themes were really Mouton's and "only the workmanship" was Morales's. After asking whether Morales was "wrong" to have borrowed so extensively,[285] he professed "the greatest respect for musical *engineers* and not only for the facile *inventors* of melodies." But Bordes was, of course, writing at the end of a century that made a shibboleth of originality. Few musicians then realized the extent of parody in the masses of even the one great sixteenth-century master whose complete works were available in 1900—Palestrina.

Trumpff, who made a special study of Morales's parody technique in his Göttingen doctoral dissertation (1938), cleared the air at once by emphasizing that Morales's very excellence and superiority consisted in: (1) the thoroughness with which he borrowed, (2) the intensity with which he combined motives from his sources, and (3) his determination to leave no significant motive in the source unworked in the parody. In a sample analysis of his technique, Trumpff minutely studied Morales's six-voice parody of Verdelot's five-voice *Si bona suscepimus*, a motet first published in 1526. His study led him to the following conclusions.[286] Verdelot's motet, like the others selected by Morales for parody, enjoyed the merit of being clearly sectionalized. Though a motet of only one *pars*, it could be divided into rhyming halves (mm. 1-60; 60-115): thus revealing its hidden reprise structure. As in *Quaeramus*, Morales began by coupling the head theme of the motet with a counterpointing theme; this time made out of the continuation in the motet of the head theme. The countersubject in turn inspired immediate imitation at the distance of only a semibreve (= minim in transcription). Obviously Morales intended here, as repeatedly elsewhere throughout this mass, to concentrate Verdelot's material by the simultaneous presentation of musical ideas that in the source were merely presented one after the other. In the Christe he attempted to concentrate his source material by another, although related, means: namely, by foreshortening the imitation that began the second half of the motet ("nudus egressus sum"), so that the time interval between subject and answer decreased from a breve to a minim. Kyrie I and Christe thus served the double purpose (1) of concentrating source material, and at the same time (2) of exposing the hidden reprise structure of the original (motives from the first half in Kyrie I and from the second half in the Christe).

Not content with the concentration and compression achieved by these means, Morales goes further in his Credo and couples Verdelot's motives with a simultaneous mensuralized presentation of the entire Credo I melody in bassus I. Jachet of Mantua, who in 1542 published a five-voice mass parodied on the same Verdelot motet, started his Patrem omnipotentem with the *initium* of the same plainsong Credo I; but failed to keep it going.[287] Morales, as if in competition, shows how to keep it alive not through just an incise or two but through the whole of Patrem and Et in Spiritum movements. To compress and at the same time unify more strongly, Morales begins each major movement with Verdelot's head motive matched differently so far as counterpoints are concerned. Jachet did not so order his beginnings that they would in themselves reflect the sequence of Verdelot's ideas. True, both Jachet's Kyrie I and Sanctus open identically, and closely resemble each other for the space of 18 breves. Also, Jachet's Agnus I resembles his Credo through 14 breves. But these paired beginnings do not counteract the impression that he regarded the source motet rather loosely and took out ore from any level of his mine rather than always from the top level down, as did Morales. Jachet's imitations run riot, and in contrast with Morales he imitates at any interval. Morales, showing the strong dominant-tonic sense found in Spanish composers generally throughout this century, imitates at the unison, fourth, fifth, or octave.

A third mass displaying Morales's parody technique is his *Aspice Domine* founded on the Gombert motet of two *partes* first published in 1532. Here the tenor starts a breve ahead of the soprano with a counterpoint from meas. 13 of the motet; while the soprano carries the head theme. The sequence of borrowed material in the Kyries (cantus 1) follows exactly the order in the source motet (meas. 37 of the mass = meas. 24 of the motet; 45 = 39; 57 = 51; and 73 = 81). Morales holds any themes from Gombert's *pars 2* in reserve until the Qui tollis, which starts with the head theme of *Muro tuo inexpugnabili*. Here he quotes the imitative point in the original, but tightens the time interval between second and third entries from four breves to two. Also, he adds two mock entries in his alto after the fourth true entry. In the polyphonic complex that starts the Patem omnipotentem, he combines the head themes of both *partes* from Gombert's source motet. The two different head themes first appear together as a tenor-bass duet; and, second, in staggered entries of alto and soprano. In the Et resurrexit, he shows a dramatic flair when he speeds the *pars 1* head theme to a double-step: a quite appropriate quickening for these words. The Et in Spiritum again brings together motives from both *partes*; meas. 195 (mass) = 51 (motet); 212 = 159. In the Sanctus he contrives a new combination of head themes from both *partes*—this time the *Muro tuo* theme moving in double-step and the Aspice at its original gait. The Benedictus brings together the same motives that he had associated at the beginning of Kyrie I, but in a new combination. For his Agnus I, Morales writes an "exposition" in which the four entries at the beginning of Gombert's *pars 1* are tightened into a "stretto." For his last Agnus he holds in reserve the combination of the head theme from *pars 1* with a melodic motive hitherto unused—namely, the motive announced for the first time in the coda of Gombert's *pars 2* (meas. 189). In summary, Morales's procedures in this mass fall under these categories: (1) presenting ideas from the source simultaneously, rather than in succession; (2) tightening imitations by closing the time span between entries; (3) highlighting the structure of the original by presenting borrowed material, at least at first appearance, in the order shown in the original; (4) zealous use of all the significant motives that were discoverable in the original. Or, in the one-word summary with which this discussion of his parody technique started, Morales's keynote is compression: his ambition is to make as many different ideas unite into a harmonious whole as can be integrated at any single moment.

In treating a borrowed secular tune, he follows various procedures. His book I *L'Homme armé* combines the techniques of cantus firmus and paraphrase. Kyries I and II show the armed-man tune lengthened into breves and semibreves, in tenor and alto II respectively. In the Sanctus, alto II isorhythmically repeats the first incise of the tune (lengthened notes) eight times: f and C alternating as starting notes of the incise. In the wordy movements, on the other hand, he paraphrases the armed-man tune, bandying it about in numerous short imitations. *Mille regretz*, we have seen, survives in two different versions. Throughout the printed version Josquin's tune is treated in every full movement as an accompanied treble—the note values being always exactly Josquin's so long as the time signature remains ₵ (the rests between phrases vary). *Mille regretz*, Morales's treble apotheosis of the secular tune, counterparts the Book II *L'Homme armé*, which can be called the tenor apotheosis of the secular tune. The three masses most consistently repeating the same "tune" throughout are these two; and *Tu es vas*, which uses for its tenor an obsolete June 29 versicle. Possibly, Morales chose the tenor and treble techniques in these three masses—as even perhaps in his other tenor mass, *Tristezas*—more to please specific dedicatees than because of any deep inner compulsions.

Magnificats   Although Morales aspired highest in his masses, his magnificats were his most popular works during his own century. No single mass was reprinted more than seven times before 1600; but some of his magnificats were published twice as frequently in the same span of years—those in Tones I, II, IV, VI, and VII. The others came only a little behind these in popularity.[288] Moreover, the magnificats were still being reprinted as late as 1614. His magnificats are his only works known to have been rearranged for equal voices (1619). So far as mere printings are concerned, the most telling evidence for the success of Morales's magnificats is the fact that the magnificats of no other European composer were reprinted more frequently before 1600.[289]

Their popularity in print is matched by the number of early manuscript copies that survive. The Hispanic Society in New York owns two handsome handwritten Spanish choirbook copies, one of which contains items by Ceballos and by Rogier as well as the Morales magnificats;[290] the Puebla Cathedral in Mexico also owns an early handwritten copy.[291] Leaving out of account those copies that are still to be found in Spain, Carl-Heinz Illing in 1936 inventoried early manuscript versions of Morales's magnificats in the following ten cities: Augsburg, Breslau, Dresden, London, Munich, Münster, Paris, Rome, Rostock, and Vienna. Even so, Illing left out of account the most interesting manuscript evidence for their popularity— Cappella Giulia MS VIII. 39. at Rome, which is a copy with *si placet* voice parts added by Palestrina.[292] Morales's magnificats thus enjoy the distinction of being the only works enriched by the greatest master of the Roman school with parts of his own contriving.

In addition to the evidence of prints and handwritten copies, another type of testimony to their continuing popularity can be mentioned—literary allusions. As late as 1592 Zacconi said Morales's magnificats were still sung "in a hundred churches."[293] In 1611 Adriano Banchieri in *L'organo suonarino* declared: "Among the numerous settings by musicians who have entwined the Song of the Blessed Virgin Mary with garlands of most fragrant flowers, using the plainsong of all the eight tones, the most grateful are those of Morales for four voices: worthy, because of their fidelity to the plainchant, of perpetual memory." This eulogy was still echoing in Padre Martini's time when Girolamo Chiti (1678-1759), chapelmaster at St. John Lateran, wrote Martini his opinion that Morales's magnificats were still "the best works in the repertory of the papal choir, and deserving of *universal* praise."

Any adequate study of the magnificats ought therefore to take account not only of (1) their relation to previous Spanish and Italian models, (2) their formal content, and (3) their influence on succeeding masters at home and abroad; but also should question the reasons for their phenomenal success in a century when every industrious composer from Ludwig Senfl in Munich to Hernando Franco in Mexico City was busy writing magnificats. Only when it is realized that well over 400 different composers between 1436 and 1620 left magnificats,[294] and that those of Morales tower above all, excepting only Lassus's (if such tangible evidences of popularity as reprints and manuscript diffusion are accepted as sufficient proof), will one be in a proper frame of mind to appreciate these particular masterworks.

Polyphonic magnificats from the fifteenth century are not frequently met. As is well known, the first exemplar that can be dated exactly—a six-verse magnificat by Johannes de Quatris preserved in the famous MS Canonici misc. 213 at the Bodleian—bears 1436 as its year of copy.[295] Unlike Dunstable's single, and Dufay's pair of magnificats, Quatris's sets only the even verses polyphonically. Those of Dunstable and Dufay employ fauxbourdon style throughout. If Icart was a Catalonian instead of a Fleming, his even-verse magnificats (two *a 4*, the other *a 3*) surviving in Faenza Codex 117 (folios 6, 7ᵛ, 44ᵛ) take pride of place as the earliest Spanish magnificats: 1480 being as reasonable a conjecture as any for their date. From Anchieta, two magnificats survive—one for four and the other for three voices. Of Peñalosa, six *a 4* are extant; three of these are copied into Toledo Codex 18 alongside magnificats by Festa, Morales, and Torrentes. Some eight or nine other Spanish magnificats antedating Morales's are preserved in Tarazona MS 2, Barcelona Biblioteca Central MS 454, and Seville Biblioteca Colombina MS 7-I-28. At Tarazona the composers named are Marleth, Porto, Segovia, Tordesillas, and Villa; at Barcelona they are Mondéjar and Quexada. At Seville the incomplete magnificat filling folios 97ᵛ-100 of the Colombina source, though anonymous, shows Spanish traits; the other sacred works in MS 7-I-28 were also composed by Spaniards. At Rome, Cappella Sistina MS 44 preserves a magnificat *a 4* in Tone VI composed before 1513 by Juan Escribano.[296] Thus a total of at least eighteen Spanish magnificats antedating 1528 survives. Although two by Brumel and one by Festa appear in early Spanish manuscripts,[297] the total number of foreign magnificats preserved in peninsular sources cannot compare with that of Spanish magnificats; nor even with the number of foreign masses and motets preserved in Spanish manuscripts.

If we take Anchieta's three-voice magnificat[298] as typical of the early Spanish output, the following contrasts with Morales's magnificats can be drawn: (1) odd or even verses were the rule in all earlier Spanish magnificats, it being understood that plainsong would always alternate with polyphony; (2) each verse tended to stop at the *mediatio*, either with a fermata or a prolonged cadence succeeded by a new beginning in all voices —this stop at the mediatio recalling Obrecht's similar practice;[299] (3) not every verse in a given magnificat needed end uniformly with the same chord; (4) fauxbourdon style, at least in short passages, was still acceptable in Anchieta's generation; (5) on the other hand, learned devices such as canon were not thought suitable; (6) no attempt was made to soar upward to a climax in the concluding *Sicut erat*.

As for likenesses: both Anchieta and Morales usually allowed at least one voice in every verse to quote or to recall the plainsong formula of the given tone. This plainsong-inspired part did not have to be the same in every verse throughout a magnificat. In Anchieta's three-voice setting, for instance, the plainsong-inspired voice is the top in Verses 2, 4, and 6, but the bottom in Verses 8 and 10, and the middle in Verse 12. Similarly, in Morales's magnificats the plainsong migrates from verse to verse: thus preventing any canticle from becoming a "tenor"-magnificat after the fashion of his "tenor"-masses, *Tu es vas* and the *L'Homme armé* for four voices. It is also worth noting that neither Anchieta nor Morales strayed from the plainsong-intonation of one tone into that of another tone during the same magnificat. Even Anchieta, who is willing enough to shift from F to G for closing chords of successive verses in a magnificat preserved at Segovia, stays with the same plainsong intonation from first to last verse.

None of Morales's Spanish predecessors wrote magnificats in all eight tones. The first publications to contain exemplars in all eight ecclesiastical tones appeared at Paris in 1534—the eighteen composers in the Attaingnant collections being Frenchmen or Flemings.[300] As opposed to collections of magnificats in the eight tones by several different composers, the first publication with such a cycle by a single composer seems to have been the *Magnificat octo tonorum* of the Swiss composer Ludwig Senfl, published by Hieronymus Formschneider at Nuremberg in 1537.[301] Morales's magnificats in all eight tones (1545) trailed therefore only a scant eight years after Senfl's. Still earlier, in 1542, Morales's earliest published magnificats had been issued by Girolamo Scotto at Venice. This collection, too, had included exemplars in all eight tones; but only the Tones I, II, IV, VI, and VII settings had been Morales's—the other tones having been eked out with canticles by Jachet, Richafort, and Tugdual. A rather important disclosure of this 1542 *Magnificat cum quatuor vocibus Moralis Hispani aliorumque authorum* (copy at Bologna in the Liceo musicale)[302] is the grouping of verses. All twelve verses are set polyphonically in each Morales magnificat, and, what is more, in serial order. On this account, as on several others, they recall Festa's *Magnificat tutti gli otti toni a quatro voce*, published by Girolamo Scotto in 1554 (but composed before 1539). Later, in a handsome folio edition of Morales's canticles to be published by Antonio Gardano in 1562 and entitled *Magnificat omnitonum cum quatuor vocibus*, the Anima mea and Et exultavit verses were to be separated: thus in effect giving Morales sixteen magnificats—eight for odd and eight for even verses. Similarly, in Spanish sources such as MS 607 at the Biblioteca Medinaceli the odd verses congregate together (pp. 86-131), as do the even (pp. 132-185). Both sumptuous choirbook copies owned by The Hispanic Society in New York credit Morales with "diez y seis magnificas," and separate odd from even verses. With the somewhat conflicting evidence of the Scotto 1542 and Rhaw 1544[303] imprints, which argue for continuous polyphonic settings, and the Gardano of 1562, which argues for discontinuous settings, the student of Morales's magnificats may find himself in some perplexity. Henceforth, I will refer to "the sixteen magnificats," eight for odd and eight for even verses. But always it will be borne in mind that the evidence of the earliest imprints argues strongly for eight continuous polyphonic settings— one for each tone.

Ludwig Senfl (1537) differed no more pronouncedly from Morales (1545) than in his concept of how to write in the eight different tones. Senfl ended all verses of his Tone II Magnificat with an A-chord; but Morales finished all his with G-chords (B♭ in signature). Senfl concluded all verses except the Fecit potentiam of his Tone III with an E-chord; but Morales halted all his with an A-chord. Senfl closed all verses except the Fecit potentiam of his Tone IV with an A-chord; but Morales chose E-chords. Senfl capped Verses 2, 4, 6, and 10 of his Tone VII with D-chords, and Verses 8 and 12 (Esurientes and Sicut erat) with A-chords; but Morales terminated every verse of his Tone VII with A-chords. To sum up the differences: Morales invariably built the chords at ends of verses in a given magnificat over the final of the appropriate plainsong formula. Senfl, though in each magnificat he tended to carve his melodies from the same Gregorian stone, did not so consistently work the plainsong formulas as to end every verse throughout his Tone II, III, IV, or VII Magnificats with chords built over the designated final notes.

It would be extremely gratifying to prove that Morales was the first composer who consistently closed every verse in any given magnificat with a chord built over the final letter-name note of the related plainsong intonation-formula. As we have just seen, Senfl cannot have originated the plan. Neither can Gombert, although he too wrote a magnificat-cycle.[304] Not only did Gombert veer between one final chord and another in successive verses of his magnificats in Tones IV and VII but also he so cavalierly disregarded tonal individuality as to write his third and sixth magnificats in mixed tones. In *El arte tripharia* (1550) Bermudo excused Gombert for writing certain motets in mixed modes.[305] Whether Bermudo knew Gombert's magnificats—which survive in a unique copy dated 1552—is uncertain. But if Gombert wilfully mixed modes in his motets he even more certainly mixed tones in his *Canticum Beatae Mariae Virginis Deiparae iuxta suos octos tonos modulatum*. That he was perfectly conscious of what he was doing is proved by the fact that he gave his third canticle the title *Magnificat tertii et octavi toni*, and his sixth the title *Magnificat sexti et primi toni*. In each, he licentiously used the formula of one tone but the final of another.

Senfl and Gombert having been struck off the list, Costanzo Festa remains as a possible forerunner. His *Magnificat tutti gli otti toni a quatro voce* resemble Morales's in providing polyphonic settings of all twelve verses. They also duplicate Morales's scheme of closing-chords. The scheme common to both Festa and Morales runs as follows: Tones I and II, all verses end on G (B♭ in signature); III, V, and VIII, all end on A; IV, all end on E; VI, all on F; VIII, all on G. These letter-name notes are the last notes of the respective plainsong intonation-formulas (*Toni solemnes*).[306] Obviously they are not always the finals of the respective modes. Only in Tone I and the even-numbered tones do they duplicate the finals of the corresponding modes. In Tones III, V, and VII, the formula always ends with the note A. Both the *initium* and the reciting note (*tuba*) differ in each of these three tones: but the last note happens to be the same. (Another way of expressing the rules for plainsong formulas is this: the reciting note in every tone is invariably the *confinalis* [=dominant] of the corresponding mode; but although the *finalis* of Mode III has always been E; of Mode V, F; and of Mode VII, G; these mode-finals do not close the corresponding magnificat-formulas. Instead, the note A enjoys this privilege.)

Morales's plan for closing-chords caught on. Every later continental composer who wrote in all the tones, from Palestrina to Monte,[307] followed the same scheme. There were, however, still other uses to which Morales put the plainsong formula besides deriving from it the clue for his closing-chords in each tone. As a fixed rule, every full movement of his magnificats cites the formula with severe exactness in at least one voice. During Verses 1 and 2 he usually cites it in the top voice. In succeeding verses scored full, it spreads to the middle voices. In Verse 12 he always spins a canon out of it, except in Tones IV and VI. Possibly Morales omitted his usual concluding canon from the Tone IV because, like Palestrina, he felt that this tone and its corresponding mode "lacked brightness."[308] Support for such a suggestion is found in the fact that among all his magnificats setting even verses, only the Tone IV never goes beyond four voices. The Tone VI, also lacking a concluding canon, augments to six voices in the Sicut erat. A reason for omitting the concluding canon from the Tone VI is found in the plainsong-formula itself: which for this particular tone is identical with that of Tone I up to the *mediatio*, and differs thereafter only in the one note after *tuba 2* and in another pair of notes appended for a close to Tone I. After having already contrived a masterful canon at the under-fourth between cantus II and altus I in his Tone I Magnificat, Morales would have been merely repeating himself had he made out of an almost identical formula another canon to conclude his Tone VI Magnificat.

It was said that Morales "cites" the plainsong formula in at least one voice during any verse scored full. In certain verses he cites it with the *ipsissima verba* accuracy of a theologian quoting scripture. In others he contents himself with paraphrase: never encrusting it, however, with so thickly ornamented an overlay as to hide the contours of the plainsong. Apart from Verses 1 and 2 and the usually canonic verse 12, *ipsissima verba* statements occur in: Tone I, Quia fecit (bass) and Esurientes (alto); Tone II, Deposuit (alto) and Suscepit Israel (tenor); Tone III, Suscepit Israel (alto), Sicut locutus (soprano), and Gloria (tenor); Tone IV, Quia fecit (tenor), Fecit potentiam (bass), Deposuit (alto), and Gloria (alto); Tone V, Quia fecit (alto) and Gloria (soprano); Tone VI, Quia fecit (alto), Deposuit (soprano), and Gloria (bass); Tone VII, Quia fecit (tenor), Fecit potentiam (alto), Deposuit (bass), Sicut locutus (soprano), and Gloria (tenor); Tone VIII, Quia fecit (bass), Fecit potentiam (alto), Esurientes (tenor), Sicut locutus (soprano), and Gloria (tenor). In movements where the formula is cited forthrightly in one voice, it may give rise to imitations in the others; or the surrounding voices may discourse imitatively upon some alien melodic idea. Morales's ingenuity is nowhere better illustrated than on the occasions when he cites the formula of the tone most rigorously. One compelling reason for the long-continuing popularity of his magnificats may well be the large number of movements in which the formula is quoted without intrusion or license of any kind.

As opposed to Festa's magnificats, Morales's may also have retained their hold on the public because they were considerably more singable. Festa's parts skip widely; they usually require greater ranges;[309] and he shifts meter within movements. As for architectural plan: (1) Morales's invariably utilized four voices or less in Verses 1-11. (2) Only in Verses 12 does he augment to six parts. Moreover, his canons are always to be found in Verses 12, rather than in previous verses. (3) These canons always take the plainsong-formula for their subject matter. Not so in Festa's case—he: (1) augments to five parts in the Deposuit of Tones V and VI, for example; (2) writes canons in the Esurientes of Tone III, in the Sicut locutus of Tones III and VII, and in the Suscepit of Tone VIII; (3) in such virtuoso exercises as the triple canon ending Tone III and the canon cancrizans concluding Tone VII, makes no attempt to construct his canon out of building-blocks from the formula. As a result, each Festa magnificat fulfills a distinctive architectural plan all its own. Morales invariably disposed his pedestals, columns, and capitals so that the last verse strikes the viewer as the crowning pediment of the whole structure. But Festa prefers the unexpected.

Just as in his masses he departed from his model and gave free rein to his fancy in the soloistic movements, so likewise in his magnificats Morales invents new material in the movements for soloists. Not only does he allow himself free rein in the duos of the magnificats, and to a considerable extent in the trios; but also the character of the voice writing differs. In the duos he often calls for extended scale-runs, spun-out sequences, and a rapid flow in crotchets (unreduced values) which contrasts pleasingly with the more restrained conduct of the voices in movements scored full. The Fecit duo of Tone III and the Esurientes of Tone VI, both of which are scored for tenor and bass, exemplify the traits just mentioned. (Festa, by way of contrast, inserted six times as many duos as Morales; but without changing his manner of writing for the voices in either his duos or trios.)

Morales consistently sets the same verses as trios. Of the fourteen trios in his magnificats, half are Et misericordia verses and four, Esurientes. The remaining three trios are a Deposuit (Tone I), a Suscepit, and a Fecit (both Tone II). The frequent choice of Et misericordia and Esurientes for trios accords well with the sense of those texts ("And his mercy is from generation to generation" and "The hungry he hath filled with good things and the rich he hath sent empty away"). Because he so consistently chooses these verses for soloistic treatment, tellingly symmetrical ground plans come into view. Not for Morales were the highly variable schemes of Gombert, who in one magnificat scored his Fecit for three voices, in another for five; or his Esurientes in Tone II for two voices, in Tone IV for three, and in Tone III for six; or his Sicut locutus in Tone III for seven, and in Tone IV for three voices. Morales's consistency in matters architectural may be yet another reason for the enduring success of his magnificats.

As an example of a Morales magnificat movement, the Fecit potentiam of Tone III has been chosen. This is one of the three magnificat movements transcribed by Fuenllana in his *Orphénica lyra* (Seville: 1554).[310] The lower

Magnificat Tertii toni

Fecit potentiam

* Fuenllana
In measures 7-8, 11, 16, 24, and 28, Fuenllana breaks the syncope dissonance into two repeated notes of this value.

staff shows Morales's duo. The seven sharps in the lower staff are those prescribed by Fuenllana. The upper staff has the *si placet* part added by Palestrina.[311] The artistry exhibited in the latter part deserves praise. Palestrina contrives an added imitation in bars 1, 10, 17, 24; and at all times conducts his part so that it seems either to grow out of, or to anticipate, a part in the Morales duo.

Palestrina's parts in the five other movements amplified by him are similarly marvels of grace and ease. His added parts contrast with Morales's: (1) in eschewing escaped dissonances;[312] (2) in always moving from the third note in a changing-note figure stepwise upward;[313] (3) in avoiding upper neighboring notes;[314] (4) in containing three times as many accidentals as the Morales movements that he amplified; (5) in containing

twice as many paired quavers (unreduced values) as the Morales movements; (6) in covering a wider vocal range than Morales usually prescribed
for upper parts[315]—Palestrina twice covering an eleventh. Even more remarkable, however, than these few contrasts (for which one has to look
diligently) are the many similarities that everywhere leap to view. It was
Charles Warren Fox who first called Morales Palestrina's closest precursor,
and who presciently remarked that in certain individual works—perhaps
his later compositions—Morales anticipated Palestrina's detail technique
so exactly as to seem an original backed by a carbon.[316]

Apart from the *Tertii toni* Fecit, two other movements from Morales's
magnificats attracted Fuenllana's attention: a Deposuit *a 3* and an *ossia*
Suscepit Israel *a 2*. Both of these belong to Tone I. They are printed in
Orphénica lyra at folios 13 and 2. Not until 1956 were the vocal parts of the
ossia Suscepit published. At that time Anglés availed himself of a manuscript copy (M.M.9) fortunately surviving at Coimbra University. (See
MME, XVII, *44-46*.) Finally, one quite free transcription should be mentioned: Enríquez de Valderrábano's *Fantasia remedando un Magnificat de
Morales* in his *Silva de sirenas* [1547] at folios 67^v-68. According to *MME*,
Volume XVII, pages *44* and *52*, this fantasia is based on Verses 1 and 3 of
an alternate Tone I preserved incomplete at Toledo Cathedral in Codex
18, folios 38^v-39. Nothing from this alternate was ever printed in Morales's
epoch. But it must have been popular in Spain if Valderrábano could
choose it for free paraphrase.

As will be shown below, Fuenllana intabulated not only the *ossia* Suscepit Israel but also a Morales lamentation that did not otherwise reach
print during the sixteenth century. The presence of all these various
individual magnificat- and lamentation-movements in Spanish tablatures
proves the viability of each as separate pieces (divorced from their
liturgical contexts). It is also at once obvious that Morales never
publicly endorsed the *ossia* versions. At least three such unpublished
alternates of magnificat or lamentation movements were preferred throughout the Spanish world to the versions printed at Venice and elsewhere in
Italy, France, and Germany.

Lamentations[317]   The *Lamentationi a quatro a cinque, et a sei voci*, which were
published simultaneously in 1564 by the two Venetian publishers, Antonio
Gardano and Francesco Rampazetto, comprise Morales's only large-scale
work issued posthumously. According to the title page of the Rampazetto
edition, these lamentations were being "newly issued" and being printed
with "scrupulous diligence."

Even so, neither Gardano nor Rampazetto claimed that his edition contained Morales's entire output: and understandably so, since Fuenllana in 1554 had already intabulated a prologue (taken over from the Septuagint into the Vulgate) and three lamentation verses that fail to concord with anything in the 1564 Venetian prints.[318] The verses transcribed by Fuenllana are distinctively Spanish. They alone of Morales's lamentations employ as *cantus firmi* the plainsong lamentation-tones that had been sung in Spain since 1200 or earlier.[319] These he threads usually through his altus; and it is these tones that Fuenllana transcribes in mensural notation—the other voices being intabulated for instrumental accompaniment. Luckily, *Orphénica lyra* is not the only source for these "Spanish" lamentations by Morales. They also survive in *Libro de coro 2*, folios 28ᵛ-37 (vocal score), at Puebla Cathedral. *Libro de coro 1* (folios 103ᵛ-108) contains still another trio of lamentation verses *a 5* (closing with a "Jerusalem convertere") that are indexed as Morales's, but which do not match with any in the 1564 Venetian prints or in the Fuenllana set.

First, however, we must study the lamentations published by Rampazetto and Gardano in 1564; since these (it is quite evident) were Morales's only complete lamentation-cycle for the last three days of Holy Week. Rampazetto claimed to have taken all due care in preparing his edition. Presumably he avoided the mistakes of Montanus and Neuber, the Nuremberg printers of lamentations, who—when they issued in 1549 their *Lamentationes Hieremiae prophetae, maxime lugubribus et querulis concentibus musicis*—ascribed to Antoine de Févin a setting of the "Jerusalem, Jerusalem, convertere ad Dominum" verse rounding off each of three lessons, which duplicates note for note the music rounding off the first lesson in Pierre de la Rue's *Lamentationes*.[320] That Rampazetto did exercise somewhat more care than had either the Nuremberg printers or Le Roy and Ballard (who issued at Paris in 1557 *Piissimae ac sacratissimae lamentationes Ieremiae prophetae*) can be inferred from the fact that when publishing Morales's *Lamentationi* he, for the first time among sixteenth-century printers, took pains to assign each lamentation to its proper lesson and its specific day. All other printers from Petrucci in 1506—with two books containing lamentations by such composers as Agricola, Icart, de Orto, Tinctoris, Tromboncino, and Gaspar van Weerbecke,— to Le Roy and Ballard—with their collection of lamentations by Arcadelt, Carpentras, Festa, Févin, and Claudin de Sermisy—had been quite content to print lamentation verses without making any attempt to inform the user on which day in Holy Week, or at what lesson, the lamentation verse in question should be sung. Rampazetto comes immediately to the user's rescue with *Feria quinta, Lectio prima*; then *Feria quinta, Lectio secunda*, and so forth, through Holy Saturday.

Rampazetto's careful assignments enable the student to learn at once (1) that Morales in his posthumously published cycle did not choose precisely the verses, and (2) did not arrange them in the exact order that was to become standard after the Council of Trent. Selections from the Book of Lamentations had, of course, been sung at matins on Thursday, Friday, and Saturday in Holy Week from at least the eighth century. The practice of moving matins from midnight to the preceding evening had long made it possible for great numbers of the laity to hear Tenebrae sung on Wednesday, Thursday, and Friday nights. But variants in local custom had determined the number and order of verses to be sung either polyphonically or in plainchant throughout any one diocese. This flexibility gave way after 1568 to a uniform usage for the whole Roman world. Lamentations 1:1-5, 1:6-9, and 1:10-14 were to be sung at the three lessons of the first nocturn in Matins of Feria V; Lamentations 2:8-11, 2:12-15, and 3:1-9 at the first three lessons of the first nocturn in Matins of Feria VI; and Lamentations 3:22-30, 4:1-6, and 5:1-11 at the first three lessons of the first nocturn in Matins of Holy Saturday. Each verse in each of these lessons, except the last on Saturday, begins with a Hebrew letter—*Aleph*, *Beth*, *Ghimel*, *Daleth*, and so forth (these letters before each Vulgate verse remind the hearer that in the original Hebrew the poetry is acrostic). For a "refrain" each lesson concludes with a verse not drawn from Lamentations: "Jerusalem, Jerusalem, convertere" (Jerusalem, Jerusalem, turn unto the Lord Thy God).

True, Morales anticipates the later uniform usage when he groups his verses into nine lessons, three for each of the three last days of Holy Week. Thirty of the verses set by him begin with Hebrew acrostic letters; he composes the Hebrew letter polyphonically in twenty-three verses. He also rounds off each of his nine lessons with the traditional "Jerusalem, Jerusalem, convertere" entreaty. But, on the other hand, more than half the verses from the Book of Lamentations which he sets were not to be retained in the revised Roman Breviary sent forth with the approval of Pope Pius V in 1568. The unrevised Vulgate available to Morales wrongly matches the Hebrew acrostic letters numerous times: with the result that the acrostic letters *Lamech* (=*Lamed*), *Ioth*, and *Gimel* in Feria quinta, Lectio secunda; *Phe* and *Res* in Feria sexta, Lectio prima; *Sade*, *Caph*, and *Vau* in Feria sexta, Lectio secunda; should read instead *Mem*, *Lamed*, *Ain*, *Sade*, *Sin*, *Aleph*, *Beth*, and *Zain*; and do so read in the revised Vulgate. Perhaps these two facts: (1) setting of eighteen verses not retained in the revised Breviary, and (2) incorrect matching of numerous acrostic letters; sufficiently account for the neglect of Morales's printed lamentation-cycle toward the end of his century. His "Spanish" lamentations—those transcribed by Fuenllana—on the other hand were still sung frequently in Spain and Mexico after 1600.[321]

Certainly the printed music is of high order. For convenience, comments will be organized under the headings of texture and structure. In comparison with Crecquillon's *Quinque vocum in lamentationes Hieremiae* and *Quatuor vocum aequalium in lamentationes* (Montanus and Neuber: 1549), Morales's texture is less imitative. When he does introduce a canon, as between tenor and alto at the acrostic letter in Verse 3 of Lesson I, it is short and unobtrusive: for that matter, all his imitations in his *Lamentationi* are inconspicuous. Crecquillon begins none of his eighteen sections full, but instead with imitation. Morales on the contrary begins the following verses full: his *Caph* in Feria quinta, Lectio tertia; his *Sin* in Feria sexta, Lectio prima; and his *Sin* in Feria sexta, Lectio tertia; not to mention many subsections.

Morales, who was always a master of counterpoint when he chose, decided in his *Lamentationi* upon a prevailingly homophonic approach, and also elected to be much more expressive than Crecquillon—if printed accidentals are a sufficient clue. Crecquillon adhered to a signature of one flat throughout. Apart from a few E♭'s in his lower voices, no accidentals crop up anywhere in the 1549 imprint of his four- and five-voice lamentations. But sharps begin appearing in the Morales lamentations as early as the tenth note in the cantus. At the mediation of his first verse we discover a printed E♭ in the bass, followed immediately by an F♯ in the tenor. In the first of his nine lessons he specifies nine sharps: 5 C♯'s and 4 F♯'s. In the second lesson, 1 F♯, 2 C♯s, 5 G♯s, and 5 B♭'s are printed; many additional ficta are mandatory. As a corollary, Morales's lamentations abound in poignant cross relations guaranteed by printed accidentals in the 1564 imprint[322] or by obligatory ficta. A survey of the nine lessons gives Morales a striking advantage over contemporary composers of lamentations so far as printed accidentals are concerned. His only near-contender is Arcadelt, who—if printed accidentals are a proper test to apply—was a more "expressive" composer of lamentations than either of his countrymen, Crecquillon or Sermisy (Arcadelt called for some 15 C♯'s and 22 F♯'s in ten verses).

In addition to his numerous accidentals, Morales induces variety by contrasting duos and trios with more heavily scored movements; duos appear, for instance, in the *Teth* of Lectio III of Feria quinta, and in the *Sin* of Lectio I of Feria sexta. As the *Lamentationi* mount to their close, he increases parts. Holy Saturday begins with five voices, mounts to six for the Jerusalem of Lectio II, and remains at six for the Prayer of Jeremy (Lectio III) through the closing Jerusalem. As the number of voice parts increases, the ranges climb. From the beginning through Lectio I of Feria sexta, the top notes in CATB are respectively g (a, very occasionally), f, d, and G. But from Lectio III of Feria sexta to the end, the upper limits of all voices rise by a third or fourth to c¹ (occasionally, d¹), a, g, and d. This shift upward of ranges (and necessarily of tessiture)—although not always made in the same verse—was a common enough occurrence in lamentations by such earlier composers as La Rue, Févin, and Carpentras. Among Morales's contemporaries, Sermisy and Arcadelt made such a shift in mid-course. However, if we seek a parallel to Morales's fuller scoring for Holy Saturday, we find that only one composer thus far named expands beyond a quartet on *Sabbato sancto*—namely, Crecquillon. Since Crecquillon also composed several verses for Feria quinta *a 5*, his over-all plan resembles more that of a trough with walls at the beginning and end; whereas Morales's plan involves a continuous ascent from a low-lying plain to a rampart.

Structurally, Morales can be shown in his published lamentation-cycle, as in his magnificats, to have sought a climax. Just as the increased number of voices, so also his choice of final chords proves him to have been thinking in architectural terms. The *Jerusalem, Jerusalem, convertere* entreaty closes each lesson. It is therefore sung three times in each matins. On Feria quinta the Jerusalem's end on F (flat in signature), E, and C. On Feria sexta they close on G, C, and E. On Sabbato Sancto they finish with A (flat in signature), F (flat in signature), and E. Thus, no adjacent lessons conclude with the same chord. Within lessons, he seeks consistency with ending chords that bear a plagal or authentic relation to the main final. But from lesson to lesson he calls for as much contrast of finals as the spectrum of "modal" colors in his paintbox will allow him to make.

Crecquillon, less interested in expressivity, ended every movement in every lesson on F through a succession of fifteen verses (five lessons); only shifting to A for the last three in his equal-voice lamentations. Arcadelt—Crecquillon's compatriot and Morales's coetanean in the papal choir—ended his Jerusalem's on A, F, and G, respectively: a plan much nearer to Morales's, although, of course, not worked out at such great length. Carpentras's Holy Week lamentations, the fame of which is great because Baini reported them to have been sung in the papal chapel until replaced by Palestrina's in 1587, similarly change finals from lesson to lesson: at least in those printed by Le Roy and Ballard in 1557.

However, Carpentras's lamentations lack any of the "harmonic" variety within individual verses which so enriches Morales's. To cite but one instance: Morales at the caesura in *Incipit* ‖ *lamentatio Jeremiae prophetae* cadences to an A-Major chord (printed c♯ in cantus); immediately after the caesura he specifies the D-Major chord (printed f♯ in altus); at the end, he cadences at "prophetae" with an F-Major chord. Carpentras, too, cadenced at the end of "prophetae" with an F-Major chord. But he had worn out its welcome by unimaginatively repeating the same F-Major chord both before and after the caesura. In consequence, his last F-Major on "prophetae" tells no new tale—but makes instead for the static, marmoreal effect that so displeased Fétis.[323] Or to say it in another way: Carpentras's tears were carved in stone, but Morales's ooze in drops as lifelike as those of *La Macarena*.

Motets and Other Liturgical Pieces

The two motets of Morales which have remained most continuously in public favor during the last century have been *Lamentabatur Jacob* and *Emendemus in melius*, both *a 5*. The first of these was anthologized several times in Germany in the nineteeth century. The second, because of its presence in the Apel-Davison *Historial Anthology of Music*, Volume I,[324] has been widely studied in university and college classes. Not content with giving *Emendemus in melius* a place in his anthology, Apel has even gone so far as to call this Morales motet "one of the greatest works in all music history" (*Harvard Dictionary of Music*, p. 705). Because of their availability, we may well begin exploration of Morales's ninety-odd motets with these very two. In describing them, Mitjana wrote somewhat as follows:[325]

The works of Morales in which his dramatic temperament burst forth in full view are his motets. In these he does not allow himself to be decoyed by any merely clever devices, but on the contrary freely expresses himself from the "depths of his heart" even when he consents to be most learned. To show how this may be true we shall begin by analyzing his portentous motet belonging to both the first Sunday in Lent and Ash Wednesday, *Emendemus in melius*—an outpouring that properly sung always produces the profoundest impression. Much of this effect is due to the truly dramatic conflict between two opposite sentiments which the composer has introduced. One sentiment finds expression in a text that entreats; the other in a text that threatens. To clothe the entreating text, four hushed voices begin by timidly murmuring the contrite sinner's prayer: "We will make amends for those sins which we have ignorantly committed." To set the threatening text, a second tenor intrudes itself on the scene at the thirteenth breve. Like a messenger of death, tenor II six successive times utters this stern warning, "Remember, man, that thou art dust, and unto dust shalt thou return," each time singing the same cantus firmus for a melody and each time resting six semibreves before the next repetition. Morales has here made of a device that could have been merely formal, a highly expressive one. The counterpoints that swirl about the cantus firmus symbolize the tumult of the penitent soul seeking forgiveness. The rigid cantus firmus is the personification of inexorable Fate. The contrast between the cry for mercy and the terrible threat of judgment (which is repeated ever more insistently) could not be more telling; nor the opposition between the two concepts more profoundly moving. The conflict reaches indeed a most pathetic extreme; even though only the inner soul is the battleground: because for a believer—and in Morales's day all were believers—this frightful duel was fought between conscience on the one hand and the awesome threat of death, judgment, and possible damnation on the other.

The symmetry of proportion in this motet is altogether remarkable. In the

following numerical scheme, italicized numbers refer to sections in which tenor
II sings its warning cry, roman numbers to sections in which tenor II rests.
The numerals in each case stand for semibreves: 24 + *24* + 6 + *24* + 6 + *24* + 6
+ *24* + 6 + *24* + 6 + *24* + 2. The dovetailing of two texts, the one of entreaty,
the other of menace, is also well thought out. In the following translation of the
supplicating text, the italicized words are those at which tenor II breaks in
with its warning cry: "Let us amend our lives, for we have ignorantly *sinned*;
lest *suddenly* the day of death overtake us; and when we seek *space* for penitence
are *not able* to obtain it. Incline Thine ear, O *Lord* and be *merciful* because
we have sinned against Thee." Each of these successive moments of entry rises
in intensity, until a true paroxysm of anguish wells up at the penultimate entry.
But thanks to the mysterious assuagement of prayer, calm slowly returns,
the warning voice is suffered to subside and to be enfolded in the trustful prayer
of the other voices as they at last find refuge in *tibi,* "Thee." "For Thou, O Lord,
will be the only hope to which the sinner can cling at the last—Thou who didst
pardon even the dying thief and whose mercy is from everlasting to everlasting."
This is probably the most powerful and stirring motet to be found in the entire
sixteenth-century repertory. Words are lacking for an adequate description of the
sublimities of this particular composition.

Hardly less dramatic and beautiful is the famous *Lamentabatur Jacob,* which Adami
da Bolsena qualified as such "a marvel of art." The atmosphere of this work
is, however, rather more intimate and melancholy, as indeed it should be since
it tells of the suffering of the aged patriarch because of the loss of his beloved
sons. Joseph was lost long ago, and now Benjamin is taken from him.
"Alas, how sorrowful I feel," complains the bereft father in a drooping phrase
(mm. 30-35). From the outset, Morales has introduced uncommonly expressive
ninth and seventh chords in long-drawn sequences of syncope dissonances
in order to capture something of the old man's desolate mood. However, the
hopes of Jacob do not altogether topple, for he trusts in the Divine Providence.
He implores God not to abandon him utterly; and the music at the end of
partes I and *II* (mm. 69-107; 154-192)[326] shifts from flaccid rhythms to
dotted and other sturdier patterns. These two works alone cannot epitomize
the whole of Morales's ninety-odd motets. But they do show to what expressive
heights he could rise. They are alternately austere, fervid, and melancholy. What
is more, he never forgets even in moments of most intense and ecstatic devotion
that his art has a twofold purpose: first, to pay his own personal tribute to the
Eternal, and, second, to induce in his fellow men an exalted mood of reverence.

Approximately a fourth of Morales's motets were published in 1953
[1954] as the second volume of his *Opera omnia.* In the preface, the editor
warned against premature judgments concerning Morales's motet style
when such a large number remain to be printed.[327] However, if we assume
that the twenty-five chosen for this volume are not unworthy of Morales
and that they form a cross-sampling, the following observations may interest the student of his style: (1) none of the twenty-five is written with
triple-meter signature, and only once in mid-course does Morales shift to

triple meter and back again (in the Christmas motet *Cum natus esset Jesus*, mm. 181-188); (2) on the other hand, short stretches of internal triple meter are frequently suggested, either by the harmonic rhythm in all parts, or by short snatches in single voice parts (e.g., *Antequam comedam*, tenor, 27₄-30; *Cum natus esset*, bass, 224₃-229₃; *Salve Regina*, tenor, 192₃-195₃); (3) the bass part is twice as "skippy" as the upper parts—analysis showing 26.4 per cent of the voice movements to be skips in Cantus I, 25.0 per cent in Cantus II, 27.4 per cent in Altus, 35.5 per cent in Tenor,[328] and 52.8 per cent in Bassus (analysis based on a "typical" five-voice motet, the *Andreas Christi famulus*); (4) individual voice-ranges are carefully circumscribed within an octave, ninth, or (rarely) a tenth, and the outside limits of highest and lowest voices never reach three octaves, even in such festal six-voice motets as *Jubilate Deo, omnis terra* and *Gaude et laetare, Ferrariensis civitas* (thus producing predominantly dense and packed sonorities); (5) no motet begins with all voices participating in the opening chord, and only one second section opens "full"; (6) voice-pairing *à la Josquin* is rare; (7) moreover, the treatment of dissonance in most cases is more mannered than Josquin's, and approaches Palestrinian usage; (8) of the 16 motets in two *partes*, 5 are in aBcB form; (9) in the 25 motets, a "key signature" of one flat occurs 18 times, of no flats 6 times, and of two flats once; (10) words control music in obvious ways, among them being these—(a) prominent words such as *Deus fortis* (*MME*, XIII, 9, mm. 35-41), *Joanne Baptista* (70, mm. 24-27), and *Ite* (88, mm. 169-173) are set off rhythmically and emphasized by homophonic treatment, (b) an aBcB musical form is never used with narrative motet texts but only with contemplative and meditative texts, (c) sad texts such as *Lamentabatur Jacob* and *Verbum iniquum* call for low voices in hypophrygian and phrygian, and exultant texts such as *Tu es Petrus* and *Andreas Christi famulus* call for high voices in hypomixolydian;[329] (11) the most impressive display of learning—a canon at the suboctave surrounding a plainsong quotation in slow notes—is reserved for the most intimate of devotional texts, the *Ave Maria;* (12) in 5 of the 25 motets an interior voice is assigned a short ostinato, which incessantly repeats a single snatch of tune and text; (13) endings of motets are always carefully prolonged, suggesting either "linkèd sweetness long drawn out" or a Jacob's ladder of mounting sonority.

In Spain itself, none of Morales's motets was printed either in partbooks or in folio during his lifetime. However, intabulated versions of the motets, just as of mass movements, are encountered frequently. To consider only those twenty-five motets in *MME*, Volume XIII, the following Spanish intabulations are known: *Sancta et immaculata*, Fuenllana [1554], folios 47ᵛ-49; *Nonne dissimulavi* (pt. 2 of *Antequam comedam*), Valderrábano [1547], folio 15; *Inter natos mulierum*, Fuenllana, folios 30ᵛ-31ᵛ; *Lamentabatur Jacob* (pt. 1), Fuenllana, folios 64-65; *Verbum iniquum* (pt. 1), Fuenllana, folios 63-64; *Quanti mercenarii* (pt. 1), Valderrábano, folios 50^V-51; *Jubilate Deo* (both parts), Fuenllana, folios 81^V-83^V, and (pt. 1 only), Valderrábano, folios 61^V-63.

The Spanish sources, since they provide not glosses but rather note-for-note reductions, give valuable clues to the ficta accidentals considered appropriate in Morales's own country and epoch. Two Spanish intabulations are known for part 1 of *Jubilate Deo*: the first being for two vihuelas (1547); the second for solo vihuela (1554). Because of their contemporaneity, these intabulations should interest not only devotees of Spanish art but also those who still hope to draw valuable clues for accidentalizing out of the vihuela or lute books published before 1600.[330] In the accompanying example, Fuenllana's accidentals are registered before the notes that they affect and Valderrábano's are shown above or below. Valderrábano's accidentals conflict in mm. 4 (A), 9 (Q), 10 (C, T), 17 (Q), 23 (Q), 32 (T), 39 (B), 40 (B), 43 (A), 50 (C), 51 (C), 55 (Q), 57 (A), 62 (Q). Only six of these conflicts however, occur on "first" beats. Five of the six involve the plainchant, which Valderrábano in conformity with ancient Spanish tradition wished occasionally to read thus: FGde♮d; rather than always thus: FGde♭d.[331]

Not only do two Spanish intabulations of *Jubilate Deo* survive but also two printed editions of the vocal parts. The first is found in *Quintus liber motettorum ad quinque et sex et septem vocum* (Lyons: Moderne, 1542); the second in *Il primo libro de motetti a sei voce* (Venice: Scotto, 1549). Valderrábano may have known the first—his *Silva de sirenas* having been published in 1547. Fuenllana could have had access to both—his *Orphénica lyra* not appearing until 1554. In the Lyons 1542 imprint, no note of the plainchant ostinato is ever flatted; whereas e♭ prefixes the penultimate note of each ostinato incise in the 1549 Venetian imprint. Valderrábano's solution, of course, lacks consistency: because so often as obligatory E♭'s appear simultaneously in the other parts, he bows to them and flats the plainsong as well. At other times he flats without any apparent necessity. As a result, his I, II, VII, and VIII repetitions of "Gaudeamus" proceed with e♮; his III, IV, V, and VI repetitions with e♭. The student may draw whatever conclusions he wishes from the fact that Valderrábano vacillated back and forth from e♭ to e♮ in the same intabulation. It would have been perfectly within his reach to have been consistent—had he valued uniformity. However, what seems more to the point for the present interpreter of Morales is the fact that the accidentals on which both Valderrábano and Fuenllana agree (mm. 20, 27, 37, 56, 63), and which are not to be found in any of the printed partbooks, are usually sharps. It is at once obvious that neither vihuelist fears the sound of cross relations: see mm. 15 (e♮ and

Jubilate Deo omnis terra*

(Pars I)

Orphénica lyra (1554), fols. 81ᵛ-83ᵛ.

[Enríquez de Valderrábano: *Silva de sirenas* (1547), fols. 61ᵛ-62]

Morales-Fuenllana

* In Fuenllana's intabulation only the voice singing the plainchant and the bass carry text. The bass sings: "Rejoice in the Lord, all ye lands; sing joyfully; rejoice and tell His praises. For through the mediation of Paul, Charles and Francis, kings of vast domains, have agreed to unite; and peace descends from Heaven."

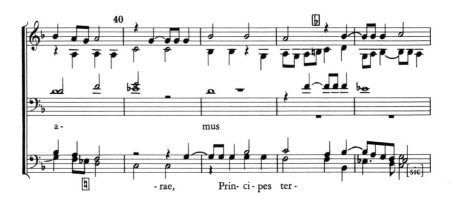

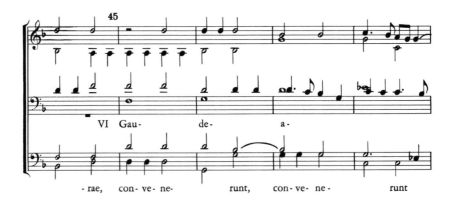

** This is the nomenclature of the voice parts in *Il primo libro de motetti a sei voce* (Venice: Girolamo Scotto, 1549), no. 25; though not in *MME*, XIII, 184-191. Anglés follows Moderne (1542) in naming voices.

E♭), 53 (e♮ and E♭), and 58 (e♮ and E♭). Fuenllana even specifies a more daring conflict when he sounds F♮ simultaneously with f♯ (meas. 50). Valderrábano does the same in meas. 63 when he specifies F♮ in his first vihuela against f♯ in his second.

As for structure: (1) Each new incise in the motet text gives rise to a new point of imitation (mm. 11$_3$, 16$_2$, 26$_3$, 39$_2$, 45$_3$, 51$_4$; mm. 83$_2$, 91$_2$, 111$_3$, 116$_2$). But these points of imitation (which are not all carried through with equal rigor) do not at any time coincide with the entries of the plainsong ostinato. (2) If the ostinato entries and the points of imitation always overlap, the counterpointing voices, on the other hand, invariably manage in part 1 of this motet to arrive at the chord of D minor whenever the Gaudeamus theme commences. (3) The head theme, which travels through five counterpointing voices in mm. 1-12, is not thereafter completely lost. In part 2 (*O felix aetas*, not shown here) it returns boldly with this new strand of text: "Qui christiano populo" (altus and bassus), thus making for a tighter unity between parts 1 and 2. (4) In part 2, which is almost exactly the same length as part 1, there are ten repetitions of Gaudeamus. But Morales builds an exciting climax by making his plainsong march at double-step the last six times that it enters. (5) This motet, although one of the earliest of Morales's datable compositions [1538], contains only two "incomplete" changing-note figures (mm. 61 and 62 in the altus), no upper neighboring notes, no escaped notes, no irregular resolutions of syncope dissonance, and no "consonant" fourths.

Jubilate Deo omnis terra enjoys the distinction of having been Morales's one motet parodied by Victoria. (See pp. 375 and 386-387.) Interestingly, Victoria in his six-voice *Gaudeamus* Mass (1576) appropriates not only Morales's themes but also the incomplete cambiata (Morales, meas. 62 = Victoria, Kyrie I, meas. 26)[332] and even the clash of F against f♯ which Valderrábano had prescribed as the proper way of accidentalizing the cadence at the end of Morales's part 1 (Morales, meas. 63 = Victoria, Kyrie I, meas. 27). So far as this one motet and the parody mass based upon it are concerned, there seems no sharp distinction to be made between the ways in which Morales (in 1538) and Victoria (in 1576) handled dissonance.

However, the tally changes when a comparison is made of Morales's motet *a 5*, *O sacrum convivium*,[333] with the parody mass *a 5* composed by Palestrina (and published for the first time in 1889 by Haberl from the unique source, *Cappella Sistina Codex 30* [copied in 1594]).[334] Morales's motet reverts to the following "archaic" usages: (1) at meas. 10 he writes a syncope that begins as a dissonance—a seventh; (2) at meas. 33 he resolves a fourth into a diminished fifth; (3) at meas. 49 he begins a syncope with a fourth; (4) at meas. 54 he writes an upper neighboring note in his top voice;

(5) at mm. 68, 70, and 73 he fails to resolve the syncope dissonance (of a seventh) stepwise downward and does not later retrieve to the required note of resolution; (6) in meas. 91 he leaps to the dissonance of a diminished fifth, second "beat." Apart from these matters, Morales writes melodic sequences in his top voice, mm. 96-97, and intrudes a Josquin triplet-figure in the midst of duple meter, meas. 104. Palestrina adheres closely to his model in many respects; but will have nothing to do with these "archaisms." Since our concern here is with Morales, not Palestrina, an exhaustive analysis cannot be undertaken. The best that can be done is to offer for comparison the following measure numbers (G.P. da Palestrina, *Werke*, ed. by F. X. Haberl, is cited as *PW*): *MME*, XIII, 115, meas. 11 = *PW*, XXIII, 71, meas. 18; *MME*, XIII, 119, mm. 67-68, 69-70, 72-73 = *PW*, XXIII, 78, meas. 2, meas. 81, mm. 21-24. Palestrina betrays himself by such other procedures as these: his running scale-lines are much longer and more frequent; he introduces a great many paired quavers (there are only two in the motet); where Morales used melodic sequences, Palestrina makes imitations of the same melodic material (in his Benedictus). As is his custom elsewhere in his parody work, Palestrina endows "motives" and fragments from the original with a power and meaning altogether unsuspected. After studying his mass, we hardly know which to admire more: Palestrina's exegetical gifts or the riches that he found lying beneath the surface of Morales's motet.

The third Morales motet parodied by a great successor, *Sancta et immaculata*, will be considered in the next chapter when Guerrero's mass of that name is discussed at length (pp. 195-198). Just as Crecquillon's motet, *Verbum iniquum et dolosum* (*Liber tertius ecclesiasticarum cantionum quatuor vocum* [Susato, 1553]) begins with a head theme near enough to that in Morales's motet of the same name to suggest a common plainsong source, so Simon Moreau's *Sancta et immaculata* (*Liber quintus ecclesiasticarum cantionum* [Antwerp: Susato, 1553]) starts with a head theme so like Morales's as to startle the unforewarned. Moreau begins his superius with a melody that plays tag with Morales's altus through a dozen notes. Since Morales's *Sancta et immaculata* was in print as early as 1541 and was again reprinted at Venice in 1546, there can be no question of his priority. What Moreau's "rewrite" proves is Morales's success in the Low Countries; as well as in Italy and Spain. His influence *per universum terrarum*[335] will indeed be devastatingly documented if many other neglected partbooks reveal such "plagiarisms" as Moreau's.

Another type of exercise that will sharpen appreciation of Morales's motets will be to compare his settings of such texts as *Pater peccavi* with Crecquillon's or Manchicourt's;[336] and of *Job tonso capite*, of *Tu es Petrus*, and of *Verbum iniquum* with Clemens non papa's.[337] The more renowned composers always etched sharply individualized profiles. Only nonentities of Moreau's stamp ignominiously borrowed other men's ideas when writing motets—this being the genre in which sixteenth-century composers were expected to show their expressive powers.

Only brief space can be allotted here to Morales's liturgical pieces not classifiable as motets. A hymn *a 4* for use at Christmas vespers and matins, *Jesu Redemptor omnium*, was printed in the *Suplemento polifónico* to the July-September, 1953, issue of *Tesoro sacro-musical*. It was Athanasius Kircher in 1650 who, while instructing sacred composers how to proceed, wrote as follows: "Renounce the trifling of such vain songs as those called ariettas and villanellas, the style of which is antithetical to that which should be used in Church hymns; . . . especially is it in opposition to the noble style of Palestrina and Morales, whose hymns always contain *cantus firmi*."[338] Morales assigns the plainsong in *Jesu Redemptor omnium* to the tenor. Its Gregorian original is not associated with that particular hymn text in the 1947 *Liber usualis*, pages 282-283, but rather with the compline hymn *Te lucis ante terminum*, as sung between December 25 and January 6. Morales brings in his tenor last, after preliminary imitation in the three other voices. The tenor quotes the notes of the plainsong original; and with the same exactitude that Morales habitually requires when citing Gregorian material. But he does not here write *Pfundnoten*. Since only one stanza—the first of seven—is clothed in polyphonic dress, it is to be suspected that the odd verses were sung polyphonically and the even verses in unaccompanied plainchant.

Another Morales hymn, recently reprinted, was transcribed for the keyboard by Venegas de Henestrosa (1557) under the title *Sacris solemniis, Joseph vir*.[339] The top voice makes a free canon at the fourth through the first ten bars with the altus. No plainsong source for this melody can be found in the *Liber usualis*. But such a source does exist. It occurs note for note as the melody for St. Thomas Aquinas's Corpus Christi hymn, *Sacris solemniis juncta sint gaudia*, in a Spanish processional dated 1526.[340] It also comes to light as the treble of two other keyboard hymns in Venegas de Henestrosa's *Libro de cifra nueva*, one of which is by Antonio [de Cabezón].[341] Since the treble reveals itself as a distinctively Spanish plainchant, then possibly the tenor is of prior origin also. Bermudo in 1555 said that Morales had written a hymn entitled *Sacris solemniis* in which he combined two plainsongs.[342] This statement could of course apply to some other hymn by Morales of the same title: if another of the same title could be found. However, none other does seem to survive. Bermudo's eulogy belongs in a section headed "Concerning some outstanding musical feats." He said: "In a stanza of *Sacris solemniis* Morales combined two plainsongs. Each goes its own way in the voice to which it is assigned; and it is a great feat for him to have carried the two all the way through to the end without their jolting each other."

Sacris solemniis, Joseph vir

Morales-Venegas de Henestrosa

MME, II, 136-137 (Libro de cifra nueva para tecla, harpa, y vihuela. 1557).

Bermudo praised still another hymn by Morales (which he did not identify by title, however: merely referring to it as a Hymn of the Holy Ghost). In this hymn, said Bermudo, Morales performs two exquisite feats. Throughout the first stanza a canon made of the plainsong engages the upper two voices; meanwhile strands of the plainsong are woven into the lower two voices. In his second stanza, according to Bermudo, Morales writes a unique kind of canon. The canonic voice, although duplicating its predecessor so far as notes are concerned, refuses in this singular type of canon to observe any of the rests found in the predecessor voice part.

To avoid controversy, we shall here abstain from "identifying" the Holy Ghost hymn to which Bermudo alluded. But a still extant Morales hymn stanza—the one copied into Toledo Cathedral Codex 25 at folios 62^V-63 —does conform with Bermudo's description of the second stanza in Morales's hitherto unidentified hymn. The title is *Solemnis urgebat dies;* the text consists of four iambic tetrameter lines, the first and third of which rhyme. The poetry tells how imminent is that solemn day, by prophecy foretold, when this present world shall be seven times folded up in presage of the coming blessed age. The altus starts before the cantus; and, because it disregards all the rests in the cantus, reverses the order of weak and strong beats during four measures (mm. 13-16 in altus = 17₄-21 in cantus). The canon is of so unusual a kind because Morales wishes it to serve as an expressive device. The day when the world will be rolled up like a scroll is fast approaching; and therefore the "rests" in the announcing cantus must be eliminated from the answering altus—to symbolize the "urgency" of that imminent event.

Still another hymn stanza preserved at Toledo (Codex 21, folios 31^V-32) illustrates Morales's skill in inventing "expressive" canons: *Salva nos, stella maris.* The text hails the Star of the Sea who bore Jesus, King of Kings: to whom earthly kings gave gifts of gold, of frankincense, and of myrrh. The canon in this setting *a 5* engages tenor and cantus at the octave. Again, in this hymn as in his *Ave maris stella* Mass, Morales has lavished his greatest art on a Marian text.

A separate class of liturgical composition can be made, if one likes, of Morales's Marian antiphons. In addition to three settings of *Regina coeli laetare* (*a 4, a 5,* and *a 6*), he left two of the *Salve Regina.* Both are easily available in modern reprint.[343] The version at the Seville Cathedral and at the Vatican in Cappella Sistina MS 17 is through-composed: verses 1-4 being set *a 5,* verse 5 *a 3,* and verses 6-7 again *a 5.* From the head notes of each successive verse in the plainsong, Morales has spun points of imitation. No one voice usurps the role of cantus firmus throughout the antiphon. Each verse ends with a clear-cut cadence—verses 1, 2, and 3 authentically, 4 and 5 plagally, 6*a* with a leading-tone cadence, 6*b* authentically, 7*a* and 7*b* authentically, and *7c* plagally. The last chord in each full verse rises over G—minor being implied at the end of verse 1; major at the ends of verses 4 and 7. The other chords lack their third. Apart from the external fact of its presence in Cappella Sistina MS 17 alongside his *Tristezas me matan* Mass, this particular Salve could be conjectured to have been a comparatively early work because of such mannerisms as the Josquin triplet (meas. 37) and the escaped notes at mm. 11 (cantus), 26 (tenor), and 93 (altus).

In his "Spanish" Salve, on the other hand, Morales adheres to untransposed dorian; sets only verses 2, 4, 6a, and 7 polyphonically; writes throughout *a 4*; never fails to assign the plainsong to the top voice toward the beginning of each polyphonic verse; and inclines to be much more repetitious so far as words and musical phrases are concerned. This is one of Morales's few pieces in which he systematically pairs voices—the upper pair alternating with the lower. The proportion of escaped notes is higher than in the other Salve. The last verse alone contains five. There are, however, no interjected Josquin triplets. A nice touch is to be seen at the endings of verses 2 and 7 when the cantus skips up from d to d^1: as if to test the "perfection" of the diapason with which the Virgin is so often compared in Spanish mystical literature.

The last among Morales's liturgical works that can be considered here is his four-voice setting of the Office for the Dead. Throughout his *Officium defunctorum*, printed by Pedrell in 1894,[344] the Gregorian melody (as in "Anglican" chant) is everywhere forthrightly harmonized *a 4*. The plain song goes either in the top voice (*1* Regem cui *2* Venite exultemus *3* Quoniam Deus *5* Hodie si vocem *8* Regem cui) or in the tenor (*4* Quoniam ipsius est mare *6* Quadriginta annos *7* Requiem aeternam). Unlike such plainly homophonic works as the Lamentations (1564), the *Officium defunctorum* makes not the slightest gesture toward imitation. Instead, Morales writes nude chords. The ending cadences in the Invitatory move to F (B♭ in signature); in the three lessons for the first nocturn, to E; and in Responsory III of the second nocturn, to F (B♭ in signature).

For more than one reason this particular Office should be of interest to students of music in the Western Hemisphere. Preserved complete in an eighteenth-century copy at Ávila in Spain, this *Officium* also survives incomplete in a seventheenth-century copy at the Puebla Cathedral in Mexico. The Puebla *Libro de coro, 3,* shows a different opening Regem cui at folios 35^v-36, but the same Venite exultemus at folios 36^v-37, Quoniam Deus at folios 37^v-38, and so forth; concluding with the Requiem aeternam and Regem cui at folios 41^v-42. A most interesting account of a performance of this *Officium* at Mexico City in 1559 can be read in Francisco Cervantes de Salazar's *Túmulo imperial* (Mexico City: Antonio de Espinosa, 1560).[345] The author, who upon arrival in New Spain (1553) first taught rhetoric and then later became Rector of the newly founded University of Mexico, had been a close friend of none other than Juan Bermudo before emigrating from Andalusia. Indeed, while still a professor in the University of Osuna he had written the preface for Bermudo's *El arte tripharia* (published at Osuna in 1550). Beyond doubt, he was a musically knowledgeable person. The events described in *Túmulo imperial* were a group of commemorative acts in the Mexican capital in honor of the deceased Charles V (d. 1558). He wrote as follows:

After all these acts were completed with utmost magnificence and authority, and after everyone was seated, the vigil then began with the chapelmaster [of Mexico City Cathedral, who was Lázaro del Álamo] dividing his choral forces into two groups for the Invitatory. One choir sang the *Circumdederunt me* and the other the *Venite exultemus* psalm: both in the polyphonic settings composed by Cristóbal de Morales. At the outset of the vigil, the hearts of all present were lifted toward heaven because of the sublimity and sweetness of the sound. . . . Upon completion of the Lord's Prayer, Morales's *Parce mihi, Domine* was sung to the great satisfaction of all present.

Here then is perhaps the first record of a polyphonic event in the New World for which exact data concerning both composer and works performed survives. On every account it deserves to be remembered. Best of all, the very works are still extant: *Circumdederunt me* in Codex 21 (folios 34ᵛ-35) at Toledo Cathedral, this being his setting of Psalm 114 (= 116):3; *Venite exultemus* (Ps. 94 [= 95]) at Puebla Cathedral; *Parce mihi, Taedet animam*, and *Manus tuae* (Job 7:16*b*-21, 10:1-7, 10:8-12) in an unnumbered eighteenth-century choirbook at Ávila Cathedral.

Compositions with Spanish and Italian Text

The sum of Morales's works with vernacular text comprises three short Spanish pieces, of which two survive in vocal parts and the third in an intabulation for solo voice and vihuela; a reasonably well authenticated Italian madrigal *a 4* and another rather doubtful one *a 5*; and a lute transcription entitled *Caronte* after the mythological ferryman who rowed the dead over the river Styx. In addition to these, Enríquez de Valderrábano in *Silva de Sirenas* (folios 92ᵛ-93) attributed to Morales a "canción," *Omni mal de amor procede*, which, however, is not Morales's at all, but is a frottola by the wife-murdering lutanist Bartolomeo Tromboncino.[346]

Of the two pieces with Spanish text which survive in vocal parts, one is Morales's four-voice setting of the initial line from the prophecy of Christ's Second Coming which St. Augustine attributed to the Erythraean Sibyl. Living either during the time of Romulus or of the Trojan War, this sibyl—according to Augustine—"certainly wrote some things concerning Christ which are quite manifest" (*De Civitate Dei*, XVIII, xxiii); her prophecy of the Second Coming, was delivered in the form of a 27-line acrostic poem, the initial letters of which spelled out in Greek, "Jesus Christ the Son of God, the Saviour."

In Toledo Cathedral, and widely elsewhere in sixteenth-century Spain, it was the custom during Christmas matins to present this sibylline prophecy in dramatic form.[347] After the *Te Deum*, a choirboy richly garbed as the oriental sibyl emerged from the sacristy followed by four other choirboys: two representing angels of judgment with swords in hand and the other two with axes. Upon mounting a specially prepared platform the choirboy dressed as the sibyl sang a Spanish translation of her 27-line prophecy. The two choirboys dressed as angels of judgment responded to each strophe by rattling their swords: whereupon a chorus of adult male singers sang in simple four-part harmony the response *Juicio fuerte será dado y muy cruel de muerte* (Severe judgment will be allotted and very cruel death). Morales's setting of this response, copied at folios 29ᵛ-30 of Toledo Codex 21, extends to only fourteen breves. It has been twice printed—first by Asenjo Barbieri in 1890;[348] second by Anglés in 1935.[349] By a strange quirk, neither of these distinguished scholars attributed it to Morales, both publishing it instead as an anonymous composition. There is a reason for this curious accident: Barbieri did not consult the original manuscript, relying instead on a hired amanuensis; Anglés in turn copied Barbieri, repeating even the small errors to be found in the transcription already printed by Barbieri. That the response printed by both as anonymous is actually ascribed in Toledo Codex 21 to Morales was, on the other hand, made known as long ago as 1925 by Trend.[350] However, Trend seems not to have noticed that it concorded with the "anonymous" item printed in Barbieri's appendix to his *Cancionero musical* at page 610.

The second of Morales's vocal pieces with Spanish text has also by an interesting coincidence been in print since 1944 as an "anonymous" item.[351] It was first published as long ago as 1556 by Girolamo Scotto at Venice: who included it among the fifty-four *Villancicos de diuersos autores, a dos, y a tres, y a quatro, y a cinco bozes*. Because the Scotto imprint was discovered in apparently unique partbooks at Uppsala, Sweden, by Rafael Mitjana, this songbook has now come to be known popularly as the *Cancionero de Upsala*. Item 13, *Si n'os huviera mirado*, concords note for note with the villancico *a 3* in MS M 454 at the Biblioteca Central in Barcelona, folios 185ᵛ-186, where it is ascribed to Morales.

The sentiment of the lyrics[352] is charming: *I* (1) Had not I beheld you, (2) I would not have suffered, (3) but neither indeed would I have beheld you. *IIa* (1) To look upon you has caused grievous sorrow, (2) but not to have seen you would have been much worse; *IIb* (1) I would not be so lost, (2) but I would have lost much more. *III* (1) What would he have seen who had not seen you? (2) What would he have missed? (3) My lady, if he had not beheld you. The music of *I* and *III* is identical; as also is the music of *IIa* and *IIb*. The spillover rhyme-scheme from *II* into *III* makes of this a classic-type villancico so far as mating of poetry and music is concerned.

On the other hand the texture is more contrapuntal than in any Encina villancico. Each of the six phrases, *I* (1) and (2), *IIa* (1) and *IIb* (1), *III* (1) and (2), starts with a point of imitation. The other phrases, *I* (3), *IIa* (2), *IIb* (2), and *III* (3), begin as dialogues in which the lowest and top voices answer each other. As for the phrase endings; Morales with his invariably keen sense of balance allows all three voices to participate in the final chord of only one authentic cadence—that cadence into A (minor) being reserved for the close of *I* (= *III*). True, the C-Major cadences at mm. 14 and 34_3 are authentic also; but the bass drops out at the moment of resolution. The A (minor) cadences at mm. 8, 17, and 22 are of the leading-tone variety. The cadence to the chord of E-Major, closing *II*, is of the phrygian type. By carefully weighting his several cadences—reserving the heaviest for the end of the *estribillo*—Morales makes even of them carefully-graded supporting pillars. Here, then, so comparatively casual a piece as a villancico gives evidences of his artistry. More than that, it is an extremely beautiful piece; long before it was discovered to be Morales's it had become a favorite with performing groups that specialize in Renaissance music.

His setting makes us wish that he had more frequently turned his hand to such gracious and neatly phrased lyrics. Perhaps he did. Only one of the fifty-four part songs in the *Cancionero de Upsala* bore an ascription when the collection was first published in 1556: namely, item 49 (*Dezilde al cavallero*) —attributed to Gombert. Now that item 13 has been discovered to be Morales's, we may hope that others in the collection will one day prove to be his also.

His third piece with Spanish words is a *romance* (*a* 4) entitled *De Antequera sale el moro*. Intabulated in Fuenllana's *Orphénica lyra* of 1554, this song was transcribed into modern notation by Count Guillermo Morphy in *Les luthistes espagnols*.[353] Subsequently, it has been reprinted several times.[354] Fuenllana's red-and-black numerals direct the vihuelist to play all four parts on his instrument, and at the same time to sing the top melody.[355] Like most romances, this one takes for its subject an incident in the wars of reconquest—here, the taking of Antequera (1410). Fuenllana printed only one strophe; but the remaining strophes have been recovered from a literary source.[356]

The first strophe reads thus: "The Moor sallied forth from Antequera carrying letters in his hand with a message." The rest of the seventeen strophes can be summarized as follows:

The letters were written in blood, and not for lack of ink. The Moor who carried them was 120 years old but looked 200 with his long beard down to his waist. . . . As he rode he would cry in a loud voice, "If you knew my sad message, King of Granada, you would tear your hair and downy beard." Thus bewailing he arrived at the gate of Elvira and thence betook himself to the king's palace. He met the king emerging from the Alhambra accompanied by 200 of his best horsemen. . . . "Allah save your Majesty!" he saluted him. "Welcome, ancient Moor. You have been many days awaited. What news do you bring from Antequera, my town?" "I must not say unless you first promise to spare my life. . . . The young prince Don Fernando has besieged the town. Everyday many of his horsemen, among them Juan de Velasco, Enríquez de Rojas, and Narváez, fight against the town. . . . Inside, the Moors are reduced to eating leather. Unless you send help quickly, O king, the town will fall."

Not only is the subject typical, but so also is Morales's homophonic setting. The anapaest rhythm of the three opening chords is a recurrent tag to be found in most traditional romances. Morales repeats this anapaest at the beginning of phrase 2. Each of the four phrases ends, typically, with the same "chord"—including the major third at the end of phrase 1; but lacking any third at the ends of phrases 2, 3, and 4. Each musical phrase sets a poetic line of eight syllables. Artfully, however, the musical phrase lengths vary, so that the "semibreve count" runs as follows: $7 + 6 + 7 + 10$.[357] Fuenllana's intabulation guarantees the accidentals: Morales ascends scalewise to his highest note using a sharped "leading tone"; but descends stepwise with a naturalized leading tone.

His madrigal *a 4, Ditemi o si o no*, appeared in Arcadelt's collection, *Il quarto libro di madrigali* (Venice: 1539). John Stafford Smith—the composer to whom is usually credited the music of "The Star-Spangled Banner"—was the first to bring it into score and reprint it in the nineteenth century.[358] Smith published it in his *Musica antiqua* of 1812, having copied it from the British Museum partbooks. Some thirty years earlier Burney had scored it from the same partbooks; in that source it shares company with thirty-eight four-part madrigals by such other composers as Berchem, Corteccia, Festa, Layolle, and Petrus Organista. Stylistically, Morales's madrigal differs in no crucial respects from Arcadelt's *O ardenti miei desiri*, *Col pensier* or *S'era forsi ripresso* in the same collection. Morales's imitations are of the lightest and most informal kind. These alternate with four-part homophony. The text dictates when a shift shall occur. The cadences are felicitously varied—a "complete" one into G [Major] rounding off the madrigal. The others alight on C or G, except at meas. 38, where E [Major] is approached with a phrygian cadence.

Because Morales so successfully emulated the style of Arcadelt in *Ditemi o si o no*, it would not pass belief that he also composed *Quando lieta sperai*, a five-part madrigal that Vincenzo Galilei ascribed to "Morales" in the 1584 edition of his *Fronimo*,[359] but which Angelo Gardano in the 1593 reprint of Cipriano de Rore's *Il secondo libro di madrigali a cinque voci* gave to Rore, the Italianized Fleming who died in 1565 at the age of forty-nine. In 1552 and 1560 this same *Quando lieta sperai* had appeared in *Il terzo* [sic] *libro di madregali dove si contengono le vergini*.[360] However, along with twenty-seven other items in these 1552 and 1560 collections, it lacked an attribution. Seven items were ascribed to Adrian [Willaert] in the 1560 edition; and one to Nicolo Dorati.

Quando lieta sperai made its final appearance in sixteenth-century imprints in 1593, in which year both Angelo Gardano and Giacomo Vincenti published it at Venice. Gardano ascribed it to Rore; Vincenti, on the other hand, published it in a collection with fifty-one other madrigals by such composers as Andrea Gabrieli, Marc' Antonio Ingegneri, Lassus, Monte, Nanino, Palestrina, Rore, Ruffo, and Wert; with this ascription: *di Morales secondo alcuni* (by Morales, according to some).[361] Vincenti in this same publication—which he entitled *Nuova spoglia amorosa*—ascribed four items to Rore. At best, then, the evidence for ascribing *Quando lieta sperai* to Morales is conflicting. Only Galilei's ascription strongly supports Morales's authorship.

Certainly, if it could be assigned to him, his reputation would be enhanced measurably: for this madrigal became the basis of parody masses by both Monte and Palestrina.[362] Van den Borren thus describes *Quando lieta sperai*: "It allies extreme technical refinement to formal beauty and expressiveness such as could hardly be surpassed."[363] Van den Borren also discovered that Lassus used it as the basis of a noble magnificat, published in 1587, but not republished in modern times. The poem of the madrigal is a sonnet; Van den Borren believed the author was, if not Petrarch, a "clever imitator of the great poet." The sense of the poem runs thus:

When I hoped to sit in the shade among the lovely purple flowers of April, and while singing to forget my sad state and not to think of a single love, behold the east and north winds bringing clouds and rain forced me to take shelter and drove away my soft hope by their raging fury. In consequence I never any longer anticipate a clear sky and a peaceful day, for the very heavens conspire against my happiness. Tears and sorrows unceasing will engulf me eternally until that day when all bitter sorrows will pass away.

Morales, if it was he who composed the setting, responded amazingly to the nuance of the Italian. The tonality is clearly "A minor," with frequent cadences to the tonic (mm. 5_3, 10_3, 20, 30_3, 34_3, 50_3, 56_3, 64_3, 69_3, 81). The few intermediate cadences come to rest on either C or E [Major] chords.

Curt Sachs, in his *Rhythm and Tempo*, first referred to the ambivalence of rhythm in *Quando lieta sperai* when he called it a piece "which, though written in *alla breve*, is an unmistakable $\frac{3}{4}$ piece and appears completely distorted in Schering's transliteration."[364] If Sachs was right, at least so far as the musical phrase used to set the first line of poetry is concerned, then it would not be so surprising to find that this madrigal was indeed Morales's rather than Rore's—rhythmic ambivalence having been a hallmark in authenticated works by the Sevillian master.

Were Galilei's attribution of *Quando lieta sperai* on page 160 of his 1584 *Fronimo* to be sustained, Morales's facility at adapting himself to changing styles in madrigal writing would be doubly demonstrated. For quite another matter, it would strengthen the case for Galilei's other attributions. On page 162 of his 1584 *Fronimo*, Galilei attributed to Morales a second piece—*Caronte* ("Charon"). If this second ascription were to be validated, we might plausibly link Morales with Diego Hurtado de Mendoza, who when he wrote his famous *Caronte* dialogue in 1547 (*Biblioteca de Autores Españoles*, XXXVI, 1-7) chose for his subject Pier Luigi Farnese's encounter with the ferryman of the Styx. From the lute intabulation, the composition seems originally to have been a four-part song starting with an imitative point; and to have included much dialogue between upper and lower voices in the middle section. For a third matter, Galilei in both the 1568 and 1584 editions of *Fronimo* presented several works by another Sevillian who spent a long time in Italy—Pedro Guerrero. These attributions all tend to stand or fall together: other sources of not only Morales's *Caronte* (p. 162 [1584]) but also of Pedro Guerrero's *Si puor biuir ardiendo* (pp. 7-8 [1568], *Biuiendo sin amar* (pp. 8-9 [1568]), and *Crainte & sospir* (pp. 112-114 [1584]), having not yet been found.[365]

Galilei was no mere practitioner as was Enríquez de Valderrábano. Indeed, he was sufficiently erudite to challenge his erstwhile teacher Zarlino on difficult points in ancient Greek theory.[366] By his own confession he had studied with the great theorist in Venice shortly before Zarlino in 1565 succeeded Rore as chapelmaster at St. Mark's. Certainly it is not beyond belief that as a lutanist already far advanced in the transcription of madrigals, Galilei should, while Zarlino's student in Venice, have interested himself in discovering the composers of anonymous items in Rore's third book—and even have picked up Morales's name from Rore himself: one of the characteristic features of the Rore publications being Rore's hospitality to other composers' madrigals. Moreover, it is an acknowledged principle of historical criticism that when ascriptions conflict—other things being equal—the less obvious attribution is usually the likelier. There were several obvious reasons that should have led Galilei to attribute *Quando lieta* to Rore. As late as 1581 he saw in Rore the crown and summation of a century and a half of musical advance; claiming that since his death there had been a steady decline.[367] In his 1568 *Fronimo* (part 1) he had intabulated for lute fourteen of Rore's madrigals—no other composer having been represented by more than five.[368] In the light of this information, the very fact that Galilei did not ascribe *Quando lieta* to Rore when he came to publish his 1584 *Fronimo* is all the more significant.

As for his transcription itself, Galilei prescribes added sharps in nearly every measure. If Morales was indeed the composer, then not only Valderrábano, Fuenllana, and Matelart but also Galilei realized his vocal music in intabulations that, by preference and not by exception, transform his stepwise progressions into what might now be anachronistically called "melodic-minor-scale" movements.

NOTES TO SECTION I

1 On the title page of Girolamo Scotto's 1541 collected edition of twenty-four motets by Gombert, Morales, Scotto himself, Ivo, Jachet, and Escobedo, this phrase appears (cantus): "excellentissimi Morales motectis."

2 George Rhaw, Luther's chosen music printer, included five Morales magnificats of twelve verses each (Tones I, II, IV, VI, VII) in his *Postremum vespertini officii opus* (Wittenberg: 1544). The title page shows woodcuts of Luther—who was still alive, Melanchthon, and the Elector John Frederick of Saxony. The next year Rhaw printed at Wittenberg a three-movement motet by Morales in his *Officiorum (ut vocant) de Nativitate, Circumcisione, Ephiphania . . . Tomus primus.*

3 François Rabelais, *La vie, faicts & dicts heroiques de Gargantua, & de son filz Panurge: Avec la prognostication Pantagrueline* (1553), p. 668: "Je ouy Adrian Willaert, Gombert . . . Morales . . . & autres joyeulx musiciens . . . mignonnement chantans."

4 Cristóbal de Villalón, *Ingeniosa comparacion entre lo antiguo y lo presente* (Madrid: Soc. de Bibliófilos Españoles, 1898), p. 176: "Biue en Roma vn español que se llama Morales, maestro de las obras del Papa, vnico en la composicion y boz."

5 Juan Bermudo, *Comiença el libro llamado declaracion de instrumentos* (Osuna: Juan de León, 1555), fol. 84^v: "Christoual de Morales, que es luz de España en la Musica."

6 Pedro Cerone, *El melopeo y maestro* (Naples: Juan Bautista Gargano, 1613), p. 144.

7 Cuzco Cathedral, *Libro de auctos capitulares 1549-1556*, fol. 44.

8 J. García Icazbalceta, *Bibliografía mexicana del siglo XVI* (México: Librería de Andrade y Morales, 1886), p. 120.

9 *Indice di tutte le opere di musica che si trovano nella stampa della pagina: di Alessandro Vincenti* (Venice: Alessandro Vincenti, 1619), p. 14: "Magnificat. . . . Morales fatti a voci pari à 4 dal Borsaro."

10 Anton Francesco Doni, *Libraria* (Venice: 1550), "La musica stampata: Madrigali, motetti, Messe, et canzoni" (appendix).

11 Giovanni Maria Artusi, *L'Arte del contraponto* (Venice: Giacomo Vincenti, 1598), p. 40.

12 Lodovico Zacconi, *Prattica di musica* (Venice: Girolamo Polo, 1592), fols. 164^v, 188, 190, 192.

13 Gustav Adolf Trumpff, "Die Messen des Cristobal de Morales," *Anuario musical*, VIII (Barcelona: Instituto Español de Musicología, 1953 [1954]), p. 120. [Hereafter *Anuario musical* is cited as *AM*.]

14 G. Baini, *Memorie storico-critiche della vita e delle opere di Giovanni Pierluigi da Palestrina* (Rome: Società Tipografica, 1828), I, 106.

15 H. Anglés, "Palestrina y los 'Magnificat' de Morales," *AM*, VIII, 153.

16 A second Guerrero mass parodied after a Morales four-voice motet occurs at fols. 109-120 of his *Liber primus Missarum* (Paris: N. du Chemin, 1566) with the title *Inter vestibulum*. The motet is printed in *MME*, XIII, 24-27.

17 Cerone, *op. cit.*, p. 89.

18 Filippo Kesperle, *Alcuni salmi et motetti di Vincenzo de Grandis posti in spartitura* (Venice: Alessandro Vincenti, 1625), dedication.

19 Athanasius Kircher, *Musurgia universalis*

(Rome: F. Corbelletti, 1650), I, 316. Kircher's ideas of these composers' dates were rather hazy. In his *Estudios* (p. 225), Mitjana declared that Kircher "inserted a Gloria Patri by Morales in Book VIII, chapter 7, of *Musurgia universalis.*" This statement, copied uncritically by Querol (*AM*, VIII, 175), cannot be verified. For another reference to Morales in Kircher see Vol. I, p. 614 ("De stylo melismatico").

20 Pedro Thalesio, *Arte de canto chão com huma breve instrucção* (Coimbra: Diego Gomez de Loureyro, 1618), fol. 12^v; Antonio Fernandez, *Arte de musica* (Lisbon: Pedro Craesbeeck, 1626), p. 19; João Alvares Frouvo, *Discursos sobre a perfeiçam do diathesaron . . . & reposta sobre os tres breves negros de Christovão de Morales* (Lisbon: Antonio Craesbeeck de Mello, 1662), p. 97; Manoel Nunes da Sylva, *Arte minima* (Lisbon: Joam Galram, 1685), p. 35.

21 Andrea Adami da Bolsena, *Osservazioni per ben regolare il Coro de i Cantori della Cappella Pontificia* (Rome: Antonio de' Rossi, 1711), p. 27: "On the third Sunday in Lent . . . the chapelmaster requires the Offertory to be sung at a diligent pace in order to allow ample time for the singing of the motet, *Lamentabatur Jacob*, by Cristóbal de Morales which follows (found at fol. 60 in choirbook 109). The whole of it is sung, both first and second parts. Since it is the most precious composition (*la più preziosa composizione*) in our entire archive, our singers are required to sing it with their best attention." On page 165 Adami called *Lamentabatur Jacob* "a marvel of art" (*una maraviglia dell'Arte*).

22 *Ibid.*, p. 11 (Prefazione Storica).

23 Fornari's manuscript account at the Vatican Library is found in Cappella Sistina MS 606. At page 18 he said: "Trovò ancora il modo di stendere le parole sotto le note con chiarezza maggiore di quella usata fino a quel tempo da tanti grandi uomini, e dallo stesso Morales; il quale nel suo libro di Magnificat stampato in Venezia l'anno 1562: ne avea mostrata la prima strada." For discussion of this passage, see *MME*, XVII, 32-33.

24 Burney's critique of Morales's style was founded on insufficient evidence; but he at least put himself to some labor. His scorings of two motets may be seen in British Museum Add. MSS 11,584 and of Morales's madrigal *Ditimi o si o no* in Add. MSS 34,071.

25 J. B. Trend, "Cristóbal Morales," *Music & Letters*, VI, 1 (Jan., 1925), 11-34.

26 Felipe Pedrell, *Hispaniae schola musica sacra*

(Barcelona: Juan B. Pujol, 1894), I, xviii (note 2). [Hereafter cited as *HSMS*.]

27 *Enciclopedia universal ilustrada*, XXXVI, 903. This article is marred by many other inaccuracies.

28 *Enciclopedia Cattolica*, VIII, 1397.

29 Mitjana, *Estudios*, p. 188; "Nuevas noticias referentes a la vida y las obras de Cristóbal de Morales," *Música sacro-hispana*, XII, 2 (Feb., 1919), 15.

30 Anglés, *Historia de la música española* (in Johannes Wolf's *Historia de la música*, Spanish translation [Barcelona: Editorial Labor, 1934]), p. 369; also A. Della Corte and G. Pannain, *Historia de la música . . . ampliada y anotada bajo la dirección de Mons. Higinio Anglés* (Barcelona: Editorial Labor, 1950), I, 290.

31 Cappella Sistina, *Diarii, 1* (1535-1540), fol. 17. [Hereafter cited as *Capp. Sist. Diar.*]

32 Toledo Cathedral, *Actos capitulares desde 1545 asta 1547* [Vol. 7], fol. 49^v.

33 Jaime Moll Roqueta, "Cristóbal de Morales en España," *AM*, VIII, 9 (lines 18-20).

34 Simón de la Rosa y López, *Los Seises de la Catedral de Sevilla* (Seville: Imp. de F. de P. Díaz, 1904), p. 76, note 1; *Documentos Americanos del Archivo de Protocolos de Sevilla: Siglo XVI* (Madrid: Tip. de Archivos, 1935), item 4; José Gestoso y Pérez, "Cristóbal de Morales: Pintor Sevillano," *Revista de Archivos, Bibliotecas y Museos*, IV, 7 (July, 1900), 385-390.

35 Seville Cathedral, *Autos capitulares. 1503-1504*, fol. 11^v.

36 *Ibid.*, fol. 12. Francisco de Morales, *canónigo*, was buried on Wednesday, July 30, 1505. See *Autos capitulares. 1505. 1506. 1507. 1510. 1523. 1524.*, fol. 131. [Hereafter *Autos* = *Actos* = *Actas Capitulares* are cited as *A.C.*]

37 *A.C., 1525-1526*, fol. 104 (Miercoles 20 de diciembre de 1525).

38 *A.C., 1538-1539*, fol. 59^v (Miercoles 25 dias de septiembre de 1538).

39 *A.C., 1540, 1541 y 1542* [*Libro 16*], fol. 61^v. The Sevillian *A.C., 1567-1569* [*Libro 28*], fol. 156^v, reveals that on May 19, 1568, a certain "Christoual de morales clerigo de seuilla" was confirmed a cathedral canon. If this person was a nephew, then his *expediente de limpieza de sangre* might tell us more about the composer.

40 Mitjana, in "Nuevas notas . . . ," *Revista de filología española*, Vol. V (1918), p. 127, suggested that this individual may have been the Palace Songbook composer, Garci Muñoz.

41 *A.C., 1503-1504*, fol. 8ᵛ (Miercoles 1 de febrero [1503]).

42 *A.C., 1505. 1506. 1507. 1510. 1523. 1524.*, fol. 88ᵛ (Miercoles 15 dias del mes de enero 1505).

43 Dedication of his *Missarum liber primus* (Rome: V. and L. Dorico, 1544). The three lower arts were grammar, dialectic, and rhetoric; the four higher ones geometry, arithmetic, music, and astronomy. Interestingly, St. Isidore of Seville, more than any other writer, influenced medieval educators to adopt this order.

44 *A.C., 1517. 1518. 1519.*, fol. 209ᵛ (Viernes 7 de enero de 1519).

45 *A.C., 1525-1526*, fol. 170ᵛ (Lunes 22 de octubre de 1526).

46 Diego Ortiz de Zuñiga, *Annales eclesiásticos y seculares de la muy noble y muy leal ciudad de Sevilla* (Madrid: Imprenta Real, 1677), p. 489, col. 1 (lines 20-24).

47 *MME*, II, *24.*

48 *A.C., 1505. 1506. 1507. 1510. 1523. 1524.*, fol. 345ᵛ.

49 *Ibid.*, fol. 359.

50 Concerning the use of the terms *clérigo de la veintena* and *veintenero* in Seville Cathedral, see Rosa y López, *op. cit.*, p. 106.

51 *A.C., 1525-1526*, fol. 45.

52 Nicolás Antonio, *Biblioteca hispana nova* (2d ed.; Madrid: Joachim de Ibarra, 1783), I, 248. Conrad Gesner, *Bibliotheca instituta et collecta . . . deinde in Epitomen redacta* (1583), p. 146, mentions Morales, but has nothing to say about his having been a Master of Arts. Two earlier Spanish composers with long records of Roman service obtained university degrees: Juan del Encina (Bachelor of Laws) and Juan Escribano (Master of Arts).

53 See *Música sacro-hispana*, XII, 2 (1919), 15-16. The archivist to whose credit the discovery should have redounded was D. Manuel Gómez Moreno.

54 Moll, *op. cit.*, p. 5. Another important document in Mitjana's hands shortly before his death at Stockholm in 1921 was Codax's *canciones de amor*. For the whereabouts of his manuscript "La capilla de música de la Catedral de Málaga" see note 191 below.

55 Ávila, *A.C., 1528-1529*, fol. 30ᵛ: "Este dia mandaron sus mercedes que ninguna obra se haga hasta que se haga el coro y se baxen los organos y los altares." This notice repeats one of like tenor dated August 3, 1528 (folio 13). For a description of Ávila Cathedral in 1526 see Gabriel M. Vergara y Martín, *Estudio histórico de Ávila y su territorio* (Madrid: Hernando, 1896), pp. 162-172.

56 Mitjana in a communication to *Le Ménestrel* (Jan. 16, 1920, p. 27) announced that he had seen a 1540 inventory of choirbooks owned by Ávila Cathedral. Among these were a book of Josquin masses, another containing two Baudouin masses, and another containing three four-part Morales masses. Like the 1526 book of Ávila capitular acts, this inventory has disappeared from view. See Moll, *op. cit.*, pp. 5-6.

57 Ávila, *A.C., 1529-1533*, fol. 8. Every year on St. Cyprian's Day (September 14) the Ávila chapter "elected" the staff for the year to come. The notice on fol. 8 begins thus: "These are the officials whom their Reverences, the Dean and Chapter of Ávila Cathedral, elected on St. Cyprian's Day, to serve during 1530." Then follows the list. First the position is designated; then the name of the individual to fill it. The musical appointees were:

Organista. Luis Lopez.
Organista de los Maytines. Miguel de Nava.
Sochantre. Alonso de Herrera.
Maestro de Canto llano. Juan Vazquez.
Maestro de Canto de Organo. Barrio Nuevo.
Tiple. Arellano.
Thenores. Oropesa y Pedro Lopez.
Contra Alta. Cevadilla. Henao. Herrera. Juan
    Carretero.

The above list fails to mention any basses. Just then the cathedral was searching for *contrabajos*. On July 3, 1530, the bass-singer Cristóbal Ruiz was appointed at an annual salary of 30,000 maravedís.

58 *A.C., 1528-1529*, unnumbered fol. at the end, dated September 3, 1529: "Este dia mandaron sus mercedes dar cuatro ducados a Juanico moço de coro de salario en cada un año. . . ."

59 What the chapelmaster was to teach his choirboys is specified in the Ávila *A.C., 1529-1533*, fol. 42ᵛ (Oct. 12, 1530): ". . . muestre [a] los niños canto de organo y contrapunto."

60 Rafael Mitjana, *Don Fernando de Las Infantas* (Madrid: Junta para ampliación de estudios, 1918), pp. 121-122. For the Ceballos-Barrionuevo song see *MME*, VIII, 89-90.

61 For Morales's starting salary at Plasencia, see Moll, *op. cit.*, p. 9 (line 30). For the yield of Plasencia diocese, see Lucio Marineo Siculo, *De rebus Hispaniae memorabilibus* (Alcalá de Henares: Miguel de Eguía, 1533), fol. 17. The bishopric at Ávila yielded 8,000 ducats annually; that at Plasencia, 15,000 ducats.

62 His father, Francisco Vargas, was a councillor of Charles V. Alonso Fernández in his *Historia y anales de la ciudad y obispado de Plasencia* (Madrid: Iuan Gonçalez, 1627) reports as follows (p. 192, col. 2): "He was a man of high aspirations. . . . He governed his diocese with admirable prudence and for its better administration retained learned advisers of first rank whom he paid large salaries. . . . He ordered the institution of archives in all the parish churches in order to conserve historic documents. . . . He was very intelligent in matters of art and architecture, a passion for which befits high nobility." Melchior de Torres dedicated his *Arte ingeniosa de Musica, con nueua manera de auisos breues y compendiosos sobre toda la facultad della* (Alcalá de Henares: 1544) to this bishop. In 1552 he was a delegate to the Council of Trent.

63 Alonso Fernández, *op. cit.*, p. 191. Clement VII confirmed this new table on April 20, 1526.

64 *Ibid.*, p. 194, col. 2.

65 Moll, *op. cit.*, p. 9.

66 *Ibid.*, p. 8.

67 *Ibid.*, p. 9.

68 *Ibid.* But it is surely a mistake to contend that the chapter gave him forty ducats "por el temor a que Morales abandonase Plasencia y no volviese" (for fear that Morales would leave Plasencia and not return). Rather, the Plasencia capitular acts state the exact purpose of the gift: "para ayudar en el casamiento de su hermana" (to help [with the expenses] at the marriage of his sister).

69 "Huérfana" does not necessarily imply that both parents were dead. The Plasencia act speaks of her being an orphan "after the death of her father." See Moll, p. 9 (line 20).

70 *Ibid.*, p. 10.

71 *Ibid.*, pp. 12-13.

72 *Ibid.*, p. 12 (line 4).

73 *Ibid.*, p. 12, note.33.

74 *Ibid.*, p. 10.

75 *Ibid.*, p. 14.

76 Mitjana, *Estudios*, p. 190.

77 Gaudio Mell was first mentioned in Antimo Liberati's *Lettera scritta . . . in risposta ad vna del Sig. Ovidio Persapegi* (Rome: Mascardi, 1685), p. 22.

78 *Le Ménestrel*, Jan. 16, 1920, p. 27.

79 Edited by Pedrell, *op. cit.*, pp. 1-20.

80 *Capp. Sist. Diar. 1*, fol. 17.

81 In the Dedication of his *Missarum liber secundus* (Rome: Dorici fratres, 1544): "quod cum me iampridem inter chori tui musicos collocaueris. . . ."

82 F. X. Haberl, "Die römische *schola cantorum* und die päpstlichen Kapellsänger," *Vierteljahrsschrift für Musikwissenschaft*, Vol. III (1887), pp. 260-261.

83 R. Casimiri, "Melchior Robledo, maestro a Saragozza: Juan Navarro, maestro ad Avila," *Note d'archivio*, XI, 3-4 (July-Dec., 1934), 203-206.

84 Haberl, *op. cit.*, pp. 249-250.

85 "Memoralia ad Summum Pontificem pro Cantoribus Cappellanis," *Capp. Sist. MS 657*, fol. 4. Six specific occasions during the year are listed when tips in the amount of two scudi are distributed by the pope.

86 Fornari, *op. cit.*, p. 48.

87 See "La obra musical de Morales," *AM*, VIII, 70.

88 See José M. Llorens, "Cristóbal de Morales, cantor en la Capilla Pontificia," *AM*, VIII, 57 (lines 13-14).

89 *Capp. Sist. Diar. 1*, fol. 28ᵛ.

90 See "Libro de decretos," Codex 72, Ambasciata di Spagna a la Santa Sede, fols. 50ᵛ, 53, 54. Other documents in the Santiago archive (now in the keeping of the Spanish Ambassador to the Holy See) which are germane: "Registro de cuentas generales, del camerlengo: 1535 [Doc. 509 bis]; 1545 [Doc. 516]"; "Capilla de música: Cantores, músicos, órgano [Doc. 2241]."

91 *Capp. Sist. Diar. 1*, fol. 36ᵛ, dated August

23, 1536; fol. 37, dated September 3, 1536.

92 R. Casimiri, "I 'Diarii Sistini'," *Note d'archivio*, XI, 1 (Jan.-March, 1934), 78 (Sept. 6, 1546).

93 *Ibid.*, p. 84 (Jan. 5, 1547).

94 *Capp. Sist. Diar. 1*, folio 120, dated January 15, 1540. A complete file on Sánchez's misconduct, which began as early as 1532, appears in *Capp. Sist. MS 678*, fols. 112-121.

95 *Capp. Sist. Diar. 2*, fols. 35 and 44 (fines for quarreling); fol. 59 (other misbehavior).

96 *Ibid.*, fol. 49, dated February 10, 1544. Another married chorister was Leonard Barré, admitted to the papal choir on July 13, 1537.

97 Léon Dorez, *La Cour du Pape Paul III d'après les registres de la trésorerie secrète* (Paris: Ernest Leroux, 1932), II, 225 (dated June 8, 1538).

98 *Ibid.*, II, 229, 223, 228.

99 Cf. the account of the Corpus Christi celebration at which it seems to have been first performed, in *Relaciones de Pedro de Gante* (1520-1544) (Madrid: Imp. de M. Rivadeneyra, 1873), p. 39.

100 *Pars 1*, only. Valderrábano did not transcribe *pars 2*. Fuenllana transcribed both *partes*.

101 *MME*, XIII, 38.

102 Felipe Rudio Piqueras, *Códices polifónicos toledanos* (Toledo: 1925), lists the date when each codex was copied. His 1554 date for Codex 13 has been verified.

103 "La obra musical de Morales," *AM*, VIII, 81-82.

104 *Ibid.*, pp. 82-83.

105 Vincenzo Pacifici, *Ippolito II d'Este: cardinale di Ferrara* (Tivoli: Soc. di storia e d'arte, 1920), p. 54.

106 *Capp. Sist. Diar. 1*, fol. 89ᵛ, shows that he was in Rome on March 9, 1539; but that he had taken a four-day trip between February 24 and 28.

107 See Pacifici, *op. cit.*, pp. 385-387, for lists of musicians patronized by Ippolito II. See also G. Radiciotti, *L'Arte musicale in Tivoli nei secoli XVI, XVII, e XVIII* (Tivoli: Stab. tip. Maiella di Aldo Chicca, 1921), pp. 9 ff.

108 In Palestrina's dedication of his *Liber primus motettorum* (Rome: 1569) to Ippolito II he alluded to "beneficia, quae in me quotidie confers."

109 *Capp. Sist. MS 688* names thirty annual feasts, in a "*Lista delle scatole che haño li sig ʳⁱ cantori di .n. .Sʳᵉ. tutto l'año dal palazzo,*" when feast boxes were customarily distributed. Morales received five such feast boxes during his decade in Rome: on April 2, 1539; March 28, 1540; May 25, 1541; May 26, 1542; and June 28, 1544.

110 *Capp. Sist. Diar. 1*, fol. 37ᵛ.

111 *Ibid.*, fols. 108ᵛ, 110.

112 Haberl, *op. cit.*, pp. 288-289 (*De licentia eundi ad partes*).

113 *Capp. Sist. MS 678*, fols. 99-101.

114 The two compositions anthologized were an eight-voice Litany and the four-voice *O Magnum Mysterium*. See Eitner, *op. cit.*, pp. 225, 268.

115 Reasons: (1) Malaria was an extremely common ailment in Rome; (2) Morales constantly hoped a change of climate would help; (3) When not suffering an attack, he could go about his business normally; (4) His condition progressively worsened, showing a chronic case; (5) He could know in advance when he would have an attack.

116 *Capp. Sist. Diar. 1*, fol. 81ᵛ: "Morales asseruit cras se esse infirmum" (Monday, November 18, 1538).

117 *Capp. Sist. Diar. 2*, fol. 35ᵛ: "D. Morales obtinuit licentiam pro vno mense eundi Ianue."

118 *MME*, II, 69. For Charles V's dates at Genoa, see Manuel de Foronda y Aguilera, *Estancias y viajes del Emperador Carlos V* (Madrid: R. Acad. de la historia, 1914), p. 546.

119 *Capp. Sist. Diar. 2*, fol. 44 (fine assessed December 22, 1543).

120 Pietro Vitali, *Le pitture di Busseto* (Parma: Stamperia ducale, 1819), p. 42.

121 On these Brescian brothers see P. Guerrini, "Per la storia della musica a Brescia: Frammenti e Documenti," *Note d'archivio*, XI, 1 (Jan.-March, 1934), 2.

122 *Capp. Sist. Diar. 2*, fol. 46 (Jan. 13, 1544).

123 Luis Zapata, *Miscelánea* (Madrid: Imp. Nacional, 1859 [Real Academia de la Historia, *Memorial histórico español*, XI]), pp. 134-135.

124 On Corteccia see F. Coradini, "Francesco Corteccia (1504-1571)," *Note d'archivio*, XI, 3-4 (July-Dec., 1934), 199-203.

125 Dorez, *op. cit.*, I, 8.

126 "Diarium Blasij de Cesena Magistri Ceremoniarum" (*Fondo Borghese*, Serie IV, 64), fols. 317, 318, 326.

127 Aulus Gellius (130-180) said in his *Noctes Atticae* (III, 10, 13) that music can distend the veins and arteries.

128 The woodcut adorning the title page of Morales's *Missarum liber secundus* shows the composer upon his knees, holding open a book that Paul III is in the act of blessing. On the two open pages of the book is printed on five-line staves the *Tu es vas* melody (concerning its source see below, note 221). In abbreviated form this serves as the tenor cantus firmus of Morales's complimentary mass.

129 José M. Llorens, *op. cit.*, p. 65.

130 *Ibid.*, pp. 62-63.

131 *Ibid.*, pp. 63-64.

132 *Ibid.*, p. 64.

133 *Ibid.*, p. 53.

134 See below, pp. 366-367.

135 See below, pp. 363, 472.

136 Llorens, *op. cit.*, p. 44.

137 Casimiri, "I 'Diarii Sistini,'" *Note d'archivio*, X, 3 (July-Sept., 1933), 274.

138 *Ibid.*, p. 270.

139 *Note d'archivio*, IX, 1 (Jan.-March, 1932), 55. The Spaniards elected to sit in the committee were Calasanz and Sánchez.

140 The original constitutions (*Capp. Sist. MS 611*) leave a blank space on page 31 (second space from the bottom) where Morales was to have signed (between the signatures of Stefanus de Toro and Antonius Capellus). The signatures descend in order of choir seniority—choir documents always listing the singers in order of senority rather than alphabetically. De Toro [Thoro] was admitted August 1, 1535; Morales, September 1, 1535; Capellus [Capello], March 28, 1536.

141 Reprinted in Haberl, *op. cit.*, pp. 284-296.

142 "Memoralia ad Summum Pontificem pro cantoribus cappellanis Cappellae Pontificiae" (*Capp. Sist. MS 657*), folio 1.

143 For a list of the twenty singers at the beginning of 1535, copied from the Sistine Diaries, see Casimiri, *Note d'archivio* (Jan.-March, 1932), 54. For the thirty-two singers at the beginning of 1545, see *ibid.* (Oct.-Dec., 1933), 333.

144 Haberl, *op. cit.*, p. 289 (cap. XXV).

145 On his September 11, 1536, trip to Viterbo he took nine singers; on his September 9, 1539, trip to Loreto, twelve; on his September 3, 1540, trip to Viterbo, twelve; on his January 11, 1543, trip, eight. While at Viterbo in the summer of 1543 he called eight singers from their vacation (August 14, 1543). Even when the pope went away for only a week or a fortnight, he insisted on carrying with him at least a double quartet.

146 On September 15, 1539, "Fuit missa lecta cum motetto." Half the singers were out of Rome on this day—twelve of them having been named to attend the pope during his Loreto trip.

147 Casimiri, *Note d'archivio*, X, 3 (July-Sept., 1933), 276: "Propter inopiam cantorum maxime supranorum ob pluuiam non fuit cantata missa, sed plane celebrata, ideo ordinatum fuit ut qui non comparauerunt punctarentur" (Aug. 30, 1545).

148 Haberl, *op. cit.*, p. 290 (cap. XXIX).

149 Casimiri, *Note d'archivio*, XI, 1 (Jan.-March, 1934), 76: "Jo. Aloysius de episcopis" received the cotta on June 28, 1546.

150 Francisco de Montalbo—admitted January 30, 1547—was a tenor. See Enrico Celani, "I cantori della Cappella Pontificia," *Rivista musicale italiana*, XIV (1907), 101.

151 Llorens, *op. cit.*, p. 46.

152 F. Rubio Piqueras, *Música y músicos toledanos* (Toledo: Suc. de J. Peláez, 1923), p. 94.

153 Toledo, *Actos Capitulares desde 1545 asta 1547* (Vol. 7), fols. 49v-50. See Moll, *op. cit.*, p. 16, for a transcription.

154 British Museum, *Egerton MS 415*, fol. 75.

155 On currency values and price movements in Spain, see Earl J. Hamilton, *American Treasure*

and the Price Revolution in Spain, 1501-1650 (Cambridge [Mass.]: Harvard University Press, 1934); especially pages 55 (note 3) and 285.

156 The Toledo *A.C.*, *1545-1547*, fol. 50, mention as one of the terms of Morales's contract: "E ansimesmo encargaron al susodicho los seyses e que se les de lo que se suele dar por el mantenimiento de ellos." On fol. 245ᵛ the chapelmaster's duties include "para que tenga cargo de enseñar y mantener los seyses." While overseeing the choirboys he must obey the instructions of the canon maestrescuela in all matters relating to their discipline and physical welfare. The chapelmaster did not choose the seises, although his advice might be heeded (*Actos capitulares desde 1548 asta 1551*, fol. 134); the maestrescuela had the last word in selecting new seises (*ibid.*, fol. 123ᵛ).

157 Toledo Capitular Library, "Expedientes de Limpieza de Sangre," Legajo 65 (Expedientes 1776-1810).

158 The maestrescuela, a canon, was the ecclesiastical superior of the *maestro de capilla*, a mere prebendary. Rank distinctions counted heavily in Spanish cathedrals.

159 *A.C.*, *1545-1547*, fols. 126ᵛ-127 (March 26, 1546). See Moll, *op. cit.*, p. 19 (lines 14-19).

160 Rubio Piqueras, *Música y músicos toledanos*, pp. 88-89, recounted a famine in January, 1546.

161 Moll, *op. cit.*, p. 18.

162 *Ibid.*, p. 19.

163 *Ibid.*, p. 20.

164 *Ibid.*, p. 18.

165 *A.C.*, *1545-1547*, fol. 244ᵛ (Dec. 10, 1547).

166 *Capp. Sist. Diar. 2*, fol. 94.

167 Francisco Sacedo, blind like Antonio de Cabezón, was elected to the organ prebend on January 22, 1541; took possession on February 9, 1541; and died shortly before August 7, 1547, on which date Cardinal Siliceo ordered thirty ducats to be paid to his indigent widow and daughters. See *A.C.*, *1545-1547*, fol. 226ᵛ. Prior to his engagement at Toledo, Sacedo was organist at Burgos (Biblioteca Nacional MS 14043). Juan de Peñalosa, "clérigo de la diocesis de Toledo," was his suborganist and succeeded him at his death. This Peñalosa later dickered unsuccessfully for the organistship at Palencia after the death of García de Baena on November 13, 1560. *Grove's Dictionary* (5th ed.), Vol. VI, p. 617, errs in citing him as

the composer of *Memorare piissima* and several other motets at Toledo (these are by Francisco de Peñalosa). Two other organists aided him at Toledo: Francisco López (*A.C.*, *1548-1551*, fol. 109) and a certain Ximénez called indiscriminately *músico de tecla* or *órgano* (*A.C.*, *1548-1551*, fols. 4ᵛ, 69ᵛ). They served irregularly on a piecework basis.

168 Rubio Piqueras, *Música y músicos toledanos*, pp. 65-66. However, the year 1509 is by no means to be taken as the first in which organs came into formal use at Toledo. As early as 1355 a certain Ruy González, queen's chaplain, was on the cathedral payroll as a *tocador de los órganos* ("player of the organs"). In 1424 Juan Rodríguez of Cordova, master organ builder, received 300 florins for repairing and tuning pipes in the "new" grand organs recently built by Fray Giraldo. Rodríguez was also paid for two keyboards to replace Fray Giraldo's, the action of which had been found much too heavy. The lowest note on the two manuals was to be C, with semitones beginning immediately in the lowest octave. He was also required to fix the leaking bellows and the pipes that ciphered; to finish before August 15, and not to depart until the Toledo chapter approved of the work done by him and his several helpers, two of whom he had brought with him from Cordova and the rest of whom were local carpenters and masons. For further details concerning the 1424 organ see Biblioteca Nacional MS 14042.

169 *A.C.*, *1548-1551*, fol. 111, lists Bernardino Çapata and Diego Ortiz as the two canons to whom "cometieron . . . los señores . . . que den orden con los musicos de organo como y quando an de tañer." Canon Ortiz was not the same individual as the Diego Ortiz of Toledo who in 1553 published *Glose sopra le cadenze*. From 1526 to 1566 a bass by the name of Alonso Ortiz was a leading singer in Toledo Cathedral. On November 4, 1547, Cardinal Siliceo recommended a salary increase in recognition of this singer's excellent work. Still another cathedral singer from *ca.* 1540 to 1561 was named Juan Ortiz. A third singer, but of less ability, was named Pedro Ortiz; he served Toledo Cathedral from *ca.* 1521 to 1561.

170 For full information concerning Gaspar de Maynete, Gerónimo de Cuéllar, and Bartolomé de Medrano, hired with a twenty-year contract on June 28, 1531, see Biblioteca Nacional MSS 14035.49, 14035.45, and 14035.47 (covering the years 1531, 1547, and 1557, respectively). Maynete was born at Osuna; his father was a French instrumentalist, "Juan de Paris." At Toledo he married Isabel de Tordesillas. Their son Francisco Maynete served as Toledo Cathedral bassoonist in 1589 (MS 14035.43). The three musicians mentioned in 1531 worked as a team; and each obligated himself to hire an assistant instrumentalist, so that an instrumental sextet would be available at all times. Moreover, they contracted to find a replacement should any of the principals or seconds fall ill or die—such replacement to be examined and approved by the Toledo chapelmaster. Gaspar de Maynete was still in service at Toledo in 1557 after twenty-six years. In that year, however, he accepted a higher bid at Seville (see below, p. 149). Many of these cathedral instrumentalists seem to have been connected by family ties and the father-son-grandson relation was common. Not so with the singers—they having been usually in orders.

171 An extremely valuable reference to the constant use of instruments at Toledo, even in accompanying plainchant, will be found in *Summi Templi Toletani*, dated 1549 (British Museum, *Egerton MS 1882*, fol. 40). The author, Dr. Blas Ortiz, who was vicar-general of the Toledo diocese, writes at length of the "ministriles, y sacabuches, y instrumentos" used at Mass and in the divine office.

172 Bermudo, *Comiença el libro primero dela declaracion de instrumentos* (Osuna: Juan de León, 1549), fol. X^v (prologue).

173 Moll, *op. cit.*, p. 19.

174 Marineo, *op. cit.*, fol. 17^v.

175 *Ibid.*, fol. 18.

176 Alonso López de Haro, *Nobiliario genealógico de los reyes y titulos de España* (Madrid: Luis Sánchez, 1622), I, 203.

177 Francisco Guerrero, *Sacrae cantiones, vulgo moteta nuncupata* (Seville: Martín Montesdoca, 1555). Guerrero hoped his own motets would recall Morales's, which the duke so loved.

178 Nicolás A. Solar-Quintes, "Morales en Sevilla y Marchena," *AM*, VIII, 29. But *clavicordio* should not be equated with "clavichord." In Joan Poblet, *Diccionario muy copiosa de la lengua española y francesa* (Paris: Matthieu Guillemot, 1604), clavicordio = espinette. In Richard Perceval, *Biblioteca hispanica* (London: John Jackson, 1591), clavicordio = virginals. John Minsheu in *A Dictionarie in Spanish and English* (London: Edm. Bollifant, 1599) and *A most copious Spanish dictionarie* (London: n.p., 1617) equates clavicordio with claricords, or virginals.

179 *AM*, VIII, 32.

180 Bermudo, *Comiença el arte tripharia* (Osuna: Juan de León, 1550), folio 3. Angel Ortega in his précis "Fray Juan Bermudo," *Archivo Ibero-Americano*, II (1915), 216-224, called Bermudo, a scion of a distinguished Écija family: he studied at Seville, entered the Minorite order at the age of fifteen and came strongly under the influence of Fray Luis de Carvajal, guardian of the Convento de Sant Francisco at Seville and representative of the order at the Council of Trent. At folio 1 in his *Declaración de instrumentos* (1555) Bermudo reveals that he was sent to Alcalá University to study mathematics. However, because of the low opinion in which music was held within the order he delayed his study of musical theory. Not until later when he was confined by a long sickness did he decide to study the subject seriously. After his illness he felt under providential compulsion to expound musical theory for the benefit of the order, as well as of the church. His mathematics provided, of course, an ideal background. Few will now dispute his 1555 *Declaración* the honor of being the best musical treatise published in Spanish during the entire century. On June 24, 1560, at a provincial meeting of the order in Baeza he was elected one of four *definidores* in the Andalusian province (see Ortega, "Las casas de estudio en la provincia de Andalucía," *Archivo Ibero-Americano*, III [1916], 189).

181 Bermudo, *El arte tripharia*, fol. 3^v.

182 Solar-Quintes, *op. cit.*, p. 33.

183 *Ibid.*, p. 35.

184 Málaga Cathedral, *A.C., 1550-1554*, fol. 193.

185 See below, pp. 138, 140, 242.

186 *El arte tripharia*, fol. 24.

187 Bermudo, *Declaración* (1555), fol. 128^v (preface to Bk. V).

188 *Ibid.*, fol. 66^v, col. 2.

189 *El arte tripharia*, fol. 24.

190 Málaga, *A.C., 1550-1554*, fol. 74. For the Spanish see R. Stevenson, "Cristóbal de Morales: A Fourth-Centenary Biography," *Journal of the American Musicological Society*, VI, 1 (Spring, 1953), 32-33.

191 For documentation, see R. Mitjana, "La capilla de música de la Catedral de Málaga / Año de 1496 al año de 1542. / Datos tomados de los libros de Actas Capitulares"—an unnumbered manuscript notebook at the Kungl. Musikaliska

Akademiens Bibliotek in Stockholm. Entries are arranged chronologically (the entry for January 5, 1535, is at page 73). The documentation referred to in notes 192-200 below was transcribed independently by the present author.

192 *A.C., 1550-1554,* fol. 75^v. Spanish in Stevenson, *op. cit.,* p. 33.

193 *A.C., 1550-1554,* fol. 105^v. Stevenson, *op. cit.,* p. 34.

194 *A.C., 1550-1554,* fol. 105^v.

195 *Ibid.,* fol. 106.

196 *Ibid.,* fol. 83. The first part of the organ-candidates' examination was given on Friday afternoon, February 5 (1552). Nuñez and then Doyz each played two vesper psalms, all in the same tone. Next they played accompaniments for a boy soloist. Doyz then played a hymn; and Nuñez, the Magnificat. On Saturday Doyz played the Mass of Our Lady; and Nuñez, the Mass of the day. At vespers Doyz and then Nuñez played the psalms. After vespers a choirbook was placed before each, opened at random, and the sight- and score-reading ability of each was tested.

197 *Ibid.,* fol. 83^v (Feb. 8, 1552). Doyz had been organist of the royal chapel at Granada. On December 9, 1536, Nuñez was designated sub-organist in Seville Cathedral. He was Jaén Cathedral organist on August 26, 1549.

198 *Ibid.,* fol. 87^v. Bermudo, in his *Declaración* (1555), fol. 60^v, col. 1, cited Doyz as one of the five best keyboardists in Spain. Even so, his appointment provoked violent opposition from a small coterie of singers—Juan de Trillo, Fernando Conversano, and Juan de Caravaca. These three banded together with certain prebendaries to protest against the manner in which the examination was given. On February 17 Trillo was dismissed for insubordination. Since he was a native of Málaga, it is possible that he was a partisan of the deceased chapelmaster's kin. Trillo was later received back, but remained a troublemaker. Doyz died on October 15, 1568.

199 *A.C., 1550-1554,* fol. 104.

200 *Ibid.,* fols. 151^v, 152.

201 Ana Ponce de León, Condesa de Feria, sister of the Duke of Arcos, was professed in religion at Santa Clara de Montilla later during this month. See López de Haro, *op. cit.,* I, 203. The mother superior, Doña Isabel Pacheco, was aunt of the Duchess of Arcos; it was for Doña Isabel that Bermudo composed *El arte tripharia.* Doña Ana Ponce de León, with her blue eyes and fair complexion, had the reputation of being not only one of the handsomest women of her time, but also of being one of the most cultivated. Her poems were published as late as 1635. Since professions were always splendid occasions and since Doña Ana was a "great" lady, her taking of the veil undoubtedly brought together not only the Arcos family but the best musicians of the time. If records of payments could be found for this convent, it might be revealed that Morales journeyed thither in late June, 1553.

202 Moll, *op. cit.,* p. 22.

203 *Ibid.,* p. 22 (lines 26-28).

204 Toledo Cathedral, *A.C., 1552-1555,* fol. 121.

205 *Ibid.* See Moll, *op. cit.,* pp. 22-23, for a transcription.

206 Toledo, *A.C., 1545-1547,* fol. 243^v: "Comision Torrentes. Este dia los dichos señores llamados por cedula ante diem encargaron mucho al Señor Don Francisco de Silva canonigo que escriba a Andres de Torrentes que venga a esta Santa Yglesia a servir el officio de maestro de Capilla" (Nov. 19, 1547).

207 Toledo, *A.C., 1548-1551,* fol. 206: Torrentes submitted a memorial requesting new beds for the seises, he also requested a change of clothing every six months (March 5, 1551). He exerted himself continuously for the physical welfare of the choirboys. No record of Morales's having so exerted himself has been discovered.

208 Moll, *op. cit.,* p. 24.

209 *Ibid.,* p. 25. He it was who eventually succeeded Morales at Málaga in December, 1554. See note 214 below.

210 Málaga, *A.C., 1550-1554,* fol. 167.

211 None of the documents thus far transcribed from Ávila, Plasencia, Rome, Toledo, and Málaga archives denominates Morales a *presbítero.* Similarly, the papal documents quoted in Llorens, *op. cit.,* refer to him only noncommittally as *clericus Hispalensis dioecesis.* During 1545-1547 the Toledo Cathedral acts, on the other hand, frequently identified other clergymen as *presbíteros.* This applied also at Málaga in 1551-1553. Juan Doyz, appointed Málaga Cathedral organist on March 5, 1552, was called *presbítero,* but not Morales. (Even so famous an ecclesiastic as Reginald Pole was still a deacon in 1551, fifteen years after he was made a cardinal. Many other important sixteenth-century clergy remained perpetual deacons.)

212 Málaga, *A.C.*, *1550-1554*, fol. 167ᵛ.

213 *Ibid.*, fol. 177: "los Racioneros y capellanes mandaron que ... se enbien edicto a muchas cibdades y a las vniversidades de Salamanca y alcala."

214 Concerning Juan de Cepa, see R. Mitjana, "La capilla de música de la Catedral de Málaga ... Año de 1543 al año de [1569]," pp. 53-54. Also Henri Collet, *Le mysticisme musical espagnol*, p. 356, and F. Rubio Piqueras, *Música y músicos toledanos*, p. 81. Cepa was a native of Descargamaría. He was ordained in the diocese of Ciudad Rodrigo and for a time served as chapelmaster in the Ciudad Rodrigo Cathedral. In 1550 he was *maestro de capilla* for Doña Mencía de Mendoza, Duchess of Calabria. Her chapel consisted in that year of 21 singers, an organist and his assistant keyboardist, a copyist, and three porters. She also kept the nine *ministriles* and six trumpeters from her husband's household until her death on January 4, 1554. Cepa through these four years, 1550-1554, was continuously searching for another post. In the spring of 1552 while residing at Valencia, he entered his name for the chapelmastership at Badajoz (see Santiago Kastner, "La música en la Catedral de Badajoz," *AM*, XII [1957], 128). On September 28, 1553, he offered himself as a candidate to succeed Torrentes at Toledo, listing himself as then "chapelmaster to the Duchess of Calabria" (Rubio Piqueras, *Música y músicos toledanos*, p. 81). Unsuccessful at Toledo, he tried out for the Málaga post sometime in the week of June 18-24, 1554. His opponents were Gonzalo Cano, Rodrigo Ceballos, Melchior Galvez, Rodrigo Ordoñez, and Francisco de Ravaneda. Voting was deferred until November 7, 1554, on which date Cepa with 14 votes in favor was declared the winner. Ceballos received 3 votes. Cepa died or retired before February 17, 1577, on which date a vacancy was announced. His successor was Pedro Periañez, elected on October 16, 1577.

Cepa seems to have been more interested in staging mystery plays (*representaciones*) in Málaga Cathedral than in music as such. See Mitjana, *op. cit.*, p. 113; but he is well represented in the Tarazona musical archive, according to Vicente de la Fuente, *Las Santas Iglesias de Tarazona y Tudela (España Sagrada*, vol. 50 [Madrid: Imp. de José Rodríguez, 1866]), p. 87.

Another nearby *maestro de capilla* who made the composition of playlets (*entremeses*) and medleys (*ensaladas*) his chief cathedral business in the 1560's was Gregorio Silvestre at Granada. See

Domingo García Peres, *Catálogo razonado de los autores portugueses que escribieron en castellano* (Madrid: Colegio Nacional, 1890), pp. 520, 531.

215 Juan B. de Elústiza and Gonzalo Castrillo Hernández, *Antología musical* (Barcelona: Rafael Casulleras, 1933), p. xxi.

216 *Declaración*, fol. 139 [actually 140].

217 Málaga, *A.C.*, *1550-1554*, fol. 148. A "concordia con el Conde de Vreña" was signed by the cathedral chapter on May 9, 1552, *A.C.*, *1550-1554*, fol. 96ᵛ).

218 López de Haro, *op. cit.*, I, 387.

219 Elzéar Genet [Carpentras] preceded Morales in such a venture when he brought out his *Liber primus missarum* at Avignon in 1532. Genet's collection, published luxuriously at his own expense, contained five masses.

220 Gombert's *Aspice, Domine* [*Motetti del fiore*, 1532]; Mouton's *Benedicta es celorum Regina* [*Motteti de la corona, libro primo*, 1514], *Gaude Barbara* [*Motteti de la corona*, 1514], *Quaeramus cum pastoribus* [*Motetti libro primo*, 1521]; Richafort's *Quem dicunt homines* [*Motetti del fiore*, 1532]. If Antoine de Févin composed the anonymous motet *Vulnerasti cor meum* [*Motteti de la corona*, 1514] his would be a fifth name in the list of Franco-Flemish composers. See note 254. Mouton's *Benedicta es celorum Regina*, although printed in *MME*, XV, 185-192, is not very clearly the source motet for Morales's mass of the same name. In the Benedictus of this mass Morales does quite plainly quote the opening of Josquin des Prez's motet *a 6*.

221 Trumpff, *op. cit.*, p. 124 (list of cantus firmus masses), p. 132 (paraphrase masses). However, on page 107 Trumpff states that Morales himself probably composed the *Tu es vas electionis* plainsong used as cantus firmus in his mass of that name. This statement must be corrected. Morales merely adapted a melody already printed in a Jeronymite *Liber processionarius* (Alcalá de Henares: Miguel de Eguía, 1526), at fol. 90. It there occurs as a versicle for use on June 29.

222 *Sur tous regretz, Philomena, Da pacem, Sancta Maria, Je suis desheritée.*

223 *Tristezas me matan* contains a duo (Agnus II).

224 *Missarum liber secundus*, fols. 14ᵛ-15, 32ᵛ-33.

225 The triple-meter Confiteor (*Missarum liber secundus*, fols. 62ᵛ-63) coming at the end of the Et in Spiritum Sanctum in the *Gaude Barbara* is not a separate movement.

226 *MME*, XI, 13.

227 *Declaración* (1555), fols. 54ᵛ-55ᵛ. See also Tapia Numantino, *Vergel de música* (Burgo de Osma: Diego Fernández de Córdova, 1570), fol. 109. (Tapia plagiarized nearly all that he wrote from Bermudo's *Declaración* of 1549).

228 *Declaración* (1555), fol. 55, col. 2.

229 In Kyrie II of Palestrina's *L'Homme armé* (1570) three breves in Φ_2^3 equal one in $\bigcirc$. See R. Casimiri, *La polifonia vocale del sec. XVI* (Rome: Ediz. "Psalterium," 1942), pp. 64, 66.

230 On the question of mensuration signs and tempo see Willi Apel, *The Notation of Polyphonic Music*, 4th ed. (Cambridge: The Mediaeval Academy of America, 1949), pp. 188-195.

231 *Declaración* (1555), fol. 52, col. 2.

232 *Ibid.*

233 *Ibid.*, fol. 55ᵛ, col. 1.

234 *MME*, Vol. XI, p. 106, shows "eleison" beneath the black breves; but just as the use of dotted minims is an incorrect method of transcribing the black breves, so the text-underlay is merely an editorial decision: and therefore subject to question.

235 Alvares Frouvo, *Discursos sobre a perfeiçam do diathesaron* (Lisbon: Antonio Craesbeeck de Mello, 1662), p. 97. In Spain as well as Portugal, Morales's black breves caused his name to be coupled with Josquin's when "difficult" rhythmic problems were discussed. In this connection see the very interesting marginal note in the New York Public Library copy of Francisco de Montanos's *Arte de música theorica y práctica* (Valladolid: Diego Fernández de Córdova, 1592) occurring at fol. 14 of the section on *canto de órgano:* "y asi son los breues negros que pone Jusquin en el credo de beata uirgine en el tiple. y morales enel criste de mile regres en el contralto que todos cantan a compas mayor y aquellos breues negros en proporçion de tres semibreues al compas sin que se mudel compas vinario. Y asi los demas que fueren negros que todos son proporçion sexquialtera."

236 *MME*, XI, 238 (meas. 9), 242 (meas. 83), 243 (meas. 99), 250 (meas. 23), 254 (meas. 88), 261 (meas. 204).

237 Trumpff, *op. cit.*, p. 105, discussed the pseudo-Crecquillon, not realizing, however, its identity with the Capp. Sist. MS 17 version. The first to identify the 1568 pseudo-Crecquillon as Morales's was Wilhelm Lueger in "Die Messen

des Thomas Crequillon" (Ph. D. dissertation, Bonn University, 1948), pp. 131-132. Lueger gave a plausible reason for the misattribution on page 132.

238 Haberl, *Bausteine für Musikgeschichte* (Leipzig: Breitkopf und Härtel, 1888), II, 7 (item 17).

239 Trend, *op. cit.*, p. 25, quoted the Spanish, but transposed lines 3-4 with 5-6. As a result, he translated differently on page 34. Trend did not have access to the original manuscript (see page 25: "copied for me by an English musical historian from the MS in the Sistine Chapel").

240 Gombert's *Aspice Domine* was published in 1532 with two flats for a "signature." But when Morales came to parody it he excluded the second flat. Bermudo suggested a reason in his *Declaración* (1555) when he said (folio 82): "In the compositions of Gombert many times mixed modes are used; for instance, in the first mode he generally uses B♭ [= E♭ in Mode I transposed] instead of B♮ ."

241 No warrant can be found in the 1544 imprint for the obligatory c♯ specified in *MME*, XI, 275 (meas. 27), although it does appear in Capp. Sist. MS 154, folio 73. In this manuscript, Kyrie I and Christe close with A-Major and D-Major chords respectively.

242 For a list of these, see pages 68-72.

243 See Jesús Bal y Gay, "Fuenllana y la transcripción de la música de los vihuelistas," *Nuestra Música*, IV, 15 (July, 1949), 180-197.

244 *El arte tripharia*, fols. 34-35.

245 Anglés, in *MME*, Vol. XI, p. 294, specifies an F at the close of the Patrem omnipotentem for the lowest note. This note should be D instead.

246 That such a shift of final was a "fault" would certainly have been Cerone's opinion. See his *El melopeo y maestro*, Lib. XII, cap. 13 (p. 687): "todas estas finales sean las mismas en la invención y terminación."

247 Morales in his *Tristezas me matan* ended his Christe on A but four other movements on the confinal, C, and ten on the final, F. See page 72 for further reference to its modal "impurity."

248 Antonio Soler, *Satisfacción a los reparos precisos* (Madrid: Antonio Marin, 1765), p. 7, assigned this mass to the "eighth tone: G without sharp." He then offered an analysis of the cadences in the Gloria, probably the first attempt ever made at a harmonic analysis of a Morales mass.

According to him, Morales cadenced successively in G. DG. GCGD. GC. GDG. CE. EAD. GF. DG. GC. CC. DG. See *AM*, VIII, 174-175. Soler's analysis cannot be checked very easily against the original (printed in *MME*, XV, 4-9), but so far as a check can be made it would seem that he came much closer to reality in his analysis of Victoria's *O vos omnes*. He ascribed the last-named work to Morales because of a misattribution in the El Escorial codex from which he copied it.

249 Strunk, *Source Readings*, p. 209.

250 Ramos, *Musica practica*, ed. by Johannes Wolf, p. 58.

251 *Declaración* (1555), fol. 122ᵛ. Ramos's dicta are here echoed exactly.

252 Mrs. Bury Palliser, *Historic Devices, Badges, and War-Cries* (London: Sampson Low, Son, and Marston, 1870), p. 248: "These words [*plus ultra*] refer to the acquisition of a world unknown to the ancients."

253 Strunk, *op. cit.*, p. 216, note r.

254 *Ibid.*, p. 206, col. 2 (last item); also p. 213, note h. Although *Vulnerasti cor meum* intervenes between two Mouton motets in the source, it shows some touches not to be found in *Quaeramus* or *Benedicta es*. In *Vulnerasti, pars 2* begins like *pars 1*, for instance. Not so in Mouton's motets of two *partes*.

255 *Declaración* (1555), fol. 122ᵛ.

256 On Gombert's mixing of modes see note 240. Also Bermudo, *El arte tripharia*, folio 33: "in the compositions of Gombert you will often find this mixing of modes. The sixth and eighth modes are for instance often mixed in his cadences."

257 Strunk, "Guglielmo Gonzaga and Palestrina's *Missa Dominicalis*," *Musical Quarterly*, XXXIII, 2 (April, 1947), 233.

258 A. W. Ambros, *Geschichte der Musik* (Breslau: F. E. C. Leuckart, 1868), III, 573-574.

259 Johann Siebmacher, *Grosses und allgemeines Wappenbuch (Wappen der deutschen Souveraine und Lände)*, ed. by Gustave A. Seyler (Nuremberg: Bauer und Raspe, 1909), Bd. I, Abt. 1, Teil 2, Taf. 8.

260 *MME*, XI, 38 (mm. 80-81), 41 (mm. 22, 26, 37), 42 (meas. 43), 45 (meas. 124), 46 (meas. 138), 49 (mm. 49-50), 50 (meas. 80), 81 (mm. 96-97), 53 (meas. 145), 55 (mm. 170-171), 57 (mm. 208, 217), 61 (meas. 48), 62 (meas. 65), 68 (meas. 63), 69 (meas. 76).

261 The last ten measures of Kyrie II in Gombert's *Quam pulchra es* Mass alone contain more "incomplete" changing-notes than the whole of Morales's *Aspice* Mass.

262 Escaped notes in the Gombert are found at mm. 46 (superius), 60 (superius), 69 (tenor), 74 (superius), 88 (bass), 101 (contra), 171 (contra). Morales's occur in this order: *MME*, XI, 44 (meas. 94), 47 (meas. 9), 50 (meas. 74), 59 (meas. 245), 60 (mm. 11, 29), 61 (meas. 32), 63 (meas. 17), 64 (meas. 29).

263 *Aspice*, mm. 60, 88.

264 Morales never forced the issue with such "harshnesses" as the simultaneous E♭ and E♮ required in Gombert's *Quam pulchra es* Mass (Agnus III, meas. 88), or the obligatory skips from B♭ to E♮ specified in the same mass (Christe eleison, mm. 66-67, and Qui tollis, mm. 182-183).

265 In the last Agnus of his six-voice *Quam pulchra es*, tenor II (voice VII) sings the *Ecce sacerdos magnus* antiphon. Tenor II sings each of the four incises twice—the second time in notes diminished in value by half. The lowest voice anticipates each incise in note values of the repetitions.

266 Trend, *op. cit.*, p. 34. See note 239.

267 *MME*, XV, 30 (note 5, 2d par.).

268 The Vogt (1568) prints the Capp. Sist. MS 17 version of *Mille regretz*, which differs significantly from the Dorico (1544) version. See *MME*, XI, 54, for a summary of the differences.

269 The Hispanic Society in New York owns a splendid choirbook copy executed in Spain during the second half of the sixteenth century. Since it has not been described in any musicological publication, the following details are offered. Bound in the original leather, now extremely worn, the volume measures 59 by 41 cm., and contains 87 paper leaves. At fols. 1ᵛ-33 is copied Palestrina's Hexachord Mass (*a 6*), at fols. 33ᵛ-55 Morales's *L'Homme armé (a 5)* from his Book I, at fols. 55ᵛ-87 his *Mille regretz*. The following movements have been excluded from the last-named work: triple-meter Osanna; Agnus I, Agnus II. The notation has been simplified and a straightforward rhythmic interpretation of 3 minims + 3 minims + 2 minims offered as the "correct" solution of the "three black breves" at the beginning of the Christe eleison.

270 The Hispanic Society in New York owns a handwritten copy. It comes last in a miscellaneous choirbook (57 by 42 cm.) bound in its original leather, consisting of 117 paper leaves, and catalogued under the title *Missae secundum ritum Toletanum cum aliis missis variorum auctorum*. Owned originally by the collegiate church of San Pedro de Lerma (near Burgos), this volume shows the arms of the Duke of Lerma (adviser to Philip III) on its front cover. The volume contains: an anonymous *Missa de duplicibus maioribus (a 4)* at fols. 1ᵛ-18; a *Missa de Beata Maria (a 4)* at fols. 18ᵛ-29 by Fray Martín de Villanueva; an anonymous Requiem Mass *(a 4)* at fols. 29ᵛ-50—*Ne recorderis* from Morales's *Officium defunctorum*, being interspersed at fols. 44ᵛ-45; Palestrina's *Missa Iste confessor (a 4)* at fols. 50ᵛ-65; his Hexachord Mass *(a 6)* at fols. 65ᵛ-84, and his *Nasce la gioia mia (a 6)* at fols. 84ᵛ-102; and Morales's *Beata* [sic] *es coelorum Regina (a 4)* at fols. 102ᵛ-117. Credo movements and triple-meter Osanna are omitted from the latter.

271 Osanna reprinted in Albert Lavignac, *Encyclopédie de la musique* (Paris: C. Delagrave, 1913–1931), II [1914], 655-656.

272 No mention seems thus far to have been made of the fact that fols. 2 and 5 of Morales's *Gaude Barbara* Mass (in manuscript copy) survive at Seville Cathedral as binding leaves in *Libro de coro 10*. These isolated leaves suggest the fate that has in the course of time overtaken other manuscript versions of his music at Seville. New manuscript copies of his works were luxuriously copied on vellum at Seville, however, as late as 1601. See the Seville *Libro de autos capitulares de los años de 1599-1600-1601-1602*, fol. 62ᵛ (Jan. 26, 1601).

273 Although it was doubtless Morales's invariable intention to use Ø for a signature in the proportioned triple-meter movements of his 1544 masses, there are two inconsistencies worthy of mention. The first Osanna of his *Gaude Barbara* shows ₵$\frac{3}{2}$ (Liber II, fol. 64ᵛ) and Ø$\frac{3}{2}$ (fol. 65) on opposite leaves. The second Osanna of *Vulnerasti cor meum* carries a signature of ₵3 in all voices (I, fols. 46ᵛ-47).

274 Cerone, *op. cit.*, p. 688 (lines 37-38).

275 Trumpff, *op. cit.*, p. 121.

276 *Da pacem* and *Tempore paschali*.

277 Reese, *Music in the Renaissance*, p. 589.

278 Josquin's *De beata Virgine* Mass is printed in Smijers's complete-works edition, *Werken*, dertigste aflevering [1952], pp. 125-150. Brumel's, which was written in old age to compete with Josquin's, is printed in H. Expert, *Les Maîtres musiciens de la Renaissance française* (Paris: A.

Leduc, 1898), VIII [*Liber quindecim missarum*, I], 1-76.

279 Peter Wagner, *Geschichte der Messe* (Leipzig: Breitkopf und Härtel, 1913), pp. 457-533.

280 Both Spanish Institute of Musicology editions err in leaving out the Marian tropes. The shape of the Gloria cannot be discerned in either issue.

281 *La Tribune de Saint-Gervais*, V, 12 (Dec., 1899), 323.

282 *Ibid.*, V, 12 (Dec., 1899), 343-348; VI, 1 (Jan., 1900), 20-22.

283 Alfred Einstein, "Cristobal de Morales: *Missa Quaeramus cum pastoribus*," *La Rassegna musicale*, X (Nov., 1937), 387. According to Einstein: "The two basses without doubt are intended to evoke the shepherds of the Bethlehem stable. Who does not recall in this connection the hundreds upon hundreds of nativity-scenes painted by Flemings, Italians, and Spaniards, in which two bearded shepherds adoring the Christ-child always appear!" Among his other interesting remarks concerning this mass were these: (1) Agnus Dei III begins with a note-for-note echo of Kyrie I, the only change being the addition of a sixth voice for greater sonority; (2) as a result, an arch-shaped unity is imposed; (3) the Credo at *et vitam venturi saeculi* mounts in "what might be called a crescendo in the modern sense of the word" reaching upward for "a grandiose conclusion." In his four short paragraphs Einstein touched on several cardinal virtues in Morales's masses: their rich symbolical content, their satisfying architecture, their amazing unity, and the splendid endings of the principal movements.

284 Michel Brenet, "Jean Mouton," *La Tribune de Saint-Gervais*, V, 12 (Dec., 1899), 323.

285 Bordes, "Étude Palestrinienne," *La Tribune de Saint-Gervais*, VI, 1 (Jan., 1900), 21: "Est-ce nous ou Moralès qui avons tort?"

286 Trumpff, *op. cit.*, pp. 132-138.

287 *Ibid.*, p. 134; the Morales and Jachet Patrem omnipotentem beginnings are shown in an almost illegible example (XIII) on page 147. The lower five staves belong to Jachet's mass.

288 Printings of all or some of the magnificats occurred in the following years: 1542 (Gardane and Scotto); 1544 (Rhaw); 1545, 1547 (Gardane); 1550 (Moderne); 1552, 1559, 1562 (Gardane); 1563 (Rampazetto); 1568 (Correggio); 1575, 1583, 1587, 1592, 1614 (Gardano).

289 For a list of magnificats printed before 1628 see Carl-Heinz Illing, *Zur Technik der Magnificat-Komposition des 16. Jahrhunderts* (Wolfenbüttel: Georg Kallmeyer, 1936), Appendix (Chronologisches Verzeichnis), pp. 6-42.

290 Copy 1 at The Hispanic Society begins at fol. 2 with the title *Siguense las 16. magnificas de morales*. In its original but rather worn leather binding this volume measures 60 by 43 cm., and contains 123 irregularly numbered paper leaves. The Index on the back of the flyleaf is dated 1608, and shows the following items: Anima mea verses at fols. 1, 8, 14, 20, 26, 33, 39, 45; Et exultavit verses at fols. 51, 58, 65, 72, 78, 85, 92, 99. In addition there occur a psalm (*Qui habitat in adiutorio*), a *Nunc dimittis*, an *In manus tuae*, all *a 4* and all by [Rodrigo] Ceballos at fols. 110, 119, and 120; and a motet *a 4* for equal voices, *Salva nos, Domine* by Philippe Rogier at fol. 122. Copy 2 at The Hispanic Society, on the other hand, contains only Morales's magnificats. The title on the flyleaf reads thus: *Canticum B. Mariae Christophori morales Hyspalensis*. Bound in its original gold-stamped leather, this choirbook measures 59 by 41 cm., and contains 107 irregularly numbered paper leaves—there being usually ten staves to the page. The Anima mea verses occur at fols. 1, 8, 15, 21, 27, 33, 38, 45; the Et exultavit verses at fols. 51, 58, 65, 72, 78, 85, 94, 101. A sampling would indicate that Copy 2 contains less copyist's mistakes than Copy 1.

291 See *Fontes artis musicae*, 1954/2, p. 74 (col. 2). The Puebla *Libro de coro, 2*, contains eight odd-verse Magnificats at folios 5-52.

292 Discovered by L. Feininger. See *AM*, VIII, 153.

293 Quoted in Llorens, *op. cit.*, p. 66. But Llorens's references are faulty. Morales is not mentioned in Lib. 1, cap. 57, nor in cap. 66; moreover, Zacconi foliated rather than paged his *Prattica de musica*.

294 Illing, *op. cit.*, Appendix, pp. 49-57.

295 Transcribed in Charles Van den Borren, *Polyphonia sacra* (Nashdom Abbey: The Plainsong and Mediaeval Music Society, 1932), pp. 137-145.

296 Haberl, *Bausteine*, II, 19 (item 44) and 166.

297 *MME*, I, *108* (item 67), *113* (item 39), (item 1).

298 *Ibid.*, *108* (item 68), *122* (item 22); for his four-voice magnificat see *123* (item 32).

299 See *Werken van Jacob Obrecht*, ed. by Johannes Wolf: *Motetten*, Bundel III (Amsterdam: G. Alsbach, n.d.), pp. 136-144. Obrecht set only even verses; the corona invariably appears at the mediatio. Although it is not so labeled, his four-voice Magnificat is in Tone VI.

300 Illing, *op. cit.*, Appendix, p. 9. Attaingnant published the anonymous *Magnificat sur les huit tons . . . mys en la tablature des orgues espinettes & manicordions* in 1530 [1530[8]].

301 *Denkmäler der Tonkunst in Bayern*, III, 2, ed. by Th. Kroyer (Leipzig: Breitkopf und Härtel, 1903).

302 Gaetano Gaspari, *Catalogo della Biblioteca del Liceo musicale di Bologna* (Bologna: Lib. Romagnoli dall'Acqua, 1892), II, 276.

303 Bibliography in *AM*, Vol. VIII.

304 Several verses printed in Th. Kroyer, *Der vollkommene Partiturspieler* (Leipzig: Breitkopf und Härtel, 1930); J. Schmidt-Görg, "Die acht Magnifikat des Nicholaus Gombert," *Gesammelte Aufsätze zur Kulturgeschichte Spaniens*, V (1935).

305 *El arte tripharia*, fol. 33.

306 Illing, *op. cit.*, p. 22 (Romanische Psalmformeln zum Magnificat).

307 Other composers: Franco, Guerrero, Kerle, Lasso, Vaet, and Victoria.

308 See above, note 257.

309 Festa's wider ranging bass and tenor parts necessitate changes of clef in such movements as the Gloria Patri of Tone I and the Quia fecit of Tone IV. Morales's ranges on the other hand are never so wide as to make a change of clef necessary in the middle of a movement.

310 The Fecit potentiam (*Orphénica lyra*, fol. 5) is one of the comparatively few polyphonic movements that Fuenllana printed wholly in black. This would mean that the movement was intended for vihuela without the intervention of a solo voice. The Deposuit potentes intabulated at folio 13, on the other hand, contains a tenor-part printed in red numerals—the purpose of the red being to show that this part should be played and sung simultaneously. The Deposuit in question is to be seen in *MME*, XVII, 4. Anglés accepts Fuenllana's suggestions for ficta accidentals everywhere except in the top voice at meas. 86. The melody in this bar should read a, b♮, c[1], b♭, according to Fuenllana, who also inserts a passing g in the top voice at meas. 80₂.

311 See *AM*, VIII, 159. The reading at meas. 20 makes Palestrina guilty of having written parallel unisons. Similarly, on page 160 by a lapse the altus II reads an octave too low, with the result that Palestrina would seem to have written consecutive perfect fifths in mm. 3, 9-10. Other mistakes in transcription are to be found in the tenor, p. 162, mm. 24-25; cantus, p. 163, meas. 5; bassus, p. 166, mm. 23-24.

312 Escaped dissonances in Morales's movements appear at the following places: pp. 157, meas. 7 (altus II; 166, meas. 14 (bassus).

313 Morales's "incomplete" cambiata: p. 162, meas. 28 (tenor).

314 Morales's upper neighbor: p. 166, meas. 24 (altus).

315 Morales reached the eleventh in altus II of his Esurientes, page 160, but this is a solo movement.

316 Charles W. Fox, "Cristóbal de Morales: Opera Omnia. Vol. II: Motetes I-XXV," *Notes of the Music Library Association*, 2d ser., XII, 1 (Dec., 1954), 140: "Is it possible that future counterpoint texts may speak of the 'mature Morales' rather than the 'Palestrina style'?"

317 For all that is contained in this section the present author is greatly indebted to G. E. Watkins's masterful study, "Three Books of Polyphonic Lamentations, 1549-1564" (Ph. D. dissertation, University of Rochester, 1953). His analysis of Morales's Lamentations is to be found in Part I of his dissertation, pages 98-113; the transcriptions, in Part II, pages 254-357.

318 Miguel de Fuenllana, *Libro de musica para vihuela intitulado Orphenica lyra* (Seville: Martín de Montesdoca, 1554), fols. 77-81.

319 R. P. Casiano Rojo, "The Gregorian Antiphonary of Silos and the Spanish Melody of the Lamentations," *Speculum: A Journal of Mediaeval Studies*, V, 3 (July, 1930), 314-317.

320 La Rue's *Lamentationes* were printed in the same Montanus and Neuber 1549 collection. For transcription into modern notation see Watkins, *op. cit.*, Pt. II, pp. 109, 115, 123 (Févin), and pp. 150-151 (La Rue).

321 The fact that they were copied into the Puebla Cathedral *Libro de coro, 2*, proves that the "Spanish" set of three lamentations for Mier-

coles Santo was sung in Mexico *ca.* 1650. As evidence for the continued popularity of the "Spanish" set in the peninsula, MSS 14045 in the Biblioteca Nacional at Madrid is conclusive. Among the loose sheets in this bundle of manuscripts is a "Memorial del estilo que se ha de guardar en esta santa Yglesia de Toledo," dated 1604. According to this memorial, on *Feria quinta* "la primera Lamentación a canto de órgano, es la de Morales." From this notice it could be inferred that Morales's Miercoles Santo verses were sung regularly for a good many years after 1604.

322 The asterisk in the following instances shows where the cross relation, guaranteed by printed accidentals, occurs. Feria V, lectio ii: *Jerusalem *cui, Magna est *velut, crudelis *quasi;* Feria V, lectio iii: *illam *quia viderunt.* These instances— which provide only the beginning of an inventory —involve respectively contiguous A Major–F Major, A Major–C Major, D Major–d minor, and A Major–a minor chords. See Watkins, *op. cit.*, II, 263, 267, 272, 274.

323 F. J. Fétis, *Biographie universelle des musiciens* (Paris: Firmin-Didot, 1878), III, 447 (col. 2).

324 A. T. Davison and W. Apel, *Historical Anthology of Music* (Cambridge: Harvard University Press, 1946), I, 138-140.

325 Mitjana, *Estudios*, pp. 206-209. Not only is an exact translation not attempted, but also at numerous places Mitjana's text has been amended, amplified, or shortened.

326 The measure count in *MME*, Vol. XIII, goes astray after meas. 90. The last measure in part 1 (p. 109) should read meas. 107. All the measure numbers in part 2 are wrong.

327 *MME*, XIII, 7.

328 The tenor takes over "bass" functions during rests in the bass part; this explains the higher rate of skips in the tenor than in cantus I, II, or alto.

329 The highest notes in *Lamentabatur Jacob* and *Verbum iniquum* are respectively c¹ and b♭. The highest note in both *Tu es Petrus* and *Andreas Christi famulus* is g¹.

330 See the extremely valuable paper on this subject: Charles W. Fox, "Accidentals in vihuela tablatures," *Bulletin of the American Musicological Society*, no. 4 (General report, 1938), 22-24.

331 See above, page 19. As late as 1618 peninsular theoreticians were still not agreed on the question of flatting the B (fifth note) in *Gaudeamus omnes in Domino*. Thalesio at page 39 of his *Arte de canto chão* (Coimbra: 1618) entered the lists against four of the best-known Spanish theorists—Guillermo de Podio (1495), Gonzalo Martínez de Bizcargui (1508), Juan de Espinosa '1514), and Juan Martínez (1532)—in a heated attempt to prove that the B should be flatted. For him, the B♮ contravenes *toda razam, & arte.* On his side was Victoria, who consistently flatted this note at its every appearance in his 1576 *Gaudeamus* Mass.

332 Thomae Ludovici Victoria, *Opera omnia*, ed. by Felipe Pedrell (Leipzig: Breitkopf und Härtel, 1905), IV, 2. [Hereafter cited as *VicO*.]

333 *MME*, XIII, 115-121.

334 Haberl, *Bausteine für Musikgeschichte*, II, 12.

335 Guerrero, in the preface to his *Magnificat octo tonorum* (Codex 4 at Toledo), alluded thus to his erstwhile teacher: "Christophorus Morales, cui per universum terrarum ob canendi peritiam in Musica primae diferuntur, praeceptor, et dux meus . . ." See Rubio Piqueras, *Códices polifónicos toledanos*, p. 19.

336 Crecquillon's in *Thesaurus musicus . . . tomi primi continentis cantiones octo vocum* (Nuremberg: Montanus and Neuber, 1564). Manichicourt's in *Liber septimus ecclesiasticarum cantionum quinque vocum* (Antwerp: T. Susato, 1553).

337 *Liber nonus ecclesiasticarum cantionum quinque vocum* (Antwerp: T. Susato, 1554); *Thesauri musici tomus quintus* (Nuremberg: Montanus and Neuber, 1564), no. 6.
   Tu es Petrus was transcribed in Charles Bordes's *Anthologie des Maîtres religieux primitifs* (Paris: Durand et fils, 1893), année 1, pp. 7-12.

338 Kircher, *op. cit.*, I, 614 (bk. 7, chap. 5: "De stylo melismatico").

339 *MME*, II, 136-137.

340 *Incipit liber processionarius secundum consuetudinem ordinis sancti patris nostri Hieronymi* (Alcalá de Henares: Miguel de Eguía, 1526), fol. 39. Hymn for Corpus Christi.

341 *MME*, II, 156-157 (hymn tune in tenor). The anonymous setting, containing transcriptionist's errors, is to be found at page 3. This hymn tune was extremely popular throughout the Spanish dominions. On its currency as far away as Peru (1598), see the *Journal of Research in Music Education* (Fall, 1960), VIII, 114 (Nicene Creed).

342 *Declaración* (1555), fol. 137 (col. 2).

343 *MME*, XIII, 137-148; Elústiza-Castrillo, *op. cit.*, pp. 73-79.

344 *HSMS*, I, 1-19. *Parce mihi Domine*, referred to by Cervantes de Salazar, is printed at pages 9-11.

345 Reprinted in Joaquín García Icazbalceta, *Bibliografía mexicana del siglo XVI*, (Mexico City: Lib. de Andrade y Morales, 1886), pp. 98-121. The passages relating to Morales occur at pages 119-120.

346 Tromboncino composed at least one frottola with Spanish text: *Quando la speranza es perdida* (*Frottole libro quarto* [Venice: Andrea Antico, 1520]).

347 Pedrell, *Cancionero musical popular español*, I (Valls [1918]), pp. 97-98. See Solange Corbin, "Le *Cantus Sibyllae*: Origines et premiers textes," *Revue de musicologie*, XXXI (July, 1952), 1-10, for references to the diffusion of this chant outside Spain.

348 Asenjo Barbieri, *Cancionero musical de los siglos XV y XVI* (Madrid: Tip. de los huérfanos, 1890), p. 610.

349 *La música a Catalunya fins al segle XIII* (Barcelona: Institut d'Estudis Catalans, 1935), Taula III [6], facing p. 298. The fifth and sixth notes of the cantus should be bracketed. The first note in the altus, meas. 10, should not show an obligatory flat.

350 *Music & Letters*, Jan., 1925, p. 30.

351 Jesús Bal y Gay, *Cancionero de Upsala* (Mexico City: El Colegio de México, 1944), pp. 25-27.

352 The lyrics are by Juan Boscan (1493-1542), the Catalonian poet. See *Las obras de Boscan y algunas de Garcilaso dela Vega repartidas en quatro libros* (Barcelona: Garles Amoros, 1543), fol. 1ᵛ. Entitled "villancico," it continues with twelve coplas (stanzas of ten lines) not to be found in the Scotto print of 1556. Juan Vásquez (1560) set a villancico that begins with the same first line (see *MME*, IV, *40* and 180), but the rest of the lyrics are different. Just as the opening lines of the Luis de Vivero and Juan Boscán lyrics are identical, so Vásquez's first phrase strongly resembles Morales's opening phrase.

353 *Les luthistes espagnols du xviᵉ siècle* (Leipzig: Breitkopf und Härtel, 1902), II, 196. Errors in transcription occur at mm. 10, 11, 16, 19 (Morphy's measure numberings).

354 Arnold Schering, *Geschichte der Musik in Beispielen* (Leipzig: Breitkopf und Härtel, 1931), p. 114. Schering transcribed correctly; and, moreover, duplicated the voice part in the accompaniment, as is proper. But he, like Westrup, did not understand the principles of elision in the Spanish language. In consequence, he was reduced to inserting an extra sung-note at his meas. 6_2, in order to eke out enough notes for what he thought to be the correct number of syllables.
J. A. Westrup, "Song," *The Oxford History of Music* (2d ed.; London: Oxford University Press, 1932), Vol. 2, pt. 2, pp. 363-364. In addition to giving a faulty matching of words with music, this transcription arbitrarily omits notes to be found in the original. Cf. the following chords: mm. 2_3, 7_2, 8_1 (Westrup's numbering).
Jesús Bal y Gay, *Romances y villancicos españoles del siglo xvi*, primera serie (Mexico City: La Casa de España, 1939), p. 16.

355 See above, note 243.

356 Bal y Gay, *Romances . . .*, pp. 42-43.

357 The last "bar" contains a breve crowned with a fermata.

358 *Musica antiqua: A collection of music of this and other countries* (London: Preston, 1812), pp. 110-113. Apart from ficta, the notes in Smith's transcription can be trusted. He would have been better advised, however, to have begun on the third instead of the first beat. A rather unusual voice-progression occurs at meas. 19: the altus skips down a fourth (crotchet-motion) to a dissonance.

359 Vincenzo Galilei, *Fronimo dialogo di Vincentio Galilei. . . . sopra l'arte del bene intavolare* (Venice: G. Scotto, 1584), p. 160.

360 Emil Vogel, *Bibliothek der gedruckten weltlichen Vocalmusik Italiens* (Berlin: A. Haack, 1892), II, 145 (item 15); 146-148 (items 18, 19/20, 21, 22, 23).

361 *Nuova spoglia amorosa, nelle quale si contengono madrigali à quattro, & cinque voci. . . . nuouamente posta in luce* (Venice: Giacomo Vincenti, 1593), p. 42 (bassus).

362 Philippe de Monte, *Missa "Quando lieta sperai,"* ed. by Ch. Van den Borren (Düsseldorf: L. Schwann, *ca.* 1933); G. P. da Palestrina, *Werke* [*Missarum liber undecimus*], ed. by F. X. Haberl, (Leipzig: Breitkopf und Härtel, 1889), XX, 50-79. Van den Borren erroneously refers to the Palestrina as a "six-part" Mass. Only the Agnus is composed *a 6*—the rest being composed *a 5*. Haberl, page II, offered his opinion that *Quando lieta sperai* was an early Palestrina mass because "the aeolian modality is inflexibly adhered to throughout, without the least concession."

363 Van den Borren, preface to Monte's *Quando lieta sperai* Mass, page 17.

364 *Rhythm and Tempo: A Study in Music History* (New York: W. W. Norton, 1953), p. 243. Sachs gave no footnote reference whereby to locate the Schering transliteration. None occurs in the *Geschichte der Musik in Beispielen;* nor in "Takt und Sinnliederung in der Musik des 16. Jahrhunderts," *Archiv für Musikwissenschaft*, II (1920), 465-498; nor in "Musikalischer Organismus oder Deklamationsrhythmik?" *Zeitschrift für Musikwissenschaft*, XI (1928-29), 212-221. The Van den Borren "transliteration" uses duple meter. Sachs's protest seems perhaps overstated when later developments in the madrigal are considered.

365 On the other hand, Pedro Guerrero's *D'un spíritu triste* intabulated in *Fronimo* (1568) at page 13, concords with the *soneto* of the same title in Fuenllana's *Orphénica lyra* (1554) at fol. 128.

366 Galilei lists 56 "errori del Zarlino" in his *Dialogo. . . . della musica antica et della moderna* (Florence: Giorgio Marescotti, 1581).

367 *Ibid.*, p. 80.

368 *Fronimo dialogo. . . . nel quale si contengono le vere, et necessarie regole del intavolare la musica nel liuto* (Venice: Girolamo Scotto, 1568-1569), p. 124. If the evidence is still not strong enough to give *Quando lieta sperai* to Morales, at least he can securely claim as his own the motet *a 5*, *Clamabat autem mulier Chananaea*, printed in Bernhard Meier's edition of Rore's *Opera Omnia*, I (Tübingen: American Institute of Musicology, 1959), pp. 143-147, as Rore's (?) from *Il Terzo Libro di Motetti a cinque Voci di Cipriano de Rore* (Venice: Antonio Gardane, 1549), where it occurs as no. 13 without ascription. This same motet was copied in Toledo MS 17 at fols. 40^v-44 (printed in *MME*, XIII, 96-101), with ten other motets, all of which are correctly ascribed to Morales.

II Francisco Guerrero (1528-1599) and Other Church Masters

II Francisco Guerrero (1528-1599) and Other Church Masters

Part I: FRANCISCO GUERRERO

Guerrero's Unique Role in Peninsular Music   Guerrero, the most purely Spanish of the triumvirate comprising for its other members Morales and Victoria, was also the most versatile of the three. Somewhat more than a dozen of his secular songs survive in Biblioteca Medinaceli MSS 13230[1] and 607.[2] Fuenllana in 1554 intabulated two of his secular songs,[3] and Daza in 1576, a further three.[4] As for sacred literature, he (like his master, Morales) published two books of masses—the first at Paris in 1566 containing nine masses;[5] the second at Rome in 1582 containing eight.[6] A mass not in either of these collections, *Saeculorum Amen (a 4)*, was printed at Venice two years before his death.[7] Although he fell somewhat short of Morales and Victoria insofar as sheer number of masses is concerned (they having each written approximately 21 while he but 18[8]), he equaled their best achievements in the other sacred categories. The number of his published hymns, 34, exactly equals Victoria's. Like Morales he composed a cycle of magnificats in every tone.[9] He bettered both Morales and Victoria by composing a *Passionarium secundum quatuor evangelistas* (1580).[10] Morales's extant motets number upward of 90; Victoria published 46. Guerrero published 32 in his first book of motets at Seville in 1555, 40 in his second at Venice in 1570, 40 in his third at Venice in 1589, and 70 in a valedictory collection at Venice in 1597.[11] Like Victoria's motet collections, Guerrero's contain duplicates, especially in the last book. Even so, we must guard against supposing that all motets of the same title appearing in successive editions are necessarily the same. For instance, the *Simile est regnum coelorum* of 1555 (*a 5*), that of 1570 (*a 4*), and that of 1589 (*a 6*); the *Ductus est Jesus* of 1555 (*a 5*) and that of 1570 (*a 4*) count as five motets. After verified duplicates are subtracted, he is left with some 115 motets: a fourth again as many as Morales, and more than twice as many as Victoria. Lastly, he touched a "sacred" category that neither of the others touched—the popular religious polyphonic song with vernacular lyrics. His *Canciones y villanescas espirituales* (33 *a 5*,[12] 20 *a 4*, and 8 *a 3*), published at Venice in 1589, contain many songs conceived originally with secular lyrics. Whether classed as secular or religious music, these *canciones* take rank with Juan Vásquez's two books—his *Villancicos i canciones* (Osuna: 1551) and *Recopilacion de sonetos y villancicos* (Seville: 1560)—as one of the three finest collections of Spanish polyphonic song published by any composer during the century.

Guerrero and Victoria were on the friendliest terms, as can be proved from: (1) the tenor of Victoria's letter to the Sevillian chapter of January 14, 1582, now preserved in the Sevillian capitular archive;[13] (2) the compliment Victoria paid Guerrero when he parodied the elder master's four-voice motet (1570) in his *Simile est regnum coelorum* Mass (1576), but more especially when he included two of Guerrero's motets in his own *Motecta Festorum Totius anni* of 1585; (3) Guerrero's efforts to have Victoria succeed him in the post of Sevillian chapelmaster.[14] What has, however, seemingly been overlooked by Guerrero's biographers up to now is the number of other composers besides Victoria who paid tribute by basing their parody masses on his motets: Géry de Ghersem (1598), Alfonso Lobo (1602), Juan Esquivel (1608), and Duarte Lobo (1621), to name only those whose parodies reached print. The *Maria Magdalena* Mass *a 6* and *Prudentes virgines* Mass *a 5*, both in Alonso Lobo's *Liber primus missarum* (Madrid: 1602), are parodied after motets in Guerrero's 1570 book (published at Venice by Antonio Gardano). Just as Guerrero honored Morales by placing the *Sancta et immaculata* Mass first in his 1566 collection, so Alonso Lobo places *Beata Dei genitrix*, parodied after Guerrero's motet of that name (1585), first among his 1602 Masses. As if three parodies by the Spanish Lobo were not enough, the Portuguese "wolf"—Duarte Lobo—also parodied Guerrero. Duarte Lobo's *Elizabeth Zachariae* Mass *a 5* in his lavish *Liber missarum IIII, V, VI et VIII vocibus* (Antwerp: 1621) is based on the like-named Guerrero motet *a 5* in the 1570 Venetian collection. Juan Esquivel based the *Ave Virgo sanctissima* (*a 5*) and *Gloriose confessor Domini* (*a 4*) Masses published in his *Missarum liber primus* (Salamanca: 1608) on motets in the same Guerrero 1570 collection.

The most pyrotechnical parody of a Guerrero motet is not Esquivel's *Ave Virgo sanctissima* Mass *a 5* (1608), but a mass *a 7* of the same title by the Flemish composer Géry de Ghersem.[15] Originally from Tournai, Ghersem arrived at Madrid in June, 1588, with a dozen other Flemish youths recruited to sing in the chapel choir of Philip II. Ghersem quickly established himself as a favorite pupil of Philip's Flemish chapelmaster, Philippe

Rogier, and was deputed after Rogier's death on February 29, 1596, to see a selection of his master's masses through the press at royal expense. Published at Madrid in 1598 with the title *Missae sex Philippi Rogerii*, this sumptuous folio concludes with a canonic tour de force entitled *Missa Ave Virgo sanctissima* (pp. 206-258). Parodied after Guerrero's motet *a 5*, the concluding mass is by Ghersem, not Rogier.

Of Guerrero's *Ave Virgo sanctissima* (first published in 1566; reprinted in 1570), Francisco Pacheco—later to become father-in-law of the painter Velázquez—wrote in 1599 as follows: "He published many motets that by reason of their excellent construction and their beauty of sound will be eternally esteemed; his *Ave Virgo sanctissima* alone has, wherever performed in Spain, brought any number of musicians fame and approbation."[16] Guerrero's motet boasts a two-in-one canon at the unison between the upper voices. Ghersem took up this cue, but went far beyond Guerrero. His first Kyrie starts with a "canon: trinitatis in unum"—cantus II being the antecedent, contralto and tenor I the consequents. Every succeeding movement up to the Crucifixus contains canons. At the Et iterum they are resumed. The Sanctus (*Missae sex*, p. 248) includes an amazingly adroit three-in-one canon.[17]

As if the musical tribute of numerous parody masses did not sufficiently honor Guerrero, Vicente Espinel (1550-1624) in *La casa de la memoria* paid him fervid literary homage: "Behold Francisco Guerrero, in whose compositions are found such elegant craftsmanship and such graceful counterpoint; whose pen has given us works of such lasting merit and universal significance; that all future ages may never produce a master who combines so many gifts. For just as in musical science he exceeds everyone else, so also he is a consummate singer and a great teacher."[18]

Sevillian Beginnings   The greatest of Sevillian painters, Diego Valázquez, was not born until the year of Guerrero's death. But painting had been a flourishing art in Seville through the whole of the sixteenth century. Guerrero's father was one of the modest painters who flourished before mid-century. Francisco Pacheco, in his *Libro de descripcion de verdaderos retratos de illustres y memorables varones*, records the father's name as Gonzalo Sánchez Guerrero. The mother's name was Leonor de Burgos. The financial position of the family must have been at least respectable if by 1521 Gonzalo Sánchez owned houses that he could rent to a bonnetmaker named Bartolomé Ruiz.[19] An elder son in the family, Pedro Guerrero, was also to choose music as a profession: the relationship between Pedro and Francisco reminding us of the similar relationship between Diego de Fermoselle and Juan del Encina.

Francisco's year of birth has been variously given. Just as Chopin's in one edition of *Grove's Dictionary* was 1809 and in the next 1810, so Guerrero's in successive editions has been 1527 and 1528. According to Pacheco (1599), Guerrero was born in May, 1527. But Guerrero himself in the prologue to his autobiographical *Viage de Hierusalem* (printed at Valencia by Joan Navarro, 1590; and often thereafter at Seville, Madrid, Cordova, Barcelona, Alcalá de Henares, Valladolid, and Lisbon) said he was sixty years of age on August 14, 1588—the day on which he sailed from Venice for the Holy Land. Two secondary authorities—Bermúdez de Pedraza (1638) and Sánchez Gordillo (1633)[20]—agree that he was born on October 4, 1528. Since October 4 is the feastday of St. Francis of Assisi, such a date is the more intrinsically probable (it was a common Spanish custom to name children after the saint on whose day they were born).

Pedro, his brother, was perhaps a decade older.[21] A composer of singular power and expressiveness in his own right, he taught the young Francisco the rudiments of music. It was Morales, however, who carried him forward to such heights in composition that he "was ready to occupy any honorable musical post" in Spain.[22] The precise months during which he studied with Morales cannot be named with dogmatic finality, but can be fixed with some probability as being in the early summer of 1545. Morales joined the papal choir on September 1, 1535. He received his first leave of absence on April 4, 1540, and reappeared in Rome on May 25, 1541. In the intervening year he presumably visited Seville. Francisco would have been eleven and twelve during his first leave. Morales departed from Rome with a second leave on May 1, 1545. On the following August 8 he was in Toledo.[23] If Morales really did prepare him to occupy any chapelmastership in Spain, then it seems likelier that Guerrero was in his seventeenth rather than twelfth year when such advanced instruction was given. Moreover, Guerrero in his *Viage de Hierusalem* said that his brother Pedro had already departed from Seville when he began to study with Morales.

Besides theoretical knowledge imparted by his brother and later by Morales, Guerrero early in life learned to play several instruments. Pacheco records that he became proficient on the seven-course vihuela—the six-course being the standard instrument. According to Pacheco, Guerrero also mastered the harp and cornett.[24] Juan Méndez Nieto, a physician who emigrated to the New World in 1559, professed to have studied organ with the *celebre organista Guerrero* before his departure from Seville.[25] This Guerrero would necessarily have been Francisco—Pedro having already departed for Italy at the time Méndez Nieto (who was born in 1535) sojourned in Seville.

Francisco's name first appears in Sevillian Cathedral documents with the *acta capitular* of April 3, 1542;[26] on that date he was received as a cathedral singer. On the same day his beginning annual salary was set at

12,000 maravedís. Presumably he already possessed the extremely beautiful *contra alto* that throughout his adult career was to win him the acclaim of all who knew him personally. The Sevillian chapelmaster was still Pedro Fernández de Castilleja (who had served since 1514). The assistant in charge of musical instruction was a certain Bernaldo de Villalva, who when appointed a cathedral singer on March 24, 1540, was asked to "help" the already aging chapelmaster teach the principles of harmony and counterpoint.[27] The cathedral chapter required that such lessons be scheduled daily, and that advanced musical instruction be always available to junior and senior members of the cathedral staff desirous of such instruction.

Guerrero continued a daily singer in Seville Cathedral from his fourteenth year until his appointment at the age of eighteen to the chapelmastership at Jaén (an Andalusian capital lying some 125 miles east of Seville and 40 miles north of Granada).

Jaén Chapelmastership Jaén, a city that passed frequently back and forth between Christian and Moorish hands in the Middle Ages, reverted finally to Spanish possession in 1449. By comparison with Seville, it was then, as now, but a secondary capital. Fortunately, the diocese was ruled during 1545-1554 by Pedro Pacheco,[28] a cardinal who exerted powerful influence at the Council of Trent.

Guerrero's predecessor in the Jaén chapelmastership was a certain Antonio de Viana.[29] The Jaén capitular acts show that during Viana's régime choral music in Jaén Cathedral—as in all other Spanish cathedrals— was (except in penitential seasons) invariably sung with accompaniment of wind, brass, and organs. When the number of shawm players (*chirimías*) so multiplied in early January, 1545, that they could not all be accommodated in the *coro*, the chapter ordered the cathedral building-superintendent to enlarge the loft where the small organs were situated, so that the various cathedral instrumentalists could be grouped together in the gallery above the choir.[30] Moreover, the canons thought the shawms would sound more brilliantly from the tribune above.

In February, 1545, the chapter censured Viana for neglecting to give the choirboys and senior singers an hour's lesson every night after vespers or compline.[31] In September of the same year he signed as surety for a loan to a singer—a practice that was later to bring the trusting Guerrero to grief.[32] Viana was also requested now and then by certain senior singers who sought cathedral chaplaincies to sign certificates guaranteeing their proficiency in plainsong and in polyphonic music.[33]

Guerrero's name first appears at Jaén in the act of April 16, 1546, entitled *Sobre la racion del maestro de capilla* ("concerning the chapelmaster's prebend").[34] Four days previously the chapter had elected him to a prebend left vacant by the death of Juan Alonso de Quadros. On July 1, 1546, his name again appears, in an act entitled "A Decision to write Morales at Toledo"; the act reads as follows:[35] "Today the canons debated whether they should write Morales, chapelmaster of Toledo Cathedral, who sends Francisco Guerrero to serve as chapelmaster in this cathedral; and they agreed to write him letting him know that they will give Guerrero the fruits of a half-prebend and entrust to his keeping six choirboys."

This notice is the most interesting of any yet recovered at Jaén. It is possible that Morales knew Cardinal Pacheco personally—Pacheco having spent much time in Rome while Morales was still in the papal choir. If Morales did not meet the cardinal in Rome, one other clue may explain the solicitude of the Jaén canons for his protégé, and also their decision to write him at Toledo telling him of Guerrero's appointment. On December 15, 1546, the Jaén chapter charged a priest named Francisco de Guzmán with the duty of celebrating the two masses before New Year's called for by a deed endowing the "chaplaincy held by Cristóbal de Morales."[36] Can it be that Morales, chapelmaster at Toledo in 1546, and the Cristóbal de Morales who was an absentee benefice-holder in Jaén Cathedral during December, 1546, were one and the same person? If so, we could better understand how Francisco Guerrero in his mid-teens inherited the chapel-mastership of a cathedral ruled by one of the grandest of Spanish prelates. Whatever grounds explain such an appointment, it is certain that Morales, the Elijah of sixteenth-century Spanish music, exerted himself valiantly in Guerrero's behalf: like Elijah and the youthful Elisha, "he passed by him and threw his mantle upon him."

The next Jaén capitular entries mentioning Guerrero reveal that his youth betrayed him into several indiscretions. For instance, he went partial surety for a new singer from Antequera on January 16, 1548. Two days later the new singer absconded, leaving him with several ducats to pay.[37] On August 30, 1548, the Jaén chapter let fall a thunderbolt on the young chapelmaster's head by voting to dismiss him. As reason, the chapter declared that "Francisco Guerrero, chapelmaster, does not fulfill his duty of teaching the choirboys." On the same day the chapter voted to distribute notices (edictos) of an immediate vacancy in "Jaén, Granada, Toledo, Seville, Cordova, Salamanca"; applications to be accepted for the vacant chapelmastership until November 1. To stimulate the most intense competition, the chapter at the same meeting decided to post a courier to Toledo, Valladolid, and Salamanca with news that the prebend would pay 150 ducats (even the Toledo chapelmastership paid ordinarily only 100 ducats); and that the new chapelmaster would enjoy an honored seat in the coro with all the rights of a prebendary: though with the duties of boarding four choirboys and of teaching all of them.[38]

This drastic action and the fear of further disgrace to follow quickly brought the soaring eaglet out of the clouds and down to earth. Guerrero, now just turned twenty, not only began immediately to teach all the boys and to look properly after "Juan de Segura, Lagartillo, Ortiz, and Pedro de Magana,"[39] his four choirboy boarders; but also he humbly submitted his own name as a contender in the competition to decide his successor. On Saturday, November 3, three days after the deadline for applications, the chapter sat to consider the qualifications of the various applicants. Because of his reformation and his manifest abilities, the chapter voted him winner of the contest to "succeed" himself—investing him at the same session with a new prebend sanctioned by a papal bull.[40]

On April 6, 1549, Guerrero received a novice choirboy boarder in place of "Lagartillo," and on May 31 a fifth boarder.[41] On June 27 he and the head organist in the cathedral were allowed the privilege of a ten-day visit to nearby Baeza (the town in which Ramos de Pareja had originated); and were permitted to take along two choirboys so that they could make up a quartet.[42] Upon their return, Guerrero was, as of July 19, voted a gift of twelve ducats "on account of his financial need at the present moment."[43] Although he probably had visited Seville previously, the first formal permission for a twenty-day leave of absence to revisit his home seems to have been voted by the chapter as late as August 26, 1549.[44] He never returned from this leave—Seville offering him inducements so powerful that he chose to remain on the banks of the Guadalquivir.

Reconciling themselves as best they could, the Jaén canons voted two months after his departure to receive Martín de Gante (Martin of Ghent), a clergyman presumably of Flemish descent, as his successor in the Jaén chapelmastership.[45]

Reëstablishment at Seville Seville would have been infinitely attractive to an ambitious young composer such as Guerrero for any number of other reasons besides the fact that it was his parental home. The cathedral itself, one of the most sublime in Europe, was substantially complete in 1549, whereas the present Jaén Cathedral had yet to be built. To add to her attractions, Seville was the richest city in Spain as a result of her New World trade monopoly. Although it is not known whether Spanish printing actually began in Seville, it is certain that more books had been published there than in any other Spanish city before 1549.

During Guerrero's absence in Jaén, certain new canons had joined the Sevillian chapter—already a group of the most cultivated ecclesiastics in Spain—among whom was Alonso Mudarra, originally a clergyman of Palencia diocese.[46] Confirmed in his canonry on October 18, 1546, Mudarra was an acknowledged virtuoso vihuelist.[47] The printing of his *Tres libros de musica en cifras para vihuela*[48] was completed in Seville soon thereafter (on December 7, 1546, by Juan de León). As all who know his *Tres libros* will subscribe, Mudarra was not only an accomplished performer but also a composer of singular excellence and taste. His tablature, for instance, includes twenty-seven original fantasias and nine tientos. In addition, he intabulated motets by Escobar and Willaert, excerpts from masses by Josquin des Prez and Antoine de Févin, and even a setting of the second epode of Horace by the German organist Paul Hofhaimer (1459-1537).[49] Within a year of his appointment as a member of the governing board of the cathedral, Mudarra had already begun his efforts to ensure the musical supremacy of Seville cathedral: efforts that were to continue unabated through three decades until his death in 1580.[50]

In explanation of his reasons for abandoning the Jaén chapelmastership and remaining in Seville, Guerrero, in the autobiographical prologue to his *Viage de Hierusalem*, cited his devotion to his parents who (he said) insisted on his remaining at home. At first, the Sevillian chapter could offer him only a singer's prebend. "But within a few months, however, I was called to the chapelmastership at Málaga," continues Guerrero in his prologue. Diego Fernández, chapelmaster at Málaga from 1507 to 1551, died there during the early part of August, 1551, after a lengthy illness.[51] Before a month was out, the Málaga chapter had offered the twenty-three-year-old Guerrero the post. This offer is certified not in Málaga cathedral documents but in a Sevillian capitular act dated September 11, 1551.[52] Copious extracts from this act must be given below.

On Friday, September 11, 1551, after prior summons the aforementioned canons met and voted by ayes and nays to accept the recommendations of the select committee whose report reads as follows. I   Because of gratitude to Pedro Fernández,[53] chapelmaster, for his long-continued services in searching out and in teaching choirboys, and in boarding, lodging, and clothing them, he shall therefore be now rewarded (1) by being relieved henceforth of all other responsibilities except that of presiding at the conductor's stand in choir; (2) he shall continue to enjoy the full honor of the chapelmaster's title; (3) but by reason of his modified service he shall be placed on half pay, both in cash and kind; during the entire remainder of his life—such pay to continue without interruption, be he sick or well. II   Since the ability of Francisco Guerrero is now abundantly known to all, since moreover he left the chapelmastership at Jaén which carried with it a prebend, *and since he is now called to the chapelmastership with prebend at Málaga*,[54] . . . and because of the evident good that he can do the choirboys in this cathedral by teaching them, be it therefore now agreed that he shall henceforth act as master of the boys so long as he attends to all the following duties: (1) he must teach them to read, write, and to sing the responsories, versicles, antiphons, lessons, and kalends, and other parts of divine service according to the use of this cathedral; (2) he shall teach them plainchant, harmony, and counterpoint, his instruction in counterpoint to include both the art of adding a melody to a plainsong and to an already existing piece of polyphonic music; he shall also teach them to compose and give instruction in any other branches needed to make them skillful musicians and singers; (3) he shall always clothe them decently and properly, see that they wear good shoes, and ensure that their beds are kept perfectly clean; (4) he shall feed them the same food that he himself eats and never take money from them for anything having to do with their services in church or their musical instruction; (5) he shall also give public lessons henceforth, in which he teaches how to add a counterpoint, either above or below any given plainchant; (6) with the income from his prebend he shall provide proper graduating clothes for a choirboy whose voice has changed, but to the chapter shall be reserved the final decision as to the time when a choirboy shall be dismissed; (7) he shall always retain a sufficient number of choirboys for any occasion that may arise; (8) the clothing, treatment, teaching, and musical improvement of the choirboys shall be examined once a month by a deputy of the chapter without advance warning; and if the boys are found to lack proper clothes and shoes they shall be bought and charged against his account; (9) since during the immediate future his cathedral income shall be made up from two sources, one source being half the chapelmaster's regular pay, the other source being the singer's salary that he had previously been receiving; and since moreover he is now promised the reversion of the chapelmastership upon Pedro Fernández's death, he shall himself therefore agree to renounce all further claim to any revenue from his singer's prebend on the day when he eventually succeeds Pedro Fernández.

Pedro Fernández's age is not disclosed in the above act. However, since he had been initially appointed some thirty-seven years earlier (1514), he cannot have been much less than sixty in 1551. Two pieces of circumstantial evidence—(1) already in 1540 Bernaldo de Villalva was deputed to teach the boys, and (2) in 1545 Luys de Villafranca was being paid to function in his stead out of funds earmarked as chapelmaster's salary[55]—suggest that in 1551 he was nearer seventy than sixty. At that, he so outlived all expectation as to die in 1574 when perhaps a nonagenarian. What started as a purely temporary sharing of salary and honors was therefore to last a quarter-century. The quite humble title of *Odei phonascus* which Guerrero gave himself when he came to publish his *Liber primus missarum* (Paris: Nicolas du Chemin, 1566)—a title that is not only unusual but can be taken to mean that he counted himself merely a music teacher instead of master— shows something of the care he exercised during all the long intervening decades never publicly to suggest in any way that he instead of Fernández was musical chief at Seville. On the other hand, the capitular acts abundantly indicate that his was the whole responsibility of the chapelmastership during at least the last two decades before Fernández died.

The first change in the musical organization after Guerrero became "prefect" occurred in the summer of 1553. At Seville, *ministriles* playing shawms, cornetts, and sackbuts had long been hired to accompany singing and to provide instrumental interludes at all church festivals and during processions. Before 1553 they were usually paid on a piecework basis. At Toledo, this piecework arrangement had been found unsatisfactory as early as 1531, in which year the chapter had signed a twenty-year contract with three virtuoso *ministriles altos* (*tiple*, *contralto*, and *sacabuche*), each of whom was in turn to pick his own assistant.[56] This contractual arrangement assured the Toledo chapter of the services of the six finest players money could buy, and guaranteed that they would always be on hand for climactic occasions, instead of being lured away on Corpus Christi and Assumption by competing bidders.

Taking their cue perhaps from Toledo, the Sevillian canons decided on July 26, 1553, that henceforth instrumentalists should be offered long-term contracts.[57] First, they agreed among themselves that all those days that according to Sevillian use were solemn festivals ought to be celebrated with the maximum apparatus and authority possible: especially since the devotion of the people was thereby increased. After deciding that the music of such instrumentalists as had previously been hired on feast days measurably increased public devotion, they agreed it to be not only "a very useful thing, but also conformable with Sacred Scripture, to make use of every kind of instrumental music in this cathedral: especially since it is so famous and splendid a temple and of such large dimensions . . . and moreover all other Spanish cathedrals, though many enjoy much smaller incomes, make constant use of instrumental music." The canons also agreed that processions both inside and outside the cathedral should as a rule move to the sound of instruments, because such music "arouses more affection and devotion and incites the people to follow the processions and to come to divine services." In view of all this, the canons therefore voted unanimously to receive the instrumentalists as long-term salaried employees of the cathedral.

In implementation of this decision Juan Peraça [= Peraza] (soprano shawmer), Andrés Deça (sackbut player), Luis de Medrano (tenor shawmer),[58] Juan Baptista (sackbut player), Antonio de San Pedro (tenor shawmer), and Martín de San Pedro (sackbut player), were hired on September 20, 1553, at the following respective amounts: 55,000 maravedís and five cahizes of wheat; 30,000 and four; 25,000 and two; 25,000 and two; 30,000 and four; 12,000 and two. The two last-named musicians, who were probably father and son—as was often so among cathedral players—were brought from Toledo. Juan Peraza, the highest paid of the group, fathered the two renowned organists, Gerónimo and Francisco. In 1556 he transferred with his family to Toledo, despite vigorous efforts to retain him at Seville.[59] (Later, however, as we shall see, his sons gravitated back to Seville.)

After thus regularizing the status of cathedral instrumentalists, the Sevillian chapter turned to the question of music books. On October 7, 1553, the canons heard "a report that the books containing polyphony are extremely old and the works copied into them also very ancient and not such as are nowadays being sung in other Spanish churches."[60] Having listened to the report (which Guerrero himself probably gave), the canons decided to commission the copying "into two or three choirbooks of the best masses that are nowadays being sung, so that the quality of the music sung in this cathedral may improve." The choice of items to be copied was left to the *maestre escuela*, Doctor Martín Gascó, whose duty it would be to consult with the finest musical authorities in Seville. The copyist, decreed the chapter, should be "Rodrigo de Ceballos, musician, who at the present moment finds himself unoccupied in this city and is competent to do the job." The chapter further promised Ceballos his living expenses and reimbursement for the cost of materials while doing the work, "provided only that he communicate with the chapter musical committee and with the chapelmasters, who are Pedro Fernández and Guerrero, before he start to copy any particular work." Ceballos must have been approximately Guerrero's age; later, he was to become a renowned chapelmaster at Cordova and Granada successively,[61] and to distinguish himself as one of the greatest Spanish composers in the reign of Philip II. Quite possibly, Guerrero started the agitation for new choirbooks because a fellow composer turned twenty needed stopgap employment; and not just because the cathedral needed new ones.

This particular notice is interesting on still other accounts. For instance, students of Sevillian musical history have often wondered why masses by such cathedral notables as Alonso de Alva, Pedro de Escobar, and Francisco de Peñalosa have not been preserved in cathedral choirbooks. The answer seems to be that the books containing their masses underwent such hard and continuous use at Seville that they finally wore out. An answer is suggested to yet another intriguing question: Of what use were the Colombina music books to the chapter? Students of Spanish musical history know that Ferdinand Columbus at his death in 1539 bequeathed his library first to his half-brother Diego, and then to the Sevillian chapter. However, on September 16, 1551, the chapter having not yet received anything more tangible than an inventory of the 15,370 books, and being already fearful that so incomparable a collection would tempt the most righteous custodians to theft, deputed two senior canons to oversee the delivery of the library "with the most scrupulous diligence."[62] A year later the books finally came into corporate possession of the cathedral, and on December

20, 1553, were being inventoried anew.[63] However, the rapid change in musical taste—causing the chapter in October, 1553, to call for the copying of fresh and up-to-date masses—meant that by the time Columbus's superb musical library (or what was left of it) reached the cathedral, the repertory in his music books was already deemed so old-fashioned by leading Sevillian musicians that no effort was made to transfer motets and masses from Petrucci and Antico prints into Sevillian choirbooks.

Guerrero, who was first invited to occupy the Málaga chapelmastership early in September, 1551, again applied after Morales's death. A formal competition for the post was announced in *edictos* publicly distributed on December 6, 1553. Six eligibles appeared in Málaga for the public trials of skill, which were held during the second week of February, 1554.[64] Juan Navarro, the second of the five who competed, tried out on Friday, February 9. Guerrero's lot fell on the next Sunday. Each contestant underwent the following tests:[65] (1) he sight-sang a plainchant picked by opening a choirbook at random; (2) his motet composed after one o'clock the previous afternoon on a prescribed text was performed before his opponents as well as the assembled Málaga chapter; (3) he sang a counterpoint first to a previously unseen solo part, next to a duo, then to a trio. No one could succeed in these trials without unusual talent, but above all, without spur-of-the-moment facility. Guerrero, who won by unanimous vote, must have possessed self-confidence that his otherwise modest demeanor hardly suggests.

Since Málaga appointments were still nominally in the royal gift, Guerrero's appointment had first to be submitted for Philip's ratification before it could be formally tendered him on April 2. Within three weeks the Málaga chapter realized that he did not aim to accept, and on April 19 announced a new competition. From the outset he may not have intended to settle in Málaga, even if such an offer were made; but rather have been interested in a renewal of the invitation first issued in 1551; so that now three years later he could stir the Sevillian chapter to make certain further concessions. With the 1551 invitation he had levered the Sevillian canons into a promise of the chapelmastership upon Pedro Fernández's decease; and an annual salary in the meantime of 50,000 maravedís. This unusual arrangement lacked papal sanction, however, so late as 1554. Without such sanction any agreement as unusual as his was a mere rope of sand. At the very least, another spectacular victory at nearby Málaga in 1554 would spur the Sevillian chapter to press for a papal bull legalizing his anomalous position. In 1551 he had been named a suffragan, as it were. In 1554 he hoped to be named coadjutor.

Even if such an interpretation credits him with too much acumen, at least it is certain that the papal bull *Pastoralis officii* was issued by Julius III on June 1, 1554;[66] and that two months would have been a quite reasonable time for the necessary fees to have gone forward through Francisco Mudarra, Sevillian procurator at Rome.[67] The bull begins as follows:

Julius, servant of the servants of God . . . for a perpetual memory. The obligations of Our Divine Office constantly impel us to protect with special favor all such proposals for the increased solemnity of Divine Worship and the better support of ministers consecrated to the same as the power given to Us from on high will allow. A recent instance has been brought to Our attention by Our dear sons, the Dean and Chapter of the Sevillian Cathedral, and by Francisco Guerrero, clergyman of that city, there having been presented to Us an act dated September 11 [1551] whose design is to enhance the splendor and prestige of that cathedral insofar as the office of chapelmaster is concerned: an office which by the consent of Our Predecessors is at the free disposition of the Dean and Chapter, and in which act is proposed the following.

The next several paragraphs of the bull contain a literal translation into Latin of the act of September 11, 1551 (see above, pages 142-143).

What then ensues must be taken as proof that on April 2, 1554—the very day on which the Málaga chapter received Philip's formal assent to Guerrero's Málaga appointment—the Sevillian chapter decided upon a counteroffer: that of lifetime tenure at Seville guaranteed by papal bull. The pertinent sentences in the bull run as follows:

And since more recently Our beloved son the esteemed Philip, Prince of the Spanish dominions, has at the earnest request of Our venerable brother, Bernardo [Manrique], bishop and Our dear sons, the Dean and Chapter of Málaga Cathedral, decreed that the said Francisco [Guerrero] shall be assigned a prebend in the said cathedral, exercising in it the office of chapelmaster; And since Bernardo, bishop of Málaga, and the Dean and Chapter of the same have offered the said Francisco other stipends and salaries, endeavoring with utmost diligence to induce his resignation from the Sevillian chapelmastership and his acceptance of that at Málaga; And since the Dean and Chapter of Seville Cathedral, taking into account his character, virtues, excellent disposition, and singular musical endowments, and the great advances already made by the choirboys entrusted to his instruction and upbringing, the future advances to be expected, the diligence that he has thus far shown in caring for them, not only insofar as musical education is concerned but also in boarding, lodging, and clothing them; And since the continued preëminence of the Sevillian Cathedral, now one of the foremost in the Spanish dominions, requires that her ministers must be similarly outstanding in all branches of their ministry; And since they have persuaded him to refuse the offers made by the Málaga Cathedral which carried lifetime guarantees; And since in view of all these transactions the Dean and Chapter in capitular session *last April 2* [1554] have in their own names and in that of their successors guaranteed to the said Francisco the following rights of succession, salaries, stipends, and other payments . . . .

What follows is an irrevocable promise of succession, a statement of his salary schedule, and a formal agreement that when he succeeds to the chapelmastership at Fernández's death he shall no longer be eligible to payments on account of his singer's appointment.

Sevillian Career (1554-1599) The chief external events in Guerrero's life after 1554 can be classified under these headings: (1) trips to nearby Spanish points and to foreign parts; (2) salary raises; (3) debts, the last of which caused him to be imprisoned; and (4) censures imposed by the Sevillian chapter. In addition, his biography should take account of: (5) his activities as "master of the boys"; (6) the hiring from time to time of new singers; (7) new instrumentalists; and (8) new cathedral organists. A review of his chapelmastership must also touch on the building of the new grand organ during the early 1570's; the constant augmenting of the cathedral musical library with new choral and instrumental books; and even such apparently peripheral matters as the shift ordered in 1575 from time-honored Sevillian use to the newly reformed Roman rite.

For all these various phases of Guerrero's Sevillian career between 1554 and his death forty-five years later in 1599, the biographer turns first to the 272 pertinent entries in the handwritten books of Sevillian *Actas capitulares* catalogued as *Libros XXI-XXXIX*. The books exist in somewhat irregularly numbered series at the Sevillian cathedral archive. Concerning two extramural phases of Guerrero's career, information must be collected elsewhere: (1) his literary activity—which took the form of a travel book, "Journey to Jerusalem," published in 1590 and reprinted frequently thereafter; and (2) the diffusion of his printed and manuscript compositions at various dates from 1555 until the year following his death.

To sharpen the focus as much as possible we shall here resort to a chronological table—such a table seeming the most convenient way to summarize information gathered from the above-mentioned books of Sevillian capitular acts. Guerrero's literary (1590) and musical publications (1555, 1563, 1566, 1570, 1582, 1584, 1589*a*, 1589*b*, 1597) will thereafter be examined separately.

1554 On May 23 he offers a handsome manuscript copy of certain unnamed compositions to the Sevillian chapter and is rewarded with a cash gift.[68]

On October 29 the cathedral chapter approves the purchase of a new organ to be built in 1555 by an organ-maker of Granada.[69]

1555   February 6: the chapter raises Guerrero's salary by 20,000 maravedís and at the same time provides him with a house near the cathedral in which to board the choirboys and give them schooling.[70]

April 22: the chapter votes to discount the salary of Anton de Armijo, Guerrero's colleague in the teaching of polyphony, at the rate of one ducat a month until a debt of thirty ducats is paid.[71]

1556   Guerrero's past year's salary being in arrears and the price of wheat high, the chapter on March 21 votes to donate ten bushels of wheat so that his choirboys may be fed properly.[72]

Alonso Mudarra, together with seven other members of the chapter, is deputed on May 29 to arrange for dances, playlets, and towering floats during the coming annual Corpus Christi parade: those who provide these entertainments being instructed to march between instrumentalists and singers in the street procession.[73]

1557   Gaspar Maynete, formerly chief instrumentalist at Toledo (see above, p. 121, n. 170), is hired on March 30 at a cash salary of 50,000 maravedís annually, plus 36 bushels of wheat.[74] On the same day three other virtuosi with the family name of Mora—a father and two sons—are hired at a collective rate of 400 ducats (150,000 maravedís) plus 8 cahizes (96 bushels) of wheat. Only a few scattered notices of this sort can be reproduced in the present chronological survey; but the cathedral continually sought, and usually obtained, the best players in Spain.

1558   May 25: the chapter orders that only grandees (and their immediate relatives), counts, marquises, and *adelantados* (provincial governors) may in future enter the choir enclosure during divine service: such a restriction being imposed so that quiet can be the better maintained during cathedral solemnities.[75]

October 3: the chapter orders the purchase of twenty-four new printed missals;[76] on December 2 Pedro Fernández, semi-retired chapelmaster, suggests that the chapter pay for the copying of certain "short masses" to be sung during celebrations outside the cathedral—these short masses being needed especially when processions are held.[77]

1560   A new sackbut player, García Gonsales, is hired on March 7 at an annual salary of 55,000 maravedís and 5 cahizes of wheat. On May 15 the chapter votes to inspect a music book "for the shawm players" to determine whether it is worth the price asked.[78]

September 30 : Canon Alonso Mudarra is a leading spirit in persuading the chapter to hire Melchor de Camargo (soprano shawmer) and Gaspar de Camargo (sackbut) at 300 ducats (112,500 maravedís) plus 10 cahizes of wheat and 150 ducats plus 6 cahizes, respectively. This father-and-son pair are invited on condition that they obtain written royal approval—they having previously been in royal service.[79]

1561   June 13: the chapter decides that henceforth neither singers nor instrumental-ists may be loaned to any outside individual or organization, any more than can the chalices or copes owned by the cathedral—this prohibition to apply on all those days of the church calendar for which polyphony is designated.[80] In this act, as in nearly all later acts making mention of polyphony in a general sense, "singers and instrumentalists" are named jointly as if belonging together irrevocably.

Toward the end of August, Guerrero visits Toledo carrying with him manuscript copies (one on paper, one on vellum) of his original compositions. He is rewarded on September 12 with a cash gift.[81]

December 3: the cathedral house formerly occupied by the now senescent chapel-master Pedro Fernández is rented to another cathedral functionary.[82]

1562   February 14: taking into account the "barrenness of the times" and the fact that Guerrero is scarcely able to feed his choirboys, the chapter decides (by a close vote) to give him money to buy new robes, surplices, and caps for his six young charges.[83]

Another cathedral functionary, a *compañero* named, coincidentally, Francisco Guerrero, departs for the New World sometime before June 8,[84] on which date the benefice held by him comes up for a split among three former choirboys whose voices have changed.

June 10: the chapter extends the prohibition of June 13, 1561, against loaning singers or instrumentalists on any account whatsoever, to include even the humblest choirboy.[85]

November 20: a vigorous search is instituted for the best tenor and bass singers to be found in the realm.[86]

Luys de Villafranca, master of the altar boys and instructor of plainchant, petitions on November 27 that the boy-bishop festivities be combined this year with those for the Feast of St. Nicholas.[87]

1563   January 29: Guerrero certifies that a certain youth has completed three years under him as a choirboy, has during all that time been a faithful student, and that now his voice has broken.[88] This certificate entitles the youth to free academic attire, free tuition, and other benefits over a specified period of time in St. Michael's, an endowed school in Seville for former choirboys of good repute and abilities. This type of certificate will be called for frequently and, as a rule, sup-plied readily by Guerrero during the remaining years of his choirmastering.

The Archdeacon of Jérez, a titular bishop, having offered a rich new endowment for singers, the chapter meets on April 16 to decide how it may best be divided.[89] New funds for singers and instrumentalists will be the order of the day in Seville during the next quarter-century.

June 2 : the chapter decides to penalize singers or instrumentalists who are tardy by a few minutes, at the same rate as if they had been absent the whole hour.[90]

June 16 : the chapter again invokes its decision of June 10, 1562, against lending singers or instrumentalists, no matter how importunate or important the would-be borrower.[91]

June 28 : a choirboy goes home with four ducats to pay his travel expenses.[92] Other similar notices show that many of Guerrero's choirboys come from afar.

July 12 : the chapter accords "Maestro Guerrero, chapelmaster of this cathedral, a month's leave of absence on account of his illness, hoping that he will during the month come to the cathedral whenever he is able."[93]

July 30: the chapter decides to offer the highest sums ever paid to cathedral singers—100,000 maravedís plus 10 cahizes of wheat (120 bushels) annually to each—in order to attract two new basses. Advertisement of the openings is to be distributed as widely as possible throughout Spain.[94]

August 18: Guerrero requests of the chapter a salary advance of 100 ducats (37,500 maravedís), this amount to be repaid in twelve monthly installments.[95]

August 23: the chapter votes to boost the salaries of five cathedral instrumentalists to the following amounts: Diego de Andrada, Juan de Rojas (soprano shawmers), and Juan Baptista (sackbut player)—50,000 maravedís and 60 bushels of wheat each; Diego López and Gaspar de Cuevas (sackbut players)—37,500 maravedís and 48 bushels each.[96]

October 6: Christóval Ximénez, a former choirboy whose voice has now changed, is approved for appointment to the first cathedral prebend that shall fall vacant among the several specifically designated for "old boys."[97] (As this notice and many another of the same type reveal, the provisions for the welfare of former choirboys in sixteenth-century Seville were exceptionally lavish and well organized.)

October 8: the chapter votes to extend the time in which the loan to Guerrero granted on August 18 must be repaid to two years, with a corresponding reduction in the amount to be withheld from his salary each month.[98]

November 5: the chapter refuses to accept a renowned bass who has come from afar to try out for one of the new 100,000-maravedí posts announced on the previous July 30. However, he is given twelve ducats toward traveling expenses.[99] Always when a major new musical appointee is to be named, he is expected to appear for a competitive trial, after which the chapter votes by secret ballot. Unsuccessful candidates are then sent on their way with a gift sufficient to take care of all traveling expenses.

November 19: the chapter orders Balthasar de Matute, a senior cathedral singer, to stop carrying around the wand that is his badge of authority in *la hermandad*.[100] He has been complained of for having abusively harangued a wheelwright in the employ of a certain cathedral prebendary. The search for even small badges of authority is extremely intense among Guerrero's singers, even when they are no better qualified than Dogberry and Verges to carry their wands.

1564   Guerrero spends the period October 3-12 away from Seville in a search for new choirboys.[101] His recruiting methods resemble those later in vogue when Georg Reutter, chapelmaster at St. Stephen's, brought the young Haydn from Hainburg to Vienna. (However, Sevillian choirboys were never castrated during the sixteenth century in order to preserve their voices.)[102]

December 13: the chapter orders Luis Martínez, a cathedral chaplain, to stay away from the choirbook-stand when the rest of the singers gather around it to sing polyphony—the reason being that "he throws the others out of tune."[103] (This notice shows that in Seville, as elsewhere, polyphonic singers clustered around a large open choirbook set on a stand in the middle of the grilled choir-enclosure.)

1565   January 19: the chapter orders Canon Luis Carrillo "to buy a new chest of recorders [*caxa de flautas*] for the instrumentalists, if necessary, but first to see if the old set can still be used and if repairs can be made.[104] The same instrumentalists who play shawms, as later notices will reveal, alternate on *flautas*.

Guerrero receives permission to take a private ten-day business trip beginning on February 2.[105]

May 25: Andrés Jacomar petitions the chapter for eight months' back payment owing him on his scholarship at St. Michael's *collegio* in Seville: this being the institution in which scholarships for former choirboys are endowed.[106] The petition further reveals that these scholarships run through four years and provide the scholar with 5,000 maravedís at the end of the course to buy the graduation cap and gown.

The chapter on June 4 authorizes an advance of twenty ducats to Mosén Roque, purportedly the best bass in Spain, in the hope of luring him to Seville.[107] On March 9, 1566, Roque receives a gratuity of forty ducats—over and above his salary—to compensate him for "damages at Ávila and the purloining of his clothing" at the time of his removal from Ávila to Seville.[108] On January 24, 1570, he is named one of four singers to accompany the Cardinal of Seville, Gaspar de Zuñiga y Avellaneda, to Santander in a journey of state.[109] On March 4, 1574, he receives a four-day sick leave. Shortly before November 3, 1581, he dies.[110]

July 6 [1565]: the chapter grants Guerrero a new loan of 100 ducats, to be repaid from his singer's salary in twelve monthly installments beginning on January 1, 1566.[111]

July 30: the chapter orders the cathedral singers to obey Pedro Fernández and Francisco Guerrero in everything connected with divine worship.[112] Both chapel-masters are expressly authorized to punish with fines any singer who errs in singing his part during divine service. Furthermore, the chapelmasters are authorized to penalize all those who talk during practice or at service, those who act in a froward or negligent manner, those who refuse to sing the part assigned (except when publicly known to be sick), those who usurp better seats than they are entitled to by virtue of their choir rank; to punish those who do not assemble for extra rehearsals of Christmas and other special music, those who murmur when called by the chapter for extra duty outside the cathedral; and to fine those who miss Masses of Our Lady and Salves sung in the Antigua Chapel of the cathedral or object to the singing of *responsorios*. This extremely detailed list of possible choir offenses has been drawn up previous to the chapter meeting by "both chapelmasters acting jointly," but from later developments it will be surmised that Guerrero is the principal compiler of the list. Already it is his announced intention that music in Seville Cathedral shall equal the best to be heard anywhere in Christendom.

August 13: Guerrero is enjoined to write down in a book the certified date of each choirboy's entry, and to provide the treasurer of the cathedral with a copy.[113] This precaution is necessary because certain youths are requesting cathedral benefits before completing the stipulated three years' service as choirboys.

September 7: the chapter orders that any cathedral singer or instrumentalist who uses a paid leave of absence to try out for a post elsewhere shall automatically forfeit his post at Seville Cathedral.[114]

Luys de Villafranca, master of the altar boys *(mozos de coro)*—who are to be distinguished from the choirboys *(seises)* because they study only plainchant whereas the choirboys live with the chapelmaster and study polyphony and counterpoint as well—is rewarded on October 17 with a salary increase of 6,000 maravedís and an extra 12 bushels of wheat.[115] Although not expressly stated, this reward is probably to be connected with the publication at Seville in this same year of Villafranca's plainchant instructor entitled *Breue Instrucion* [sic] *de canto llano*—undoubtedly the best of its type published in sixteenth-century Spain. In addition to approbations signed by Pedro Fernández and Guerrero, Villafranca's instructor commands attention because of its skillful digest of information from such other authorities as Guillermo Despuig (folio 5ᵛ), Andreas Ornithoparchus (folio 10ᵛ), Juan de Espinosa (folio 13), and Juan Bermudo (folio 13).

October 22: the chapter reinforces its enactment of the previous August 13—adding weight to it by requiring Guerrero to record the birthplace and the parents' names alongside each choirboy's date of entry.[116]

October 29: the chapter instructs its auditors to fine Guerrero for "certain laxnesses."[117] On November 14 it orders a raise for the sopranist Bartolomé de Victoria on condition that he "repay the total added amount" if he at any later time takes employment outside Seville Cathedral. This type of proviso attached to salary raises will recur rather frequently during the next few years.

December 5: the chapter decrees that any cathedral singer or instrumentalist who performs in a street serenade at night shall be fined a month's pay.[118]

December 17: Guerrero's salary is boosted by a further 20,000 maravedís annually.[119] His salary continues to derive from two sources—singer's prebend (now worth 90,000 maravedís annually) plus half the chapelmaster's prebend. Although not expressly stated, his total cash salary (both sources) must now range annually in the neighborhood of 150,000 maravedís.

1566   January 2: the chapter accords Guerrero a fifty-day leave of absence (to start on January 7).[120] This leave is granted so that he may visit Lisbon and personally place a copy of his *Liber primus missarum* in the young Portuguese king's hands.

January 9: the chapter instructs Luis Carrillo to purchase the chest of recorders that was under discussion the previous January 19, and to buy the set "quickly."[121]

March 16: the chapter authorizes Canon Alonso Mudarra and two others to sit as an organ committee, their duty being "to inform themselves concerning the ability of Maestre Jox, Flemish organ builder, and to discover if he be competent to build a new grand organ for the cathedral."[122]

March 23: the chapter secretary is authorized to write a letter beseeching a royal pardon for Gaspar de Cuevas, cathedral sackbut player, who is imprisoned on a murder charge.

1567   January 3: the dean of the cathedral (Cristóbal de Padilla) and the prior (Pedro Vélez de Guevara) are requested by the chapter to sift out the cause of the dispute raging between the archdeacon of Seville (Rodrigo Ximénez) and Guerrero; "and if they find Guerrero at fault to punish him severely."[123] This controversy arises from charges brought by Ximénez that Guerrero neglects his choirboys shamefully.

Saturday, February 15: Guerrero is temporarily in disgrace: Pedro Fernández (now surely senile) is entrusted with disbursing all special gifts to the choristers such as those they receive when they sing outside the cathedral at authorized fiestas. To make the sting more painful, the chapters orders that neither "Francisco Guerrero nor any other singer shall sit in any seat anywhere in the choir enclosure, nor on any bench[124] that is reserved for beneficed clergymen during sermons." In thus downgrading Guerrero to a mere singer, the chapter of course disgraces him in the eyes of the very singers whom he has hitherto conducted.

Tuesday, February 18: the chapter enters on a more lenient course. Dean Padilla and Canon Carrillo are deputed to visit Guerrero with an official scolding. But he is not to be demoted, nor fined 300 ducats, as the chapter had in anger decided upon doing the previous Saturday.[125]

April 9: the "organ committee" is augmented to include the dean, Doctor Ramírez, and the cathedral organist, Pedro de Villada.[126] Canon Alonso Mudarra
still remains the musical "authority" on the committee, which is now instructed to
obtain specifications for the proposed new grand organ from the visiting Flemish
master builder, Maestre Juan [Jox]. On April 23 the latter and a competitor
newly arrived in Seville are instructed to build portables.[127] He who is adjudged to
have built the better portable will be awarded the contract for the large organ, and
his portable purchased for use during processions. On May 21, Jox's organette
having been accepted as the superior, the four-man organ committee is instructed
to draw up a contract.[128] Work starts, but some nine months later (March 6, 1568)
the chapter asks the dean to report the reasons for an unaccountable delay.[129] On
May 5, 1568, Maestre Jors [*sic*] is instructed not to exceed his contract, and in
the dean's place three other chapter members are deputed to consult with the
Flemish maestre concerning the place where the organ shall be installed.[130] On
June 16 the chapter votes to place it in the tribune where the great clock now
hangs, and to move the great clock to the tribune above the red door.[131] Quarreling over various details in the construction continues rife, however, and on Monday, June 21 [1568] the chapter decides to revoke the contract.[132] As reasons,
the chapter secretary records the following: (1) the organ promises to cost much
more than the contract called for; (2) the Flemish maestre's chief assistant has been
quoted as saying that there is no certainty the organ under construction will match
in tone and in mechanism the instruments at Toledo, Cordova, Pilar of Saragossa,
or San Salvador of Seville: these being the four most-admired organs in Spain.
On July 9 the chapter commits to the organ committee the unpleasant task of
"concerting as best they can with the Flemish organ builder and paying him for
what he has done already: provided that he agrees to revoking the contract."[133]
But Maestre Jox [= Jos, Jors—all three spellings occur] will not be bought off so
peremptorily. On September 3 he sends in a written letter of expostulation against
breaking the contract.[134] He wins his point, for on November 12 [1568] after a
four-month stoppage the chapter orders "that the work on the large organ shall
be resumed according to the original specifications and the contract drawn up with
Maestre Jos."[135] He may continue his work either somewhere in the "Granada"
nave, or in a vacant classroom of the adjoining St. Michael's *collegio*. Henceforth
"he is not to be disturbed nor any account taken of idle rumors until the new organ
is completed." The work proceeds and is still in progress on August 11, 1570; on
which date the organ is being installed.[136] On May 16, 1572, the chapter requests
the cathedral treasurer to bring the contract forward for reëxamination.[137] On
February 14, 1573, the installation is nearly complete and the chapter accepts a
suggestion from the constructors that a protective grille be added.[138] On September
1, 1573, a brilliant new organist—Gerónimo de Peraça (= Peraza)— is engaged[139]
and henceforth an exciting new chapter in Sevillian organ history begins to unfold.

Upon written request from the Cordova Cathedral chapter, the Sevillian chapter
on April 16, 1567, grants Guerrero a short leave of absence to visit the neighboring Andalusian city—he having been invited to serve as member of an examining
jury[140] called together by the Cordovan chapter to elect a successor to Andrés Villalar, chapelmaster at Cordova from July 5, 1563, until December 16, 1566.[141] As a

kindly gesture the Sevillian chapter votes to pay him full salary and allowances during his absence. On Thursday, April 24, the Cordovan chapter votes Guerrero an honorarium of sixty ducats for his services on the jury.

September 17 [1567]: Guerrero has sufficiently regained favor at Seville to be again called "chapelmaster." Indeed, the chapter is ready on this date to back him up in a disciplinary case by threatening dismissal of an impudent baritone named Juan Vaca who refuses to sing *chançonetas* (vernacular spiritual songs) with the choirboys when they march in outside processions.[142]

1568   Guerrero's "forgiveness" is complete on January 5; on which date the chapter votes to pay him for all the days that he was on suspension during the previous year, or absent on leave. He shall, however, use this money to clothe his choirboys and to buy them new surplices.[143]

Wednesday, February 4; the chapter "irrevocably" expels a choirboy named Camacho, decreeing that he shall never be permitted to return. Nine days later (Friday, February 13) he is received back, "despite the previous expulsion."[144] In this disciplinary case, as in others, the chapter shows admirable willingness to reconsider even an "irrevocable" decision.

Also on February 13, Guerrero receives a back payment of 5,100 maravedís (150 reales) in compensation for 10 fanegas (16 bushels) of wheat that were not delivered to him while he was on suspension the previous year.[145]

March 20: Canon Alonso Mudarra is elected major-domo of the cathedral[146]—a post analogous to that of bursar in a university. During the next dozen years he will have much to say on the apportionment of cathedral income: and usually to Guerrero's great advantage.

May 19: *Christoual de morales clerigo de seuilla* is installed as a canon of Seville Cathedral.[147]

May 28: the chapter votes to remit fines assessed earlier in the month against "Guerrero and Victoria."[148] The latter is to be identified as Bartolomé de Victoria, prominent sopranist in Seville Cathedral from approximately 1565 to 1586. (Whether Bartolomé belonged to the same Victoria family as Tomás Luis, the composer, is not yet known.)

July 14: Guerrero for a third time borrows a substantial sum from the cathedral treasury—100 ducats.[149] The plan of repayment is again the discounting of his future salary at the rate of 4 ducats a month over a two-year stretch.

October 25: the chapter approves Mudarra's purchase of two dozen new robes and surplices for the altar boys and the giving away of the old robes to serve as swaddling bands for orphans.[150] Under ordinary circumstances Villafranca himself would have been responsible for buying new robes and surplices.

1570 Monday, January 2: the chapter grants Guerrero a twelve-day paid leave of absence "so that he may visit Jérez [just above Cádiz] to dispatch certain private business."[151]

January 24: the chapter responds to news that their own archbishop, Don Gaspar de Zuñiga y Avellaneda, has been chosen to solemnize the impending nuptials of Philip II with the Princess Anne (daughter of the Emperor Maximilian), by promising him the most impressive retinue that the cathedral can muster.[152] Among the accoutrements offered are these: the best silver candlesticks, gold cross and chalice, and brocade canopy; any mitre except the rich one left by Don Diego Hurtado de Mendoza; and a set of jewels. All six instrumentalists shall accompany the archbishop during his trip north to receive the princess, and in addition these four singers: Francisco Guerrero, *contraalto;* Mosén Roque, *contrabaxo;* Juan Baptista, *tenor;* and Bartolomé de Victoria, *tiple*—or if the last-named cannot go, then Ribilla. Moreover, all the instrumentalists and singers shall be continued on full salary during their absence.

Saturday, April 29: the president of the Royal Council, Cardinal Espinosa, reaches Seville, to be followed into the city on May 1 by Philip II.[153] The king makes his ceremonial entry into the cathedral through an archway of cedar and orange-tree branches laden with sweet-smelling flowers.[154] In opposite niches of this floral archway thirteen instrumentalists are stationed: on one side six shawmers and sackbut players wearing blue robes and hats bordered with gold; on the other side seven specially hired viol players wearing crimson and gold. The procession includes sixteen cathedral boys dressed in scarlet, turquoise, and gold—eight singing and the other eight dancing.[155] After Philip has sworn to observe the ancient privileges of the cathedral, all the singers and instrumentalists stationed in the various parts of the huge edifice burst into a hymn of acclamation. On May 14 the chapter rewards the instrumentalists with special gifts.[156] On May 15 Philip leaves Seville after a fortnight of the most intense festivity since the marriage of Charles V in 1526. Meanwhile Don Gaspar de Zuñiga y Avellaneda (created a cardinal on May 16) has proceeded north with his train to Santander. Guerrero belongs to his retinue. At Santander, however, they are obliged to wait several months for the arrival by sea of the Princess Anne. She finally disembarks on October 5; on Monday, October 23, she reaches Las Huelgas convent and the next day makes a ceremonial entry into Burgos.[157] She reaches Segovia on Sunday, November 12. Two days later the Sevillian cardinal pronounces the marriage ceremony in Segovia cathedral.[158] The cardinal then proceeds south toward his own see. While detained temporarily in Jaén, however, he is stricken and dies on Tuesday, January 2, 1571. During all this long trip Guerrero and his fellow musicians have followed in his train, participating in the utmost panoply of which Spain was capable at the moment of her highest glory.

Anton de Armijo, Guerrero's deputy during his trip to Santander and Segovia, annoys the chapter by reason of his inefficiency. However, on June 7 the canons decide to excuse him from a reprimand, because of his "old age and illness."[159]

1571 January 3: Anton de Armijo is still acting as *maestro de capilla* during Guerrero's absence.[160]

January 26: the chapter orders special payments to the six instrumentalists who have just returned from Jaén with the cadaver of the cardinal (d. January 2). This notice lists each player by his full name, identifying each with his principal instrument: Juan de Rojas and Diego de Andrada (soprano shawmers); Gaspar de Cuevas (tenor); Juan Baptista, Diego López, and Gerónimo de Medina (sackbuts).[161]

March 3: Guerrero obtains a fourth loan, although he has not yet finished paying back the third (July 14, 1568).[162] The present one is for 70,000 maravedís (approximately 187 ducats). Until the previous debt is repaid this new one shall be amortized at the rate of 4 ducats monthly; and thereafter at the monthly rate of 6 ducats. Special precautions must be taken that this present loan be fully secured.

April 5: Anton de Armijo borrows thirty ducats from the chapter, to be repaid at one ducat a month.[163]

June 15: Guerrero is allowed a three-day leave of absence to dispatch some private business.[164]

July 20: the chapter entrusts Canon Antonio del Corro with the purchase of more *flautas* for the cathedral instrumentalists: Baptista, sackbut player, to take them in charge after purchase.[165]

Monday, July 23: the chapter allows Guerrero another six-day leave to dispatch certain "important" private business.[166] On Friday, August 31, he is granted leave until September 7.

1572 April 16: the chapter commissions Canon Alonso Mudarra to buy a book of Guerrero's masses "which is needed by the instrumentalists," and also to oversee the repair of the book out of which they play *venites* at matins.[167]

April 23: the chapter allows Guerrero a fifth loan, this time of thirty ducats.[168] With it he shall buy proper clothing for the choirboys. Repayment shall be exacted at the rate of two ducats monthly.

1573 March 4: the previous organist, Pedro de Villada, having just died,[169] the chapter meets to discuss what is now to be done. The archbishop is unavoidably absent. The secretary goes out of the meeting and returns with the archbishop's advice: do whatever seems best for the glory of God and for the service of the cathedral; but if you wish to decide upon a successor I leave my vote with Canon Alonso Mudarra. (In this instance, as in others, Mudarra's opinion shapes musical policy in the cathedral.)

September 1: Gerónimo de Peraça (= Peraza) is installed in the organist's half-prebend, "he having in public competition with other contenders demonstrated his superiority; and proofs of the purity of his lineage having been adduced."[170] His full name is given several times thus: Gerónimo de Peraça de Sotomaior.

October 25: the chapter requires the presence of all the singers at the evening burial service for Don Luis Cristóbal Ponce de León, Duke of Arcos—the service to be held in St. Augustine's.[171] Their assistance is also required the following morning: an appropriate gesture of respect, he having been one of the most generous musical patrons of his age.[172]

November 4: Canon Mudarra is charged with preparing all arrangements in San Francisco Plaza for the forthcoming *aucto de la fee*. One week later "the singers are ordered to assist in the usual manner on Sunday, November 15, at the *aucto de la fee*."[173]

1574 Friday, January 8: Guerrero receives a six-day leave of absence so that he can attend to some private affairs.[174]

March 9: Pedro Fernández having died on March 5, the chapter appoints a commission of four to look over the papal bull and other accessory documents from the cathedral archive touching on Guerrero, and to examine the promises contained therein.[175] After waiting two decades for the post he at last becomes sole titular chapelmaster.

March 23: Alonso Mudarra and two others are requested to study the contract for the new organ (drawn up in May, 1567) and not to make further payments.[176] On March 30[1574] Mudarra, Gerónimo Peraza, and Canon Corro are authorized to prod Maestre Jox into finishing as soon as possible.[177] Jox is to stop working on the organ case and must finish installing the rest of the pipes. On July 7 Cristóbal de León, the cathedral organ tuner, is asked to finish tuning it.[178]

1575 January 7: the chapter decrees that henceforth the Roman rite, as reformed by the Council of Trent, is to be used exclusively.[179] At a stroke this decree renders obsolete such a troped mass as Guerrero's *De beata Virgine* (*Liber primus missarum* [1566], folios 79ᵛ-95) or polytextual mass as his *Beata Mater* ([1566] folios 119ᵛ-133).

April 8: the chapter requests Peraza to arrange meetings with the Flemish Maestre Joz [*sic*] for the purpose of studying the stops, and to make up two books describing them, so that if one is lost the other will be available in the archive.[180] On

April 11 the chapter repeats this same request.[181] On April 27, with a new note of urgency, the chapter directs Peraza to meet Maestre Joz daily in order to acquaint himself with all the registers of the new organ.

In early June, Peraza goes on leave, turning his job over to a deputy who soon proves the veriest tyro. The chapter on June 6 therefore orders the substitute to hand back the organ keys. Another substitute is engaged and it is decided to mulct Peraza's salary.[182]

November 11: Guerrero is directed not to set any lyrics for the approaching Christmas festivities without first consulting with Canon Alonso Mudarra, who shall look them over and after deliberation decide whether they are sufficiently decorous to sing.[183]

December 12: the chapter again stops payment on the Flemish organ-builder's contract until he finishes installing the rest of the large organ-pipes that Mudarra notes are still missing.[184]

1578 Certain oversights in Guerrero's attentions to his choirboys cause the chapter to decide on January 29 that he shall be paid the 600 ducats owing him this year as chapelmaster's salary and be given his annual allowance of wheat (secured by a bond of 400 ducats) only on condition that he move close to the cathedral, tighten discipline among his choirboys, and attend properly to their material wants.[185]

Peraza is directed as of February 13 to sell the old organ in the Antigua chapel and with the proceeds to buy a new one.[186]

Miguel Fernández, a sopranist from Segovia who is visiting in Seville in February, hears that a sopranist's prebend in the cathedral is open, even though no public announcement has yet been made. Since he must shortly return to Segovia, he petitions to be heard before leaving Seville. The chapter on February 18 responds that he is on no account to be considered before the formal announcement of the vacancy.[187] He must apply then, and then only. The whole system of filling vacant musical posts will be placed in jeopardy if roving singers start intriguing themselves into unadvertised positions.

March 22: Juan Peraza, brother of Gerónimo, is appointed instrumentalist at 100,000 maravedís annually and 60 fanegas of wheat.[188] On May 8, 1579, his salary is raised to 131,250 maravedís and 100 fanegas on the conditions that he bring his wife to Seville and that Gerónimo post a bond of 500 ducats that his married brother will not depart before completing four years' service to the cathedral.[189]

April 5 [1578]: Gerónimo is granted leave until Pentecost, provided that this time he engages a properly qualified substitute during his absence.[190]

July 14: the chapter orders the papal bull affecting the Guerrero prebend (*Pastoralis officii*, June 1, 1554) to be reëxamined.[191]

Armijo, Guerrero's colleague in teaching the choirboys polyphonic singing since 1555, having quit, his post is advertised.[192]

September 3: the chapter meets to discuss the amount that shall be sent Tomás Luis de Victoria, "chapelmaster at Rome,"[193] in recompense for the present that he has made of his *Liber Primus. Qui Missas, Psalmos, Magnificat . . . Complectitur* [Venice: Angelo Gardano, 1576]. Victoria has done two Sevillian composers the honor of parody in this publication. The *Simile est regnum celorum* Mass is parodied after Guerrero's motet (1570), and the *Gaudeamus* after Morales's *Jubilate Deo omnis terra.*

1579 January 7: the chapter grants Guerrero a one-year leave of absence with regular pay, minus only the amount required to administer and feed the choirboys during his absence.[194] The conductor during his leave shall be the most senior choir singer. Guerrero's destination will be Rome. On January 16 he and a committee from the chapter have agreed upon the amount to deduct during his absence.

Constantly troubled by the absence of singers who prefer to lose a day's pay whenever a more lucrative engagement offers itself elsewhere, the chapter on April 11 rules that any singer who takes part in an outside procession shall be fined eight ducats. Any cathedral clergyman whose official duties include singing shall be fined eight days' pay.[195]

June 1: the chapter passes a rule that anyone ascending to the new organ without official permission shall be fined a month's pay.[196]

June 5: Luys de Villafranca, master of the altar boys (*mozos de coro*), is nearing retirement age. He receives a loan of eighty ducats, to be repaid the treasury within a year.[197]

September 28: the chapter requests the new cathedral major-domo Pedro Vélez to meet Maestre Jox and to talk over a price settlement. Vélez and another canon are to seek some sort of reduction in the maestre's latest bill.[198]

October 26: Villafranca quits[199] and on November 6 Gaspar Delgadillo is engaged as master of the altar boys to succeed him.[200] Delgadillo continues master of altar boys until 1586 whereupon he is succeeded by Mosén Blanco, *presbítero*, who in turn holds office until his death on November 8, 1596. The altar boys remain always separate and distinct from choirboys—the one group learning only plainchant and assisting at the altar, the other living with the chapelmaster and studying counterpoint and polyphony as well.

Guerrero postpones his departure for Rome and instead spends the entire year in Seville making ready for the trip.[201] In the meantime he neglects his choirboys. On November 16, after considerable complaint against their unruliness and ignorance, he engages an assistant, Bartolomé Farfán.[202] The chapter reminds him that the papal bull instituting him emphasized the boys.

1580   Friday, January 22: the choirboys are remitted to the charge of Alexandro de la Serna.[203]

April 1: Alonso Mudarra dies, leaving "sisters and other relatives" in his house. On April 8 his effects are announced for public sale.[204] Two years later—on May 25, 1582—a final accounting of his estate is ordered[205] and on the following June 1 the sum realized from the sale of his personal goods is listed at 92,000 maravedís.[206] On June 6 [1582] this sum is by the terms of his will distributed among the poor.[207]

June 13, 1580: the chapter requests Guerrero to resume the giving of a daily counterpoint lesson. Singers who miss shall be fined.[208]

July 27 [1580]: the chapter votes to seek papal sanction for downgrading the organist's prebend to the level of mere singers' prebends.

Wednesday, August 3: Hernando Tapia is named temporarily to succeed Gerónimo Peraza[209]—the latter having been elected organist at Toledo Cathedral on the previous November 27 and having been inducted in the post on March 21 [1580].[210] On August 31 the Sevillian chapter votes not to pay Peraza a single maravedí of certain back salary that he is demanding: the reason being that "he has deceived us."[211]

September 12: the chapter votes to buy a book proposed for the instrumentalists, but as cheaply as possible.[212] One month later the position of sackbut player left open by the recent death of the colorful Gaspar de Cuevas (in service since ca. 1563; accused of murder in 1566; attendant to the cardinal during the Santander trip in 1570) is offered to Luis de Alvánchez of Plasencia at 60,000 maravedís and 4 cahizes of wheat annually. However, his pay is not to begin until the day he marries the deceased Cuevas's daughter.

1581   February 14: the chapter authorizes the expenditure of 30,000 maravedís to buy new clothes for Guerrero's choirboys.[213]

March 16: Guerrero still having failed to start the Roman trip for which a year's leave was granted on January 7, 1579, the chapter announces that only four months further grace remain for him to start the trip.[214] He leaves Seville the next month but along the way is delayed six months for some strange reason.[215]

March 28: the surplices and hoods of the altar boys can no longer be worn because of an outbreak of plague in Seville.[216]

April 28: Diego del Castillo, the victor in a duly announced competition, is installed as cathedral organist.[217] His prebend conforms with the reduced status recommended by the chapter after Gerónimo Peraza's deceitful conduct of the previous year.

June 26: the chapter receives a request from Philip II, currently at Lisbon for his Portuguese coronation, that the cathedral "lend" him two of its best singers. Antolin de Paredes (sopranist) and Juan Baptista (tenor) are selected.[218] On July 3, however, the cathedral finds itself so depleted of good singers that the chapter authorizes a "paid expenses" trip for a scout, who must not be a regular employee of the cathedral, nor himself a singer. Juan de Navarrete is engaged as a tenor on July 12. On November 3 Andrés Hernández is named to a bass's prebend.[219]

In October, Guerrero finally reaches Rome. He starts negotiating immediately for the publication of his second book of masses. On November 13 he addresses a letter to the Sevillian chapter in the following terms.[220]

Most Illustrious Sirs: Although desirous of writing some news of myself and more especially of expressing my eagerness to return once again to your service, still I have heretofore feared intruding upon your time with my letters. But now I must importune you for your kindness. Your Excellencies were gracious enough to allow me a leave of absence so that I might visit Rome, my principal business here being the printing of two books: a Missarum liber secundus *and a* Liber vesperarum. *The masses are already in the process of being printed, thanks to the help of certain kind folk with business connections in Seville. But, to come to the point. I must now beg of Your Excellencies two further favors: first (since we were detained along the way six months), added time, so that I will not have to leave uncompleted that which has just been started; second, continued income from my prebend to pay for my personal expenses while here and for the costs of printing. I have the better hope that Your Excellencies will bestow on me these additional favors because certain most illustrious cardinals have taken me under their protection and have opened doors that would have been shut to me but are now opened out of respect for such lofty personages. All these ambitious compositions were written while in your service; and even in affairs of lesser scope your disposition to succor your servants is well known. I would not be so outspoken, however, without adding my deepest thanks for favors already granted. Not to be more lengthy, I here close with a prayer for your healths and long lives.*

December 6: the above letter reaches Seville and a chapter meeting is called to discuss its contents.[221]

1582   January 5: the chapter decides to advance Guerrero 200 ducats, which shall be charged against his prebend's income for 1582.[222] On January 31 the chapter extends his leave of absence until the coming October 31.[223]

Victoria writes a letter to the Sevillian chapter on January 14 in which he mentions Guerrero.[224] His letter accompanies a new gift to the Sevillian chapter, this time of his *Cantica B. Virginis* and *Hymni totius anni*, both published in 1581 by the same firm now printing Guerrero's masses.

April 20: Guerrero acknowledges the chapter's new kindnesses in the following letter.[225]

Illustrious Sirs: I take your decision to advance me 200 ducats from the income of my preb-

end as an extremely kind favor; and the extension of my leave of absence as a no less gracious deed. For the one and the other kindness I bow in gratitude to Your Excellencies. You will be interested to know that I recently had the opportunity of personally presenting the newly printed book of masses to His Holiness [Gregory XIII: 1572-1585]. *He received me most kindly and after having looked it over and having read the preface to the* Ecce sacerdos *Mass written in his honor*[226] *then detained me a quarter of an hour making very minute enquiries concerning Seville Cathedral, the number of beneficed clergymen, their income, and the income of the cathedral foundation. I replied as best I knew how, but His Holiness's knowledge far exceeded mine.*[227] *I told him of Your Excellencies' continual prayers in his behalf. He took great pleasure in knowing of your zeal and imparted his Apostolic blessing, whereupon I left his most venerable presence overwhelmed with joy. I am now hoping speedily to return to Seville and to resume my accustomed service in the cathedral. I wish no other good fortune than now to have the opportunity of paying back some small part of my great debt to Your Excellencies. If then it please God, I shall leave the Roman court toward the beginning of June, proceed to Genoa, and there take the first ship that sails. I have already forwarded the newly printed book of masses. I beg of you to receive it and have it added to the cathedral music library. Our Lord guard and save Your Excellencies during many years to come.*

November 3: Diego del Castillo, the cathedral organist hired eighteen months earlier, is instructed to prepare "libros de las mixturas y tonos del horgano grande" (books of the mixtures and tones of the large organ), and to see that the organ is kept clean and properly covered.[228]

1583   Wednesday, June 8: the instrumentalists are instructed henceforth to play a *marchee* whenever the singers gather at the choirbook-stand in the middle of the choir enclosure to sing polyphony.[229]

August 31: the chapter reminds Guerrero that whenever he receives a new choir-boy he must register the day and year with the cathedral accountant.[230]

September 16: the salaries of each of three instrumentalists—Juan Baptista, Diego López, and Gerónimo de Medina—are raised to 200 ducats annually.[231]

September 23: the salary of Andrés López, *maestro de capilla del claustro*, is raised by 6,000 maravedís to a total of 40,000.[232]

Early in December, Diego del Castillo serves notice of his imminent departure. On December 14 the chapter votes to reëxamine both the old and new papal bulls affecting the organistship.[233] On December 16 the organist's half-prebend is advertised.[234]

1584   January 9: the chapter votes to enforce the terms of the dean's agreement with Maestre Jorge [= Jors, Jos, Jox] and to so notify the cathedral treasurer.[235]

The chapter rules that for their better safekeeping Guerrero's books shall henceforth be chained in the library of the upper church.

Now in his fifty-sixth year and eager to devote himself more fully to other enter-prises, Guerrero in March petitions the chapter to divide the chapelmaster's prebend (worth 600 ducats and 80 fanegas of wheat) after the fashion that was approved when he first took over the choirboys in 1549. This time, however, he shall be the one who remains titular chapelmaster and continues to conduct. A younger man shall take over the ungrateful task of boarding and rearing the choir-boys. The chapter agrees in principle on March 15, but entrusts him with the task of finding his own assistant.[236] On March 17 he names the same Bartolomé Farfán who in 1579 was temporarily in charge of the boys.[237] On November 5 a formal agreement is reached, Guerrero retaining half the salary (300 ducats and 40 fane-gas) and the other half going to Farfán (who in addition is to receive 100 ducats and 40 fanegas to make up a total annual salary of 400 ducats and 80 fanegas of wheat).[238] Farfán's salary in cash and kind will therefore be larger than Guer-rero's. But he must board, lodge, and clothe at least six boys with his proceeds.

May 16:[239] Francisco Peraza (1564-1598), younger brother of Gerónimo (organist at Seville from 1573 to 1580; organist at Toledo from 1580 to 1617; d. 1617) is in-stalled as organ prebendary in succession to Castillo (who has left Seville to enter royal service). At the competition that preceded his election, Francisco Peraza has already shown himself to be the most gifted of the entire Peraza clan. "At his examination the most illustrious cardinal, Rodrigo de Castro [archbishop of Seville; 1582-1600; created cardinal, 1583],[240] an extremely well-informed person in musical matters and a princely protector of artists, was present. Finding that Guerrero was confronting the competitors with some of the hardest tests of skill known to musicians—but that scarcely had he announced a task before Francisco Peraza had accomplished it to perfection, even adding his solution of variants to the problem—the cardinal was overwhelmed with admiration of such skill, which he supposed must be the result of that natural genius found only in prodigies. Without more ado the cardinal therefore requested that the chapter confer the 200-ducat prebend upon him: to which the chapter unanimously agreed." This Francisco Peraza is to be the organist whose fingers Guerrero kisses, saying that "he has an angel in every finger" and who is similarly to excite the admiration of Philippe Rogier, chapelmaster to Philip II.[241]

July 6, 1584: Luis de Coçar [= Cózar], bass singer of Jaén, is nominated to a singer's prebend but does not accept immediately.[242] On January 13, 1586, he is singing at Salamanca, from which cathedral the Sevillian chapter receives him with an equal salary.

December 17: the singer Miranda is ordered to bring his wife to town and to live with her through the entire month of January or be dismissed from the cathedral. On the ensuing January 28 she still has not arrived and the chapter gives him only two more weeks grace.[243]

1586   Thursday, March 20: two cathedral officials are enjoined to discuss with Guer-rero his proposal that the chapter pay for the copying of a book of Josquin's music, and to report back.[244] (This notice, coming as late as 1586, is but one of many proofs showing the extraordinary popularity of Josquin's music in Spain throughout the sixteenth century.)[245]

April 21: Alonso López, *menestril corneta* (cornettist), is granted a fifteen-day leave to visit Sanlúcar.[246] This is one of the few instances in which the cornett is listed as a player's principal instrument: *chirimías* (shawms) and *sacabuches* (sackbuts) being usually the principal instruments; *cornetas* and *flautas*, alternating instruments.

May 30: Francisco Peraza's petition for a salary raise is approved.[247] On June 4 he is instructed henceforth to play the organ every Sunday, on all days within an octave, at all semidouble feasts, on all Saturdays when Our Lady's office is recited, and at capitular vespers of any feast of Our Lady.[248] Two days later his salary is raised by a further 1,000 reales (34,000 maravedís), but he is required to post a 500-ducat bond that he will never leave his Sevillian post, no matter what inducements are offered elsewhere.[249] With this new raise he is now making within a few ducats of what Guerrero is earning from his chapelmaster's divided prebend: even though he has been in cathedral service only two years whereas Guerrero is approaching his fortieth year of service.

June 18: word is sent to Maestre Jorge [*sic*] to "finish the book [describing the stops] of the large organ immediately; pending the completion of which his salary will be withheld."[250]

Saturday, July 5: the chapter permits "some singers" to accompany the cardinal during his next day's visit to a Jesuit church for Mass,[251] provided that there are enough singers left in the cathedral to perform part music. The chapter does not accede even to the possibility of a Sunday celebration of Mass in the cathedral in which only plainchant is sung; but on the contrary insists that polyphony must be sung.

July 7: the chapter meets to discuss a petition offered by certain instrumentalists for a raise of salary.[252] Guerrero is sent for to give his recommendation. He does not regularly attend meetings of the chapter, since he is not a member. However, his opinion is consulted on all matters concerning the cathedral musical establishment.

July 11: the chapter orders Francisco Peraza to transcribe for organ "some motets appropriate to diverse feasts" and to play them. Furthermore, he must himself perform and not send any substitute; if he disobeys he shall be fined.[253]

On the same day, the chapter receives from Guerrero a written declaration of the "Order which must be observed by the instrumentalists in playing."[254] The chapter adopts his memorial *in toto* and instructs the *chantre* and a senior canon to inform the instrumentalists that they must abide by Guerrero's rules in every detail or be fined whatever amount he recommends. His list of rules reads as follows:

First, Rojas and López shall always play the treble parts: ordinarily on shawms. They must carefully observe some order when they improvise glosses, both as to places and to times.[255] *When the one player adds glosses to his part, the other must yield to him and play simply the written notes; for when both together gloss at the same time, they produce absurdities that stop one's ears. Second, the same Rojas and López when they at appropriate moments play on cornetts must again each observe the same moderation in glossing: the one deferring to the other; because, as has been previously said, for both simultaneously to add improvised glosses creates insufferable dissonance. As for Juan de Medina, he shall ordinarily play the contralto part, not obscuring the trebles nor disturbing them by exceeding the glosses that belong to a contralto. When on the other hand his part becomes the top above the sackbuts, then he is left an open field in which to glory and is free to add all the glosses that he desires and knows so well how to execute on his instrument. As for Alvánchez, he shall play tenors and the bassoon.*[256] *At greater feasts there shall always be a verse played on recorders.*[257] *At Salves, one of the three verses that are played shall be on shawms, one on cornetts, and the other on recorders; because always hearing the same instrument annoys the listener.*

August 4: the two treble singers, Bartolomé de Victoria and Antolin de Paredes, and the bass, Andrés Hernández, are warned to stop hiring themselves out for fiestas not sponsored by the cathedral: on pain of ten ducats fine for each violation.[258] On August 18 the same penalty is imposed on the masters of the boys if acolytes or choirboys assist at outside fiestas. Any boy who assists shall be expelled and may not be readmitted to the service of the cathedral without the chapter's express permission.

August 22: the major-domo is authorized to go to Maestre Jorge's house, and seize all plans, tracings, tools, and whatever else can be found having anything to do with the large organ.[259] On September 5 Andrés Jacomar—now a cathedral prebendary (formerly a choirboy, and from 1561 to 1565 a scholar at St. Michael's) —is delegated to see Francisco Peraza and find out what has happened to *el libro del organo grande* (the book of the large organ).[260] Two weeks later (September 22) —Peraza having in the meantime produced the book—the chapter orders two copies to be made: one for the cathedral archive, and one to deliver back to Peraza, but only for the length of time he remains organ prebendary.[261] Four days later Diego López is hired as a full-time organ tuner;[262] the organs that he must keep tuned are the large organ and smaller organs in the main body of the cathedral; those in the sacristy and in the Antigua chapel. Withn a month López is to transcribe the "two books of the large organ" ordered to be copied on September 22.

September 24: the chapter meets to consider Guerrero's request for superannuation.[263] Most of the members approve, but the major-domo ("who knows not Joseph") rises up to protest. According to him, Guerrero is at full liberty to search on his own for a substitute. But if he finds one, the substitute must still meet with the chapter's approval. Furthermore, all the trouble and expense of finding and then retaining the substitute ought, says the major-domo, to be Guerrero's responsibility. In effect, of course, any such conditions as these would utterly prevent

Guerrero from retiring: it being out of the question that a successor of his own calibre would even think of living in Seville without a formal chapter appointment. Fortunately for Guerrero, some of his own former choirboys have now risen to membership of the chapter; his devoted friends among the other members are many; and, best of all, Cardinal de Castro is his warm admirer.[264] His petition therefore overrides the major-domo's protest. The latter—unable to prevent Guerrero's petition from succeeding—then speaks out against the chapter's appointment only the week previously of a new sopranist, Juan de Haro, at an annual salary of 100,000 maravedís and 50 fanegas of wheat. He threatens to "contradict and appeal" the chapter's decision, "because this cathedral already has four sopranists, which are enough"; and, moreover, "the new sopranist's voice is not so excellent as it ought to be." Finally, he declares, the cathedral treasury cannot stand the strain of so many new salaries. If the chapter does not reconsider, he promises to carry his appeal up to the pope himself.

October 6: Farfán still acts as Guerrero's assistant in charge of choirboys,[265] but on December 19 Alexandro de la Serna succeeds him—he being the same singer who had inherited them from Farfán in 1580.[266]

November 26: Bartolomé de Espinosa is received as bassoonist at a salary of 82,000 maravedís plus 60 fanegas.[267] He succeeds Alvánchez, and is to serve every day with the other instrumentalists "at the choirbook-stand." A few weeks later the chapter grants him leave and travel money to bring his wife from Segovia.[268]

1587 February 4: the chapter meets to consider the major-domo's demand that Juan de Haro, sopranist, be dismissed. The chapter not only votes to retain him but one canon even suggests that the sum of 200 ducats be given Haro should he voluntarily leave Seville in order to escape the major-domo's harassment.[269]

Ten days later, Serna is confirmed as Farfán's successor.[270]

Guerrero's request that a new book of motets be copied on vellum at cathedral expense (perhaps those he is to publish at Venice in 1589) wins chapter approval on February 26.[271]

Monday, May 11: a commission of five chapter-members is instructed to sit with Guerrero.[272] Working as a team they are to draw up a written memorial outlining the duties of the new master, who is to be named when Guerrero's superannuation becomes effective. This same commission is delegated to start an immediate search for boys with fine voices. All prospects shall be auditioned by the assembled chapter prior to their appointment.

The chapter having decided that this time the submaster shall not automatically enjoy the right of succession held by Guerrero when Fernández de Castilleja died, the difficulty of finding a submaster is somewhat increased. On August 14 the chapter sends an invitation to Sebastián de Vivanco, a native of Ávila, who is "chapelmaster at Segovia." He is assured that he will be paid his traveling expenses if he does not decide to stay. He is moreover urged to bring with him "two or three boys with outstanding voices."[273]

Friday, September 18: the chapter recommends purchase of Victoria's *Motecta Festorum Totius anni* [Rome: Alessandro Gardano, 1585], which shall then be bound in boards, "placed among the other music books, and not handed over to the instrumentalists."[274] Evidently it is the custom to hand over new books to the shawmers and sackbut players, but Victoria's motets are to be treated as an exception.

October 7: the chapter is ready to crystallize its invitation to Vivanco. He will be paid 500 ducats plus 90 fanegas of wheat, but he will be a *substituto del Maestro Guerrero sin futura suçession*.[275] His appointment shall terminate when Guerrero dies, or sooner if the chapter so pleases. He is again urged to bring along from Segovia "two or three boys with exceptional voices."

1588   Friday, January 29: Guerrero is voted a payment of 300 reales (10,200 maravedís) for books that he has presented, and which are now to be bound in calf and placed in the cathedral archive.[276]

Wednesday, February 10: all incompetent singers in the cathedral are warned that they must immediately begin to improve themselves or be fined. Regularly scheduled practice hours shall be announced, and all incompetents must attend. No one shall henceforth sing anything by way of a solo except those whose names the dean communicates to Guerrero.[277] Ten days later, the dean and chapter decide that a procession with sung litany shall be undertaken through the cathedral cloisters in order to invoke blessing upon the Armada gathering at the moment in Lisbon harbor[278] (sailed against England on May 18).

Monday, February 29: Vivanco has arrived, and the choirboys are delivered to his keeping.[279] He requests an advance for the purpose of renting a house plus something extra for his moving expenses. With him he has brought only one choirboy; and that one now wishes to go home to Castile. Four days later (March 3), Vivanco is voted a loan of 200 ducats upon surety and a gift of 30 ducats for his unforeseen expenses to date.[280] However, only a little over a week later (Saturday, March 12) he petitions for money to take him back home to Ávila.[281] The next Thursday, the chapter accommodates him with 100 ducats.[282] On Saturday, March 26, after Vivanco has been lured back to his home town, the Sevillian chapter requests Farfán to resume control of the choirboys.[283]

Cardinal de Castro having been invited to visit Rome, Guerrero petitions to go in his train. During a stopover at court, Guerrero "kisses His Majesty's hand" and receives permission to proceed directly to Venice to oversee publication of his compositions.[284] He boards ship at Cartagena, disembarks at Genoa, and passes thence to Venice.[285] After a week in Venice, he sails on August 14 for the Holy Land. He visits the sacred sites in Palestine and Syria, regains Venice on January 9, 1589, and after a six-week stopover proceeds home by way of Marseilles and Barcelona. His trip is filled with dramatic episodes that are to be vividly narrated in his forthcoming travel book, *Viage de Hierusalem* (1590).

1589   August 9: Guerrero having returned for duty, the chapter decides that Farfán shall continue to board and lodge the choirboys and that Guerrero's urgent petition for more money—even if he has to resume boarding and lodging the choirboys—be denied.[286] On Friday, September 22, however, the chapter does agree to his sleeping at nights in a private room inside the cathedral.[287]

1590   Francisco Peraza having departed without leave, the chapter votes on June 27 to revoke his prebend and for other just causes to stop his salary as of the day he left Seville.[288] In due time he returns, however, and is reinstated.

November 28: Farfán—in charge of the choirboys during the past two and a half years—again quits.[289] Guerrero eagerly offers to take the choirboys back because of his penury. The chapter on December 7 proposes restoring to him the other half of the chapelmaster's prebend which he relinquished six years earlier. In addition he shall receive a cost-of-living allowance of an extra 150 ducats with 40 fanegas of wheat. He shall now again "board, lodge, clothe, and teach" the choirboys in his own house. The dean at once contradicts the "extra 150 ducats," saying it should be an "extra 100"—Farfán having received only the extra 100 ducats as cost-of-living allowance.[290]

1591   Guerrero's attentions to the choirboys, however, prove extremely inadequate. Now in his sixty-third year, he is too old for the task of wet-nursing any half-dozen or more squirming choirboys. On August 21 the chapter votes to take them away from him, even though he sorely needs the money.[291] Some other master is to be found. At best, Guerrero shall continue to be one of their teachers. Andrés de Jacomar—former choirboy,[292] now a member of the chapter—is delegated to write Alonso Lobo, a canon in the collegiate church at Osuna who simultaneously serves as chapelmaster, inviting him to take charge of the choirboys for the same sum formerly paid Farfán.

On the same day, the chapter learns that Guerrero's debts have finally overwhelmed him and that he is now in prison for sums owed at Rome, backed by Sevillian guarantors.[293] This particular debt was incurred in 1584 for the printing of his *Liber vesperarum* (dedicated to the Sevillian chapter). The chapter deputes a canon named Pedro de Santander to find out how Guerrero fares in his dark and miserable debtors' prison; to find out just how much he owes; and to see what, if any, money can be eked from his prebend to bail him out. On Monday, August 26, the chapter learns that he owes 200 ducats; and thereupon authorizes Pedro de Santander to pay off the debt so that he can be released from prison.[294] Two days later the chapter appoints a three-member committee whose duty it shall be to see that all legal processes against Guerrero are stopped before they hand over the cash to his impatient creditors. Upon further investigation the committee discovers the total sum to be 280, not 200 ducats. By an open vote taken in the chapter meeting of September 2, it is decided to pay off the whole amount, which equals 105,000 maravedís.[295] For the moment this sum is listed simply as "remuneration for services." On September 9, however, the committee of three is instructed to draw up an agreement with Guerrero: the implication being that he shall now attempt to repay the chapter.[296]

Alonso Lobo on September 2 is confirmed as master of the boys at 400 ducats a year plus 80 fanegas of wheat—this being what Farfán had received.[297] Jacomar and the *chantre* are to attend to all details connected with the transfer of the boys. On November 29 Lobo is authorized to conduct while Guerrero is on leave.[298] Lobo is also allowed to wear a mantle in recognition of the fact that while at Osuna he was a canon. He shall accompany the choirboys whenever they arrive or leave the cathedral.

November 11: the large organ needs repairing.[299] On January 5, 1594, the chapter forbids anyone to mount to the console without the chapter's express permission.[300]

1593 Alonso Lobo is elected chapelmaster at Toledo on September 22 and installed on December 3.[301]

1594 Francisco Peraza, reinstated at Seville, is on January 7 granted leave to visit Sanlúcar de Barrameda (above Cádiz) until January 31.[302]

January 24: some 1,800 clergy and professed accompany the remains of Don Gonzalo de Mena, former archbishop of Seville (d. 1401), from the cathedral to a new resting-place across the river—the Convento de las Cuevas. During the procession, Guerrero's psalms and hymns composed especially for the occasion make a thrilling impression.[303]

February 9: Guerrero borrows another 200 ducats from the chapter.[304] On May 25 this sum is called a gift. On May 27 the chapter—realizing that he cannot live on any mere 300 ducats a year—decides to raise his salary to 400 ducats, beginning in 1595.[305]

Alexandro de la Serna, *contralto*, is sent away to scout for new boys with fine voices on July 20.[306] Two months later (September 26) he has located two prospects.

October 19: another member of the Peraza clan—Gerónimo by name (perhaps a nephew of his namesake who is organist at Toledo)—is appointed to be suborganist at Seville.[307]

1595 Francisco Peraza on February 14 is granted leave of absence from Seville until Easter.[308] On July 28 the chapter decides that he ought to reduce the number of his engagements elsewhere.[309]

1596   March 21: the chapter informs Peraza that he exceeds his rights when he sallies forth with bands of pilgrims bound for local saints' celebrations. Should be desire to attend a *romería*, he must ask permission of the chapter.[310] He goes to these affairs as if a pilgrim himself, but always ends by displaying his digital prowess. However, to mollify him, the chapter votes on April 22 to raise his salary.[311]

June 28: Diego Sánchez—already a chaplain in the cathedral—is named temporary custodian of the choirboys (*seises*) but on November 27 wins permanent appointment as master of the altar boys (*mozos de coro*).[312] He continues as master of the altar boys until July 1, 1598: his successor (named on July 13, 1598) is Pedro Suárez.[313]

November 29: the chapter starts searching for a new master of the choirboys. The appointment shall continue in effect only until Guerrero's death. The opening shall be advertised publicly, but not outside Andalusia. The towns to which notice shall be posted are Granada, Cordova, Jaén, Ubeda, and Baeza.[314]

1597   Although the chapter would like to hold the position open a little longer in the hope of attracting better competitors, a scheduled competition is held on January 10 from which Gil de Ávila emerges the victor.[315]

January 24: the chapter gives Francisco Peraza permission to attend a *romería* at the famous Jeronymite monastery of Guadalupe (Estremadura).[316]

March 4: Gil de Ávila, new master of the choirboys, borrows 500 reales (17,000 maravedís) from the chapter. But the chapter's misgivings are borne out. On September 15 Juan Vaca—perhaps the same as the singer rebuked by the chapter on September 17, 1567—is named master of choirboys to succeed Gil de Ávila.[317]

1598   Francisco Peraza dies on June 24, aged only thirty-four.[318]

September 9: Juan de Vargas succeeds Andrés López as teaching assistant in polyphonic music.[319]

1599   January 11: the chapter makes Guerrero a last gift—this time of 100 ducats. On May 14 he is allowed a one-year leave of absence to revisit Rome.

May 14: Alexandro [de la Serna], being worn out with age, is dispensed from coming to the cathedral except when he feels able to do so.[320] On the same day Pedro Guerrero—possibly a nephew—is engaged as a *contrabajo* (bass): his salary is to be 200 ducats and 36 bushels of wheat.[321]

One of the periodic outbreaks of plague devastates Seville in the late summer. On September 1 "the plague has not abated" and cathedral business is disrupted.[322] Guerrero, having delayed his departure, falls ill. On Wednesday, November 3, his death is expected and the chapter votes to accord him the honors of a prebendary at interment.[323] On Monday, November 8, decision is taken that he shall be buried in the Antigua chapel of the cathedral with a novena "because of his services." On Wednesday, November 10, the singers are authorized to celebrate a Requiem Mass in his honor at the conclusion of the daily office.[324]

December 20: Andrés López is recalled to replace Juan de Vargas as teaching assistant in polyphony. He shall also become interim conductor, his salary to be 40,000 maravedís plus 36 fanegas of wheat annually.[325]

1600 Candidates of sufficient worth having failed to offer themselves for the vacant chapelmastership, the chapter twice (April 26 and May 17) prorogues the competition. On September 22 Ambrosio Cotes wins the post.[326] He causes trouble, however, and to the great relief of the chapter is soon (1604) succeeded by the famous Alonso Lobo who served Toledo Cathedral as chapelmaster from 1593 to 1604.

Guerrero's Personality

No known portrait of Victoria survives, but of Guerrero there exists a likeness painted by Francisco Pacheco,[327] the father-in-law of Velázquez. To accompany the portrait, Pacheco wrote a biographical summary that adds materially to our knowledge of Guerrero's later years. According to Pacheco:[328]

The regard and appreciation which everyone—the highest nobility included, and particularly Cardinal de Castro—bestowed on Guerrero was made manifest in many ways. The cardinal knew that he was in the habit of spending most of the income from his prebend in works of charity and therefore wished him to dine at his own table. But the cathedral was Guerrero's habitation day and night, and the most that Guerrero would accept were dinners sent each evening from the archiepiscopal palace after the doors of the cathedral were closed, and delivered through a small aperture filed in one of the iron screens that protect the lower windows of the cathedral.

In every respect he was the most outstanding musician of his epoch. His compositions were so numerous that for every day of his long life there exist several handwritten pages. His works always make an impressive sound, and the voice parts always fuse agreeably. He wrote a great quantity of Masses, Magnificats, and Psalms—among the last-named an *In exitu Israel de Aegypto* [*Liber vesperarum* (1584), folios 12ᵛ-18] which those who are best informed declare he must have composed while swept aloft in contemplative ecstasy.

Pacheco next refers to Guerrero's printed motets, singling out the *Ave Virgo sanctissima* for special praise. He claims that no one is able to move the listener with a *Pange lingua* like Guerrero. The fame of Guerrero has travelled everywhere, avers Pacheco—who may well have known of the Nuremberg reprints. Hardly a church in Christendom lacks his works or fails to appreciate them, continues Pacheco. Of his personality, Pacheco writes:

He was a man of wide sympathies and understanding, always affable and patient with his musical subordinates. His presence was dignified and imposing, his conversation and public discourse beautiful to hear. Above all, he was charitable to the poor. . . . He indeed gave so freely of his own clothing and shoes that he was often on the point of going barefoot himself. . . . Shortly before his death he proposed to make a second pilgrimage to the Holy Land. But God choosing to reward him betimes took him from this life in his 72d year and in the 44th of his chapelmastership [1554-1599]. His death was enviable in every respect: his last words being those of Psalm 121 [= 122]: "I rejoiced, because they said unto me, We shall go into the house of the Lord."

The chapter honored him with greater tokens of respect than any of his predecessors and agreed that he should be buried in the Antigua Lady Chapel: his priestly garments being covered with the palmer's weed that had been sewn for him to wear during his second trip to Palestine. Above his resting-place was inscribed on stone an epitaph in Spanish. . . . Not the least of his distinctions was the honor conferred upon him by Gioseffo Zarlino, chapelmaster of Venice, when he called him "the most eminent of all musicians whom he had heretofore known." At his death Jacome Barbosa, the renowned Portuguese poet, wrote a Latin poetic eulogy, which translated into the vernacular . . . reads as follows.

Pacheco then gives a 45-line Spanish translation of Barbosa's Latin eulogy: which amidst many classical allusions voices the not unwarranted claim that Guerrero's music is "known from the English Channel to faraway Isthmuses." Since repertory lists found at Mexico City Cathedral assure us that his works were being already sung there during Hernando Franco's régime as chapelmaster (1575-1585),[329] it is reasonable to suppose that they may also have been sung at Panamá—which was founded as early as 1519, and before 1600 was one of the wealthiest cities in the Spanish empire. Cuba so rang with his praises the year after Jamestown was founded that Silvestre de Balboa's Cuban poem *Espejo de Pacienca* (1608) ends with a stanza making Guerrero Orpheus's only worthy competitor. In the cathedral music archive at Lima, a worn copy of Guerrero's *Liber vesperarum* (Rome: 1584) still survives today, with inked annotations that attest his continuing fame in distant Peru for a century after his death.

"Journey to Jerusalem" Guerrero's account of his 1588-1589 trip to the Holy Land begins with a short autobiographical prologue. During his long life as chapelmaster he had continually harbored a desire to see Bethlehem, he says. Especially had he felt his urge at Christmases when he composed *chançonetas* and *villancicos* lauding Christ's birth. His trip in 1588 took him first to court in Cardinal de Castro's train. With the cardinal's permission he then proceeded independently to Venice. There, he tells us: "My first business . . . was to arrange for the printing of two music books [*Canciones y villanescas espirituales* and *Mottecta . . . liber secundus*]. When the printer told me that he would need more than five months I asked a friend: can I make a trip to Jerusalem in that length of time?"[330]

His friend told him that indeed such a trip would be possible: whereupon he found a ship. The fare amounted to five scudi for passage and seven for meals at the captain's table. Francisco Sánchez, one of his Sevillian pupils, accompanied him during the trip. Before their departure, Gioseffo Zarlino kindly offered to correct any proof that the printer might submit during his absence.[331]

Departing from Venice on August 14, 1588, they reached Jaffa thirty-seven days later. The longest stopover was at the Ionian isle of Zante where he heard a Greek Mass—several clergy and numerous laity assisting during the celebration. "Their chant is very simple and crude but they celebrate Mass devoutly and with many ceremonies," remarked Guerrero. He found it surprising that the Greeks knelt before the consecration.[332]

In Jerusalem his touring party was escorted by an Italian-speaking Franciscan who had spent two decades in Palestine and whose advice to his travellers included such homely items as this: refrain from coughing or spitting; otherwise the Moslems will think you are ridiculing them. The friars in procession sang a Te Deum. At both Jerusalem and Bethlehem, Guerrero confesses that: "As a musician I had a burning desire to bring together all the best musicians from over the whole world—singers and instrumentalists—so that they could unite in singing a thousand songs."[333]

After a month in Jerusalem he visited Damascus, "a city slightly smaller than Seville but with four hundred mosques." During the journey he ate only bread and grapes. A drunk Janizary on horseback rode by and slit open a Turk's head, "and would doubtless have liked doing the same to me, but I got away." At Damascus, where he remained five days, his host was the Venetian consul.[334]

Upon regaining Venice (January 9, 1589), he found hospitality in the house of a Spanish singer employed by the seigniory, Antonio Ribera,[335] who treated him "as a member of the family." He spent a month and a half in correcting proof; then departed for Genoa whence he took ship for Marseilles. Shortly after sailing from Marseilles, where he spent Holy Week, the ship was forced into a cove by bad weather. Their ship was soon joined by a vessel manned by ruffians who robbed them at harquebus-point and imprisoned Guerrero with six other passengers in a nearby fort-ress. After three days one resourceful prisoner offered the captain's wife a bribe. At first a ransom of 100 scudi was demanded from each prisoner, but Guerrero was eventually released upon payment of only 25 scudi. Their ship then put to sea again but a second time ran afoul of pirates. In the course of the fight to ward them off, Guerrero this time vowed to visit Montserrat.[336]

After paying his vow when the ship touched Barcelona, Guerrero thence proceeded overland to Seville, stopping en route at Valencia, Murcia, and Granada. "The distance of the outward journey was 1,400 leagues, that of the return by way of Damascus 1,600. . . . But I declare for a matter of sober fact that in all our journey, which took us among Turks, Moors, and Arabs, we never encountered molestation nor harm, except in France."

Guerrero, like Encina (1519), inserts lengthy catalogues of biblical scenes. Both dwell on any small detail of peculiar interest to Spaniards. Guerrero, for instance, itemizes Spanish gifts sent to St. Saviour's monastery. Both disappoint a modern reader who hopes to find either of them a kindred spirit with Salinas. Apart from a few scanty and unsympathetic references, such as the one in which Guerrero calls Greek chant *simple è ignorante*, nothing of ethnomusical moment is to be found in his prose narrative, anymore than in Encina's poetic account. That Guerrero's account, on the other hand, achieved its end is proved by the large number of reprints it enjoyed during the next century. As late as 1801 it was still in sufficiently wide demand to make profitable a commercial reprinting at Madrid.[337]

Diffusion of Guerrero's Music Guerrero's compositions were dispersed in two principal ways during his lifetime. One method involved the preparation of beautiful manuscript copies, which were then presented either by Guerrero or by an agent to potentially interested individuals or organizations. The second method was publication. Lacking the advantage of long years in a pivotal center such as Rome, Guerrero had to bestir himself to see that his publications reached the hands of chapelmasters in significant cathedrals. His achievement seems all the more granitic when it is realized that he alone of Spanish composers who lived at home—not travelling abroad except for short tours—overcame all the problems inherent in his geographical isolation from international centers and music presses.

To consider first the dispersion of his music in manuscript copies. He began with presentations to his own chapter. As early as May 26, 1554, he was able to offer a luxurious manuscript copy of certain unnamed compositions to the Sevillian cabildo; and was duly rewarded with a cash payment.[338] The copyist may have been Rodrigo de Ceballos, who was engaged on the previous October 7 (1553) to prepare "two or three new choirbooks." Or it may well have been Guerrero himself: who came, it will be remembered, of a family in which painting was a profession.

Sometime between February 3, 1557, and September 21, 1558, he presented a manuscript copy of certain masses he had composed, along with a book of his motets (perhaps his 1555 *Sacrae cantiones*), to the Emperor Charles V—then living in retirement at Yuste (in nearby Estremadura).[339] Charles, at whose request fourteen or fifteen of the best musicians in the

Jeronymite order had been transferred to the cloister at Yuste, called for the singing of one of the presentation masses. An alert listener who could readily tell when a singer erred, and the kind of amateur who liked to beat time with his own hand during a performance, Charles immediately recognized certain borrowed passages in the new mass of Guerrero. It is not likely that any of the friars, on the other hand, had heard much foreign polyphony. At all events, none was so tactless as to claim that he had recognized some chanson or madrigal as Guerrero's source. Instead, they were willing to allow Charles the joy of discovery; when the emperor spoke out they all united in admiring his vast musical knowledge.

Guerrero ranged widely in his choice of models—his *Congratulamini mihi*, for instance, having been parodied after Guillaume Le Heurteur's five-voice motet of that name,[340] his *Della batalla escoutez* after Janequin's *Bat-taille de Marignan*,[341] and his *Dormendo un giorno* after Verdelot's madrigal *Dormend'un giorn'a Bai*.[342] Modern exegetes happening upon the above-mentioned anecdote in Sandoval's biography of Charles V have shown a curious tendency to apologize for Guerrero, as if he had been detected in some disgraceful thievery. But Bishop Sandoval, on the other hand, distinctly specifies the composition as having been a mass: not a motet. It is, of course, true (at least according to Sandoval) that Charles detected borrowings from more than one source. But even if the mass in question did parody more than one source, Guerrero had distinguished precedent for so doing. Morales before him had already shown the way in his *Benedicta es coelorum Regina* Mass, the sources having been both Mouton's and Josquin's motets of the same name. What is more, Victoria followed suit—parodying two different original antiphons of the same name in each of his two Marian masses, *Alma Redemptoris* and *Ave Regina* (1600).

The next presentation of which a record survives took Guerrero to Toledo: where he arrived toward the end of August, 1561, with two handsomely bound volumes in hand for delivery to the cathedral chapter. These were immediately shunted to the official cathedral copyist of liturgical books, who was requested to evaluate them with the chapter secretary.[343] In their report, which was ready on September 10, they declared that the books could be used because the plainchant quoted throughout conformed with Toledan usage. One book of 188 leaves had been copied on the finest paper purchasable and the other of 100 leaves on vellum; 70 spendid initials together with numerous illuminations in gold and in various colors embellished the leaves of the latter book. On September 12 the dean of Toledo Cathedral suggested that Guerrero, "chapelmaster of Seville Cathedral," be rewarded for his pains with 112,500 maravedís (300 ducats). The chapter secretary protested, claiming that Toledo "already possesses better polyphonic books than those which Francisco Guerrero has brought along and presented to us." But the dean's motion carried the day. On September 15 Guerrero signed a first receipt for 100 ducats. Shortly afterward he left Toledo. The remaining 200 ducats were forwarded to him at Seville, his second receipt being dated November 24. This transaction is important not only because one of these 1561 presentation copies—the vellum *Libro de Magníficat a cuatro voces*—survives today at Toledo as Codex 4;[344] but also because this type of unsolicited presentation was to become a Spanish chapelmaster's accepted method of recovering costs of handwritten as well as published copies during the next half-century or more. In addition, the transaction throws welcome light on Guerrero's relationship to Morales. He alludes to Morales so adroitly that at one and the same time he establishes himself and makes it hard for the Toledo chapter to refuse his books. After offering his Magnificats, he says, for instance, that he is moved to do so because Cristóbal de Morales, his erstwhile teacher whose fame now extends to the four corners of the earth on account of his supreme ability, "was while exercising his art amongst you treated with the greatest liberality." He is moved to dedicate his compositions because the "example of his teacher" has taught him that any acceptance by the Toledo chapter is a guarantee of fame through all eternity. If evidence previously gathered has been correctly interpreted, Morales was not *liberalissime* received at Toledo. But Guerrero's diplomacy, always untinctured with guile, served him well in this instance as in many another to follow.

The next dated manuscript (1580) survives at Seville and consists of 68 vellum leaves. At folio 68ᵛ *Franciscus Guerrerus faciebat anno Domini.1.5.8.0.* appears as a colophon: giving reason to think that it may have been copied by Guerrero himself. This manuscript (beautifully lettered with Mudéjar-style initials) bears *Passionarium secundum quatuor Evangelistas . musicis modulis variatum* for its title and contains chordal settings of the turba parts in the four passions.[345]

If the Toledo chapter was slow to acknowledge the magnificats presented in 1561, their reaction some thirty years later was on an entirely different cast. Not only during the intervening years had Guerroro's fame spread far and wide but also copies of his 1570 motets printed at Venice—and endorsed by Pope Pius V—had been purchased on the recommendation of Ginés de Boluda, currently the chapelmaster at Toledo. Best of all, Cardinal de Castro in 1592 personally intervened with a letter to the Toledo primate and cardinal, Don Gaspar de Quiroga. Cardinal de Quiroga's letter of reply survives and deserves quotation:[346]

Most Reverend and beloved brother: We have received your kind letter of the 6th instant [May 6, 1592]. The polyphonic books that Guerrero sent have now reached Toledo Cathedral and have been deposited; 2,384 reales [81,056 maravedís] will be paid for them from cathedral funds, that being the amount

that you graciously say represents the whole cost of having prepared them.
May Our Lord guard your Reverence many years.

Madrid, May 9, 1592   *G. Cardinalis Toletanus*

The Toledan cardinal's letter speaks of *libros de canto*. Guerrero had sent two
such books copied on vellum, their contents being ten masses. Francisco
Sánchez, who had made the 1588-1589 journey to the Holy Land with him,
personally undertook the trip to Toledo in order to present these masses.[347]
Ginés de Boluda (chapelmaster from March 14, 1581, until succeeded by
Alonso Lobo on September 22, 1593) was the intermediary through whom
the 2,164 reales authorized by Cardinal de Quiroga reached Guerrero. In
addition, the Toledo chapter voted Francisco Sánchez 220 reales (7,480
maravedís) towards the cost of his journey.

Both these 1592 vellum manuscripts survive in the Toledo capitular
library: the first as Codex 11 (six masses *a 4*) and the second as Codex 26
(four masses *a 5*).[348] Significantly, both codices contain only masses that
had already been printed in 1566 and 1582. This fact of itself would
strongly suggest that the printed editions (Paris: 1566; Rome: 1582) were
exhausted as early as 1592. This supposition grows to a moral certainty
when MS 110 in the Seville Cathedral music archive is discovered to contain masses already printed in 1566 and 1582. The date of Sevillian MS
110, which like MSS 11 and 26 at Toledo is luxuriously copied on vellum,
is given on the flyleaf as 1595.[349]

To come now to Guerrero's nine publications. The first was issued in
1555 by the same Martín Montesdoca[350] of Seville who had in 1554 printed
what many scholars now concede to be premier among the seven known
Spanish vihuela tablatures—Miguel de Fuenllana's *Orphénica lyra*. Guerrero's *Sacrae cantiones* of 1555 appeared in five small but exquisite partbooks
that by reason of their accuracy and beauty would do credit to a Scotto
or a Gardano. The Latin dedication contains more information than is
usually to be found in such formal epistles and may therefore profitably
be paraphrased here:

To the most illustrious and excellent Don Luis Cristóbal Ponce de León
[1518-1573], Duke of Arcos, Marquis of Zahara, Count of Casares, Lord of
Marchena and other dependencies: greetings from Francisco Guerrero. Having
sometime ago decided, most illustrious Sir, to publish certain songs suited for
use during divine worship, I thought only of you among the many who delight
in such pleasures as the lofty person to whom I should wish to dedicate
the fruits of my vigils. First among the reasons for so desiring to dedicate these
sacred songs was the knowledge that if you with your excellent taste approved,

public approbation would necessarily follow. Then again I knew that it has
been a long-honored custom in your family to devote such time as remained
after serious pursuits, to the enjoyment of music. For, leaving out of account still
earlier ancestors, no one needs to be reminded that your father[351] nurtured
you from your earliest years in all those subjects that belong to the education
of a truly noble prince such as you: who are now the ornament of this age. In
addition to being a valiant warrior he was so consummate a scholar that he
undertook narratives in Latin, the style of which is above censure. Moreover,
he so enjoyed music that not only did he listen long and lovingly to skilled singers
with beautiful voices but also he learned to sing himself in a very creditable
manner. He was incited to pursue music by the examples of such renowned
heroes of old as Achilles, who acknowledged its healing powers, and Alexander,
who sought no other recreation from cares of state. I could go on with praises
of your father but conclude with his having engendered so accomplished and
courageous a prince as you, who are like him in every way. I well know,
most learned Sir, how eagerly you pursue all those humane studies in which you
were initiated by the erudite Greek preceptor of your youth, Alphonsus of
Molyvo [island of Lesbos], and would not now entice you from these other
studies did not I know that any after-hours spent with music will not interfere
with them. Receive, then, most illustrious duke, these small songbooks with
my best wishes that they may alleviate the sadness of any unoccupied hour,
and in so doing recall to your mind Cristóbal de Morales, who received the
greatest benefits at your hands.   Farewell.

Copies of this, Guerrero's maiden publication, are now almost nowhere
to be found. The Hispanic Society in New York possesses as one of its most
valued treasures a complete set of the partbooks. These—unlike the *superius*
and *tenor* partbooks of his 1570 motets owned by the same Society—are still
in perfect condition, even as regards the original limp bindings. The importance of this treasure may be estimated from the fact that no other
known exemplars have been brought to the New World. What is still more
interesting is the fact that none of the following repositories possesses so
much as a single partbook: British Museum, Bibliothèque Nationale,
Biblioteca Nacional; not to mention libraries in Italy and Germany.

As for England, the 1555 partbooks are not in any known collection,
public or private; nor are any later Guerrero partbooks or folios preserved
in even so famous a library as the British Museum or the Bodleian. Such
lacunae in their otherwise admirable collections ought surely to be taken
account of by anyone inclined to puzzle over the strange neglect of his
masterworks in standard English reference manuals. True, Christ Church
library at Oxford came into possession of two Guerrero motets before
1600;[352] but they easily escape attention because they are embedded in
a copy of Victoria's *Motecta Festorum Totius anni* (Rome: Domenico Basa,
1585)—this being, of course, the volume in which the younger honored

the elder master by including his *Pastores loquebantur* and *Beata Dei genetrix*. So effectively, indeed, are these two motets buried amidst the Victoria motets that Aloys Hiff could publish his catalogue of printed music in Christ Church library (1919) without noticing Guerrero as the composer of the Christmas motet; and what he as a cataloguer missed, earlier historians can hardly be presumed to have noticed. Certainly, Burney and Hawkins should not be censured for neglecting Guerrero by comparison with Morales and Victoria, when neither historian enjoyed access to Guerrero's publications.

The second of Guerrero's published chefs-d'oeuvre, his *Canticum Beatae Mariae, quod Magnificat nuncupatur per octo musicae modos variatum* (1563), was published in the Low Countries rather than in the peninsula. For his choice of Pierre Phalèse at Louvain[353] as the printer instead of Montesdoca of Seville, such reasons as these can be advanced: (1) Montesdoca had printed only one choirbook of the *libro de facistol* type—Juan Vásquez's *Agenda defunctorum* (1556)—a small one at that (31.5 by 21 cm.); (2) any volume published by Phalèse, a renowned polyphonic specialist, could be depended upon to reach international markets more quickly and win wider fame for the composer.

Dedicated to Philip II, Guerrero's magnificats can by no means have been new, since they concord with those in the collection delivered to Toledo Cathedral in 1561. The dedication, unlike the preface to the Toledo manuscript copy, is impersonal and therefore less interesting. In the main, Guerrero confines himself to praises of music. He ends with an appeal to Philip for protection of the sacred branches.

If F. J. Fétis was right in calling Guerrero's magnificats "one of the most precious collections of the old Spanish school," the next of his publications is certainly one of the most monumental—*Liber primus Missarum Francisco Guerrero Hispalensis Odei phonasco Authore* (Nicolas du Chemin: Paris, 1566).[354] Unlike Morales and Victoria, Guerrero placed his four masses *a 5* first, following them with his five *a 4*. Whether he adopted this order so that he could begin with a mass parodied after a motet by his master Morales cannot be proved. But in any event his *Sancta et immaculata (a 5)* does pay tribute to Morales's 1541 motet *a 4*. Still another parody in this 1566 collection acknowledges a Morales motet *a 4* as its source—*Inter vestibulum*. Among the other masses in Guerrero's *Liber primus* (besides the parodies of Le Heurteur and Verdelot already mentioned) are a *De beata Virgine (a 4)* beginning with the Rex virginum trope; and a lengthy Requiem in twenty-one polyphonic sections. As an appendix, Guerrero adds three motets: the ineffably beautiful *Ave Virgo sanctissima (a 5)*, *Usquequo Domine oblivisceris (a 6)*, and a *Pater noster (a 8)*. The last is a group canon, four voices taking their rise out of the other four.

For a dedicatee, Guerrero picked a monarch of whom much was hoped, but who was yet in his nonage—Sebastian of Portugal (1554-1578). The regency was still securely in the grip of Sebastian's mother when Guerrero made his Lisbon journey in January, 1566. The preface (dated May 1, 1565, at Seville) contains a number of remarkably prescient phrases when the later events of Sebastian's short reign are taken into account. Though the boy was only in his twelfth year, Guerrero dwelt on the recent Portuguese victories over the Moors in Morocco as a matter of great moment: extolling the warlike disposition of the young king. Above all, he lauded Sebastian's religious zeal. According to Guerrero, Portugal exceeded every other nation in religious fervor; and also stood in the international forefront because sacred music received there her most generous support.

Guerrero's next dedicatee was Pope Pius V, the Dominican (later canonized) during whose pontificate the reforming decrees of the Council of Trent first began to take churchwide effect. Published by Antonio Gardano at Venice in 1570, the *Motteta Francisci Guerreri in Hispalensi Ecclesia Musicorum Praefecti* open with a dedication in which he deplores the efforts of those malicious persons who wish all sacred music to be curtailed. He notes, however, that extremely erudite men have resisted their attacks. He hopes that such compositions as those in the present collection will show his devout disposition. "If they win the approbation of Your Holiness in like manner as in times past you were pleased to bestow approval upon my other modest efforts—as was shown in your letter [June 22, 1566] (which I count my richest treasure)—you will encourage your servant Francisco to continue with his efforts at speaking to the hearts of pious men and at constantly improving upon his former works." *Pastores loquebantur* (pars 2 : *Videntes autem*), the Christmas motet later to be printed in Victoria's 1585 *Motecta Festorum Totius anni*, survives in Cappella Sistina MS 29 at folios 22^v-28.[355] Verses of a *Miserere mei, Deus* occupy folios 10^v-12 in MS 205, with attribution to "F. G." The *meas nugas* to which he refers, however, were the masses in his *Liber primus* [Paris: 1566]. Pius V had received a gift copy and had sent Guerrero a letter of congratulation dated June 22, 1566, in which he not only lauded the masses but said that he had ordered them to be sung by the pontifical choir (*AM*, IX, 70).

Guerrero's second book of masses—*Missarum liber secundus*, published at Rome in 1582 by Francesco Zanetto—saluted both the then reigning pontiff, Gregory XIII, and the Blessed Virgin. To the pope was dedicated the *Ecce sacerdos magnus* Mass *a 5*, but to the Blessed Virgin the remaining seven masses. This sumptuous folio is not only one of the largest but is one of the most luxurious of sixteenth-century publications. Guerrero, as has already been shown, went to Rome to proofread; upon its issue from Domenico Basa's press he personally placed a presentation copy in the hands of Gregory XIII. The letter from Guerrero to the Sevillian chapter in which he describes his half-hour audience with the pope has already been quoted at pages 163-164.

The *Liber vesperarum* published at Rome in 1584 by Alessandro Gardano contains psalms, vesper hymns, magnificats, and Marian antiphons. In his dedication to the Sevillian chapter, dated December 1, 1584,[356] Guerrero volubly thanks the canons for their benefits: which, as has been amply shown in the chronological table, were many. Although he may have lacked the lucrative absentee benefices that Victoria received from Gregory XIII and Sixtus V; or the munificent protection of such rulers as those of the House of Bavaria; or the income from a prosperous fur business; the Sevillian chapter supported him in his publishing ventures no less lavishly: even if sometimes belatedly (as in 1591 when he went to prison for debt).

The preface to the 1584 book of vespers music sets forth as idealistic a philosophy of church music as do any of the prefaces written by Morales or Victoria—or, for that matter any of the manifestos written by such lesser composers as Las Infantas; it may therefore be appropriately paraphrased here.

To the most illustrious fathers of the Cathedral of Seville: Francisco Guerrero, prebendary and master of the choristers, conveys wishes for unending felicity. Just as Almighty God has always found it more desirable and acceptable that worship ceremonies should be celebrated with song and for that reason required sacrifices at the Temple in Jerusalem to be offered with a large ensemble of singers accompanied by various types of instrumental music (and I would not forget that with equal ceremony His worship is even now offered by the most reverend fathers of this temple), so He finds the more detestable that abuse of lascivious and effeminate singing the only purpose of which is to caress the ears. Such abuse not only fails to lift the mind to contemplation of the Almighty but even profanes those very sanctuaries where it is heard, catering as does such music to the baser affections and the more vulgar emotions. How malicious this corruption can become no devout soul would dispute. . . . But our holy fathers, the Roman Pontiffs . . . have ordained an austere and holy music for the Church, and have safeguarded the chant with most prudent laws that banish far from the Church all the caressings of those songs that corrupt the purity and majesty of divine worship: taking care that all music used in sacred ceremonies shall be of a more austere and solemn kind, differing as regards essential spirit nowise from the original Gregorian chant. They have moreover taken due measures against lascivious inflections and any noise without meaning.

Whether I have myself cultivated with any success this devout and sober style in my own modest publications up until the present moment must be left for others to judge. But I have truly held it as my goal and desire from the very beginning not to flatter the ears of the devout so much as to predispose their minds the better toward a right regard for the sacred mysteries. I have striven toward the same goal in the present work: in which are to be found psalms in the several tones together with hymns suitable for the several seasons esteemed of greatest consequence in the year. To these have been added settings of the canticle of the Blessed Virgin in which she magnificently magnifies and praises God; and also settings of the Salve Regina in which she is saluted as queen and merciful mother.

All of these settings, my most worthy and esteemed Fathers and Patrons, are dedicated to you: to whom I am already indebted for all that I am, having served your cathedral church since infancy. You moreover took me under protection after ordination to the noble and elevated order of priest. For all your beneficence I shall never cease giving thanks to Heaven.

. . . Seville, December 1, 1584.

In 1589 a collection of spiritual part-songs, appeared, many of which had been composed originally to secular lyrics but were now refitted to sacred texts. The flavor throughout all sixty-one items remains distinctly popular. The cardinal to whom *Canciones y villanescas espirituales* was dedicated— Rodrigo de Castro,[357] ruler of the Sevillian see during Guerrero's last seventeen years—has already been mentioned several times as a consistently staunch friend and supporter. The preface by Cristóbal Mosquera de Figueroa (d. 1610), auditor-general of the fleet commanded by the Marqués de Santa Cruz, contains several valuable observations.

Just as Aristoxenus was preëminent among the Greeks, Boethius among the Romans, Morales among the Italians [*sic*], Josquin among the French and Picards, and Gombert among the Flemish, so among the Spanish Francisco Guerrero stands out. In his copious and elegant polyphonic compositions he has ornamented our Spain; for so widely has his fame traveled among all discerning musicians that no collector thinks his library complete without works by the celebrated Guerrero. Among his merits that deserve applause are his pioneering success in fitting music to Spanish verse so that the very life and rhythm of the poetry are preserved.

Mosquera de Figueroa, even though a well-informed amateur, makes of his fellow-Sevillian Morales, an Italian. But he is on solid ground when he bespeaks the enthusiasm of the high-born amateurs of his time for Guerrero's Spanish songs, which he avers were among the works Guerrero composed first (even if among his latest in reaching print). Moreover, he typifies the sentiment of his contemporaries in placing Guerrero above all other Spaniards alive or dead.

In the same year, 1589, a second collection was published by the same printer, Giacomo Vincentio, at Venice: *Mottecta Francisci Guerreri in Hispalensi Ecclesia musicorum praefecti. . . . Liber secundus.*[358] This second book of Venetian motets is, by contrast with its predecessor, offered to Christ Himself. The dedication concludes with this devout hope: "I would not seek the transitory gifts of mortal kings nor their fleeting riches. My sole desire is to continue singing Thy praises in Heavenly Courts which I now everyday sing in Thy temples here below." A reprint of this same dedication stands at the front of Guerrero's valedictory publication, his *Motecta Francisci Guerreri* published by Giacomo Vincentio at Venice in 1597. In this farewell collection of seventy items he repeats thirty-four of the forty motets published in 1570, adding thereto the harvest of his later years. When Guerrero in 1582, 1589, and 1597 dedicated his final masses and motets either to the Virgin Mary or to Christ, he was caught up in the same fervor that caused Victoria to turn aside from kings and princes for three of his later dedications (the junior master offered his 1583 *Motecta* to the Virgin, his *Officium Hebdomadae Sanctae* to the Blessed Trinity, and his 1589 *Motecta* [published at Milan] to the Virgin.)

The above nine publications span forty-two years and represent the sum of Guerrero's works known to have been issued under his personal supervision. However, two other publications must be added to the list of sixteenth-century imprints containing his music:[359] (1) *Magnificat, Beatissimae Deiparaeque Virginis Mariae Canticum* (Nuremberg: Friedrich Lindner, 1591) and (2) *Sacrarum symphoniarum continuatio. Diversorum excellentissimorum authorum Quaternis, v. vi. vii. viii. x. & xii. vocibus tam vivis, quam instrumentalibus accommodata* (Nuremberg: Paul Kaufmann, 1600). Neither of these German prints contains anything not already encountered in Guerrero's personally supervised publications, but both serve neatly to prove the geographic spread of his reputation and the viability of his music outside the peninsula. In the Lindner publication his magnificats appear beside Vincenzo Ruffo's. In the Kaufmann, his two motets *O Domine Jesu Christe* and *Ibant Apostoli gaudentes* (*a 4*) occupy positions of honor as items 1 and 2 in the collection; *Gaudent in coelis animae sanctorum* (*a 5*) stands apart as item 14. Guerrero wrote two different motets *a 4* with *O Domine Jesu Christe* as text: one occurring on page 19 of his 1570 motets as a motet for Palm Sunday, the other as item 12 in his 1589 *Mottecta . . . Liber secundus*. It was the first of these which Kaufmann extracted for publication in 1600, a generation having elapsed since the original imprint. In the long Kaufmann title the editor promises that the motets to follow will be found equally suited for voices or instruments. In view of the important role allotted instruments in the Seville Cathedral during the entirety of Guerrero's service, we cannot be surprised that in Kaufmann's collection "for voices or instruments," two

Guerrero motets should stand first. Just which instruments were used during his incumbency at Seville, as well as the manner of their combination or alternation with voices, will be discussed presently.

Still a third and final class of publication—in addition to the nine personally supervised, and two alien, imprints thus far mentioned—must now be examined: namely, the vihuela tablatures of Fuenllana (1554) and Daza (1576). These contain a total of thirteen Guerrero items—five of which are secular songs. Fuenllana's *Orphénica lyra* accounts for nine items (two of which are secular). Daza's *El Parnasso* accounts for four (three of which are secular; one—*Esclarecida Juana*—being misattributed to Villalar). Fuenllana's tablature lists all nine simply as by Guerrero without any identifying "Francisco." But since concordances for the *Pater noster* (folios 96ᵛ-98) and *Ojos claros* [y] *serenos* (folios 143-144) have been found in his 1555 *Sacrae cantiones* and in Biblioteca Medinaceli MS 13230 respectively, it seems probable that when Fuenllana attributed anything to "Guerrero" rather than "Pedro Guerrero," he meant Francisco. Furthermore, all seven items attributed in *Orphénica lyra* to "Pedro Guerrero" are secular *sonetos*, whereas but two of those ascribed to "Guerrero" are secular.

The sacred items in *Orphénica lyra* include the following: (1) *fabordones* in each church mode at folios 108ᵛ-111—all eight being set throughout *a 4* except the festal Tone VI *fabordón* that augments to five voices in the last *verso;* (2) *Fecit potentiam (a 2)* at folio 3ᵛ; (3) and (4) two *Pange lingua's*, one *a 3* at folios 94ᵛ-95ᵛ and the other *a 4* at folio 95;[360] (5) *Pater noster (a 4)* at folios 96ᵛ-98; (6) *Sacris solemniis (a 3)* at folios 95ᵛ-96; (7) *Suscepit Israel (a 2)* at folio 3. The secular items are *Ojos claros* at folios 143-144 and *Torna Mingo a enamorarte* at folios 144-145 (both *a 4*).[361]

The sacred item in *El Parnasso*, an *Ave Maria*, occupies folios 49-52. The secular items include the following: (1) *Adios, verde ribera* at folios 87ᵛ-88ᵛ; (2) *Esclarecida Juana* at folios 90ᵛ-91ᵛ; (3) *Prado verde y florido* at folios 83-84. All four of these *Parnasso* items are for vocal quartet. The *Ave Maria* concords with the Hail Mary to be found in Guerrero's 1555 *Sacrae canciones*.

Masses   Although only two leaves of one mass (*Gaude Barbara*) by Morales—the most renowned of Sevillian composers—have been found at Seville, four complete masses by Guerrero survive in the Seville Cathedral music archive in manuscript copy: *Dormendo un giorno*, *Iste sanctus*, *Saeculorum Amen*, and *Surge propera amica mea*. These four, like the ten preserved in manuscript copy at Toledo, duplicate masses to be found in imprints (1566, 1582, and 1597). One may therefore suppose that Guerrero's masses, like Victoria's, extend only to the number printed during his lifetime. It is true that a Guerrero *L'Homme armé (a 4)* not printed in any sixteenth-century edition was reported to have been seen at the Real Monasterio de Santa Ana in

Ávila during the early 1930's,[362] but in 1950 the pertinent manuscript could not be found at Ávila. Until the existence of such a Guerrero *L'Homme armé* can be verified, the number of his masses must be set down as eighteen: eleven of which are *a 4*, six *a 5*, and one *a 6*.

In alphabetical order those for four voices may be listed thus: *Beata Mater* (1566),[363] *De beata Virgine* (1566 and 1582), *Dormendo un giorno* (1566), *Inter vestibulum* (1566), *Iste sanctus* (1582), *Pro defunctis* (1566 and 1582), *Puer qui natus est nobis* (1582),[364] *Saeculorum Amen* (1597), *Simile est regnum coelorum* (1582); those for five voices; *Congratulamini mihi* (1566), *Della batalla escoutez* (1582), *Ecce sacerdos magnus* (1582), *In te Domine speravi* (1566), *Sancta et immaculata* (1566), *Super flumina Babylonis* (1566); and the one for six voices: *Surge propera amica mea* (1582). Since the latest mass in the above list, *Saeculorum Amen* (1597), still calls for only four voices, Guerrero stands in marked contrast with Victoria, who—following the polychoral trend of the times—published an eight-voice mass in 1592, and two *a 8*, one *a 9*, and one *a 12* in 1600; or, for that matter, with Palestrina, who began with an eight-voice in 1585, and three of whose later masses *a 8* were issued in 1601. Guerrero does, however, customarily augment with one or two added voices in his last Agnuses: *Della batalla* reaching eight, for instance. Indeed, he augments so uniformly in his four-voice masses that the apparent breaking of the rule in Hilarión Eslava's transcription of *Simile est regnum coelorum* (*Lira sacro-hispana* [1869], I, ii, 111-131) would in itself cast doubt over his version; since in his edition this mass would seem to end lamely with a single Agnus *a 4*. Comparison with the original, however, immediately discloses that Eslava omitted the last Agnus; to say nothing of the other respects in which his—the first modern reprint of a Guerrero mass —belies the original.

Guerrero's masses may also be contrasted with Victoria's by reason of the number of voice parts that each composer is willing to accept in individual movements as his irreducible minimum. The younger composer, usually the richer harmonist, never reduces below a trio in his masses. But the elder, whose effects are as often achieved by his *gallardo contrapunto*[365] as by his juxtaposition of chords, reduces in the Crucifixus of his *Congratulamini mihi* Mass (one of the most successful movements in this mass) to a duo between first treble and tenor.[366] The dramatic quality of this duo is all the more poignantly felt because the preceding section, Et incarnatus est, was scored full. After the sonorous solidly packed chords *a 5* used to set the words "Et homo factus est," the sudden bareness of the duo as strikingly reminds the hearer of the nakedness of Christ stretched on a cross between two thieves as does a *paso* carried about during Holy Week. For a Flemish composer of Josquin's generation the Pleni was an appropriate movement for a duo; but Guerrero insists on putting even a change of vocal texture to dramatic account. In still other ways he manifests his extraordinary sensitivity to the changes of tone color which result from shifts in vocal registration. When he adds a voice part, he may simultaneously change the vocal combination—as, for instance, in the Agnuses of his *Ecce sacerdos* Mass: the first of which ("miserere nobis") lachrymosely congeals in the middle registers (CAATB); whereas the second ("dona nobis pacem") brilliantly expands at both vocal extremes (CCATBB). Even when he retains the same number of voice parts in successive movements, he not infrequently changes his voice combination for a clearly recognizable expressive purpose; and not merely for the aesthetic value of contrast.

As for the general character of the vocal lines, Guerrero—himself a singer of *escogida voz*[367]—soars with melodies of markedly individual contour and grace; whereas Victoria—himself primarily an organist—contrives more interesting and novel chord-progressions. If an attempt is made to count the number of accidentals appearing in their printed masses, Guerrero is found to occupy a halfway house between Morales's penury and Victoria's prodigality. However, obligatory chromaticisms are specified in the imprints as early as Kyrie II of the first mass in his *Liber primus* (1566), altus II being in this instance directed to sing e♭, d, c♯, to set the word *eleison* (mm. 73-74).

All three composers—Morales, Guerrero, and Victoria—published bitextual masses. Allusion has already been made to Morales's *Ave Maria* and *De beata Virgine* (*a 5*) Masses, in both of which are to be found certain movements during which the tenor sings the angelical salutation while the remaining voices sing the appropriate texts of the Credo- or Sanctus-movements. Below, at pages 377 and 474 (n. 138), are mentioned the *Ave maris stella* and *Gaudeamus* Masses of Victoria, both of which were published in his first volume of masses (1576) and both of which contain bitextual movements. But Morales and Victoria, each with two published masses containing bitextual movements, are both exceeded by Guerrero in this respect. During the Benedictus of the opening mass in his *Liber primus* (1566) he pits the tenor singing "Sancta et immaculata" against the three other voices singing "Benedictus qui venit in nomine Domini." During the Sanctus of his *Beata Mater* Mass in this same 1566 book he requires the superius to sing "Beata Mater, et innupta Virgo, gloriosa Regina mundi: intercede pro nobis ad Dominum"; during the Osanna of the same mass the altus apostrophizes "Beata Mater" four times (in breves and longs) while the other voices sing the prescribed liturgical text. Undeterred by any change of custom, Guerrero continued to indulge in the same bitextual practice as late as his *Liber secundus* (1582). The second mass in this collection—the one mass in the entire collection dedicated specifically to Pope Gregory XIII—is bitextual in Kyries, Sanctus, and Agnus movements.

During Kyrie I the tenor sings the entire *Ecce sacerdos* antiphon in notes of various values. During Kyrie III the three words "Ecce sacerdos magnus" are four times repeated by altus I (singing breves). During the Sanctus (folio 34), altus I sings the antiphon text: here treated, as during Kyrie III, in cantus firmus fashion. Throughout Agnus I, at a distance of two breves, altus II and tenor make a canon at the fifth (words and melody, as before, deriving from the antiphon). During Agnus II, cantus II sings the entire text of the antiphon through the word "justus": then sings "dona nobis pacem" three times.

Was Guerrero the least progressive of the three because he had not yet given up this type of composition in 1582—thirty-eight years after Palestrina had published a similarly entitled mass that was to be his one and only bitextual essay? In Guerrero's favor was the national custom. Among Spanish composers, not only bitextual masses but also polytextual magnificats continued in vogue long after Guerrero's death. Indeed, this was a custom to which even distinguished foreigners acceded while residing in Spain. Philippe Rogier's *Missae sex* (Madrid: 1598) opens with such a mass: one voice singing the acclamation, "Philippus secundus Rex Hispaniae," in unremitting breves during all except a few solo movements (Crucifixus, Et iterum, and Benedictus). For his cantus firmus he employs in this instance a soggetto cavato derived as rigorously from the vowels as the cantus firmus of Josquin's notorious *Hercules dux Ferrariae* Mass. Among polytextual magnificats (which seem to have been published only in Spain), Sebastián de Vivanco's 1607 collection published at Salamanca provides the most noteworthy example: the Gloria Patri *(a 8)* of his fourth tone Magnificat combining no less than three different Marian texts with the ascription of praise.

Closely akin to the bitextual interludes of Guerrero's masses are those sections in which he takes one or more words of the ordinary, weds the word (or words) to a concise melodic figure, and then repeats that figure incessantly throughout the entire movement (after the manner of an ostinato). This was of course a unifying principle already used by Morales in the Benedictus of his *Quem dicunt homines* Mass (see above, page 62). Guerrero uses it during the Sanctus of his *Sancta et immaculata* Mass: in which movement the second treble repeats a figure comprising the first six notes of the head motive in the source motet. Only the one word "Sanctus" is sung to the melodic figure (a-d-a-f-b♭-a); this motto-phrase then serves as a five-times-repeated ostinato during the course of the movement. In the Sanctus of his second mass *In te Domine speravi* he makes use of precisely the same unifying device. From the head motive of the source motet he derives a six-note ostinato (g-g-b♭-f-g-d) that altus II repeats three times. In Agnus I of his third mass, *Congratulamini mihi*, superius II repeats another ostinato (g-c¹-d¹-e¹): again made from the head motive of the source motet. The

Osanna of the *Beata Mater* Mass in his 1566 collection has already been cited as a movement with double text.[368] Throughout, the altus sings an ostinato that becomes a fourfold repetition of the words, "Beata Mater." In his second collection (1582), Guerrero continues to exploit ostinati of diverse types: as, for instance, in Agnus I of *Della batalla escoutez*, during which cantus II sings a four-note figure (c^1-a-a-g; g-e-e-d); and in Agnus I of his *Simile est regnum coelorum* Mass. During the latter, the tenor sings G-A-B-G-c-d-e in semibreves; then, after a breve's rest, recites the same figure backward, thus—e-d-c-G-B-A-G. Above his cancrizans initium he inserts this legend: *Vado et venio ad vos* ("I go away and I am coming to you").[369] These are, of course, Jesus's words at John 14:28. The whole verse reads: "Ye have heard how I said unto you, I go away, and come again unto you; if ye loved me, ye would rejoice because I said, I go unto the Father: for the Father is greater than I." Since the transformation of every learned device into a symbol is so characteristic not only of Guerrero's art but of Spanish *renacimiento* music in general, Guerrero may well have intended his cancrizans as an allusion to the gospel for Whitsunday; and this mass for Pentecost.

Even more patently, symbols inspire Guerrero's last mass, his *Saeculorum Amen*. For his motto in this mass (copied into MS 110 at Seville in 1595; published at Venice two years later) he selects not a plainsong initium, but the close of the Tone VIII ascription of praise. The *hypermixolydius*, according to Ramos de Pareja and Bermudo, is the "stellar" mode.[370] Properly, it belongs to the heavens beyond the planets: those regions to be reached only by mortals who loving "vertue, she alone is free," have learned to "clime / Higher than the Spheary chime." So early as 1410 Guerrero's Sevillian predecessor Fernand Esteban had in his *Reglas de Canto Plano* further individualized this mode by declaring it suited to the "manner of the aged."[371] Now approaching the biblical span of three score and ten, Guerrero rightly chooses this mode, this formula. His plainsong— c-A-B-c-A-G—is found in any early Spanish plainsong instructor among *euouae* for Tone VIII. (Alonso Spañon, in his *Introducion muy util y breue* printed at Seville *ca.* 1500, gives it as the penultimate *saeculorum amen* on the last page of musical examples.)

In Guerrero's Kyrie I, this plainsong euouae serves as the treble initium; in intermediate movements the euouae migrates to other voices; in the Agnus it becomes a tenor cantus firmus. It is in the last-named movement that Guerrero transforms the euouae into an ostinato: first in longs (repeated twice), then in breves (twice). Unto few composers has it been given to close a lifetime with so apropos a work of art. Pacheco said that his last words appropriately ended a well-nigh flawless life ("I rejoiced, because they said unto me, We shall go into the house of the Lord"). When we take into account the various musical and liturgical presuppositions that he accepted, then a "World without end, Amen" Mass based on an eighth mode euouae makes a perfect coda to a career such as no other composer was able to achieve solely on Spanish soil during his century.

Just as the quality of Guerrero's art cannot be appreciated without studying his use of symbols, so also his message cannot be fully understood without a close analysis of his learned devices. His imitations are often quite subtle. For instance, the Sanctus of his *Simile est regnum coelorum* Mass (*Lira sacro-hispana*, I, ii, 129) opens with a pair of mirror imitations—first between alto and soprano, next between tenor and bass. His canons often go beyond the usual two-in-one variety. In the *Pater noster, a 8,* included in his 1555 *Sacrae cantiones* and reprinted at the close of his *Liber primus missarum* (by way of an appendix), he does not rest content until he has made of the Lord's Prayer a canonic *tour de force* (four-in-eight variety). His *Inter vestibulum* Mass in the same 1566 *Liber primus* closes with a three-in-one canon that is

Missa Inter vestibulum
Agnus Dei
Liber primus missarum (Paris: 1566), fols. 118ᵛ-119.   Francisco Guerrero

no less to be admired. Here he simultaneously contrives to quote the source motet (Morales's *Inter vestibulum et altare*) in the three other voices, while spinning a *trinitas in unitate* canon in altus, superius II, and tenor I—the threads of which canon are always twisted from filaments of Morales's cantus. Properly to appreciate Guerrero's remarkable though unobtrusive feat, one should compare Morales's four-voice *Inter vestibulum et altare* motet, phrase by phrase, with Guerrero's six-voice Agnus. In the accompanying example only the Agnus appears; but since Morales's motet has been at least twice reprinted with modern clefs, a more thorough comparison can easily be made by having recourse to Anglés's or Rubio's 1953 editions of the motet.[372] The aesthetic of the source motet and the parody mass will also be the better appreciated if some attention is given to Morales's penitential text (Joel 2:17): "Let the priests, the ministers of the Lord, weep between the porch and the altar, and let them say, Spare thy people, O Lord, and give not thine inheritance to reproach, that the heathen should rule over them; why should they say among the nations: Where is their God?" In his last Agnus, Guerrero's three-in-one canon dramatizes the insistent entreaties of those "ministers of the Lord who weep between the porch and the altar"; while the three outer voices perhaps symbolize the people who stand outside the sacred enclosure.

Another *Liber primus* mass in which formal canon recurs frequently is the four-voice *Beata Mater*. The Credo movements are composed throughout "ad fugam in diathessaron." The order of entries appropriately symbolizes the ideas of raising and lowering: in the Patrem, the altus is answered by superius; in the Et incarnatus, the superius by altus; in the Crucifixus, the altus by superius; in the Et in spiritum, the altus by superius. The final Agnus (*a 5*) of this mass includes canon, but here at the unison between two trebles. As for *Liber secundus* masses, the *Ecce sacerdos* dons formal canon at the fifth between altus II and tenor in Agnus I; the *Iste sanctus* wears one at the union in the last Agnus (*a 5*); and the *De beata Virgine* boasts one between tenor and cantus II at the octave: again in the concluding five-voice Agnus.

Guerrero's technique of parody shows certain individual facets. Just as he yields to no other Spaniard in contrapuntal mastery, so also his virtuosity as parodist equals his best sixteenth-century compatriots'. True, Morales staked out the path that he was to follow. Above, at pages 74-79, we saw that Morales delighted in finding ways to entwine in a new parti-colored braid, melodic strands that in the source motet by no means counterpointed with each other but were, on the contrary, spun out one after the other. From the moment of printing his first mass, Guerrero proves his mastery of just this same art—that of weaving loose threads drawn out of a source motet into a new, tightly meshed web. Appropriately, he begins by using this parody technique—learned from Morales—upon one of his master's own motets, the winsome four-voice *Sancta et immaculata virginitas*. So eager is he to use Morales's head motive in as many new combinations as possible that in Kyrie I he introduces it a dozen times within 30 breves (= bars in the transcription). Since this head motive normally occupies 3 breves, the net result is a continuous overlapping of "entries" in the manner of a baroque fugue-stretto. What happens in Guerrero's "parodies" is marvelously proleptic: he becomes so excited with the numerous combinations possible when using only a limited number of motives from his source motet that he begins to write contrapuntal movements of the baroque type (in which subject and countersubject dominate a whole movement). This is not to say that Guerrero consciously decided to embark upon new seas any more than those who first sailed for the "Indies": but rather that he became so engrossed in his master's method as to write, without premeditation, contrapuntal movements in which a single subject keeps turning up in one voice after another throughout the whole movement. In Kyrie I of his *Sancta et immaculata*—shown here as an example—the "subject" dominating

Missa Sancta et immaculata
Kyrie I

Liber primus missarum (Paris: 1566), fols. 2ᵛ-3.

Francisco Guerrero

the whole movement duplicates the head motive of the source motet. Guerrero makes his "countersubject" from the continuation of the head motive
found in Morales's bassus at mm. 7-9. In the Kyrie above, roman numerals

designate "subject" and "countersubject." (If Morales was his musical godfather, the likeness of motive I to the beginning of Josquin's *Missa Sine nomine* establishes beyond dispute who was Guerrero's "grandfather."

Since in the rest of the *Sancta et immaculata* Guerrero's parody technique is revealed as admirably as in any of his eighteen masses, his procedures in the other movements are summarized here. Morales divided his reprise-motet into two *partes* of approximately equal length (71 and 70 bars). Measures 33-66 duplicate mm. 105-138. The motet supplies Guerrero with seven motives (the head motive remains the one most frequently quoted throughout the entire mass). These several motives first appear in the motet at the following measures: II (bassus, mm. 7-9); III (altus, mm. 15_4-17, and bassus, mm. 17_4-21_3); IV (bassus, mm. 33_2-35_3, and cantus, mm. 37_2-40_1; V (cantus, mm. 44_3-46_3, and tenor, mm. 45_4-48_3); VI (tenor, mm. 72-73_4); VII (bassus, mm. 86_3-89_1). Morales himself develops each of motives III-VII in a distinct point of imitation—bandying III in six entries, IV in four, V in forty-four (twenty-two in *pars 1* and twenty-two in *pars 2* [reprise]), VI in seven entries, and VII in six. But having developed each motive in its own point, he passes on to the next without harking back to III, IV, VI, or VII in any later point of imitation. Guerrero, with a larger canvas, does just the opposite. In the Et in terra pax he starts with I, moves to III, then harks back to I. In the Qui tollis he develops VI and VII; then reverts to I and V. In the Patrem he starts with I, moves to V, then reverts to I, III, and II, and finally again to I. In the Crucifixus (a trio) only I and III are worked. In the Et iterum (the first section in this mass to open full) he develops I, II, VI, IV, VII, V, in approximately that order. The Sanctus (which includes an ostinato for second superius) hugs I: as does also the Pleni. The Osanna opens with a point bandying V, but reverts to I (V and I being combined in the last few measures). At the opening of the Benedictus, VII and I are made to combine. In the Agnus *a 6*, I, IV, and V are imitated successively: V being chosen to close the mass, in deference to the source motet where it similarly closes *partes 1* and *2*.

What this brief summary reveals is not only Guerrero's tendency to double back on himself (he harks back to I in the Et in terra, Qui tollis, Patrem, and Osanna), not only his interest in combining I with other motives (Kyrie I, Osanna, Benedictus), but also just as importantly his commitment to motives from the source motet in every section and subsection throughout the entire mass. Even when he constructs a point of imitation using melodic material of his own invention, he always sees to it that his point successfully counterpoints with some motive drawn from Morales: instances of this occurring both in the Crucifixus (in which he again dramatically reduces his number of voices after a preceding section scored full) and in the Sanctus.

Because he quotes motives from his source anywhere and everywhere, objection might be taken that Guerrero shows even less originality than the sixteenth-century composer of parody masses had a right to exhibit. This objection collapses, however, if account is taken of the uses to which he puts motives drawn from his sources. In the *Sancta et immaculata*, for instance, he never quotes Morales's polyphonic *complex*. Rather, he always excerpts Morales's motives, and of them devises new and unforseen combinations. Strictly speaking, indeed, such a mass as the *Sancta et immaculata*, because of this procedure, does not even exemplify the classic concept of parody; for, according to the classical definition, the whole polyphonic complex itself (and not just motives drawn out of that complex) should be quoted at least occasionally in a parody mass. If an excursion into semantics be allowed, a better classification for a mass such as this one of Guerrero's would be in a category, then, of new name—*permutation* mass. It is significant, moreover, that such a type should have developed in a Spanish milieu —tentatively sprouting in Morales's masses and luxuriantly blossoming in Guerrero's—Spain being the nation above every other one in sixteenth-century Europe where the *glosa* and the *diferencia* enjoyed their heyday.

Account having now been taken of Guerrero's procedures in his parody— or, better, permutation—masses, our next concern must be to examine his masses of plainsong derivation. Again as in Morales's two books, Guerrero includes a *De beata Virgine* in both his 1566 and 1582 collections. The 1566 is perhaps the more interesting because of its text, which in Kyrie and Gloria movements is as heavily troped as Anchieta's movements in the *Missa de Nuestra Señora* (= *de beata Virgine*) composed cooperatively with Escobar some half-century earlier.[373] It is the more interesting also because when placed side by side, Anchieta's treatment of the same melody is found to differ pronouncedly from Guerrero's. The accompanying illustrations therefore include: (1) the tenth-century plainsong Kyrie, as edited by the Solesmes Benedictines; (2) Anchieta's discantus, *ca.* 1500; (3) the initium of the troped Kyrie as printed (with sharps) in Luys de Villafranca's *Breue instrucion de canto llano* (published at Seville in 1565 with approbations signed by Pedro Fernández and Francisco Guerrero); (4) Guerrero's superius (*Rex virginum*), tenor (*Christe*), and superius (*O Paraclite*), 1566. In Anchieta's Kyries, every phrase except the first begins on the "downbeat" of the measure. Small note-values occur only toward the ends of phrases. Seven of the nine phrases close with the same syncopated tag. Guerrero, a half-century or so later, eliminates all traces of the static, posed marble to be seen in the earlier art-work, and instead dissolves the chant into fluid rhythms. He divides the plainsong into a greater number of phrases—eleven—without changing the total number of measures. Each successive phrase within sections (except the last two in *O Paraclite*) begins on a different "beat" of

Missa de beata Virgine

Cunctipotens Genitor Deus   *Liber usualis* (1947 ed.), p. 25.

Ky- ri- e   e-   le- i- son. *iij.*

Chri- ste   e-   le- i- son. *iij.*

Ky- ri- e   e-   le- i- son. *ij.*

Ky- ri- e   le- i- son.

Juan de Anchieta *(Missa de Nuestra Señora).* MME, I, 35 -37.

Rex, vir- gi- num a- ma- tor, De- us, Ma- ri- æ de-

- cus   e- le-   i- son.

Chri- ste, De- us de Pa-   tre,   ho- mo na- tus Ma- ri-

a Ma- tre, e- le-   i- son.

O Pa- ra- cli- te ob- umbrans cor- pus Ma- ri-   æ,

Ma- ri-   æ, e- le-   - i- son.

Luys de Villafranca, *Breue instrucion* (1565), fol. 13ᵛ.

Rex, vir- gi- num a- ma- tor De- us

Francisco Guerrero, *Liber primus missarum* (1566), fols. 79ᵛ-80ᵛ.

the measure from its predecessor; and the rhythms at the ends of phrases are quite different at each of the eleven cadences. As would be expected, the cadences themselves are much more varied in their harmonic implications. Whereas Anchieta parsimoniously restricts himself to V-I and IV-I cadences, Guerrero begins (1) with a leading-tone cadence; and then proceeds in this order: (2) phrygian, (3) authentic, (4) authentic, (5) leading-tone, (6) authentic, (7) deceptive, (8) IV-V, (9) leading-tone, (10) half, (11) authentic. Though a categorical comparison of the accidentals that they require cannot be attempted, it is significant that Guerrero inserts a printed sharp before the third note in both tenor (meas. 2) and superius (meas. 4). This sharp, as Villafranca's instructor (1565) reveals, was considered obligatory at Seville when the *Rex virginum* was sung even as a plainchant. (Present evidence would tend to show that the Gregorian repertory never received a richer overlay of accidentals—sharps, especially—than at Seville, *ca.* 1565.)

Guerrero's two Requiems (1566 and 1582) differ pronouncedly in their lengths, the second being extended with the *Libera me* responsory and its versicle which belong to the Burial Service (after Mass).[374] Among the unusual movements chosen in his 1582 Requiem for polyphonic setting is the *Hei mihi Domine* that belongs to the second nocturn of matins in the Office of the Dead.[375] This particular portion of the 1582 *Missa pro defunctis* seems to be the only movement of either Requiem as yet available in modern reprint—Pedrell having elected to include it (all voices being transposed down a fourth) in his *Hispaniae schola musica sacra*, Volume II (pp. 8-12). In contrast with most of the movements in his second Requiem, this noble *Hei mihi* quotes the plainsong prototype in current Roman use only sporadically. At best, only one or two phrases—"Quid faciam miser" in trebles and "ubi fugiam" in tenor—recall the plainsong. Even then they seem to do so more by coincidence than by design. Also by way of distinction, *Hei mihi* calls for six voices: a greater number than any other movement throughout either Requiem (both of which are for the most part scored *a 4*). Lastly, it differs from the generality of his Requiem movements because it is composed in motet style (series of imitative points), rather than as paraphrased chant with accompaniment scored for the three lower voices.

As Morales had done in 1544, Guerrero in both his 1566 and 1582 Requiems consistently alternated short monodic passages with polyphony. The three Agnuses in both 1566 and 1582 Requiems are each, for instance, composed as alternating movements: with the words "Agnus Dei" being sung each time in plainsong. This alternation between monody and polyphony also distinguishes the Libera me responsory appended to the 1582 *Pro defunctis* (Quando caeli movendi, Dum veneris, and the last Libera me are each sung as plainchant; whereas the first Libera me [*a 4*]—as well as the three versicles, Tremens factus [*a 3*], Dies illa [*a 3*], and final Requiem aeternam [*a 4*]—are each set polyphonically).

Guerrero's second Requiem can be shown to have been sung in the New World as late as 1650. In the same decade that his *Liber vesperarum* was in daily use at the Lima Cathedral his second Requiem was being copied into both Choirbook 3 (folios 6[v]-28) and loose partbooks at the Puebla Cathedral in Mexico. For the sentimental reason that it obviously belonged to the "American" repertory in an earlier day, as well as for its intrinsic musical value, a sample from this 1582 Requiem merits reproduction here. The *Dies illa* versicle enjoys a further advantage: it typifies Guerrero's treatment of plainsong in most movements of his Requiems. Crosses above treble notes (accompanying example) indicate those quoted from the plainchant.

Missa pro defunctis (1582)
Dies illa *

Puebla Choirbook 3, fols. 26ᵛ-27.

Francisco Guerrero

*That day is a day of wrath, calamity, and misery: that great and very bitter day.

Still another interesting discovery awaiting the student of Guerrero's masses must be mentioned in connnection with this excerpt. Guerrero is the first peninsular composer who consistently observed Zarlino's ten rules for setting Latin text (broached in *Le istitutioni harmoniche* [quarta parte, cap. 33] of 1558 and repeated in his *Istitutioni harmoniche* of 1573[376]). Lastly, it will be worth noting that Guerrero uses in this example, as elsewhere in his Requiems, a number of ligatures not often encountered in the works of other Spanish composers after 1550—the *cum proprietate et sine perfectione* two-note ligature, and the three-note type beginning as a *ligatura cum opposita proprietate*, for instance.[377]

Motets   Guerrero's best known motet, *Ave Virgo sanctissima* (*a 5*), has already been mentioned several times. Not only did it serve as the source for Géry de Ghersem's 1598 mass but also for Juan Esquivel's 1608 mass (see below, page 290). There can be little doubt that the uninformed estimate that makes of Guerrero a merely mellifluous composer of Marian praises owes something of its origin to the excessive popularity of this one motet—which to judge from Pacheco's praise must have become a veritable Rachmaninoff C♯ minor Prélude shortly before 1600. The words set by Guerrero belong to that of an antiphon sung in sixteenth-century Spain on June 24 (Nativity of John the Baptist) but now no longer retained in Roman usage. The *Ave Virgo sanctissima* plainsong had already been printed in a *Liber processionarius* at Alcalá de Henares as early as 1526, and was therefore no parvenu melody in Guerrero's day.[378] Unlike Juan Navarro, who composed a setting of the same antiphon text, Guerrero chose to adopt only the words and to ignore the traditional melody associated with them: contenting himself instead with a passing allusion at mm. 24-33 to quite another plainsong, the *Salve Regina*. Because of the high order of Navarro's creative gift, a comparison of his *Ave Virgo sanctissima*[379] with Guerrero's should prove instructive.

The plainsong itself is in Mode VIII. Navarro, who treats it in cantus firmus style, is therefore committed to the hypomixolydian; whereas Guerrero chooses Mode I. Navarro assigns the first three plainsong incises to his tenor, the fourth and sixth to cantus, fifth to altus, and seventh (and last) again to tenor. The first few notes of each plainsong incise are heavily weighted with *Pfundnoten*—notes of small value being reserved for the ends of each incise. Guerrero, however, dislikes the knottiness of such long notes in motets, reserving them exclusively for vespers music. In magnificats and hymns he will frequently draw a plainsong strand through his skein, but in motets he prefers to thread every part with free-flowing lines. Navarro introduces five wide leaps within the first half-dozen bars and makes of the octave an expressive interval, using it within words. But Guerrero never leaps upward in either of his trebles a greater distance than a fourth throughout his 74-bar motet; and five of the six octave skips in inner voice parts coincide with punctuation in the text. Navarro's motet demands for its successful execution trebles of crystalline purity who can rise repeatedly to g¹ in the first space above the clef without strain and without a loss of pitch. In spacing his four voices, he occasionally submerges the three lower voices below Middle c while the trebles soar to a distance of an octave and a third, fourth, or even sixth above the nearest voice. Guerrero, who chooses d¹ for his highest treble note, keeps all five voices grouped so compactly that no gap wider than an octave ever separates any two adjacent voices throughout all 74 measures.

Guerrero's motet has been admired for its "sweetness" by every critic who has studied it. If Ornithoparchus—whom John Dowland translated in 1609—had it correctly, then: "Euery Song is so much the *sweeter*, by how much the fuller it is of formall *Closes*."[380] In defining his terms, Ornithoparchus (as translated by Dowland) wrote as follows: "Being that euery Song is graced with formall *Closes*, we will tell what a *Close* is. Wherefore a *Close* is . . . a little part of a Song in whose end is found either rest or perfection. Or it is the coniunction of voices (going diuersely) in perfect *Concords*."[381] If Ornithoparchus and Dowland were right in believing that "sweetness" depends on the frequency of "formall Closes," then Guerrero's *Ave Virgo sanctissima* is indeed "sweeter than the honeycomb." His nineteen V-I cadences, not to speak of his half-dozen leading-tone cadences (VII$^6_3$-I), make a dramatic contrast with Navarro's slim total of six V-I cadences. To solidify the harmonies, Guerrero's bass always participates in the closes; whereas Navarro's frequently drops out just at the moment of resolution: the tenor being left with the duty of singing the lowest note in the resolving chord. Not only does Guerrero cadence frequently, but also in every instance his cadences are so deployed as to further his overall harmonic scheme. For instance, the first five cadences are all authentic—G minor serving as the resolving chord. The next three are leading-tone cadences; and again resolve each time to G minor. Following these, he writes five more V-I cadences (mm. 25-33), each of which still resolves to the G-minor chord. Thus, he confines himself exclusively to G minor as the flowerbed over which to sip his honey during the first 33 bars. Only at meas. 34 does he move into another field. However, having abandoned the old he stays out of it through the whole of the second section (mm. 34-61); never once writing another cadence that resolves into G minor until he reaches meas. 62. The remaining strains (mm. 62-74) serve as a coda. As for the cadences in his second section: these resolve successively to chords of D minor (meas. 36), F Major (meas. 44), B♭ Major (mm. 50-51), and D minor (mm. 55-56). In the "coda" he recapitulates his over-all harmonic scheme by writing in close series three authentic cadences that resolve successively to chords of G minor (mm. 63-64), F Major (meas. 66), and D minor (mm. 69-70). The last four measures conclude with the only plagal cadence in the motet. It is for his *vale* that he saves his linked sweetness, "long drawn out." (D Major serves as the ending chord in the amen cadence.)

In contrast with this ordered scheme, Navarro not only shies away from authentic cadences—writing as few as possible—but surrounds his leading-tone F's with such frequent skips of a fourth or fifth that ficta sharps can only now and then be intruded. If by printing frequent sharps in both the 1566 and 1570 editions of his motet Guerrero showed in which direction his sympathies lay, Navarro, on the other hand, by his voice-leading counter-manded any close approach to modern major or minor syntax. To sum up: Guerrero's setting won later-day sympathies because his *Ave Virgo* is essentially a "G-minor" piece (which happens to end on the "dominant" chord); Navarro's, although it communes in high and holy places, is more removed, more abstracted, and more reticent. Guerrero's exhibits more virtuostic contriving with its canon between the upper two voices. But the leaven of "learning" never causes his sweet dough to turn into sour any more than does, for instance, the equally felicitous canon at the octave in the last movement of Franck's sonata.

Ave Virgo sanctissima seems to have been recognized for its full worth by Guerrero himself from the first moment of publication. Not only did he give it pride of place among the three motets that he elected to include in an appendix to his *Liber primus missarum* but also he twice republished it, first in his 1570 and second in his 1597 motet collection. *Usquequo Domine oblivisceris*[382] and the eight-voice *Pater noster*, the companion motets published with *Ave Virgo sanctissima* in the 1566 *Liber primus missarum*, were also to be repeated in other collections—both recurring in his 1570 collection, and the *Pater noster* having already appeared in his 1555 *Sacrae cantiones* as well. If we go beyond the three motets in the 1566 *Liber*, still further arresting instances of such reprinting await us. To take only the concordances between the 1555 and 1570 collections for an introduction to the problem: *Ambulans Jesus* (a 5), *Dedisti Domine habitaculum* (a 4), *Et post dies sex* (a 5), *Gloriose confessor* (a 4),[383] *Pater noster* (a 8), and *Regina coeli* (a 4) are carried over from one collection into the other. But the four-voice settings of the *Salve Regina* in both 1555 and 1570 collections differ, as do the two four-voice settings of Luke 11:14 entitled *In illo tempore* (1570 adds Luke 11:27b). It goes without saying that the *Ave Maria, Beatus es, Ductus est Jesus,* and *Simile est regnum coelorum* motets found in the two books differ—since in each instance the number of voice parts conflicts. In summary, twelve motets of the same title occur in the 1555 and 1570 collections. Six are duplicates; the other six differ.

The problem of duplicates having been introduced by reference to the 1555 and 1570 imprints, one next asks: Why did Guerrero—and he alone among the principal Spanish composers—reset the same motet texts in so considerable a number of instances? Both Morales and Victoria did, it is true, compose more than one setting of such Marian antiphons as the *Salve Regina*. Victoria composed two settings of the half-verse found at Lamentations 1:12*a*. The first version (1572) is a motet and the second (1585) a responsory. He also composed two settings of the Corpus Christi text *O sacrum convivium*: one *a 6*, the other *a 4*. But these are solitary examples in comparison with Guerrero's many. Would it be correct to infer that with some texts—the *Ave Virgo sanctissima* (1566, 1570, 1597) affording as good an example as any—Guerrero felt that his first try could not be improved upon; but with certain other texts, such as the *O Domine Jesu Christe* (which appears as a four-voice motet in both the 1570 and 1589 collections, the music being different in each instance), he felt dissatisfied with his earlier setting and therefore returned for a second time to the same words?

If any satisfactory answer is to be found, it should be sought through an analysis of two diverse settings: preferably with the same number of voices, of equal length, and in similar contrapuntal style. Furthermore, the text should belong to a specific occasion in the liturgical year rather than being one so general in character as to suit almost any day in the calendar. For such an analysis, the above-mentioned settings of *O Domine Jesu Christe* suggest themselves as a suitable test case. Both the 1570 version and the 1589 call for the same number of voices; both use ₵ for a "time signature"; both are of approximately equal length (65 breves [1570] and 63 [1589]); and both are composed as a series of loose imitative points. Indeed, so conspicuous are the likenesses between the setting that appears at page 19 of the 1570 partbooks headed *Dominica Palmarum*, and the version that appears as number 12 in the 1589 partbooks, that after a superficial glance at the two a critic might declare no artistic problem to be involved. Guerrero, such a critic might say, wrote a second setting of this Palm Sunday motet text—just as some such Romantic composer as Schubert composed two settings of Goethe's *Am Flusse* (1815 and 1822) or even three of Schiller's *Der Jüngling am Bache* (1812, 1815, 1819)—not in the hope of succeeding better the second time, but because he found certain texts particularly congenial. Moreover, to contend that he did succeed better with this text the second time than the first finds no support in any judgment delivered by his contemporaries; for it was the 1570, rather than the 1589, version that was chosen for reprint in *Sacrarum symphoniarum continuatio. Diversorum excellentissimorum authorum* published at Nuremberg by Paul Kaufmann in 1600.

But to proceed with a more detailed examination of the two settings. First: although the text is the same and the over-all length nearly equal, Guerrero emphasizes certain phrases in the one motet as compared with the other. The translated text will clarify this distinction: (1) O Lord Jesus Christ, (2) I adore Thee, (3) wounded on the cross, (4) drinking gall and vinegar. (5) I entreat Thee (6) that Thy wounds be (7) the remedy of my soul. In the 1570 version he allots the following number of measures to these seven successive phrases: $21 + 6 + 7 + 7 + 7 + 3 + 14 = 65$. In the 1589 version his scheme runs as follows: $15 + 7 + 4 + 14 + 6 + 6 + 11 = 63$. The most striking difference in proportion is to be found in his treatment of phrase (4). In the 1570 motet, "drinking gall and vinegar" occupies only half the number of bars allotted this clause in the 1589 version. For a second distinction, only the 1589 motet contains any lengthy melismas; and those are appropriately assigned the word "drinking" (mm. 37-39). For a third difference, the 1570 motet is in Mode IV, the 1589 in Mode I. If in his 1570 motet he is to stay within his mode, he may then use no accidentals other than sharps (G♯, C♯, F♯). His "harmonic" vocabulary cannot go beyond the following chords: E Major and minor, F Major, G Major, A Major and minor, C Major, and D Major and minor—a total of nine. Missing from this group is the major chord built over B. Because of the limitation on accidentals, the all-important chord built over the final of the mode can be approached only by a plagal cadence. The 1589 motet, on the other hand, is cast in Mode I. As a result it becomes at once possible to use flats (B♭, E♭) as well as sharps (C♯, F♯)—the "harmonic" vocabulary being significantly enlarged to include the following twelve chords (several of which are related to each other only remotely): D Major and minor, E minor, E♭ Major, F Major, G Major and minor, A Major and minor, B♭ Major, C Major and minor. More importantly, he can with the accidentals at his disposal "modulate" (transitorily) as far afield as the "keys" of E♭ Major and C minor. Analysis of the 1589 motet discloses that he indeed puts to fullest use all these added "harmonic" possibilities. Best of all, he uses them with unmistakable dramatic intent. Throughout phrases (1) and (2) he specifies only B♭'s, F♯'s, and C♯'s. But suddenly, at the appearance of the word *vulneratum* in phrase (3), he specifies an E♭ chord. During only seven semibreves (his values) he travels at mm. 23–26 through this succession of chords: A Major – D minor – B♭ Major – E♭ Major – C minor – G Major; these chords being used to set the phrase "wounded on the cross." Palestrina when setting the first phrase of his eight-voice *Stabat Mater* conceived no more poignant succession.

Guerrero in 1570 set the words *in cruce vulneratum* with a gently drooping series of first-inversion chords. The words that follow—*felle et aceto*—received scarcely less neutral treatment. No radically new "key"-area was explored when the words "gall and vinegar" were mentioned, nor did any change of pace, of vocal registration, or of contrapuntal manner, stab the listener into awareness. On the contrary, the harmonies continued to revolve closely within the orbit of A minor throughout mm. 28-38, veering off toward D minor only momentarily in meas. 35. When setting the same clauses in his 1589 motet, he explores not only a hitherto unheard key-area, but more particularly that of E♭: this being the area which stands in so-called Neapolitan relationship to the dorian D-minor tonality established during the first 15 bars of the 1589 motet. Having terminated the section setting the words *felle et aceto potatum* at meas. 40 in his 1589 motet, he thereafter excludes E♭-Major and C-minor chords from any further participation, thus proving the Neapolitan effect not to have been introduced haphazardly. In the 1589 version, the progression of the harmonies remains continually interesting, moreover, until the very end. An especially fine touch graces meas. 46, where he transitorily modulates to F Major territory when arriving at the word *te* in the phrase "I entreat *Thee.*"

If our analysis is valid, then Guerrero in his second setting chose these expressive devices in order to stress the words "drinking gall and vinegar": (1) he doubled the number of measures allotted this phrase; (2) he emphasized the word "drinking" with melismas elsewhere absent from either setting; (3) he introduced in the 1589 motet a sudden flatted supertonic at mm. 24-25 and 28-29—this being a harmonic relation that was not yet to have lost its "pathetic" quality when Beethoven came to write the opening page of his Opus 57. The new concern with expressivity in Guerrero's 1589 motets follows, of course, the trend manifest in Marenzio's *Motecta festorum totius anni* (Rome: 1585) and in the publications of lesser madrigalists. Because of his consummate mastery of traditional motet techniques, Guerrero succeeds better than his juniors, however, in infusing passion without breaking the old molds. Just because it is more the spirit than the letter which quickens in his later motets, it would be easy to pass over in silence the 1589 motets in four and five parts as if they were conservative throwbacks,[384] and to consider only his twelve-voice *Duo Seraphim*, his eight-voice hymns, *Te Deum* and *Pange lingua*, his eight-voice antiphon, *Regina coeli*, and eight-voice motet, *Ego flos campi*, as truly progressive specimens. But should our analysis be accepted, such is not the case. What lastly must be observed of his 1589 *O Domine Jesu Christe*, and by implication of certain companion motets in the 1589 set, is its peculiarly Ignatian tendency to dwell on just those physical details of Christ's passion which are physically harrowing. The *Spiritual Exercises* with their emphasis on the tears, the perspiration, and the blood, are counterparted by Guerrero's emphasis in 1589 on the "drinking of the gall and vinegar."

Another aspect of Guerrero's motet style which will repay study is his use of learned devices. Morales introduced formal canons more sparingly in his motets than in his magnificats and masses. Victoria wrote three motets *a 5* in which the two trebles follow each other in a canon at the unison: *Gaude Maria* (1572), *O lux et decus Hispaniae* (1583), and *Resplenduit facies ejus* (1585). In addition, he included a four-in-two canon in his six-voice motet *Trahe me post te* (1583). For the rest, he neglected formal canon in this branch of his repertory. Guerrero, the most distinctively Spanish of the trinity, contrasts sharply with both Morales and Victoria in the frequency with which he introduces formal canon in his motets. Already in his maiden publication at Seville, he begins with eight canonic motets *a 5*. The first is labelled *fuga ad unisonum*, the second *fuga ad secundam*, the third *fuga ad tertiam*, the fourth *fuga ad quartam*, and so forth through the eighth. But—typically Spanish in his treatment of any learned device—he chooses scriptural texts that in each instance express the ideas of following, returning, or sending. The first, *Dixit Dominus Petro*, sets John 21:19*b*-22. To show how apt is the sense of this passage for canonic treatment, it must here be quoted verbatim: "The Lord said unto Peter, 'Follow me.' Turning round, Peter saw following them the disciple whom Jesus loved, the one who, at the supper, had leaned back upon his breast, and said, 'Lord, who is it that will betray thee?' Peter therefore, seeing him, said to Jesus, 'Lord, and what of this man?' Jesus said to him, 'If I wish him to remain until I come, what is it to thee? Do thou follow me.'"

Each of the remaining canonic texts is as aptly chosen to illustrate the mandates of following, returning, sending. In *Ambulans Jesus* (Matthew 4:18-20), Jesus walking beside the sea of Galilee, sees two brothers, Simon Peter and Andrew, and says to them, "Come follow me, and I will make you fishers of men": at once they leave their nets and follow him. In *Trahe me post te* (Song of Songs 1:3a [Vulgate]; 7:6-8), the single verse, "Draw me: we will run after thee," is matched with three others describing the beauties of the mystic spouse. In the fourth motet, *In illo tempore* (John 17:1-3), Jesus prays that the Father will glorify the Son so that he may in turn glorify the Father. In *Dum complerentur* (Acts 2:1-4), the Holy Spirit prompts the apostles to tell the mighty works of God in various tongues. In *Et post dies sex* (Mark 9:1-5), Jesus takes Peter, John, and James up to the Mount of Transfiguration. In *Hoc enim bonum est* (1 Timothy 2:3-7a), God wishes all men to be saved and to come to the knowledge of the truth. In *Simile est coelorum regnum* (pt. 1: Matthew 21:1-2; pt. 2: Matthew 20:3-4), a householder sends laborers into his vineyard.

As if it were insufficient for him to have composed his first canonic motet at the unison, second at the second, third at the third, and so forth; to have chosen none but scriptural texts; and, what is more, to have set only texts that express the mandates of following, returning, sending; Guerrero went even further in such instances as *Ambulans Jesus* and *Et post dies sex* by setting *Ambulans* as a canon at the second because Jesus sees "two" brothers, and *Et post* at the sixth because after "six" days Jesus takes his disciples to a high mountain. True, he cannot always be quite so exact. *Dum complerentur* for Pentecost ("Fiftieth day") is set as a canon at the fifth, and *Trahe me post te* (the Virgin who is mother, daughter, spouse) as a canon at the third. But when an exact number is not mentioned in the text itself, Guerrero's canonic number can be rationalized.

All this planning may seem extremely schematic and even "Gothic" in the opprobrious sense that peninsular scholars such as Pedrell have been wont to give that adjective. These 1555 canonic motets, however, stand at the forefront of Guerrero's one collection of motets published in Spain and dominate his only motet collection dedicated to a Spaniard. At the time of publishing them he had never traveled beyond Andalusia and can have known at first hand only the repertories sung in the Seville, Jaén, and Málaga cathedrals. Pedrell, interestingly enough, published one of these very canonic motets of 1555—*Trahe me post te*. However, neither in his analytical notes nor in his transcription[385] did he betray the fact that Guerrero headed this motet *fuga ad tertiam*. Rather, Pedrell seems to have missed the canon between the two trebles in *Trahe me* just as he had in *Ave Virgo sanctissima*, another motet printed in the same 1894 volume of *Hispaniae schola musica sacra*. And it is just here, of course, that Guerrero's great art that conceals art must be admired. One of the anomalies of Spanish musical criticism has been the categorizing of Guerrero's style as merely tender and graceful when his was so consummate a mastery of counterpoint that Zarlino could call him the "most eminent" musician of their generation. If others attempt such feats as an eight-in-four canon the listener feels a sense of strain. But because Guerrero solves even the hardest problems with the ease of Bach's *Canonische Veränderungen*, he can deceive an unwary editor into believing that he has written simply an expressive piece of music.

Trahe me post te hides its learning, then, so successfully that only the forewarned student is likely to notice the canon at the third. What seizes the listener's attention is not the learned device, but such bold strokes as the sweeping contrapuntal lines during the first 24 breves contrasted with the sudden delicious serenity of the music at mm. 25-38; or, again, the exulting urgency of the ascending passage that leads to the words *palmae* and *palmam* in mm. 39-41 and 53-56; or, further, the extraordinarily suave sonority obtained at mm. 22, 38, 43, 46-49, 55-56, 58-60, and 62-64 by lacing the outer parts in a succession of parallel tenths while inner parts move freely in various types of contrary and oblique motion. As in his music generally, Guerrero accepts every change of sentiment in the text as a signal to vary the rhythmic pattern, "key"-area, or vocal registration. These shifts occur at moments of punctuation in the text, and in *Trahe me post te* result in the following musical divisions: I, mm. 1-9; II, mm. 10-15*a*; III, mm. 15*b*-24; IV, mm. 25-38; V, mm. 39-50; VI, mm. 51-65; VII, mm. 66-77; VIII, 78-87. Any discussion of "key"-area will confuse the student who must rely on the 1894 reprint (Pedrell chose to transpose this motet down a whole tone). Recourse should therefore be had to Eslava's edition (*Lira sacro-hispana*, I, ii, 105-110), where the original pitches are retained. Sections I, III, V, VI, VII cadence to A minor; II, IV, to C Major; and VIII to A Major. Within sections the harmonies remain continually lithesome. At his most expansive climax Guerrero modulates transitorily to G (meas. 44).

When using Eslava's edition, the student should remember that even he was not wholly faithful to the composer. The 1555 partbooks certify that Guerrero did not write consecutive fifths between "altus" and "bassus" at mm. 23*b*-24; nor did he break his canon at meas. 31*b* in "cantus 1"; nor did he skip to and from a dissonance in the "tenor" at meas. 49*a*—of which solecisms in grammar he is accused in Eslava's edition. In the first instance, the semibreve in the bass at meas. 23*b* should have read F rather than D; the notes in meas. 23*a* should have read A (dotted minim) followed by G (crotchet). In the second instance, the cantus should have read e[1] instead of c[1]. In the third, the tenor should have read c (crotchet), B (crotchet), e (minim). Eslava's text-underlay also calls for animadversion —he having made it appear that Guerrero frequently violated Zarlino's rules. The underlay in the original 1555 edition proves that at even so early a date Guerrero did not begin a new syllable after four running crotchets (unreduced values); nor did he intrude new syllables into the middle of a group of running crotchets.

Both Eslava in 1869 and Pedrell in 1894 chose from Guerrero's more than one hundred motets precisely the same two for publication—*Ave Virgo sanctissima* and *Trahe me post te*. Since these both treat of Marian subjects, and since for a known fact *Ave Virgo* did enjoy astounding popularity around 1600, foreign scholars, with no more support than is provided by these nineteenth-century editions and Pacheco's testimony, have concluded that this particular pair of motets must be Guerrero's twin pearls; and that they can justly be taken as representative of his total achievement.[386] The dangers of making any value-judgments based solely on the editions of Eslava and Pedrell become all too apparent when other hitherto unmentioned lapses in these two editions are acknowledged. In the first place, Pedrell slavishly followed Eslava's errors of transcription—in *Trahe me post te*, for example. Pedrell did, it is true, transpose both *Ave Virgo* and *Trahe me*. He also added expression marks. Although these editorial labors do change somewhat the appearance of the music, they cannot be used to prove that he consulted original sources. In the second place, *Ave Virgo* and *Trahe me* are not representative of Guerrero's entire motet repertory, since they are both canonic. For a third objection, neither *Ave Virgo* nor *Trahe me* is in two *partes*. On the other hand, not only are two of the canonic motets in the 1555 collection—*Simile est regnum* and the eight-voice *Pater noster*—each divided into two *partes;* but, more importantly, eleven of the twenty-three non-canonic motets in this collection are in two *partes*. (The Salve is in three.) As for the 1570 collection: twenty-two out of a total of thirty-nine[387] are in two *partes*. (The Salve is again in three, but differs from the 1555 setting because of the alternate-verse treatment found in the 1570 setting.) For a fourth objection, *Ave Virgo* and *Trahe me* are not representative: in that they are the only Marian canonic motets in either the 1555 or 1570 collections. Of a total of thirty-two canonic and non-canonic motets in the 1555 collection, eight treat of Marian subjects; of a total of thirty-nine in the 1570, ten treat of Marian subjects. In making these counts, any text that mentions the Blessed Virgin, even such a one as *Elizabeth Zachariae*, is included. *Surge propera* is also counted, since traditional exegesis applies its Song of Songs text to Mary. Without for a moment questioning Guerrero's devotion, it still seems an exaggeration to distinguish him from Morales and Victoria (or even from Palestrina) with some such sobriquet as *el cantor de María*, when in sober reality three-fourths of his motets are devoted to quite other sacred subjects.

Although Pedrell in 1894 contented himself with merely duplicating Eslava's limited choices of a quarter-century earlier, he did unwittingly add one new item to the sum of Guerrero's motets now to be found in modern reprint when in 1902 he published the first volume of Victoria's *Opera omina*. In his 1585 *Motecta Festorum Totius anni*, Victoria had extended hospitality to two six-voice motets by Guerrero—*Pastores loquebantur* (folios 7ᵛ-10) and *Beata Dei genetrix* (folios 36ᵛ-40). Both these were plainly labeled as Francisco Guerrero's at recto leaves in Victoria's sumptuous Roman folio. The first, a Christmas motet (*In eodem festo natalis Domini*), comprises a single *pars*. The second, for September 8 (*In nativitate Beatae Mariae*), continues with a second *pars*—*Ora pro populo*. By an oversight, Pedrell caught Guerrero's name at the top of folios 37-40, but missed it at the top of folios 8-10. In consequence, he published Guerrero's *Pastores loquebantur* as Victoria's (*Opera omnia*, I, 142-146). Though misattributed, this motet does at least enjoy the distinction of having been transcribed accurately (so far as notes are concerned) from an original sixteenth-century source, rather than from a secondary nineteenth-century source.

Guerrero himself reprinted this motet in his 1589 *Liber secundus*. In addition, it survives in Cappella Sistina MS 29. In the Vatican copy, *Pastores loquebantur* continues, however, with a second *pars*—*Videntes autem*. It is perhaps not this knowledge alone which causes the listener to feel a certain sense of incompleteness in the single *pars* chosen by Victoria. Even so, a study of this *pars* in the Pedrell transcription should temper the notion that Guerrero reached his apogee only when treating languid or sentimental texts. Here he gives us instead a brilliant and forthrightly jubilant setting of Luke 2:15*b*-16. The vocal scoring calls for CCATBB—the two trebles constantly crossing each other as do also the two "bearded shepherd" basses. The top melody that one hears, and also the lowest bass line, cannot therefore be read out of any single voice part. Instead, the sounding lowest and top lines are both synthetic. When he arrives at the word *festinantes* ("rejoicing") the pace quickens into a paroxysm of crotchets—Guerrero's energies here for the first time in the motet bursting forth in a series of sharply accented syncopations (mm. 43-46). But immediately upon reaching the word *invenerunt* ("they found"), he suddenly broadens out into spacious breves and semibreves. As so frequently occurs in his other motets, he holds his most striking chordal sequence in reserve for the climactic clause in the motet text. In *Pastores loquebantur*, he reaches his climax when the shepherds who have hastened from the hillside to the stable find Mary and Joseph and the Christ-child. Up to this moment the cadences have succeeded each other in this order: (1) authentic to G Major, meas. 15; (2) authentic to D minor, meas. 19; (3) complete to C Major, mm. 24-25; (4) authentic to C Major, meas. 42. When the pace slackens suddenly at *invenerunt* he veers into a new chordal area and at meas. 53 for the first time makes an authentic cadence to A Major. His precise intent can by no means be doubted; the 1585 imprint specifies both G♯'s and C♯'s at mm. 53-54. During the phrase "infant lying in a manger" he writes this succession of chords: A Major, D Major, G Major, C Major, F Major, G Major, A Major (mm. 54-57). During mm. 58-61 he repeats the same progression, except that he substitutes the D-minor chord for the penultimate G-Major. Since this particular group of measures, 54-61, marks his only use of any such colorful harmonic progression, Guerrero's dramatic intent shines through with unusual clarity. In the last dozen bars (which set the word *Alleluia*) he rings changes on I, IV, and V chords in what may anachronistically be called the key of C Major: with a half cadence to close the *pars* (the final chord is built over G).

As if Pedrell's 1902 reprint were insufficient, still another motet was reprinted with a misattribution in the Elústiza-Castrillo Hernández *Antología musical* (Barcelona: 1933). By an oversight the first of Francisco Guerrero's two motets in this volume was at page 86 attributed to his brother Pedro Guerrero. The Valladolid codex from which the transcription was made does, however, correctly attribute *Gloriose confessor Domini* to Francisco. That the younger brother was indeed the composer can under no circumstances be doubted; both the 1555 and 1570 imprints (Seville and Venice) include it at folios 8ᵛ-9 and pages 22-23 respectively. In the imprints, this motet continues with a second *pars* not to be found in the Elústiza-Castrillo Hernández 1933 transcription. The omission of second *pars* and even the misattribution are inconsequential, however, when compared with the bad luck in transcribing the notes. As early as meas. 6, the cantus in the transcription has a semibreve on the third beat ($\frac{4}{2}$ time signature); whereas both manuscript and prints call for only a minim. As a result, the cantus during mm. 7-8 lags a minim behind the three lower parts. At mm. 19-20 the tenor goes wildly astray. Guerrero's intentions are further traduced in this 1933 edition by the omission of numerous obligatory accidentals. True, the "key-signature" of one flat is correctly shown. On the other hand, the six obligatory sharps (= naturals) before B's and an E which are to be found in the 1570 printed edition are all omitted from the 1933 transcription of the motet.

Like thirty-one of the thirty-nine motets published in the 1570 collection, *Gloriose confessor Domini* is assigned by Guerrero to a specific day in the calendar—in this instance, August 4 (Feast of St. Dominic). The other three nonscriptural saints for whose feasts he provides specific motets in the same collection are: Jerome (*Quasi stella*), Sebastian (*Beatus es*), and Clement (*Dedisti Domine habitaculum*; 2nd *pars*, *Vidit supra montem*). He groups these saints' motets between his Easter (*Regina coeli laetare*) and his Common of One Martyr motets (*Iste sanctus*). Guerrero's over-all plan for the 1570 collection calls for an introductory motet, then eleven covering the year from Advent to Easter; next, four honoring nonscriptural saints,[388] then five for various commons. A sheaf of miscellaneous motets for Rogation Day, November 30, August 6, June 24, and other more general occasions brings the collection to a close. Unlike his masses, the motets in the 1570, 1589, and 1597 collections always begin with those *a 4*, proceeding thence to those *a 5* and *a 6* (*a 8* and *a 12* in 1589 and 1597).

As a rule, his motets of two *partes* do not adhere to an aBcB pattern. Among the twenty-two of two *partes* in the 1570 collection only two (*Canite tuba* and *Dedisti Domine*) are in responsory form. He sets duple signatures at the head of every motet in both the 1555 and 1570 collections, but does occasionally lapse into triple meter in mid-course: as, for instance, during second *partes* of *Hic vir despiciens*, *Prudentes virgines*, and *Virgo divina* (1570, pp. 35, 37, 45). In each instance, the change of meter coincides with a changed viewpoint in the text. To illustrate: the words *media autem nocte* (p. 37), and they alone, are set in triple meter during *Prudentes virgines*. Only black notes are used in this triple-meter passage. Obviously they signalize the darkness of midnight (*media nocte*) when the Bridegroom's approach is announced to the waiting wise and foolish virgins. In four of the 1570 motets—*O Domine Jesu Christe*, *Dedisti Domine*, *Ambulans Jesus*, and *Usquequo Domine*—Guerrero heads the motet with C (instead of the usual ₵). In each instance C implies a slower pace than ₵.

Throughout the 1570 set, two flats appear in the "key" signature of only *Clamabat autem mulier Cananea*. The 38 other motets carry no signature, or call for the single flat. Twenty of the 32 motets in the 1555 collection have a signature of one flat. The remaining 12 lack any accidental in the signature. Of the 20 with B♭, 15 end on G and 5 on F. Of the dozen without accidental, 4 end on G, 3 each on A and E, and 1 each on D and C. Among the 13 motets of two *partes* in the 1555 collection, the first and second *partes* usually conclude with chords built over the same final (nine motets); occasionally with authentically related chords (three); and only once with plagally related chords. The final cadence at the end of any *pars* always involves a V-I or IV-I progression in the 1555 collection, except in *Virgo prudentissima*. In two of the fourth-tone motets, *Beatus Achacius* and *In illo tempore*, the bassus several times touch E_1, a lower note than any in Morales's motets. Only one of Guerrero's 1555 motets confides a constantly reiterated ostinato to a single part, namely, no. 11, *Veni Domine et noli tardare* (*a 5*). In this Advent motet, superius II sings no other text than the words found in the title. Guerrero repeats the ostinato four times; and inserts rests of three breves between each repetition. Morales in his motet *a 6* of like title (published at Venice in 1549 and at Nuremberg in 1554) assigned a similar ostinato to a tenor voice (which, however, descends a step in pitch at each of its five successive recurrences in each *pars* of the motet). Both the responsory (aBcB) and the ostinato motet loom so large in Morales's repertory that Guerrero's reluctance to write these two types makes a strong contrast.

Only a few accidentals are to be seen in the 1555 Sevillian edition of Guerrero's motets. Fuenllana's 1554 intabulation of the opening *Pater noster* (*a 4*) discloses, however, that sharped leading-tones were invariably added at cadences; and frequently within phrases. Guerrero himself specified numerous sharps in later editions of those 1555 motets that he chose to reprint at Venice in 1570 and 1589. *Ambulans Jesus* in the 1555 print (folios 18ᵛ-19), for example, shows no sharps. The 1570 reprint (p. 41) specifies five sharps in cantus and tenor. *Et post dies sex* shows none in the 1555 (folios 22ᵛ-23). Two sharps are to be found in the cantus of the 1570 (pp. 42-43). In Victoria's 1585 *Motecta*, Guerrero's six-voice *Beata Dei genetrix* (folios 36ᵛ-40) contains no less than twenty-six flats and sharps.

Canciones y villanescas espirituales (1589)

If Guerrero's masses, magnificats, and motets merely equal but do not surpass Morales's and Victoria's in quality and substance, his 61 Spanish songs (33 *a 5*, 20 *a 4*, and 8 *a 3*) published at Venice in 1589 demonstrate, on the other hand, his superiority to all other sixteenth-century peninsular composers when the setting of vernacular poetry is the task in hand.

The title itself is unique. *Canciones*, of course, means "songs" in the generic sense. But *villanesca* was a term that had made its first peninsular appearances in the vihuela tablatures of Pisador (Salamanca: 1552) and Fuenllana (Seville: 1554).[389] In these imprints the term had been applied exclusively to examples of Italian origin. Pisador had intabulated ten *canzoni villanesche* by Vincenzo Fontana and Willaert; Fuenllana had intabulated three—one each by Giovane Domenico da Nola, Fontana, and a hitherto unidentified composer. Since it is to be presumed that Guerrero knew at least the Nola and Fontana examples in Fuenllana's tablature, he cannot have failed to observe the musical characteristics of this light and frolicsome Italian type. True, Nola and Fontana had disagreed on the question of writing consecutive fifths (only Nola gave way to this license). On the other hand, both had agreed to set their texts (always with refrain) syllabically, to eschew imitation, to embrace a chordal style (usually *a 3*) throughout, and to choose light, patter-like rhythms. However, by the time that Esteban Daza published his *El Parnasso* (Valladolid: 1576), the term had lost its vogue in Italy—where *villanella* replaced it after 1570—and had become domesticated in Spain to mean a thoroughly madrigalian Spanish song: preferably *a 4*. Eight part songs—three by Rodrigo Ceballos, two each by Francisco Guerrero and Juan Navarro, and one by an anonymous composer—were intabulated in Daza's 1576 imprint under the heading of villanescas.[390] In place of Nola's deliberate *gaucheries* of part writing, Daza's examples show closely worked imitation alternating with finely wrought homophonic passages. Not only is the subject always amatory but the treatment is always serious: mere banter being forgone. Further to distinguish the lyrics, the verse includes no burdens. Just as it is obvious that the term had been domesticated by 1576, so also it is immediately apparent to anyone who studies Guerrero's *Canciones y villanescas espirituales* that in 1589 he understood the term wholly in the Spanish sense that Daza gave "villanesca" —even if he did publish his collection at Venice.

Early lexicographers frequently knew so little about music as to lead dictionary-users astray when technical terms are at stake. But still further to prove that the term *villanesca* had lost all its Italian associations before 1600, the definitions in both Covarruvias's *Tesoro de la lengua castellana* (Madrid: 1611) and John Minsheu's *A most copious Spanish dictionarie* (London: 1617) may be cited. Covarruvias writes: "Villanescas are those songs which country folk are wont to sing when at leisure. But courtiers, changing them for the better, have composed happy little songs in the same mode and measure. Villancicos, so well known at Christmas and Corpus Christi, have the same origin." John Minsheu writes: "Villanescas. *Cantiones quas canunt rustici*. A Carol or Countrie Song." Villancico is Minsheu's next term. He defines it with the one word: *Idem*. Richard Perceval in his

Bibliotheca hispanica (London: John Jackson, 1591) defined villancico as "a sonet"—which is probably as near an equivalent as one is likely to find, if "sonet" be taken in the loose sense that Byrd had given it when three years previous to the issue of Perceval's dictionary he had published his *Psalmes, Sonets, and songs of sadnes and pietie* (London: 1588).

Guerrero went on to qualify his 1589 songs as "espirituales." According to Mosquera de Figueroa, writer of the 1589 prologue,[391] the verse of Guerrero's canciones had many times been originally secular. Where the lyrics had been amatory, changes were necessary to fit the songs for sacred use. That such textual revisions were made in at least ten songs would be known even if Mosquera de Figueroa had not forewarned us. At the Medinaceli library (Madrid) in MS 13230 the music belonging to items 34, 36, 38, 40, 42, and 54 of *Canciones y villanescas espirituales* recurs with secular texts. In their original amatory guise they have been printed in the modern edition of the *Cancionero musical de la Casa de Medinaceli* at nos. 1, 79, 92, 44, 90, and 59 (*MME*, VIII and IX). Still another concordance is to be seen between item 45, *Huyd huyd*, of *Canciones y villanescas espirituales* and no. 70 in the modern edition of the Medinaceli songbook. In this one song, however, it was not necessary to change the words—they having been moralistic to begin with. At the Museo Lázaro Galdiano (Madrid) a single soprano manuscript partbook inventoried as item 15411 shows at folio 15ᵛ a secular song, *Acaba de matarme*, which in *Canciones y villanescas espirituales* is printed with revised text as item 41. At Valladolid Cathedral an alto partbook (MS 255) contains at folios 17, 18, 18ᵛ, 21, 106ᵛ, 107ᵛ, and 108ᵛ songs entitled respectively: *Divina ninfa mía*, *Prado verde y florido*, *Dexó la venda*, *Vana esperança*, *Claros y hermosos ojos*, *Baxásteme señora*, and *Mi ofensa es grande*. These reappear in *Canciones y villanescas espirituales* with revised texts (except *Vana esperança*, which is textless at Valladolid, and *Mi ofensa*, the lyrics of which required no changing) as items 42, 40, 36, 44, 2, 3, and 11. Lastly, *Adios verde ribera* (item 37 in Guerrero's 1589 imprint) had been intabulated for solo voice and vihuela (with secular text) in Daza's *El Parnasso* of 1576. Thus disregarding *Mi ofensa es grande* and *Huyd huyd* (items 11 and 45 in the 1589 imprint) because the original texts were of sufficiently moralistic nature not to require revision, and eliminating duplicates, we discover a total of ten purely secular songs in Spanish sources which were in 1589 printed as sacred songs in *Canciones y villanescas espirituales*.

In one of these ten songs such drastic textual changes were made that Guerrero had to revise the music as well. The secular lyrics of *Ojos claros, serenos* were by Gutierre de Cetina (1520-1557), a Sevillian who travelled first to Italy (where he translated Petrarch to perfection) and later to Mexico.[392] The poet asks his lady why she turns her "clear and serene eyes" upon him with such fury that he is consumed in rabid torments. He wishes her nonetheless to continue at least glancing at him. First published in Fuenllana's *Orphénica lyra* of 1554 with secular text, Guerrero's music had to be revised considerably before the sacred version could be printed in 1589: the reason being that the "clear and serene eyes" become those of Christ which Peter offended by his thrice-repeated denial. In the sacred version, the penitent beseeches Christ to cast a pitying glance of forgiveness upon him even as Peter was once forgiven: "for I too bitterly weep . . . and, besides, You died for me." The words "I weep" occur at the same juncture in the sacred version as "Alas, Alas, what rabid torments" in the secular; and the words "and besides, You died for me" at the same juncture as "and even though you [angrily] behold me." In the rest of the 1589 rewrites, no such drastic change of sentiment was involved; and therefore identical music could be used for sacred and secular versions. Item 4 in the 1589 imprint sets a sonnet by Garcilaso de la Vega (1501-1536), *En tanto que de rosa y azucena*, of which only two lines have been changed. Item 5 sets a 15-line madrigal by the Sevillian poet Baltasar de Alcázar (1530–1606). Among seventy-six words only fourteen have been changed. In one instance he selected an entirely new poem to replace the secular original. At item 54, Lope de Vega's *Si tus penas no pruebo* replaces *Tu dorado cabello*.[393] Here, the over-all mood does not change. In consequence, Guerrero feels himself under no obligation to recast the original music—the changes being limited to slight rhythmic adjustments at mm. 10-11, 28, and 39 which in no wise affect pitches; and the addition of certain accidentals. In the Medinaceli songbook, *Tu dorado cabello* was copied with a mixed signature—two flats prefixing the tenor part while single flats prefixed each of the two upper parts. In *Si tus penas*, on the other hand, all three voices carry the single flat: printed e♭'s being added where required in the tenor voice (mm. 3 and 14). Printed f♯'s are shown at mm. 1, 4, 9, 12, and a printed b♯ (= b♮) at meas. 20. But in the Medinaceli manuscript no sharps were inserted anywhere in *Tu dorado cabello*. Summarizing: the printed versions differ from the secular originals (1) because of certain slight rhythmic adjustments made in order to improve the declamation of the sacred verse, and (2) because a copious supply of sharps has been added. They do not differ significantly from the secular originals so far as pitches or note values are concerned—except in *Ojos claros, serenos*.

In his prologue to *Canciones y villanescas espirituales*, Mosquera de Figueroa not only tells us of the number originally composed to secular texts; he says, also, that Guerrero wrote the 1589 songs at the beginning of his career. So far as *Ojos claros, serenos* is concerned this statement can be corroborated from the fact that Fuenllana published an intabulated version of the secular original as early as 1554. The secular song can hardly have been composed, therefore, much later than 1550; in which year Guerrero was only twenty-two years of age. As for the other songs, no equally objective proof can be brought forward. But what should be of interest, if the majority were indeed composed before 1555, is the immediate contemporaneity of the poems he set. In 1550 neither Gutierre de Cetina (item 34) nor Gregorio de Silvestre (item 10) can have been over thirty; nor can Baltasar de Alcázar (items 5 and 36) have been over twenty. Guerrero's secular poets, with the exception of Garcilaso de la Vega (d. 1536), would therefore have been yeasty Andalusian personalities who had not yet broken into print when he set their verse. Or at least this would be so if Mosquera de Figueroa was correctly informed when he declared at the end of his prologue that *Canciones y villanescas espirituales*, although the most recently published of Guerrero's collections, contained his earliest compositions.

As for the forms in which verse and music are cast, Guerrero divides the contents of the 1589 imprint into a first bloc of songs *a 5*, a second bloc *a 4*, and a third *a 3*; he also divides each of the three blocs into (1) songs without initial refrain and (2) songs with initial refrain. Type 1 songs are through-composed, even when the poetic original comprises several strophes. If the poem is long (items 9, 10 and 39, for instance), he may articulate his setting in two *partes*. Not only do Type 1 songs lack opening refrains, but also repeated passages of any kind are rare. Exceptions to this rule are found in items 38 (*Esclarecida madre = Esclarecida Juana*) and 54 (*Si tus penas = Tu dorado cabello*). In item 38, the last 16 bars are repeated; in item 54, the first 13. Type 2 songs are all *da capo* or *dal segno* villancicos. In the majority, the coplas—like the trios of classic minuets—reduce parts. In the 20 five-part villancicos, for instance (items 13, 15-33), 8 reduce to three parts (items 15, 19, 21, 27, 29, 30, 31, 33); 5 reduce to solo voice (items 16, 18, 25, 26, 28); and 2 to four parts (items 22, 24). The rhyme-scheme of the coplas usually has nothing to do with that of the estribillo. Only in items 18, 19, 23, and 30 of the five-part villancicos, for instance, does the rhyme spill over into that of the da capo section. It does not spill over in any of the three-part villancicos (items 58-61).

The order in which Type 1 songs are arranged, at least insofar as the five-part examples are concerned, seems quite logical. Those seven with B♭ in their signatures come first. The next five lack signatures. The first seven are all susceptible of classification as major or minor in the modern sense. The next four can be classified as phrygian, or phrygian transposed up a fourth. The last is a mixolydian example. The two "major" examples (items 4 and 5) mention such delights as roses, lilies, a clear fountain, a green walk, larks, and nightingales. The phrygian, or transposed phrygian, examples begin with one in which the poet implores Fortune not to plunge him into an abyss by turning her wheel (item 8); continue with one in which the poet execrates Death for his theft of a promising youth (item 9);

another in which the poet passionately cries that he cannot love God (item 10). In the next (item 11) the poet confesses an enormous sin. It can hardly be doubted that Guerrero, who turns even a time signature to expressive account, intended to catch the flavor of bitter dregs with the phrygian mode. In the villancicos (Type 2 songs), on the other hand, he rejoices perpetually. Therefore he never uses an E-mode in the twenty Type 2 five-part items. He casts his Type 2 songs in the F-mode with B♭ in the signature eight times (items 17, 21-26, 31-32); in the C-mode four times (items 13, 19, 28, 29); and in D-modes (♮ or ♭), G-modes (♮ or ♭), and A-mode (♮) the remaining eight times (15, 24; 18; 16; 27, 23; 20, 30).

That Guerrero was indeed self-conscious in his choice of modes could be inferred from the texts associated with each. But, in addition, Mosquera de Figueroa in his prologue explicitly affirms as much:

There are some who use Tone IV (which is suited for laments), saying that it assuages equally the sorrow of those who by nature are merry and bustling, and of those who by nature are sluggish and retarded; of those whose disposition is gross and of those whose disposition is attenuated. The composer of this collection eschews this particular mode because he himself is on the whole of a cheerful and mild disposition, and tends to pursue moderation in all things. There is another mode called the phrygian [Mode III] which distracts and harasses the mind. The ancients abhorred it. Porphyry called it barbaric because it so easily provokes fighting instincts and a bestial fury. Others have characterized it as bacchic, frantic, headlong, perturbed. . . . This also is a mode not favored by the composer of the present collection—whose style tends to be quieter and more self-controlled, although he always rises to sublime artistic heights. As is at once apparent, our composer himself prefers the ionian mode (which some have characterized as florid, brilliant, and pleasing), and the dorian (which is a more profound, chaste, and controlled mode).

If by ionian we understand the C-mode or the F with flat; and if by the dorian we mean the D-modes or the G with flat; then Mosquera's remarks on Guerrero's modal preferences in *Canciones y villanescas* are not only apt but also illuminating. With the self-consciousness of a painter choosing his colors, Guerrero chose his modes to express different emotions.

Just as he selects his modes with an expressive goal in mind, so also he freely "modulates" to strengthen the emotional impact of the lyrics. When temporal blessings cause the poet's spiritual damnation and God's day-by-day favors make him hard and stiff-necked, Guerrero responds by modulating through the following chords at "favor, punishment" (*Baxóme mi descuydo*, mm. 32-33): A Major – D minor – C minor; at "gracious, hard" (mm. 36-39) he writes the following chordal succession: F Major – A minor – G Major – C minor – G Major – F Major – A minor. When, in another song, the poet pauses after asking the rhetorical question, "Where is now that happy time when I pressed smooth and delicate flowers and drank cool water?" to complain, "A cruel grief and bitter hour has intervened," Guerrero changes mood not only with a pause followed by slow chords for the beginning of the reply, but also with these harmonies for the words ". . . cool water? There intervened a cruel grief . . ." (*Dezidme fuente clara*, mm. 60-63): G Major – C Major – F Major – E♭ Major – G minor – [B♭ Major]. When the poet turned metaphysician in *Pluguiera a Dios* admits the excellency of God but immediately confesses that he loves Him not and is instead a great sinner, Guerrero seizes upon the words "I am a great sinner" to write this astonishing succession of chords (mm. 50-59): A minor – D Major – G Major – C Major – A minor – B Major – E Major – A Major – F♯ minor (first inversion) – B minor – G Major (first inversion) – C Major – B Major – E Major – A Major (first inversion) – D Major – D minor – E Major – F Major – D minor – E Major – A major – F Major – [D minor]. That Guerrero went to extravagant harmonic lengths in this last passage would be known even without analyzing the chords. In this passage, Guerrero not only pits f♯ against f♮ (meas. 57) and calls for c♯ followed by c♮ in the same voice (meas. 59) but even dares to specify printed d♯'s[394]—the most "inharmonious" of all accidentals—in the inner voices (mm. 53, 55). This bold succession is but one of several such passages in *Pluguiera a Dios*. For instance, at the words "my very great guilt" (mm. 61–62) he writes an F♯ minor – G Major – F Major sequence.

To summarize: (1) Guerrero picked his modes with expressive intent, just as Mosquera de Figueroa forewarned in his prologue; (2) he freely modulates within the entire range of what would now be called "related keys"; (3) secondary dominants are his escalators from key to key; (4) even more remote "modulations" sometimes occur—these more violent wrenches in the harmonies invariably illustrating a changed viewpoint in the text. His poets shift their sentiments frequently in Type I songs, but much less often in Type II; corollarily, Type I *canciones* contain the boldest harmonic experiments. Both types abound in false relations. On principal beats in both types he frequently writes unprepared augmented-sixth chords (d–f♯–b♭; E–G♯–c). He also proves in *Canciones y villanescas espirituales* to have been one of the earliest composers who specified in print, and with clear harmonic intent, an Italian-sixth chord (e♭–g–c^1♯: *Pues la guía d'una estrella* [item 27], meas. 13).

Guerrero's other ways of adumbrating text are less exceptional but still of sufficient interest to be worth enumerating. When the poet asks to be humbled (*Baxóme mi descuydo*, mm. 1-3), a descending scale-figure passes imitatively through each of the five voices at the word "abase." Later in the same song Guerrero word-paints *cumbre* (= crest) with a leap of an octave in the bass to d, and in the top voice to a high g^1. When the poet beseeches Fortune "not to cast me down into the depths with your wheel" (*O dulçe y gran contento*, mm. 31-35), the several parts—and especially the conspicuous outer parts—plummet scalewise downward tenths, or less. Still other types of word-painting can be listed. To objectify such abstract ideas as "happiness, glory, heaven" (*A un niño llorando*, mm. 35-42, for instance, he calls for brisk syncopation in the fastest triple meter possible, C 3.

All the villancicos (Type II songs) teem with pert, frisky rhythmic figures. Triple meter, absent from Type I songs, is frequently to be found in Type II. The entire villancico may be set in C3 (items 15, 20, 25, 26, 27, 28, 30, 31), or in ₵3 (items 17, 23). Shifts back and forth into triple meter may enliven the villancico in mid-course (items 19, 21, 24). Certainly, the C3 songs never suggest a tempo of less than presto; nor the ₵3 of less than allegro. The sharp and frequently displaced accents heard in the triple-meter songs later were to become the stock-in-trade of every Spanish baroque composer of villancicos. As far away as Peru and Mexico, Juan de Araujo (*ca.* 1646-1714) and Antonio de Salazar (fl. 1690) were still imitating Guerrero's triple-meter mannerisms at the turn of the century. Another tag that later composers imitated to excess was the "hark-hark" beginning. One voice starts with a "hear, hear" figure which the others take up imitatively (items 13, 16, 19, 22). In still other ways Guerrero's technique of villancico composition obtained so widespread and long-continuing a hold on Spanish successors that even today his villancicos are often called the most typical pieces in his entire repertory—perhaps because echoes of them are still heard at Christmas and Epiphany in Spanish cathedrals.

Although Guerrero's villancico style can be proved to have become essentially popular, he forbears using folk melodies. Even when for a stretch someone sings a solo in his Type II songs, the melodies seem to have been composed for the occasion. *Cantus firmi* are not employed, nor are plainsongs quoted. Unlike the majority of villancicos composed in the century to follow, Guerrero's never divide neatly into four-bar phrases, nor do they cadence at regular intervals. Only rarely does he call for repeats within either the estribillo or the coplas. Where by way of exception he does condescend to repeat within the estribillo, as in *Hombres, victoria* (item 22), he disguises the repetition rather cleverly. In this one song, mm. 10_3-15 equal 21-26. But the two top voices interchange their parts at the repeat. Also, he switches beats: notes taking a principal stress in mm. 10_3-15 come on a secondary stress in mm. 21-16. This same technique of switching stresses can be studied in an even better-known item, *Si tus penas no pruebo*, at mm. 20_4-30 and 30_2-42. During the repeat, the principal and secondary stresses are reversed, just as in *Hombres, victoria*.

Juan Vásquez—who among Guerrero's contemporaries most nearly approaches him when the Spanish language is being set—as early as 1560 acknowledged that "Francisco Guerrero has so penetrated the secret, and has so demonstrated how to vivify the meaning of a text" that he stands as the climax of the age. Mosquera de Figueroa praised Guerrero in still more glowing terms when he called him the foremost of his epoch in knowing how to identify the rhythm of music with that of poetry, the emotional connotations of music with the sense of the lyrics: no one else knows so well how to devise musicial figures that with true-to-life fidelity proclaim the inner meaning of the text, said Mosquera. As means of doing all this, Mosquera cited Guerrero's opposition of "swiftness to slowness, harshness to softness, sweetness to bitterness, wrangling to repose."

The *Canciones y villanescas espirituales*, even if originally wedded to secular lyrics, exemplify in sure ways the Spanish religious temperament. No foreign sixteenth-century composer of Latin church music who turned aside to write vernacular sacred music approaches him in the vividness and life-likeness of his settings. Their earnestness and intensity befit the religious temper of a land where every truly popular poem was always changed sooner or later *a lo divino*. The tradition reached at least as far back as Alfonso X, who could not rest content until he had poured all the ardor and zeal of an earthly love into a heavenly love.

NOTES TO SECTION II, PART 1

1 J. B. Trend, "Catalogue of the music in the Biblioteca Medinaceli, Madrid," *Revue hispanique*, LXXI, 160 (Dec., 1927), 492-493. Corrections and additions in *Cancionero musical de la Casa de Medinaceli*, I, ed. by Miguel Querol Gavaldá (*MME*, VIII [Barcelona: Instituto Español de Musicología, 1949]), pp. 27-28.

2 R. Stevenson, "Music research in Spanish libraries," *Notes of the Music Library Association*, 2d ser., X, i (Dec., 1952), 54.

3 Miguel de Fuenllana, *Libro de musica para vihuela, intitulado Orphenica lyra* (Seville: Martín de Montesdoca, 1554), fols. 143-144 and 144-145 (*Ojos claros* and *Torna Mingo*).

4 Esteban Daza, *Libro de musica en cifras para Vihuela, intitulado el Parnasso* (Valladolid: Diego Fernández de Córdova, 1576), fols. 83-84, 87ᵛ-88ᵛ, 89-90ᵛ (*Prado verde*, *Adios verde ribera*, and *Esclarecida Juana* [the last-named work attributed erroneously by Daza to Villalar]).

5 For bibliographical details see F. Lesure and G. Thibault, "Bibliographie des éditions musicales publiées par Nicolas du Chemin," *Annales musicologiques*, I (1953), 334.

6 See Samuel Rubio, "El archivo de música de la Catedral de Plasencia," *AM*, V (1950), 163-164.

7 H. Anglés, "La música conservada en la Biblioteca Colombina y en la Catedral de Sevilla," *AM*, II (1947), 23 (item 80). Corrections must be made, however. Only one motet *a 12* is to be found in the 1597 *Motecta*: Namely, *Duo Seraphim*. Anglés makes no mention of the *Missa Seculorum Amen, a 4;* nor of the four hymns *Te Deum laudamus*, *Ave maris stella*, *Veni Creator*, and *Pange lingua;* nor of the *Magnificat Primi toni* (even verses); which succeed the motets in this 1597 publication.

8 The number of Victoria's masses printed in the *Opera omnia* and accepted as his total output in *Grove's Dictionary* (5th ed.; 1954), Vol. VIII, p. 773, will have to be reduced if we accept R. Casimiri's conclusions in his "Una 'Missa Dominicalis' falsamente attribuita a Tommaso Ludovico de Victoria," *Note d'archivio*, X, 3 (July-Sept., 1933), 185-188.

9 Rubio, *op. cit.*, p. 166.

10 Anglés, *op. cit.*, p. 33 (item 3). Otto Kade in *Die ältere Passionskomposition bis zum Jahre 1631* (Gütersloh: C. Bertelsmann, 1893), pp. 153-157, printed excerpts from Guerrero's Passions according to SS. Matthew and John, using as source Eslava's *Lira sacro-hispana*, I, ii, 77-89 and 90-98. Unfortunately Kade left the impression that Guerrero composed only these two passions; whereas he composed four.

11 Bibliography (subject to numerous corrections) in *Hispaniae schola musica sacra*, ed. by Felipe Pedrell, II, xxix-xlv [Hereafter cited as *HSMS*].

12 *MME*, Vol. XVI, reprints the *Canciones y villanescas espirituales* a 5.

13 Juan B. de Elústiza, *Estudios musicales*, Tomo I (Seville: Imp. de la "Guía Oficial," 1917), p. 197.

14 "Libro de Memorias de las cosas que en la Iglesia del Asseo de Çaragoça se han offrecido tocantes a ella desde el Agosto del año 1579 hasta el año 1601 inclusive. Hecho por el Doctor Pascual de Mandura Canonigo de dicha Iglesia," Biblioteca Nacional, *MS 14047* (Dec. 23, 1587). See below, pages 326 (n. 26), 363, 472-473 (n. 91).

15 João IV, *Difesa della musica moderna* (Venice: n.p., 1666), pages 40, 49 and 51, voiced his high opinion of Géry de Ghersem's lamentations, motets, *canciones*, and, at page 54, of the *Ave*

Virgo sanctissima Mass parodied after Guerrero's motet.

16 Francisco Pacheco, *Libro de descripcion de verdaderos Retratos de Illustres y Memorables varones . . . En Sevilla 1599.*, facs. ed. (Seville: Rafael Tarascó, 1881-1885), fol. 95.

17 For further comment on Géry de Ghersem's mass, see Manuel Joaquim, *Vinte livros de música polifónica do Paço Ducal de Vila Viçosa* (Lisbon: Ramos, Afonso & Moita, 1953), pp. 24-26.

18 Vicente Espinel, *Diversas rimas* (Madrid: Luis Sánchez, 1591), fol. 46^V.

19 José Gestoso y Pérez, *Ensayo de un diccionario de los artífices que florecieron en Sevilla desde el siglo XIII al XVIII inclusive*, III (Seville: Of. tip. de la Andalucía Moderna, 1909), p. 395.

20 Alonso Sánchez Gordillo, "Historia eclesiástica de Sevilla." Extracts printed in Francisco Ariño, *Sucesos de Sevilla de 1592 á 1604* (Seville: Imp. de Rafael Tarascó y Lassa, 1873). Guerrero's birthdate at page 159.

21 Biographical information below at page 315, note 13.

22 *Viage de Hierusalem, que hizo Francisco Guerrero, Racionero y Maestro de Capilla de la Santa Iglesia de Sevilla. Dirigido al Ilustrissimo, y Reverendissimo Señor Don Rodrigo de Castro, Cardenal, y Arçobispo de la Santa Iglesia de Sevilla* (Seville: Francisco de Leefdael [1690]), p. 2.

23 Jaime Moll Roqueta, "Morales en España," *AM*, VIII (1953), 16.

24 Pacheco, *op. cit.*, fol. 94^V (line 8): "por si aprendio viguela de Siete ordenes, harpa, i Corneta, i otros varios instrumentos."

25 Juan Méndez Nieto, "Discursos medicinales," Biblioteca Nacional, *MS 14036. 76.*

26 Simón de la Rosa y López, *Los seises de la Catedral de Sevilla* (Seville: Imp. de Francisco de P. Díaz, 1904), p. 80.

27 *Ibid.*, p. 77, n. 1.

28 Biographical data in C. Gutiérrez, *Españoles en Trento* (Valladolid: Inst. "Jerónimo Zurita," 1951), pp. 976-983: also Pedro Sainz de Baranda, "Noticia de los españoles que asistieron al Concilio de Trento," *Colección de documentos inéditos para la historia de España*, IX (Madrid: Viuda de Calero, 1846), pp. 53-54.

29 Jaén Cathedral, *Libro de Actos Capitulares. Desde XXIII de agosto de 1540 [hasta el año de 1545]*, fol. 40^V (July 13, 1541).

30 *Ibid.*, fol. 154^V (Jan. 14, 1545).

31 Jaén Cathedral, *Registro de los actos capitulares. Años de 1545-1546*, fol. 1^V (Feb. 25, 1545).

32 *Ibid.*, fol. 22 (Sept. 9, 1545).

33 Jaén, *A. C., 1540-1545*, fol. 40^V (July 13, 1541).

34 Jaén, *A. C., 1545-1546*, fol. 43.

35 *Ibid.*, fol. 46: "Que se escriua a Morales a Toledo. Este dia los dichos señores platicaron sobre escreuir a morales maestro de capilla de la santa iglesia de toledo que enbie a francisco guerrero para que sirua de maestro de capilla en esta santa iglesia e acordaron que se le escriua faziendole saber como se le daran los frutos de la media racion e que ha de tener a su cargo seys moços de coro e asy se le escriuia."

36 *Ibid.*, fol. 62^V.

37 Jaén, [*A. C.*] *Desde el año de 1548 hasta 1568.*, fol. 3 (Jan. 18, 1548).

38 *Ibid.*, fol. 15^V.

39 *Ibid.*, fol. 14^V (July 20, 1548).

40 *Ibid.*, fol. 17^V.

41 *Ibid.*, fols. 22^V, 24.

42 *Ibid.*, fol. 26.

43 *Ibid.*, fol. 26^V.

44 *Ibid.*, fol. 28.

45 *Ibid.*, fol. 37^V (Tuesday, Oct. 29, 1549).

46 Seville Cathedral, *Autos capitulares de 1542 y 1546*, fol. 101^V.

47 Juan Bermudo, *Declaración de instrumentos* (1555), fol. 29^V, col. 2: "I consider the best performers to be Narváez, Martín de Jaén and Hernando de Jaén, dwellers in the city of Granada; López, a musician in the service of the Duke of Arcos, Fuenllana in that of the *marquesa* of Tarifa, Mudarra, a canon in Seville Cathedral, Enríquez [de Valderrábano], in the service of the Count of Miranda." Luys Narváez and Hernando de Jaén served Philip II and João III, respectively, as court *vihuelistas*. See Francisco Bermúdez de Pedraza, *Antiguedad y Excelencias de Granada* (Madrid: Luis Sánchez, 1608), fol. 132.

48 *MME*, Vol. VII, transcribed by Emilio Pujol. Note that Pujol gives the sixth word in the singular. Mudarra, whom I prefer to follow, gave it in the plural. Juan de León, the printer, later brought out Vásquez's and Bermudo's publications (1551 and 1549, 1555), ostensibly in Osuna —though there is reason to believe that he continued to reside all the time in Seville.

49 For the original see H. J. Moser, *Paul Hofhaimer* (Stuttgart: J. G. Cottasche Buchhandlung, 1929), p. 123, no. 24 (Beatus ille = *MME*, Vol. VII, p. 108, no. 64). John Ward discovered this borrowing.

50 Mudarra—like Narváez (1538), Enríquez de Valderrábano (1547), Pisador (1552), Fuenllana (1554), and Daza (1576)—published only the one tablature. After working his "end upon the Sences, that This Ayrie-charme is for," Mudarra adjured his "Magicke" and drowned his "book deeper then did ever Plummet sound." He thenceforth exchanged the role of performer for that of patron.

51 R. Mitjana, "La capilla de música de la Catedral de Málaga / Año de 1543 al año de [1569]," MS notebook in Kungl. Musikaliska Akademiens Bibliotek, Stockholm, page 28. Guerrero seems to have anticipated the decease. As early as August 5, 1551, the Málaga chapter had received a manuscript book of his music— sent doubtless as an earnest of his talents. On that day the chapter decided to post him a cash award.

52 Extracts in Rosa y López, *op. cit.*, pp. 81-83.

53 Interestingly enough, the "de Castilleja" that all modern writers seem ever bent on adding to "Fernández" is not met with in the Sevillian capitular acts: even in a rather formal entry such as the present one.

54 See note 51. Italics mine.

55 Juan B. de Elústiza and Gonzalo Castrillo Hernández, *Antología musical* (Barcelona: Rafael Casulleras, 1933), p. LVII (line 32).

56 See above, pages 121-122, note 170.

57 Seville Cathedral, *A. C., 1553-1554*, fol. 56[v].

58 Luis de Medrano later transferred to Cordova. Through him Guerrero sent a copy of his *Liber primus missarum* (Paris: N. du Chemin, 1566) to the Cordova chapter on March 5, 1566; the chapter responding on April 2 with a *gratificación* of seven ducats. See R. Mitjana, *Don Fernando de Las Infantas* (Madrid: Imp. de los Sucs. de Hernando, 1918), p. 122, n. 5. He and his son were still in service at Cordova on August 20, 1574 (*ibid.*, p. 123).

59 The elder Juan Peraza was in such demand that Toledo and Seville vied for his services. On October 7, 1551, Andrés de Torrentes, chapelmaster at Toledo, promised to repay his cathedral chapter the large sum of 15,000 maravedís on the December 7 following if by that date Juan Peraza, *menestril* of Seville, had not brought his wife to Toledo and settled. At Torrentes's instance the money had been advanced to Peraza for moving expenses. This testimony should of itself suffice to prove that before 1551 the family had been living in Seville. Pacheco, *Libro de descripción*, fol. 92[v], said that the Peraza family followed this itinerary: (1) Salamanca, (2) Valencia, where Juan was in the service of the Duke of Calabria, (3) Seville, (4) Toledo. But if the family did move to Toledo in 1551, they were again at Seville in 1553: as the act of September 20 indicates. According to Pacheco, both Juan *senior* and his wife were virtuoso instrumentalists—to say nothing of the several children.

60 Seville Cathedral, *A. C., 1553-1554*, fol. 74.

61 See below, pages 304-307, note 5.

62 Seville Cathedral, *A. C., 1549, 1551, 1552*, fol. 56[v]. For the history of this library see Henry Harrisse, *Grandeza y decadencia de la Colombina* (Seville: Imp. de "El Universal," 1896). See also Dragan Plamenac, "A Reconstruction of the French Chansonnier in the Biblioteca Colombina, Seville," *Musical Quarterly*, XXXVII, 4 (Oct., 1951), 502-514.

63 *A. C., 1553-1554*, fol. 93.

64 Rafael Mitjana, *Francisco Guerrero (1528-1599): Estudio crítico-biográfico* (Madrid: Talleres poligráficos, 1922), pp. 26-27.

65 *HSMS*, Vol. II, p. viii. Pedrell leaves the reader in some doubt concerning the events of April 2, 1554. According to Mitjana, "La capilla ... 1543 al año de [1569]," page 49, Guerrero took possession by proxy—Canon Diego González Quintero of Málaga acting for him. The legal instrument entitling this canon to act in Guerrero's stead had been notarized in Seville a few days previously by a certain Alonso Guerrero, *bachiller* and *notario apostólico*. The last-named individual may well have been a relative of the composer.

66 Spanish translation in Rosa y López, *op. cit.*, pages 91-96. But observe that on page 91 (line 12) he gives a wrong date. That this particular date should read "1554" can be proved by consulting the actual text of the bull at page 96 (line 6).

67 Francisco Mudarra was *procurador del cabildo en Roma* at least as early as 1539, five years before his brother became canon. See *A. C., 1538-1539*, fol. 288ᵛ (Sept. 26, 1539). In 1555, or shortly before, he confessed to heresy. See *A. C., 1555-1556*, fol. 62ᵛ (July 26, 1555). Having admitted his Lutheran errors to the Roman Inquisition he lost, at least temporarily, the right to enjoy any of his *benefiçios, especialmente para en esta sancta iglesia.*

68 *A. C., 1553-1554*, fol. 149.

69 Probably Pedro Vázquez. See Gestoso y Pérez, Vol. I, p. 354. In 1561 this organ builder was paid 5,984 maravedís by the Sevillian chapter "porque vino de Granada a Sevilla á dar orden para hacer un organo."

70 Elústiza-Castrillo, *op. cit.*, p. LX.

71 *A. C., 1555-1556*, fol. 34.

72 *A. C.*, fol. 23ᵛ.

73 *Ibid.*, fol. 64. Simón de la Rosa y López, *op. cit.*, pages 183-195, describes Sevillian methods of celebrating Corpus Christi between 1477 and 1613. For an interesting description of the *modo de celebrar la procesion del Corpus Christi* in Málaga, see the act of August 7, 1535, in Mitjana's "La capilla . . . 1496 al año de 1542," pages 93-94. This festival was celebrated everywhere in sixteenth-century Spain with dances, floats, *representaciones, gigantes*, and *castillos.*

74 Biblioteca Nacional, *MS 14036.39*, contains a list of the six instrumentalists in service at Toledo Cathedral on October 21, 1559: namely, Bartolomé de Medrano, Antonio de Sanpedro, Tomás López, Juan del Castillo, Juan de Cordova, and Nicolás de Figueroa. By a cathedral act of that date, each was granted a temporary cost-of-living adjustment of 2,500 maravedís for the year. Only Bartolomé de Medrano remained of the group hired originally in 1531.

75 *A. C., 1558-1559*, fol. 35ᵛ.

76 *Ibid.*, fol. 64ᵛ.

77 *Ibid.*, fol. 80ᵛ.

78 *A. C., 1560-1561*, fol. 43.

79 *Ibid.*, fol. 71ᵛ.

80 *Ibid.*, fol. 191ᵛ.

81 "En Toledo doze dias del mes de setiembre de mill y quinientos y sesenta y un años . . . don Gomez Tello Giron governador y general administrador en la sancta iglesia y Arçobispado de Toledo declare . . . que por quanto Francisco Guerrero maestro de capilla de la iglesia mayor de Sevilla avia presentado dos cuerpos de libros puntados de canto de organo a los SS. de la dicha santa iglesia de Toledo que su señoria le advertia que por el trabajo y costa que tenian los dichos dos cuerpos de libros era justo de la gratificar y dar de los maravedis que la obra de la dicha santa iglesia tenia de renta ciento y doze mill y quinientos maravedis."

82 *A. C., 1560-1561*, fol. 250ᵛ.

83 *A. C., 1562-1563*, fol. 18ᵛ.

84 This homonymous person may be the "Guerrero of La Rinconada" (a hamlet above Seville) mentioned in *A. C., 1540, 1541, 1542*, folio 31 (May 21, 1540).

85 *A. C., 1562-1563*, fols. 57ᵛ-58.

86 *Ibid.*, fol. 111.

87 *Ibid.*, fol. 113.

88 *Ibid.*, fol. 131ᵛ.

89 *Ibid.*, fol. 157.

90 *Ibid.*, fol. 174.

91 *Ibid.*, fol. 183ᵛ.

92 *Ibid.*, fol. 190.

93 *Ibid.*, fol. 195.

94 *Ibid.*, fol. 202ᵛ.

95 *Ibid.*, fol. 209.

96 *Ibid.*, fol. 210ᵛ.

97 *Ibid.*, fol. 228.

98 *Ibid.*, fol. 229ᵛ.

99 *Ibid.*, fol. 237.

100 *Ibid.*, fol. 242.

101 *A. C.*, *1564-1565-1566*, fol. 103.

102 Rosa y López, *op. cit.*, p. 137. The earliest of these Farinelli's and Senesino's joined the Sevillian choir in 1620. Eleven such served as Sevillian singers at one time or another before 1635. The first *castrato* hired in overseas Spanish dominions seems to have been Francisco de Otal, who after singing at Guamanga Cathedral in 1614 was hired at La Plata (= present-day Sucre) in 1618. See Sucre Cathedral, *A. C.* II (1616-1619), folio 266 (Aug. 3, 1618). But Spanish opinion always lagged far behind Italian insofar as the acceptance of *castrati* was concerned. If Eximeno's viewpoint was typical (he poured contempt on Italian capons in his witty *Don Lazarillo Vizcardi*), they were more often ridiculed than admired.

103 Seville Cathedral, *A. C.*, *1564-1565-1566*, fol. 109ᵛ.

104 *Ibid.*, fol. 122.

105 *Ibid.*, fol. 124ᵛ.

106 *Ibid.*, fol. 145ᵛ.

107 *Ibid.*, fol. 147.

108 *Ibid.*, fol. 215ᵛ.

109 *A. C. 1570-1571*, fol. 6.

110 *A. C.*, *1580-1581*, fol. 123ᵛ.

111 *A. C.*, *1564-1565-1566*, fol. 153ᵛ.

112 *Ibid.*, fol. 157.

113 *Ibid.*, fol. 159ᵛ.

114 *Ibid.*, fol. 164.

115 *Ibid.*, fol. 175.

116 *Ibid.*, fol. 176ᵛ.

117 *Ibid.*, fol. 179ᵛ.

118 *Ibid.*, fol. 185ᵛ.

119 *Ibid.*, fol. 191.

120 *Ibid.*, fol. 193ᵛ.

121 *Ibid.*, fol. 195ᵛ.

122 *Ibid.*, fol. 218.

123 *A. C.*, *1567-1568-1569*, fol. 1.

124 *Ibid.*, fol. 18. Elústiza (*Estudios musicales*, p. 179, n. 1) mistook *danzas* for *bancas* in the phrase: "ni por las bancas donde se sientan los señores beneficiados en los sermones." This error recurs in the Elústiza-Castrillo *Antología musical*, page LX (line 21).

125 *A. C.*, *1567-1568-1569*, fol. 18ᵛ.

126 Villada was already a Sevillian organ prebendary on November 29, 1540. Juan Bermudo, in his *El arte tripharia* (Osuna: Juan de León, 1550) at folio 24 and again in his *Declaración de instrumentos* (1555) at fol. 60ᵛ, ranked Villada as a stellar keyboardist, worthy of comparison with such other stars as Antonio de Cabezón and Gregorio Silvestre. Although none of his compositions seems to survive, Bermudo vouched for their excellence and their "progressivism." Villada died in early March, 1573. See below, notes 169, 182.

127 *A. C.*, *1567-1568-1569*, fol. 32.

128 *Ibid.*, fol. 39. José Gestoso y Pérez, *op. cit.*, I ("A-O" [1899]), p. 353, states that Jox (= Jos and Joez on p. 353, Joz on p. 355) received an advance payment of 400 ducats as early as May 10, 1567, "on account of the large organ that he is to make." His competitor for the contract, a certain Juan Sunsier according to documents discovered by Gestoso y Pérez (*op. cit.*, I, 354), was—like Jox—a *flamenco* (Fleming). But Spanish organ builders were not idle during this epoch. For documents concerning Sevillian organ builders see Gestoso y Pérez, *op. cit.*, II, 253-259. In 1549 an organ for distant Cuzco, Peru, was constructed at Seville (*op. cit.*, III, 256).

129 *A. C.*, *1567-1568-1569*, fol. 139.

130 *Ibid.*, fol. 151ᵛ.

131 *Ibid.*, fol. 170.

132 *Ibid.*, fol. 172ᵛ.

133 *Ibid.*, fol. 178.

134 *Ibid.*, fol. 193ᵛ.

135 *Ibid.*, fol. 209ᵛ.

136 *A. C.*, *1570-1571*, fol. 57.

137 *A. C.*, *1571-1572-1573*, fol. 89.

138 *Ibid.*, fol. 13 (new foliation).

139 *A. C.*, *1573-1574-1575*, fol. 2^v.

140 Elústiza, in *Estudios musicales*, page 179, note 1, erroneously stated that Guerrero himself intended to try out at Cordova. This mistake recurs in the Elústiza-Castrillo *Antología musical* at page LX. For refutation, see Rafael Mitjana, *Don Fernando de Las Infantas*, page 122, note 5.

141 *Ibid.*, pp. 121-122. Mitjana erroneously gave "junio" instead of "julio" on page 121 at line 29.

142 *A. C.*, *1567-1568-1569*, fol. 80^v.

143 *Ibid.*, fol. 124.

144 *Ibid.*, fols. 131^v, 135.

145 *Ibid.*, fol. 134^v.

146 *Ibid.*, fol. 142. Interestingly enough, Luys de Peñalosa, nephew of the great Francisco, also enjoyed at one time the office of *mayordomo* in Seville Cathedral. See *A. C.*, *1536-1537-1538*, fol. 25^v (April 24, 1536).

147 *A. C.*, *1567-1568-1569*, fol. 156^v.

148 *Ibid.*, fol. 159^v.

149 *Ibid.*, fol. 179^v.

150 *Ibid.*, fol. 204^v.

151 *A. C.*, *1570-1571*, fol. 1^v.

152 *Ibid.*, fol. 6.

153 Diego Ortiz de Zuñiga, *Annales eclesiásticos, y seculares, . . . de Sevilla* (Madrid: Juan Garcia Infançon, 1677), p. 536, col. 2.

154 Juan de Mallara, *Recebimiento que hizo la muy noble y muy leal Ciudad de Seuilla* (Seville: Alonso Escrivano, 1570), fol. 170.

155 *Ibid.*, fol. 171^v. Presumably the altar boys danced while the choirboys sang. Guerrero's absence during all this solemnity was keenly felt, according to Mallara (fol. 170, lines 4-8).

156 *A. C.*, *1570-1571*, fol. 34^v. These instrumentalists were replacements for the regular group (which was en route to Santander).

157 *Relacion verdadera, del recebimiento, que la muy noble y muy mas leal ciudad de Burgos . . . hizo a la Magestad Real de la Reyna nuestra señora doña Anna de Austria* (Burgos: Philippe de Iunta, 1571). On October 24 she entered Las Huelgas by the royal door, friars in white forming part of the welcoming group. Near them stood the singers of the convent and the *menestriles altos* (fol. 4). Mass was celebrated with *mucha musica de cantores, y menestriles*. Other interesting musical references at fol. 41^v (*muy dulce y acordada musica, que de diferentes instrumentos, y excellentes vozes en el auia*), 42-43, and 46^v (*los cantores cantaron muchos motetes y composiciones, . . . y los menestriles tocaron sus instrumentos, con gran suauidad: por ser los de esta yglesia* [Burgos Cathedral] *muchos, y muy esmerados*).

158 *Relacion verdadera del recibimiento que hizo la ciudad de Segouia a la magestad de la reyna nuestra señora doña Anna de Austria* (Alcalá de Henares: Juan Gracián, 1572). At fol. C 2 is found an interesting description of the ceremonies in Valverde. The author makes it quite clear that the rustic music performed on *gaytas y tamborinos y panderos, instrumentos de la musica aldeana* differed both in quality and kind from the cultivated music gracing the bride's entry into nearby Segovia. Other musical references are to be seen at folios T 3 (*mucha musica de vozes y menestriles, cantando, Te Deum laudamus*), T 3^v (*el villancico era compuesto muy prima y graciosamente en canto de organo*), V (*no tenia menos gracia en la composicion de la musica este villancico que el primero*), V^v (*los villancicos entrambos fueron contrahechos por seruir a las sonadas, que era lo principal que se requeria para la musica*), Y 4^v, and Z 2^v.

159 *A. C.*, *1570-1571*, fol. 38.

160 *Ibid.*, fol. 92.

161 *Ibid.*, fol. 99^v. Almost contemporaneously at Toledo the names of ten—instead of six—instrumentalists are encountered in the cathedral payrolls (Dec. 19, 1573). See Biblioteca Nacional, *MS 14036.130*.

162 *A. C.*, *1570-1571*, fol. 109.

163 *Ibid.*, fol. 117.

164 *A. C.*, *1571-1572-1573*, fol. 9^v.

165 *Ibid.*, fol. 24.

166 *Ibid.*, fol. 25^v.

167 *Ibid.*, fol. 82^v.

168 *Ibid.*, fol. 84^v.

169 *Ibid.*, fol. 16.

170 *A. C.*, *1573-1574-1575*, fol. 2^v. Guarantees of "pure" lineage were exacted of all appointees. On April 12, 1554, a royal order had gone forth in the names of Charles, his mother (still alive), and Prince Philip (signed at Valladolid). Henceforth—according to this decree—all candidates for cathedral posts were not only to meet previously imposed conditions for appointment but also to offer proof of the purity of their lineage and of their Christian ancestry (*probar limpieza de sangre y ser cristianos viejos*). See Mitjana, "La capilla . . . Año de 1543 al año de [1569]," page 51a.

171 A.C., *1573-1574-1575*, fol. 20.

172 See pages 33-35 and 179-180, for data concerning this duke's munificence.

173 A. C., *1573-1574-1575*, fol. 22^V.

174 *Ibid.*, fol. 44.

175 *Ibid.*, fol. 77^V.

176 *Ibid.*, fol. 82.

177 *Ibid.*, fol. 84.

178 *Ibid.*, fol. 127^V. This Cristóbal de León may have been the son of a like-named senior who tuned the Sevillian organs at Christmas, 1538. See *A. C.*, *1538-1539*, fol. 125 (Dec. 20, 1538). The junior namesake made a trip as far afield as Peru to repair the organs in Cuzco Cathedral in 1583. See Cuzco Cathedral, *A. C.*, I, fol. 57 (July 2, 1583).

179 Seville Cathedral, *A. C.*, *1573-1574-1575*, fol. 205.

180 *Ibid.*, fol. 219^V. Some idea of the stops included in the Seville organ may be obtained by studying the specifications of the Toledo "imperial" organ. See Santiago Kastner, *Música Hispànica* (Lisbon: Ed. Ática, 1936), pp. 140-141.

181 *Ibid.*, fol. 223.

182 *Ibid.*, fol. 232^V. Mudarra was on this date instructed to employ the heir (*heredero*) of the former organist Villada (d. 1573) until Peraza's return.

183 *Ibid.*, fol. 279^V.

184 *Ibid.*, fol. 289^V.

185 A. C., *1578-1579*, fol. 10^V.

186 *Ibid.*, fol. 14.

187 *Ibid.*, fol. 15. On July 16, 1578, the chapter hired Antolin de Paredes, reputedly the finest

tiple in Spain (*ibid.*, fol. 51^V). See also note 218 below.

188 *Ibid.*, fol. 25.

189 *Ibid.*, fol. 108^V.

190 *Ibid.*, fol. 27.

191 *Ibid.*, fol. 51.

192 *Ibid.*, fol. 55 (Aug. 5, 1578).

193 *Ibid.*, fol. 63.

194 *Ibid.*, fol. 85.

195 *Ibid.*, fol. 105.

196 *Ibid.*, fol. 115.

197 *Ibid.*, fol. 116^V.

198 *Ibid.*, fol. 134. The chapter consulted the opinion of several outstanding organists in 1579 to determine the merits of the new organ. An organist from Toledo, Ximénez (cf. Felipe Pedrell, *Antología de organistas clásicos españoles* [Madrid: Ildefonso Alier, 1908], pp. III and 40-54), was paid two ducats for his opinion; Gerónimo de León and Sebastián de Maldonado, eight ducats for theirs (Gestoso y Pérez, *op. cit.*, I, 355). Quite possibly the opinions of these visitors convinced the chapter that Jox wished too much money for his finished product.

199 A. C., *1578-1579*, fol. 140.

200 *Ibid.*, fol. 141^V.

201 Upon arriving at Rome Guerrero had in hand sufficient copy for two collections—his second book of masses and a complete cycle of vesper music. In 1580 he prepared copy for a third important opus—choral settings of the four passions. See page 178; also notes 10 and 345.

202 A. C., *1578-1579*, fol. 144.

203 A. C., *1580-1581*, fol. 4. Further information concerning Alexandro de la Serna below at page 334, note 50.

204 A. C., *1580-1581*, fol. 16.

205 A. C., *1582-1583-1584 y parte de 1585*, fol. 28.

206 *Ibid.*, fol. 30.

207 *Ibid.*, fol. 30^V.

208 *A. C.*, *1580-1581*, fol. 54.

209 *Ibid.*, fol. 24. Either Tapia transferred to some such Sevillian church as San Salvador or became suborganist in the cathedral after Diego del Castillo's appointment to the organ prebend (April 29, 1581). On April 4, 1584, he was momentarily expected in Palencia, where a competition for the organ prebend of that cathedral had been announced. As of that date, he is referred to in a Palencia capitular act as a *músico de tecla de Sevilla*. Canon Zapata of Palencia had invited him to compete. But eventually it became apparent that Tapia was not even sufficiently interested in making a change from Seville to take a paid-expenses trip to Palencia for the trial. See Elústiza-Castrillo, *Antología musical*, page LXXX.

210 Felipe Rubio Piqueras, *Música y músicos toledanos* (Toledo: Suc. de J. Peláez, 1923), p. 66. Gerónimo [de] Peraza died on June 26, 1617, and was buried in San Lorenzo parish.

211 *A. C.*, *1580-1581*, fol. 30^v.

212 *Ibid.*, fol. 32^v.

213 *Ibid.*, fol. 84.

214 *Ibid.*, fol. 88^v.

215 See his letter from Rome dated November 13, 1581 (printed in Elústiza-Castrillo, *op. cit.*, page LXIII): "por abernos detenido seys meses en el camino . . ."

216 *A. C.*, *1580-1581*, fol. 89^v.

217 *Ibid.*, fol. 93^v. According to *Diccionario de la Música Labor* (Barcelona: Ed. Labor, 1954), Vol. I, p. 479 [hereafter cited as *DML*], Diego del Castillo became organist at Seville *ca.* 1560. Even if one lacked access to the capitular acts, his date of appointment could be known to have occurred much later. Correa de Arauxo, in his *Facultad orgánica* (Alcalá de Henares: 1626), recorded that Castillo succeeded [Gerónimo] Peraza. Further on Castillo below at pages 302-304, note 3.

218 *A. C.*, *1580-1581*, fol. 102. Vicente Espinel in his *La casa de la memoria* cited this singer as one of the two best whom he had heard: "Con boz suaue, y con veloz garganta, / Pura, distinta, dulce, y claro pecho / En regalado canto se leuanta / Primo, y el coro dexa satisfecho: / En competencia suya Antolin canta / Pretendiendo el assiento por derecho." (*Diversas rimas*, fol. 47^v).

219 *A. C.*, *1580-1581*, fol. 123^v.

220 Elústiza, *Estudios*, p. 195.

221 *A. C. 1580-1581*, fol. 128^v.

222 *A. C.*, *1582-1583-1584 y parte de 1585*, fol. 1^v.

223 *Ibid.*, fol. 9.

224 Letter printed in Elústiza, *Estudios*, page 197.

225 *Ibid.*, p. 196.

226 Guerrero's *Missarum liber secundus* is, as a whole, dedicated to the Blessed Virgin; this one mass in it (fols. 21^v-40) to the reigning pope.

227 Such a phrase was more than a mere compliment. Before becoming pope, Gregory XIII had served as legate in Spain (1557). See Ludwig von Pastor, *The History of the Popes*, trans. by R. F. Kerr, Vol. XIX, p. 19.

228 *A. C.*, *1582-1583-1584 y parte de 1585*, fol. 57.

229 *Ibid.*, fol. 94.

230 *Ibid.*, fol. 105.

231 *Ibid.*, fol. 107^v.

232 *Ibid.*, fol. 108. More information on Andrés López below at page 318, note 15.

233 *Ibid.*, fol. 119.

234 *Ibid.*, fol. 119^v.

235 *Ibid.*, fol. 122.

236 *Ibid.*, fol. 133.

237 *Ibid.*, fol. 133^v.

238 *Ibid.*, fol. 170.

239 *Ibid.*, fol. 141.

240 P. B. Gams, *Series episcoporum* (Regensburg: G. J. Manz, 1873), p. 73, col. 2. Castro was not a cardinal, nor even for that matter archbishop of Seville, in 1554 as Querol Gavaldá erroneously supposed in *MME*, VIII, 26 (line 30).

241 Biographical data in Francisco Pacheco, *op. cit.*, fol. 92^v.

242 *A. C.*, *1582-1583-1584 y parte de 1585*, fol. 150.

243 *Ibid.*, fol. 176^v.

244 A. C., *1586-1587*, fol. 23ᵛ.

245 Josquin enjoyed the cachet of theorists' as well as practitioners' approval. Francisco Salinas in his *De musica libri septem* (1577), page 56, wrote thus: "Iodocus Pratensis inter Symphonetas sui temporis facile princeps." An inventory of the chapel choirbooks of Philip II made at the close of the century shows that 77 years after his death Josquin was still represented by more choirbooks than any other composer but one. Nine were devoted exclusively to his works; in several others he was anthologized liberally. See Alfonso Andrés, "Libros de canto de la capilla de Felipe II," *Musica sacro-hispana*, Vol. X (1917), pp. 94 (item 7), 109 (item 30), 111 (item 65), 123 (item 81), 124 (item 83), 126 (item 127), 154 (item 146), 155 (item 152), 156 (item 173). Even more remarkable, however, was the prestige that Josquin enjoyed in Spain as late as 1626—Correa de Arauxo in that year using Josquin's authority to justify his own use of B♮ against b♭, and of F♯ against f. Correa's manner of citing a *Pleni sunt*, *a 3*, allows us not only to infer that he was familiar with the whole body of Josquin's works but also that he considered one ciphered example from so universally respected a master enough to stop the mouths of all his own adverse critics. See *MME*, VI, *50*.

246 A. C., *1586-1587*, fol. 29ᵛ.

247 *Quadernos de Autos Capitulares Antiguos. 1586. Desde Abril 1587*, fol. 16ᵛ. [Hereafter cited as *Quadernos*.]

248 *Ibid.*, fol. 18.

249 *Ibid.*, fol. 18ᵛ.

250 A. C., *1586-1587*, fol. 40.

251 *Quadernos* [1586-1587], fol. 27 ᵛ.

252 *Ibid.*, fol. 30.

253 A. C., *1586-1587*, fol. 46ᵛ.

254 *Ibid.*

255 The *glosas* at folios 89-91ᵛ (Mouton's *Quaeramus cum pastoribus*), 131-133ᵛ (Josquin's *Stabat mater*), and 134-136 (Josquin's *Inviolata*) in Antonio de Cabezón's *Obras de musica para tecla arpa y vihuela* (Madrid: Francisco Sánchez, 1578) give an accurate clue to actual performance practice so far as instrumental glossing is concerned. Or at least Hernando de Cabezón certified as much when he inserted a paragraph on the penultimate page of the *Declaración* which serves as a preface to his father's book. He declared that instrumentalists would find the *glosas* in his father's book to be models that they could safely follow. He advised them to extract the individual lines in these *glosas* for their own instruments. The paragraph is worth reproduction here: "Tambien se podran aprouechar del libro los curiosos menestriles, en ver inuenciones de glosas tratadas con verdad sobre lo compuesto, y ver la licencia que tiene cada voz, sin perjuyzio de las otras partes, y esto toparan en muchos motetes canciones y fabordones que ellos tañen, que con poca dificultad podran sacar desta cifra en canto de organo."

Further on the subject of *glosas* see Bermudo, *Declaración* (1555), fols. 29ᵛ, col. 2; 84ᵛ, col. 2. Bermudo inveighed heavily against glossing, unless the written music were of poor quality. He was in sufficiently close contact with Morales to reflect enlightened opinion. Guerrero perhaps allowed glossing of purely chordal music such as *fabordones*.

256 *baxon.*

257 *flautas.*

258 A. C. *1586-1587*, fol. 51ᵛ.

259 *Ibid.*, fol. 55ᵛ.

260 *Ibid.*, fol. 59.

261 *Ibid.*, fol. 62ᵛ.

262 *Quadernos* [1586-1587], fol. 60. Gestoso y Pérez, *op. cit.*, Vol. I, p. 353, records further interesting details. In 1592 the chapter guaranteed López 250 ducats for repairs on the large organ. These repairs were still going forward in 1593, during which year López's assistant was a certain Enrique Franco of Cádiz. Coming so soon after completion of the organ, these repairs might seem to indicate Jox's faulty workmanship. However, major repairs were a recurring expense in all the larger Spanish cathedrals during this century. On average, the Toledo chapter, for instance, was obliged to spend large sums every dozen years from 1550 to 1600 for the overhauling of the large organ built by Juan Gaytán (1549).

263 *Quadernos* [1586-1587], fols. 58ᵛ-59.

264 Pacheco, *op. cit.*, fol. 94ᵛ (line 33). Concerning Cardinal de Castro's own superior musical background see fol. 92ᵛ (line 12). While still bishop of Zamora he accepted the dedication of Francisco Salinas's *De musica libri septem* (Salamanca: M. Gastius, 1577), probably underwriting at least a part of the printing expenses. For biographical details, see Antonio Domínguez Ortiz, "Un informe sobre el estado de la Sede hispalense en 1581," *Hispania Sacra*, VI, 11

(1953), 182 (especially n. 5).

265 *Quadernos* [1586-1587], fol. 63^V.

266 *A. C.*, *1586-1587*, fol. 82.

267 *Ibid.*, fol. 77.

268 *Ibid.*, fol. 85.

269 *Quadernos* [1586-1587], fol. 105^V.

270 *A. C.*, *1586-1587*, fol. 92^V.

271 *Ibid.*, fol. 95.

272 *Ibid.*, fol. 107.

273 *Ibid.*, fol. 122^V.

274 *Quadernos* [1586-1587], fol. 160.

275 *Ibid.*, fol. 165.

276 *A. C.*, *1588-1589*, fol. 4^V.

277 *Ibid.*, fol. 5^V.

278 *Ibid.*, fol. 7.

279 *Ibid.*, fol. 7^V.

280 *Ibid.*, fol. 8.

281 *Ibid.*, fol. 9^V.

282 *Ibid.*, fol. 10.

283 *Ibid.*, fol. 11.

284 Pacheco, *op. cit.*, fol. 94^V.

285 Mitjana, *Francisco Guerrero*, p. 45.

286 *A. C.*, *1588-1589*, fol. 60^V.

287 *Ibid.*, fol. 65.

288 *A. C.*, *1590-1591*, fol. 23.

289 *Ibid.*, fol. 38^V.

290 *Ibid.*, fol. 39^V.

291 *Ibid.*, fol. 69^V.

292 For data on Jacomar's service as choirboy, see above, page 152 (May 25, 1565).

293 Since the debt had been incurred for the publication of his *Liber vesperarum*—a volume dedicated to the Sevillian chapter—he justly expected aid from the chapter toward liquidating it. A badly worn copy of this very book is today the proudest polyphonic possession of Lima Cathedral (Peru).

294 *A.C.*, *1590-1591*, fol. 70^V.

295 Act printed in Elústiza, *Estudios*, page 198.

296 *A.C.*, *1590-1591*, fol. 74.

297 *Ibid.*, fol. 72.

298 *Ibid.*, fol. 87.

299 *Ibid.*, fol. 84^V. See also note 262 above.

300 *A.C.*, *1594-1595-1596*, fol. 1.

301 Rubio Piqueras, *Música y músicos toledanos*, pp. 58-59.

302 *A.C.*, *1595-1595-1596*, fol. 1^V.

303 Francisco de Ariño, *Sucesos de Sevilla de 1592 á 1604*, pp. 18-19, 159.

304 *A.C.*, *1594-1595-1596*, fol. 5.

305 *Ibid.*, fol. 11^V.

306 *Ibid.*, fol. 16.

307 *Ibid.*, fol. 25.

308 *Ibid.*, fol. 37^V.

309 *Ibid.*, fol. 53^V.

310 *Ibid.*, fol. 83^V.

311 *Ibid.*, fol. 86^V.

312 *Ibid.*, fols. 94^V, 112. See also Elústiza-Castrillo, *op. cit.*, page XXI.

313 *A.C.*, *1597-1598*, fols. 78, 80.

314 *A.C.*, *1594-1595-1596*, fols. 112^V.

315 *A.C.*, *1597-1598*, fol. 2.

316 *Ibid.*, fol. 4^V.

317 *Ibid.*, fol. 40^V.

318 Pacheco, *op. cit.*, fol. 93.

319 *Quadernos de Autos Capitulares Antiguos. Años de 1599. 1600. 1601. 1602. 1603. 1604. 1605. 1606.*, fol. 33. (The entry in this instance is a cumulative salary record.)

320 *A.C., 1599-1600-1601-1602*, fol. 18ᵛ.

321 *Ibid.* In the Elústiza-Castrillo *Antología musical* at page LIII is to be seen the suggestion that the Pedro Guerrero who was Francisco's elder brother returned from Rome to occupy a singer's post in Seville Cathedral. Elústiza confessed, however, that he did not know the date of the said Pedro's engagement as singer in Seville Cathedral. It seems quite possible that he somewhere saw a reference to the *contrabajo* engaged in 1599 and thenceforth confused the two Pedros. The Pedro Guerrero mentioned in the act of May 14, 1599, later transferred from Seville to Toledo.

322 *A.C., 1599-1600-1601-1602*, fol. 28ᵛ.

323 *Ibid.*, fol. 33ᵛ.

324 *Ibid.*, fol. 34ᵛ.

325 *Ibid.*, fol. 37.

326 *Ibid.*, fol. 53.

327 *Libro de descripción*, no. 48.

328 *Ibid.*, fols. 94ᵛ-95.

329 Lota M. Spell, "Music in the Cathedral of Mexico in the Sixteenth Century," *Hispanic American Historical Review*, XXVI, 3 (Aug., 1946), 317. See also note 293 above. Cuzco Cathedral still counts among her musical treasures the *Missae sex* that concludes with Géry de Ghersem's parody Mass based on Guerrero's *Ave Virgo sanctissima*.

330 *Viage de Hierusalem*, p. 5.

331 *Ibid.*: "Tomando à su cuenta la correccion de la Estampa el Maestro Joseph Zerlino, Maestro de Capilla de San Marcos."

332 *Ibid.*, p. 7.

333 *Ibid.*, p. 43.

334 *Ibid.*, p. 68.

335 *Ibid.*, p. 74. This may have been the Antonio Ribera to whom the Mystery of Elche music should rightfully be attributed.

336 *Ibid.*, p. 78.

337 For a partial bibliography of later reprints,

see *HSMS*, Vol. II, p. iv. See also Manuel Serrano y Sanz, *Autobiografías y memorias* (Madrid: Lib. ed. de Bailly-Bailliére é Hijos, 1905 [*Nueva Bibl. de Aut. Esp.*, II]), pp. LV-LVI.

338 *A.C., 1553-1554*, fol. 149.

339 Prudencio de Sandoval, *Historia de la vida y hechos del emperador Carlos V* (Pamplona: Bartolomé Paris, 1614), II, 828 (col. 2). Sandoval, bishop of Pamplona, said he had enjoyed Guerrero's personal acquaintance.

340 Reprinted in *Treize livres de motets parus chez Pierre Attaingnant en 1534 et 1545*, ed. by A. Smijers (Paris: Éditions de l'Oiseau Lyre, 1936), Vol. III, p. 104.

341 Janequin's own *Missa La Bataille* (Lyons: Jacques Moderne, 1532; repr. Paris: Salabert, 1947 [ed. by Henry Expert]) seems to have been the only French parody. In Spain, Morales was perhaps the first to compose a *Batalla*—now apparently lost (unless the anonymous *Batalla* Mass at pages 260-279 in Biblioteca Medinaceli MS 607 is his). In 1626 Correa de Arauxo in his *Facultad orgánica* (*MME*, VI, 129-137) published a *tiento* based on Morales's *Batalla*. However, the best proof of the long vogue of the chanson in Spain is to be found in the Guerrero, Victoria, and Esquivel parodies. Ximénez (see note 198 above) left two strongly indebted organ "battles." The Janequin moreover continued a parody source in Spanish dominions even after 1608. See *Fontes artis musicae*, 1954/2, p. 77. For instance, as far away as Mexico City an organist named Fabián Ximeno (fl. 1648) was still at mid-century parodying the chanson in a *Missa De la batalla, a 8*. The many Spanish parodies ought to be assembled and studied as a group. Just as the many *L'Homme armé* masses are better understood when compared with each other, so also would be the Spanish *Batallas*.

342 Gustave Reese, *Music in the Renaissance*, p. 595.

343 See above, note 81.

344 Rubio Piqueras, *Códices polifónicos toledanos*, pp. 18-20.

345 Excerpts in Kade, *op. cit.*, pp. 153-157. See above, note 10.

346 Cardinal de Castro not only interceded for Guerrero on this occasion but even addressed the primate on another occasion (September 10, 1582, in a letter written from Lisbon) asking for favors to Ginés de Boluda, chapelmaster of Toledo from March 14, 1581, to September 22,

1593. Castro, from the evidence presently at hand, interested himself more actively in the welfare of musicians than did any other contemporary Spanish prelate. Cf. note 264 above.

347 Francisco Sánchez was Guerrero's pupil. See Pacheco, *op. cit.*, fol. 94ᵛ.

348 Rubio Piqueras, *Códices polifónicos toledanos*, pp. 27, 52.

349 Further details concerning MS 110 at pages 190, 264, and 272.

350 Although only three musical publications by Martín Montesdoca have been found—namely, the Fuenllana of 1554, Guerrero of 1555, and Vásquez of 1556—each was epoch-making. He himself was an exceptionally enthusiastic amateur. Two of his Latin poems—one of 12, the other of 8 lines—appear on the recto of the leaf preceding folio 1 in *Orphénica lyra*. He knew Fuenllana personally, admired him extravagantly, and expended his utmost printer's art on the 1554 tablature.

351 Rodrigo Ponce de León (succeeded to the title in 1492).

352 Aloys Hiff, *Catalogue of Printed Music published prior to 1801 now in the Library of Christ Church, Oxford* (Oxford University Press: 1919), pp. 34, 71-72.

353 Alphonse Goovaerts, *Histoire et bibliographie de la typographie musicale dans les Pays-Bas* (Antwerp: Pierre Kockx, 1880), pp. 35-36, 230.

354 See above, note 5.

355 F. X. Haberl, *Bibliographischer und thematischer Musikkatalog des päpstlichen Kapellarchives* (Leipzig: Breitkopf und Härtel, 1888), p. 142.

356 *HSMS*, II, xxxvii-xxxviii.

357 See above, notes 240, 264, 346. *Cf.* also Alonso Morgado, *Historia de Sevilla* (1587, repr. for *Archivo Hispalense*, 1887), pp. 303, 307.

358 Contents listed in Anglés-Subirá, *Catálogo Musical de la Biblioteca Nacional de Madrid* (Barcelona: 1951), Vol. III, pp. 4-5.

359 Eitner, *Bibliographie der Musik-Sammelwerke* (Berlin: Leo Liepmannssohn, 1877), p. 615.

360 In the imprint, fol. xcv should read xciv.

361 Apparently a unicum in Fuenllana.

362 *Grove's Dictionary*, 3d ed., ed. by H. C. Colles (1935), II, 477.

363 Printed in *Tesoro de la música polifónica en México: El Códice del Convento del Carmen*, ed. by Jesús Bal y Gay, (Mexico City: Instituto Nacional de Bellas Artes, 1952), I, 114-144 and 223-226.

364 Printed in *Anthologie des maîtres religieux primitifs*, ed. by Charles Bordes, deuxième année: *Messes* (Paris: Schola Cantorum, 1894), pp. 159-182.

365 Espinel, *Diversas rimas*, fol. 46ᵛ.

366 *Liber primus missarum*, fols. 50ᵛ-51.

367 Pacheco, *op. cit.*, fol. 95.

368 See *Tesoro*, ed. by Bal y Gay, I, 223-224.

369 Pedro Cerone, *El melopeo y maestro* (Naples: Jaun Bautista Gargano, 1613), page 1118, alludes to a Vado et venio ad vos canon in the last Agnus of Guerrero's *Puer qui natus est* Mass. Unless Cerone enjoyed access to some other version than the 1582 printed copy, his memory must have tricked him into confusing Guerrero's *Puer qui* with the *Simile est* Mass. Cerone carried the allusion somewhat further, mentioning a similar "going-and-coming" canon in an unspecified Orazio Vecchi (1550-1605) motet. Since the earliest known imprint containing any Vecchi motet appeared as late as 1587, Guerrero's *Simile est* Mass (if not the *Puer qui*) was first in the field with a Vado et venio ad vos scheme.

370 Ramos de Pareja, *Musica practica*, ed. by Johannes Wolf, pp. 58-59.

371 Toledo: Biblioteca Provincial, *MS 329*, fol. 18: *la manera delos ançianos*.

372 *MME*, XIII, 17-23; *Tesoro sacro-musical: Suplemento polifónico*, 39 (July-Sept., 1953), 52-59.

373 *MME*, I, 35-61.

374 *Liber usualis*, 1947 ed., pp. 1126-1128.

375 *Ibid.*, pp. 1150-1151. Guerrero's *Hei mihi* is in his 1589 and 1597 motet publications. In motets as such, Guerrero refrained from quoting plainsong. The fact that *Hei mihi* found its way into the 1589 and 1597 collections strongly suggests that any faint resemblances to a plainsong source discernible in the motet were merely the result of chance.

376 Gioseffo Zarlino, *Le istitutioni harmoniche*

(Venice: 1558), pp. 340-341; *Istitutioni harmoniche* (Venice: Francesco de i Franceschi Senese, 1573), pp. 421-422.

377 See Willi Apel, *The Notation of Polyphonic Music, 900-1600* (4th ed.; Cambridge, Mass.: The Mediaeval Academy of America, 1949), pp. 90-91.

378 Copies of Miguel de Eguía's Jeronymite processional of 1526 may be seen at both The Hispanic Society (complete) and The New York Public Library (imperfect). Indiana University owns a third copy (perfect). The *Ave Virgo sanctissima* antiphon occurs at fols. 85^v-86.

379 Printed (with flaws) in Elústiza-Castrillo, *op. cit.*, pages 116-118. Corrections: meas. 17$_4$, bassus, should read A, not F; meas. 18, cantus, eliminate dot after semibreve d^1, and lengthen minim b to semibreve; meas. 42$_{2,4}$, altus, eliminate notes with descending stems. No account is taken of necessary ficta at such places as meas. 25$_2$, altus; nor at cadences.

380 Andreas Ornithoparchus, *Micrologus, or Introduction: containing the art of singing*, trans. by John Dowland (London: T. Adams, 1609), p. 85.

381 *Ibid.*, p. 84.

382 Psalm 12.

383 In *Sacrae cantiones* (1555) the text honors Jerome; in the *Motteta* (1570), Dominic; in the Santiago Codex at Valladolid, "N" (the name of any desired saint). This motet, as printed in both 1555 and 1570 versions, extended to two *partes* (*Pars 2: Et ideo*). Elústiza-Castrillo, *op. cit.*, pages 86-88, printed only *Pars 1*. For further comments on the Elústiza-Castrillo transcription, see page 214.

384 P. Samuel Rubio reprinted the following items *a 4* from the 1589 *Mottecta* in his *Antología polifónica sacra*, Vol. II (Madrid: Ed. Coculsa, 1956), at pages 313-318, 95-101, 205-212: *Dum aurora finem daret* (St. Cecilia), *Exaltata est*, *Sancta et immaculata* (2d pars, *Benedicta tu*). He transposed *Exaltata est* (TTBB becoming CCAT).

385 *HSMS*, II, xxv-xxvi and 18-23. Reese (*Music in the Renaissance*, p. 595) printed a short excerpt, using Pedrell's transposed version as source.

386 Mitjana, *Francisco Guerrero*, pages 64-66, showed no broader acquaintance with Guerrero's motet repertory than these two items. What is more, he knew only the Pedrell transposition of

Trahe me and therefore ignorantly classified it as a "seventh-tone" motet (*ibid.*, p. 66).

387 Pedrell, *HSMS*, Vol. II, p. xxxv, counts 40. His no. 6 should be *pars 2* of his no. 5.

388 The *Salve Regina* (Ad te, Et Jesum, O clemens) breaks the scheme somewhat, since it occurs as an interpolation between *Gloriose confessor* (De sancto Dominico) and *Beatus es et bene tibi* (De sancto Sebastiano).

389 Diego Pisador classed the following items as "villanescas" in his *Libro de música de vihuela* (Salamanca, 1552): (1) *A quand' haveva*, a 4 (Willaert), fol. 89; (2) *La cortesia*, a 3 (Fontana), fol. 88; (3) *Lagrime mesti & voi sospir dolenti*, a 4 (Willaert), fols. 89^v-90; (4) *Madonna mia fa*, a 4 (Willaert), fol. 90-90^v; (5) *Madonna mia la vostra*, a 3 (Fontana), fol. 87^v; (6) *O bene mio fa*, a 4 (Willaert), fols. 90^v-91; (7) *O dolce vita mia*, a 3 (Fontana), fol. 87; (8) *Quanto debb'allegrarse*, a 3 (Fontana), fol. 87^v; (9) *Sempre me fing'o*, a 4 (anonymous), fols. 88^v-89; (10) *Tutta s'arissi*, a 3 (Fontana), fol. 88. In addition to these items (traced by Professor John Ward) Pisador ciphers at fol. 87. *Io ti vorria contare* from Fontana's same *Canzone villanesche* of 1545. Miguel de Fuenllana's *Orphénica lyra* of 1554 contains three items classed as "villanescas": (1) *Madonna mia* (Fontana [same as (5) above]), fol. 131^v; (2) *Oymé, oymé dolente*, a 3 (Nola), fol. 131; (3) *Quando ti veggio*, a 3 (anonymous), fol. 131-131^v.

390 Esteban Daza classed the following as "villanescas" in his *El Parnasso* (1576): (1) *Adios verde ribera*, a 4 (F. Guerrero), fols. 87^v-88^v; (2) *Ay de mi, sin ventura*, a 4 (Navarro), fols. 85^v-87^v; (3) *Callese ya Mercurio*, a 4 (anonymous), fols. 94-95^v; (4) *Dime, manso viento*, a 4 (Ceballos), fols. 93-94; (5) *Duro mal, terrible llanto*, a 4 (Ceballos), fols. 91^v-93; (6) *Esclarecida Juana*, a 4 (Villalar [but *recte*, F. Guerrero]), fols. 90^v-91^v; (7) *No vez amor*, a 4 (Navarro), fols. 89-90^v; (8) *Pues ya las claras fuentes*, a 4 (Ceballos), fols. 84-85.

391 Pacheco, *op. cit.*, fols. 43-44, states that Cristoval Moxquera was born in Seville. His parents were *licenciado* Pedro Moxquera de Moxcoso and Leonor de Figueroa. He studied at Salamanca where he graduated a bachelor of canon laws (*Bachiller en los Sagrados Canones*); then became a licentiate in jurisprudence at the University of Osuna. An extremely versatile student, he mastered not only the classic tongues but Italian as well. Meanwhile, he diligently pursued music, eventually becoming an adept vihuelist (*tocando gallardamente una viguela*). Upon completing his university courses he served successively as *alcalde mayor* at Utrera and *corregidor* at Puerto Santa María.

392 Pacheco, *op. cit.*, sketches Gutierre de Cetina's biography at fols. 70-71.

393 Lope de Vega's exquisitely sensitive poem must have been composed while he was still a student at Alcalá. Certainly it was among his earliest pieces to reach print. It occurs with Guerrero's music as item 27 in *Il secondo Libro delle Laude spirituali* (Rome: Alessandro Gardano, 1583). During this same year Lope embarked upon a military career that was to take him first to the Azores. The poem can hardly be called, therefore, "the effusion of a mystical crisis."

Fortunately the *Laude spirituali* version may be seen in a modern reprint (*Musica sacro-hispano*, V, 8 [Aug., 1912], 116-117). Soto de Langa is generally recognized to have been the editor of

Il secondo Libro. Exercising his editorial prerogative he somewhat simplified Guerrero's rhythms— as comparison of the 1583 with the 1589 imprint discloses immediately. Guerrero's own version is, of course, artistically much the superior: because more subtle and refined.

394 A century later, Andrés Lorente in his *El porqué de la música* (Alcalá de Henares: Nicolás de Xamares, 1672), page 218, thought one of the most remarkable features of an organ constructed at Alcalá in 1670 (by a builder from Navarre) to be the keyboard; because to the customary black keys for E♭'s and G♯'s were added others for D♯'s and A♭'s. As late, then, as 1670 most Spanish organs lacked D♯'s and A♭'s—according to Lorente. If organs lacked them, their occurrence in Spanish sacred vocal polyphony continued to be just as exceptional.

Part 2: OTHER CHURCH MASTERS

Church Masters Active during the Reign of Philip II   Just as Tallis and
Byrd stand at the heads of their generations in English music, so Guerrero
and Victoria tower above contemporary Spanish composers. But the scales
are not equally balanced when English is compared with Spanish music
during the reigns of Elizabeth I and Philip II because of the sheer weight
of numbers in the peninsula. For a Christopher Tye there was a Juan Navarro; for a Robert White, an Alonso Lobo; for a Peter Philips, a Sebastián
de Vivanco; for a Richard Deering, a Juan Esquivel. However, only a very
ingenious Plutarch bent on writing "parallel lives" at any cost would find
enough figures to pit against all the following composers: (1) José Bernal,[1]
(2) Ginés de Boluda,[2] (3) Diego del Castillo,[3] (4) and (5) Francisco[4] and
Rodrigo de Ceballos,[5] (6) Bernardo Clavijo del Castillo,[6] (7) Juan Bautista
Cómes,[7] (8) Ambrosio Cotes,[8] (9) Bartolomé de Escobedo,[9] (10) Bartolomé
Farfán,[10] (11) Mateo Flecha the Younger,[11] (12) Juan García de Basurto,[12]
(13) Pedro Guerrero,[13] (14) Fernando de las Infantas,[14] (15) Andrés
López,[15] (16) Francisco de Montanos,[16] (17) and (18) Alonso[17] and Pedro
Ordoñez,[18] (19) Diego Ortiz,[19] (20) Pedro de Pastrana,[20] (21) Juan Ginés
Pérez,[21] (22) Pedro Periañez,[22] (23) Juan Pujol,[23] (24) Sebastián Raval,[24]
(25) Bernardino de Ribera,[25] (26) Melchor Robledo,[26] (27) Francisco de
Sepúlveda,[27] (28) Francisco Soto de Langa,[28] (29) Andrés de Torrentes,[29]
(30) Luis de Vargas,[30] (31) Juan Vásquez,[31] (32) Pedro Alberch Vila,[32]
(33) Andrés Villalar,[33] (34) Martín de Villanueva,[34] and (35) Nicasio
Zorita.[35] And even this list of thirty-five composers, all of whom were active
in the sacred field during the reign of Philip II, can by no means pretend to
completeness. It fails, for instance, to include any vihuelist or any composer
who emigrated to the New World.

Some of the reasons for the difference in numbers are sufficiently obvious.
In England the disparaging attitude of the Reformers adversely affected the
musical careers of such composers as John Taverner and John Marbeck.
There are no comparable instances of blight caused by Bishop Cirillo
Franco's influence in Spain.[36] For another matter, artistic life was more
centralized in London than at Madrid, Valladolid, or any other Spanish
capital. In sixteenth-century Spain the provincial capitals were jealous

of their own cultural traditions to an extent hardly matched elsewhere. Upon entering capitals such as Saragossa, Segovia, or Seville, Philip II always began with the ritual of swearing to uphold all the local exemptions and privileges. He, moreover, was king of *las Españas*. Elizabeth I was never queen of "the Englands"; nor was there ever any doubt that London, or its environs, was the center of her government. She can hardly be imagined upon entering some great English cathedral (as Philip did upon entering Seville Cathedral in 1570) to have made an elaborate bow to the whole body of "privileges" extended the cathedral by her royal ancestors.[37] Neither would she have gone through the motions of humbly "praying" permission of some mere bishop (as Philip did of the Bishop of Segovia in 1570) to marry in his cathedral. Nor would she have assuaged any such mere bishop's feelings by promising that all the ceremonies would be conducted strictly according to local diocesan use[38]—even had there been a local use to observe anywhere in England as late as 1570.

Local pride incited Seville to complete with Toledo, Ávila with Salamanca, Saragossa with Burgos, Cordova with Málaga, and Plasencia with Palencia. As a result, the movements of such composers as Navarro, Lobo, and Vivanco read like American Express tours of Spain, with a master such as Vivanco, for instance, moving from Lérida to Segovia, to Seville, to Ávila, and to Salamanca, in succession. In England, on the other hand, if Thomas Weelkes was appointed to Chichester, there he remained; even though, relatively speaking, Chichester was second-class and Weelkes first-class. The same applied to Francis Pilkington at Chester. Public announcement of vacancies distributed far and wide, public description of salaries and duties, public competitions in which any reasonably qualified entrant could take part—but secret balloting to decide the winner—were all typical of the Spanish system. True, these features of the system made for frequent moves, but at the same time they made it easy for the abler men to rise.

Sixteenth-century Spanish music differs also from English, French, and even Italian music in that only the Spanish royal house maintained two royal chapels: one of which was called the chapel of the House of Burgundy; the other, that of the House of Castile. The first chapel was made up entirely of Charles's and Philip's Low Countries subjects. The second, which was usually smaller, comprised Spaniards. Historically, this double establishment harked back to the union of the houses of Burgundy and Castile at the marriage of Philip the Fair with Joanna, daughter of Ferdinand and Isabella (1496). Charles V, son of this pair, always kept the House of Burgundy chapel for his own. The House of Castile chapel, on the other hand, belonged successively to his wife, Isabella of Portugal (whom he married in 1526 and who died in 1539), and to his children (while still in their minorities).[39] After Charles's abdication in 1556, Philip II was served by this succession of Flemish chapelmasters: (1) Nicolas Payen (1556-1559);

(2) Pierre de Manchicourt (1560-1564); (3) Jean Bonmarchais (1564-1569); (4) Gérard de Turnhout (1572-1580); (5) Georges de La Hèle (1581-1586); (6) Philippe Rogier[40] (1587-1596). As for the House of Castile chapel during the reign of Philip II,[41] its numbers dwindled from 14 adult singers, 4 boys, an organist (Juan de Cabezón) and a tuner (Cristóbal de León) in 1562; to only 8 singers in 1587 (a year in which the Flemish chapel enrolled 21 singers. However, during the next decade it "revived markedly." At the end of his reign, just as at the beginning, Philip II with his two chapels of singers and players—the one Flemish, the other Spanish—outdistanced every contemporary sovereign in his support of music. Though it is not to our present purpose, we could also add to his credit the support (after 1582) of a third musical chapel—with headquarters at Lisbon. Indeed, only after Philip's accession to the Portuguese crown did Lusitanian polyphonic achievement begin to match Spanish, as evinced, for instance, in the music of Duarte Lobo, Manuel Coelho, and Felipe de Magalhães.

Philip was also the only monarch of his time who patronized Italian, Spanish, and Flemish composers with impartial largesse. He was the only patron to whom Palestrina dedicated two books of masses (1567 and 1570). Guerrero found him an equally ready patron for his first foreign publication—his magnificats published at Louvain by Phalèse in 1563. Victoria dedicated his most lavish single publication to Philip—the *Missarum Libri Duo* of 1583. Or, to turn to Flemings: La Hèle dedicated to him "one of the most magnificent specimens of music typography" in existence—his *Octo Missae* of 1578 (published at Antwerp by Plantin). Finally, it was Philip's generosity that made possible in 1598 the posthumous publication of Rogier's *Missae sex*.

Not only was Philip II the leading international music patron of his age, but also at his court foreign and domestic music mixed on impartial terms. With his approbation, Morales and Guerrero were composers whose masses and magnificats were performed frequently. Despite the evident clannishness of his Flemish singers, motets by the two Spaniards were also marked out for the intensive study required to produce parody masses. In Rogier's case, his first three parody masses were based respectively on motets by Clemens non papa, Crecquillon, and Gombert. But his last parody mass, *Inclina Domine*, was based on Morales's motet *a 4*. Ghersem (as has already been noted) chose Guerrero's *Ave Virgo sanctissima*. We find (1) in the repertory sung at court and (2) in the parody sources used by the Flemings themselves, the strongest proofs that the music of these two composers—and for that matter, of such other composers performed at court as Rodrigo Ceballos, Escobedo, Infantas, and Pastrana—won esteem not for merely particularistic or patriotic reasons but because even Flemings found their music no less meritorious than the best Flemish product.[42]

The task of deciding who the ablest peninsular composers were between

1550-1600, leaving out of account Victoria and Guerrero, poses difficulties: (1) on account of the sheer numbers; (2) because during the reign of Philip II such a clear-cut test as membership of a court chapel was never permitted to determine a composer's superiority. The Tallises, Byrds, and Morleys of Spain, while enjoying Philip's favor, pursued their careers entirely outside the "Chapels Royal." A fortiori, the eminence of the lesser men is not to be gauged by such tokens of royal favor. Somewhat arbitrarily, then, the following four have been chosen for special study: Navarro, Lobo, Vivanco, and Esquivel. The criteria for this selection included: (1) extensive publication before 1611 (the year of Victoria's death and the terminal year adopted for the present study); (2) activity in Spain rather than in Italy; (3) centralization of activity in the sacred rather than in the secular field.

Juan Navarro (ca. 1530-1580)

In existing biographies, Seville and Marchena vie for the honor of having been Navarro's birthplace.[43] The title page of his posthumously published *Psalmi, Hymni ac Magnificat* (Rome: Francesco Coattino, 1590)[44] begins thus: *Joannis Navarri Hispalen.* Since *Hispalensis* means "Sevillian," the case would seem to be settled. The fact that Navarro while at Salamanca was on August 17, 1569, granted leave of absence to visit his father, then living in Seville, strengthens Sevillian claims. But, on the other hand, he registered as a native of Marchena when inducted as chapelmaster at Ciudad Rodrigo, after leaving Salamanca at the beginning of 1574.[45] Furthermore, a singer by the name of Juan Navarro belonged to the chapel of the Duke of Arcos at Marchena in 1549. These seeming contradictions will best be resolved by accepting the dictum of Gilbert Chase, who, in his article "Juan Navarro *Hispalensis* and Juan Navarro *Gaditanus*" (*The Musical Quarterly*, XXXI, 2 [April, 1945], 189), wrote as follows: "It appears that Navarro was born in Marchena. . . . At all events, since Marchena is a town in the province of Seville [lying 30 miles east of Seville], our composer could have been born there and still be called *Hispalensis.*"

Morales was chapelmaster to the Duke of Arcos from at least May, 1548, until February, 1551. He was thereafter chapelmaster at Málaga Cathedral (from November 27, 1551, until his death 22 months later). Juan Navarro, if the thesis of his Marchena origin is accepted, sang in the chapels conducted by Morales at both places. The evidence for his presence at Marchena survives in the form of a pay voucher dated September 6, 1549.[46] In this voucher his annual salary for singing in the Duke's chapel is listed as 10,000 maravedís. Obviously if this Juan Navarro is our composer he, like Francisco Guerrero, enjoyed Morales's tutelage. Furthermore, Morales seems to have done what he could to help Navarro, just as he had already helped Guerrero. Morales's efforts in behalf of the young Guerrero are certified by a Jaén Cathedral capitular act dated July 1, 1546. His efforts in behalf of the young Juan Navarro—or another youthful singer of the same name—are certified by two Málaga Cathedral capitular acts. On July 12, 1553, the succentor at Málaga persuaded the chapter to hear an "excellent tenor who had been singing at Jaén Cathedral." The chapter postponed decision until July 14, on which date Juan Navarro was hired at an annual salary of 25,000 maravedís.[47] Although again near Morales, Navarro was not to enjoy the privilege of renewed association for more than a few weeks (Morales died suddenly in early autumn). Navarro's next step was to submit his name as a contender in the competition to decide Morales's successor. Failing in his tests on February 9, 1554, he continued as a mere singer in the cathedral until October 2, 1555. On the latter date he asked permission to resign from his post and for a month's "terminal leave" pay.[48]

His trail vanishes during the next decade and is not picked up again until September 12, 1565, when he is found in service at Ávila Cathedral as chapelmaster. The *Actas Capitulares, 1565-1566-1567-1568* at Ávila reveal him to have been Bernardino de Ribera's successor. According to the act of Wednesday, September 12, 1565, he had been missing appointments in the cathedral on account of a protracted illness.[49] Because of an imminent *fiesta de música*, the chapter on that day urgently requests his presence in the cathedral. The bishop, Álvaro de Mendoza (who is something of a musical connoisseur), himself hopes that Navarro can attend the necessary practice sessions. On September 17 the chapter authorizes Navarro to write Alexandro de la Serna, *contralto*, a letter offering that renowned singer a half-prebend on condition that he agree to ordination *in sacris*.[50] On Saturday, December 8, 1565, the chapter authorizes the dean and precentor to offer another even more famous singer, Mosén Roque, *contrabaxo*, the best salary that it is within their power to give.[51] (Within three months, however, Roque yields to the lure of a higher salary at Seville.[52])

In the meantime Navarro has begun to attract nationwide attention. On September 27, 1566—the Salamanca chapelmastership having fallen vacant recently—the Salamanca chapter decides to invite him to occupy it without undergoing any formal trial of skill.[53] On Wednesday, October 9, the Ávila chapter grants him a fortnight's leave of absence.[54] Presumably he visits Salamanca during this leave and returns to Ávila ready to pack his bags and depart. Faced with an emergency, the Ávila chapter in special session on October 23 votes to increase his salary by an amount to be specified at a meeting on the morrow.[55] Already having recently raised his salary by 30,000 maravedís, the chapter on October 24 agrees to raise it by another 30,000 annually, provided that he bind himself to remain at Ávila for life.[56] To assure themselves, the chapter decrees that he must post bond guaranteeing repayment of the entire salary raise of 60,000 maravedís

annually—times the number of years he shall have enjoyed the raise—
in the event that he at any later time decides to renege the lifetime agreement. So eager is one canon, Cristóbal de Sedano, to keep Navarro at
Ávila that of his own free will he immediately offers in the same chapter
meeting to go surety for Navarro. However, the raise, bringing Navarro's
salary from the level of a mere half-prebend to that of a whole, fails to fulfill
all his demands now that the Salamanca Cathedral has offered him a more
desirable post. He wishes the chapter also to decree that he shall take prece-
dence over every other musician employed at Ávila, even those who have
occupied their prebends longer than he. The chapter can reply only tentatively to this last demand, and decides instead that the senior musicians
must first themselves agree to such a leap over the conventional hurdles of
cathedral seniority before the chapter can formally accede to this request.
For a few days Navarro wavers in his decision to move. But at last on
Thursday, November 7, he does depart.[57] In order to avoid a last-minute
flurry of protests and recriminations he goes off without formal leave-
takings. Next day the chapter reprehends both him and his aider and abet-
tor in the getaway—Juan Sánchez, cathedral succentor.

Navarro remains at Salamanca from the autumn of 1566 until January 2,
1574—a period of slightly more than seven years. During this epoch, Sala-
mancan music reaches unprecedented heights. Francisco Salinas, professor
from 1567 until 1587, governs music in the university and reaps the praise
of such discerning lovers of music as the great poet Luis de León.[58] Of
Salinas's researches during this epoch (culminating in his *De musica libri
septem* published at Salamanca in 1577), Vicente Espinel was to write
thus:[59]

That prince of music, Salinas, who revived the enharmonic genus, could
obtain it only by means of a keyboard instrument. Apparently singers cannot
conform to that particular genus except with superhuman effort and difficulty.
I have seen him playing his specially tuned keyboard instrument in Salamanca.
On it he performed miracles with his hands. But I never found that even
he had reclaimed the genus so that human voices could sing in it; although
there were then at Salamanca in the cathedral choir expert soloists with
splendid voices; and their master was the great composer, Juan Navarro.

Salinas, immediately before coming to Salamanca in 1567, had spent five
years as cathedral organist at León (1562-1567);[60] on other accounts he
enjoyed warmest respect at Salamanca, as both a practical and a theoretical musician. Espinel's first-hand account allows us to believe that Salinas
communicated his research results to Navarro and used Navarro's choir
as a laboratory in which to test his discoveries.

From Salamanca capitular acts the following further details concerning
Navarro's career have been recovered. On April 18, 1567, the contracts

let by the chapter for the repair of certain houses in the Calle de San Millán formerly occupied by Doctor Luis Pérez are made over to Navarro. Probably it is in one of these houses that Navarro is to be found during the next year boarding four choirboys "with beautiful voices."[61] On August 17, 1569, the chapter authorizes him to take a trip to Seville.[62] While there he is to look over the sopranists in Sevillian churches and to offer the best-qualified singer the half-prebend in Salamanca Cathedral left vacant by Martín de Herrera.[63] The replacement whom Navarro selects is to be guaranteed reimbursement for his travelling expenses from Seville to Salamanca. But since the primary purpose of Navarro's trip is to see his father at Seville, he must take care of his personal expenses out of private pocket.

Immediately upon his return, a grave disciplinary problem arises with Pedro Ricardo, cathedral organist. Discovered drunk while on duty, Ricardo is fined 20 ducats on October 1, 1569, and warned not to touch wine henceforth on pain of irrevocable dismissal.[64] In 1570 the chapter secretary draws up a revealing list of salaried musicians. As in all other Spanish cathedral lists of this period, the names of *cantores y ministriles* run parallel in such fashion as to prove that singers and instrumentalists enjoyed equal importance in the making of cathedral music. Among the cathedral singers in 1570, interestingly enough, is another Navarro—a *cantor contrabaxo*, whom the chapter minutes designate as a licenciado.[65] A second homonymous official in this year is the cathedral succentor, Rodrigo Ordoñez (d. 1572). By an interesting coincidence a Rodrigo Ordoñez is summoned to succeed Navarro in 1574.

In early September, 1570, Navarro shows signs of being overworked, perhaps venting his fatigue in outbursts of temper. On September 11 the chapter therefore acts favorably on his petition for a leave of absence, granting him the remainder of the month on full pay with permission to "recreate" himself.[66] On January 31, 1571, Bernardino de Villel relieves him by taking charge of the choirboys.[67] On February 19, 1571, the chapter requests Navarro to arrange for the immediate tuning of the cathedral organs.[68] On March 23, 1571, Francisco López, formerly a chaplain at Granada, joins the choir as a sopranist. But the search for better sopranists still goes vigorously forward. On October 11, 1572, the chapter authorizes an absentee canon, Antonio de Soria (detained in Rome while sick), to treat with Francisco Soto de Langa.[69] Canon Soria is to discuss with Soto, "sopranist at Rome in the pope's chapel," the possibility of his accepting a half-prebend at Salamanca; and if he shows interest to hand him an official letter inviting him to take up his duties at Salamanca in May, 1573. Before delivering the Salamanca chapter's letter of invitation, however, Canon Soria is first to ascertain whether or not Soto keeps his voice—and whether it is as beautiful as reported.

Navarro's departure from Salamanca comes as suddenly as it is dramatic.

On New Year's Eve he strikes the succentor. The full details cannot be reconstructed, but on January 2, 1574, the chapter meets to "discuss the transgression committed by the chapelmaster during Vespers on New Year's Eve when in the choir enclosure he dealt Juan Sánchez, cathedral chaplain and succentor, a violent blow on the face, thereby causing a grave scandal."[70] After some discussion, the chapter votes that Navarro's contract must be cancelled, his salary withdrawn, and his name crossed off the list of cathedral officials. On January 4 the chapter decides to distribute public announcements of the vacancy, with Ash Wednesday set as the terminal date for receiving applications.[71] Within a little more than three weeks the chapter agrees not to await the public competition but to offer the post straightway to Rodrigo Ordoñez at an annual salary of 300 ducats and 50 fanegas of wheat. (Born probably *ca.* 1530, Rodrigo Ordoñez was in 1553 a chapelmaster at Zamora and a *clérigo de la primera tonsura*. In November, 1554, he entered the competition to succeed Morales at Málaga, but was disqualified. In 1567 Villalar became chapelmaster at Zamora. In 1574 Rodrigo Ordoñez was chapelmaster at Murcia. Vicente Espinel lauded him in *La casa de la memoria* [1591].)[72] On February 4, the further enticement is offered Ordoñez of placing a house at his disposal. Eventually, however, the chapter finds its lures have been to no avail and decides to search elsewhere.

Ironically enough, Navarro's fame at the very moment of his dismissal had traveled so widely that on June 29, 1574, he was one of only two Spanish chapelmasters whose opinion the nuncio in Spain was advised to consult on candidacies for the papal choir.[73] Antonio Boccapaduli, master of the papal choir, forwarded a letter on that date asking that the nuncio in Spain seek out three or four Spanish singers. But Boccapaduli in his letter showed himself behind the times when he thought Navarro was still at Ávila. With irrefutable finality the Ávila capitular acts reveal that Navarro never regained the chapelmastership after leaving Ávila in 1566. Indeed, his relations with the Ávila chapter were so strained that in 1572 when he tried to retrieve some money still owing, the Ávila cathedral chapter refused him or his representatives so much as an opportunity to review the disputed accounts.[74] Not Ávila, then, but the less opulent cathedral at Ciudad Rodrigo (50 miles southwest of Salamanca) was to be Navarro's next stopping-place. That despite his troublous departure from Salamanca he was not to be treated with contumely during his four years (1574-1578) at Ciudad Rodrigo is proved by the fact that while there he was given the honor of a "high seat" in the choir and the right to vote at cathedral chapter meetings.[75] Moreover, his stay was fruitful, musically. While there he instructed the youthful Juan Esquivel, a native of Ciudad Rodrigo.[76] Esquivel in turn later rose to the dignity of the Ciudad Rodrigo chapelmastership, and by virtue of his publication of masses and motets at Salamanca shortly after the turn of the century established himself as one of the two or three worthiest sacred composers active during the reign of Philip III.

Navarro's last halting-place was to be Palencia. The aging former papal chorister Pedro Ordoñez (a native of Palencia) was in service there as chapelmaster during 1576-1578; but because of his infirmities a committee was appointed on October 26, 1577, to find a successor.[77] Matters dragged somewhat slowly, because adequate financial provision had first to be made for the retiring Pedro Ordoñez. A prebend was found for him on April 9, 1578, and on the following September 10 the Palencia chapter voted to receive Navarro—"of whose abilities and talent an excellent report had been given." He took six weeks to wind up his affairs at Ciudad Rodrigo; and on October 17 reported for duty at Palencia.[78] The cathedral act announcing his arrival is of interest for several reasons. First, it shows that he brought into the chapter meeting of that date an effusive letter written in his behalf by the new Bishop of Palencia, Álvaro de Mendoza. This bishop had governed the diocese of Ávila from 1563 until 1577. His term at Palencia was to last from 1577 until 1586. Beyond doubt, the new bishop's interest dated from the days of Navarro's chapelmastership at Ávila— Navarro's last two years there (1563-1564) having coincided with the bishop's first two. Second, the act of October 17, 1578, is of interest because it proves that Navarro coveted certain evidences of respect for his profession, among them (1) the right to wear the same brocade as that worn by canons, and (2) the right to a high seat in choir. The act itself deserves at least partial quotation.

On Friday, October 17, 1578, Juan Navarro, chapelmaster of Ciudad Rodrigo, brought in a recommendatory letter written by His Excellency the Bishop: in which after warmly urging the chapter to accord Navarro all possible honor the bishop stated that everything done for the chapelmaster would be interpreted as a kindness done him personally, his reason being that Navarro's talents did not fall short of the best recognition that the chapter could give them. Navarro, after presenting the letter, offered his services to the cathedral with every mark of appreciation for the chapter's kindness in inviting him to Palencia. Having paid his devoirs, he left. The Archdeacon of Campos and the precentor then made mention of the fact that Navarro did not ask for more than he had been previously conceded in other cathedrals; and that while His Excellency was now asking the chapter to assign him an altar and a high seat in choir, Navarro had been enjoying even greater honors at Ciudad Rodrigo, where in addition to these tokens of respect he had had the privilege of a vote at chapter meetings. This privilege he was not now requesting in our cathedral. Navarro's petition having been heard, his many fine qualities explained, his preëminence as an artist bespoken, but principally the bishop's letter having been taken into consideration, it was proposed that a vote be taken. Juan Alonso de Torres, prebendary, intruded at this juncture to protest (in his own name, and in that of the other cathedral prebendaries who had authorized him to speak for them) that the proposal clearly prejudiced the rights of the titular prebendaries in elevating Navarro over them in the seating plan; and that he must therefore denounce the proposal and was prepared to do so at great length, given time and place; and that he would himself petition His Excellency not to approve any action taken by the chapter. His protest having been heard and his notice of intention to appeal to the bishop duly recorded, the chapter proceeded to vote. Scrutiny of the tallies showed 27 for the bishop's proposal, 10 against. The chapter then ordered that because of his personal merits Navarro should during the time of his service in Palencia Cathedral be allowed the privilege of his own altar in weeks chosen by him, provided that they did not encroach on double or semidouble feasts marked in the calendar for polyphonic celebration. Also he might wear the same silk brocade worn by canons, and enjoy a high seat in choir: all of this by express permission of the chapter.

The next capitular act mentioning Navarro is dated May 22, 1579. Having just completed his seventh month of service he waited on the chapter that day with a request, made "in his own name and in that of the musical prebendaries and twelve singing chaplains," for permission to establish a Brotherhood dedicated especially to the praise of Our Lady and of the cathedral patron Saint Antolín (French third-century saint thought to have been buried on the site of Palencia Cathedral). At the same time he brought in the constitutions of the proposed brotherhood and asked the chapter to reserve a special chapel for their religious exercises. The chapter agreed to study the proposed constitutions.

That Navarro continued to enjoy the bishop's high favor throughout his stay at Palencia is borne out by the personal letter that the bishop wrote in his behalf to the chapter in April, 1580, asking that he be granted a salary raise. But he had not long to enjoy it, for he died at two on Sunday afternoon, September 25 of the same year. As a mark of honor he was buried in the cathedral. On the following Saturday, October 1, the chapter met to consider how his place, and also several other musical vacancies, might best be filled. Because of the difficulty of luring first-rate musicians to Palencia, the chapter decided that the next chapelmaster must be offered the same privileges as Navarro: namely, "brocade and an altar in addition to all the rest." Villalar of Zamora (whose name they mistook for Villacampa) was their first choice. He refused, whereupon the chapter voted (December 19, 1580) to write Melchor Robledo—who had for a decade been serving as chapelmaster at Saragossa. Their letter to Robledo proved a futile gesture—he having recently moved from Saragossa. When news that he had transferred to Calahorra "for just and sufficient reasons" reached the Palencia chapter on February 6, 1581, nought remained but to hire a contender who suffered from the twin disadvantages of being a layman and married—Bricio Gandí.

Like Guerrero, Navarro first bursts into print in a vihuela tablature. Guerrero was represented by intabulations of nine items in Fuenllana's *Orphénica lyra* (1554); Navarro is represented by three in Daza's *El Parnasso* (1576). Two of these are labeled villanescas, *No vez amor* (folios 89-90^V) and *Ay de mí, sin ventura* (folios 85^V-87^V). Daza classifies the third as a villancico, *Que razón podeys vos* (folios 99-100^V). These three are, of course, secular items: just as are the six in the Medinaceli cancionero (*MME*, Vol. VIII, items 26,[79] 35, 45, 50; Vol. IX, items 55, 76), two of which (items 35 [= 89], 76) concord with the second and first Daza intabulations. Apart from these secular pieces, Navarro seems not to have reached print during his lifetime.

On the other hand, his *Psalmi, Hymni ac Magnificat*, published at Rome ten years after his death, establishes him as a unique figure among Spanish sixteenth-century composers in that his was the only such monumental collection (177 leaves) for which publication was engineered not by the composer himself, but by an admirer willing to defray the costs. Moreover, it was the only such publication that rose, phoenix-like, above a composer's ashes. True, individual motets by this or that Spanish composer reached a first printing posthumously. But only in the instance of Navarro did such a collected edition comprised entirely of a single composer's works appear after his death.

The patron at whose charges the collection was printed, Canon Francisco Reinoso, bore the title of *abad* (abbot) *de Husillos*—this being a dignity in Palencia Cathedral. Husillos, a small village five miles north of Palencia, gives its name to this cathedral dignity.[80] Later, when Reinoso became bishop of Cordova (1597-1601) he patronized Victoria (see below, p. 366). It was he also whom Antonio Ortiz in his *A Relation of the Solemnetie wherewith the Catholike Princes K. Phillip the III. and Quene Margaret were receyued in the Inglish Colledge of Valladolid the 22. of August. 1600* (published 1601) came to extol for the gift of a "payre of virginales of an excellent sound" used to "accompany the other instruments which the schollers vse with great dexteritie in the solemnities of Masse and Euensong vpon feastiuall dayes, which they sing with no lesse deuotion and proprietie of Ecclesiasticall ceremonies as the Institution and statutes of these Seminaries ordayne." Such largesse proves that Reinoso was an unusually cultivated music lover and a patron of informed taste. At his solicitation, Fernando Navarro Salazar (himself a distinguished canonist) submitted manuscript copies of his uncle's vespers music (perhaps identical with the two large manuscript collections still existing in 1933, although in deteriorated condition, at Palencia Cathedral). Reinoso, who had visited Rome *ca.* 1580, in turn transmitted these to Francisco Soto (1534-1619), the singer in the papal chapel for whose services the Salamanca chapter had vied unsuccessfully in 1572-1573 while Navarro was still chapelmaster. Soto was an experienced editor. Before 1590 he had already edited three books of *Laudi spiri-tuali*. In the third he had even changed *a lo divino* the secular words of a villanesca—*No ves amor*—that Daza had in his *El Parnasso* (1576) attributed

No ves mi Dios *

Il terzo libro delle laudi spirituali (Rome: 1588), fol. 35ᵛ.　　　　　　　[Juan Navarro]**

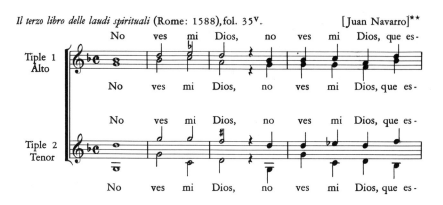

* Do not regard, O God, how this soul diverts himself among vain pleasures of such kind that despite Thy redemption he hugs destruction: forgetful of Thee, the highest good. Since Thou art vexed by the provocation offered Thee, cast an arrow at this soul that will pain it.

** The secular original, *No ves amor*, is anonymous in Biblioteca Medinaceli MS 13230 at fols. 136ᵛ-137ᵛ, but as a *villanesca a quatro* entitled *No vez amor* is accredited to Navarro at fol. 89 of Esteban Daza's *El Parnasso* (Valladolid: 1576). Tiples 1 and 2 are interchanged in the secular and sacred versions. Our suggested accidentals duplicate Daza's required accidentals in his intabulation (fols. 89-90ᵛ).

to Navarro: the new sacred lyrics bearing as title, *No ves mi Dios* (*Il terzo libro delle laudi spirituali* [Rome: 1588]). Obviously, Soto already knew and therefore admired Navarro's music before Reinoso commissioned him to see the 1590 selection through the press.

In his 1590 preface Soto begins with an expression of thanks to Reinoso for assigning him such an editorial task.[81] He declares that Navarro's art

... lacks nothing that the most erudite musician might desire, but that at the same time Navarro knows how to transport the hearer with the incredible sweetness of his music. . . . Therefore, notwithstanding the pressure of innumerable other duties from every side, I most willingly undertook the task of seeing these works through the press at the earliest possible moment; for not only am I certain that those who are expert in the art, as well as that larger general public which shall in future have an opportunity of hearing these works sung, will be grateful to me for having completed this editorial task; but more especially do I know that this collection ought to be published for the honor and glory of God and of Our Lady.

So far as actual contents are concerned, Navarro's 1590 posthumous publication closely parallels Guerrero's *Liber vesperarum* published at Rome six years earlier. Both books begin with vesper psalms, continue with vesper hymns (arranged in church-year sequence), proceed next to magnificats in each of the eight tones, and conclude with settings of four Marian antiphons. Apart from the similarity of liturgical types—psalms, hymns, magnificats, and Marian antiphons—the two collections deserve comparison because: (1) the same seven psalms with which Guerrero commences his *Liber vesperarum* (nos. 109-113, 116, 147) are to be found among Navarro's dozen psalms; (2) every one of the twenty-four hymn texts set in Guerrero's second section occurs among Navarro's twenty-eight, and always in connection with the same feasts; (3) in both Guerrero's set of ten and in Navarro's of nine magnificats is to be found a series of alternate-verse settings in all eight tones; (4) both composers chose to conclude their collections with the same four Marian antiphons, namely, *Alma Redemptoris, Ave Regina coelorum, Regina coeli,* and *Salve Regina* (Vita, Ad te suspiramus, Et Jesum through ventris tui, O clemens through the end, in polyphony). Actual performance of almost every item in both the Guerrero and Navarro books presupposes the alternation of verses in plainsong with those in polyphony *a 4.*

Navarro's psalms bear these numbers (Vulgate numbering): 109-113, 115-116, 121, 126, 131, 138, 147. In Psalms 109-112, 115-116, 121, 126, and 147 he sets the even verses polyphonically (*Liber usualis* numbering). On the other hand, in Psalms 113, 131, and 138—each of which extends to more than twenty verses—he sets only every third verse polyphonically:[82] begin-

Laudate pueri (Psalm 112 [=113])

Quarti toni

Psalmi, Hymni ac Magnificat (Rome: 1590), fols. 8ᵛ-9.

* Blessed be the name of the Lord, both now and for evermore.

† High above all nations is the Lord, His glory is above the heavens.

ning with verse 2 (*Liber usualis* numbering). Since he commits himself to the use of the same psalm tone in every polyphonic verse during a given psalm, a rather severe test is imposed upon his artistry. He avoids monotony by shifting the psalm-tone formula from one voice to another; by reducing (verses 8 of Ps. 109 and 9 of Ps. 138) or augmenting the number of voice parts (Gloria Patri in Pss. 121, 147); by changing the vocal combination from a mixed quartet to four equal voices (verses 21 of Ps. 113, 8 of Ps. 115, 6 of Ps. 121, 4 of Ps. 126, 14 of Ps. 131, 6 of Ps. 147); and occasionally by culminating in a canon (tenor with altus II at the fifth in Ps. 147). As for the order in which they are printed, the first eight (109, 110, 111, 112, 116, 121, 147, 126) adhere respectively to the eight psalm tones. The remaining four (138, 115, 131, 113) follow no such predetermined tonal scheme (Tones II, V, III, and III, respectively).

Navarro contrives canons of one sort or another in ten of the twenty-eight hymns (*Ad caenam Agni providi, Jesu nostra redemptio, Ave maris stella, Ut queant laxis, Lauda mater ecclesia, Christe Redemptor omnium, Tristes erant Apostoli, Deus tuorum militum, Urbs beata Jerusalem,* and *Te Deum laudamus*). The second of these boasts an enigma canon, as does also the solmization hymn. In that only notes of designated time value in the dux are to be sung by the comes, the *Jesu nostra redemptio* canon foreshadows feats of like kind in Alonso Lobo's *Prudentes virgines* Mass (Osanna I) and in Vivanco's first magnificat (Gloria Patri *a 8*).[83]

The most "Spanish" hymns are the Passion Sunday *Vexilla Regis prodeunt* and the Corpus Christi *Pange lingua gloriosi*. In each, Navarro has polyphonically dressed "more hispano" melodies. The *Vexilla Regis prodeunt* at folio 46^V opens with a plainsong intonation (the first three words) succeeded by polyphony during the rest of the strophe. Either because the Spanish plainsong would not have been known elsewhere, or because this is the only hymn in which Navarro breaks into polyphony in the middle of a strophe, this one hymn alone of the twenty-eight is headed by its appropriate plainsong intonation printed in black semibreves. Such an exception stands out all the more boldly because Navarro provides another polyphonic setting of two strophes from Venantius Fortunatus's identical hymn at folios 70^V-72. The second *Vexilla Regis* (In festo S. Crucis) differs musically from the first (Dominica in Passione) because: (1) no allusion is made to the "more hispano" melody; (2) Navarro breaks into polyphony not in the middle of the strophe, but at the beginning of a stanza; (3) no printed intonation stands at the head of the superius. Venantius Fortunatus's is the only hymn set twice in Navarro's collection. He provides polyphony for strophes 1, 4, 6, and 8 in the Passion Sunday version; for strophes 3 and 7 in the Holy Cross version.

The second specifically Spanish hymn tune that he chooses for polyphonic treatment is the *Pange lingua gloriosi* at folio 60^V-65. Here he assigns the borrowed melody—which he quotes with scrupulous exactness—to his superius throughout all three strophes (2, 4, and 6). Since Guerrero uses the same "more hispano" melody when setting the same hymn text by St. Thomas Aquinas (*Liber vesperarum*, folios 45^v-48), a comparison of Navarro's with Guerrero's setting is in order. Instead of confining the borrowed melody to the superius, Guerrero allots the first, second, third, and sixth incises of the borrowed melody to his cantus, but the fourth and fifth incises to his tenor in the *Nobis natus* strophe; all incises to the lowest of four equal voices in the *Verbum caro* strophe; the first pair of incises to the cantus, and the last four to the tenor, in the *Tantum ergo* strophe. Guerrero, in addition to shifting his vocal combination from mixed voices in the outer strophes to equal in the middle strophe, veers from the triple meter in which the Spanish plainsong was traditionally sung to unconventional duple during his final *Tantum ergo* strophe; and does not hesitate to embellish the borrowed melody with passing notes, especially at final cadences. Navarro, by reason of his literal quotation, rigid placement in the superius, and unvarying meter, achieves the elegant stiffness of finely embroidered brocade. Guerrero, because of his willingness to paraphrase, his shifting of borrowed material from one voice to another, his unexpected abandonment in the last strophe of triple for duple meter, and his preference for motet rather than strict cantus firmus treatment, weaves a more pliable silken fabric that shines with different-hued iridescence at every stirring of the atmosphere. Both settings are works of high art. Navarro, by virtue of the more straightforward design in this as in other of his hymns, seems to have provided a setting that chapelmasters in the smaller Spanish cathedrals could perform with greater assurance of success.[84]

Although only a third of Navarro's twenty-eight hymns vaunt canons, every final Gloria Patri of his first eight magnificats (found at folios 109^v-157) contains them. Interestingly enough, the canonic interval corresponds with the number of the tone. The first Gloria Patri (Magnificat in Tone I) exhibits a canon at the unison, second (Tone II) at the second, third (Tone III) at the third, and so forth, through the eighth (Tone VIII) with its canon at the octave. This highly schematic arrangement—so typically Spanish, in that the learned device (1) answers to the beck and call of an exterior authority and (2) is applied to a series of magnificats (rather than to movements of a *Missa Prolationum* or *Repleatur os meum*)—caught the fancy of the slightly later peninsular composer, Sebastián Aguilera de Heredia. But instead of a canon at the number of the tone in only the Gloria Patri of each five-voice magnificat (*Canticum Beatissimae Virginis Deiparae Mariae octo modis, seu tonis compositum* [Saragossa: Pedro Cabart, 1608], folios 1^v-49), Aguilera propounded canons at the respective interval in all six polyphonic movements of each magnificat.[85] Navarro's canons appear always in odd-verse (*Anima mea*) magnificats; so do Aguilera's. In all eight of his *Anima mea* magnificats, Navarro reduces to three voices in the Et misericordia movement (SSA, ATB, SAT, SAB, SAA, AAT, SSA, STB in Tone I through Tone VIII, respectively). Aguilera similarly reduces to four voices in every Et misericordia movement of his canonic magnificats. The basic number of voices in Navarro's magnificats (like his psalms and hymns) is, on the other hand, always a quartet; whereas Aguilera's canonic exemplars are all composed *a 5*.

For a postscript to his series of eight odd-verse magnificats, Navarro's 1590 publication includes a ninth even-verse magnificat (Tone I). Just as in the Gloria Patri of each *Anima mea* magnificat, so also in the Sicut erat of this *Et exultavit* magnificat he augments to five voices. However, in the Sicut erat of this ninth magnificat he refuses to extend his scheme by constructing a canon at the ninth.

The four Marian antiphons—*Alma Redemptoris (a 5)*, *Ave Regina coelorum (a 5)*, *Regina coeli (a 6)*, and *Salve Regina (a 4)*—are designated respectively for use in the following seasons: (1) Advent until Septuagesima; (2) Septuagesima until Easter; (3) Easter until Trinity; (4) Trinity until Advent. The highly wrought scheme visible in both the parts and the whole of Navarro's 1590 *Psalmi, Hymni ac Magnificat* strongly suggests that before his death he had planned the publication of his "works" in just such a collected form. In this one volume he supplied choristers with a complete body of polyphony for the most important of the office hours—vespers: it alone among the hours being a service at which polyphonic singing has ever enjoyed general encouragement. Indeed, nothing in the book, except the last two hymns—*Te lucis ante terminum* being the compline hymn sung indiscriminately throughout every season of the church year and *Te Deum* being the thanksgiving hymn admitted at matins of the greater feasts and on other occasions for celebration—belongs in any service other than that of vespers.[86]

Navarro's vespers music enjoyed a remarkably widespread vogue. Manuscript copies made long after the exhaustion of the printed book are still to be encountered today in such unfrequented and widely separated places as Puebla, Mexico, and Vila Viçosa, Portugal. Whatever the other reasons for the wide popularity of his vespers music, these excellencies should be mentioned: (1) his succinctness, (2) his ability to capture a mood immediately, (3) his fidelity to the plainchant source, (4) his presentation of the source melody in as conspicuous a way as possible, and (5) his preference for rational rather than esoteric devices.

In Spain itself the continued vogue can be adduced from the survival in both east (Murcia) and west (Plasencia) Spain of manuscript copies made as late as the eighteenth century.[87] Such continued popularity after 1632, when radically revised texts for fourteen of the twenty-eight hymns

included in Navarro's printed collection were approved by Pope Urban
VIII (in an effort to improve the Latinity of medieval hymnology), meant
that Navarro's 1590 texts had to be changed. One such revised text is to
be found in a 1933 reprint of his Low Sunday hymn *Ad caenam Agni providi*
(*Psalmi, Hymni ac Magnificat* [1590], folios 50ᵛ-54). Elústiza and Castrillo
Hernández, when they republished this hymn in their *Antología musical*,
took for their source a late Burgos Cathedral manuscript rather than Navarro's 1590 printed version.[88] In consequence, they adhered to the revised
text of this hymn, which begins *Ad regias Agni dapes*. This title alone would
warn any informed hymnist that the rest of the Ambrosian text has been
made to conform with the more "classically correct" version approved
by the last humanist pope.

In this particular hymn, although not quite so faithfully as in the Spanish
Pange lingua already alluded to, Navarro adheres to the plainsong in every
polyphonic strophe—those polyphonically set being strophes 2, 4, 6, and 8.
In strophes 2 and 4 he places the plainsong in the top voice of the mixed
quartet. In strophe 6, for SAB trio, the plainsong still travels in the top
part. In the concluding strophe *a 5* (SSATB) he devises a canon at the
unison between superius I and II: meanwhile confiding the plainsong to the
tenor. Whether in the top voice or in the tenor, the plainsong shades off
into a chiaroscuro, by reason of an added note or two, only at cadences.
Because of his tendency to quote plainsong literally and to pace the
plainsong-bearing voice slower than those surrounding it in the polyphonic
complex, Navarro more nearly approaches his teacher Morales—at least
so far as the treatment of plainchant is concerned—than does his fellow
pupil Guerrero.

Navarro, unlike most sixteenth-century Spanish masters, seems to have
avoided composing masses. However, ten motets not classifiable as vespers
music are preserved in the Santiago codex at Valladolid. One of these,
his *Ave Virgo sanctissima*, has already been compared with Guerrero's more
famous motet of the same title (above at pp. 204-206). Two others from the
same codex were reprinted in the 1933 Elústiza-Castrillo anthology that
contains the Low Sunday hymn described in the two previous paragraphs.
Though neither is edited satisfactorily—wrong notes cropping up in both—
the edition does not so belie the originals as wholly to obscure Navarro's
great expressive powers. The study of both is of value because they prove
that Navarro's motet style departed radically from his vespers style. The
phrases in both are expansively drawn. If not the proleptic master of tonic-
dominant harmony that Guerrero proves to have been, Navarro does use
the shifts of harmony implied by new obligatory accidentals to underline
sharp turns of thought in the motet texts. For instance, in his Maundy
Thursday *In passione positus*, a fourth-tone motet in two *partes a 6*,[89] he re-

serves the use of B♭'s for the dramatic moment when Jesus begins to cry out in agony, "My soul is sorrowful even unto death." Flats, which would be of such commonplace occurrence in all other modes as not to deserve notice, make a strange and telling effect at this juncture: especially since only when Jesus begins to speak do they adorn either treble or bass lines in this motet of 96 breves duration. In *Laboravi in gemitu*, a single-*pars* motet *a 5*, he sets verses 7-9 from Psalm 6.[90] But Navarro makes no allusion to a psalm tone, does not divide the verses for alternate polyphonic and plainsong rendition, and instead constructs his music as a series of imitative points. His lines are extremely poignant. The drooping thirds at mm. 1-13$_3$ aptly evoke the sigh of the psalmist, "I am weary with my moaning." When the psalmist rouses himself and suddenly shouts, "Depart from me, all you workers of iniquity," Navarro responds musically with swift upward leaps to an accented octave, followed by downward thirds, in a point of imitation at mm. 50-54. Not only by the contour of his lines but also by harmonic juxtapositions he finds ways to reinforce the text. When the psalmist complains, "Every night I flood my bed with tears," Navarro at the word "tears" (meas. 23) moves directly from a D-Major chord (obligatory f♯) to an F-Major chord (obligatory F♮). He again repeats this shift at mm. 63-64. The cross relations are by no means Navarro's only harmonic expedients. At mm. 40-41 he moves from A minor to B♭ Major and thence to E♭ Major chords in quick succession when setting the words "troubled with indignation."

Alonso [= Alfonso] Lobo (ca. 1555-1617)

After mid-century it became the custom at Toledo to require that a biographical sketch of each important new cathedral appointee be filed in the cathedral archives. These sketches do not always reveal date of birth, but they do state the names of the parents and the place of birth. Alonso Lobo, who became chapelmaster at Toledo in 1593, is known from his *expediente de limpieza de sangre* to have been born in Osuna (50 miles east of Seville). His father's name was Alonso Lobo, and his mother's, Jerónima de Borja.[91] It would be tempting to suppose that Alonso Lobo the father of the composer was the same *alonso lovo moço de coro del qual le hazian e hizieron merçed e limosna porque sirue vien el coro* in Seville Cathedral on February 18, 1538.[92] (The composer himself can hardly have been the choirboy commended in the Sevillian capitular acts for his outstanding service, because he would then have turned seventy when named chapelmaster at Seville in succession to Cotes—a superannuate's age.)

Not only does the Toledo *expediente* reveal the name of the composer's father, but also that of his paternal grandfather, which was Alonso Lobo as well; it further certifies that each of the four grandparents was a native of

Osuna. If the composer was born in 1555, as Eslava suggested, he rose to a canonry in the collegiate church at Osuna before he was thirty-five. Whatever his exact age, it is certain that the surroundings in which Lobo came to maturity were culturally as stimulating as any to be found in Spain during the reign of Philip II. The collegiate church—endowed by Juan Téllez Girón, fourth count of Ureña, the amateur composer who was a patron of Morales[93]—had been erected on a sumptuous scale in 1531-1535. Situated near the peak of a windswept hill and flanked by an imposing tower (now fallen), this *Iglesia colegial* enjoyed all the pretensions of a major cathedral.[94] Adjacent to it stood the buildings of the University of Osuna, founded in 1549. That Lobo was himself a graduate with the degree of *licenciado* is to be learned from a document that he signed in 1602.[95]

His reputation had spread sufficiently for the Sevillian chapter to invite him by a letter dated August 21, 1591, to become Guerrero's aide and probable successor.[96] Since contrary to custom he was not asked to undergo any formal tests, he must have enjoyed Guerrero's complete confidence before the letter was sent. Indeed, it seems likely that he was Guerrero's former pupil: especially in view of the number of Lobo's parody masses based on Guerrero's motets. Wasting no time, Lobo reported for duty in Seville on September 2.[97] His salary was set at 400 ducats annually, with 80 fanegas of wheat. His duties included care and feeding of the choirboys, in addition to their musical instruction. On November 29, 1591, the Sevillian chapter authorized him to wear a mantle: this privilege being extended in recognition of his previous rank at Osuna.[98] On the same day, he was invited to conduct while the aging Guerrero (with whom he was obviously on the most intimate of terms) took extended leave from official cathedral duties.

Lobo's talents were such that he could not long be suffered to remain in a subordinate position, even to Guerrero. On September 22, 1593, he was elected chapelmaster at Toledo Cathedral in succession to Ginés de Boluda, and on the following December 3 formally installed in *Ración 44 de tenor*. By an anomaly and not by deliberate planning, the chapelmaster's salary at Toledo during the sixteenth century had derived from a mere tenor's prebend. Before Lobo, such Toledo chapelmasters as Andrés de Torrentes (December 9, 1539; December 16, 1547; February 9, 1571), Cristóbal de Morales (September 1, 1545), Bartolomé de Quebedo (December 5, 1553), and Ginés de Boluda (December 7, 1580) had each occupied the same tenor's prebend. But during Lobo's term a proposal was made to normalize matters by assigning him *Ración 35*, the prebend that anciently had been designated for the chapelmaster. This shift was not confirmed without an acrimonious debate that ended in an appeal to the primate. At last, however, the change was ratified (September 18, 1601).[99] In consequence,

Lobo's successors for the first time in Toledo history can be found occupying a prebend officially made over not to a mere singer, but more properly to the *maestro de capilla*.

Soon after induction at Toledo, Lobo suggested the purchase of Guerrero's *Mottecta liber secundus* and *Canciones y villanescas espirituales*, both of which had been published in partbooks at Venice in 1589. Lobo signed for 200 reales on September 3, 1594, an amount which he then forwarded to Guerrero. This sum of 6,800 maravedís (200 reales) for both Guerrero's 1589 publications may seem small, especially when it is remembered that in 1592 Lobo's predecessor at Toledo, Ginés de Boluda, had paid 81,056 maravedís (2,384 reales) for certain *libros de canto de órgano* of Guerrero— presumably the 1582 masses and 1584 vespers. But an explanation can be found in the fact that both the 1582 and 1584 books were *libros de facistol* whereas both the 1589 publications, on the other hand, were issued in hand-size partbooks. In payment for his Christmas villancicos composed in 1593 and 1596, Lobo received 4 ducats (1,500 maravedís) each time.

Like his predecessor Ginés de Boluda, Lobo boarded six specially selected boy choristers in his own house. His wheat ration amounted to approximately 42 English bushels in 1596. Since the portrait (front view) on his *Liber primus missarum* published at Madrid in 1602 shows him still in the full prime of manhood, his success with his boyish charges at both Seville and Toledo was probably measured by his own youthful vigor. As for adult singers under his charge, four extra clergy at nine reales each had to be hired to chant psalms during *Tenebrae* in 1600. In consequence, the chapter specially commissioned him on April 18, 1600, to go in search of new clergy adept at singing psalms; and on the same day budgeted 20,000 maravedís for the trip. Certain phrases in the dedication of his *Liber primus missarum* to the Toledo chapter suggest that his singers (as well as instrumentalists) were at other times accounted the best in Spain, both in numbers and in quality.

It was toward the close of Lobo's decade in Toledo that he undertook to publish six of his own masses: *Beata Dei genitrix* a 6, *Maria Magdalena* a 6, *Prudentes virgines* a 5, *Petre ego pro te rogavi* a 4, *Simile est regnum coelorum* a 4, and *O Rex gloriae* a 4. Like Guerrero, who added three of his choicest motets to his first volume of masses (Paris: 1566), Lobo concluded his *Liber primus missarum* with a section of motets suitable for "devout singing during the celebration of Mass." Of the seven added motets, the *Ave Maria* calls for double quartet, the others for four, five, and six voices.[100] Lobo's contract with his printer has been recovered;[101] as has also a *carta de pago* dated March 4, 1603. From these sources he is known on August 30, 1602, to have signed a contract before a Madrid notary with the same royal printer, "John the Fleming," who had already in 1598 done so well by the deceased

Philippe Rogier (chapelmaster to Philip II from 1587 to 1596) when publishing *Missae sex* in elegant folio.[102] Lobo's contract with Juan Flamenco (= Joannes Flandrus) specified the printing of 130 copies of 137 leaves each. On February 28, 1603, he wrote a letter from Toledo to his good friend Victoria in Madrid authorizing final settlement with the printer. Five days later Juan Flamenco made out a receipt to Victoria, Lobo's proxy. In order to appreciate how much the printing actually cost Lobo, we can draw some comparisons. Hernando de Cabezón in 1576 had agreed upon only 5,000 reales for 1,200 copies of 127 leaves.[103] True, the *Obras de musica para tecla arpa y vihuela* (1578) did not reach maximum folio size. But it was printed in tablature; and by terms of the contract, Francisco Sánchez (the Madrid printer with whom Hernando Cabezón bargained) was required to provide new matrices and type. Victoria, whose *Missae, Magnificat, Motecta, Psalmi, et alia quam plurima* was issued in 1600 by the same royal firm that in 1602 undertook to print 130 copies of Lobo's *Liber primus missarum* for $5936\frac{2}{3}$ reales, had moreover paid less than half Lobo's amount: his bill amounting to only 2,500 reales for 200 sets of nine vocal partbooks and a tenth book for organ.[104]

Lobo's superb title page alone must have added considerably to production costs. Centered on the page is an engraving of Mary surrounded by angels. She is in the act of enduing Ildephonsus (606-667),[105] apologist for her perpetual virginity, with a rich chasuble. Since Lobo dedicated his book to the Toledan chapter, such an engraving was, of course, especially appropriate—Ildephonsus having been the most famous bishop of Toledo during the Visigothic era. The engraving is surrounded by a border filled with such diverse musical instruments as viol, vihuela, lute, harp, small stringed keyboard instrument, portative organ, trombone, cornett, and drum. Although it is improbable that all these instruments were used at Toledo conjointly on any single occasion, the frequent references to *menestriles* in the primatial records vouch for complete sets of wind instruments on all festive days. A small oval vignette at the bottom of the title page shows the composer. In his right hand he holds a sheet of music paper inscribed with a three-in-one canon. He wears his hair, mustache, and beard, close-cropped; out of his deep-set eyes flashes a bright gleam. Altogether, his regular features and broad forehead would deserve to be called, if not handsome, at least prepossessing.

After publication of his masses, Lobo decided that his task at Toledo was done, and thenceforth turned his eyes southward. On September 9, 1603, Ambrosio Cotes (chapelmaster at Seville since September 22, 1600) opportunely died. In a matter of months Lobo exchanged Toledo for Seville. On March 9, 1604, the Sevillian capitular secretary jotted this marginal entry: "The chapter received Maestro Lobo for chapelmaster and decided that he should be paid prebend's salary from January 1, plus 40,000 mara-vedís and 40 fanegas of wheat for taking charge of the choirboys."[106] On April 1 (1604) the chapter voted him a further gift of 300 reales to buy bread.[107] On July 1, 1605, the canons acceded to his request for a loan of 300 ducats provided that proper surety was given.[108] On March 16, 1606, the chapter notified the cathedral corps of instrumentalists that they must continue to discharge their most onerous obligation—that of marching in processions.[109] On April 10, 1606, Baltasar de Torres succeeded to the mas-tership of the altar boys (*maestro de los moços de coro*). As during Guerrero's time, the *mozos de coro* sang only plainchant, polyphony being reserved for the *seises* who boarded with the chapelmaster. Lobo's last years have not yet been so thoroughly explored as they deserve; but it is known that the choirboys remained in his charge from February 10, 1604, until August 1, 1610; and that he died on April 5, 1617.[110] Burial took place at chapter expense in the Antigua chapel. The full complement of cathedral singing clergy accompanied his body to the grave. Since at his death he was still Sevillian chapelmaster, his whole career is accounted for, and there is no unoccupied time left for the period of service in Lisbon hypothecated by the enthusiastic Portuguese musical historian Joaquim de Vasconcellos in his uncritical *Os musicos portuguezes* (Oporto: Imp. Portugueza, 1870), Volume I, page 199. Neither is it any longer possible to hold that Lobo died in 1601, as was affirmed by Higinio Anglés in *MME*, Volume IV, page 5.

The latter's "La música conservada en la Biblioteca Colombina y en la Catedral de Sevilla" (*AM*, II [1947]) also stands in need of correction. Though in this article a complete catalogue is attempted, no mention is made of such music in the Sevillian cathedral archive as Lobo's two masses *a 4*, *Petre ego pro te rogavi* and *O Rex gloriae*, copied into MS 110 at folios 1ᵛ-16 and 46ᵛ-62. Nor is this perfectly preserved large vellum choirbook the only Lobo source overlooked in the 1947 catalogue: MS 115, another large choirbook (31 by 21 inches) sumptuously copied on vellum, opens with three hymns *a 4* by Lobo: the first for St. Isidore's feast, the second for the feast of SS. Justa and Rufina, and the third for the feast of Hermene-gild.[111] To these hymns for Visigothic saints should be added Lobo's hymn for San Diego at folios 11ᵛ-14, and for the Apostle James at folios 14ᵛ-16 in this same choirbook. An unnumbered choirbook copied at Seville as late as 1772 and reaching 41 leaves also goes unmentioned in the 1947 catalogue. This choirbook, devoted entirely to Lobo's lamentations, bears the title *Lect. Prima de Ieremie Propheta. Christus factus est. Et Miserere. In Officio Tenebrarum. Sabbati Sancti. Ildephonso Lupo, Auctore.* Far from being wholly neglected in the Sevillian Cathedral archive, as "La música conservada" would lead one to believe, Lobo is still represented in at least three manuscripts, the latest of which is not only given over *in toto* to his works but was even copied within a decade of the invitation given Haydn by nearby Cádiz Cathedral to compose *The Seven Last Words*.

From the Sevillian capitular acts of 1648, without reference to the music manuscripts just mentioned, it would be known that Lobo enjoyed peculiar favor at Seville long after his decease. On August 12, 1648, the chapter met on special call to consider the proposal of Don Mateo Vázquez de Leca, archdeacon of Carmona. The chapter minutes merit quotation:[112]

The archdeacon proposed that henceforth the *Credo Romano* be sung in Maestro Lobo's polyphonic setting every Sunday, except during Lent, Advent, and Septuagesima . . . and also on Corpus Christi, throughout its octave, and on the Feasts of Assumption and Conception; because it is an extremely devout and solemn setting, and most beautiful to hear. After having talked over the archdeacon's proposition, the chapter then took a vote: white tallies being cast by those in favor of, black by those opposed to, the proposal. The scrutiny revealed 32 for, and 12 against: whereupon the diocesan ordered that since the proposition had carried, the chapelmaster must be notified that from henceforth Lobo's *Credo Romano* would be sung regularly, because the chapter considers his setting especially fine and lovely. The archdeacon was so pleased at this favorable action that he immediately gave 100 ducats to the cathedral foundation [fábrica]. The chapter accepted the gift for deposit in the cathedral treasury, and expressed thanks to the said archdeacon.

Nor was this all. Some six weeks later the chapter ordered that Lobo's *Credo Romano* should, in addition, be sung at all first-class feasts of Our Lady. But to bring the story to a still more interesting denouement, this setting alone of all Lobo's compositions seems thus far to have reached the United States, in manuscript. It is to be found at folios 8^V-15 of a hitherto uncatalogued Spanish choirbook purchased before World War I through a Leipzig antiquarian for The Hispanic Society in New York. The choirbook bears as its present factitious title, *Missae secundum ritum Toletanum cum aliis missis variorum auctorum*.[113] Heading Lobo's creed at folio 8^V appears this rubric: "Con el canto llano del credo Romano Del maestro Alonso Lobo." The choirbook itself belonged originally to the collegiate church of San Pedro de Lerma (near Burgos). The *Credo Romano* is an independent item, not belonging to any mass. No other composition by Lobo occurs in this book. His creed is followed by a *Missa de beata Virgine* (folios 18^V-30) of Fray Martín de Villanueva—the Jeronymite from Granada who served as chapelmaster at El Escorial *ca.* 1605.

As for Lobo's creed, his tenor sings a mensuralized version of the fifteenth-century plainsong enumerated as Credo IV in the 1947 *Liber usualis* (pp. 75-78); but not in *Pfundnoten*. Instead, the tenor always moves lithely in semibreves and minims. For a "key signature" Lobo has added B♭—and quite properly since he has transposed the plainsong up a fourth.

In addition to the sharps invariably necessary at cadences, Lobo specifies numerous other f♯'s and c♯'s in the tenor: with the result that the plainsong-bearing voice is as often degree-inflected as any of the other three making up the CATB quartet. With the exception of the "Credo in unum Deum" intonation, he has composed the entire creed polyphonically. He divides the text among eighteen musical phrases, each ending with a fermata. The coronas coincide with double-bars in the present-day *Liber usualis* edition of the plainchant. Lobo has so long been known primarily as a learned composer (perhaps because Antonio Soler in his *Llave de la modulación* [1762] advertised two of Lobo's canons as the most difficult enigmas in old Spanish polyphony)[114] that this *Credo Romano* deserves to be studied —if only as a corrective to so one-sided a judgment of his genius.

His reputation as an exceptionally skilled contrapuntist has been upheld also by the *Ave Maria* (*a 8*) reprinted by Eslava in *Lira sacro-hispana* (s. XVII, I, i, 27-47). In this ingenious motet Lobo attacked a problem that Guerrero had already solved successfully in his *Pater noster* (*a 8*) printed in 1555 and again in 1566: namely, that of an eight-in-four canon—one quartet giving birth to the other quartet. Victoria had closed his early mass, *Simile est regnum coelorum* (1576), with a similar canon. In the *Pater noster* of 1555 Guerrero specified the fifth above for the answer; in the *Simile est regnum coelorum* Mass Victoria chose the unison as answering interval; in the *Ave Maria* of 1602 Lobo selected the fourth below or fifth above. The time lag between each dux and its comes in Guerrero's canonic *Pater noster* always amounts to two breves. But since the "leading" voices do not start singing simultaneously, the entries of the "answering" voices are similarly staggered. Victoria, on the other hand, brings in all four leading voices together. In consequence, the four answering voices also start together. Lobo follows Victoria's bloc-entry plan—his $C_I A_I T_I B_I$ commencing together, thus forcing his $A_{II} C_{II} C_{III} B_{II}$ answering voices to enter together also.

To come, however, to the two canons from Lobo's *Liber primus missarum* which so intrigued Soler as to occupy him from pages 192 to 234 of his *Llave de la modulación*: both are, significantly, Osanna movements; and both belong to the same mass, *Prudentes virgines*. The parody source in this instance was Guerrero's motet *a 5*, *Prudentes virgines* (published with dedication to Pope Pius V in 1570). As has already been shown above at page 215, Guerrero—ever the symbolist—resorted to so literal an expedient as blacks and a momentary switch from ₵ to 3 for the nonce when setting these three words: *media autem nocte* ("And at midnight"). Immediately thereafter he returned to his customary ₵ and to note values mostly in voids for the rest of the sentence, "a cry arose, Behold the Bridegroom is coming, go forth to meet him!" (Matt. 25:6). Since Guerrero resorted to so literal an expedient as eye-music, Lobo the parodist ought not to be accused of musical exhibitionism for having resorted to the much subtler symbolism of enigma canons in his two Osannas. Usually considered the most joyful movements of any mass, the Osannas after the Sanctus and again after the Benedictus were particularly appropriate movements in which to exemplify the *Prudentes virgines* title. The "wise virgins" were ready to shout Osannas when the Bridegroom arrived. Lobo symbolized their superior wisdom with his exceptionally learned canons. That such a symbolical interpretation does not strain against fact can be the more confidently assumed, because Lobo in none other of his masses brandished so much learning. For another matter, enigma canons were in vogue even in Italy at this time for similarly symbolical purposes. Giovanni Maria Nanino (*ca.* 1545–1606) left a four-in-one canon headed (in Latin) "He who is not with me is against me" (Matt. 12:30). The second consequent voice follows in unison, but the first and third go in contrary motion at a dissonant interval of imitation.

At the head of Osanna I in his *Prudentes virgines* Mass, Lobo inserts this rubric: *Cantus secundus vadit et venit, sed de minimis non curat. Idem Thenor in Octauam cancrizando.* In effect these directions mean that cantus II is to sing only the semibreves found in cantus I—next, to sing them in reverse order. Upon completion of one forward-and-backward cycle, cantus II repeats the whole cycle several times over. The tenor meanwhile must imitate cantus II at the suboctave, crabwise. At the head of Osanna II in the same Mass, Lobo places this rubric: *Currebant duo simul. Sed Basis praecucurrit citius.* Tenor and bass are therefore to sing from the same part. But the bass carries ₵ for its time signature whereas the tenor carries O. In addition the clefs differ, with the result that although the tenor starts simultaneously with the bass it commences a fifth higher. So much for Lobo's rubrics. The exhibition of learning does not end with these verbal canons, however. In Osanna II the singers must be constantly on the alert against confusing points of division with those of alteration. Color as a means of alteration also plays its role. Not because these two Osannas are the best things that Lobo ever composed, but because of the fame that Soler gave them, they must both be shown here in compressed score. In the first, plus signs have been used to show the notes in cantus I which were semibreves in the original. In the second, a time signature of $\frac{6}{8}$ for the bass and $\frac{3}{4}$ for the tenor would be technically the more correct solution. The following incipit serves for both voices:

Thenor.   *Basis supra Thenorem.*

Missa Prudentes Virgines

Osanna I

Liber primus missarum (Madrid: 1602), fols. 61ᵛ-62.

Alonso Lobo

Osanna II

[Alonso Lobo]

Liber primus missarum, fols. 63ᵛ-64.

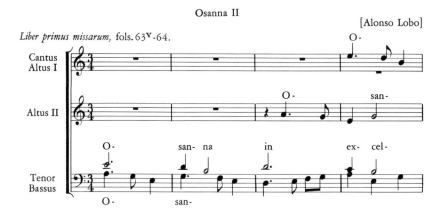

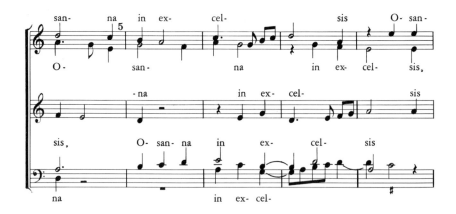

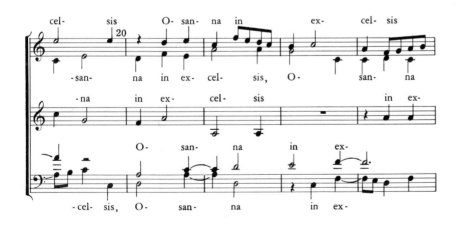

As for the other movements of *Prudentes virgines*, the Crucifixus contains a forward-and-backward canon in the tenor (folio 55ᵛ). Beginning at *Et iterum* the tenor sings in reverse motion all that had been sung in direct motion up to those words. In the Agnus (folio 66ᵛ), the cantus carries two time signatures, one above the other. The top signature C applies to the cantus voice part; the bottom O, to the tenor, which sings the same notes in proportion at the lower octave. Agnus Dei I also deserves attention because of its polytextuality—the words "Prudentes virgines" being pitted in the tenor voice part against "Agnus Dei" in the others.

The earliest dated manuscript copies of Lobo's masses seem to be the already mentioned pair *a 4* found in MS 110 at Seville Cathedral.[115] This manuscript bears 1595 as its date of copy. Since each of the three other masses in this source was composed by Guerrero—*Dormendo un giorno* (1566) at folios 30ᵛ-46, *Surge propera amica mea* (1582) at folios 62ᵛ-81, and *Saeculorum Amen* (1597) at folios 16ᵛ-30—Lobo's companion masses eking out the manuscript might appropriately have been chosen from among his masses that parody Guerrero's motets. However, *O Rex gloriae* in this manuscript parodies not Guerrero but the Pentecost motet of that name published in Palestrina's *Motecta festorum totius anni liber primus* (1563). In his last Agnus, Lobo lengthens the first five notes of Palestrina's head motive; and makes of them a sequencing ostinato in the tenor (after Morales's manner in his *Veni Domine et noli tardare* motet). The tenor here carries two time signatures: C above ₵. These mean that after singing the thrice-sequenced ostinato in notes of written value, the tenor is to sing the same sequencing ostinato again, but now at double-quick. This double-quickening of a sequencing ostinato in the last Agnus was an idea that appealed to Guerrero as well as to Lobo: as can be discovered by referring to Guerrero's *Saeculorum Amen* Mass *a 4* in this same Sevillian choirbook (MS 110). But Lobo went one better than his mentor by introducing in this last Agnus of *O Rex gloriae* a canon at the lower eleventh between the two outer voices (1602, folios 116^V-117).[116]

The identical two masses *a 4*, *Petre ego pro te rogavi* and *O Rex gloriae*, that are copied in Sevillian MS 110 at folios 1^V-16 and 46^V-62, respectively, are also to be found in another manuscript antedating the 1602 publication of Lobo's *Liber primus missarum*. This other manuscript source, surprisingly enough, was encountered not in Spain but in Mexico. Its owner at the time of writing is the distinguished Canon Octaviano Valdés of Mexico City Cathedral. Among the nine other masses in this codex are one by Juan Esquivel, four by Patestrina, and still another ascribed to the latter but actually Pierre Colin's *Christus resurgens*.[117] The only date in the Valdés codex is 1599. It occurs at folio 87, where in the upper right-hand margin is to be descried "1599. Años." Of the eleven masses in this Mexican source, *O Rex gloriae* shows the signs of most intensive use. Lobo, whose name is now known by only a few historians, and who is by some of them confused with his Portuguese namesake Duarte Lobo,[118] clearly enjoyed not only fame but even popularity in the New World at about the time Jamestown was founded. Such signs of frequent and unremitting use as the frayed leaves, mending, and excessive dirt at folios 46^V-56 of the Valdés codex are by no means the only evidence. The fact that printed copies of his *Liber primus missarum* are so widely distribued in Mexico—at least five being known to exist in the following places: Mexico City, Guadalajara, Puebla, Morelia, and Oaxaca—must also be taken into consideration. If for no other reason than because of a desire to scan the repertory of a composer who early became a favorite in the Western Hemisphere, the reprinting of Lobo's 1602 book would therefore serve a useful purpose. So many contemporary copies of any other printed collection of early masses have not thus far been discovered in the New World.

Among the more characteristic features of Lobo's style which such a reprint can be expected to reveal, the following should be named: (1) frequent recourse to rather subtle types of imitation such as by contrary motion, or to the type that involves a change of time values in the head motive; (2) fondness for double and even triple expositions (in which two or three subjects introduced simultaneously at the opening are immediately thereafter switched between voice and voice); (3) reluctance, however, to repeat or to sequence a head motive in any single melodic line; (4) profuse insertion of printed sharps (f♯, c♯, g♯) and flats (b♭ and e♭); (5) a liking for successions that involve cross relations and for linear movements that oppose an accidental to its opposite in quick succession (e.g., b♮ c¹ b♭, f♯ g f♮); (6) skillful use of modulations to closely related keys as a structural device (he usually times his shifts from one key into another to coincide with punctuation in the text).

The spiritual qualities of Lobo's art cannot be localized so easily. But mere craftsmanship—his mastery of which will be disputed by no serious student—must not be allowed to divert attention from the yearning emotional intensity of his best work. He was perhaps the first Spanish composer who timed his climaxes to coincide with high notes. For instance, as early as the opening Kyrie of his *Beata Dei genitrix* Mass (meas. 20),[119] the moment of climax is timed to coincide with a¹, followed immediately by the resolution of a first-inversion F♯-minor into a root-position G-minor chord. If geography counts for anything in determining an artist's spiritual outlook, then it is perhaps significant that Ginés de Boluda and Alonso Lobo were the two chapelmasters (of whom any considerable repertory survives) active in Toledo simultaneously with the production of the most admired achievements in Spanish Renaissance painting—namely, the canvases of El Greco (*ca.* 1542-1614). Should Lobo's Lamentations one day be sung in the Toledo, Ohio, gallery where now hangs an El Greco *Christ in Gethsemane*, or his *Petre ego rogavi pro te* Mass in the Washington gallery where hangs an El Greco *St. Peter*, closer spiritual ties between the two than have hitherto been suspected may be revealed.

Sebastián de Vivanco (ca. 1550-1622)

That Vivanco—like Victoria—was a native of Ávila comes to light in certain Ávila Cathedral capitular acts, which will later be quoted. He would also be known to have been *Abulensis* from the title page of his 1607 book of magnificats printed at Salamanca. Nevertheless, the earliest biographical documentation thus far adduced comes not from Castile but from Catalonia. On July 4, 1576, the Lérida Cathedral chapter passed the following resolution:[120] "For certain just causes, which do not however affect his honor, the chapter revokes and Lérida Cathedral chapter passed the following resolution:[120] "For certain just causes, which do not however affect his honor, the chapter revokes and declares terminated the appointment of the reverend Sebastián de Vivanco, choirmaster and chapelmaster of the said cathedral; and removes him from his office of singing teacher." Two days later, an inventory of the effects left in his house was submitted to the chapter. This list names certain gatherings of paper of the sort used in music copying, four hand-size and four large songbooks, a few Latin grammars, miscellaneous song sheets, and an index to the cathedral collection of music books. Two months later, on September 7, the Lérida chapter appointed a committee of canons to investigate the dispute between Sebastián de Vivanco, "recently chapelmaster," and Joan Torrent, a clergyman of Lérida diocese who had been a sopranist in the cathedral since July 19, 1560. Vivanco had already departed. But he asserted that he had left behind certain possessions to which Torrent was now laying claim.

Catalonia, then as at present, was a province with its own proud cultural traditions, its own literature, and its own language. Since Spanish was not spoken, Vivanco's effects were inventoried in the Catalonian language, on July 6, 1576. A Castilian, he cannot have been particularly happy in a province with such pronounced separatist leanings. Even Andalusia seems not to have appealed to him when a decade later he was invited to become master of the boys at Seville. Ávila was his desired haven, just as Seville was Guerrero's—and for the same reason.

The first inkling that the Sevillian chapter intended to invite Vivanco is given not in Sevillian documents but in an Ávila Cathedral capitular act. On Wednesday, July 8, 1587, the Ávila chapter "decided that the office and ministry of chapelmaster in this cathedral stand in great need of rehabilitation; because Hernando de Ysassi, the present occupant, is old and tired, and does not heed the requirements of his office." The pertinent act continues as follows:[121]

Just now Sebastián de Vivanco, who has been serving as chapelmaster at Segovia, is reported ready to move from Segovia to Seville. But he is a native of Ávila and it is understood that he would be quite eager to join our staff if he could be promised a sufficient salary, even though it did not match the salary that he has been offered at Seville. After discussing the matter the chapter resolved that (1) since the said Vivanco has already quit Segovia with the intention of moving to Seville, and (2) since the Segovia Cathedral authorities will therefore have no objection to our offering him a prebend, such an offer of a chapelmaster's prebend with the obligation of boarding certain boys ought now to be made, always on condition that his release from Segovia Cathedral is duly confirmed.

This signed release from Segovia arrived nine days later. On July 31 Ysassi was instructed to take a long rest; and on August 7 Vivanco's monthly salary in Ávila Cathedral was set at 4,000 maravedís.[122]

At last, on August 14, his name crops up for the first time in a Sevillian

Cathedral capitular act. On that day three Sevillian chapter members were instructed to write an official letter "inviting Vivanco, *chapelmaster at Segovia*, to come here; and promising him the kind of salary that a person of his eminence deserves; and also inviting him to bring with him two or three choirboys with excellent voices."[123] However, the letter of invitation stipulated that any appointment in Seville Cathedral was not to be construed as a guarantee of succession to Guerrero. The letter did promise him ample expense money, should he decide not to stay after arriving. The Sevillian dean proposed more concrete terms at the chapter meeting of October 7, 1587: namely, 500 ducats annually and 90 fanegas of wheat. His duties were to include "rearing, teaching, and boarding the choirboys, on a level that meets with the chapter's approval."[124] But he was to be warned again that no guarantee of succession could be given. Again he was urged to bring with him two or three boys with fine voices.

Repercussions soon began sounding at Ávila. On Friday, October 23, Vivanco came into the Ávila chapter meeting with the signed offers from Seville in hand.[125] Immediately, he asseverated that "he esteemed the kindness already done him in this cathedral to be of greater moment than any other that could be done him anywhere else." He therefore asked the Ávila Cathedral authorities to consider matching the Sevillian offer. A week later the Ávila chapter learned that the total value of the Sevillian post would be 900 ducats (counting half-prebend's salary, an additional 200 ducats, and an allowance of wheat). After looking over the signed offers, the Ávila chapter decided that everything possible must be done to hold Vivanco, "because he has proved already to be not only an ornament to the cathedral but also a most necessary servant." Moreover, the chapter thought it just to take account of "the eminence that he enjoys as a musician, his natural tendency to exceed his contractual obligations in coming to additional services and in teaching singing, the great respect accorded him by other musicians, the advantage that all of this promises to celebrations and solemn festivals." Not being able to boost his salary as high as Seville Cathedral could pay, the Ávila chapter proposed instead to give him a high seat in the section reserved for senior prebendaries.

With this satisfaction and the promise of better things to come, Vivanco made himself content during the Christmas season. So acceptable was his conduct that on January 13, 1588, the chapter took a vote to determine whether a present ought to be given. This was not approved;[126] but he did receive a handsome present on February 1. On the same day he asked for a month's leave to visit Seville. Toward the end of February he arrived in Seville, bringing with him only one of the "two or three choirboys with fine voices" requested by the Sevillian chapter. This boy immediately became homesick, and had to be sent back. On February 29 Vivanco formally took charge of the Sevillian boys.[127] Since he asked on this same date for a loan so that he could engage a house it cannot be doubted that he intended to stay. He asked also for expense money to cover the costs of moving. On March 3 the chapter agreed to a 200-ducat loan and a 30-ducat gift, to cover the expenses of moving "from Ávila."[128] Nine days later, he petitioned for more money so that he might return to Ávila. On March 17 the chapter acceded with another 100 ducats,[129] thus fulfilling the original bargain: namely, that should Vivanco decide not to stay he would be amply reimbursed for the whole cost of the inspection trip.

Vivanco thereafter remained at Ávila until 1602, on October 2 of which year he was appointed chapelmaster at Salamanca. Soon after the next New Year's, Bernardo Clavijo del Castillo, occupant of the Salamanca music chair since April 3, 1593, resigned to accept the higher paying post of chapel organist for Philip III. On January 10, 1603, the chair was declared vacant. Vivanco immediately entered his name. At the formal examination on February 19, Clavijo served as one of the judges. Victorious in the trial, Vivanco henceforth held two posts—the cathedral chapelmastership and the university professorship. On March 4, 1603, he was incorporated a Master of Arts. In 1607 he published his *Liber Magnificarum*, a 269-page maximum-size folio. Three years later he published a volume of motets: a mutilated copy of which is today preserved in the Toledo capitular archive. According to Saldoni, he also published in 1608 a volume of masses (see below, p. 287). He retired from the Salamanca chair in January, 1621, and died the next year on October 26.[130] His substitute in 1621-1622, Roque Martínez, succeeded him in the chair on December 9, 1622; continuing to occupy it until 1642.

In the engraving to be found on the title page of his *Liber Magnificarum* (published at Salamanca, 1607),[131] Vivanco's two posts—those of chapelmaster and of professor—are each symbolized by a different type of headcovering. The engraving shows Vivanco on his knees before a crucifix. In his outstretched hand is a book inscribed with the words "Give me of Thy gifts." Through the open door behind him appear trees in full leaf. Vivanco is ceremoniously attired in full clericals, and on the floor beside him lie both his biretta and his academic cap. This collection of magnificats has grown so rare that even bibliographical details are hard to come by and must be given here as a preliminary to discussion of its contents. The title runs: *Liber Magnificarum Sebastiani de Vivanco Abulensis in summo templo Salmanticensi portionarii, et a musicis praefecti: in eiusdemq. urbis academia artium et philosophiae magistri, ac primariam musices cathedram moderantis.* The meaning is clear enough: "Book of Magnificats by Sebastián de Vivanco of Ávila, prebendary in Salamanca Cathedral and chapelmaster: master of arts and philosophy in the university of the same city, and morning professor[132] of music." The dedication, like that of Guerrero's 1597 motets, reads to Christ Himself. Below the engraving is printed a three-in-one canon with "O come, let us adore Christ the King, hanging upon a cross for us" as text. Around the three other sides of the engraving are to be seen three perpetual canons: at the top a four-in-one, at the left a five-in-one, and at the right a six-in-one. These three, unlike the canon below the engraving, lack texts. At the bottom of the title page appears *Superiorum permissu*—a legend not found frequently in Spanish musical publications—followed by *Salmanticae, Ex Officina typographica Arti Taberniel Antuerpiani. Anno a Christo nato M.DC.VII.*

Artus [= Arthur] Taberniel, a printer from Antwerp active at Salamanca from 1602 until his death in 1610,[133] produced for Vivanco a choirbook that by virtue of its luxury and accuracy rivals the best Plantin publications. Since the music has not been studied, Vivanco's endowments are as yet but little recognized. This neglect is unfortunate, for certainly Vivanco's *Liber Magnificarum* exceeds any work of its class published in Castile during his generation. To list some distinctions of the collection: (1) the canons approach the outer limits of adroitness and complexity; (2) for the first time a polytextual magnificat is encountered—the Gloria Patri *a 8* of one fourth-tone magnificat combining, for instance, four different texts; (3) the ostinato technique favored by Morales in such motets as *Jubilate Deo omnis terra* and *Gaude et laetare* makes a telling appearance in at least two magnificats; (4) he proves to be the first and apparently the only composer who made a foray into "polytonality"—the Gloria at pages 170-171 inscribed *Super octo tonis cum octo vocibus* consigning a different tone to each of the eight different voices; (5) in another magnificat, the tenor sings all eight tones in numerical sequence; (6) his dexterity as a contrapuntist is such that on occasion he can even produce a four-voice *Benedicamus* in quadruply invertible counterpoint. However, side by side with all this display he inserts exquisite movements *a 3* of the most tender simplicity. His contrapuntal resource never masters him. Rather, he is so completely the master of device that astonishing feats seem no more difficult than the composition of a free fantasia.

Because imaginative use of learned devices, "polytonality," and polytextuality make interesting news, these features cannot but loom large in any analysis of Vivanco's magnificats. Just as the best-intentioned of dictionary writers when discussing J. S. Bach's *Die Kunst der Fuge* neglect the earlier counterpoints for the augmentations; inversions; mirrors; and the "two quadruple fugues, one with four invertible subjects of which one is at the 12th; and the other a totally invertible fugue with four subjects" —which, according to Tovey, was to have crowned the whole series: so also in a discussion of Vivanco's "The Art of the Magnificat" a due proportion will not easily be achieved.

Vivanco published eighteen magnificats. In conformity with widespread custom his 1607 book included a setting of both the odd verses (*Anima mea*) and the even (*Et exultavit*) for each of the eight church tones. Bringing the total number of magnificats to eighteen are an extra *Anima mea* in Tones I and VIII. Eleven magnificats call for four voices (Tones I, II, III, and VII, odd-verse exemplars; Tones I, III, IV, V, VI, VII, and VIII, even-verse); four for six voices (Tones I, V, and VI, odd-verse; Tone II, even-verse); two for five voices (Tones IV and VIII, odd-verse); and one for eight voices (Tone VIII, odd-verse). In only the Tone VIII odd-verse *a 8* does he exploit the antiphony of two quartets. Although in several other magnificats he expands to eight voices in the concluding Gloria, in none of these other Glorias *a 8* does he employ double-choir techniques. Vivanco was the first peninsular composer to make a regular habit of printing two alternate Glorias at the ends of his *Anima mea* magnificats: the first Gloria not increasing the number of voices nor displaying the composer's contrapuntal prowess; the second increasing voices and spurting with contrapuntal geysers. Such alternate Glorias end these seven magnificats: Tones I *a 6*, II *a 4*, III *a 4*, IV *a 5*, V *a 6*, VI *a 6*, VII *a 4*. A printed rubric always appears at the end of the simpler Gloria and usually reads as follows: *Verte folium et alteram videbis* ("Turn the leaf and you will see another [Gloria]"). The smallest number of voices that Vivanco consents to use in any interior movement of a magnificat is three. The Et misericordia movements of the Tones III *a 4*, IV *a 5*, V *a 6*, VII *a 4*, VIII *a 5*, the Esurientes of the Tone IV *a 4*, and the Fecit potentiam of the Tone VI *a 4*, all reduce to a trio. As a rule, the *Et exultavit* magnificats wear less learning than their companion *Anima mea* exemplars. Only in the Tone VIII *Et exultavit* (*a 4*) does he conclude with two alternate Sicut erat movements. The simplest among all eighteen are the *Et exultavit* magnificats belonging to Tones V and VII (both *a 4*). He rarely cites the plainsong formulas in *Pfundnoten*. By way of exception, the plainsong creeps at slow speed in the top voice of the Deposuit's belonging to Tones III and VI. He confides the formula to the altus of the Tone III Sicut erat, but to the bass of the Tone VII Sicut erat. Throughout all eighteen magnificats Vivanco eschews triple meter. He carefully differentiates between C and ₵. His printer does occasionally lapse, heading some voice parts in a movement with C and others in the same movement with ₵ —when manifestly the signatures of all voices in the movement should have read either C or ₵; as, for instance, at pages 150–151 of the 1607 book. Accidentals, although not supplied so profusely as in Victoria's 1600 and 1605 Madrid imprints, are given sufficiently frequently for the composer's intentions to be clear throughout. His combined vocal limits reach from E_1 to a^1.

To come now to the more spectacular, and therefore more newsworthy, aspects of Vivanco's magnificat technique. The most adroit canons are invariably to be found in the *ossia* Glorias. In these he makes a specialty of combining several different types of canon in one and the same movement. Therefore it will not do merely to list types, such as canon by inversion, by cancrizans, and by augmentation; and then next to enumerate the movements in which he uses each type. Rather, it will be necessary to study each *ossia* Gloria individually and to name the types combined in that particular Gloria.

In the Tone I magnificat (pp. 14-15) three types join hands. Superius II answers the altus a fourth above. Superius III answers tenor II an octave above in augmentation—but disregards all black notes (and dots equal to a black) in the dux. Bassus II answers bassus I an octave above; but in contrary motion. Superius II enters a breve after the altus; superius III, five semibreves after tenor I; and bassus II, three breves after bassus I. So intricate did the famous Spanish scholar Federico Olmeda find this virtuostic Gloria that he wrote two penciled notes at page 15 of his copy calling attention to fancied errors in Vivanco's notation. Fortunately for Vivanco's reputation, a latter-day transcription adhering rigorously to his precise directions absolves him of any errors whatsoever. True, on page 14 at what corresponds to meas. 20 in a transcription, tenor I shows traces of a superfluous minim (d). But this printer's error has been carefully whited out in both The Hispanic Society and the Puebla copies—The Hispanic Society copy being that which originally belonged to Olmeda before it was purchased for the Society from a German representative of his heirs *ca.* 1912.

The *ossia* Gloria at the close of the *Anima mea* Magnificat in Tone II boasts a three-in-one canon—superius I being answered by the bassus at the twelfth below and by altus II at the fifth below. In the Gloria at the close of the Tone III, tenor I answers superius I at the fourth below and tenor II altus I at the fifth below, while tenor III repeats a nine-note ostinato four times (with five breves rest between each repetition). In the Gloria at the close of the Tone VII, tenor II answers tenor I in unison, altus II likewise follows altus I at the unison, while tenor III answers superius II in cancrizans.

The combination of three favorite plainsongs praising the author of the Magnificat, which occurs in the Gloria of the Tone IV, would in itself be a feat of very high order. But of tenor III Vivanco declares: *Hic Tenor in ordine decantat octo tonos;* which means that together with the quodlibet—during which bassus I sings *Ave Maria*, bassus II *O gloriosa Domina*, and the altus *Ave maris stella*—Vivanco makes tenor III simultaneously sing (in numerical sequence) the plainsong formulas for the words "anima mea Dominum" belonging to Tones I through VIII. So far as quodlibet is concerned, Vivanco could have found it exemplified in the repertories of such Spanish predecessors as Triana (*Non puedo dexar querer* in the Colombina Songbook, no. 28), Peñalosa (*Por las sierras de Madrid* in the Palace Songbook, no. 312), and even Fuenllana (whose abortive attempt at combining four villancicos—*De donde venis amores* in black ink for the soprano, *Si me llaman a mi llaman* in red ink for the contralto, *Con que la lavare* in blue ink for the tenor, and *Por una vez que mis ojos alçe* in green ink for the bass—is advertised at the bottom of canceled folio 169^V in his 1554 *Orphénica lyra*). But these particular precedents, reaching back more than a century, were exclusively secular in their intent. Moreover, no previous Spanish quodlibet had brought together preëxisting melodies that so intimately share the same topic as do the three Marian plainsongs selected by Vivanco. For such reasons as the following it must be shown here in open score: (1) its polytextuality; (2) the quotation of preëxistent melodies; (3) the "catalogue-aria" in tenor III (every plainsong formula from I through VIII is recited in numerical order); (4) the welding of diversities into an extraordinarily compact unity.

To clarify the picture, roman numerals I-VIII are inserted above the third tenor part throughout the accompanying example. These numerals show the moments at which the corresponding formula commences (in the third tenor Vivanco quotes only so much of each formula as comes after the mediation). Meanwhile, he cites not just the second half of a formula in his superius I but the whole of the formula for Tone IV—this being the tone to which this particular magnificat belongs. Tone IV starts in the top voice at mm. 7-25. Notes of large value add weight to this initial statement. At mm. 29-38 the same formula is paraphrased. As for tenors I and II, Vivanco not only brings them in in imitation but also has superius II imitate their head motive (in augmentation so far as the first three notes are concerned). Among later references to the head motive, the following can be studied: superius II, mm. 13-14; tenor I, mm. 7-8, 17-18; tenor II, mm. 12-13. It should also be noted that the two Marian hymns combine with the angelical salutation to make a quite self-sufficient trio. Lastly, mention should be made of Vivanco's scrupulous attention here, as elsewhere in his music, to Zarlino's rules for text-underlay. In conformity with these rules Vivanco consistently avoids a new syllable on a minim or semibreve after two or more running crotchets (unreduced values).

When in 1936 Carl-Heinz Illing drew up his *Chronologisches Verzeichnis der Magnificat-Komposition bis 1620*, Vivanco's 1607 publication was not so much as mentioned.[134] But, on the other hand, the fact that Vivanco published a large selection of motets (Salamanca: Artus Taberniel, 1610) has been known since at least 1925, in which year Felipe Rubio Piqueras called attention to Codex 23 at Toledo Cathedral. In the Toledo exemplar, the title and index pages, pages 16-37, and several after page 234, have been lost. Nevertheless, some 36 motets survive in the mutilated

Magnificat Quarti toni
Gloria Patri

Liber Magnificarum (Salamanca: 1607), pp. 112-113.

Sebastián de Vivanco

* *Hic Tenor in ordine decantat octo tonos* ("This tenor sings in succession the eight tones").

Toledo copy: 15 *a* 5, 14 *a* 4, 4 *a* 6, 2 *a* 8, and 1 *a* 12 (Rubio Piqueras's count).

As was customary in motet collections of the period, Vivanco inserts a bloc that runs through the church year in chronological order: this series begins with *Fratres hora est jam* for First Sunday in Advent. But before he reaches his Advent to Ascension series he gives us quite another group: Commons of Saints motets. In addition to breaking the rule of beginning with *proprium de tempore* motets, he also selects texts that for the most part had not been set by previous Spanish composers. To take, for instance, his twenty Pre-Lenten to Palm Sunday motets—all with scriptural texts— only five or six make use of passages utilized previously by Morales or Guerrero. A simple explanation can be given: Vivanco always chose for his text a passage from the Gospel for the Day. A new and revised missal went forth with the approval of Pius V in 1570. By 1575 it had come into general use within the dominions of Philip II. Not only all of Morales's but also all of Guerrero's motets in his 1555 and 1570 collections (and even the thirty-three in Victoria's classic 1572 collection) were composed at a time when local-use missals still prevailed throughout Spain. Because Vivanco's choice of texts, on the other hand, always agrees with the Gospel for the Day in the revised missal, his source passages agree closely with the texts as they have continued to be printed to the present day. The only slight disagreements between his texts and those printed in such a compendium as the *Liber usualis* reflect the changes in the wording of the Vulgate authorized by Clement VIII.

Domine Pater et Deus vitae meae, the four-voice motet at pages 12-15 in Vivanco's book, was transcribed by Theodor Kroyer from the Toledo copy and reprinted in his tendentious *Der vollkommene Partiturspieler* (Leipzig: Breitkopf und Härtel, 1930). To name some of the more interesting facets of Vivanco's technique exhibited in this motet: (1) change of time values in the answers to the head motive (mm. 1-8); (2) unmistakable augmented chords at the word "Father" (meas. 8); (3) false relations between the words "evildoer" and "nor" (mm. 41-42); (4) deceptive cadence between the words "forsake" and "me" (mm. 43-44); (5) sudden octave-leaps upward to the word "far" (mm. 55, 59-60, 63-65, 67-68); (6) resort to sequence in the upper voice (mm. 29-30 = 32-34; mm. 35-38 = 38-41)— not to mention less conspicuous instances in the lower voices; (7) unprepared second inversion chord (meas. 30_4).

In addition, eight other Vivanco motets, a hymn (*Ave maris stella*), and a set of lamentations for Holy Saturday have reached print recently in Samuel Rubio's *Antología polifónica sacra*, Volumes I and II (Madrid: Ed. Coculsa, 1954 and 1956). Two of the five motets published in 1954 (*Ecce apparebit Dominus*, a 5, and *O quam suavis*, a 4) and the three published in 1956 (*Dulcissima Maria*, a 4, *Iste est qui ante alios Apostolos*, a 5 [a stirring

tribute to St. James, patron of Spain], and *Stabat Mater*, a 4) were transcribed from a Salamanca Cathedral manuscript. The Holy Saturday
lamentations and the other three motets published in 1954 (*Ante diem festum*,
Petite et accipietis, and *Spiritus Sanctus*, each a 4) were copied from Choirbook 2 at the famed Guadalupe monastery in Estremadura. The hymn
(1956) was drawn from Choirbook 1 at the same monastery.

In contrast with his magnificats, Vivanco's recently published motets
and lamentations are simpler music. As for their plan, he constructs his
motets as a series of imitative points alternating with homophony. But he
veers from routine by changing at will the rhythm of a head motive
throughout any given point of imitation. He laces sections together so ingeniously that clear-cut divisions are usually hard to establish. His dramatic
instinct only awaits such phrases as "King of Kings and Lord of Lords"
in *Ecce apparebit Dominus* (Rev: 19.16), or "knock, and it shall be
opened unto you" in *Petite et accipietis* (Matt. 7:7), to respond with bold
tableaux. In his Second Coming motet the cantus ascends to g^1 twice: the
first time when Jesus's coming on a cloud is prophesied (meas. 12), and
the second time for a full-blooded climax (meas. 56) at the word "King."
During the build-up the text reads: "and he hath on his vesture and on
his thigh a name written." The heroism of this climax thrills the hearer
the more because of the sudden G-Major chord and block harmony after
a swift surge from B♭ (meas. 52) to D Major (meas. 55). A dramatic silence
precedes the shout of acclamation in all voices. As for the word "knock,"
which Vivanco repeats with mounting insistence at mm. 30-34 in *Petite et
accipietis*, the upper pair of voices interlock in imitations of a bacchiac figure; the lower pair develop a figure that after dipping a fifth, spurts upward
in rivulets of scales.

At least four Vivanco masses are extant in MS 1 at Valladolid Cathedral.
Each takes its title from its tone (I at folio 7, IV at folio 21, V at folio 33,
VI at folio 45). Although they have not yet been transcribed, their importance is suggested by the company kept by these four masses in a manuscript
still in use as late as 1792. Morales, Guerrero, Victoria, and Alonso Lobo
are the other named composers in this choirbook. These masses were
probably copied from a 268-page Salamanca imprint of 1608. As with
Vivanco's magnificats, Artus Taberniel was the printer. A mutilated copy
survives at Granada, and José López Calo lists the contents in his article
"El Archivo de Música de la Capilla Real de Granada" (*AM*, XIII [1958],
119). The ten masses follow each other in this order, according to López
Calo: *Crux fidelis* a 6 (5), *Assumpsit Jesus* a 5 (34), *Doctor bonus* a 4 (66), *Super
octo tonos* a 4 (88), *O quam suavis es, Domine* a 4 (112), *In festo B. M. V.* a 4
(140), *B. M. V. in Sabbato* a 4 (168), *Quarti toni* (188), *Sexti toni* (208), *In
manus tuas* a 8 (228).

At the outset it was said that Vivanco, like Victoria, was a native of Ávila. Even if Vivanco died eleven years later, he cannot have been much younger (in view of the fact that he was old enough to be in major orders and a chapelmaster at Lérida in 1576). Indeed, the best informed estimate would have it that not five years separate their years of birth. Both grew up, therefore, in the same musical environment. They may even have shared the same teachers. So far as career is concerned, Vivanco made a record as distinguished as any achieved solely in Spain during his lifetime. The best chapelmasterships were offered him. Guerrero wanted him for a colleague. He published extensively. His ambition even led him into some completely new and untried paths so far as magnificat composition was concerned. In such motets as his *Stabat Mater* he used plangent, new harmonies. Anyone who has ever taken time to examine their works cannot in conscience hail Victoria as so vastly superior that he should be called the greatest of all Spanish composers while Vivanco's name begs admittance to such exhaustive works of reference as *Grove's Dictionary*.[135]

Some months before the tercentenary of St. Theresa of Ávila (1515-1582), the townspeople of Ávila decided to erect a statue to her memory. Around its pedestal were to be inscribed the names of those various other natives who were in 1882 thought most worthily to have represented Ávila in letters and the arts. To avoid all partiality, the citizens' committee appealed to the Royal Academy of History for a panel of names.[136] Vivanco was the only musician chosen. Victoria's name—whatever its worldwide implications—was in 1882 considered of less moment in his own country by a national historical commission. At the very least, it can be said in his behalf that Vivanco was the more truly Spanish of the two: for only he made his career in Spain. Whatever elements of strength can be found in his music—like those to be discerned in the music of Francisco Guerrero, Juan Navarro, and Alonso Lobo—all the more truly redound therefore to the glory of peninsular art.

Juan Esquivel (fl. 1608) Esquivel, a native of Ciudad Rodrigo, published three important folios at nearby Salamanca: the first two in 1608 (printed by Artus Taberniel) and the third in 1613 (Francisco de Cea Tesa). A pupil of Juan Navarro during the latter's incumbency in the mid-1570's, Esquivel himself was appointed to the Ciudad Rodrigo chapelmastership before 1608. He still occupied it in 1613. His Maecenas was Pedro Ponce de León, son of the same Duke of Arcos who engaged Morales as chapelmaster from 1548 until 1551 and upon Morales's death befriended Guerrero. After studying at Salamanca University and rising to become rector of the university, the son took the Dominican habit. Consecrated in 1605 for the diocese of Ciudad Rodrigo, he administered that cathedral from 1605 until his translation to the see of Zamora in 1609. Esquivel in his 1613 dedication explicitly cites this eminent Dominican bishop as the protector who after 1605 underwrote the cost of his publications.

The first of these contained six masses preceded by an *Asperges me*. In his article for the Sandberger *Festschrift* (Munich: 1918), "Juan Esquivel: Ein unbekannter spanische Meister des 16. Jahrhunderts," Albert Geiger reproduced the title in full: *Missarum Ioannis Esquivelis in alma ecclesia Civitatensi portionarii, et cantorum praefecti, liber primus*.[137] At the bottom of Esquivel's title page appears this legend: *Superiorum permissu, Salmanticae, ex officina typographica Arti Taberniel Antverpiani, anno a Christo nato* MDCVIII. The title reveals, of course, that this was Esquivel's first book of masses; and that he was prebendary and chapelmaster in the cathedral of Ciudad Rodrigo—*Civitatensis* being the adjectival form of the Latin place-name. As for the legend at the bottom, the printer discloses himself as the same Taberniel—originally from Antwerp—who had published Vivanco's *Liber Magnificarum* at Salamanca in the previous year. Between the title and the legend is an engraving that closely resembles that on the title page of Vivanco's 1607 magnificats. Esquivel, like Vivanco, kneels in an attitude of prayer. Like Vivanco he wears full clericals; but instead of the two head-coverings on the floor in the Vivanco engraving, Esquivel possesses only one head-covering (the biretta). Vivanco knelt before a crucifix. Esquivel, a man in his youthful prime, kneels before a painting of the Virgin with Child. At the bottom of her picture is engraved St. Jerome's well-known response, *Sancta et immaculata*.

In the Asperges *a 4* heading the Esquivel volume, the plainsong (*Liber usualis*, p. 11) travels in the soprano voice. As a precedent for thus opening a volume of masses with a polyphonic Asperges, Esquivel could have looked to Morales's volume of masses published by Moderne at Lyons in 1551 or the du Chemin miscellaneous collection, *Missarum musicalium*, published at Paris in 1568. Esquivel went far beyond either of these imprints, however, in the number of obligatory accidentals called for at cadences. The six masses that make up the main body of Esquivel's *Missarum . . . liber primus* lean so heavily upon Guerrero for their parody sources that he, like Lobo, would seem to have admired the Sevillian chapelmaster above all other composers. The Hexachord *a 8* and the Requiem *a 5* do not parody Guerrero. Neither does the *Missa Batalla, a 6*. All the rest do. Even the *Batalla* recalls Guerrero's five-voice *Della batalla escoutez* (1582)—not to mention Victoria's nine-voice *Missa pro victoria* (1600). For all three masses Clément Janequin's *La bataille de Marignan* (1529) served as the parody source. In addition to knowing the chanson, Esquivel must be presumed to have been acquainted with Janequin's parody of his own chanson, the *Missa La bataille* (Lyons: Jacques Moderne, 1532). Both composers develop a head motive in Kyrie

II which is not to be found in the chanson itself. In comparison with Janequin's loose and discursive treatment of motives in his own parody *a 4* of
1532, Esquivel in 1608 compresses motives, works them in double harness,
and subjects them to much more intensive development. The *Agnus Dei* of
the Esquivel shows some originality in the disposition of voice parts. Opening *a 3*, the number of parts increases successively to 8 and 9, and finally
to 12 (SSSSAAATTTBB).

If position in a series means anything, then the facts that in their first
books of masses (1544, 1566, 1576, 1602, 1608) Morales's first parody chose
Gombert; Guerrero's first parody chose Morales; and Victoria's, Lobo's,
and Esquivel's chose Guerrero for their source; should prove how high was
the esteem in which the seniors were held by the juniors. Such priority is
all the more worthy of notice because in all five collections the composers
themselves had the right to dictate the order in which their masses would
be printed. In Esquivel's volume, the order deserves even closer attention
because, unlike other collections, his does not group masses according to the
number of voice parts. The opening *Ave Virgo sanctissima* calls for 5, the
Batalla for 6, the Hexachord for 8, the *Ductus est Jesus* for 4,[138] the *Gloriose
confessor Domini* for 4, and the Requiem for 5.

Taking his cue from the source motet, Esquivel makes his *Ave Virgo sanctissima* a canonic mass: spinning unison canons between cantus I and II in
every movement except the three-voice Crucifixus and Benedictus.
Throughout, he tirelessly works Guerrero's motives. The excerpts printed
by Geiger can be associated with passages in the source thus: the Christe
develops the melodic incise associated with the words "margarita pretiosa"
(mm. 40-42); at Qui tollis peccata mundi, Esquivel utilizes Guerrero's
melodic incise, "Dei mater piissima" (mm. 9-13); the concluding Amen of
the Gloria recalls "nitens olens, velut rosa" (mm. 67-69). Tenor and bass
open the Patrem omnipotentem with the same imitation to be found at
mm. 1-3 in the source motet. Esquivel's homophony at Et ex Patre natum
recalls Guerrero's "salve" (mm. 24-26); his lumen de lumine, Guerrero's
"Ave Virgo" (mm. 1-2); his descendit de coelis, Guerrero's "margarita
pretiosa" (mm. 40-42); his et conglorificatur, Guerrero's "Dei mater
piissima" (mm. 9-12); his Osanna in excelsis, Guerrero's "maris stella"
(mm. 17-20). In Agnus Dei II, Esquivel augments to six voices and becomes polytextual: Guerrero's opening incise (mm. 3-8) here being quoted
not only literally as regards melody in the top voice, but also Guerrero's
very text being set beneath this particular incise.

In closing his collection with a Requiem, Esquivel followed precedents
already set in Morales's *Liber II* as well as in both of Guerrero's books (1566
and 1582). The penultimate mass in Esquivel's collection is a parody of
another Guerrero motet, *Gloriose confessor Domini*, which was probably com-

posed after 1605. The reason for this opinion has nothing to do with its style. Indeed, from a stylistic standpoint the *Gloriose confessor Domini* contains cadential tags that were in vogue when *Nunca fue pena mayor* was composed. What seems to make *Gloriose confessor* not only the last parody but also the latest mass of the six in Esquivel's 1608 collection is the subject of the source motet. In the version published by Guerrero in 1570 (*Motteta*, pp. 22-23), the source motet carried the inscription *De sancto Dominico;* and the name of St. Dominic (the Castilian founder of the Dominican order) recurs frequently in the motet text. Pedro Ponce de León, consecrated bishop of Ciudad Rodrigo in 1605, was a Dominican. He had in all probability known Guerrero's motet *Gloriose confessor Domini* from childhood, since (in an earlier version) it had appeared at folios 8ᵛ-9 of the *Sacrae cantiones* dedicated by Guerrero to his father in 1555. Since it was he who made possible the publication of the 1608 book, what more gracious or fitting a compliment to a patron? Especially to one who was so ardently a Dominican that he insisted on being consecrated in a house of the order (St. Stephen's at Salamanca) rather than in a cathedral.

Of this last parody, Geiger wrote as follows.[139] "The head-motive [*Thema*] is carried through all parts of the mass with great mastery. Most of the movements begin imitatively. Since various stylistic turns belong more properly to the previous century, certain passages may perhaps seem austere. But neither Morales nor Victoria in any of their compositions more intimately penetrated the inner sanctum of Beauty than Esquivel in this mass." Geiger then illustrated with an excerpt: "the splendid Osanna." The motet text travels in the top voice while altus II follows in canon at the lower fourth and simultaneously the tenor follows the bass in canon at the fifth. Geiger found the "soul-stirring ending" of this Osanna particularly affecting. He also admired Esquivel's gift for individualizing each voice part. Altus I, for instance, moves exclusively in syncopated semibreves (= minims).

A copy of Esquivel's next publication, *Motecta festorum et dominicarum cum communi sanctorum 4, 5, 6, et 8 vocibus concinnanda*, has fortunately found its way to The Hispanic Society in New York City. Another copy, according to Anglés, has been preserved at Burgo de Osma. Both Trend and Anglés unite in declaring this motet collection to have been published at Salamanca by Taberniel in 1612.[140] On the other hand, the colophon of the copy in The Hispanic Society reads: *Salmanticae excudebat Artus Tabernelius Antverpianus quinto kalendarum Julii M.DC.IIX.* That IIX here means "8" rather than "12" can under no circumstances be doubted: the reason being that Taberniel died in 1610. Henceforth books were published by the "Viuda [widow] de Artus Taberniel." Indeed, such a book appeared in the year of his death.[141]

The 1608 motet collection reaches 272 pages. Twelve staves are always printed on each page, even though the bottom half-dozen or so often go empty. The Hispanic Society copy begins at page 12; the first eleven having been lost from it—as have also pages 107-110, 225-228, 255-256, and 263-266. Since the total loss amounts to 24 pages, the following remarks concerning the collection cannot pretend to finality. It is sufficiently obvious, however, that Esquivel intended to divide his collection into three parts: (1) specific feasts, (2) commons of saints, (3) Sundays from Advent I through Lent. At page 12 comes the Easter motet *a 5, Surrexit Dominus*. In the next 130 pages he runs through a cycle of 38 motets for 37 church feasts, arranged in chronological sequence. The last in this first cycle is an *Ecce ancilla, a 5*, for the Feast of the Annunciation (March 25). No motets specifically honoring Spanish saints are to be found except *O Ildephonsus* (pp. 128-129). A motet in St. Lawrence's honor is included (pp. 66-69), perhaps because of the special favors Philip II ascribed to this saint (prompting him to build El Escorial). By way of exception, two motets are provided for October 4 (St. Francis): but only one each for other feasts. At page 142 Esquivel begins a second cycle of a dozen motets, for commons of saints. Then at page 182 he starts a third cycle of thirteen motets: for Sundays from Advent I through Palm Sunday. Extras are provided for Ash Wednesday (*Emendemus in melius*, pp. 216-219) and at the end for Maundy Thursday (*Christus factus est*, pp. 254-255). Three other motets bring the collection to a close—one "for any necessity" and two for burial services. The *In paradisum, a 6*, at pages 266-271 duplicates the *In paradisum* with which the Requiem in his *Missarum . . . liber primus* ended.[142]

Esquivel, like both Lobo and Vivanco, frequently writes imitative points in which the lower pair either proceed in opposite direction to the upper pair; or two different head motives are imitated simultaneously—one in upper voices, another quite different head motive in lower voices. Examples of either the first or second procedures can be seen at the beginnings of his *Gloria in excelsis Deo, a 4* (pp. 116-117), *Suscipiens Simon, a 5* (pp. 134-135), *Sancti angeli, a 6* (pp. 136-139), and *Vox clamantis, a 4* (pp. 192-195). Whenever his motets open with such words as "Salve" or "Ave"—as, for instance, in the *Salve sancte pater, a 4* (pp. 88-91, the *Salve crux, a 5* (pp. 102-105), and the *Ave Maria, a 5* (pp. 106-109)—he appropriately constructs his imitative point upon a head motive recalling the *Salve Regina* or *Ave Maria* plainsong incipits. In still other motets he threads plainsong in notes of greater value through an inner voice, thus paying his respects to the most time-honored of techniques. *Tria sunt munera, a 5* (pp. 122-123), for Ephiphany; *Ecce ancilla, a 5* (pp. 141-142), for Annunciation; *Ecce sacerdos, a 4* (pp. 156-157), for Commons of a Confessor Bishop; *Sacerdos et pontifex, a 4* (pp. 158-159), for the same; and *In paradisum, a 6* (pp. 266-271), for the Commemoration of the Faithful Departed; are only five among a total of seventy motets in the collection. Not even all of these can be classed strictly as cantus firmus motets—there being a free admixture of other unifying devices in the last three. But even if only *Tria sunt munera* and *Ecce ancilla* are accepted as pure specimens, their presence in the collection deserves remark.

Another motet harks after precedent: *Veni Domine et noli tardare, a 5* (pp. 186-191). In this Advent II motet the second soprano repeats the following phrase six times. After each statement he interposes rests, the value of

which alternates between two breves (unreduced) and three semibreves. Even-numbered statements of the melodic ostinato are pitched a fourth higher than odd-numbered statements. Esquivel's constructivism in this particular motet recalls Morales's procedure in *Gaude et laetare, Ferrariensis civitas*. But an even more obvious predecessor is at hand: Guerrero's Advent motet of the same name occurring as item 11 in his *Sacrae cantiones* (Seville: 1555). Identical voices carry the ostinato in the Guerrero and in the Esquivel—namely, superius II; and both motets are in the same mode. Even the melodic contours in the Guerrero and Esquivel are strikingly similar. The Guerrero ostinato (four times repeated with three breves rest intervening between each statement) reads thus:

Since mode, melody, and method are so alike, Esquivel may well have trodden familiar ground to pay Guerrero a funerary tribute in 1599.

Veni Domine et noli tardare, along with four other motets in Esquivel's 1608 motet collection, has been reprinted recently—in Samuel Rubio's *Antología polifónica sacra*, I (Madrid: 1954). What the reprint does not reveal, however, is the chromaticism specified in the 1608 edition as early as the first incise of the altus: d–e♭–d–c♯–d. Rubio used a manuscript copy rather than the printed source.[143] Whether or not he suppressed the chromaticism— thinking such a progression to have been a scribal blunder—need not perhaps be asked here. But what can be asserted dogmatically is that the imprint shows the chromaticism. As such "daring" at the very outset ought to suggest, Esquivel was no mere epigone. Even in this one motet, palpably modeled on the 1555 motet of like name, he set about competing with his model rather than merely copying it.

Esquivel seems deliberately to have entered the lists with previous Spanish masters on still other occasions. Unlike Vivanco, he chose texts already set with outstanding success. In each of the following, for instance: *O quam gloriosum* (pp. 92-95), *Ecce sacerdos*, (pp. 156-157), *Emendemus in melius*, (pp. 216-219), and *O vos omnes* (pp. 250-253); he chose a text that Victoria or Morales had already set to perfection. His later settings were not to be dismissed as altogether inferior, either in Spain or abroad. Long after printed copies of his 1608 collection were exhausted, handwritten copies of his motets continued to be made. Choirbook 1 at Plasencia contains both Esquivel's *Emendemus in melius* and *O vos omnes* (folios 106[v]-108 and 123[v]-125); but none of the Plasencia books contains Morales's or Victoria's settings of these texts.[144] The *Officium majoris hebdomadae*, a choirbook copied at Lisbon in 1735 and today preserved at Vila Viçosa, contains Esquivel's *O vos omnes* at folios 18[v]-19. Victoria is heavily represented in the same manuscript, but not with his far more famous setting of the same antiphon.[145]

Five years after his first books of masses and motets, Esquivel returned to print with a third publication containing 8 vesper psalms, 30 hymns, 8 odd-verse and 8 even-verse magnificats, 4 Marian antiphons, 8 Masses, a Requiem, additional burial service music, and 5 miscellaneous items. That an exemplar does survive (or at least did in 1894) cannot be doubted; even if the copy cannot now be located. Felipe Pedrell's *Diccionario biográfico y bibliográfico de músicos y escritores de música españoles* (Barcelona: Tip. de V. Berdós y Feliu, 1897), Volume I, pages 594-596, vouches for its existence. Pedrell recorded its complete table of contents. He also transcribed or translated all the preliminary matter. But he seems to have feared that other scholars using his dictionary would reap a premature harvest from fields that he had sown.[146] For that reason (or another) he cited Esquivel's title not in the original Latin but in a Spanish translation. Further to confound the student, he refused to divulge the name of the "diligent friend" who had copied the approbation, licence, and dedication that precede Esquivel's index. Nor would he tell where the atlas-size choirbook printed at Salamanca in 1613 by Francisco de Cea Tesa had been encountered.[147] If Pedrell's Spanish translation of the title may be trusted, then presumptively the Latin began thus: *Liber secundus psalmorum, hymnorum, magnificarum.* In a footnote he did record the Latin original of one questionable phrase in the title: *necnon T missarum.*[148] Obviously, he had the Latin before him at the time he compiled his dictionary. He himself was baffled by the *T*. He rightly remarked that it could not stand for Trium (= three)—the reason being that Esquivel's 1613 publication contains not three but eight masses. For what it may be worth, Pedrell's Spanish translation of the Latin title is here rendered into English. No account is taken of the T, which according to Pedrell stood before the genitive plural, "of masses." This puzzling letter may even have been some other character. With this proviso, the title reads: "Second volume of psalms, hymns, magnificats, and the four antiphons of Our Lady appropriate to the season; and in addition of masses. By Juan Esquivel, a native of Ciudad Rodrigo and prebendary in the cathedral of the same. The entire contents conformable with the revised Breviary of Pope Clement [VIII]. Dedicated to the most illustrious and most reverend Fray don Pedro Ponce de León, bishop of Zamora and member of the royal council." Below this title, according to Pedrell, came a large engraving (probably the bishop's coat of arms). Then at the bottom was added this legend: "With approval of higher authorities, printed at Salamanca by Francisco de Cea Tesa, native of Cordova, in the year 1613."

On the verso of the title page was printed Vicente Espinel's "approbation," dated December 7, 1611. Pedrell quotes it in full. Espinel, one of the most highly regarded poets and novelists of his day, was also so consummate a musician that Lope de Vega wished to nominate him "father of music." *Diversas rimas* (Madrid: 1591) included Espinel's well-known poem "The House of Memory," which because of its allusions to contemporary musicians has been as often quoted as Martin le Franc's earlier poem "The Champion of Women" (*ca.* 1441). From 1599 until 1623 Espinel was nominally a chapelmaster himself, of Plasencia Cathedral. However, he spent much of this time in Madrid; and it was at Madrid that he signed his "approbation": which reads somewhat as follows:

By order of Don Martín de Córdova [inspector of liturgical books] . . .
I have examined three gatherings of music composed by Juan Esquivel Bárahona, prebendary and chapelmaster at Ciudad Rodrigo Cathedral: the which comprise (1) masses (2) magnificats (3) hymns, psalms, motets, and other miscellaneous sacred items—all of which conform with the new liturgy. This deliciously sweet and gracefully made music everywhere proclaims its fine breeding, not only in its sound but also by reason of its correct theoretical foundations. The printing will redound to the glory of God and of the Church.

Espinel's approbation, and also the printing licence that follows, were, according to Pedrell, orginally in Spanish. The licensor, Don Martín de Córdova, first lists his various offices (the most important of which for Esquivel's purpose would have been his right to inspect new liturgical books); and then decrees:

For the present we allow Joan de Esquivel Barahona . . . the privilege of
printing three books of music composed by him (1) Masses (2) Magnificats
(3) Hymns and Psalms; in any printery of the realm. . . . Likewise we stipulate that
after printing the said books he shall give two copies to the Royal Monastery of
San Lorenzo [El Escorial] in return for our benevolence. Given at Madrid,
March 9, 1612. This licence shall be printed at the beginning of the said books.

Three questions arise. First, why "Juan Esquivel Barahona" in the
approbation and "Joan de Esquivel Barahona" in the licence? The "Barahona" was doubtless the name of Esquivel's mother, just as "Borja"
(Alonso Lobo de Borja) was also the mother's name. The "de" between
Juan (or Joan) and Esquivel was probably a courtesy. The second query
relates to the contents of the book. The licence certainly itemizes
three books. If *Liber secundus* in the 1613 title means that Pedrell's "diligent" friend saw only the second of three volumes printed in that year,
perhaps it was a truncated copy containing only magnificats. The third
question that both Espinel's approbation and the printing licence pose has
to do with the *rezo nuevo* (literally, new prayer) or *nuevo rezado* (new divine
service) that they both mention. On May 10, 1602, Pope Clement VIII
sent forth a newly revised breviary; and on July 7, 1604, a newly revised
missal.[149] It was doubtless to these revisions, especially the first, that Espinel
and the inspector general of new books were referring when they spoke of
rezo nuevo or *nuevo rezado*.

In his dedication (which, as noted above, reads to Pedro Ponce de León)
Esquivel begins by lauding the deeds of earlier Dukes of Arcos. In so doing,
Esquivel follows the course sailed by Guerrero, who in 1555 inscribed his
Sacrae cantiones to Luis Cristóbal Ponce de León, father of Esquivel's patron.
The 1613 dedication then tries this new tack: "But lest these prior glories
should in time be dimmed, your family's fame has in more recent years
been illumined by the valiant deeds of your illustrious brother, Duke
Roderick. For while the other Andalusian nobility cowered beneath the
onslaughts of the perfidious English, he led a courageous cohort of his own
retainers during the sack of Cádiz [1596], and by his heroic exertions succeeded in exacting a measure of vengeance for their desecration of shrines
and dedicated virgins." Next, Esquivel praises his patron for having chosen
the demanding life of a Dominican friar in St. Stephen's house at Salamanca. Finally, he promises that his present publication contains his most
conscientiously elaborated compositions; he hopes that it wiil be found an
improvement over anything that he has published previously.

According to the index, the eight vesper psalms (two settings of 109, one
each of 111, 116, 121, 147, 115, 113 [Vulgate numbering]) and thirty
hymns (arranged in church-year sequence) were in every instance com-

posed *a 4*. All eight odd-verse magnificats (I-IV *a 5*, V *a 6*, VI-VIII *a 4*) were for first vespers; all eight even-verse (always *a 4*) , for second vespers. The titles of the eight masses suggest that they were usually parodied on motets: *Tu es Petrus* (*a 5*), *Quarti toni* (*a 5*), *B. Mariae in Sabbatho* (*a 4*), *Surge propera* (*a 3*), *Hoc est praeceptum meum* (*a 4*), *Quasi cedrus* (*a 4*), *Hortus conclusus* (*a 4*), and *Deo gratias* (*a 4*). Any mass *a 3* composed as late as 1610 would be enough of an atavism to whet interest in a search for its present-day whereabouts: especially when it is remembered that none of Victoria's masses published in 1600 calls for less than eight voices, and the *Laetatus sum* Mass for as many as twelve.

Sacred Polyphony in Review (1550-1600)   The limited amount of sacred music now in print, not to mention the still incomplete documentation in the hands of musical historians, warns us against offering any set of generalizations without insisting upon their provisional character. However, for what such a set of a dozen may be worth, the following are submitted.

I   Sacred vocal polyphony was sung at court by a Flemish choir led by Flemish masters. But the presence of such a choir, which was more the result of a political accident than of any derogation from Spanish talent, did not for a moment preclude the singing at court of masterworks by Morales and Guerrero.

II   Throughout Spain, Josquin des Prez seems to have outdistanced all other foreigners in popularity, even as late as 1586. Morales remained by all odds the most esteemed peninsular composer even in 1601.[150]

III   Unlike England and France, Spain in the sixteenth century was dotted with more than two dozen vigorous local centers, each with its own liturgical traditions (until 1575) and own particularistic cultural pride. The least "Spanish" of these local centers was Barcelona. Composers in one locality disseminated their works by sending (usually on their initiative) manuscript or printed copies to performing organizations in other centers.

IV   The two areas in which sacred music flourished most vigorously were Andalusia, and Old and New Castile. If any one city is allowed preëminence above all others, Seville must be given the palm.

V   In the various cathedrals, the direction of music was always vested in a chapelmaster whose rank hardly ever rose to that of a canon. He was, instead, a mere prebendary. Vila at Barcelona and Mudarra at Seville did become canons. But Mudarra was no chapelmaster, and neither Mudarra nor Vila produced sacred masterpieces. High quality was arrived at and maintained because individual prelates and chapter members could discriminate; not because this or that chapelmaster was given much power or rank.

VI   The chapelmasters, organists, and important singers were chosen in open competitions, publicly announced throughout the realm and rigorously staged. Except in the most unusual circumstances, the chapelmaster was personally responsible for the boarding, lodging, clothing, education, health and welfare of from six to a dozen choirboys. He also trained the rest of the singers. In actual performances he was expected to beat time—speed being determined by such variable factors as the solemnity of the feast and the character of the texts sung.

VII   In addition to singing personnel, who were usually celibate clergymen, the major cathedrals hired six or eight instrumentalists to eke out their music staffs. These were family men, and passed on their craft from father to son. Their favorite instruments were *chirimías*, *cornetas*, *flautas*, and *sacabuches*—in other words, wind instruments. They were as a rule expected to double on winds other than their principal instruments. When glossing, they were not allowed to add improvised ornaments merely at random but were required to adhere to plan and to gloss at predetermined moments. The more "artful" the music, the less scope was offered for their glossing. Though on occasion individual parts were copied for them, they often read their parts from the same large choirbooks used by the singers.

VIII   From a foreigner's viewpoint, the most distinctive aspect of Spanish sacred music was the role of instruments.[151] According to Marguerite de Valois, *une messe à la façon d'Espagne* (a mass in the Spanish manner) meant in 1577 a mass with *violons et cornets*.[152] In France, on the other hand, instruments began to invade church ceremonies only at the very end of the century, and even then were usually reserved for state occasions. Not until the reigns of Louis XIII and Louis XIV did instruments become rife.[153]

IX   Learned devices continued to link, almost always, with expressive purpose. The exaltation of expressivity to a principle—more than the framing of such local melodies as the Spanish *Pange lingua* in a polyphonic context, or the composition of Lamentations and Passions "in the Spanish manner," or even excessive accidentalizing—gives Philippic sacred music its individual flavor.

X   Despite Victoria's greater fame at the present moment, the true "guru" during the reign of Philip II was Francisco Guerrero. The latter was, moreover, the only one of the Spanish trinity who made his career in Spain, whose versatility enabled him to compose with equal success in all current genres—sacred and secular—and who adapted successfully to the demands of a chapelmastership. He it was above all others whom his contemporaries and successors—Victoria, Alonso and Duarte Lobo, Géry de Ghersem, Esquivel—delighted in honoring by composing parody masses based on his motets.

XI   Not all the principal Spanish composers wrote masses. All did compose magnificats. Nearly all composed Marian antiphons. Music for Vespers looms relatively larger in the Spanish sacred repertory than in the French or Italian.

XII   Relatively speaking, fewer of the principal Spanish sacred composers reached print than did their major French and Italian counterparts. From the beginning, the paucity of music presses has been a lamented but universal fact in Spanish musical history. Fortunately, however, we need not believe that during the sixteenth century the number of Spanish musical imprints was coterminous with the sacred repertory.

1 Eslava (*Lira sacro-hispana*, I, i, 167-170) printed a motet *a 4*, *Ave sanctissimum et gloriosum corpus*, by "Antonio" Bernal (the opening strongly resembles Victoria's *O magnum mysterium*). Collet (*Le mysticisme musical espagnol*, pp. 261-262) claimed that Bernal's Christian name should be "José" and said that after singing in the chapel of Charles V, Bernal became chapelmaster of San Salvador, the collegiate church in Seville. At Toledo, Codices 12 (not 40 as erroneously reported in *MME*, VIII, *22*) and 24 contain the Pentecost hymns *a 4*, *Qui Paraclitus diceris* and *Veni Domine*, by Bernal [= Vernal] González. MS 13230 at the Biblioteca Medinaceli (Madrid) contains a ferial Mass *a 4*, a motet *a 4*, *Domine memento mei*, and a passion *a 4* beginning *Non in die festo*—all ascribed to Bernal; and at fol. 40ᵛ a secular song, *Navego en hondo mar*, attributed to Bernal Gonçales. A *romance* by Bernal, *A las armas moriscote*, keeps company with Morales's *De Antequera sale el moro* in Fuenllana's vihuela tablature *Orphénica lyra* (1554). Among the unsuccessful contenders for the Cordova chapelmastership in April, 1567, was a certain Bernal (Mitjana, *Don Fernando de Las Infantas*, p. 122).

2 Ginés de Boluda, son of Gaspar de Boluda and Catalina de Yniesta, was born at Hellín. His parents were natives of this historic town in Albacete province. On March 14, 1581, he became chapelmaster at Toledo Cathedral with an annual salary of 44,000 maravedís. Shortly thereafter he asked the elderly primate Gaspar de Quiroga to raise his salary to 100,000 maravedís—the amount paid his predecessor Andrés de Torrentes (d. September 4, 1580). He felt it unjust for some mere singers to receive more than 44,000 maravedís. On September 10, 1582, the cardinal of Seville, Rodrigo de Castro, came to his rescue with a personal letter to the primate from Lisbon, whither Philip II had summoned him on state affairs. Castro's personal intervention suggests some previous link. Possibly Boluda had attended

Castro while the latter was still bishop of Zamora or Cuenca. The contact cannot have been made in Seville—Castro having taken possession of the Sevillian see after Boluda's induction at Toledo. While at Zamora, Castro had accepted the dedication of Salinas's *De musica libri septem*; his musical refinement exceeded that of any Spanish prelate of the age, if his patronage of Salinas, Guerrero, Francisco Peraza, and Boluda measures his intelligence.

In his letter to the primate, Cardinal de Castro reminds the senior prelate that a request was made for a salary raise on a previous occasion. Previously, Cardinal de Castro had said that such a raise would be accounted a personal favor to himself as well as to Boluda. Castro reminds the aged primate that others have been granted pay increases and that Boluda obviously merits one.

Some two months before Torrentes's death an inventory of all the music books belonging to Toledo Cathedral had been ordered. When completed on August 13, 1580, the inventory showed a total of only twenty-one polyphonic choirbooks; no. 8 was Victoria's 1576 book of masses and magnificats, nos. 9 and 11 were hand copies of Guerrero's works, and no. 10 contained magnificats and motets by Ceballos. Boluda immediately set about enlarging the polyphonic collection. On March 2, 1582, George de La Hèle's 1578 book of masses luxuriously printed by Plantin at Antwerp was purchased. In October, 1583, Guerrero's 1570 motets were added. On September 9, 1585, he recommended payment of 200 reales (6,800 maravedís) for Victoria's *Missarum libri duo* (Rome: 1583). See Biblioteca Nacional MS 14047 for further details. On April 28, 1586, for his *buen servicio* to the cathedral, Boluda was rewarded with 10,000 maravedís; and was paid 35,118 maravedís plus 42 fanegas of wheat for the board, lodging, and instruction of six cathedral choirboys. In 1587 he received an honorarium for his composition of villancicos; in the same year he took a one-month tour through the

Castilian provinces in search of new singers. He stopped in Palencia, Burgos, Logroño, and Valladolid. After his certifying that a new volume of Victoria's motets (probably that of 1585) would be of great use, the chapter on September 13, 1588, approved paying Victoria 100 reales—such sum to be personally transmitted by Boluda. On September 24, 1590, he recommended paying 29,580 maravedís to a certain cathedral instrumentalist, Alonso Gascón, who was also an expert copyist. Gascón had copied 73 leaves of *canciones* and motets *a 5* and *a 6* for the cornetts to play, and 55 leaves of vocal polyphony (including Victoria's *Ascendens Christus* Mass *a 5*) for the *capilla* to sing. Other Toledo notices prove that instrumentalists took no less active a part in music at the primatial cathedral than at Seville during this epoch. The instrumentalists mentioned by name played *chirimías*, *sacabuches*, and *cornetas*. Much documentation also survives concerning dancers in religious processions during Boluda's and Lobo's incumbencies of the Toledo chapelmastership.

During 1590-1591, Boluda acted as an intermediary in negotiations for the purchase of two large carpets for Toledo Cathedral. These were woven in the hamlet of Lietor near his birthplace Hellín. Meanwhile, however, efforts to increase the Toledo polyphonic collection did not lag. Francisco Sánchez, who had accompanied Guerrero to the Holy Land (1588), came in the spring of 1592 bearing two books of his teacher's masses luxuriously copied on vellum. In a covering intercessory letter, Rodrigo de Castro, the Sevillian cardinal who had intervened for Boluda a decade earlier, recommended the manuscript copies to the Toledan primate in the warmest terms. Cardinal Quiroga replied on May 9 with a very courteous offer of 2,384 reales (81,056 maravedís) for Guerrero's ten masses. Ginés de Boluda was again the intermediary through whom the money was transmitted. During the next year Alonso Lobo, transferring from the vice-chapelmastership at Seville, replaced Boluda. Lobo was confirmed in the Toledan chapelmastership on September 22, 1593. Allowing time for *edictos*, a public competition, and the required check of each candidate's purity of lineage, one would suppose that Boluda died or retired at the end of 1592 or the beginning of 1593.

Vicente Espinel lauded Voluda [= Boluda] in his *La casa de la memoria* (Madrid: 1591), claiming that his fame would live eternally because of his conquest of the *nuevo estilo* (new style). Toledo Codex 8 (in a handwritten appendix) shows at page 92 Boluda's setting *a 4* of *A solis ortu usque ad occasum* (Ps. 112:3 [Liber usualis numbering]) followed by a Gloria Patri, *a 5*. Four motets and a set of lamentations follow. These, although unattributed, may be his. Codex 22 contains a Holy Week fabordón, *Quoniam ipse liberavit me*; Codex

25 an *Asperges me*, a *Miserere mei, Domine*, and a Gloria Patri. Trumpff in 1953 announced the preservation of a Hexachord Mass *a 5* and a psalm *a 4*, *In exitu Israel de Aegypto*, in a large choirbook now in Germany but copied (on paper) at Toledo in 1696. See *AM*, VIII, 121.

3 Diego del Castillo, a brother of the equally famous organist Bernardo Clavijo del Castillo, was appointed organ prebendary in the Seville Cathedral on April 28, 1581. The sumptuous grand organ built by the Flemish *organero* Maestre Jox between 1567 and 1579 imposed certain difficulties so far as registration was concerned. Therefore, Castillo was instructed by the chapter on November 3, 1583, to prepare some guidebooks describing its stops (*libros de las mixturas y tonos del horgano grande*).

Francisco Correa de Arauxo in his *Facultad orgánica* (Alcalá: 1626) referred to Castillo at fol. 3ᵛ in the following terms: "When I began to study music in this city [Seville], not a trace of anything for organ using accidental [sharp] signatures was to be found. It was not until some years later that I saw the first examples of such music in cipher: they being certain Verses in Tone VIII transposed to D. The earliest to cipher these was Peraza [Sevillian organist, 1573-1580]; and then a little later Diego del Castillo, organ prebendary at Seville [1581-1583] and afterward organist in the royal chapel. Both of these [Peraza and Castillo] —like various others—inserted sharps every time F's occurred [in such Tone VIII transposed Verses]. After considering, however, the philosopher's dictum that it is foolish to make many gestures when but a few will do, and after pondering also on the commonly accepted method of avoiding the constant repetition of B♭'s solely by prefacing a piece in which such occur with a capital B—thus eliminating the tiresome repetition of flats every time the note B appears—I thought it advisable to place at the beginning of pieces with sharp signatures a single ♮ if only F's are to be sharped throughout, ♮ ♮ if both F's and C's are to be sharped, ♮ ♮ ♮ if F's, C's and G's are to be sharped." This long abstract from the *Facultad orgánica* should serve three purposes. First, it should clarify Correa's meaning when he says that nothing ciphered for organ with *accidental* signatures was to be seen at Seville in his early youth. By *accidental* he meant in this connection sharp accidentals. The Verses in Tone VIII ciphered by Peraza, and ending on D, ran through the following octave: D-E-F♯-G-A-B-C-D. Peraza and Castillo, following the current Spanish system, would have ciphered F's with 1's, G's with 2's, A's with 3's, and so on, through E's with 7's. In Tone VIII verses ending on D, they were therefore obliged to cipher thus: 1♯, 1˙♯, 1'♯, in order to designate the notes F♯, f♯, or f¹♯. Correa, on the other hand, found a way to avoid such repetitiousness. Second, the quotation shows clearly that organ tablatures were already in vogue at Seville (as elsewhere) long before either Gerónimo Peraza or Diego del Castillo appeared on the Sevillian scene. Third, the quotation from Correa's *Facultad orgánica* deserves study because his words were interpreted by Pedrell (*Diccionario biográfico y bibliográfico*, p. 323, col. 2) to mean that Castillo himself published an organ tablature. Actually, the word *rastro* in Correa's text means "trace" or "sign." Other scholars have therefore been rather reluctant to infer from Correa's text that Castillo necessarily *published* his tablature: especially since Pedrell never adduced any supporting evidence for such an interesting claim.

Castillo occupied the Sevillian organ prebend for approximately thirty-two months. Shortly before December 14, 1583, he was appointed organist in the royal chapel. At the order of Philip II he was paid on December 16 an initial sum of 73,000 maravedís for salary plus 29,200 for *ayuda de costa* (cost-of-living allowance). On February 24, 1584, his annual cost-of-living allowance was raised to 114,500 maravedís—his stated annual salary remaining at 219,000. On April 4, 1588, Philip granted him an annual pension of 400 ducats (150,000 maravedís) in place of the previous cost-of-living allowance: this pension to be charged against income from the diocese of Cuenca. Henceforth until death he was carried in fiscal records of the House of Castile as "nuestro capellán y músico de tecla"—*tecla* being the generic term in sixteenth-century Spanish for keyboard instrument just as *Klavier* was in eighteenth-century German. Hernando de Cabezón, son of the great Antonio, shared with Castillo the title of royal *músico de tecla*. As early as May 29, 1584, their signatures begin appearing conjointly on salary receipts (Biblioteca Nacional, MS 14024.9).

One other manuscript at the National Library in Madrid deserves mention because of the light that it throws on Castillo, as well as upon the four organs at El Escorial which he was asked to examine in 1587: *Relacion delo que declaro Diego del Castillo se deuia remediar en los quatro organos de S. Lorenzo el Real . . . 1587 años* (MS 14025.194). In this *relación*, Castillo itemizes the few improvements that he thinks might be made. At the time of his visit one organ had been tuned a minor third lower than the others. Both Castillo and Melchor de Miranda, chief organist at Toledo, suggested that a fourth would be preferable. They counseled the prior not to worry over the stiffness of the action so long as it was even. Castillo's other suggestions were equally practical.

The earliest imprint containing a description of Castillo's art seems to be Vicente Espinel's *Diversas rimas* of 1591 (fol. 47ᵛ). In *La casa de la memoria*, Espinel characterizes Castillo as a "pure

and unique talent who dominates his instrument completely," adding that "his is a learned and discreet temperament"; and that "both as performer and as composer he scales lofty heights." After Espinel's 1591 imprint the next published description of Castillo's art is found in *Discursos sobre la filosofia moral de Aristoteles* by Antonio de Obregón y Cerezeda, a canon of León and a royal chaplain. Although dedicated to Philip III while he was still a prince, and therefore written before 1598, this didactic work was not published until five years after he ascended the throne (Valladolid: Luis Sánchez, 1603). At pages 181–182 Obregón writes thus: "A *claviórgano* had arrived the day before from Germany, a gift from a great sovereign to His Highness. It proved to be a most rare and right royal instrument both on account of its wide variety of cunningly devised mixtures, string and flute stops; as well as for its rich workmanship and the beautiful ornamentation of its exterior. Diego del Castillo, His Majesty's chaplain and organist, was summoned to demonstrate to His Highness the potentialities of the instrument. He proceeded first to test the full organ with a series of quite solemn chords [*algunas consonancias muy graves*], then with several florid passages [*flores*], and lastly with various modulations [*passos peregrinos*] such as he who was most singular in his art knew how to introduce with excellent effect. His Highness showed that he was greatly pleased with the instrument, and said that he would enjoy hearing Castillo accompany a singer. Luis Honguero, an eminent member of the royal chapel and chamber musician was called for; he sang with such a naturally reposeful countenance, such admirable virtuosity, such suaveness, sweetness, breath control, and evenness . . . that His Highness was delighted beyond measure."

Still another revealing allusion to Castillo's art is made in Fray José de Sigüenza's *Historia de la Orden de San Jerónimo*, tercera parte, libro quarto, discurso XXIII (Madrid: Imp. Real, 1605). According to Sigüenza, a young friar named Diego de la Concepción—a rank amateur—was frequently asked to play the grand organ at El Escorial; "though he knew very little, what he did play sounded admirably"; at least to some of the friars. Sigüenza continues thus: "I recall that once Diego del Castillo, the renowned royal keyboardist, upon hearing him play, asked me if his own playing sounded like that of this young friar? Laughingly I replied, No, because your flights are beyond our comprehension, but what our friar does sounds very well indeed to us." Sigüenza admits that the young friar knew enough to sense his own defects. This anecdote deserves study in the original Spanish (see *Nueva Biblioteca de Autores Españoles*, XII, 673, col. 2). One infers that Castillo's art was caviar to the general.

Probably still under fifty, Castillo died on

May 11, 1601. His mother, who was his survivor and legatee, collected on June 7, 1602, the back pay still owing him. In 1623 his estate—which included a considerable amount of property in Guadalajara (35 miles northeast of Madrid)—passed to his brother Bernardo Clavijo del Castillo: three years later to be inherited by the latter's two sons, Antonio and Francisco (see below, p. 309, col. 2).

Castillo belongs in the present company of vocal polyphonists by virtue of the two motets *a 5, Quis enim cognovit* and *O altitudo divitiarum,* published by Eslava in *Lira sacro-hispana,* I, ii, 165-169, 171-173. The first is in transposed dorian, and the second in transposed phrygian; both set impersonal scriptural texts. Each is conceived as a series of closely worked imitative points. Castillo tightly braids these points; as a rule threading in a new strand before time has been given for the previous subject to be woven through all parts. Analysis that would divide the motets into clearly articulated sections is made the more difficult because of his parsimonious use of V-I cadences. In *Quis enim cognovit,* mm. 94-106 = 116-128. But even this repetition fails to sectionalize the motet (the repeated bars are neither prefaced by, nor concluded with, a clear-cut cadence).

4 Francisco and Rodrigo Ceballos have been confused frequently. According to Pedrell (*Diccionario biográfico y bibliográfico,* pp. 334-335), Francisco served as chapelmaster at Burgos from 1535 to *ca.* 1572. Although this much may well be true, it is on the other hand now certain that both Eslava in *Lira sacro-hispana* (I, i, 96-108 [transcribed from Toledo Codex 7]) and Pedrell in the dictionary just cited erred in attributing three motets to Francisco which are by Rodrigo (see *MME,* VIII, 23). At present no single composition is indubitably by Francisco—all extant "Ceballos" compositions either lacking a Christian name or bearing Rodrigo for a *nombre de pila.* Because of the generation to which he belonged, if for no other reason, *el gran çauallos, cuyas obras | Dieron tal resplandor en toda España* ("the great Ceballos, whose works shine so brightly throughout all Spain" [Vicente Espinel, *La casa de la memoria,* 1591]) would have had to be Rodrigo, not Francisco. The biographical data assembled (1918) by Mitjana indicates that Rodrigo was not even likely to have been Francisco's relative (*Don Fernando de Las Infantas,* p. 119).

5 Rodrigo Ceballos was born about 1530 in Aracena, a town 50 miles northwest of Seville with a history reaching back to classical times (Elústiza-Castrillo, *Antología musical,* p. LXXXV). On October 7, 1553, he was commissioned by the Sevillian cathedral chapter to copy two or three choirbooks in which would be contained several up-to-date masses. At that time he was residing in the city but was without employment. To accommodate him, the chapter decided on a pay-as-you-go financial arrangement. He was given some latitude in choosing the repertory: a fact which in itself suggests that his musical opinions were already considered trustworthy (see above, page 145).

Rodrigo Ceballos is next heard of as a competitor for the chapelmastership at Málaga which, after falling vacant upon Morales's death in the early autumn of 1553, was again vacant on April 19, 1554—this time because of Guerrero's renunciation of the appointment (see Mitjana, "La capilla de Música de la Catedral de Málaga [1543-1569]," pp. 48, 52-54). The six competitors in the new trials held during the week beginning Monday, June 18, 1554, were Juan de Cepa, Rodrigo Ceballos, Rodrigo Ordoñez, Francisco de Ravaneda, Gonzalo Cano, and Melchor Galvez. Cepa, originally from Ciudad Rodrigo diocese, had served the Duchess of Calabria as chapelmaster. Rodrigo Ordoñez, maestro de capilla at Zamora in 1553 (Rubio Piqueras, *Música y músicos toledanos,* p. 81), was to be eminently desired at Salamanca in 1574 and highly praised by Vicente Espinel in 1591. Ravaneda—a contributor to Fuenllana's *Orphénica lyra* (1554)—was a sacred composer of distinct merit, if the preservation of his first-tone Magnificat alongside other settings of the canticle by Jean L'Héritier, Gascogne, Peñalosa, Torrentes, and Morales are considered sufficiently eminent company (Rubio Piqueras, *Códices polifónicos toledanos,* p. 37).

The week-long competition ended on June 24. A vote could not be taken immediately however. On the preceding April 12 a royal decree had required all cathedral chapters to examine henceforth the family background of each candidate prior to naming the winner. At last, on November 5, the required information had been gathered, whereupon Cepa was voted first choice and Ceballos second. These two names were forwarded to court: Cepa was approved, and formally inducted on Christmas Eve.

Ceballos had in the meantime returned to Seville, where in January, 1556, he was found singing, either in the cathedral or in some such church as San Salvador, by the treasurer of Cordova Cathedral (acting as a scout). On Friday, January 31, the Cordovan chapter met to discuss a letter from the treasurer to the archdeacon describing his discovery of an "excellent sopranist (*cantor tiple*) of both ability and character who has agreed to come here at the same salary of 1,000 reales (34,000 maravedís) and two cahizes of wheat which he has been receiving in Seville." The chapter at once invited Ceballos to appear for a personal interview; and on June 1 voted to set his salary at 30,000 maravedís plus 17 fanegas of wheat. Ten days later the appointment took effect. By its terms he was to assist the elderly Alonso de Vieras, who had been chapelmaster at Cordova during the previous quarter-century. His contract also stipulated that he should board and instruct two choirboys (the rest apparently residing with a certain Pedro de Blancas), that he should conduct only in the chapelmaster's absence, and that he should give regular lessons in plainsong, counterpoint, and harmony to all the singing clergy in Cordova Cathedral. At that epoch, the cathedral hired no more than four adult professional singers—one for each part. The highest paid of these was the contralto, who received twice as much as the tenor. In addition, the adult music staff included an organist and four or five *menestriles* (Mitjana, *Don Fernando de Las Infantas*, p. 120).

Ceballos's next step was to seek holy orders. To obtain these he needed to show the ordinary a certificate of appointment to some chaplaincy. The same Cordovan treasurer who had sponsored his coming now induced the chapter to name him to a chaplaincy, but upon the condition that he resign it immediately after being ordained. The chapter acceded to the request and on October 14, 1556, granted him a fortnight's leave of absence to visit Seville for his ordination (*ibid.*, p. 119, n. 2). Upon returning he continued to find even greater favor in the eyes of the Cordovan bishop and chapter. On May 21, 1557, the chapter decided "that two chapelmasters having proved a superfluity, their worships ought to terminate Alonso de Vieras's contract, and to install Rodrigo de Ceballos as sole chapelmaster" (*ibid.*, p. 118).

The next three years proved a period of intense creative activity. In the spring of 1560 Ceballos was able to send the Málaga chapter a book containing his first fruits (Gerónimo de Barrionuevo carried it to the port city). The Málaga chapter, remembering Ceballos's excellent account of himself in 1554, voted to send him a letter of thanks as well as six ducats. Meanwhile the Cordovan chapter gave further tokens of approval. On August 2, 1560, the canons voted him a lifetime lease on certain houses *enfrente de Santa Ana*—generously fixing the annual rental at less than half the usual figure (4,000 maravedís and 4 pairs of chickens instead of the accustomed 9,210 and 9 pairs). Even this concession could not sway him, however, when in the next year he received an offer to become *maestro de capilla* of the royal chapel at Granada. On October 1, 1561, he handed in his resignation. Two weeks later Diego Ximénez was offered the succession—occupying it for but a short time, however; after which the senile Alonso de Vieras was called back as an interim appointee. On June 21, 1563, Ceballos was invited to sit as judge during a set of examinations in Cordova to select a worthy successor to himself. After a series of tests, Andrés Villalar was elected

on July 5, 1563 (*ibid.*, pp. 121-122). Nine years later Ceballos was appointed a royal chaplain (on January 29, 1572; see Elústiza-Castrillo, *Antología musical*, p. LXXXVII).

A year before the death of Philip II, a volume of Ceballos's magnificats, hymns, and *fabordones* belonged to the library of the royal chapel at Madrid (*Música sacro-hispana*, Vol. X [1917], p. 155, item 157). In the capitular library at Toledo, Codex 7—reaching 336 leaves—is prefaced with a table of contents listing 52 motets (*22 a 4, 24 a 5, 6 a 6*), a Salve Regina, and finally 3 masses by Ceballos. According to the compiler of the table of contents, "this book contains all the motets that Ceballos composed" (Rubio Piqueras, *Códices polifónicos toledanos*, p. 23). Unfortunately, the "ink has so corroded the paper that it is impossible to transcribe so much as a single composition in the volume" (Pedrell, *Diccionario biográfico y bibliográfico*, Vol. I, p. 336, col. 2). Whether this last quoted judgment would be held as true now as when Pedrell uttered it in 1897 will not be guessed here. But at least the titles can be read. Comparing these with the six preserved in the Santiago codex at Valladolid and the dozen in the private collection of Pedrell's friend Monasterio (*Diccionario*, Vol. I, p. 336, col. 2), we find that the Toledo codex makes good its claims to completeness.

The Santiago Codex at Valladolid contains these motets (each *a 4*): (1) *Dicebat Jesus turbis* (fol. 28ᵛ); (2) *Ductus est Jesus* (fol. 23ᵛ); (3) *Erat Jesus ejiciens* (fol. 33ᵛ); (4) *Hortus conclusus* (fol. 54ᵛ); (5) *Inter vestibulum et altare* (fol. 30ᵛ); (6) *Posuerunt super caput ejus causam ipsius* (fol. 27ᵛ). Item 4 is a motet in two *partes* (2d pars: *Veni sponsa mea*). The Monasterio partbooks (*Superius, Altus, Tenor*) mentioned by Pedrell in his *Diccionario*, page 336, included the following: (1) *Ad Dominum cum tribularer* (2d pars: *Heu mihi quia incolatus sum*); (2) *Clamabat autem mulier cananea*; (3) *Cum accipisset Jesus panes*; (4) *Ductus est Jesus*; (5) *Ego quasi vitis fructificavi*; (6) *Et factum est postquam in captivitatem* (Lamentation); (7) *Exaltata est Sancta Dei genetrix* (2d pars: *Virgo Dei genetrix*); (8) *Hortus conclusus soror mea* (= item 4 in the Santiago list); (9) *In illo tempore descendens Petrus de navicula*; (10) *In mense autem sexto missus est angelus Gabriel*; (11) *Posuerunt super caput ejus* (= item 6 in the Santiago list); (12) *Regina coeli*. Lastly, a Sevillian source contains several of Ceballos's motets— MS 1 in the cathedral music archive. At fols. 21ᵛ-25, 87ᵛ-91, 91ᵛ-93, 93ᵛ-95, and 95ᵛ-96, respectively, in this handsome 15 by 22-inch vellum choirbook are to be seen the following works of "Roderici Çeuallos": Salve Regina *a 4*, concordances for items 8, 5, and 7 in the Pedrell list, and a *Deo dicamus a 5*.

The first and last of Ceballos's masses in Toledo Codex 7—each *a 4*—bore *Simile est regnum coelorum* and *Veni Domine* for titles. The second, also *a 4*, lacked a title. A *Missa mi fa la fa sol la* (*a 4*) by Ceballos in a Toledo choirbook copied in 1696, but carried to Germany, was announced by G. A. Trumpff without specifying the present location of the manuscript (*AM*, Vol. VIII [1953], p. 121, n. 150).

Outside Spain, three further Ceballos sources have thus far been inventoried: one at Vila Viçosa (Portugal) in Choirbook 8, the second at Puebla (Mexico) in Choirbook 20, and the third in an unnumbered choirbook at The Hispanic Society (New York City). A page from Ceballos's *Nunc dimittis* in the last-named source may be seen (reduced facsimile) at page 392, item 290, in *A History of The Hispanic Society of America: Museum and Library* (New York: 1954).

Ceballos favored motet texts that had already been set by composers born at, or lengthily associated with, Seville. Such a text as *Clamabat autem mulier cananea*, for instance, is to be found among Escobar's, Morales's, Farfán's, and Guerrero's motets; and also set for solo voice with vihuela accompaniment in Mudarra's *Tres libros* (Seville: 1546). Ceballos's *Et factum est postquam in captivitatem* immediately recalls Morales's version of the same unscriptural prologue to Lamentations. Morales's setting of this prologue (intabulated by Fuenllana) has already been characterized above at page 90 as peculiarly Spanish. As for links with Guerrero: Ceballos imitates him by writing a canon at the sixth in a motet entitled "And the angel Gabriel was sent in the *sixth* month." In Ceballos's motet describing Peter's descent from the ship to meet Jesus walking on the waves, the watch of the night and the interval of the canon agree. These agreements immediately recall the opening series of canonic motets *a 5* in Guerrero's *Sacrae cantiones* (1555). Ceballos is, of course, known from contemporary records to have been living in Seville during 1553-1556.

His secular pieces include six items in Biblioteca Medinaceli, MS 13230 (see *MME*, VIII, *24*). *Ojos hermosos* (*MME*, VIII, 89-90), includes a fourth voice by "Varrionuevo," who may have been the Gerónimo de Barrionuevo entrusted with delivering a book of Ceballos's sacred compositions to the Málaga cathedral chapter in the spring of 1560. Two others concord with intabulations in Esteban Daza's *El Parnasso* of 1576 (*MME*, Vol. IX, items 74 and 75). At Valladolid Cathedral, MS 17 (= 255) contains a single voice part of Ceballos's *Quán bienaventurado aquel puede llamarse* (conflicting details concerning this source are to be found in *AM*, III, 83; and *MME*, VIII, *19* [item 122], *54* [line 2], *56* [line 20]). Daza, in addition to intabulating *Díme manso viento*, *Duro mal terrible llanto* and *Quán bienaventurado*—concordances for each of which are to be found in Biblioteca Medinaceli MS 13230—intabulated an otherwise unknown villanesca,

Pues ya las claras fuentes.

Transcriptions of all Ceballos's motets in the Santiago codex (Valladolid), except *Ductus est Jesus*, are printed in the Elústiza-Castrillo *Antología musical*, 1933. (*Hortus conclusus* and *Veni sponsa mea* [*ibid.*, pp. 144-146, 147-150], although first and second *partes* of the same motet, are in this anthology treated, incorrectly, as independent motets.) Ceballos, like Guerrero, knows how to invent head motives that stick in the memory. More frequently, perhaps, than Guerrero's motets, his exploit pert—even jaunty—rhythmic figures. Repeated notes, ornamented resolutions of syncopations, and wide melodic skips, in such motets as *Hortus conclusus* (Song of Songs 4:12, 8) and *Erat Jesus ejiciens*, emphasize the ictus. Although he did undoubtedly learn much from Guerrero, Ceballos's personal mannerisms give his motets an individual flavor. For one thing, he reveled in melodic repetitions and sequences—going beyond any other Andalusian, if the available repertory can be taken as representative. These repetitions and sequences stand out the more boldly because he favors the top voice (he was himself a tiple). *Hortus conclusus* (both *partes*) and *Dicebat Jesus* are cases in point. Ceballos obviously liked sweeping and dramatic gestures. The sections that begin "aperi mihi" in *Hortus conclusus*, "parce" in *Inter vestibulum et altare*, and "in nomine Jesus" in *Posuerunt super caput* provide telling instances.

Two of the five motets in the Elústiza-Castrillo anthology concord with those in *Lira sacro-hispana*, I, i, 96-105. The third in the Eslava edition—*Exaudiat Dominus*—boasts a typically repetitious and sequential tiple. Its several sections are marked off by authentic cadences (mm. 1-26; 27-43, 44-55₁, 55₃-62₁; 62₃-71₁, 71₃-93; 93-119) that clarify its structure. In each of the four principal sections (separated by semicolons in the measure analysis) a new melodic subject is developed by imitation, as well as by repetition and by sequence. In this *Exaudiat*, as in his other now available motets, Ceballos adjusts words to text so aptly that he would seem to be setting his native Spanish rather than ecclesiastical Latin.

Fétis was the first international scholar to pass critical judgment on Ceballos. In the second edition of his *Biographie universelle des musiciens* he classed Ceballos as a truly important master "because of his elegant sense of form and his limpid style." On the basis of just the single motet *Inter vestibulum et altare* (Eslava, I, i, 102-105 = Elústiza-Castrillo, pp. 141-143) he was willing to give him a place beside Morales, Guerrero, and Victoria (*Biographie universelle des musiciens* [1878], II, 243). Had Fétis's knowledge of the repertory ranged more widely he would no doubt have found Ceballos equally persuasive in *Erat Jesus ejiciens* and *Dicebat Jesus*. Were spontaneity any sufficient criterion, he might indeed have called

Hortus conclusus—which is in every known Spanish manuscript containing his motets—one of the finest things in the Spanish repertory. Morales knew how to be more profound, Guerrero more suavely sensuous, Victoria more soulful. But none of these knew how to be more naïvely charming than Ceballos in this motet of two *partes*: nor have Song of Songs texts (4:12,8) been treated so captivatingly anywhere else in the Spanish literature.

6 Like Juan Doyz, the renowned organist from Navarre who after playing at Granada joined the cathedral staff at Málaga, Bernardo Clavijo del Castillo seems to have originated in the extreme north of Spain. Two reasons can be advanced for such a presumption: (1) Esteban Álvarez, chapelmaster at Pamplona (capital of Navarre) testified on April 2, 1593, that he had known Clavijo personally for twenty years; (2) Clavijo enjoyed such friendly connections at the nearby University of Oñate (province of Guipúzcoa) that he was able to obtain a licentiateship from that university in 1594 without fulfilling any residence requirements.

As a youth Clavijo followed Spanish arms to Italy; but, according to Ottavio Tiby, "La musica nella Real Cappella Palatina di Palermo," *AM*, Volume VII (1952), page 184, began serving as a musician in the R. Chiesa di San Pietro at Palermo as early as December 6, 1569. If so, then at least twenty years intervened before his definitive return to Spain in 1589. His annual salary in 1589 amounted to 200 scudi, whereas that of Canon Luis Ruiz the chapelmaster amounted to 240. In addition, seven singers were paid a total of 1,236 scudi (*ibid.*, p. 183). In 1588 he published at Rome a motet collection dedicated to the new viceroy of Sicily, the Count of Alba de Liste (appointed 1585). "Suitable for instruments as well as voices," the 19 items in this imprint included 6 each *a 4*, *a 5*, and *a 6*, and one *a 8* (*Die Musik in Geschichte und Gegenwart*, II, 1474 [hereafter cited as *MGG*]).

In the fall of 1589 while Clavijo was visiting Spain, Juan Alonso, a canon of Salamanca Cathedral, met him at Madrid to discuss the possibility of his abandoning the Palermo position (from which he was on leave) and of coming to Salamanca at an annual salary of 25,000 maravedís. On November 14, 1589, the Salamanca cathedral chapter voted to engage him, but on condition *que traya habito largo de clerigo y que se escriuiese al canonigo Juan Alonso la prouision* (that he wear a clerical habit—a letter being written to inform Canon Juan Alonso of this proviso). Clavijo accepted. Soon after reaching Salamanca, however, he appeared before the assembled chapter—on January 24, 1590—protesting that the amount of required *residencia* exceeded his expectation and left him no time *para poder estu-*

diar en su Arte lo que le combenja (for needed practice and study). He therefore pleaded for a reduction of his duty hours. The chapter refused such a reduction: whereupon he decided that he would not stay. In May, 1590, he was again in Madrid, whence he wrote Don Roque—who was simultaneously chapelmaster in the cathedral and professor of music in the university—protesting that the Salamanca organ prebend lacked the expected attractions *por su mucha Residencia y obligacion de Rezar*; and declaring his intention of returning to Palermo. This letter was read publicly in chapter meeting on May 25. The canons then enquired *si convendria hacer alguna commodidad al dicho Bernardo del Castillo por ser tan perito en el Arte del organo y tan benemerito* (whether some adjustment might legitimately be made since he is so skilled an organist and so worthy). Mention was made of the fact that *en ninguna delas yglesias de españa hay mejor* (there is no better organist in any church in Spain), and that much searching had preceded the appointment. The canons thereupon decided that some relaxation of his duties might be allowed *con condicion que quando entrare en el choro y subiere a tocar el organo entre con sobre pelliz* (on condition that he wear a surplice when he enters the choir enclosure and ascends to play the organ).

The desired concessions having been at last formally granted, Clavijo "solicited and obtained" royal approval not only for his resignation from the Palermo post but also for the collection of three months' back pay still owing at the time of his departure for Spain the year previously (*pagamento di tre mesi di stipendio per il permesso ottenuto di poter ritornare in Spagna*, dated October 15, 1590 [Palermo: *Archivio di Stato, Cancelleria*, Vol. 513, p. 191]).

On February 8, 1593, Roque de Salamanca having just died, *Yo Bartolome Sanchez, notario y secretario desta Universidad de Salamanca . . . publique por vaca la catedra de propriedad de canto desta Universidad con termino de treinta dias* (the secretary of the university announced the chair of music theory to be vacant, with thirty days allowed for the submission of contenders' names [*Libro de Claustros de 1592 a 1593*, fol. 42]). Two days later, Clavijo, who had already been playing at university functions for over a year, entered his name (*ibid.*, fol. 45ᵛ). On March 26 he underwent the formality of receiving a bachelor's degree—Francisco Sánchez, who was a cathedral canon and at the same time a philosophy professor in the university, proposing him for the degree (*Libro de Bachilleramientos desde Abril de 1591 a id. de 1594*, fol. 154ᵛ). No other contenders for the vacant music chair having entered their names in the meantime, the question was raised on March 30 whether an examination for appointment to the professorship ought yet to be held (*Libro de Claustros*, fol. 63). On April 2, 1593, the university authorities decided to proceed even though Clavijo was the only applicant. Don Roque had been cathedral chapelmaster as well, and three candidates for succession to the chapelmastership were fortunately in town on that very day. These three and Manuel Castro, a singing clergyman (sopranist) in the cathedral, were invited to witness the examination.

The jury consisted of twenty-three members of diverse university faculties, plus the four invited musical guests. Only one of the twenty-three faculty members was a musician—Maestro Çumel, teacher of plainchant—his post corresponding to that of university choragus (and the vacant one to Heather Professor). After the jury and all the interested spectators who could crowd into the examination room had assembled, the Rector of the university handed Clavijo a familiar textbook—Pedro Ciruelo's *Cursus quattuor mathematicarum*. Three paragraphs from the section on music were marked. Clavijo was asked to choose any one of the three and translate it from Latin into Spanish. After having made his choice and having given an oral translation, he was then questioned on the meaning of the passage by various members of the jury. Next, a *monachordio* (spinet) was brought into the examination room. The partbooks of Clavijo's own *Motecta* published at Rome five years earlier were brought out, whereupon he was asked to sing and play one of his six-part motets. Having concluded, he went out, together with all the spectators in the room, so that the jury might freely discuss his qualifications before taking a vote.

Maestro Çumel opened the discussion, averring that whatever else Clavijo might know he certainly did not know Latin. "If he himself doesn't understand the book that he is to expound in his half-hour lectures on speculative music, nor Boethian theory, how can he teach others?" asked Çumel. Others as vehement against Clavijo's appointment spoke at great length. To appease them, the Rector suggested that perhaps some of those present who had known Clavijo over a period of several years might be willing to testify. Of the two clergymen present who had known Clavijo, the first—Francisco Sánchez—immediately responded that on oath he would rate Clavijo's ability to read Latin as fully the equal of Roque's (who had just died). The second declared that from a three-year acquaintance he would rate Clavijo as *sufficientissimo para leer la dicha catedra*. Esteban Álvarez, chapelmaster from Pamplona and one of the four invited musicians, stated that he had known Clavijo for twenty years and that although he dared not estimate his ability as a Latinist, because he had never tested him, of this one thing he was sure: namely, that Clavijo was *muy heminente en la musica*. When the ballots were finally cast, 13 voted for appointment, 7 against, 4 refused to express an opinion,

2 wished further information before casting their ballots, and 1 held aloof on the ground that he had entered after the examination had started (*Libro de Claustros de 1592 a 1593*, fol. 67ᵛ). Although without an absolute majority, Clavijo was declared elected (*ibid.*, fol. 68) and the next morning (April 3) formally inducted at ten o'clock. He himself joined with such other musicians present for the ceremony in the *Escuelas menores* as an instrumentalist named Morales and an organist named Salas in singing a motet.

Somewhat over a year later, on August 27, 1594, Clavijo appeared before the university vice-chancellor with a petition to be incorporated as a Master of Arts. As evidence of sufficiency he produced a diploma dated July 29, 1594, certifying that he had been named *licenciado* by the University of Oñate (*Libro de Doctoramientos, Magisterios y Licenciamientos desde 1588 à 1595*, fol. 212ᵛ). The very fact, of course, that he should have enjoyed connections at the recently founded University of Oñate which enabled him without residence to become a *licenciado*—not to refer again to the testimony of Esteban Álvarez, chapelmaster from Pamplona—makes it extremely likely that Clavijo originated in either the province of Guipúzcoa or of Navarre. His name next appears in Salamanca University records on October 28, 1595, when he asked for a salary raise, reminding the administration that he had been playing the organ at university functions for the past four years *con muy poco estipendio*. Eight years later, he forfeited his university post.

From the previous December 9, 1602, Clavijo had been away at court playing the Christmas services. When his month's leave expired on January 10, 1603, the university authorities declared the music chair vacant. Inasmuch as he was not yet entirely sure of his new appointment, his wife's brother came forward the next day asking that a further two-month leave be granted. Simultaneously, the brother-in-law produced evidence to show that "his Highness very much desires Clavijo's presence this coming Lent in his chapel." Since Clavijo still held his house in Salamanca as proof of his intention to return, the university authorities granted the desired leave extension. But within a few days Clavijo learned that he would be advanced to a permanent appointment in the royal chapel, and that he would thus succeed his brother Diego del Castillo (d. May 11, 1601). On February 19, 1603, Sebastián de Vivanco underwent examination for the university chair—Clavijo being present to act as a member of the jury (cf. p. 277). Clavijo again visited Salamanca on May 10, 1603. On the following October 31, the same pupil Tomé Hernández who had succeeded him at the cathedral became university organist.

Doña Maria Carrión, Clavijo's first wife, having died, he married his second wife on August 3, 1618—Doña Ana del Valle. His house in Madrid became a resort for *literati* and musicians alike. Vicente Espinel in his *Vida del Escudero Marcos de Obregón* (Madrid: 1618) gave an animated description of such a reunion of keyboard, harp, and vihuela virtuosi. In the garden adjoining his house the greatest performers alive— Clavijo at the keyboard, his daughter Bernardina on the harp, and Lucas de Matos on the seven-course vihuela—"discoursed with each other in profound and highly original movements" (*Relación tercera, Descanso quinto*). This Bernardina was the daughter who had entered religion (Santo Domingo el Real). Don Francisco was the son whom Lázaro Díaz del Valle mentioned as gentleman of the royal house, keyboardist and organist to Philip IV from 1633 to 1637. Clavijo drew his will, which is generally considered to coincide with his death, on February 1, 1626. By its terms he left property in Guadalajara (inherited from his brother, Diego del Castillo) and other property in Salamanca to his two sons.

P. Luis Villalba—the first to unearth a Clavijo *tiento*—announced his discovery in the June 5, 1896, issue of *La Ciudad de Dios* (no. 111; published at Madrid). He had found it in an eighteenth-century manuscript preserved at El Escorial (sign. 56 – 67 – ñ. *Archivo Vicarial*); the title (at fol. 104ᵛ) reads thus: *Tiento de 2°. tono, por Jesolreud, Clabijo.* Later twice reprinted, this one tiento would not of itself justify Clavijo's reputation, thought Pedrell (*Diccionario*, p. 367). One year later, however, Pedrell announced the discovery of a truly important printed collection of Clavijo's motets: *Bernardi Clabixi del Castello in Regia Capella Sicula organici musici Motecta ad canendum tam cum quattuor, quinque, sex, et octo vocibus, quam cum instrumentis composita. Permissu superiorum. Romae. Apud Alexandrum Gardanum.* M.D.LXXXVIII. (1588).

The dedication reads: "To the most illustrious and excellent Don Diego Enríquez de Guzmán, Count of Alba de Liste, Viceroy, Senior Member of the Royal Council, . . . Governor General of Sicily: Just as, most illustrious Sir, your renown has spread throughout the whole viceroyalty of Sicily because of your puissant administration of secular affairs, so also you have not forgotten spiritual concerns but have even gone to the length of endowing the music of the royal chapel [at Palermo] so that divine praises may more fittingly be offered. For that same purpose I who am now organist and was formerly chapelmaster of the same chapel have composed some modest musical works that are dedicated to Your Excellency and to the Countess of Alba, your very dear spouse, and have arranged to have them printed in partial acknowledgment of my infinite debt." (Pedrell, *Diccionario*, pp. 367-368.)

The partbooks seen by Pedrell lacked a tenor— the CAB partbooks "being bound with another

Spanish sixteenth-century imprint" in a private library to which he enjoyed access. But since for fear of anticipation he refused to divulge any other details (*ibid.*, p. 368), a pall was cast over further Clavijo research: only to be lifted fifty years later when, in his "El Archivo Musical de la Catedral de Valladolid" (*AM*, III, 103), Anglés revealed the existence of another—presumably complete—set of six partbooks at Valladolid Cathedral.

The dictionary article in *MGG*, Volume II (pp. 1473-1475), is accompanied by a facsimile of the dedication; but calls for the following corrections: (1) the dedicatee was Viceroy of Sicily rather than of Naples—his seat of government being Palermo; (2) the succession of chapelmasters at Naples (col. 1473) has no bearing on Clavijo's career; (3) Clavijo was not licentiate of the "University of Oña" (col. 1474), but rather of the University of Oñate, public classes at which were first held in 1545; (4) at his death, three children survived: the daughter in religion, Bernardina, and two sons, Antonio and Francisco —both sons having shared in the bequest of Guadalajara property from Diego del Castillo's estate in 1623, and both sons being mentioned in Clavijo's will of February 1, 1626.

7 Mosen Juan Bautista Cómes, chief of the Valencia school of composers, was born at Valencia in February, 1568; baptized in the parish church of Santa Cruz in that city; entered the Colegio de Seises de Valencia Cathedral as a choirboy; and studied with Juan Ginés Pérez— founder of the Valencian school. His date of ordination is not known. After a period as chapelmaster in Lérida, he was recalled to Valencia and in 1605 named *maestro de capilla* at the Colegio de Corpus Christi—later known as the Colegio del Patriarca in deference to its founder, Juan de Ribera, Patriarch of Valencia (d. January 6, 1611). For Ribera's funeral ceremonies Cómes composed a motet *a 6, Si morte praeoccupatus fuerit.* On April 20, 1613, Cómes was advanced to the *magisterio* of the Valencian cathedral. Six years later, on January 6, 1619, he was named *teniente de maestro* (vice-chapelmaster) of the royal chapel. In 1627 he was offered a salary raise. Already, however, he wished to return to his native Valencia. In May, 1629, he was again named to the post he had held from 1605 to 1613 at the Colegio del Patriarca. On October 16, 1632, he resumed the chapelmastership of the Valencian Cathedral. On June 9, 1638, he had reached seventy, and the care and instruction of the choirboys was transferred to other shoulders. As a token of respect, his salary was not reduced. He died five years later, on January 5, 1643, a month short of his seventy-fifth birthday. He was buried the next evening in the *panteón de sacerdotes* of Valencia

Cathedral.

From Cómes's pen a total of 216 sacred pieces survive, usually for more than four voices. Although aged thirty in the year that Philip II died, he belongs with such baroque composers as Carlos Patiño, Bernardo de Peralta, Juan Pujol, and Manuel Correa, rather than with the generation of Rogier and Ghersem. His favorite mode of expression, if the selection of his works published at Madrid in 1888 is accepted as typical, was polychoral antiphony, often involving as many as four choirs. See *Obras musicales del insigne maestro español del siglo XVII, Juan Bautista Cómes, escogidas, puestas en partitura é ilustradas por D. Juan Bautista Guzmán, presbítero y maestro de capilla de la Santa Iglesia Catedral de Valencia. Publicadas de Real Orden.* (Madrid: Imprenta del Colegio nacional de Sordomudos y de Ciegos, 1888). Henri Collet in *Le mysticisme musical espagnol*, pages 304-306, described Cómes's style at length, paying particular attention to a *Miserere* for four choirs which Pedrell had praised lavishly after studying Guzmán's anthology.

This anthology is prefaced, first, by an engraving from a portrait in oils by Juan de Ribalta, the renowned Valencian painter (1597-1628), and, second, by a biography from which the above details have been extracted. Cómes, like Correa, has been the subject of some confusion because a Fray Miguel Cómes from Barcelona (studied at Montserrat, took the habit in June, 1627, became a respected organist, died in 1659) has not always been distinguished from the Valencian composer.

8 Ambrosio [Coronado de] Cotes, one of the more colorful Spanish chapelmasters, became *maestro de capilla* of the royal chapel at Granada during 1580 or 1581. Soon after appointment he ran afoul of Francisco Palero, organist since at least 1568. Palero objected violently to Cotes's exercising any superior authority—feeling himself of equal consequence. In 1591, when called upon to explain the difficulties that had arisen with Palero, Cotes wrote as follows: "It is true that on numerous occasions Palero has irritated me; he is without doubt the most ambitious man alive, and desires to be reverenced above all others." After a bass's prebend had gone unfilled for fifteen years, a competition was finally held over Palero's protest. By insults and threats Palero forced the best contender to desist, so that he could inveigle the appointment for a crony. His plan miscarried, however, and a new competition was held. On another occasion Cotes refused to name Palero chairman of Holy Week arrangements, because it was not his turn; whereupon Palero intrigued to have Cotes ousted from his time-honored prerogative of naming such officials. On still another occasion Palero entered the sacristy where Cotes was directing a

rehearsal of his own *Ave Maria, a 8*, and forthwith ordered Cotes and his colleagues out of the sacristy, "just as if we were mere altar boys." Palero's reason for ordering them out, said Cotes, was patent: the elderly organist *no poder sufrir qualquier genero de musica que sea mia* (could not abide any kind of music that I write). Palero had become such a lover of mediocrity as he grew older that "during the past eight years he has done everything in his power to bring in a string of incompetents." To make things doubly hard for Cotes after the appointment of a new *capellán mayor* (Pedro Ruiz Puente), Palero artfully wheedled the new official into accepting his own musical judgment as superior to that of the youthful chapelmaster. Once, after particularly harsh words, Cotes sought reconciliation through the intercession of a third party. Palero pretended that he was willing to let bygones be bygones. But no sooner had the third party to their public reconciliation departed than Palero again began to rail.

Palero simultaneously held an organistship in the nearby Church of St. Jerome. In order to retain both posts, he insisted on performing everything as fast as possible in the Capilla Real—forcing the succentor to rush through the plainchant, and chopping off his own responses, even at vespers and on solemn feasts—*por salir presto y poderse ir a tañer a San Gerónimo* (so that he could leave quickly and run over to St. Jerome's to play). Because at the same time his vanity forbade his suffering the chapelmaster to demonstrate any ability superior to his own, Palero strenuously objected when Cotes improvised a florid upper fourth part in falsetto—even though others enjoyed the added part and "while in Seville both the cardinal [Rodrigo de Castro] and Guerrero desired that I add such a part."

All these difficulties came to a head in 1591: in which year Palero, Ruiz Puente, and a few abettors drew up a list of twenty-four charges against Cotes which they then lodged with the Bishop of Guadix and Baza, a deputy appointed to visit the royal chapel and to maintain discipline. The charges reached such extravagant lengths that they fell of their own weight. Cotes was charged with being a gamester, a trifler with women, a malingerer, a disrespecter of authority, and a faker. The fact that Cotes was not impeded in his career, but rather that he rose successively to the chapelmasterships of Valencia Cathedral, 1596-1600 (Collet, *Le mysticisme*, p. 289), and of Seville Cathedral, September 22, 1600 – September 9, 1603, speaks for itself.

Collet, though an enthusiastic admirer of Cotes's *Missa de Plagis, a 5* (preserved in manuscript at Valencia Cathedral), did somewhat naïvely accept the charges brought against Cotes at their face value (*ibid.*, pp. 302-303). In an epoch when ecclesiastical discipline throughout

Spain was being tightened, Cotes could not have held his place at Granada, or gained higher posts at Valencia and Seville, had his name not been cleared of the charges brought by his intriguing enemies.

Cotes gained the Sevillian *magisterio* in an open competition against Juan de Riscos, chapelmaster at Jaén (uncle of the Juan de Riscos [b. Antequera, 1590] who after serving as chapelmaster at Cordova became *maestro* at Toledo, 1617-1619). On September 20, 1600, his right to wear a cloak and to occupy a seat of honor in the *coro* was acknowledged. On the following October 2 his preëminence over all other members of the Sevillian musical establishment was officially recognized. On November 17 he was admonished to obtain a *patitur* when absent on account of sickness. On January 3 his right to fine singers in the same amounts that Guerrero had mulcted their salaries was confirmed. On the following October 5 he was warned to fulfill his duties exactly as they were prescribed in the *tabla*. On February 25, 1603, his health had so deteriorated that the chapter voted a drastic reduction of his duties and placed him on half-pay. He died the succeeding September 9.

Although one recent scholar would have Cotes successively a chapelmaster at Seville, at the royal chapel in Granada, and after 1581 a maestrescuela at Valencia (*MME*, II, *174*), the chronological data to be found at the Archivo General de Simancas (Patronato Eclesiástico, Legajo 282, fols. 2-12) forbid any such chronological succession. Cotes, in his own *petición* contained in the above Legajo (dated 1591), distinctly stated not once but several times that he had been chapelmaster of the Real Capilla "diez años y mas" (paragraphs 9 and 10). Moreover, this same information reached print as long ago as 1896 (see *HSMS*, Vol. V, p. xvi, n. 1). As for his service at Seville, the capitular acts of that cathedral reveal beyond question the dates of Cotes's initial appointment and of his death in the Andalusian capital.

The largest cache of short works by Cotes thus far catalogued is at Granada. José López Calo lists 25 motets and lamentations of Cotes in five partbooks (see "El Archivo de Música de la Capilla Real de Granada," *AM*, XIII [1958], 112-113). These same partbooks contain four Morales motets *a 4*, the titles of which are unknown elsewhere in his repertory.

9 If previously assembled data may be trusted (Pedrell, *Tomás Luis de Victoria* [Valencia: Manuel Villar, 1918], pp. 20-21), Bartolomé de Escobedo was born *ca.* 1510. He studied at Salamanca, there becoming a cathedral singer. He was the next Spanish singer after Morales to be admitted into the papal choir. At the moment of his entrance on Wednesday, August 23, 1536, he was listed in the Sistine Diary (*Note d'archivio*, I, 3-4 [July-Dec., 1924], 268) as *clericus Zamorensis*, a clergyman of Zamora diocese. The French faction (perhaps because the ratio of French, Italian, and Spanish singers was disturbed) protested violently against his acceptance, even refusing to sing the next day. Escobedo was not deterred, however, from paying his entrance fees—ten ducats *pro omnibus ragalibus* [= *regalibus*] and two ducats *pro Cotta*.

The record of Escobedo's two periods of choir service—the first lasting from August 23, 1536, to June 5, 1541; the second from May 1, 1545, to October 25, 1554—is preserved in Sistine Diaries numbered 1, 2, 3, and 4. The only gap in this record comes between January 7, 1550, and January 5, 1553. (As early as May 1, 1554, the diary that covered 1550, 1551, and 1552 was carried away by the *magister capellae*, never to be returned: see *Note d'archivio*, XIII, 3-4 [May-Aug., 1936], 148 [col. 1]). These four diaries contain a record of Escobedo's frequent illnesses. Unlike Morales, he was never sick for several weeks at a stretch. His longest absence on account of illness seems to have occurred during the late winter of 1541; on February 14 (1541): *Scobedo infirmus et excusatus pro toto mense*. During his second term, he suffered from gout. For November 17, 1547, the diary reads: *Scopedus podagrosus*. On the preceding July 3, 1547, the diarist recorded that *Scopedus dolens pedem* (Escobedo was in pain because of his foot). The other notations relating to his illnesses include: *male habet* (Oct. 9, 1540), *in medicinis* (May 12, 1541), *sirupans exemptus est* (April 21, 1547), and *medicinatus* (Nov. 28, 1547). Like Nuñez, Ordoñez, and Sánchez, Escobedo occasionally malingered. On January 24, 1540, for instance, he was reported sick; but was later seen during the course of the day *in plateis*. On August 18, 1549, after being excused he was seen walking about in the city near the *templum pacis*.

Escobedo's voice being of the same range as Morales's, he could substitute for Morales (Feb. 2, 1540). In turn, Giovanni Abbate and Antonio Capello substituted for him (June 12 and July 29, 1540). It was with the latter, the favorite private musician of Pope Paul III (see Léon Dorez, *La cour du Pape Paul III d'après les registres de la trésorie secrète* [Paris: Ernest Leroux, 1932], I, 223), that Escobedo traded insults at vespers on Epiphany eve (Jan. 5), 1547. Escobedo called Capello an ass (see *Note d'archivio*, Vol. XI, no. 1 [Jan.-May, 1934], p. 84, n. 3). The Savoyard singer replied: "You're lying in your teeth." Both were fined ten julii.

On Wednesday, April 7, 1546, Escobedo was excommunicated. The next day he was absolved. On Monday, September 6, 1546, he called his fellow singer Leonard Barré (entered 1537) a "fat pig." On August 6, 1548, he was fined for wearing a short cassock. Later this particular fine was remitted. The following four notices in the diaries specifically mentioning him: *ad instantiam Bartholomei Schobedo sex sotij vadant pro celebranda certa missa pro quodam defuncto* (Oct. 29, 1538); *habuit scatulam* (April 4, 1539; July 29, 1548; May 31, 1553); *ad septem ecclesias* (Oct. 30, 1540; June 1, 1541); *mutauit domicilium* (Aug. 22, 1547); may be translated thus: (1) at Bartolomé de Escobedo's request six colleagues went to celebrate a Mass for a certain deceased individual; (2) he had the feast box (distributed in rotation from the pope's kitchen to his singers); (3) he visited the seven churches (as a one-day pilgrimage); (4) he changed his dwelling.

Francisco Salinas, who accompanied Pedro de Sarmiento to Rome for his investiture with the purple on October 18, 1538, and who remained in Italy until approximately 1562, became well acquainted with Escobedo. In his *De musica libri septem* (1577), page 228, he called Escobedo "an extremely learned musician and a very dear personal friend." Salinas continued thus: "Many prior theorists have labeled the major third as a 5:4 and the minor as a 6:5, the major sixth as a 5:3 and the minor as an 8:5 consonance—among them Bartolomé Ramos the Spaniard, whom a little while ago we said that Franchino [Gaffurio] so severely reprehended because such ratios did not correspond with those given by Boethius. But again [Ludovico] Fogliano, without reading the ancients, experimentally discovered the validity of the same disputed ratios: the validity of which will become apparent to anyone who properly investigates the subject. Long before myself reading his text or any other writings on the subject, I indeed turned over in my own mind these problems, discussing them frequently with Bartolomé Escobedo, *viro in vtraque Musices parte exercitatissimo, atque mihi amicissimo*. He told me that all these matters [of ratio] upon which I had been pondering had been treated of by Fogliano, just as I was later to be told by still another friend."

It was this well-deserved reputation for theoretical learning which no doubt caused Escobedo to be selected a judge (along with Ghiselin Danckerts) when in May, 1551, Nicola Vicentino challenged Vincenzo Lusitano to a public debate on the meaning of the ancient genera. The Portuguese theorist promised "in the name of all musicians to prove that I know what genus is used in the music composed nowadays and commonly sung." The rigidly doctrinaire Vicentino pretended to have acquired sufficient arcane lore to rout his rival. The first trial was held on June 4 in a large room of Cardinal Ippolito d'Este's palace. Because Danckerts could not attend, and because Escobedo refused to give his single opinion, a second trial was scheduled for the morning of June 7. At this second trial both judges united in upholding the Portuguese theo-

rist's contention that the genus "in which music is composed today" and which is "commonly sung" is the diatonic. Danckerts informed the heady protégé of Cardinal Ippolito that to be in enharmonic or chromatic genus, a piece must contain the diesis or major semitone. Vicentino had argued valiantly that the interval of a minor third was borrowed from the chromatic tetrachord. (For further details, see Giuseppe Baini, *Memorie storico-critiche della vita e delle opere di Giovanni Pierluigi da Palestrina* [Rome: Soc. Tipografica, 1828], I, 342-347 [note 424]. Baini's account, although impugned by Trend, agrees closely with the manuscript version in Biblioteca Casanatense [MS 2880]. See Claude V. Palisca, "The Beginnings of Baroque Music" [Ph.D. Dissertation, Harvard University, 1953], pp. 105-110).

Escobedo retired from the papal choir on October 25, 1554: *Eodem die congregatis dominis Cantoribus dominus Bartholomeus de Scouedo petiit licentiam eundi in partibus et obtinuit cum bona voluntate Summi Pontificis et mastro* [sic] *Capelle ut moris est (Note d'archivio*, XIII, 5-6 [Sept.-Dec., 1936], 202-203). Upon returning to Spain he enjoyed a benefice at Segovia. According to *Capp. Sist. Diar.*, no. 7, fol. 45^v, three Spanish sopranists selected by Escobedo as worthy candidates for the papal choir were auditioned on March 21, 1563 (he had previously been given a general commission to search for such candidates). Juan Figueroa was declared the winner (joined the choir on April 17, 1563). Escobedo died before the following August 11. Under date of Wednesday, August 11, a notice of *beneficia vacantia per obitum Bartholomei Scobedo* enters the diary (fol. 61^v).

In *MME*, Vol. II, p. *80*, Anglés said that Escobedo *regresó a España en 1545* (returned to Spain in 1545) and later became chapelmaster to the princess Doña Juana. Seven years after his "return" (*MME*, II, *81*), Anglés wished to identify Escobedo as Doña Juana's "former chapelmaster." Anglés repeats the claim that Escobedo served Doña Juana in *MGG*, Vol. III, p. 1518, and in his edition of Mateo Flecha's *Ensaladas* (Barcelona: Biblioteca Central, 1955), pages 28-29; and the claim that *Escobedo regresó a España en 1545* in *Diccionario de la Música Labor* (Barcelona: 1945) [hereafter cited as *DML*], in the Spanish version of the Wolf *Geschichte der Musik*, and in the Spanish translation of the Della Corte and Pannain *Storia della musica*. However, the Sistine Diaries irrefutably establish the fact that Escobedo returned not to Spain, but to Rome, in 1545. The attempt to identify Escobedo as Doña Juana's chapelmaster prior to her departure for Portugal is a similar lapse—Anglés having mistaken "Bartolomé de Escobedo" for "Bartolomé de Quebedo" in the Simancas legajo that served as his source of information. Quebedo—a native of Sahagún who became chapelmaster at Toledo after Morales's death—might not have been confused with Escobedo if recourse had been had to the Toledo documents first made known by Rubio Piqueras in his *Música y músicos toledanos* (p. 80) and subsequently reprinted in *AM*, Vol. VIII (1953), pp. 25-26.

The earliest allusion to one of Escobedo's compositions descends to us in a letter written by the same Antonio Capello with whom Escobedo exchanged insults on January 5, 1547. On November 6, 1538, Capello—who, prior to papal service, had been a singer at Ferrara in the chapel of Duke Hercules II—forwarded his erstwhile employer a mass *a 5* and a motet *a 6* by Morales; together with an unnamed motet *a 6* by Escobedo *(AM*, VIII, 82-83). Whatever the name of the Escobedo motet, it seems not to have been preserved—his surviving motets in the Cappella Sistina archive and at the Toledo capitular library all requiring fewer voices. Two masses are extant: the first, *Philippus Rex Hispaniae*, being a solmization mass through the soft hexachord. Composed for the coronation of Philip II, this *mi mi ut re mi fa mi re* Mass *a 6* pits tenor II, singing the soggetto cavato in every full movement (cancrizans in Et in Spiritum) against the other voices. In keeping with Escobedo's renown for learning, the mensuration problems in such movements as Et in terra pax (Φ in tenor II versus ₵ in the other voices), Qui tollis (₵ above ₵ 2 in tenor II, ₵ in the rest), Et incarnatus est, ends of Credo and Sanctus, Osanna (Φ 3 and ₵ ³⁄₂), and Agnus I (O in tenor II against C 2 in the other voices) admirably test the singers' knowledge of proportions. In the Pleni, the singers must find their intervals of imitation in a three-in-one canon. The two *si placet* parts in this movement are obviously for virtuoso soloists. To climax the acclamations, Escobedo inserts an Agnus Dei with *Clama ne cesses* for a rubric (Cabezón's *Obras* [1577], fol. 91ᵛ, has Josquin's *Clama ne cesses*). These words are written in above the liturgical text. This tributary mass was copied into Codex 39 in 1563, the year of Escobedo's death. Philip II evidently relished the tribute; his Flemish chapelmaster Philippe Rogier later opened his *Missae sex* (1598) with the same kind of mass. A second Escobedo mass *(a 5)* preserved in Rome (Cappella Sistina Codex 13, copied before 1550) is entitled *Ad te levavi*. This same Codex 13 preserves two Escobedo motets: *Immutemur* (2d *pars: Juxta vestibulum)*, *a 4;* and *Hodie completi sunt* (2d *pars: Loquebantur), a 5*. Codex 24, copied in 1545, contains his motet in three *partes (a 3* and *a 4): Domine non secundum* (2d *pars: Domine ne memineris;* 3d *pars: Adjuva nos)*.

Eslava printed the first *pars* of *Immutemur habitu in cinere (Lira sacro-hispana*, I, i, 143-147). In addition, he published Escobedo's *Exurge quare obdormis Domine* (1st *pars)* and *Erravi sicut ovis quae periit*—each *a 4 (ibid.*, I, i, 148-151, 152-155).

For these last two he used as his source Codex 13 at Toledo *(Códices polifónicos toledanos*, p. 29); *Erravi sicut* bears 1554 for its date of copy. For *Immutemur*, he used as source Codex 17 *(Cod. pol. tol.*, p. 34), which was copied in 1550. This last-named codex opens with a Josquin motet; but is in the main devoted to eleven of Morales's motets. *Exurge* seems to have been Escobedo's only motet printed during his lifetime; Gombert's *Musica quatuor vocum (vulgo Motecta nuncupatur)* (Venice: Girolamo Scotto, 1541) includes both *partes* (2d *pars: Quoniam humiliata est)*, at nos. 21 and 22.

If Escobedo's other motets are as surcharged with emotion as *Exurge* (Ps. 43 [Vulgate = 44 A. V.]: 23-24; 25-26), he was a remarkably expressive composer. To capture something of the pent-up, distraught feeling of the psalmist, he contrived melodic lines that skip widely (cantus, mm. 7, 29-31; altus, meas. 91; tenor, mm. 5, 126-127; bass, mm. 13-14, 27-30, 78-80, 115) but do not later fill in the skip with returning stepwise movements. He also blurred cadences by dropping out the bass at resolutions (mm. 33-34, 56-57, 67-68, 92-93, 125-126), by resolving deceptively (meas. 13) or to the first inversion (mm. 52-53, 64-65, 65-66, 76-77, 133), and by writing a number of leading-tone instead of V-I cadences (mm. 26-27, 42, 93). To reinforce the emotional quality of the word "humiliata" (mm. 73-81) Escobedo pushes all voices down into the depths. At the return of "exurge Domine" (mm. 103-106, 110) he hypostasizes his rhythms and reaches for the highest note to be found in either *pars*. In *pars 2* he indulges in several melodic repetitions (bass, mm. 83-84, 131-140; cantus, mm. 95-99). As for his "detail technique" in this particular motet: (1) he frequently has recourse to the *nota cambiata*—nine instances occurring in *pars 1* alone (mm. 6, 15, 19, 24, 31, 41, 49-50, 56, 60)—but never omits the upward step after the third note in the figure (this is a "modern" nicety that in itself would stamp him as junior to Morales); (2) he employs the escaped-note figure so parsimoniously that only one instance has been found in 140 bars (at meas. 31); (3) he uses dissonant anticipations, on the other hand, rather freely (mm. 20, 40, 41, 67, 123); (4) the "consonant" fourth enters twice (mm. 12-13, 101); (5) two upper neighboring notes intrude—both involving a fourth on weak crotchets (mm. 53, 79).

So far as this Sexagesima motet is concerned, Escobedo shows much firmer control of his technical resources than do the majority of his Spanish contemporaries. The wider spacing of cadences, their variety, the richer vocabulary of "chord-progressions," the tenser melodic contours, and above all his effective use of device to reinforce text, bespeak the past master of his art.

10 Bartolomé Farfán became master of the seises in Seville Cathedral on March 17, 1584. His annual salary was fixed at 300 ducats and 40 fanegas of wheat. His duties included boarding, lodging, clothing, and teaching the boys who sang polyphony; for these services he received the income of a half-prebend. Further financial details are recorded in acts dated September 14 and November 5, 1584. On December 19, 1586, Alexandre de la Serna resumed control of the boys on an interim basis. Farfán was again temporarily in charge on August 9, 1589; but remained master of the choirboys until only November 28, 1590. Farfán's motet *a 4, Clamavit autem mulier cananea*, appears at fols. 51ᵛ-52 in MS 13230, Biblioteca Medinaceli (Madrid). This text, a favorite with Sevillian composers, was first set by Escobar, and thereafter by Morales and Guerrero.

11 Of Mateo Flecha the Elder, unrivaled master of musical motley, eight rollicking numbers were published posthumously in *Las ensaladas de Flecha, maestro de capilla que fue de las Serenissimas Infantas de Castilla* (Prague: Jorge Negrino, 1581). Although he must be classed as primarily a secular composer, his career was that of a chapelmaster. On September 30, 1523, he became *maestro de capilla* at Lérida Cathedral. He was succeeded on October 31, 1525, by Joannes Molló, who had been a tenor singer in the cathedral since 1506. José Romeu Figueras, in his article "Mateo Flecha el Viejo, la corte literariomusical del duque de Calabria y el Cancionero llamado de Upsala" (*AM*, XIII [1958], 36), suggests that Morales and Flecha were more intimately connected than the parody *Caça* implies. At about the time Morales's books of Masses were being published at Lyons by Moderne, Flecha's *La Justa* (*La Batailla, en spagnol*) was being issued in *Le difficile de chansons. Second livre* by the same publisher. Romeu Figueras works out an elaborate itinerary for Flecha, on the strength of supposed autobiographical allusions in an ensalada comparing music to a widow bereft of protectors such as Ferdinand V, Pope Leo X, Archbishop Fonseca of Toledo, and the Duke of Calabria residing at Valencia. Romeu Figueras suggests that Flecha's "service" under these protectors antedated 1540. Later, he served as chapelmaster to the Princesses Maria and Juana, his term lasting from 1544 to 1548, in which latter year Maria married Maximilian II. He is thought to have died at Poblet (Catalonia) in 1553, aged seventy-two. His *El fuego* urges sinners to quench the eternal fire in store for them by prompt *penitencia* and a return to God. For transcriptions of this charming "sacred" ensalada *a 4*, see F. Pedrell, *Catàlech de la Biblioteca Musical de la Diputació de Barcelona* (1909), II, 210-232; Mateo Flecha, *Las Ensaladas*, ed. by H. Anglés (1954), pp. 62-80. Fuenllana

intabulated three Flecha ensaladas (*Jubilate, La bomba, La justa*) and four villancicos, one of which —*Que faran del pobre Juan*—was ciphered in 1552 by Pisador (fols. 87ᵛ-88ᵛ: "es a manera de villanesca") and anthologized in 1556 by Scotto (*Villancicos de diuersos Authores*).

Flecha the Younger, born at Prades *ca.* 1530, became a boy chorister in the chapel of the infantas in 1543. He continued as a singer until the marriage of Doña Juana in 1552. He chose not to accompany her to Portugal but rather to enter religion, taking the Carmelite habit in the Valencia house of the order. After an intermediate period in Italy he followed Doña Maria to Vienna and Prague—she having become empress at her marriage to Maximilian II. The latter died in 1576. Soon thereafter the dowager empress returned to Spain. Flecha continued in imperial service, however, until approximately 1599, in which year Philip III named him *abad* of the Benedictine monastery at Portella (Lérida). He died on February 20, 1604. See *MME*, II, 71-74. In 1568 Antonio Gardano published at Venice his *Il libro primo di madrigali*. Three of the ensaladas in the 1581 collection published at Prague are his. See *Catàlech*, II, 180. None of the three—*La feria, Las cañas*, and *Ben convene Madona* —found its way, however, into the manuscript collection itemized as no. 968 in Pedrell's *Catàlech* (II, 208). In the sacred field he published *Divinarum Completarum Psalmi, Lectio brevis, et Salve Regina cum aliquibus motettis* at Prague (Negrino) in 1581. Incomplete partbooks survive at Breslau. For further details concerning both elder and younger Flechas, see *MGG*, IV, 292-299. In *La música española desde la edad media hasta nuestros dias* (Barcelona: Biblioteca Central, 1941), Anglés offered as Facsimile 24 a Flecha *Miserere, a 4*, the original of which is to be seen in Barcelona Biblioteca Central MS 587 at fols. 81ᵛ-82. The other composers in this manuscript include Palestrina, Victoria, Vila, and Rafael Coloma (fl. 1588). Whether the Flecha in question should be identified as uncle or nephew can scarcely be decided from internal evidence—the *Miserere* in question being a mere *fabordón*.

12 García de Basurto, a native of Calahorra diocese, served Cardinal Ximénez de Cisneros as chapelmaster during 1504. On March 1 of that year he signed a receipt at Madrid in the amount of 144 reales for four choirbooks. Two were service books (psalter and vesperal) but the other two contained polyphony (the one Christmas *chanzonetas*, the other masses). Payment was made by the cardinal's treasurer, Rodrigo de Quiroga. See Biblioteca Nacional MS 14030.286. On April 15, 1517, after the cardinal's death at the age of eighty-two, García de Basurto was appointed *cantor* in Tarazona Cathedral. See *MME*, II, 92. From *cantor* he was advanced to *maestro de capilla* the year following. The Tarazona capitular acts record that on May 14, 1518, his annual salary was raised to 100 gold florins. The chapter simultaneously praised his musical ability in the most extravagant terms. According to *DML*, Vol. I, p. 213, he remained at Tarazona until March 1, 1521, on which date he assumed the chapelmastership at the new cathedral, *el Pilar*, in Saragossa. Elústiza-Castrillo in their *Antología musical*, page XLV, claim that on September 28, 1521, he moved to Palencia, where he continued as chapelmaster until January, 1525. *DML* has it that in 1529 he was named a royal chaplain and shortly thereafter chapelmaster to Isabella (Charles' consort). On October 15, 1539, he was appointed chapelmaster to Juan Tavera, cardinal and archbishop of Toledo (*AM*, VI [1951], 163). He retained this post for two years and was in 1543 earning an annual salary of 50,000 maravedís (*MME*, II, 143). Toward the close of the same year Tavera's entire body of singers was transferred to Prince Philip's household. Basurto continued chapelmaster of the group until his death in 1547.

Among Basurto's extant pieces are two motets in Biblioteca Medinaceli MS 607, *Regina coeli* and *Resurrexit sicut dixit* (pp. 66-69). A Requiem and various motets survive at Tarazona Cathedral and at the Seo in Saragossa; and a Magnificat (Tone I) in Codex 18 at Toledo (fol. 30; see Rubio Piqueras, *Códices polifónicos toledanos*, p. 37). Pisador, in his *Libro de música de vihuela* (Salamanca: 1552), intabulated two motets *a 4: Dum complerentur* (Pentecost) and *Angelus Domini locutus est* (Easter). Esteban Daza repeated the latter in his *El Parnaso* (1576) at folios 69-71.

13 Pedro Guerrero, elder brother and teacher of Francisco, made his way to Italy before 1545. According to the eighteenth-century Jesuit historian Esteban Arteaga, Pedro was active in Rome. Arteaga, however, did not claim that he sang in the papal choir. Since no evidence from the Sistine Diaries supports such an assertion, *MME*, Vol. VIII, p. 25 stands in need of correction. Anglés has suggested that Pedro sang at S. Maria Maggiore (during 1560-1561). See *AM*, IX, 61. In the Elústiza-Castrillo *Antología musical*, at page LIII, the editors claim that later Pedro Guerrero returned from Italy to become a singer in Seville Cathedral. The singer in question was indeed named Pedro Guerrero, but he was not inducted until May 14, 1599 (*Actas capitulares, 1599-1602*, fol. 18ᵛ). On February 15, 1600, this homonymous individual's salary was raised (*ibid.*, fol. 40ᵛ). A bass, he tried for a prebend at Toledo Cathedral in 1603 and received on August 26 a travel grant of 3,750 maravedís.

The items in the following list, except no. 4, were intabulated by Fuenllana in *Orphénica lyra* (Seville: 1554). Pisador, in his *Libro de música de vihuela* (Salamanca: 1552), repeated no. 6. Item no. 4 was intabulated by Daza in *El Parnasso* (Valladolid: 1576). (1) *Amor es voluntad*, a 4 (text by Boscán); (2) *D'un spiritu triste*, a 4 (also intabulated in Vincenzo Galilei's *Fronimo dialogo*, 1568 and 1584); (3) *Mi coraçon fatigado*, a 4; pt. 2, *Agora cobrando acuerdo* (text by Boscán); (4) *O beata Maria*, a 4; pt. 2, *Accipe quod offerimus* (pt. 1 copied in Santiago Codex at Valladolid); (5) *O más dura que mármol*, a 4; pt. 2, *Tu dulce habla* (text by Garcilaso de la Vega; see *MME*, VIII, 112-116); (6) *Pasando el mar Leandro*, a 4 (text by Garcilaso; see *MME*, IX, 96-99); (7) *Por do començaré*, a 4 (*MME*, VIII, 100-103); (8) *Quien podrá creer*, a 3. Galilei's predilection for Pedro "Gherrero" comes to view in both editions of his *Fronimo*. In addition to *D'un spiritu triste*, both the 1568 and the 1584 editions contain *Biuiendo sin amar* and *Si puor biuir ardiendo*. *Crainte & Sospir* is to be found in the 1584 edition. A source catalogued as item 201 in João IV, *Primeira Parte do Index da Livraria de Musica* (1649), bore for its title *Liber primus Epigramatum Petri Gerrero Hispalensis, a 4. 5. & 6*.

Some half-dozen of Pedro Guerrero's motets *a 4* survive. In Codex 7 at Toledo Cathedral are found *Gloria et honore*, *Haec est Virgo sapiens*, *Pulcra facie*, and *Quinque prudentes virgines*. In the Diego Sánchez codex preserved at Santiago parish church in Valladolid are to be seen *Domine meus* and *O beata Maria (pars 1)*: these were transcribed for the Elústiza-Castrillo *Antología musical*. Each of his secular pieces in Biblioteca Medinaceli MS 13230 begins with homophony. The motets in the Santiago codex both begin with points of imitation. They relapse into homophony only at a single climactic moment (*Domine meus*, meas. 36; *O beata Maria*, meas. 35). The points are monothematic, but the answers in both motets are "tonal" rather than "real." *Domine meus* is a quarti toni motet. *O beata Maria* continues with a second *pars* (intabulated by Daza but not transcribed by Sánchez). *Pars 2* concludes with a C-Major chord. Although *pars 1* comes to rest on G Major, this motet should in view of its *pars 2* be classed as ionian. The crystalline purity of the text is mirrored in the translucent musical setting. Daza in his intabulation (*El Parnasso*, fols. 45ᵛ-47; 47-49) designates the tiple as the solo voice. Not a single accidental is to be seen in the top part of either the Valladolid vocal copy or Daza's intabulation. For that matter, the vocal copy shows but a single accidental in any of the other parts. Daza specifies only the scantiest number of f♯'s (mm. 6₂, 14₄, 46₂, 47₃, 48₂). By contrast, Pedro Guerrero's *D'un spiritu triste*, in both the Fuenllana intabulation (1554) and the Galilei (1568), reeks with accidentals. The tortured harmonies that result, to say nothing of the rhythmic agitation, befit the tale of an "anguished soul." All doubt and confusion have been left behind in *O beata Maria*.

14 Fernando de las Infantas (1534-*ca.* 1610) owed the appellation *de las Infantas* to his great-grandfather's great-grandfather, Juan Fernández de Córdoba, who accompanied two of Peter the Cruel's daughters to England after that Castilian king's violent death at Montiel in 1369. These two young princesses espoused sons of Edward III—John of Gaunt (Duke of Lancaster) and Edmund of Langley (Earl of Cambridge, afterward Duke of York). Edward III bestowed on the composer's ancestor the coat of arms that is to be seen at the foot of the title pages in each of the composer's publications. As for his more immediate ancestors, the composer's grandfather Antonio de las Infantas (d. 1516)—called *el Comendador* on account of a dignity to which he rose in the military order of Santiago—was a principal citizen of Cordova. The composer, born in this same Andalusian capital, was third son of *el Comendador's* fourth son. Although somewhat reduced from its former status, the composer's family seems still to have possessed sufficient means to give him a fine classical education, and to bequeath to him a patrimony that obviated the necessity of earning a livelihood. On his own confession in the dedication of his *Plura modulationum genera* (Venice: Girolamo Scotto, 1579), Infantas began his musical studies while still a child. Fourteen of the contrapuntal exercises standing at the head of his 1579 publication were completed when he was a mere student. His earliest motet that can be closely dated commemorates the death of Charles V in 1558—*Parce mihi Domine*. The rubric standing before this motet *a 5* (no. 28 in *Sacrarum varii styli cantionum . . . Liber II cum quinque vocibus* (Venice: Girolamo Scotto, 1578) reads thus: *In exequijs foeliciis memoriae Caroli quinti, Imperatoris.* He was therefore approximately twenty-four when he composed this funerary motet. A phrase in the dedication of *Plura modulationum genera* can be taken to mean that Charles V while at Yuste either received the young Infantas or bestowed some other mark of favor upon the young Cordovan.

Among Infantas's other datable motets the following deserve mention: *In oppressione inimicorum: Pro victoria in turcas Mellite obsedionis, A., 1565* (no. 20 in his *Liber III*), *Pro victoria nauali contra Turcas Sacri foederis classe parta, A., 1571* (no. 5 in *Liber II*), and *Anno Jubilei 1575, Psalmus XCIX. Jubilate Deo* (no. 14 in *Liber III*). In the first of these three he prays for victory against the Turks who besiege Malta; in the second he celebrates the triumph over the Turkish fleet at Lepanto; and in the third he proclaims the year of jubilee. It would seem that Infantas alone among Spanish composers commemorated the greatest Spanish naval victory—that of October 7, 1571. Lepanto was, of course, the engagement in which Cervantes's left arm was maimed.

Philip II entrusted Infantas with some kind of minor mission in the viceroyalty of Naples shortly before 1572, granting him a pension for his services. Or at least so Infantas inferred in a memorial addressed to Philip III, *ca.* 1608, when he wrote: "Don Fernando de las Infantas Sacerdote de Cordoba con ocasion que tuvo de cierta pinsion que la dichosa memoria de Phelipo segundo le mando dar en el Reyno de Napoles por servicios de lego. . . ." From 1572 until *ca.* 1597, Infantas resided at Rome. First he voluntarily gave his services in a hospital for the poor. Later, after ordination to the priesthood (1584), he served a small church on the outskirts of the city. During these twenty-five years he lived on his *patrimonio*.

In 1578, after waiting five years to find a suitable opportunity, Infantas published two collections, both consisting of partbooks and both bearing the title *Sacrarum varii styli Cantionum tituli Spiritus Sancti. Liber I* contains motets *a 4; Liber II*, motets *a 5.* On the title page of each partbook the arms of Philip II are borne aloft by two angels: at their feet cartouches contain Infantas's coat. In the large oval flies a dove symbolizing the Holy Ghost. Around the oval circles a canon constructed of incises from *Veni Creator Spiritus.* Angelo Gardano published *Liber I* at Venice, Girolamo Scotto *Liber II.* Book I contains thirty-seven motets *a 4;* Book II, thirty motets *a 5.* Psalm texts recur freely in both books. Infantas was later to claim that the reading of the psalms converted him to a desire for holy orders. His *Liber III,* containing motets *a 6,* was published by Girolamo Scotto at Venice in 1579. The first item in Book III, *Missus est Gabriel* (in three *partes*), and the sixth, *Domine, ostende nobis Patrem* (in two *partes,* for St. Philip's day), were reprinted at Nuremberg in 1585 by Friedrich Lindner (nos. 11 and 22 in *Sacrae Cantiones cum quinque, sex et pluribus vocibus*). The seventh item, *Victimae paschali laudes* (in two *partes,* based on the Easter plainsong sequence), was reprinted at Nuremberg in 1583 by Leonard Lechner (*Harmoniae miscellae Cantionum Sacrarum, a sex exquisitissimis aetatis nostrae musicis cum quinque et sex vocibus concinnatae*). In the Lechner miscellany, Infantas shares company with Andrea Gabrieli, Marc' Antonio Ingegneri, Orlandus Lassus, Philippe de Monte, Costanzo Porta, Cipriano de Rore, and Palestrina.

In 1579 Infantas published his last volume, a manual of counterpoint exercises, *Plura modulationum genera quae vulgo contrapuncta appellantur super excelso Gregoriano cantu* (Venice: Girolamo Scotto). This collection of 100 (actually 101) exercises in two to eight parts against a ten-note Gregorian initium (Ps. 116:1) begins with the set of 14 dating from his student epoch. The rest were composed between 1576 and 1579. From 15 through 47, he offers exercises *a 3,* from 58 through 89 *a 4,* from 93 through 95 *a 5,* from 96 through 98 *a 6.* Exercise 99 is composed *a 7,* and 100 *a 8*. This vast set rivals the *Cento cin-quantasette contrapunti sopra del canto fermo intitolato la Base di Costanzo Festa* by G. M. Nanino. The 157 exercises were completed, however, at a later date: October 23, 1602 (at Mantua). For an appendix to his collection Infantas adds three extra canons, independent of the cantus firmus used in the 100 (= 101) previous exercises. Two of these were reprinted in Adam Gumpeltzhaimer's *Compendium musicae* (1591) at pages 40 and 43. The third, an enigmatic canon, caught Cerone's eye, and was reprinted in *El melopeo y maestro* at pages 1082-1083. Cerone solved the enigma with the suggestion that Infantas intended a *moto contrario* canon beginning at the lower seventh. Rafael Mitjana in *Don Fernando de Las Infantas: Teólogo y Músico* (Madrid: Imp. de los Sucs. de Hernando, 1918) reprinted this particular mirror canon at page 124, solving the enigma along the lines suggested by Cerone in 1613. He erred, however, at meas. 15 when he flatted the lower voice. If this canon is an exact mirror the b should read natural, not flat. Reese transcribes the first 20 measures (= 10 in reduced values) at page 610 in his *Music in the Renaissance*.

Mitjana intended originally to complete his splendid monograph—perhaps the best ever devoted to a single Spanish composer—with a selection of motets as well as canons. He was prevented from adding the musical supplement, however. Analysis of Infantas's style suffers today from the want of such a supplement. Neither Pedrell nor Anglés supplies reprints. The only motet reprinted in Eslava's *Lira sacro-hispana*, I, ii, 175-183, is the *Victimae paschali laudes, a 6*, already alluded to as having been republished by Lechner at Nuremberg in 1583. A study of this superb motet should serve as a corrective to the impression that Infantas was primarily a contrapuntal juggler. Like most of his motets, this one is based on the plainsong. He does not treat it as a cantus firmus, however. Instead, he allows fragments to permeate all voices. Near the close of *pars 1* he bursts into joyful triple meter. Only at the Amen of *pars 2* does he return to duple. The part writing—despite Mitjana's acknowledgment that when hard-pressed in his contrapuntal exercises Infantas occasionally allowed fifths to intrude—cannot be impugned on any count. By reason of the rich harmonic palette, the vigor of the independent lines, the admirable juxtaposition of contrasting rhythms, the balance of low and high sonorities, and the constant attention to textual meanings, this motet ranks with the major Spanish achievements of the epoch.

More recently, P. Samuel Rubio has reprinted ten additional Infantas motets in his *Antología polifónica sacra*, Volume II (Madrid: Ed. Coculsa, 1956). All were transcribed from *Sacrarum varii styli Cantionum, Liber I*. Except for the Petrine

motet *Tu es pastor ovium* (2d *pars: Quodcumque ligaveris*) these ten do not go beyond one *pars*. In aBcB form, *Tu es pastor ovium* extends to 79 + 85 breves—the "B" portion in each *pars* reaching 23 breves. *Hodie Maria Virgo*, a motet of single *pars*, is an "introduced" couplet (aBB: 16 + 23 + 23). Half of the ten are headed with the highly characteristic Infantas label, *super excelso Gregoriano cantu*. Two others, his *Ave Maria* and *O lux et decus Hispaniae*, quote plainsong in *Pfundnoten*, even though not thus headed. *O lux*, honoring St. James, contains a tenor cantus firmus 24 breves in length. First quoted *per motum contrarium* during mm. 5-28, this *O lux* plainsong is next heard in identical rhythm but straightforward motion at mm. 31-54, and, lastly, again *per motum contrarium* at mm. 57-81.

Infantas, if the eleven motets now in print are typical, was obviously still under the spell of Des Prez. He even adopted such mannerisms as the Josquin triplet. In contrast with Morales he reveled in changing-note figures to an extent hardly matched elsewhere in the Spanish motet repertory. He wrote vocal lines of extraordinary range. He liked running scales. He specified chromaticisms, at least occasionally (*O lux*, meas. 37, for instance). When we compare his registration of such a Marian motet as *Virgo prudentissima* for four trebles with his disposal of voices in the Petrine *Tu es pastor ovium* and in *Beatus es et bene tibi erat* (honoring St. Sebastian) for four men's voices, we admire his skillful use of vocal color to capture moods appropriate to his texts.

Infantas struggled successfully to delay publication of the Gradual that finally appeared in 1614-1615 as the Medicean. On November 25, 1577, he wrote Philip II from Rome, advising the king that a new edition was contemplated—Palestrina and Zoilo having undertaken the task of revision at the behest of Pope Gregory XIII. Infantas complained that the melismas were to be retrenched, ligatures revised to conform with accent, and certain chants to be rewritten so that they would remain within a single tone. Philip II became genuinely alarmed. He not only wrote the Spanish ambassador, instructing him to intercede with the pope, but even despatched a personal missive to Gregory XIII. Infantas, meanwhile, sent the pope a memorial in Italian in which he said that even Palestrina, after conversation on the matter, agreed that what he had previously deemed "errors" in the chant were not so in reality. "Far from being errors, they were actually admirable musical artifice, which the maestro to whom Your Holiness entrusted the task [of revision], after further study, agreed should in no wise be altered." Infantas appealed to the new Gregory not to undo the work of his great namesake Gregory I.

Heartened perhaps unduly by his success in combating Roman opinion so far as revised chantbooks were concerned, Infantas in later life rushed into two of the most delicate theological controversies of the epoch—the regalist and the Molinist. His undoing proved to be his *Tractatus de praedestinatione. Secundum Scripturam Sacram* (Paris: n.p., 1601). He thenceforth bore the brand of being an illuminist if not a quietist. He spent his entire career after ordination in theological speculation. At the close of his life, overwhelmed by his theological enemies, he was reduced to beggary. For further details, consult Mitjana's monograph, which has served as the source of all biobibliographical information offered in the present note.

15 According to the Sevillian cathedral *Actas Capitulares, 1571-1572-1573*, folio *4*, an Andrés López—possibly the composer with whom we are concerned—completed three years of choirboy service on January 5, 1573, and in that year entered St. Michael's on an alumni scholarship. On January 10, 1582, the Sevillian cathedral chapter presented "Andrés López" with twenty ducats as a reward for his services during Guerrero's absence at Rome. Upon Guerrero's return, López was named *maestro de capilla del claustro*. On September 23, 1583, his annual salary was raised to 40,000 maravedís. Guerrero died on November 8, 1599. On December 20, 1599, the Sevillian chapter named López *maestro del exercicio del canto de órgano*. His salary, previously reduced, was in the same year again raised by 6,000 to a total of 40,000 maravedís. As of January 28, 1600, he was listed interim conductor *(tenia cargo del facistol)*. This interim appointment lasted until the seating of Ambrosio Cotes as Guerrero's successor on September 22, 1600. López died during the week preceding June 22, 1601. On that date the Sevillian chapter announced a competition to decide his successor in the *magisterio de canto de órgano*. Just as MS 13230 in the Biblioteca Medinaceli contains Farfán's only known surviving work, so MS 607 in the same library contains Andreas [= Andrés] López's unique extant pieces: (1) *Ave Maria*, a 4 (pp. 32-33); (2) *Ay, ay, que no ay amor*, a 4 (p. 803); (3) *Ay que el alma*, a 4 (p. 806); (4) *Hero del alta torre*, a 4 (pp. 804-805).

16 Francisco de Montanos's permanent reputation rests on his treatise in six books *Arte de musica theorica y pratica* (Valladolid: Diego Fernández de Córdova y Oviedo, 1592). In the dedication to Don Fernando de Castro, Count of Lemos, of Andrade, of Villalva, and Marquis of Sarria (father of Cervantes's principal patron), Montanos professes to have spent many years in the count's household. These no doubt preceded his ecclesiastical career.

The earliest notice of Montanos's churchly career makes him chapelmaster of the Valladolid *iglesia mayor* on September 24, 1564: with half-prebend. On June 8, 1571, the chapter adjured him to give two hours of daily instruction (one hour in the morning and the other in the afternoon) to the fifty-five singers and choirboys forming the musical establishment of the *iglesia mayor*. Qualified outsiders who wished to sing were also admitted to his public lessons. For each hour that he should miss, he was to be fined one real. On June 13, 1572, he was instructed to release all the choirboys from his personal care, and to forfeit all payment in kind for their sustenance. On April 2, 1576, he was dismissed from the chapelmastership.

At fol. 5^v in his *Arte de musica*, Montanos says that in the year that saw the end of his services as chapelmaster he decided to compose a treatise in six books. "Various distractions prevented my completing the task so soon as I could have desired," he adds. However, the treatise was ready for the press sooner than the 1592 year of publication would suggest. Since the *preuilegio* that stands at fols. 2^v-3 bears July 31, 1587, as its date, he must have spent some ten years writing his *Arte*. During this decade he continued to occupy a half-prebend in the Valladolid *iglesia mayor*. In 1587 (and therefore probably in 1592 as well) he held the added title of chapelmaster in the *yglesia collegial de Valladolid* (fol. 2^v). As for other sources of income, it is probable that he came of a sufficiently well-to-do family not to need any. At fol. 27^v of "De proporcione" (in his *Arte*) appears an *epigramma* by Alonso Bezerra, linking him with several ancient families renowned by reason of their military prowess. One of these relatives—Bernardo Prego de Montanos—contributed his own *epigramma* at fol. 26 of "Compostura." This poem concludes with a salute: "Your learning, dear Montanos, which seems almost more than human, covers us with glory."

Montanos's last book was his *Arte de cantollano con entonaciones comunes de Coro y Altar y otras cosas diversas* (2d ed.; Salamanca: Francisco de Cea Tesa, 1610). This plainsong instructor, issued with an approbation signed (in 1593 at Madrid) by Hernando de Cabezón (d. 1602), was later to be revised by Sebastián López de Velasco (editions: 1648, 1693, 1756) and José de Torres (editions: 1705, 1711, 1712, 1728, 1734).

Two of Montanos's motets *a 4* were published by Elústiza-Castrillo in their *Antología musical: O Domine Jesu Christe* and *Interveniat pro nobis*. Transcribed from the Santiago codex at Valladolid (fols. 2^v-4), both are soulful pieces, innocent of learned contrivance and akin in spirit to Victoria's *Vere languores*. Cerone, on the other hand, in *El melopeo y maestro* (Naples: 1613) printed at pages 1080-1081 a four-in-one canon by "Francisco de Montanos" which reaches virtuostic extremes. A single voice part bears four clefs. The bass, tenor, alto, and tiple enter successively—each a fifth above the starting pitch of the preceding (G, d, a, e[1]). Cerone concludes by remarking that Palestrina accomplished a like feat in the final Agnus of his canonic *Sine nomine* Mass (1599).

17 Alonso Ordoñez, a native of Plasencia, may possibly have studied with Morales (known to have served as chapelmaster at Plasencia from 1528 to 1531). From 1530 to 1536 he occupied the chapelmastership at Santiago de Galicia, whence he was called on April 3 (1536) to take up the chapelmastership at Palencia. His predecessor at Palencia was a clergyman of Toledo diocese named Diego del Castillo (not to be confused with the homonymous individual discussed above in note 3). Of Alonso [= Alfonso] Ordoñez, a Magnificat *a 4*, a *Salve Regina a 4*, and two motets *a 4* —*Iste est* and *Vias tuas, Domine, demonstra mihi*— survive in the cathedral archive at Valladolid (MS 5, fols. 132ᵛ-135, 45ᵛ-51, 43ᵛ-45, 55ᵛ-57). See *AM*, III, 67.

18 Pedro Ordoñez, younger brother of the preceding, may likewise have studied with Morales. That he followed Alonso to Palencia can be surmised from the fact that he was ordained in Palencia rather than Plasencia diocese. On April 29, 1539, he was admitted to the papal choir. He so quickly became a recognized leader of the Spanish contingent (Calasanz, Escobedo, Morales, Sánchez) that they deputized him on January 15, 1540, to visit the pope in Sánchez's behalf after the latter had been imprisoned for striking a fellow singer. On November 4, 1540, Ordoñez reported himself sick, but was seen about town. As a result he was fined heavily. On March 30, 1541, and again on October 17, 1543, he substituted for Calasanz. In turn, Calasanz substituted for him on November 24, 1543. Charles d'Argentilly substituted for him on November 6, 1543. These interchanges establish beyond doubt the fact that Ordoñez was a bass.

Harsh words between him and Abbate resulted in the fining of Ordoñez on May 2, 1543. A similarly angry exchange with Sánchez brought a fine on December 22, 1543. On June 19, 1542, he was granted a leave of absence to see to certain private affairs. Again on September 4, 1544, he was allowed a leave, this time of ten days. On January 11, 1545, he was elected *abbas* (treasurer) of the choir for one year. His predecessor in this office was Arcadelt. Ordoñez remained in Rome, singing daily in the choir throughout the whole of 1545 and until the end of January, 1546. He certainly did not attend the opening sessions of the Council of Trent in December, 1545—common allegation notwithstanding. See *Note d' archivio*, X, 4 (Oct.-Dec., 1933), 329-336. He may, however, have been sent to Trent after Jan-

uary 27, 1546. Thereafter his name fails to appear in the Sistine Diaries until March 11, 1548. On this date he with four other papal singers is mentioned as absent in Bologna, whither the council had transferred in March, 1547. See *Note d'archivio*, XI, 3-4 (July-Dec., 1934), 313. On May 30, 1549, he was licensed to leave Bologna for a visit to the baths at Padua. At the moment he suffered from sciatica. On November 17, 1549, he arrived at Rome from Bologna. He continued in Rome until at least January 5, 1550. The Sistine Diaries unfortunately break at January 7, 1550, and do not resume until January 1, 1553. This lacuna was caused by the chapelmaster's carrying away of the *liber punctorum* for the intervening years on May 1, 1554, and never returning it. When the diaries resume, Ordoñez has already departed from the choir. The common opinion that he died in 1550 was founded on nothing more substantial than the absence of his name from the choir list in 1553 and thereafter.

A quarter-century later he is to be found at Palencia, functioning as chapelmaster in succession to his deceased brother Alonso. His whereabouts in the intervening years have not been traced. Following Morales's route, he possibly spent the interim as chapelmaster in some prominent Spanish cathedral, the capitular acts of which have not been explored. However, he was certainly Palencia chapelmaster in 1576. On June 7, 1577, the chapter urged him to look after the choirboys with the same zealous care given them by his deceased brother. On August 30, 1577, he was appointed diocesan examiner of all Palencia clergymen in *canto eclesiástico*. On October 26, 1577, a chapter committee was instructed to search for an able assistant "on account of the age and infirmity of the chapelmaster, Pedro Ordoñez." The fact that on April 9, 1578, he was rewarded with a prebend "on account of his merits and his many years of service, in addition to his age and sickness" strongly suggests that he had been Palencia chapelmaster since perhaps 1565. See Elústiza-Castrillo, *Antología musical*, pages LXXIX, LXXX. He died on May 5, 1585.

Just as Juan Escribano, one of the leading Spaniards in the papal choir from *ca.* 1507 to 1539, reached print only as a secular composer, so also the only works by Pedro Ordoñez to be published during his lifetime were unashamedly secular—the two *sonetos (a 4)* intabulated at fols. 75-77 and 77ᵛ-79 in Esteban Daza's *El Parnasso* (1576): *Ay mudo soy hablar non puedo* and *Ay fortuna cruel* (pt. 2, *Lebantaron muy alto*). The first voices the plaint of a suffering but silent swain. In the second, the poet reproaches Fortune and Cupid. The first is a G-minor piece of treble-dominated homophony. The second (an A-minor piece), although it opens with an imitative point, is just as surely an accompanied song with melody in the treble.

Concerning another Ordoñez, named Rodrigo, see pages 41, 124 (n. 214), and 246.

19 The number of Spanish musicians who sojourned temporarily in Italy during the sixteenth century is so large as to include nearly every important composer of the epoch. But Diego Ortiz and Sebastián Raval stand apart from such other composers in the group as Escribano, Morales, Escobedo, Infantas, Victoria, and Clavijo del Castillo, because these two alone seem to have pursued their adult careers entirely in Italy. Diego Ortiz, despite his designating himself a native of Toledo, belongs as surely to Neapolitan musical history as Domingo Terradellas. Engaged as chapelmaster while Pedro de Toledo was still viceroy at Naples, Ortiz published his epoch-making "treatise on the ornamentation of cadences and other types of passages in the music of viols" at Rome in 1553. Two editions, one with the text in Italian, the other with the text in Castilian, emerged simultaneously from the press of the Dorico brothers. The very fact that Ortiz discussed ornamentation in viol music would in itself alienate his treatise from peninsular tradition. No instructor published in sixteenth-century Spain devotes any appreciable amount of attention to bowed instruments.

Ortiz's treatise, edited by Max Schneider at Berlin in 1913 (2d; ed.; Bärenreiter [Cassel]: 1936) cannot be analyzed here. It must for the moment suffice to say that numerous false impressions concerning its character and purpose have been disseminated. Ortiz was not primarily interested in teaching "how to improvise," nor even in teaching how to add ornamentation "at sight." He specifically counseled taking the voice that one desired to ornament and "writing it out anew" (*yrla escriuiendo de nueuo*). When in the course of copying it, one arrived at cadences or other passages that one wished to ornament, Ortiz advised looking at all the ornamental formulas in his treatise covering the notes in question (*mire alli todas las diferencias que estan escritas sobre aquellos puntos*) and picking the best for insertion in the written copy.

Another widely held false impression concerns Ortiz's use of accidentals. After examining the Schneider edition one might suppose that Ortiz never calls for sharps in his ornamented cadences (Book I). Nothing could be further from the truth. Ortiz, like a grammarian, always begins his paradigms with an uninflected verb: that is, he always begins with a plain cadence and then proceeds to show a dozen or more ornamented forms that will fit exactly within the aggregate time value of the notes in the plain cadence. When sharps appear in the plain cadences before the notes f, c, g (or b♭), these notes are to be sharped (or naturalized) wherever they appear in the ornamented cadences: so he plainly directs

in the last paragraph of his introduction. Schneider not only defeats Ortiz's intentions in his 1913 and 1936 editions, but even places Ortiz's sharps before the wrong notes in the plain cadences.

A new and better-informed study of Ortiz's treatise is long overdue. Ortiz deserves attention, moreover, as a sacred composer. He published at Venice in 1565 (Antonio Gardano) a folio miscellany of hymns, magnificats, motets, psalms and other vespers music under the title *Didaci Ortiz Toletani Regiae Cappellae Neapolitanae. Moderatoris et Magistri. Musices Liber primus Hymnos. Magnificas. Salves. Motecta. Psalmos. Aliaque Diversa Cantica Complectens.* No authoritative study of this collection has yet been attempted.

There are thirty-four hymns in the collection. Two of the thirty-four are alternates for stanzas 2 and 4 of *Hostis Herodes impie* and 2, 4, and 6 of *Ave maris stella*. In every hymn Ortiz seems to have hewed to a plainsong source, paraphrasing it oftenest in the top voice. As a rule he (like Victoria in 1581) sets even stanzas. Exceptions are found in the Apostles' and Evangelists' hymn, *Tristes erant Apostoli*, and in those for January 18 and 25, July 22, August 1, and November 1. In one instance, *Pange lingua gloriosi* (for Corpus Christi), he provides both odd- and even-verse settings. The odd-verse setting enshrines the Roman melody; the even-verse, the Spanish melody. Ortiz does not seem to have drawn upon any specifically Spanish plainsong source anywhere else in his anthology. (Victoria, not to mention such stay-at-home composers as Guerrero and Navarro, used the same *more hispano* melody. See item 32 in Victoria's *Hymni totius anni.*) In a dozen instances, Ortiz directs that stanzas 1 and 3, or 2 and 4, be sung to the same music. This is the more interesting because as a master of the *glosa* it would have been supposed he would always have preferred variants in successive polyphonic stanzas. Both Palestrina and Victoria follow another path—always devising new treatments of the plainsong source in successive polyphonic stanzas. As a usual practice, Ortiz concludes each stanza of a given hymn with the same final chord, no matter how radically he varies his treatment of the plainsong source in successive stanzas. (He transgresses this rule in *Christe Redemptor omnium*, *Veni Redemptor gentium*, and *Vexilla Regis prodeunt*.) In only one hymn does he seem to have resorted to the kind of sequential figuration that everywhere characterizes his ornamental patterns in the *Trattado de Glosas sobre Clausulas*. See mm. 16-17 of the stanza *Ubi patres* (altus) in his Transfiguration hymn, for such a mechanical sequence.

Ortiz's 1565 miscellany contains a magnificat for each of the eight Tones. The number of the magnificat corresponds with the number of the Tone. Thus, the fourth magnificat in his collection is in Tone IV. The magnificats in Tones I, III, V, VI, and VIII set odd-numbered verses; those in Tones II, IV, and VII, even-numbered verses. With one exception, the successive verses in any given magnificat end on the same chord. Tone I (transposed) ends on G; II, III, V, and VII, on A; IV, on E; VI, on F; VIII, on G. Tones I and VI carry B♭ in the signature. The one exception to his rule that successive verses must end on the same chord is the Et misericordia of his Tone VIII, which—carrying the Tone VIII formula in the altus a fifth below normal pitch—closes on the C-Major instead of G-Major chord. Canonic verses conclude his Tones I, II, III, IV, and VII magnificats. Whether or not the last verse breaks into canon, it invariably augments. Tones I, II, III, IV, VI, and VII augment to six voice parts; Tones V and VIII, to five. The normal number of voices in every magnificat is four. Usually one or two interior verses reduces parts. The Et misericordia of Tone III and the Fecit of Tone VII reduce to a duo. Although Morales's influence is everywhere to be seen in Ortiz's magnificats, he does strike out on a new line with his paired imitations in verses 1, 3, and 7 of Tone I, and in verse 10 of Tone II. (Paired imitations will often be found in Victoria's magnificats.) A stylistic comparison of Ortiz's with Hernando Franco's magnificats should prove rewarding—one having been chapelmaster in the viceroyalty of Naples, 1565, and the other chapelmaster in the viceroyalty of Mexico, 1575-1585; the one a native of Toledo, and the other having been born near Alcántara in the extreme west of Spain.

Although in his hymns Ortiz as a rule sets even stanzas, in his psalms he invariably sets odd verses. Five of his nine psalms belong to vespers (Pss. 109, 110, 111, 112, 116), and one to compline (Ps. 4). These each begin with a plainsong initium for the first half-verse; and conclude with homophony for the last half of verse 1. Of the remaining three psalms, 70 belongs to Maundy Thursday, and 90 and 133 to Holy Saturday. These, unlike the other five, forgo any plainsong initium. In all the psalms he eschews imitation, contenting himself with simple four-part chordal writing. For the vesper psalms he uses Tones I, IV, VI, IV, and VIII, respectively. The compline and Holy Week psalms belong to Tone VIII.

Pay vouchers signed in February, 1558, show that Ortiz's singers then numbered twelve. In the same year Francisco Salinas served as viceregal organist. See José Subirá, La música en la Casa de Alba (Madrid: Sucs. de Rivadeneyra, 1927), pages 26-28. Although Salinas returned to Spain before 1565 (he served as organist in the cathedral of León from 1562 to 1567), Ortiz may have obliquely referred to Salinas when he complained in his dedication to Pedro Afán de Ribera (viceroy, 1559-1571) of the controversy then raging at

Naples over the exact relationship of music to mathematics. For Ortiz the true doctors of music were not Boethius, Gaffurio, Le Fèvre d'Étaples, and Ciruelo, but rather Ockeghem, Josquin, Mouton, and Lupus. No Spaniard enters his list. Cerone later testified that Ortiz was an ardent admirer of Morales (see above, page 4). Even so, he slighted Spaniards and peninsular music in his Trattado of 1553 when he composed four ricercadas on Arcadelt's madrigal O felici occhi miei and four on Pierre Sandrin's chanson Douce memoire, but none on an Iberian air. One further reference in the 1565 dedication casts some light on his career. He voiced a desire to publish a book of masses. The fact that no such book appeared lends weight to the presumption that he died in 1570.

Not only the tirelessly skipping bass line in such a Marian antiphon as his Ave Regina coelorum, a 6, the generally instrumental character of his vocal lines in such another Marian piece as the Benedicta tu in mulieribus, a 6, but also Ortiz's own explicit testimony in his dedication gives us reason to presume that he expected everything in his Musices Liber primus, 1565, to be performed with instrumental accompaniment. He asked, for instance, these rhetorical questions in his dedication: An non in antiquo & nouo testamento, diuinus cultus, in catholica Ecclesia, non solum humanis vocibus, sed etiam musicis instrumentis: ex diuino praecepto, & sanctorum patrum ordinatione: deo optimo maximo exhibetur ac celebratur? Ecquid admirabilius ac magnificentius hac in re excogitari potest? Although aware of the arguments against both instruments and excessive elaboration of polyphonic music, he ranged himself squarely in his dedication with the instrumental and the "artificial" party. His reasoning is important, not only because it teaches us to conceive his music in its proper instrumental context, but also because it throws light on performance practice at the Spanish chapel at Naples. Evidently the Spaniards, wherever they emigrated, always expected instruments to play a dominant role in any performance of sacred music.

Apart from "Diego" Ortiz, another sacred composer with the same surname calls for mention. To "Miguel" Ortiz are attributed two items in Enríquez de Valderrábano's 1547 tablature, Silva de sirenas. In the first, a motet a 4, Ut fidelium propagatione, Valderrábano intabulates STB, but mensurally notates the supple alto part (fols. 31ᵛ-32). Again, in the concluding section of a Lamentation (at fols. 32ᵛ-33), Valderrábano intabulates STB, but mensurally notates the alto part (the text for which reads, "Hierusalem, Hierusalem, convertere ad Dominum Deum"). Both items belong to Mode I (motet in transposed dorian). Still another two items ascribed to "Ortiz" (no Christian name) survive in Biblioteca Medinaceli MS 607 at pages 74-79: an Ave *maris stella* and a *Pange lingua gloriosi* (both *a 4*). The funerary motet *a 5*, *Pereat dies*, published in Eslava's *Lira sacro-hispana*, I, ii, 191-195, must also be added to the "Ortiz" repertory. Contrary to *Grove's Dictionary*, 5th ed. Vol. VI, p. 455, it concords with nothing in the 1565 imprint. Among the other corrections that should be made in the same article the following can be named: Valderrábano intabulated nothing by "Diego" Ortiz in his 1547 *Silva de sirenas;* Diego Ortiz was not called to Naples by the great Duke of Alva; He did not begin service at Naples in the year 1555; The *glosas* in his 1553 *Trattado* are not designed exclusively for the bass viol; The title of his 1565 publication does not read *Musicae Liber I.*

Three long motets by Ortiz *a 6*, each in two *partes*, survive in Cappella Sistina Codex 24 (copied in 1545)—*Paulus apostolus, Omnes in regnum Dei* (fols. 109ᵛ-115); *In illo tempore assumpsit Jesus duodecim discipulos, Ecce ascendimus* (115ᵛ-120); and *In illo tempore assumpsit Jesus Petrum et Jacobum, Hic est filius meus* (133ᵛ-141). Stylistically, all three motets demand an earlier Ortiz than Diego— perhaps the Miguel intabulated by Valderrábano.

Vicente Lusitano, putative author of *Un tratado de Canto de Órgano*, edited by Henri Collet from a Bibliothèque Nationale sixteenth-century manuscript (Madrid: Ruiz hnos., 1913), alluded familiarly to a *L'Homme armé* Mass by Ortiz (p. 48: no first name). This is the only mass by a Spanish composer anywhere mentioned in "Lusitano's" immensely learned treatise.

20 According to *DML*, Vol. II, p. 1724, Pedro de Pastrana was inducted as a singer in the Aragonese chapel of Ferdinand V as early as September 20, 1500. On July 12, 1527, he was appointed a royal chaplain. He became chapelmaster to the Duke and Duchess of Calabria (Fernando de Aragon and Doña Germana) at the end of 1534 or in 1535. They named him *abbad de San Bernardo.* Later he had to give up the emoluments of this *abbadía*, but he held on to the title of *abbad* even after 1544, when he accepted the papal decision taking away the preferment. Upon the death of García de Basurto in 1547, he was named successor in the post of chapelmaster to the twenty-year-old Prince Philip: formal appointment being tendered on December 28, 1547 (he had served since the preceding October). Toward the middle of 1548 the adult singers under Pastrana's direction numbered 11—3 sopranists, 4 contraltos, 3 tenors, and 4 basses. In addition, the House of Castile chapel carried on its rolls the two brothers Antonio and Juan de Cabezón, organists. The elder members of the chapel were permitted to remain in Spain during Philip's extensive journeys abroad initiated in that year. Pastrana, one of the seniors, thereafter served Doña Maria and her consort Maximilian II of

Austria, whose court was situated temporarily at Valladolid. In addition to his chapelmaster's pay, Pastrana was allowed to retain the emoluments due him on account of his appointment in 1527 as royal chaplain. His petition to the young prince asking this financial favor (March 5, 1548) survives. Pastrana was still alive in 1559, in which year he wrote a letter endorsing Tapia's *Vergel de música* (published 1570). In so doing, however, Pastrana lent the treatise more weight than it deserves (Tapia plagiarized outright from Juan Bermudo's *Declaración* [Osuna: 1549], changing only first and last sentences of chapters to throw unwary readers off the scent).

Of Pastrana's works, seven psalms *a 4* are extant in a Saragossa choirbook alongside psalms by Jean Mouton and Pierre de Manchicourt. At Valladolid, MS 5, folios 129ᵛ-132, contains a Magnificat *a 4*; and at Tarazona, MS 4 contains three Magnificats *a 4*, three motets *a 4* (*Sicut cervus, Pater dimitte illis, Miserere mei Deus*), and a *Benedicamus, a 4*. According to *DML*, MS 5 at Tarazona embodies still other of Pastrana's compositions; and MS 454 at the Barcelona Biblioteca Central contains two Spanish songs, *Ay de mí, señora (a 3)* and *Llenos de lágrimas tristes (a 3)*. Among the 204 choirbooks belonging to the chapel choir of Philip II in 1597 were two inventoried as items 101 and 184; the first of which contained several Pastrana psalms beginning with *Dixit Dominus*, the second a Magnificat, and certain unnamed motets (*Musica sacro-hispana*, X [1917], 124-125, 156).

21 Juan Ginés Pérez, founder of the so-called Valencian school of composers, was baptized in Orihuela, thirteen miles northeast of Murcia, on October 7, 1548. His father was a basketmaker, his godparents a notary public, a lacemaker, and a blacksmith (*HSMS*, V, iv). His early musical education can have been only fragmentary—Orihuela during his youth still lacking a chapelmaster and its university not yet having been founded (1568). However, his natural aptitude was such that when at last on October 15, 1562, decision was taken to add a *maestro de capilla* to the cathedral staff—a staff that was still in an embryo stage because the diocese of Orihuela had been created only recently—he was named to the post at the age of fourteen, with an annual salary of 60 libras (30,600 maravedís). He held this post somewhat longer than eighteen years. In that period a bishop of Orihuela was at last seated (1566) and the formal organization of the cathedral staff completed. At the age of thirty or thereabouts he was named to a cathedral chaplaincy, but for some reason he failed of advancement beyond deacon's orders while at Orihuela. On February 3, 1581, after demonstrating his talents in a public competition, he was elected chapelmaster of Valencia Cathedral. Here he remained some fourteen years, disappearing from the capitular records in May, 1595 (*HSMS*, V, x). From Valencia he returned to Orihuela, where he held a canonry within the royal gift until October 5, 1600. His trail then disappears. The fact that Canon Alenda in his manuscript history of Orihuela Cathedral (*ca.* 1636) refers to Pérez's death as a recent event gives grounds, however, for supposing that he did not die at fifty-two but lived perhaps twenty years longer (*HSMS*, V, xii).

According to Don Julio Blasco, who wrote a biography at the turn of the last century, Pérez lacked serenity and poise, and was dropped from the Orihuela Cathedral rolls in 1600 because he failed to discharge his canonical duties. However, the esteem in which his musical gift was held by his fellow townsmen caused the Orihuela chapter to collect his *opera omnia* with a view to publishing them. Or at least so Alenda testified *ca.* 1636 when he said: *Las obras de Pérez están en este Archivo y con el favor de Dios saldrán a luz por lo mucho que se estiman.*

Unfortunately, Pérez's works were lost later from the Orihuela archive and are now but fragmentarily represented in such other musical libraries as those at Valencia (some thirty pieces), Málaga, and Segorbe Cathedrals (*HSMS*, V, xx). Pedrell, who devoted Volume V of *Hispaniae schola musica sacra* to Ginés Pérez, admired his style—writing as follows (p. xviii): "It cannot be denied that his works are instinct with devotion and solemnity. . . . On principle, he undertook to evoke the over-all mood suggested by a text, rather than trying to paint any single, precise word—rightly believing that the latter technique produces deplorable results. . . . He used not only 'chords' and harmonic intervals but also allowed himself other licenses that were not yet sanctioned in his epoch. . . . He thus developed an original style, perhaps because of the isolation that he had to endure in an out-of-the-way cathedral where he was cut off from any contact with musical life in the one center where religious music shone most brightly—Rome."

Pérez's repertory in *HSMS*, Vol. V, includes two canticles (Magnificat and Benedictus), six psalms (113, 114, 119, 120, 129, 137), a Palm Sunday hymn (*Gloria, laus, et honor*), a *Parce mihi* belonging to the Office of the Dead, and two funerary motets. The canticles and psalms, all *a 4*, are alternate-verse settings. The remaining pieces, *a 5*, are through-composed. It is obvious to anyone who undertakes a comparison of Pérez's *Parce mihi* (*HSMS*, V, 45-49) with Morales's (*HSMS*, I, 9-11), that the junior composer vented a "romantic" grief, but the elder a "classical." Pérez uses the drooping fifth for affect ("peccavi," mm. 77-83), but Morales used it because it belongs to the plainsong formula (mm. 11-12, 40-42, 60-64). Pérez modulates (in the modern

sense) from his home key of F Major to the dominant (mm. 23, 51, 126), the subdominant (meas. 105), and submediant (meas. 131); but Morales never for a moment forgot that he was in Tone IV, the "chordal" vocabulary of which is narrowly restricted. Pérez neither quotes a plainsong formula nor does he submit to any rigid scheme of imitations. Morales, on the other hand, considered himself honor-bound to adhere to the intonation-formula from beginning to end of his 131-bar setting.

Among the freedoms that Pérez allowed himself was the right to change at will the rhythms of the several answers in a point of imitation. In the opening points of both *Miseremini fideles animarum* (*HSMS*, V, 50-54) and *Domine Deus* (55-59), for instance, not one answer duplicates the rhythm of the subject. The melodic lines are always plangently expressive. The popular appeal of these two motets *a 5* is increased by his frequent use of melodic repetition and sequence. Neither exhibits Pérez's "learning." Both are ostensibly motets in Tone IV. But for all practical purposes they deserve to be called A-minor pieces that end on the dominant. In the second motet, Pérez even reaches the Neapolitan chord at the word "angustiis."

22 Pedro Periañez, whose *Ave Domina Maria, a 5*, was printed by Eslava in *Lira sacro-hispana*, I, ii, 197-201 (using for his source an El Escorial choirbook), was born *ca.* 1540 at Babilafuente. This village lies some ten miles east of Salamanca. See *AM*, IX, 68 (Anglés mistook the place name). In February, 1558, a singer named Periañez was employed in the Duke of Alba's chapel at Naples. See José Subirá, *La música en la Casa de Alba* (Madrid: 1927), page 27. Periañez's first chapelmaster's appointment took him to Almería (*AM*, IX, 68). In the week beginning Monday, September 30, 1577, he competed for the Málaga chapelmastership left vacant by Juan Cepa. On Tuesday morning he and his three rivals were instructed to compose within the space of twenty-four hours an imitative motet using as text, "Holy Father, keep them in thy name whom thou hast given me" (John 17:11b). At the same time the competitors were each required to add two voices to a given cantus firmus, a third voice to *un duo de la oposición de Morales* (a duo used in Morales's trial), and a fourth voice to a trio. The four motets were sung before the Dean and chapter on Wednesday afternoon. At the same session each contender was required to improvise counterpoints above a plainsong and above a given piece of polyphony. Last, each was given a *soneto* with *copla* to set before the morrow. On Thursday afternoon at half-past two the final session began with the singing of the four villancicos composed overnight by the four contenders. Various other tests culminated in Periañez's conducting of a

Benedictus qui venit. While conducting, he sang the tenor part. Periañez was declared winner by a vote taken on October 16. However, in the intervening two weeks he had competed for the Cordovan chapelmastership. After some weeks of vacillation he accepted the Málaga appointment. On January 21, 1578, he was formally inducted. Some six years later (October 28, 1583) he transferred from Málaga to Santiago de Compostela. His successor at Málaga, Francisco Carrillo, served from 1584 to 1585. (His predecessors seem to have been Francisco Logroño, Santiago chapelmaster from 1536 to 1578, canon after 1563; and A. N. Villar de Hecesso from Valladolid, who served as Santiago chapelmaster for only two years, 1579-1581. See Biblioteca Nacional MS 14033.258.)

23 Juan Pujol (*ca.* 1573-1626) occupied the chapelmastership at Tarragona Cathedral from November 29, 1593 to January 23, 1596 (*DML,* II, 1811); whence he passed to the Pilar at Saragossa. There he sang his first Mass in August, 1600. For other details of his career at Saragossa, see Antonio Lozano González, *La música popular, religiosa y dramática en Zaragoza* (Saragossa: Julián Sanz y Navarro, 1895), pp. 22-23. At the death of Jaime Ángel Tapias in 1612, he was appointed chapelmaster at the Barcelona Seo. The first two volumes of his *Opera omnia* were published in 1926-1932. His editor, Anglés, considers him a *gran maestro*; and regrets the loss of his Tarragona motets. His entire repertory now in print dates from his Barcelona period, and cannot be studied in the present volume.

24 Sebastián Raval, like both Diego Ortiz and Mateo Flecha the Younger, spent his productive years abroad. No documentation showing that he returned to Spain after his early departure to fight in the Low Countries has thus far been adduced. He published two books of madrigals and one of *canzonette,* but every item in these three collections uses an Italian text. He ended his career at Palermo (d. October, 1604) in the service of the Spanish viceroy, the Duke of Maqueda. That so late as the year before his death he wished to identify himself culturally with Sicily may be learned from the dedication that he wrote for *Infidi lumi* (Palermo: G. B. Maringo, 1603), the last imprint to contain his music. Accounts of his life are to be seen in Raffaele Casimiri's "Sebastiano Raval: musicista spagnolo del sec. XVI," *Note d'archivio,* Vol. VIII, no. 1 (Jan., 1931), pp. 1-20; and in Ottavio Tiby's "Sebastian Raval: A 16th century Spanish musician in Italy," *Musica disciplina,* Vol. II, fasc. 3 and 4 (1948), pp. 217-223. In addition to the bibliography of Raval's publications in the Casimiri article, pages 8-12, H. Anglés's "El Archivo Musical de la Catedral de Valladolid," *AM,*

Vol. III (1948), pp. 105-107, may be consulted.

Raval's three sacred publications—*Motectorum quinque vocum* (Rome: 1593), *Lamentationes Hieremiae prophetae quinque vocum* (Rome: 1594), and *Motecta selecta organo accommodata* (Palermo: 1600) —must be transcribed before his powers can be assessed. The last parallels Victoria's 1600 Madrid publication by virtue of its organ part.

In Raval's dedication of the 1600 Palermo motets to the Duchess of Maqueda, wife of the viceroy, he makes several interesting allusions. He says that on Fridays during Lent she has caused polychoral works accompanied by instruments to be sung "en Oratorio." Raval dedicated the last of his 1595 *Madrigali a tre voci* to Emilio de' Cavalieri; in all likelihood he knew Cavalieri's *Rappresentazione di anima e di corpo* (Rome: 1600). It seems therefore at least possible that Raval had in mind not just a "prayer room" but a musical genre when he wrote: "Sin las demas obras de muchos coros, y instrumentos, que en los viernes de quaresma por deuoçion de V. E. se han selebrado *en Oratorio,* quales plaçiendo a Nuestro Señor pretendo dirigillas con mayor opportunidad à V. E. entanto suplico a V. E. accepte lo mucho, que en mi animo deseo, aunque poco lo que en publico offrezco . . . " Whatever else is uncertain, this much at least is clear: the polychoral works with instruments which had been performed on Fridays in Lent were not being published in the present imprint, although, please God, he hoped to publish them when opportunity offered. In the meantime, he begged her to accept that which in heart he wished to be a large gift, but which in the public eye he knew to be small.

Only a single piece *a 8* has been included, he says in the dedication: *Super flumina Babilonis*—composed entirely for "*tiples* which in Italy are called *suprani.*" Raval includes this piece for eight sopranos because he "has heard that from the Duke's estates have come forth excellent musicians, and more especially, choice *tiples.*"

25 Bernardino de Ribera, son of Pedro de Ribera, was born *ca.* 1520 at Játiva. This was the town in which both the Spanish popes were born. It was also the native town of the distinguished painter José de Ribera (*ca.* 1581-1652). Whether this painter came of the same family as the composer remains to be determined. What is known for certain is that Pedro de Ribera, the composer's father, was a chapelmaster in Játiva, and that the composer's paternal grandparents came from Seville. On April 14, 1559, the Ávila Cathedral chapter decided to seek an *honbre prençipal en su profesion* for chapelmaster. Gerónimo de Espinar, the previous chapelmaster, had died the preceding autumn. On June 2, 1559, the chapter voted to invest "Vernaldino" [= Bernardino] de Ribera with a full prebend, even though he was absent and had not given assurance that he would accept the Ávila chapel-mastership. The next day, the chapter secretary was instructed to write him a letter of invitation. On June 17, 1559, negotiations were still in progress. Before September 18, 1559, he had arrived and was on that date admonished to give lessons. On January 8, 1560, the chapter ordered "that boys with voices suitable for polyphonic singing be exempted from matins and paid an extra three ducats annually." For further details consult the Ávila *Actas Capitulares*, 1556-1560, especially fols. 88ᵛ, 91, 92ᵛ, 93, 101, and 109ᵛ. Ribera's term extended until 1563, on April 15 of which year he was inducted as chapelmaster at Toledo. His four years of service at Ávila coincided with Victoria's eleventh through fifteenth years. Since it is now known that Victoria was a choirboy at Ávila Cathedral (see below, p. 351), Ribera deserves special consideration. Of the three Ávila chapel-masters—Espinar, Ribera, and Navarro—Ribera probably exerted the most decisive influence. Only two years after Ribera left Ávila, Victoria had departed for Rome.

At Toledo, Ribera succeeded the disreputable Bartolomé de Quebedo (who was dismissed for misconduct). He brought with him a dozen large choirbooks for sale to the Toledo chapter. Of these, seven contained masses; three, magnificats; and four, motets. He was allowed to retain the books after sale, so that he might use them during singing lessons. Two of these were Morales's printed Masses, books I and II. The bill of sale to the chapter listed these two books as "old and with leaves pulled out." One of the two was at the moment of sale kept at the house of a certain assistant named Gómez. Ribera had given it to Gómez *para exercicio delos seyses* (so that the choirboys could use it during practice sessions).

Unlike such other Toledan chapelmasters as Morales, Boluda, and Torrentes, Ribera occupied Ración 45, which was the prebend designated for a contralto singer. Apparently Ribera held office for eight years. Andrés de Torrentes, who had already twice before occupied the primatial chapelmastership, returned for a third term on February 9, 1571. See Rubio Piqueras, *Música y músicos toledanos*, pp. 58, 60.

Codex 6 in the Toledo musical archive contains two *De beata Virgine* Masses by Ribera, both *a 4*. Six motets *a 8, a 6,* and *a 5* follow. Last, this vellum choirbook, "the calligraphy of which is superb," contains eight magnificats, two each for Tones I-IV. It is to be supposed that the remaining magnificats in a Tone I-VIII series have been lost. Rubio Piqueras (*Códices polifónicos toledanos,* pp. 21-22) describes this manuscript thus:

"Bound in boards, this unindexed manuscript is devoted to Bernardino de Ribera's masses, motets, and magnificats. Throughout are to be seen handsomely illuminated initials. The codex opens with a *De beata Virgine* Mass *a 4*, based on

plainchant. Since folio 1 has been lost, cantus and tenor of Kyrie I are unfortunately missing. In the Gloria the usual tropes are encountered. The Crucifixus reduces to three voices (Bassus silent). The verbal canon in the Benedictus *a 5* requires the upper voices to reverse themselves and sing backward in notes half the value of those written. Although fols. 28 and 29 have been torn out, it can be seen that the last Agnus augmented to five voices. At fol. 28ᵛ was to have begun another *De beata Virgine* Mass, also *a 4*. All of Kyrie I has been lost as well as cantus and tenor of the Christe. In the Gloria are to be found the same Marian tropes as in the preceding mass. The loss of fol. 40 impedes somewhat our knowledge of the Credo. Obviously, however, this movement is polytextual from Patrem to Crucifixus, a fifth voice during the interim singing in cantus firmus fashion the plainsong hymn *Ave maris stella.* The Et resurrexit reduces to three voices. The polytextual Et in Spiritum augments to five (the fifth voice here singing the angelical salutation). The Pleni sunt again reduces to three. In the Osanna, Ribera writes a canon at the octave. The final Agnus expands to six voices.

"The section of motets opens with a six-voice *Ascendens Christus* for Ascension. At fol. 69 is to be seen *Ortum dignissimum* for the Nativity of Our Lady. The loss of fol. 68 makes it impossible to transcribe the beginning of this, or the end of the preceding, motet. At fol. 75 occurs the psalm *Conserva me Domine, a 6.* There next follows a motet for the Translation of St. Eugenius, also *a 6, O quam speciosa festivitas.* But a missing leaf again makes transcription of the opening impossible. At fol. 85 is copied the motet *a 6* for festivals of the Virgin—*Beata Mater et innupta Virgo gloriosa, Regina mundi.* A responsory copied much later than the main body of the codex precedes the next motet: *Regina coeli, a 5,* for Easter. Pentecost, Assumption, and Octave of Corpus Christi motets come next—*Hodie completi sunt dies, Virgo prudentissima,* and *Rex autem David* (each *a 5*)."

Ribera is represented in a tenor partbook at Valladolid Cathedral with a motet *a 6, Dimitte me ergo* (MS 17, fols. 184ᵛ-185). See *AM,* III, 86. At Plasencia in MS 2 (fols. 47ᵛ-49) is to be seen Ribera's hymn *a 4* in honor of St. James, *Huic caeli ab altis sedibus* (pt. 2, *Tu ceca nos atque impia*). The music for part 2 exactly repeats that for part 1. In this hymn, each of the four lines of verse is set in a new point of imitation—all four voices participating in the first three points. There is no sign of a cantus firmus.

26 An untitled Mass *a 5* by Melchor Robledo survives in Cappella Sistina Codex 22 at Rome. Kyrie I is composed *a 4*, Agnus II *a 6*. In the "O" of the Osanna is inscribed the year in which the codex was copied—1568. The head motive in Kyrie I consists of the same *fa re ut fa sol la* theme on which Morales based his *Missa cortilla*, and which was to be used again as a motto by Juan de Lienas in his five-part *Convento del Carmen* mass. The Lienas Mass comes closer to the Robledo, because it is scored for the same high voices and ends throughout on the A chord (rather than the D chord chosen by Morales). Robledo throughout his Mass treats the head motive as an ostinato (*Pfundnoten*) threaded through the top voice of every movement except the Crudifixus *a 4* and Et in Spiritum (even in these, he uses the head motive, but modifies it slightly). It is vehemently to be suspected that the *Missa fa re ut fa sol la* attributed to Melchor de Aragon in a manuscript of Toledo provenience (copied in 1696) concords with the mass by Robledo in Cappella Sistina Codex 22. See *AM*, VIII (1953), 121 (n. 150).

During 1549 Robledo served as chapelmaster in Tarragona Cathedral. He occupied the same post at the Seo in Saragossa (with an interruption) from July 2, 1569, until his death in April, 1587. Saragossa was, of course, the capital of the Kingdom of Aragon; hence "Melchor de Aragon." He spent several years at Rome between the Tarragona and Saragossa appointments.

Motets by Robledo are preserved at Rome and at Valladolid. As yet, however, no conscientious effort has been made to assemble either biographical or bibliographical data. Cappella Sistina Codex 38 (copied 1563) contains his polytextual motet *a 5*, *Simile est* (pt. 2, *Inventa autem*). The fifth voice sings the *Veni sponsa Christi* antiphon (second vespers) in cantus firmus style, each note lasting three semibreves. MS 17 at Valladolid—a tenor partbook—contains both a motet, *Concussum est mare et contremuit* (*a 5*), and a secular song, *Recuerde el alma dormida* (*a 6*). The Diego Sánchez codex at Valladolid shows all four parts of *Hoc corpus*. Elústiza-Castrillo printed the last-named work in their *Antología musical* at pages 130-133. At meas. 36 and again at meas. 53₄, Robledo breaks (after a general pause) into homophony. Attention is thereby focused on *Hoc facite* (This do, as oft as ye shall drink it, in remembrance of me).

At Puebla, Mexico, Robledo is represented in *Libro de coro 1* by a "G minor" *Salve Regina*, *a 6* (SSAATB; fols. 47ᵛ-52). If this is a typical work, he liked to repeat or sequence expressive melodic incises, especially with such emotion-fraught words as "vale of tears."

In 1571 (January 12 and August 7), the canons at Saragossa presented Robledo with two extra *raciones* as tangible marks of their favor (see Lozano González, *op. cit.*, p. 20). Robledo's continuing fame at Rome after his return to Spain is attested in a letter drafted June 29, 1574, by Antonio Boccapaduli, *maestro della cappella pontificia* (see *Note d'archivio*, XI, 3-4 [July-Dec., 1934], 203-206). But even though renowned at home and abroad, he did not always enjoy smooth sailing in Saragossa. He moved to Calahorra "for

good reasons" *ca.* 1580 (see Elústiza-Castrillo, *Antología musical*, p. LXXIX). In 1581 Palencia Cathedral wished to engage him. The acrimony that caused him to seek a temporary haven in Calahorra turned into real appreciation of his greatness at his death (April, 1587). The entire Seo chapter accompanied his body to the grave. Later, a rule was made that on great occasions at Saragossa only the music of Morales, Palestrina, Victoria, and Robledo should be sung. Contrary to Elústiza-Castrillo, *op. cit.*, page LXXXII, his successor was not Bernardo Peralta, but rather José Gay (three months). Gay was succeeded by Cristóbal Téllez, who prior to gaining the Saragossa appointment on December 23, 1587, had been chapelmaster of the collegiate church at Berlanga. Téllez served at the Seo in Saragossa until 1593. For further details concerning the competition, see Biblioteca Nacional MS 14047, "Libro de Memorias de las cosas que en la Iglesia del Asseo de Çaragoça se han offrecido tocantes a ella desde el Agosto del año 1579 hasta el año 1601 inclusive." The author of these cathedral memoirs was Doctor Pascual de Mandura, canon of the Seo (the Seo being the older of the two cathedrals in Saragossa). The Peralta whom Elústiza-Castrillo mention did not arrive from Burgos to take up the chapelmastership of the Seo until December 9, 1611.

27 Francisco de Sepúlveda succeeded Morales as chapelmaster at Ávila Cathedral on October 12, 1530. A singer named Barrionuevo had substituted as an interim appointee after Morales's departure for Plasencia. Gerónimo de Espinar succeeded Sepúlveda. See *AM*, VIII (1953 [1954]), 5-6. Manuscripts 2 and 4 in the Plasencia musical archive contain hymns with music by Sepúlveda. In MS 2 are two Christmas, a Circumcision, and two Epiphany hymns; in MS 4 a Holy Innocents. Although the texts differ, each stanza in each of these six hymns is set to the same music *a 4*. See *AM*, V (1950), 152-153, 155-156. Enríque de Valderrábano published an intabulation of Sepúlveda's Apostles and Evangelists hymn *a 3*, *Exultet celum laudibus*, at fol. 10ᵛ in *Silva de sirenas* (Valladolid: 1547). The tenor (ciphered in red) sings the complete text. In the opening point, the tenor is imitated by the soprano (meas. 2₃) and then by the bass (meas. 6₃). The rhythms are boldly accentual; the mode is major; the key is F. The chord progressions are everywhere amenable to modern tonic-dominant analysis. In this environment, the "Landini" cadence at mm. 7-8, and escaped notes in the soprano at meas. 14₁₋₂ sound atavistic. That the tempo moves briskly could be surmised from text and rhythmic patterns. Valderrábano confirms such a surmise with the sign ₵: (= fast).

28 In 1911-1912 Rafael Mitjana published his monograph "El Padre Francisco Soto de Langa" in seven instalments (*Musica sacro-hispana*, Vol. IV, nos. 8-10; Vol. V, nos. 1, 3, 8, 9 [Aug.-Oct., 1911; Jan., March, Aug., Sept., 1912], pp. 125-129, 142-144, 156-163; 1-5, 33-38, 115-121, 131-133). Because he dealt exhaustively with this expatriate, a large chapter would be needed for an adequate exposition of his biographical and bibliographical results. Here, however, his monograph must be reduced to a mere note. The reason for doing so is that Soto de Langa, although born in Spain, spent his entire adult life in Rome.

Mitjana, against the authority of others, selected 1534 as Soto's year of birth. Langa is a town lying somewhat west of Burgo de Osma in the province of Soria. Paolo Aringhi, who became an Oratorian in 1622, wrote a life of Soto—to be seen in his *Vitae, Sententiae, Gesta et Dicta Patrum Congregationis Oratorii de Urbe a S. Philippio Nerio fundatae*, a manuscript collection in the Biblioteca Vallicelliana at Rome (sign. O. 58-60). The biography begins thus (Cod. O. 58, pp. 245, 249): "Having from earliest childhood manifested extraordinary musical ability and in particular a marvellous voice, he soon won the plaudits of the most discerning critics of his time. Arriving in Rome while still a youth he here came under the instruction of the best masters. Quickly he gained the same renown as in Spain. Not much time passed before a vacancy for a sopranist in the papal choir was announced. (The choir at that time comprised representatives of four nations: Spanish, French, German, and Italian.) After submitting to a competition he was unanimously declared the best candidate, elected by acclamation, and forthwith admitted to the choir [June 8, 1562]. Throughout many years he continued to be always beloved and favored by a long succession of popes on account of his exquisite voice and his dignified deportment" (quoted in *Musica sacro-hispana*, Vol. IV, no. 10, p. 158).

Four years after entering the choir, Soto came under the spell of St. Philip Neri, founder of the Oratorian congregation. Aringhi provides a detailed description of the circumstances of Soto's entry into the society. Struck by the brotherly spirit that animated the new group, Soto decided to choose one of St. Philip's associates for his own confessor. He then underwent the spiritual exercises enjoined by Neri. His zeal caught Neri's attention. Since the plan of the infant community called for the preaching of four sermons every day at the church to which the group was assigned from 1564 until 1575—S. Giovanni de' Fiorentini —and since each homely half-hour homily was followed by the singing of *laudi spirituali* and other popular devotions, the services of so eminent a vocalist as Soto were especially welcome. After a visit to his native land to put his affairs in order so that he need never return to Spain again, Soto placed himself as completely at Neri's disposal as his continuing duties in the papal choir would allow. At Neri's request, Giovanni Animuccia, chapelmaster of St. Peter's and a friend of the new group, composed *diverse laudi e canzonette spirituali* to be sung by Soto. Enthusiastic crowds were drawn to the Oratory by Soto's singing, just as in a later epoch crowds were to be drawn to similarly popular religious meetings by the singing of Sankey and Shea. Soto's performance on festival days in particular helped to draw out the youth whom Neri desired to attract.

The infant community was as yet a purely informal association of secular priests bound by no vows, although under obedience. Not until July 15, 1575, did Pope Gregory XIII give the community S. Maria in Vallicella for its own church. Soto formally joined the group on the December 17 following (*Musica sacro-hispana*, Vol. IV, no. 10, p. 160). He still continued as a papal chorister, however. In 1590 he was elected interim *maestro* of the pontifical choir. During his term in office Cappella Sistina Codex 29 was copied. All three of the greatest Spanish composers were represented in this codex: Morales with *Lamentabatur Jacob*, Guerrero with *Pastores loquebantur*, and Victoria with *Vidi speciosam*. Aringhi concludes his account of Soto's career in the choir with the following tribute: "He was always looked upon in later years as an oracle, and when time came for his superannuation the occasion was treated as a great festival in his honor." The year of superannuation, according to Mitjana, cannot have preceded 1617 (*ibid.*, p. 161).

During his long Roman sojourn, Soto amassed a sizable fortune. On December 10, 1591, he purchased a house on the outskirts of the city. By a series of financial transactions dated November 2, 1595, and April 30, July 1, and November 16, 1596, he added certain small nearby orchards to this property at a cost of 2,360 scudi. Between 1596 and 1598 a church and convent were built on the combined grounds—the approval of Pope Clement VIII having been won for the establishment at Rome of a house of discalced Carmelites subscribing to the reform of St. Theresa of Ávila. By the bull of erection (1598), Soto was named patron, and the house was conceded exceptional exemptions and privileges. He was also allowed to name his successor. In 1611 he passed on his rights as patron to the president and congregation of Santiago parish in Rome. He died on September 25, 1619, at the age of eighty-five. He was buried in the Chiesa Nuova chapel set aside for founders of the Oratorian congregation.

Soto's name is nowhere blazoned as editor of *Il primo, Il secondo, Il terzo*, or *Il quarto libro delle laude spirituali* (Rome: 1583, 1583, 1588, 1591), but it does appear in *Il quinto libro* published at Ferrara in 1598. Nevertheless, the first four books were as certainly as the fifth edited by Soto. From concordances in Giovenale Ancina's *Templo armonico* (1599) seven unattributed items in these books are known to have been composed by Soto. Ancina's *Templo armonico* attributes another six laudi to him which are not to be found in any of his five editions of *laude spirituali*. Giovanne Arascione's *Nuove laudi ariosi* (1600) attributes to him a further ten items. Lastly, the laude *a 3, Jesu dulcedo cordium,* found at fol. 105 in *Il quarto libro* (Rome: Alessandro Gardano, 1591) is Soto's because of a concordance in E. Frober's *Jubilus rhythmicus de nomine Jesu* (see *Musica sacro-hispana*, Vol. V, no. 3, p. 36). Thus, Soto's identifiable original laudi total twenty-four. Only one of these sets a Latin text—the remaining twenty-three setting Italian poems. Musically, the entire group is characterized by (1) block chords, (2) treble-dominated harmony, and (3) symmetrical phrases. Those reprinted by Ancina were composed *a 3;* those by Arascione, *a 4.* About them all hang the charms of devout simplicity, homely fervor, and unaffected commonness which gave the Oratorians their distinctive hold on the populace.

The following is Mitjana's list of the laudi in Soto's editions identifiable as his own original compositions because of concordances in Ancina's *Templo armonico:* (1) *E. natto il gran'Iddio,* (2) *Vergine se ti calse,* (3) *Beneditt'il Signor,* (4) *Donna celeste,* (5) *Ond'è che l'aureo crine,* (6) *Il pietoso Giesu,* (7) *Per aspri monti.* Items 1 and 2 appear in Soto's *Secondo libro;* 3, 4, and 5 in his *Terzo;* 6 and 7 in his *Quarto* (*Musica sacro-hispana,* Vol. V, no. 3, p. 34).

29 Even though Andrés de Torrentes's services at Toledo were divided into three short terms: December 9, 1539-September 1, 1545; December 16, 1547-July 26, 1553; February 9, 1571-September 4, 1580 (he died on the last date); he exceeded every other sixteenth-century Toledan chapelmaster in the total number of years that he served—eighteen.

His compositions have not been transcribed, with the exception of a Magnificat in Tone VII (*Lira sacro-hispana,* I, i, 87-94). At Toledo, Codices 10 (two motets *a 4*), 12 (seven vesper psalms, ten hymns, eight magnificats), 18 (*fabordones,* hymns, lamentations, magnificats), 21 (*fabordones* and hymns), 33 (*Missa De beata Virgine*), and 34 (four magnificats) entitle him to the rank of a major composer. See Rubio Piqueras, *Música y músicos toledanos,* p. 58; and *Códices polifónicos toledanos,* pp. 26-28, 35-37, 43-44, 58-59.

30 Luis de Vargas of Seville (1502-1568), although primarily a painter, was also an accomplished musician. So testified Francisco Pacheco, his first biographer, in the *Libro de descripción de verdaderos retratos* (Seville: 1599) when he declared that Vargas *fué músico fundado y ecelente.* See R. Mitjana, *Estudios sobre algunos músicos españoles*

(Madrid: 1918), p. 122. Vargas's most admired painting, *Generación temporal de Cristo,* belongs to a retable in the Seville Cathedral, the upper inside panels of which show angels as musicians. In the left inside panel four angels sing out of an open book, the music of which can be read and has been transcribed. In the right inside panel an angel plays the organ: a choirbook on the organ rack is open at the same music that the angels on the left are singing. The interlined text reads *Tota pulchra es amica mea et maculata non est in te* (Song of Songs 4:7). Vargas, if he is the composer of this short motet *a 4,* well exemplified the Renaissance ideal of a universal artist. See the transcription in Mitjana, *op. cit.,* pages 123-124. Vargas is also represented in the Tarazona Cathedral archive; see *España sagrada,* vol. 50 (1866), p. 87, col. 2.

31 Juan Vásquez, a native of Badajoz, published two secular collections: *Villancicos i canciones . . . A tres y a quatro* (Osuna: Juan de León, 1551) and *Recopilacion de Sonetos y villancicos a quatro y a cinco* (Seville: Juan Guttiérrez, 1560). He published also an *Agenda defunctorum* (Seville: Martín de Montesdoca, 1556), in the dedication of which he subscribed himself *sacerdos.*

Either he or his homonym was *Maestro de Canto llano* in Ávila Cathedral during 1530 (see p. 117, note 57); toward the end of the decade he was a singer in Palencia Cathedral, and on April 19, 1541, was voted traveling-expense money to Madrid, where he was hired the next month to sing in Cardinal Tavera's chapel choir (see Jaime Moll Roqueta, "Músicos de la Corte del Cardenal Juan Tavera [1523-1545]," *AM,* VI [1951], 165-166). In October, 1543, Cardinal Tavera's chapel choir was transferred to Prince Philip, but Juan Vásquez seems to have left the choir at this time to return home. He succeeded Luis de Quiñones as chapelmaster of the Badajoz Cathedral in mid-1545, and was receiving an annual salary of 25,000 maravedís from the cathedral in 1546—5,000 less than the organist, Juan de Trejo (who served the cathedral from 1525 to 1572). Vásquez was still chapelmaster at Badajoz during 1549, but in the first half of 1550 left to enter the private household of the Andalusian magnate Antonio de Zuñiga (for details of his career at Badajoz, see Santiago Kastner, "La música en la Catedral de Badajoz [años 1520-1603]," *AM,* XII [1957], 127).

Both in his own century and in ours, Vásquez has won recognition primarily as a composer of delightfully fresh villancicos. Nineteen secular items by Vásquez were ciphered in Enríquez de Valderrábano's *Silva de sirenas* (1547), Pisador's *Libro de música de vihuela* (1552), and Fuenllana's *Orphénica lyra* (1554)—but not any sacred items. No other Spanish composer except Morales was intabulated so frequently. If only secular items intabulated at home and abroad are considered, Vásquez stands first with 19, Pedro Guerrero second with 10, Mateo Flecha the Elder third with 7, Francisco Guerrero fourth with 5, Rodrigo de Ceballos fifth with 4, and Navarro sixth with 3 items.

The title page of Vásquez's *Agenda defunctorum* (1556) may be seen in facsimile at page 282 of Pedrell's *Catàlech de la Biblioteca Musical de la Diputació de Barcelona*, I. Anglés, in *MME*, Vol. IV, pp. *16-18*, suggests that Vásquez dedicated the *Agenda* not to an actual person named Juan Bravo, but "symbolically" to Juan Téllez Girón, Count of Ureña. This suggestion must be rejected. The bearings charged on the escutcheon in the sinister chief quarter belong to the Bravo family, not to the Téllez Girón house. See Julio de Atienza, *Nobiliario español* (Madrid: M. Águilar, 1948), p. 490, col. 1. Moreover, the helmet on the title page of *Agenda defunctorum* is that of an hidalgo rather than that of a *conde*.

Both the dedication and the Latin poem prefacing the *Agenda* are in Latin. In the one, Vásquez admits that the dedication of such a book to a secular person may seem inappropriate. But Bravo is given to meditation on Eternity. The words, by their very nature, cannot be "dedicated"—only the music—and Bravo has repeatedly shown himself an outstanding patron of the art. Bravo's continued favor will sheathe him from the attacks of the envious. In the 18-line Latin poem that follows, he recalls Orpheus's success in assuaging the torments of the dead. His *Agenda defunctorum* will not console the dead but is meant to comfort the living (*Conciliantque animis vota benigna Deum*).

In general, the music of the *Agenda* shows these traits: (1) exquisitely sensitive contrast of high and low groupings of voices, for expressive purposes; (2) liberal use of the higher accidentals, especially C♯ and G♯; (3) frequent recourse to the nota cambiata; (4) occasional lightening of texture with trellises of fleetly running scales through an octave or more in the top voice; (5) harmonic treatment of the bass—which skips freely in fourths and fifths; (6) exploitation of such extreme notes as D_1 for dramatic effect; (7) free use of cross relations for expressive purposes; (8) use not only of consonant fourths at cadences, but of consonant sevenths as well; (9) frequent use of repetition and sequence in successive melodic incises. This last trait, of course, is a hallmark of Morales's style as well as of Vásquez's.

Vásquez's *Agenda* culminates in a Mass for the Dead. Among its other distinctions, this volume is the first printed in Spain to contain such a polyphonic Mass. Throughout the *Agenda*, Vásquez adopts a much more richly figurative style than is customary in Office for the Dead music. The first Requiem aeterna even includes a canon between soprano 1 and the alto (at the lower fourth). He also pays greater heed to pace-distinctions than the usual composer of funerary music. The Dirige, Domine ne in furore, and Nequando of the First Nocturn choose, for instance, C for their time signature; but the lessons from Job which immediately follow are composed with ₵ for their signature. He also varies the voice part to which he entrusts the cantus firmus. As if changes from soprano to tenor were insufficient, he even allots the cantus firmus to the bass in both second and third antiphons of the Third Nocturn. The lessons, as a rule, veer away from Gregorian quotation; indeed, such an item as Psalm 41 (= 40 A.V.) after the Gradual proceeds throughout in motet style, that is, as a series of imitative points.

In contradistinction to Morales, Vásquez does not feel obligated to start every movement of his *Missa pro defunctis* with a plainsong intonation. Both composers do set the In memoria versicle *a 3* for male voices, but Vásquez omits the Hostias versicle that Morales chose to set polyphonically. As for their quoted Gregorian material, Morales seems bent on interpolating perhaps a greater number of under-notes at cadences than Vásquez. Vásquez's plainsong in the Sanctus and Agnus I of his *Missa pro defunctis* does not correspond with the plainsong for these movements in either Morales's 1544 Requiem Mass or in the presently used *Liber usualis*. Instead, his Sanctus quotes a chant that resembles, if it does not quote in its entirety, the Sanctus of Mass XI in the *Liber usualis*; and his Agnus quotes at length the Agnus in Mass XV.

His choice of modes shows exquisite sensitivity to the demands of a large canvas. Up to the Dirige of the First Nocturn he clings to the sixth mode (flat in signature); the three lessons Parce, Taedet, and Manus tuae move successively, however, from finals G and A with flat in the signature to G without flat for the responsory after Lectio I; to G with flat for Taedet but E for the accompanying responsory; and finally to E for the Manus tuae with which this Nocturn ends.

Analysis cannot be prolonged; but the Agenda should be published entire at the earliest possible date. Just as surely as his secular music, it shows Vásquez to have been one of the rarest musical geniuses that Spain has produced.

32 Pedro Alberch [y] Vila (1517-1582 [November 16]) was born at Vich and died at Barcelona. He became organist in Barcelona Cathedral as early as 1538. In 1559 he was promoted to a canonry in the same cathedral. One of the few Catalonian artists whose fame exceeded provincial boundaries, Vila was lauded by Bermudo as a compeer of Juan Doyz (Málaga Cathedral), Antonio de Cabezón, Francisco de Soto (royal organists), and Pedro Villada (Seville Cathedral).

See *Declaración de instrumentos* (1555), fol. 60ᵛ, col. 1. The first works of Vila to reach print were two keyboard *tientos* published in Venegas de Henestrosa's *Libro de cifra nueva para tecla, harpa, y vihuela* (Alcalá de Henares: Juan de Brocar, 1557). See *MME*, II, *172*, 43-46. Four years later (1561), a printer in Barcelona, Jaume Cortey (= Jacobus Cortesius), issued a collection of Vila's secular and sacred vocal pieces under the title *Odarum (quas vulgo madrigales appellamus) diuersis linguis decantatarum Harmonica, noua, & excellenti modulatione compositarum, Liber primus*. Book 1 comprises secular items with Catalonian and Castilian texts. Book 2 (*Liber secundus*) contains eight sacred pieces, six of which extend to two *partes*. All the sacred pieces set Castilian lyrics. Unfortunately, only the printed altus part survives. However, several individual numbers were copied in manuscript partbooks in the late sixteenth century. Use of one such set (SAB) has made possible the reconstruction of the first six numbers in *Liber secundus*. For notices of the printed and manuscript versions see Pedrell, *Catàlech de la Biblioteca Musical de la Diputació de Barcelona*, II, 174-175, 233. A third publication containing Vila's vocal music came out at Prague only a year before his death: *Las ensaladas de Flecha*. See above, note 11. In this last collection, Vila is represented with two ensaladas, *Bon jorn* and *La lucha*. The first, with its macaronic text (Castilian, Catalonian, French, and Latin), tends toward burlesque. See Pedrell, *Catàlech*, II, 180, 182, 208, 233. Details concerning Vila's now-lost works, which were preserved in manuscript at Lisbon before 1755 (library of João IV), are given in *Catàlech*, II, 177. A Lamentation, *a 3*, photographed from the Orfeón Catalán MS 6 (Barcelona), was presented as Facsimile 25 in Anglés's *La música española desde la edad media*. Transcription of this Maundy Thursday Lamentation (*Lamech* [= Lamed], *O vos omnes, Hierusalem*) reveals, however, a turgid approach to the Latin text (especially when comparison is made with Morales's noble ventures) and suggests that Vila chose wisely when he specialized in the instrumental and secular fields.

33 According to Rafael Mitjana, *Don Fernando de Las Infantas* (Madrid: Imp. de los Sucs. de Hernando, 1918), pages 121-122, Andrés de Villalar competed successfully for the chapelmastership at Cordova in the early summer of 1563. In a secret chapter ballot cast on July 5 [1563] he received 30 votes; the two other candidates—Diego Ximénez (interim Cordovan chapelmaster since October 15, 1561) and Gerónimo de Barrionuevo —18 and 1, respectively. Villalar hankered after his native Zamora during his triennium in Cordova. On October 30, 1566, he petitioned the Cordovan chapter for leave to visit his sick mother at Zamora. Once granted the leave, he

departed—never to return. On December 16 [1566] the Cordovan chapter received his letter of resignation from Zamora. His successor at Cordova, Gerónimo Durán de la Cueva—a native of Granada—was elected on April 24, 1567, and held office until death (January 7, 1615). Villalar, although invited to Palencia in 1580, chose to remain at Zamora: where he was still chapelmaster as late as 1593. The Diego Sánchez Codex at Valladolid (Santiago parish) contains a *Regina coeli, a 4*, by Villalar. Although constructed as a series of overlapping imitative points, each of which introduces a new incise of the plainsong Marian antiphon for Eastertide, this motet nevertheless should be called a treble-dominated piece. Only the treble consistently paraphrases the plainsong. The other voices do not allude to the plainsong except during imitative points. The tonality can hardly be denominated anything but F Major. Authentic cadences debouch into F-Major chords of resolution at mm. 8, 30, 51, 69, 79, 86, 104, 113. An interesting chain of "consonant" fourths is to be seen at mm. 6, 37, 39, 41, 49. Elústiza-Castrillo show this piece at pages 134-137 in their *Antología musical* (Barcelona: 1933). They print Villalar's altus an octave too high, however, and belie his counterpoint with parallel fifths (in semibreves) at mm. 77-78.

The only printed piece ascribed to Villalar during his lifetime, *Esclarecida Juana*, is found in Esteban Daza's *El Parnasso* (Valladolid: 1576) at fol. 90. Trend accepted Daza's attribution in his article, "Catalogue of the music in the Biblioteca Medinaceli, Madrid," *Revue hispanique*, LXXI (1927), 499. On the other hand, Francisco Guerrero at no. 38 in his *Canciones y villanescas espirituales* (Venice: 1589) printed as his own the same music that Daza ascribed to Villalar. It is unthinkable that Guerrero should have thus misappropriated music by Villalar. Daza must therefore have erred in his attribution. See *MME*, VIII, *21* (item 163 = 92).

34 P. Samuel Rubio, writing for *La Ciudad de Dios*, CLXIII, nos. 1-3 (Jan.-Dec., 1951), traced the early history of music at El Escorial in an article entitled "La Capilla de Música del Monasterio de El Escorial." At pages 89-90 of this article he showed that Martín de Villanueva, before his arrival at El Escorial in 1586, had been a Jeronymite friar in the Granada house of this distinctively Spanish religious order. Since it was only in 1586 that the Office first began to be chanted in the basilica of the monument to St. Lawrence built by Philip II, skilled musical talent began to be needed in that year. But Villanueva was already known as a *gran polifonista y diestro tañedor de órgano* (fine polyphonic musician and accomplished organ player). His transfer from Granada to El Escorial was therefore in all probability prompted by his known musical talent. Rubio considers him to have been the second chapelmaster at El Escorial—probably the first having been Fray Gaspar de León. Villanueva served also as *corrector mayor del coro*. At El Escorial the hours were timed so exactly that every minute was accounted for. In a letter to the general of the order written in the year of Philip's decease, it is revealed that three masses were sung every day; that the religious occupied their choir stalls from 5 A.M. until 12 noon without respite; and that the afternoon was similarly occupied with continuous exercises. Philip II himself frequently spent as many as fourteen hours daily in devotions— "a thing that seems impossible." See *La Ciudad de Dios*, XXVIII, 133. It was Villanueva's duty as *corrector mayor* to see that such tempi were chosen as would enable every hymn, psalm, lesson, and responsory to fit into a foreordained schedule. The organist's interludes had similarly to be timed with the kind of precision now expected only in radio and television programs. See *La Ciudad de Dios*, CLXIII, 113-114 (note 1). Just as the capitular acts at such a cathedral as Málaga reveal that no such thing as a "correct" tempo for any particular chant was then known, but only a "correct" tempo for a particular event, so at El Escorial the speed at which everything was sung depended upon the ceremony within which the chant in question was expected to fit. See R. Mitjana, "La capilla de Música de la Catedral de Málaga. Año de 1543 al año de . . . ," page 22 (May 5, 1548): *Que se diga al sochantre* [Pedro González, bass singer and succentor] *que lleve el compas segun la fiesta, si mayor, mayor, si menor, menor*. A similar idea is expressed in the "Directorio del corrector mayor del canto," a manuscript guidebook for the regulator of plainchant tempi in El Escorial. Villanueva filled this office, as well as that of polyphonic conductor, until his death. Sent to Valladolid on monastery business, he died there in June, 1605. See *La Ciudad de Dios*, CLXIII, 114-115, for further biographical details. His extant compositions at El Escorial are considerably less interesting than his Mass of Our Lady preserved at The Hispanic Society in New York. The El Escorial repertory includes Passions according to Matthew and John, each *a 4*, a Kyrie *a 3;* the opening Lessons for Good Friday and Holy Saturday, each *a 4; Miserere mei Deus* and *Positus Jesus in agonia*, each also *a 4*. At The Hispanic Society a manuscript of 117 paper leaves, *Missae secundum ritum Toletanum cum aliis missis variorum auctorum* (57 by 42 cm.), copied at the end of the sixteenth century contains at fols. 18ᵛ-30 a *Misa de N. Señora con el canto llano de fray Martin de Villa nueba*. This alternation mass deserves transcription and study not only because it testifies to the musical culture of the Jeronymites who sang it, but also because such masses do not enter the repertories of Villanueva's Spanish contemporaries. Even the method of copying departs from that found in any other known contemporary peninsular manuscript. Throughout Kyries and Gloria the tenor sings black breves, which must, however, be transcribed as semibreves (unreduced) or minims, common time. Throughout Gloria and Credo, unaccompanied plainsong alternates with polyphony. Thus, Laudamus te, Adoramus te, and Gratias agimus are set polyphonically. The intervening phrases—Benedicimus te, Glorificamus te, and so forth—are to be plainchanted. Still more interesting is the fact that in the polyphonic passages the tenor continues to sing the plainchant, without making the slightest concessions to the three other voices. Not that the tenor sustains notes lengthily: notes of even longer value appear frequently in other parts. But the tread of the tenor is inflexible. True, the tenor in the Credo does occasionally include a few notes of minim-value (= crotchets). However, in the Agnus Dei the tenor again resumes its pendulum-like regularity of motion. In this last movement 40 semibreves (= minims in transcription) succeed without pause or relief of any kind. All the more to be admired under these circumstances are the supple and finely wrought CAB parts that Villanueva has invented to encase, as it were, with velvet and pearls the hard bone of the martyr's relic that is the tenor part.

The following subtitle for the mass, *Tenor primero tono de nuestra señora*, appears in the manuscript. But actually the tenor throughout the Kyries sings the plainchant belonging in the present-day *Liber usualis* to Mass IV (Cunctipotens Genitor Deus); in the Gloria, the plainchant belonging to Mass III (Kyrie Deus sempiterne); and in the Credo, the plainchant belonging to Credo II. Only in the Agnus Dei does Villanueva assign his tenor a plainchant belonging to Mass IX (In Festis B. Mariae Virginis [Cum jubilo]). One must therefore conclude that the several chants comprising a plainsong Mass of Our Lady as sung at El Escorial during the last decade of Philip II departed widely from what would now constitute such a plainsong mass. For further information on plainchanting at El Escorial in the sixteenth century, see *La Ciudad de Dios*, Vol. CLXIII, p. 112, n. 3. Since Villanueva's musical procedures in his mass correspond so closely with norms known to have been prescribed by Philip II, perhaps royal rather than personal tastes dictated the character of the mass now under consideration. For a contemporary description of the *modo de cantar . . . en las fiestas en el coro de san Lorenzo el Real* which Philip himself prescribed for the Jeronymites at El Escorial, see *La Ciudad de Dios*, CLXIII, 63. The king desired that *sobre el canto llano que canto el coro, se echasen otras voces*. The commonly held opinion that he desired only the singing of plainchant in the monastery that he endowed so richly cannot be sustained in the face of either literary evidence supplied by Fray Martín de la Vera, or the musical evidence available in Villanueva's extant Holy Week music and Mass of Our Lady. The best proof of Philip's tastes is the character of this very music. Villanueva was constrained to compose a tenor alternation Lady Mass for use in El Escorial which departs radically from the style of any known masses composed during his epoch for performance in Spanish cathedrals; and that perhaps for that very reason realizes the more aptly those sober ideals of plainsong-dominated polyphony which today receive official ecclesiastical sanction. Much more than the instrumentally accompanied masses of Boluda, Esquivel, Lobo, Ribera, or Vivanco, Villanueva's *a cappella* mass might today win the kind of approval that would justify commercial, rather than merely scholarly, publication.

35 Nicasio Zorita [= Çorita], an Aragonese, was admitted chapelmaster at Tarragona Cathedral on September 9, 1578—he previously having served at Valencia. His beginning salary at Tarragona was unusually large: 75 libras annually (15 being added to the accustomed stipend of 60 in order to induce him to accept). Soon after his appointment he was permitted to return to Valencia for his effects. He also promised to bring back with him a talented boy chorister, an adult contralto, and a *castrato*. The offer to bring back a *castrato* shows that the Italian vogue of the eunuch invaded the east coast of Spain a full generation before other parts of Spain succumbed. (The first eunuchs to sing at the Seville Cathedral, for instance, were not employed until 1620 in Fray Francisco de Santiago's first term as chapelmaster. See Simón de la Rosa y López, *Los seises de la Catedral de Sevilla*, pp. 137, 145.) Upon Zorita's return to Tarragona he obligated himself to care for six boy choristers in his house. Zorita was still chapelmaster on March 4, 1589. An assistant named Peruga was appointed *maestro de canto* on April 21, 1587.

Pedrell was the first to examine Zorita's motets, published at Barcelona in 1584. His lengthy article describing the set of four partbooks discovered by him in the music archive of the Colegiata de Gandía appeared under the title "Libros de música españoles raros ó desconocidos" in two successive issues of the *Revista crítica de historia y literatura españolas, portuguesas é hispano-americanas*, Vol. IV, nos. 7 and 8; nos. 9 and 10 (July-Aug., 1899; Sept.-Oct.), pp. 302-308, 420-425. Part II of this article deals primarily with the Zorita publication: *Nicasii Çorita Chori, Sancte, metropolitane, Ecclesie Tarraconensis, Magistri Motectorum quae partim quaternis partim quinis vocibus concinnantur. Barcinonae Cum licencia & Priuilegio apud Hubertum Gotardum*. Because of its date and its

printer, Zorita's collection invites comparison with Joan Brudieu's well-known set of madrigals printed in Barcelona by the same Hubert Gotard only one year later. Zorita's set contains 32 four-voice and 20 five-voice motets. Among the latter is to be found one entitled *Virgo Dei Tecla* in honor of the patroness of Tarragona, St. Thecla. The collection is prefaced by a Latin dedication to Don Rafael Doms, archdeacon and canon in Tarragona Cathedral. The terms of the preface are by no means unusual. Zorita praises the art of music; declares that modesty forbade publication of his motets until the importuning of friends caused his resolution to change; and vows that if Doms will look benignly on the collection, he will be inspired to better labors in future. Next comes a Latin eulogy of Zorita's work by a friend filled with such commonplace mythological conceits as: "Zorita knows better how to move the listener than Orpheus how to move Galathea." Two poetic paeans in Spanish conclude the stiff introductory formalities.

Apart from this publication, Zorita will be remembered because of an altercation with Cerone, duly recorded in the latter's *El melopeo y maestro* (1613) at pages 109-110. While making a pilgrimage to Santiago de Compostela in 1593, Cerone stopped briefly at Tarragona. A meddling third party carried the tale to Zorita that his distinguished Italian guest had discovered plagiarisms in a certain motet. The next day they ran into each other by chance. But Zorita ostentatiously pretended not to see Cerone. When they again ran into each other a day or so later, Zorita this time vented his spleen, even "wishing to eat me alive for having said such a thing." After being tongue-lashed, Cerone felt that he had no other recourse except to substantiate his accusation and to add to it yet another—namely, that Zorita not once but twice had been guilty of plagiarism. A second motet had been shamelessly copied from *Noé, Noé, psallite Noé, Noé, a 4*, by the master of Cremona, Marc' Antonio Ingegneri. This citing of chapter-and-verse temporarily silenced Zorita, "who for a while remained as mute as a disciple of Pythagoras." He soon recovered spirit, however, and began to grumble that Cerone was not only a slanderer but was also trying to wreck the school he had laboriously established in Tarragona. Upon looking about in the city, Cerone did find that Zorita was considered by everyone to be a man of parts, and even a rather learned individual. "I could add a number of other particulars concerning our dealings, but since they transgress the limits of decency, I shall simply add that the spite and rage which he conceived against me pass the bounds of belief."

According to Pedrell, the Bergamo theoretician was indeed just what Zorita called him—a liar. Pedrell believed that the motet to which Cerone alluded can be found at number 14 in Zorita's collection. Working from that assumption, he concluded that Zorita had not by any means copied Ingegneri blindly, but had on the contrary merely made use of certain progressions that were the common property of all polyphonists in the epoch.

A *Credo, a 4*, by Zorita survives at Barcelona in Orfeón Catalán MS 6 (fols. 92ᵛ-93). Nine motets for Pre-Lent and Lenten seasons are to be seen in a manuscript catalogued as item 382 in Pedrell's *Catàlech de la Biblioteca Musical de la Diputació de Barcelona*, I, 243. Rubio, in his *Antología polifónica Sacra*, I (1954), published one of these—the Palm Sunday motet *a 4*, *Pueri Hebraeorum*.

36 Bishop Cirillo Franco's attack on "modern" church music, first published in *Lettere volgari di diversi nobilissimi huomini . . . terzo libro* (ed. by Aldo Manuzio [Venice: 1567]), took the form of a letter (dated February 16, 1549, at Loreto) to Ugolino Gualteruzzi *sopra l'improprietà delli musici moderni nelle loro compositioni delle messe e canto ecclesiastico*. This letter, which was promptly translated into Spanish, began with a frontal assault on Josquin's Hercules Mass. As late as 1649 the king of Portugal, João IV, felt the necessity of parrying Franco's thrusts with a *Difensa de la musica moderna contra la errada opinion del Obispo Cirillo Franco*. An Italian translation of João's "Defense of modern music" was published at Venice in 1666. No such defense of church composers from Josquin to Palestrina would have been required, however, had not the Italian bishop's animadversions found their echo in the writings of certain Spanish moralists. Typical of these "echoes" was a treatise entitled *Ynconvenientes, y gravisimos daños que se siguen de que las Religiones tengan Musica de canto de Organo* ("Troubles and very great mischiefs which arise from the use of polyphonic music by religious orders"). This tract, which belonged to a collection formed by the historian Gil González Dávila (*ca.* 1578–1658), dates from the first decade or so of the seventeenth century. A copy is to be seen in MS 14059.11 at the Madrid Biblioteca Nacional. Because of its intimate bearing on the decline of church music after Victoria's death, this tract is summarized in the following long paragraph.

"Although the use of plainchant is a laudable custom, polyphony should not be allowed in religious houses under any circumstances. *First:* the singing of polyphony requires special talent of a sort that is quite unrelated to the religious vocation. Then again where part-music is sung, novices are all too often given the habit solely because of their fine voices. Moreover they often rise to positions of authority. But both SS. Gregory and Thomas inveighed against entrusting musicians with such responsibility. The better the singer, the more unlikely he is to be himself either an acceptable preacher, teacher, or exhorter. At best, he attracts other singers into a house, rather than preachers and exhorters. *Second:* polyphony of the kind nowadays sung contravenes the very object for which music was first introduced into the church, which purpose is to convert rather than to entertain. SS. Augustine and Bernard considered it sinful to give ear to church music on account of its beauty rather than because of its call to contrition. Navarro [Martín de Azpilcueta Navarro (1491-1586), professor at Salamanca and Coimbra; author of *De musica et cantu figurato*] has treated of the same sin most learnedly and piously. Singers interested in beauty of sound never pay much heed to the sense of a text and indeed scarcely ever care whether the words can be understood or not. Villancicos sung in the vernacular are a still worse abuse. The kind now popular mix Castillian, Portuguese, Basque, and Galician in an unconscionable farrago. What is more, characters such as Negroes, Moors, and others just as hostile to the Christian religion, are introduced solely to divert, to cause laughter, and to turn the House of God into a playhouse. What shall we say of the cornetts, the sackbuts, and all the other wind instruments that some religious orders today permit on every occasion? Their use ought also to be extirpated. St. Thomas expressly condemned such instruments. Religious who allow the glossing, the embellishment, the disfiguration, that these and other like instruments frequently add, should blush for shame. Then to further compound the abuses that polyphony engenders, the majority of religious must invariably sit mute as statues while only a select few gargle their runs. Heaven is better pleased with the sound of a plainchant, even if 'there is no beauty in it nor comeliness.' Doctor Navarro made the same point when he told of an old raucous religious who dared to open his mouth at a principal feast. The polyphonic singers stood aghast because of the ugliness of his voice. Suddenly, however, a voice from Heaven interrupted, saying: *solus raucus auditur* ['only the raucous voice is heard']. Now, if someone should aver that we would exclude all polyphonic singing from churches administered by secular clergy, we deny the charge. Let the secular brethren have their polyphony if they insist. But religious orders must aspire to higher ideals. They should be nearer angels than men. *Third:* religious houses that allow polyphony must usually admit outside singers to eke out parts on important feast-days, at special thanksgivings and the like. These outsiders never fail to sully the purity of the cloister. *Fourth:* musicians who inveigle their way into religious orders are for the most part silly, idle, vacillating, vain, effeminate, and even vicious individuals. Ovid well knew the pernicious influence of music when in his *Remedia amoris*, lines 753-754, he wrote: 'The sound of

citharas, lyres, flutes, and voices has an ener-
vating influence.' The Greeks always required
that instruction in gymnastics be joined to music
in order to overcome the effeminacy that music
alone induces. When musicians wheedle their
way into religious orders they always shy away
from work, refuse to arise betimes (especially in
winter), insist on favored treatment such as delicate food and other special privileges 'in order to
preserve their voices.' If not coddled, they aposta-
size, or desist from their vocation. In any event
they never fail to make nuisances of themselves.
Fifth: the strictest groups such as Carthusians,
Recollects, and Discalced Friars, have never
known such a thing as polyphony. Several Franciscan generals have proposed its abolition. At
the recent Friars Minor chapter meeting in Segovia its use was utterly condemned. The Domini-
cans long ago gave it up absolutely so that they
might devote themselves without let or hindrance
to sacred learning and to the preaching of the
Gospel."

Perhaps the most important official pronounce-
ment on church music, so far as sixteenth-century
Spain is concerned, was delivered at the Toledo
Provincial Council of 1565. The *Actio de Reforma-
tione* passed at this council (which brought together prelates from all of Spain) may be seen in
Joseph Sáenz de Aguirre's *Collectio maxima conciliorum omnium Hispaniae*, Vol. IV (Rome: J. J.
Komarek, 1693), p. 50 (par. 11). "Whatever is
sung in church must redound to the glory of God
and be understood by the people. Words must
not be obscured. Polyphonic singing may be
retained but the text must be clearly intelligible.
Above all, theatrical music (*sonus quid theatrale*)
and any type that arouses the venereal or warlike
passions or those sentiments associated with certain classic modes (*classicos modulos*) must be
rigorously excluded."

37 Juan de Mallara, *Recebimiento que hizo la muy
noble y muy leal Ciudad de Seuilla* (Seville: Alonso
Escrivano, 1570), fol. 172: "Alli se le tomo el
juramento de guardar las ·immunidades y priui-
legios de la yglesia."

38 *Relacion verdadera del recibimiento que hizo la
ciudad de Segouia a la magestad de la reyna nuestra
señora doña Anna de Austria* (Alcalá de Henares:
Juan Gracián, 1572), fol. Y 3ᵛ: "Y para que todos
entiendan con quanto miramiento guarda su
magestad las disposiciones de la yglesia, sepan
que el dia antes del matrimonio . . ."

39 *MME*, II, *29, 85* (last paragraph).

40 Anglés's explanation of the term *Rugier*,
which he connects with the name Rogier (*MME*,
II, *181*), must be rejected. John Ward in his "The
Vihuela de mano and its Music (1536-1576)" [Ph.D.

dissertation, New York University, April, 1953],
pages 189-190, pointed to the similarity between
the alto melody in *Ruggier qual sempre fui tal esser
voglio*, intabulated by Enríquez de Valderrábano
in *Silva de sirenas* (1547) at fol. 24, and Antonio's
Rugier ciphered by Venegas de Henestrosa in his
Libro de cifra (1557) at fol. 67.

41 Isabel Pope, "The 'Spanish Chapel' of
Philip II," *Renaissance News*, V, 1 and 2 (Spring
and Summer, 1952), 2-5, 34-37.

42 Edmond Van der Straeten, *La musique aux
Pays-Bas avant le XIXᵉ siècle* (Brussels: Schott
frères, 1888), VIII, 361 [Ceballos]; 358 [Esco-
bedo]; 363-364 [Guerrero]; 358 [Las Infantas];
371, 380 [Morales]; 358 [Pastrana].

43 Gilbert Chase, "Juan Navarro *Hispalensis*
and Juan Navarro *Gaditanus*," *Musical Quarterly*,
XXXI, 2 (April, 1945), 191.

44 The printer was Giacomo Tornieri.

45 Elústiza-Castrillo, *Antología musical*, p.
LXXIII.

46 Nicolás A. Solar-Quintes, "Morales en Sevilla y Marchena," *AM*, VIII (1953 [1954]), 35.

47 R. Mitjana, "La capilla de Música de la
Catedral de Málaga. Año de 1543 al año de . . .",
p. 45.

48 *Ibid.*, p. 62.

49 Ávila Cathedral, *A. C., 1565-1566-1567-1568*,
fol. 21.

50 *Ibid.*, fol. 22. Francisco Alexandre [= Alex-
andro] de la Serna was installed on June 24, 1548,
as singer in Toledo Cathedral, by direct order of
Cardinal Siliceo. His duties were to include both
the playing of organs and polyphonic singing. His
last years were spent at Seville. On September 13,
1581, the Sevillian chapter authorized a bread
allowance. At the moment he was boarding the
choirboys. Bartolomé Farfán took charge of them
on March 17, 1584. On December 19, 1586,
Alexandre de la Serna was recalled for temporary duty while the chapter looked about for a
permanent master. On February 14, 1587, the
chapter voted to continue him in the post and to
pay him the income of a half-prebend. This arrangement lasted until Vivanco took temporary
charge of the boys on February 29, 1588. On
July 20, 1594, the chapter commissioned him to
travel in search of new choirboys. As of September 26, 1594, the chapter voted to receive two
whom he had sent. On May 14, 1599, the chapter
decreed that he need no longer sing, march in

processions, nor even attend services, except when he felt able to do so, "on account of his age and illnesses."

51 Ávila, *A. C., 1565-1566-1567-1568*, fol. 35.

52 For details concerning Mosén Roque's career at Seville see above, page 152.

53 A direct invitation saved the cathedral the expense of *edictos*. See the capitular act at Salamanca dated September 27, 1566 (fol. 495ᵛ). The minutes of the *cabildo ordinario* held on this day state: "por quanto estaban informados de la abilidad e suficiencia de Juan Navarro maestro de capilla que esta en Avila e la prevenda de esta santa iglesia de maestro de capilla esta vaca que acordaban e acordaron que se fuese a llamar al dicho Juan Navarro y le proveen y proveyeron desde agora la dicha prevenda de maestro de capilla si aceptare de venir."

54 Ávila, *A. C., 1565-1566-1567-1568*, fol. 66.

55 *Ibid.*, fol. 66ᵛ.

56 *Ibid.*, fol. 67.

57 *Ibid.*, fol. 69ᵛ.

58 *Biblioteca de autores españoles*, XXXVII (Madrid: M. Rivadeneyra, 1855), pp. 2-3.

59 *Bibl. de aut. esp.*, XVIII (1851), p. 431, col. 2 [Relación tercera, Descanso quinto].

60 Elústiza-Castrillo, *Antología musical*, p. LXXIII.

61 Salamanca Cathedral, *A. C., 1568-1574*, fol. 6 (June 7, 1568).

62 *Ibid.*, fols. 47ᵛ-48: El diez y siete de agosto 1569 los dichos señores mandaron que el maestro de capilla fuese a Sevilla y viese los tiples que en aquellas iglesias hay y el que le paresciese mejor se le diesse la media racion quen la dicha iglesia esta vaca e tenia Martin de Herrera y el gasto que hiciese en yr se le pagase a costa del proveido en la dicha media racion e el demas gasto que hiciese en ir a Sevilla atento que abia de yr a ver a su padre que le hiciese a su costa.

63 Vicente Espinel, in *La casa de la memoria* [1591], fol. 47ᵛ, cited this singer as the cynosure of the age: Mas Martin de Herrera, que es del alma, / Al uno ecede, al otro lleva palma.

64 Salamanca, *A. C., 1568-1574*, fol. 53ᵛ.

65 Still other homonymous contemporaries must be distinguished from the composer. *Gadi-* *tanus* emigrated to Mexico, where he published *Quatuor passiones* in 1604 (105 leaves of monody). In 1580 the *capiscol* in Toledo Cathedral bore the name of Juan Navarra. A canon as well as cathedral precentor, he had visited Rome two or three years previously, had met Victoria, and had received from the latter a copy of the *Liber primus. Qui Missas, Psalmos, Magnificat . . . Aliaq. Complectitur* (published at Rome in 1576) for presentation to the Toledo chapter.

66 Salamanca, *A. C., 1568-1574*, fol. 106ᵛ.

67 *Ibid.*, fol. 126ᵛ.

68 *Ibid.*, fol. 132.

69 Further on Soto de Langa above at pages 326-328 (note 28).

70 *A. C., 1568-1574*, fol. 212: En Salamanca este dicho dia dos dias del mes de enero del dicho año de 1574 años estando juntos y congregados los illustres señores dean e cabildo de la dicha yglesia cathedral de Salamanca los dichos señores trataron del delito que la vispera de año de este año cometio estando en el choro en visperas el maestro de capilla contra Juan Sanchez capellan de la dicha iglesia e sochantre della en dalle un bofeton de que hizo grande escandolo en la dicha iglesia y choro e haviendo votado sobre ello parescio al cabildo que le debia de quitar de salario e partido que tenia e la prevenda de maestro de capilla de la dicha iglesia e ansi se la quitaron y mandaron no fuese mas avido por maestro de capilla de la dicha iglesia de aqui adelante e le borrasen de los libros de la iglesia. / Testigos / Pedro Sanchez / pertiguero de la dicha iglesia / e Francisco Maldonado de Toro / e yo el dicho notario secretario.

71 *Ibid.*, fol. 213ᵛ.

72 (1) *AM*, VIII (1953 [1954]), 25. (2) R. Mitjana, "La capilla de Música de la Catedral de Málaga. Año de 1543 al año de . . .," p. 54 (Nov. 5, 1554). (3) Vicente Espinel, *La casa de la memoria* [1591], fol. 47.

73 R. Casimiri, "Melchor Robledo, maestro a Saragozza: Juan Navarro, maestro ad Avila nel 1574," *Note d'archivio*, XI, 3-4 (July-Dec., 1934), 203-206.

74 Ávila Cathedral, *A. C., 1572-1573-1574-1575*, fol. 9ᵛ (Oct. 24, 1572).

75 Elústiza-Castrillo, *Antología musical*, p. LXXIV (line 31).

76 *Ibid.*, p. LXXIII (lines 7-8).

77 *Ibid.*, p. LXXIX.

78 *Ibid.*, pp. LXXIV-LXXV.

79 In *MME*, Vol. VIII, item 26 at page 53 of the "parte musical" is listed as anonymous. At pages *17* (item 35 = 26) and *29* (line 14) the same item is ascribed to Navarro. Cf. J. B. Trend, "Catalogue of the music in the Biblioteca Medinaceli, Madrid," *Revue hispanique*, LXXI (1927), p. 497, line 27.

80 Further concerning Husillos in Joseph Saenz de Aguirre's *Collectio maxima conciliorum omnium Hispaniae*, III (Rome: J. J. Komarek, 1694), p. 317: "Concilium Fusselense." Elústiza-Castrillo in their *Antología musical*, page LXXV, journeyed to an Alice-in-Wonderland "Fusel" in their search for a place name. But see Sta. Teresa de Jesús, *Obras*, ed. by P. Silverio de Santa Teresa, IX (Burgos: Tip. de "El Monte Carmelo," 1924), p. 185, n. 2: "D. Francisco Reinoso, *abad de Husillos en la catedral palentina . . .* conoció en Roma al general de la Compañía . . ." In Rome *ca.* 1580 Reinoso doubtless met both Soto and Victoria, as well as Aquaviva.

81 For the Latin original (though unfortunately in a faulty transcript) see Gaetano Gaspari, *Catalogo della Biblioteca del Liceo musicale di Bologna* (Bologna: Lib. Romagnoli dall'Acqua, 1892), II, 279-280.

82 By contrast, Guerrero in his Tone VIII setting of Psalm 131, *Memento Domine David*, composed all ten even verses polyphonically. Navarro's three psalms, 113, 131, 138 (and these only), are prefixed by the rubric *Cum tribus choris:* which means that the choral forces were divided into three groups—the first singing plainsong, the second polyphony, and the third again plainsong. *Cum tribus choris* does not in these instances mean "three polyphonic choirs."

83 Sebastián de Vivanco, *Liber Magnificarum* (Salamanca: Artus Taberniel, 1607), pp. 15-16.

84 A late fifteenth-century two-part setting of *Nobis natus* was copied at fol. 64ᵛ of Toledo Codex 25. The clumsy added parts (copied at fol. 65) are of late seventeenth- or early eighteenth-century facture. Theodor Kroyer in his unfortunate article "Zur Chiavetten-Frage," *Studien zur Musikgeschichte* (Vienna: Universal Edition, 1930), offered a transcription and facsimile (at pp. 114-115). In meas. 25, the last note in the tenor should have read B♭, not d. See the facsimile.

85 Another composer who acted on Navarro's cue was the Portuguese, Filipe de Magalhães. In

each of his eight even-verse *Cantica Beatissimae Virginis* (Lisbon: Laurens Craesbeck, 1636) he also devised canons at the interval of the tone-number.

86 Psalm 131, *Memento Domine David*, fols. 28ᵛ-30, is assigned *In secundis Vesperis*.

87 *MME*, VIII, *29*; *AM*, V, 153, 155-156.

88 Elústiza-Castrillo, *op. cit.*, pp. 124-129. As happens often in this anthology, wrong notes abound. See mm. 19_3, 41_2, 63_4, and 75-76 for obvious errors. Even if Navarro uses the "consonant" fourth at cadences he does not treat the unprepared fourth or seventh on other occasions as a consonance. Nor does he write consecutive octaves and fifths. He does make occasional use of both escaped- and changing-notes.

89 *Ibid.*, pp. 108-115. Again in this example, a number of wrong notes mar the composer's intentions. See mm. 9_2, 22_1, 35_3, 41_3, 44_3, 72_1, 87_2, 89_2. At meas. 92 the rhythm of cantus II must be corrected; and in meas. 94 the impossible leap of an augmented second in tenor II. Cf. *In passione positus*, no. 14 of the five-part motets in Guerrero's *Sacrae cantiones* (1555). In *pars 1* Guerrero sets the whole of the text divided by Navarro between *partes 1* and 2. For *pars 2*, Guerrero selects Jesus's words on the cross, *Deus meus*.

90 Wrong notes intrude at mm. 18_2, 22_1, and 52 of *Laboravi in gemitu* (pp. 119-123). Necessary ficta accidentals have been omitted at mm. 12_4, 13_{2-4}, 14_1, 18_4, 19_{1-2}, and 61_3. In the bass part at meas. 5, D (breve) must be supplied.

91 The "Borja" which appears as the seventh word on the title page of his 1602 Masses (*Liber primus missarum Alphonsi Lobo de Borja*) is his mother's name, not a place name. He was born at Osuna. Nor were there two composers named Alfonso [Alonso] Lobo. Both José Subirá, in his *Historia de la música española e hispanoamericana* (Barcelona: Salvat editores, 1953), pages 258, 433 (see *índice onomástico*, p. 989, for double listing), and Higinio Anglés, in his *Historia de la música española* (3d ed.; Barcelona: Editorial Labor, 1949), pages 376 and 403, leave such an impression. That Anglés in 1949 still thought there had been two Alonso Lobo's—one of whom served at Toledo, the other at Seville—is proved by his dating of the Toledo chapelmaster's death at 1601 and the Seville chapelmaster's death at 1617. The 1617 date was extracted from Simón de la Rosa y López, *Los seises de la Catedral de Sevilla* (1904), page 145. On page 144 of the same book, however, Rosa y López stated that Lobo returned to Seville after serving at Toledo.

Lobo enjoyed the esteem of Lope de Vega, who

eulogized him in *El peregrino en su patria* (published 1604; approbation 1603). See Lope de Vega, *Colección de las obras sueltas*, V (Madrid: Imp. de D. Antonio de Sancha, 1776), p. 346, lines 4-5.

92 Seville Cathedral, *Autos capitulares de 1538–1539*, fol. 20.

93 Gerónimo Gudiel, *Compendio de algunas historias de España* (Alcalá de Henares: I. Iñiguez de Lequerica, 1577), fol. 115 (musical ability of the Count of Ureña = Urueña).

94 *Ibid.*, fol. 116ᵛ: *dizen las horas canonicas con tanta deuocion y solennidad, como en la metropolitana de Seuilla.*

95 R. Mitjana, *Para música vamos* (Valencia: F. Sempere y Cia, 1909), p. 223, n. 1. See also Cristóbal Pérez Pastor, *Bibliografía madrileña* (Madrid: Tip. de la "Rev. de Archivos, Bibliotecas y Museos," 1906), Vol. II, p. 39, col. 2, line 36.

96 Seville Cathedral, *Libro de Autos Capitulares de los años de 1590-1591*, fol. 69ᵛ.

97 *Ibid.*, fol. 72.

98 *Ibid.*, fol. 87.

99 Felipe Rubio Piqueras, *Música y músicos toledanos* (Toledo: J. Peláez, 1923), p. 53.
Added light is thrown on Lobo's Toledan career in a "Memorial del estilo que se ha de guardar en esta santa iglesia de Toledo en todas las fiestas del año que se celebran con solennidad de canto de organo" preserved in the Barbieri collection at the Biblioteca Nacional in Madrid. This *memorial*, dated 1604, bears directly on his activities at Toledo, in that it describes the method of celebrating the principal feasts of the year. Since this memorial is too prolix to translate in full, it is here summarized. (1) Polyphony is to be sung on 140 days in the year. (2) Sixty-seven of these will be the calendar days, January 1, 6, 18, 20, 23, 24; February 2, 3, 12; March 1, 19, 25; April 25, 26; May 3, 6, 8; June 11, 24, 29; July 2, 16, 22, 25, 26; August 1, 4, 5, 6, 10, 12, 15, 20, 22, 24, 28, 29; September 8, 14, 21, 29, 30; October 4, 7, 18, 23, 28, 30; November 1, 2, 15, 18, 21, 25, 30; December 6, 8, 9, 15, 18, 19, 20, 21, 25, 26, 27, 28. (3) Fifty-two will be Sundays of the year. (4) Twenty will be the Saturdays in Advent, Rogation Days, the last four days in Holy Week, Ascension and the day following, Saturday before Pentecost, Whitmonday, Wednesday after Pentecost, Corpus Christi, and its Octave. Samples of the specific directions for such principal occasions as Christmas vespers and the last four day of Holy Week are here offered:

"At first vespers (*In Nativitate Domini*) the organ shall accompany the singing of the stanzas beginning *Veni, redemptor gentium* which come at the end of the book of *Ave maris stella* settings and other hymns by Morales." "On Wednesday in Holy Week, the first Lamentation is to be Morales's polyphonic setting. The Miserere shall be sung antiphonally, one choir at the high altar, another in the tribunes of the *coro del arzobispo*. One choir shall consist of the boys and a tenor." "On Maundy Thursday at High Mass the introit shall be sung in a contrapuntal setting, the Kyrie, Gloria, Credo, and Sanctus polyphonically, the Agnus in plainchant." "On Good Friday the Passion shall be sung as a solo [on Palm Sunday, the *turba* parts were sung polyphonically by a complete choir, and on Tuesday and Wednesday by a trio]. The first Lamentation shall be sung polyphonically." "On Holy Saturday the Gloria shall be sung in plainchant with counterpoint above. The same for the Alleluia. At Vespers the same for Psalm 150. The Magnificat must be in Tone VIII, odd-verses plainchanted, even- sung polyphonically. At solemn compline in the evening, two choirs shall sit on the benches of the cope-bearers and two bands of instrumentalists shall play. The portable organ shall be lowered into the *coro* to accompany the singers, who shall sing solos in their order of seniority, with organ and, if desired, instrumental support. Psalm 133 shall be sung in *fabordón*, Tone VIII." On Easter, the *prosa* "must be the one composed by Morales."
This 1604 *memorial* reveals far more concerning Alonso Lobo's daily duties in Toledo Cathedral, the character of the repertory, and the choral and instrumental resources at his command, than the perfunctory notices that tell of his trips or of the music books that he bought.

100 Four of these 1602 motets were reprinted in Eslava's *Lira sacro-hispana*, I, i: *Versa est in luctum* (a 6), *Credo quod redemptor* (a 4), *Vivo ego* (a 4), *Ave Maria* (a 8). *Versa est in luctum* was again reprinted, though with numerous errors, in *Tesoro sacro-musical*, XXII, 2 (March-April, 1955), 22-28.

101 See Cristóbal Pérez Pastor, *Bibliografía madrileña*, II (1906), p. 39, col. 2; III (1907); p. 415, col. 2; for details concerning the impression. Each three leaves were to cost one real. Since the total number of leaves (130 copies of 137 leaves each) reached 17,810, the delivery price amounted to 5,936⅔ reales. The original contract specified that only two hours were to be allowed for proof corrections on each leaf. A surcharge was to be levied for any extra time. Evidently Lobo submitted such excellent copy that surcharges were not necessary. He paid a first instalment of 2,000 reales to "start the work" on August 30, 1602. By the succeeding February 28 the job was finished, and the books ready for delivery. Juan Flamenco signed a receipt for full payment on March 4, 1603 (in Julio Junti's name).

102 Details concerning Rogier imprint in Pérez Pastor, *op. cit.*, Vol. I (1891), p. 320 (item 602). See also Manuel Joaquim, *Vinte livros de música polifónica do Paço Ducal de Vila Viçosa* (Lisbon: Ramos, Afonso & Moita, Lda., 1953), pp. 21–28. For Rogier's parody sources see *Primeira parte do Index da Livraria de Musica do Muyto Alto, e Poderoso Rey Dom Ioão o IV* (ed. by Joaquim de Vasconcelos), p. 373. *Inclyta styrps Jesse*, a 4, is modeled after Clemens non Papa; *Dirige gressus meos*, a 5, after Crecquillon; *Ego sum qui sum*, a 6, after Gombert; *Inclina Domine*, a 6, after Morales.

103 Pedrell, *HSMS*, VIII, xvi.

104 Pedrell, *Tomás Luis de Victoria* (Valencia: Manuel Villar, 1919), p. 168.

105 For reproduction, see Anglés, *La música española desde la edad media*, facsimile 42. Ildephonsus is the Latin form of Lobo's own Christian name, Alfonso. Significantly, Lobo's collection starts with the Marian mass *Beata Dei genitrix*.

106 Seville, *Quadernos de Autos Capitulares Antiguos. Años de 1599. 1600. 1601. 1602. 1603. 1604. 1605. 1606.*, fol. 174 (margin).

107 *Ibid.*, fol. 178.

108 *Ibid.*, fol. 224.

109 *Ibid.*, fol. 247ᵛ.

110 Rosa y López, *op. cit.*, p. 145.

111 The hymn a 4 for St. Isidore's feast at folios 1ᵛ-5 divides into two *partes:* (1) *Dulce facundi sunt hoc leporis;* (2) *Pater cleri populique*. During each *pars*, Lobo quotes in his cantus the same plainsong (with small variants). Fragments of this plainsong occasionally filter into ATB. Because Isidore belongs so peculiarly to Sevillian hagiology, the plainsong may itself mount to Visigothic antiquity. The initium reads: [d e] c d [d a] a [cⁱ a] g . . . d. The hymn a 4 for St. Hermenegild, on the other hand, consists of a single *pars: Carceris squalor nec acerba patris*. Beginning with paired imitation, this mixolydian hymn supports a cantus that moves more slowly than the other parts. A derivation from plainsong, however, is more difficult to establish—there being no second *pars* in which an alternate paraphrase can be viewed. The cantus repeats notes of minim (= crotchet) value (mm. 10, 15, 17); and lacks ligatures. By

way of contrast, ten such are to be seen in the cantus of St. Isidore's hymn (mm. 3-4, 6, 14, 19-20, 25, 32-33, 38, 40, 41-42, 54-55).

The local character of both hymns, so far as text is concerned, can be proved. Ulysse Chevalier in his *Repertorium hymnologicum* (Louvain: Imp. Polleunis & Ceuterick, 1892-1897) listed neither text. Nor were they listed in Faustino Arévalo's *Hymnodia hispanica* (Rome: E. Typ. Salamoniana, 1786).

112 Rosa y López, *op. cit.*, p. 354.

113 Further details concerning this manuscript above at pages 126-127 (note 270).

114 Antonio Soler, *Llave de la modulacion, y antiguedades de la musica* (Madrid: Joachin Ibarra, 1762), pp. *39-40* (unnumbered) in the introduction. Still earlier in the eighteenth century, Joseph de Torres, when editing Francisco Montanos's *Arte de canto llano* (Madrid: Miguel de Rezola, 1728), pages 154-155 and 158-159, had reprinted two Benedictus qui venit movements a 3 by Lobo. Obviously Alonso Lobo was no "forgotten" composer, exhumed merely for antiquarians to marvel at, when Soler in 1762 transcribed two of his canons. At least two of Lobo's masses, *Petre ego pro te rogavi* a 4, and *O Rex gloriae*, also a 4, continued to be sung in the royal chapel as late as the reign of Charles III. See José García Marcellan, *Catálogo del Archivo de Música del Palacio Nacional* (Madrid: Gráficas Reunidas, 1938), p. 92. The manuscript parts included an extra one for *fagot* (= bassoon).

115 Further details concerning Seville Cathedral MS 110 above at pages 179, 190, 264, 273.

116 The tenor in *O Rex gloriae* sings a forward-and-backward canon. See the 1602 imprint, folio 115ᵛ. Cf. also the Crucifixus of the *Prudentes Virgines* Mass, folio 55ᵛ.

117 See the present author's "Sixteenth- and Seventeenth-Century Resources in Mexico" (part II), *Fontes artis musicae*, 1955/1, pp. 11-15.

118 Cf. *Enciclopedia universal ilustrada* (Barcelona: Hijos de J. Espasa, n.d.), XXX, 1246-1247; and VI [Apéndice], 1249. Both articles must be impugned. Concerning Duarte Lobo see Manuel Joaquim, *op. cit.*, pp. 57-59. The birthyear given for Duarte Lobo in *Grove's Dictionary*, 5th ed., V, 351 (like that given for Antonio de Cabezón), must be revised. A baptismal certificate was issued at Alcáçovas (Portugal) on September 19, 1575 (not 1565), for a homonymous Duarte Lobo.

119 *Liber primus missarum Alphonsi Lobo de Borja*, fols. 2ᵛ-3.

120 Mateo Flecha, *Las Ensaladas*, ed. by H. Anglés (Barcelona: Biblioteca Central, 1955), fol. 123ᵛ.

121 Ávila Cathedral, *A.C., 1587-1588-1589*, fol. 46ᵛ.

122 *Ibid.*, fol. 59. Vivanco's "contract" with the cathedral allowed him thirty days "de Requien" (vacation) each year, besides an extra day every two months. According to the rules of residence he could not leave Ávila without the express permission of the chapter. He was allowed neither voice nor vote in chapter meetings. See *A. C., 1587-1588-1589*, fol. 53ᵛ.

123 Seville, *A. C., 1586-1587*, fol. 122ᵛ.

124 Seville, *Quadernos de Autos Capitulares Antiguos. 1586. Desde Abril 1587*, fol. 165.

125 Ávila, *A. C., 1587-1588-1589*, fols. 59ᵛ-60.

126 *Ibid.*, fol. 84.

127 Seville, *A. C., 1588-1589*, fol. 7ᵛ.

128 *Ibid.*, fol. 8.

129 *Ibid.*, fol. 10.

130 Enrique Esperabé Arteaga, *Historia de la Universidad de Salamanca* (Salamanca: Imp. y lib. de Francisco Nuñez, 1917), II, 512. See also Vol. II, p. 457. Data concerning Roque Martínez, Vivanco's substitute (Jan. 9, 1621) and successor (Dec. 9, 1622), at Vol. II, p. 488. Martínez, a native of Salamanca, served as cathedral organist before his university appointments. He was incorporated M. A. in 1623.

131 Facsimile of the engraving (not the entire page) in *A History of The Hispanic Society of America . . . 1904-1954* (New York: 1954), p. 393 (no. 295).

132 On the connotations of the term "morning professor" at Salamanca, see Caro Lynn, *A College Professor of the Renaissance* (Chicago: University of Chicago Press, 1937), page 89. Vivanco's chair was a *cathedra de propriedad*.

133 Concerning the printer Artus Taberniel [= Tavernier], see Académie royale des sciences, des lettres et des beaux-arts de Belgique, *Biographie nationale* (Brussels: Émile Bruylant, 1928-1929), XXIV, ii, 417. Probably the son of Aimé Tavernier, Artus Taberniel published his first book at Antwerp *ca.* 1580—*Premier livre des Hymnes mis en vers français.* At Salamanca he used a printer's device that included the anagram *Arte*

natus liber. The earliest of his Salamanca imprints in possession of The Hispanic Society, New York, is dated 1603; the latest 1608. At Salamanca he was official university printer. He cannot have survived 1610—his widow in that year already publishing a book in her own right. See Clara Louise Penney, *List of books printed 1601-1700 in the library of The Hispanic Society of America* (New York City: The Hispanic Society, 1938), pages 558-559 (Alonso de Salazar, *Fiestas que hizo . . .*) and 832. From 1630 to 1632, and possibly longer, Hyacinthe [= Jacinto] Tabernier, son of Artus Taberniel, was official printer for Salamanca University.

134 Illing's chronological list occurs as an appendix to his *Zur Technik der Magnificat-Komposition des 16. Jahrhunderts* (Wolfenbüttel: Georg Kallmeyer, 1936).

135 Mrs. Walter Carr does recite Vivanco's name in the table of contents she gives for Hilarión Eslava's *Lira sacro-hispana*. See *Grove's Dictionary*, 5th ed., Vol. II, p. 970, col. 1 (17th cent., i, I). Unfortunately, she did not take time to collate her "table" with the actual contents of Eslava's Tomo I, serie 1a, siglo XVII. In Eslava's own table of contents (at page III of his volume) he itemizes a motet, *O Domine*, as Vivanco's: giving 121 as its page number. But upon turning to page 121 the reader discovers not the promised motet, *O Domine*, by Vivanco; but rather the *Vivo ego* by Lobo which has already been printed at pages 37-39 in the same volume. Of course, it is extremely disillusioning to find that Eslava could have been so lax as to send forth a volume in which on pages 37-39 he printed *Vivo ego* as by Lobo and at pages 121-124 as by Vivanco. (The *Vivo ego* motet is indeed Lobo's, on evidence of the 1602 imprint.)

136 Pedrell, *Tomás Luis de Victoria* (Valencia: 1919), pp. 153-155.

137 *Festschrift zum 50. Geburtstag* (Munich: Ferdinand Zierfuss, 1918), p. 138.

138 The Valdés Codex at Mexico City contains this mass at folios 27ᵛ-36. Above the cantus at folio 27ᵛ one reads *Missa. Ductus est Iesus. Quatuor vocibus.* and above the altus at folio 28 *Ioannis Exquivel*. Immediately preceding the *Ductus est* Mass come Palestrina's *Quem dicunt homines* and *Già fu chi m'ebbe cara* Masses (fols. 5ᵛ-18, 18ᵛ-27). Following the *Ductus est* are copied Alfonso Lobo's *Petre ego pro te rogavi* (fols. 36ᵛ-46) and *O Rex gloriae* (fols. 46ᵛ-56). Then at folios 56ᵛ-65 intervenes Palestrina's *Aeterna Christi munera* (fols. 56ᵛ-65) followed by *Ave Regina coelorum* (fols. 86ᵛ-101). The Valdés Codex also contains the only two surviving part songs with

Nahuatl texts (fols. 121ᵛ-123). Nahuatl was the language spoken by the Aztecs. The transfusion of so much sixteenth-century art-music into Aztec veins cannot but seem startling. Whatever the origin of the codex, the presence of these two Nahuatl hymns assures us that at one time the manuscript was used by singers whose native language was Nahuatl.

139 *Festschrift* (Sandberger), p. 164.

140 *DML*, I, 843 (col. 1). *Grove's Dictionary* (5th ed.), II, 973.

141 See above, note 133.

142 Superius II sings a mensuralized version of the plainsong versicle that belongs to the Office of the Dead, *Requiescant in pace*. This is repeated six times—three times beginning on a, another three on d¹ (half-step instead of whole step between first two notes of the mensuralized chant). Such an ostinato at once reminds us of Morales. Moreover, the motet harks back a century because of its polytextuality.

143 In *AM*, Vol. V (1950), pp. 149-151, Rubio first announced discovery at Plasencia Cathedral of the manuscript source—a paper volume of 128 leaves, copied in 1776. Only two of the sixty-four motets in this MS 1 at Plasencia Cathedral are by composers other than Esquivel. At folios 9ᵛ-11 will be found Fray Manuel de León's *Domine, Jesu Christe, a 4;* at 39ᵛ-41, Victoria's *Vere languores.* Fray Manuel de León, born at Segovia toward the end of the sixteenth century, took the Jeronymite habit at El Escorial on December 4, 1623. He died in the same monastery on August 23, 1632. Several works of his are conserved at El Escorial, where for several years he was chapelmaster. See *La Ciudad de Dios,* Vol. CLXIII, no. 1, pp. 92-93. With the exception of the two motets in the 1608 Esquivel imprint which these replace, and some seven others, the manuscript collection duplicates the printed book. The copyist has even followed the precise order of the 1608 Salamanca imprint. His nos. 7 and 8 reverse Esquivel's order. Between his nos. 8 and 9, 36 and 37, 40 and 41, 42 and 43, and 63 and 64, he has omitted motets to be found in Esquivel's printed collection. He has also excluded the last two motets ("for the dead") found in the printed collection. Otherwise the correspondence between MS 1 at Plasencia and the 1608 imprint is exact; even the feast to which each motet is assigned concords. However, in one instance the copyist has forgotten to copy the title of the feast. His no. 12 should have been headed with "In f. visitationis B. M. V."

Since the contents of MS 1 at Plasencia and of the 1608 imprint match so well, all that is needed here by way of a bibliographical addendum is a list of those motets in the imprint that are excluded from the manuscript. The numbers in parentheses in this list indicate the place in the table of contents for the manuscript (*AM*, V, 149-151) where an insertion or replacement should be made. (5) "In f. S. Crucis": *O crux benedicta,* a 4; (8a) "In f. SS. Trinitatis": *Duo seraphin,* a 6; (19) "In nativitate B.M.V.": *Sancta Maria,* a 8; (36a) "In f. angeli custodis": *Sancti angeli,* a 6; (40a) "In f. plurimorum martyrum": *Istorum est,* a 4; (42a) "Commune confess. pontif.": *Sacerdos et pontifex,* a 4; (63a) "In coena Domini": *Christus factus est,* a 4; (64a) "Pro defunctis": *Delicta iuuentutis,* a 4; (64b) "Pro defunctis": *In paradisum,* a 6. The total number of items in Esquivel's 1608 imprint can be presumed to have been seventy-one. The 1776 copyist at Plasencia excluded or replaced all six- and eight-part motets (items 8a, 19, 36a, 64b), besides alternate motets for the same feast (items 40a, 42a).

144 MS 2 at Plasencia (dated 1784) contains at fols. 106ᵛ-109 two motets by Victoria: *Resplenduit facies eius,* a 5 (canon at unison between cantus I and II); and *Doctor bonus,* a 4. Nothing by Morales seems to have been preserved, despite his term as chapelmaster. Guerrero is heavily represented: in manuscript and also by virtue of his 1582 printed Masses and 1584 *Liber vesperarum.* See *AM*, V, 149-168.

145 Compositions by Victoria in choirbooks 10, 12, 15, and 16 at Vila Viçosa.

146 On the other hand, Pedrell did not give Asenjo Barbieri due credit for the hundreds of notes now in the Barbieri collection at the Madrid Biblioteca Nacional which he copied verbatim into this selfsame dictionary. José Subirá, in his article "Manuscritos de Barbieri existentes en la Biblioteca Nacional" for *Las Ciencias,* Vol. III, no. 2 (Madrid: C. Bermejo, 1936), exposed some of the pilfering that has disgraced users of these laboriously assembled notes; but forbore mentioning Pedrell by name.

147 Pedrell, *Diccionario,* p. 594, col. 1.

148 *Ibid.,* p. 594, n. 1.

149 *Bullarium Magnum Romanum,* X (Turin: Sebastiano Franco, 1865), pp. 788-790 ("Cum in Ecclesia"); XI (1867), pp. 88-90 ("Cum sanctissimum").

150 At Ávila (*A. C., 1572-1575,* fol. 247), for instance, on December 23, 1575, the chapter ordered that two books of polyphonic music—one by Josquin—be repaired so that his music could still be sung: *que adereço dos libros de canto de organo uno de Jusquin.* Although Des Prez remained the most popular intermural composer, Morales remained the intramural composer most frequently copied—and presumably most popular. As late as March 20, 1586—sixty-five years after Josquin's death—the Sevillian cathedral chapter decided to undergo the expense of having his music copied anew for choir use. Equally significant is the fact that the Sevillian chapter on January 26, 1601—forty-eight years after Morales's death—decided to underwrite the high cost of transcribing Morales's works anew—this time *en pergamino* (on vellum). See Seville Cathedral, *Libros de autos capitulares de los años de 1599-1600-1601-1602,* fol. 62$^\mathrm{v}$.

151 Manuscript 14018.19 at the Biblioteca Nacional (Madrid) is a "Consulta del bureo sobre lo de los menestriles de su magestad" dated July 26, 1589. *Vajones y cornetas* (bassoons and cornetts) were, according to this *consulta,* entitled to extra pay for their services in the royal chapel "on very solemn days." A *Memoria de los ministriles de Su Magestad* dated May 13, 1592, reveals

that the number of royal instrumentalists had swollen on that date to twenty-two. Seven of the veterans wanted the newcomers dismissed so that their own pay might be increased. Information from such sources as these proves that in the royal chapel, as elsewhere, instrumental accompaniments and interludes were the rule on solemn days in the church calendar—even though Philip's own tastes inclined toward liturgical austerity.

152 *Collection complète des mémoires relatifs a l'histoire de France,* ed. by M. Petitot (Paris: Foucault, Librairie, 1823), p. 117: "Le matin estant venu, dom Jean nous fit ouïr une messe à la façon d'Espagne, avec musique, violons et cornets."

153 Michel Brenet, "Notes sur l'introduction des instruments dans l'églises de France," *Riemann-Festschrift* (Leipzig: Max Hesses Verlag, 1909), p. 283. She records as an exceptional event a Christmas Mass celebrated at Rouen in 1596 "en musique, cornetz, bucines et autres instruments musicaux, par les chantres de la chapelle du Roi avec ceulx de l'église et enfans de choeur."

III Tomás Luis de Victoria (ca. 1548-1611)

III Tomás Luis de Victoria (ca. 1548-1611)

Family Connections   Whereas the parentage of Morales must be conjectured, and nothing beyond the names of Guerrero's parents, together with his father's occupation, is at present known, Victoria's family connections[1] can be traced with gratifying fullness. The names of both paternal grandparents have been established, as well as the grandfather's occupation. The names of his father and mother are likewise known, as are also the locales in which each was born and the exact date of his father's death. The names of his father's five brothers and sisters are known. The same can be said of his own ten brothers and sisters, and of his eldest brother's and sister's children. Indeed, so rich a record of his family connections has come to light in recent years that a a genealogical tree can be drawn. Such a tree is the more necessary because in the composer's family, as in most Spanish families, the repetition of names in different generations can puzzle and confuse the unwary Anglo-Saxon reader. Throughout the next several pages, the reader is therefore advised to refer constantly to the accompanying family chart.

In the accompanying tree, the composer's name is italicized. To elucidate his family connections as precisely as possible, each individual of whom anything of interest is known will be mentioned in this order: grandfather; father, uncles; brothers and sisters (in chronological sequence).

Hernán Luis Dávila [= de Ávila] is first heard of at Ávila in 1509. In that year he followed the trade of tailor. Later he began to buy and sell wool; then wheat, barley, salt, and oxen. He made his will in 1545. In part, the will read: "I hereby depose, inasmuch as I am much beholden and obligated to Francisco Luis, my eldest and my legitimate son, both on account of his numerous and faithful services, past, present, and anticipated, and for many other just causes and reasons thereunto moving me, that I have intended and do intend to enrich him with a third of all my property, real and corporal, and a third of my credits outstanding and receivable. And, besides the third of my property, I do also bestow upon my son, Francisco Luis, the houses that I purchased of

GENEALOGICAL CHART

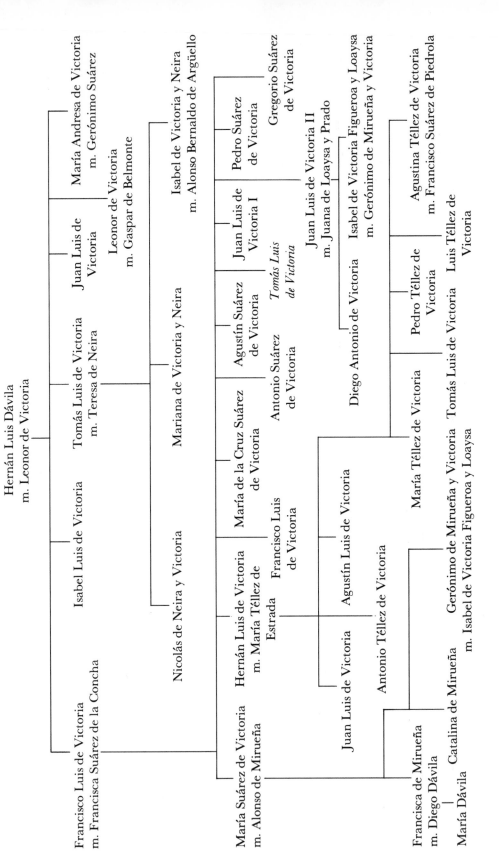

Alonso de Cogollos, former inhabitant of this city, in which dwellings I now live and which are situated on Caballeros Street."[2]

Francisco Luis de Victoria, eldest in a family of six children, married Francisca Suárez de la Concha of Segovia in 1540. To this couple were born eleven children, ten of whom reached maturity. Francisco Luis died prematurely on August 29, 1557.

Tomás Luis de Victoria, uncle of the composer (who was possibly named after him), obtained the degree of *licenciado*. He settled at the erstwhile capital, Valladolid (70 miles north of Ávila), and there practiced law before the Real Chancilleria (royal chancery). He seems to have married twice—his eldest son (not shown on the chart) who bore the name of Gerónimo de Victoria[3] having been born *ca.* 1545. On December 14, 1565, Philip II conceded to "Maestro Tomé de Victoria" an annual pension of 45,000 maravedís, chargeable against fees due the crown for the passage of cattle from one province to another. This pension continued to be paid his son and surviving heir Nicolás de Neira y Victoria[4] as late as 1620: so testifies a receipt signed April 23, 1624, at Madrid. Formerly, this royal pension was thought to have been conceded to the composer himself, but Casimiri in 1934 demonstrated irrefutably that it had been granted to the composer's namesake uncle.[5] As for his younger children, Isabel de Victoria y Neira married an important individual, Alonso Bernaldo de Argüello, *regidor perpetuo* (permanent alderman) of Valladolid. In 1575 or thereabouts his wife, Teresa de Neira, died, whereupon he took holy orders in the diocese of Ávila. In the Ávila Cathedral *Actas Capitulares* for 1576-1577 will be found notices showing that although still residing at Valladolid (where he frequently represented the cathedral in legal disputes carried before the royal chancery) he was at the end of 1577 elevated to a canonry in Ávila Cathedral. As a widower he not only took orders, just as did, for instance, Francisco de Borja, third Jesuit general—but also like Borja he rose immediately to a responsible position in the church. Juan Luis de Victoria, his next younger brother, acted as his proxy on Friday, December 27, 1577, when the Ávila chapter formally made him a cathedral canon. See folios 208[V] and 211 of the Ávila capitular acts for 1576-1577.

Juan Luis de Victoria, fourth in the family of the composer's father, took priest's orders in Ávila diocese when still a youth. He it was who acted as guardian of the brood of ten surviving children after the composer's father died prematurely on August 29, 1557. Fortunately he lived nearby, on the same Caballeros Street (in a house bequeathed by the head of the clan, Hernán Luis Dávila). He frequently intervened in the composer's behalf—even after the latter's departure for Rome. It was he, for instance, who on April 15, 1573, and again on January 9 and September 6, 1577,[6] presented to the Ávila cathedral chapter in the composer's behalf the *Motecta* of 1572 and the *Liber Primus. Qui Missas, Psalmos, Magnificat . . . Aliaque Complectitur* of 1576.

The composer's eldest sister married Alonso de Mirueña. This couple reared at least three children. One of these, Francisca de Mirueña, and her daughter, María Dávila, received exquisite praise in a will dated September 1, 1610.[7] The kindly disposition of Francisca de Mirueña must have exceeded all usual bounds if María de la Cruz Suárez de Victoria in 1610 could exclaim upon her desire to leave Francisca 2,000 ducats. One of the other children, Gerónimo de Mirueña y Victoria, became a licenciado, practiced law, and rose to considerable eminence. He was the only member of the immediate family to witness the composer's last will and testament in August, 1611. He married his cousin Isabel de Victoria Figueroa y Loaysa, niece and goddaughter of the composer. From their marriage proceeded illustrious issue, a genealogical tree for which is (or was) preserved in the Archivo Histórico Nacional, Sección de Calatrava, number 2818.[8]

Hernán Luis de Victoria, eldest of the composer's brothers, was born in 1542; and was therefore only fifteen at the time of the father's untimely death. Juan Luis, who assumed the guardianship, later praised the lad highly for turning over to the widowed mother all income from an entailed inheritance— until such time as the younger members could fend for themselves.[9] The fact that uncle Juan Luis could so laud Hernán Luis suggests that such self-sacrifice was rare. In honor of his uncle, Hernán Luis in turn named his first child Juan Luis. The latter took the degree of licenciado;[10] and as eldest son of the eldest son of the eldest son of Hernán Luis Dávila, founder of the family fortunes, inherited the entailed bequest. The other children in this fourth generation included Agustín Luis de Victoria, who became a priest; María Téllez de Victoria, who became a nun at Santa Catalina in Ávila; Tomás Luis de Victoria, who may perhaps have been the priest of this name who at Rome in 1603 joined with his nephew in the early work of the Piarists;[11] and, last in a family of eight children, Agustina Téllez de Victoria, whom María de la Cruz Suárez de Victoria (composer's sister) made her universal legatee in her will of September 1, 1610.[12]

Francisco Luis de Victoria, third in the composer's immediate family, emigrated "to the Indies"—probably to Peru. He must not be confused, however, with the homonymous Dominican friar who became bishop of Tucumán. See Robert Levillier, *Gobernacíon del Tucumán* (Madrid: Juan Pueyo, 1920), page 178 and *passim*.

María de la Cruz Suárez de Victoria, born *ca.* 1544, seems to have remained a spinster. She made Valladolid her home and resided there as late as 1601.[13] On November 13, 1603, the composer ceded to her certain rents in the diocese of León.[14] In her will, signed at Madrid on September 1, 1610, she still called herself a resident of Valladolid. Her major bequest was a demonstrative legacy to her niece Isabel de Victoria Figueroa y Loaysa (b. 1591). She again confirmed this bequest to her niece on March 13, 1611. On this date her brother the composer signed the confirmation in her behalf—she being at the point of death

and too weak to sign. In the will of September 1, 1610, she bequeathed to
her brother the composer some white lace pillows and embroidered towels. She
also named him one of her executors. Her will, which Pedrell printed in
Tomás Luis de Victoria (Valencia: Manuel Villar, 1918) at pages 193-200, itemizes
bequests to fifteen relatives, not all of whom can be listed in the family tree,
because each is not described at sufficient length to assure his or her identity.
In addition, she requested that María Herraz, a domestic in the employ of
her brother the composer, be given a small gift by her executors.[15] Her major
bequest—that of the demonstrative legacy to her niece—consisted of an annual
income of 32,812 maravedís. The niece was to enjoy this annual income until
death, even if she became a nun. If the niece married, the income was to
pass to the children. If she had none, it was to be divided upon the niece's death
between the following two relatives—Juan Luis, son of Hernán Luis, and
Gerónimo de Mirueña, son of María Suárez. This annual income, deriving from
duty levied on merchandise passing through inland ports of entry into Portugal,
had been purchased from the crown for a fixed sum in the first year of the
reign of Philip III. Her uncle the licenciado was doubtless the one who advised
her to make so wise an investment. Or he may have himself bequeathed it
to her if he died *ca.* 1599.

Antonio Suárez de Victoria entered commerce and with his younger brother,
Juan Luis de Victoria (II) opened a bank in 1575 at Medina del Campo, 50
miles north of Ávila. Juan López Ossorio's "Principio, grandezas y caida
de la noble villa de Medina del Campo," a manuscript account written *ca.*
1630 and printed in Ildefonso Rodríguez y Fernández's *Historia de Medina del
Campo* (Madrid: 1903), contains an interesting description of these two brothers'
banking activities. Translated, the account runs somewhat as follows: "Seeing
that the realm was prospering and that creditors were able to pay promptly,
Antonio Juárez [= Suárez] de Victoria and his brother Juan Luis de Victoria
—men of great prudence and with lifelong experience in business matters
(both in these kingdoms and elsewhere), men as it were born for such financial
enterprises because of their extremely sympathetic and accommodating
disposition toward persons in need of credit—opened a new bank [in Medina del
Campo] during 1575. Their business prospered greatly until the decree of 1596
which required the closing of money exchanges and the shutting of a number of
banks, especially those run by Spaniards." After the closing of their bank in
1596, Antonio Suárez moved 20 miles north to Valladolid. On November 23,
1604, he collected in his composer brother's behalf the sum of 100 ducats
bestowed by Archduke Albert of the Netherlands[16] (son of the deceased Empress
María, former cardinal archbishop of Toledo, and dedicatee of Victoria's 1592
book of Masses). He was still alive in 1610, when María de la Cruz Suárez
de Victoria made her will. In it she left him a small rug for his bedroom and
some yellow pillows.

Agustín Suárez de Victoria, born *ca.* 1546, studied at Salamanca, there earning a doctorate in sacred sciences. He became a priest, served Jorge de Almeida, the archbishop of Lisbon (1570-1585) who espoused the cause of Philip II, and after Almeida's death he became a personal chaplain to the Dowager Empress María at Madrid.[17] From at least 1599 (and probably much earlier) until 1603 the composer and his elder brother were thus in daily contact.[18] The doctor's honorific titles included *abad de Toro*—Toro being an ancient town 20 miles east of Zamora. María de la Cruz left him a silver image of the fifth sorrow of Our Lady in her will of 1610.

The composer—next in the family line after Agustín—was followed by a brother, Juan Luis de Victoria, who died as an infant. The following child was given the same name. Juan Luis II can therefore not have been born before 1550. As was mentioned above, he became a businessman, and in 1575 opened a bank in partnership with his elder brother Antonio at Medina del Campo. He spent most of his time in Madrid, however, after 1590. The composer became godfather to his daughter Isabel de Victoria Figueroa y Loaysa at a baptismal ceremony in San Ginés Church, Madrid, on March 4, 1591.[19] The parents were listed as parishioners of the same church. On February 17, 1596, Juan Luis (acting as agent for his brother the composer) signed an authorization to collect the large sum of 315,000 maravedís, due his brother from various benefices.[20] Juan Luis executed his will at Madrid on August 4, 1599. He died soon thereafter. In it he called himself an inhabitant of the small village of Sanchidrián, 15 miles north-northeast of Ávila, but a resident of Madrid.[21] Sanchidrián, though certainly not the birthplace of the composer, nor of any of his brothers and sisters, seems to have been the village in which their youngest aunt, Maria Andresa, settled with her husband Gerónimo Suárez: or at least Doña Francisca Nuñez Suárez, the composer's cousin, was living there in 1610 when María de la Cruz, the composer's sister, made her will.[22] Juan Luis at his death in 1599 was survived not only by his eight-year-old daughter, of whom the composer had become godfather in 1591; but also by a son, Diego Antonio, who was soon thereafter to take the Augustinian habit. María de la Cruz excluded this son from her will "because he was a man, and it was not needful." She remembered the daughter, Isabel de Victoria Figueroa y Loaysa; because without a dowry doubtless it would have been difficult for Isabel even to enter a convent. María de la Cruz's memory of her own father's untimely death in 1557 (and the hardships resulting thereby) probably excited her sympathy for Isabel, orphaned at an even earlier age.

Gregorio Suárez de Victoria, the composer's cadet brother, cannot have been older than five when their father died in August, 1557. He spent his career in the service of the "Ilustre Señor Secretario, Saganta" (Crown secretary).[23]

Beginnings at Ávila Born *ca.* 1548, the seventh child of Francisco Luis de Victoria and Francisca Suárez de la Concha, the composer was nine when his father died on August 29, 1557. His uncle Juan Luis thenceforth served as guardian. Because his elder brother financially assisted their widowed mother with the fruits of an inheritance from their paternal grandfather, the lot of the younger brothers and sisters was made more bearable in the years immediately following their father's death. In 1558 or thereabouts the composer became a choirboy in Ávila Cathedral. The proof of his having been thus reared in Ávila Cathedral is to be found in a capitular act dated January 9, 1577.[24] On that day his uncle Juan Luis presented to the cathedral chapter Victoria's *Liber Primus* published at Venice in 1576, simultaneously reminding them that the composer had been reared in Ávila Cathedral.

The young choirboy—composer-to-be—would have found the aging Gerónimo de Espinar chapelmaster, if he began to sing in 1558. Espinar's activities from 1550 until 1558 (in which latter year he died) can be exemplified in the following notations from the Ávila capitular acts. On March 3, 1550, Espinar was admonished to give daily lessons in counterpoint and harmony.[25] On March 26, 1550, he was authorized to pay three ducats for Morales's "sixteen" magnificats.[26] Again on August 4, 1550, he was urged to exert himself to the utmost in teaching the choirboys *canto de órgano* (polyphony) and *contrapunto*.[27] On November 24, 1553, he was admonished not to start teaching any prospective choirboy until surety had been posted that the new boy would serve out his full time, in return for his free board, lodging, and lessons.[28] On September 12, 1554, he was ordered not to receive any new boy who did not furnish his own surplices and other necessary vestments.[29] On January 3, 1558, the chapter decreed that each seise be paid a ducat every four months, but only at the expiry of each fourth month.[30] Toward the close of the summer—certainly before October 21, 1558—Espinar died. The first choice for a successor fell on Chacón, then chapelmaster at Sigüenza.[31] Chacón proved unavailable, however. On February 6, 1559, *edictos* were published offering the post of chapelmaster for 100,000 maravedís annually.[32] But not until June 2, 1559, was a successor to Espinar finally named—Bernardino de Ribera. On June 17, the chapter agreed to name Ribera to a whole- instead of a half-prebend.[33]

Ribera stayed at Ávila until 1563, in which year he transferred to Toledo. As is shown above at pages 324-325, Ribera was truly an *honbre prençipal en su profesion*. His masterworks remain unedited. But his obvious preëminence makes Victoria's precocious achievements in 1572 and 1576 the more easily understandable. What is more, even if as choirboy Victoria did not reside in the cathedral house provided Ribera by the chapter, he lived always within earshot of the master. The Victoria family dwellings stood only a tenth of a mile west of the cathedral on Caballeros Street. Ribera was succeeded by Juan Navarro. See pages 243-244. Navarro's successor was Hernando de

Yssasi, inducted on January 7, 1567. Yssasi held office for twenty years.[34]

Victoria's later accomplishments as organist suggest that he may first have begun keyboard study in his early youth with one of the masters of this instrument hired at Ávila. Damián de Bolea served as cathedral organist until October 22, 1556, on which date the post was declared vacant: Bolea having elected to transfer elsewhere (to Saragossa).[35] His successor, Bernabé del Águila, an Ávila clergyman, was appointed on November 27, 1556.[36] But a greater organist than these played in the cathedral at least twice during Victoria's boyish years. Antonio de Cabezón, glory of the age, appeared during November, 1552,[37] and again during June, 1556.[38] On each occasion the Ávila cathedral chapter voted him a cash reward. His wife, Luisa Nuñez, came of a prominent local family. They maintained a home within easy walking distance of Victoria's birthplace from *ca.* 1538 to 1560.[39]

If the presence in Ávila of Ribera, of Navarro, and of Cabezón do not sufficiently account for the musical advantages that Victoria enjoyed at home long before he left for Italy, then mention should be made of the possible contact that the young musician could have made with Bartolomé de Escobedo. Victoria's mother came from nearby Segovia. After completing eighteen years of service in the papal choir, Escobedo departed from Rome in the autumn of 1554. Upon his return to Spain he enjoyed a Segovian benefice. The young Victoria may have met Escobedo in the course of a visit to his mother's relatives, and even perhaps have received encouragement and instruction. Or at least so Pedrell suggested.[40] But Pedrell never studied the capitular acts at Ávila Cathedral, did not know even the names of the Ávila chapelmasters, and was wholly unaware of Cabezón's sojourns.[41]

In 1554 the newly organized Society of Jesus established a boy's school at Ávila, St. Giles's.[42] As with many early ventures of the Society, the Colegio de San Gil enjoyed immediate success. Numerous contemporary testimonials survive. Julián de Ávila, chaplain of the first house subscribing to the Theresan reform (St. Joseph's at Ávila), praised their impartial treatment of students.[43] Luis Muñoz, a Jesuit with many years experience as a teacher at St. Giles's, declared to the general of the society in 1573 that peace and harmony had always reigned in the school and that the townspeople had never wavered in their support.[44] St. Theresa, who from the first moment of her contact with the *compañía* extolled its educational system, lauded this school highly. Not only did she insist that her nephews attend this school and none other, but she expressly wrote to her brother Don Lorenzo de Cepeda while he was still in South America (at Quito) —recommending it in these terms: "The Jesuits have an academy [at Ávila] in which they teach grammar, send the boys to confession every week, and make them so virtuous that Our Lord is to be praised for it; the boys also read philosophy."[45] Because of such schools as St. Giles's, she said, the city was an academy of virtue. "People who come from elsewhere are always edified by the spectacle at Ávila," she maintained. It was this school in which with all probability Victoria began his classical studies.

Roman Period   After his voice broke, Victoria was sent (perhaps on the recommendation of his masters at St. Giles's) to the Jesuit *collegium* founded at Rome in 1552 by Loyola for the express purpose of training missionaries to win back Germany—the Collegium Germanicum. The young Victoria, only sixteen or seventeen when he enrolled in 1565 at Rome,[46] found among his fellow freshman classmates two English enrollees—Thomas Evans and Thomas Cottam.[47] Cottam, born in 1549, came of Lancashire stock. He returned to England and proceeded B. A. of Brasenose College at Oxford on March 23, 1569.[48] After various further sojourns on the continent he again landed in England, this time to share with Edmund Campion the rigors of execution at Tyburn (May 13, 1582) for priestly activities. His brother John taught grammar school at Stratford in Shakespeare's youth. At the very least, Shakespeare knew who Thomas Cottam was—even if Victoria's old classmate reached neither Stratford nor Shottery during his last missionary journey.[49]

Victoria's English classmates deserve mention. Only he among prominent Spanish composers of his century was thrust into so cosmopolitan an environment: not to mention the fact that he was still an impressionable sixteen or seventeen when he enrolled. The constitutions of the Collegium Germanicum (August 31, 1552) specified that only youths between the ages of fifteen and twenty-one could be admitted. Thus, all those entering in 1565 would necessarily have been born not earlier than 1544 nor later than 1550. The total number of students in the collegium in 1565 reached approximately 200. They lived and studied at the Cesi-Mellini (= Vitelli) palace in the Corso—this fifteenth-century edifice (enlarged and renovated in 1537) having become Jesuit property in 1563.[50] Two kinds of student lived side by side in the Collegium Germanicum during Victoria's three years of enrollment—a small minority of Germans in training for the missionary priesthood; and a much larger group of paying boarders. The latter included English, Spanish, and Italian students, some of whom had declared their priestly vocations. Victoria belonged to the paying-boarder group (*convittori*).

The two principal benefactors of the Collegium Germanicum from its start had been Philip II of Spain and the cardinal-archbishop of Augsburg, Otto von Truchsess von Waldburg.[51] Cardinal Truchsess early signaled youthful Victoria for his protection. Although the precise year in which the cardinal first took an interest in Victoria must be conjectured, it is worth noting that Truchsess visited Spain in March, 1564, only a year before Victoria entered the Collegium Germanicum.[52] An interview at Barcelona between March 17-28 would not have been impossible (even if it is ruled unlikely). Whatever the background of their first meeting, Victoria acknowledged his indebtedness to Truchsess for everything that he had become or done when in 1572 he dedicated to the cardinal his first publication —the *Motecta* printed by Antonio Gardano at Venice.

Casimiri, who must be thanked for having clarified the circumstances of Victoria's career at Rome, suggested that Tomás Luis while still a student at the German College may simultaneously have profited from contacts with Palestrina at the nearby Roman Seminary (founded by Pius V in 1564, and entrusted to the Jesuits). From April, 1566, until September 20, 1571, Palestrina's two sons, Angelo and Rodolfo, studied at the latter institution. To pay their expenses Palestrina served as *maestro di cappella* of the seminary. His boys, who were both extremely musical, may well— thought Casimiri—have introduced their Spanish coetanean to their illustrious father.[53]

What Victoria later said of his own student days in his dedications to Pope Gregory XIII (*Hymni totius anni*, 1581) and to Philip II (*Missarum Libri Duo*, 1583) should prove beyond cavil that he studied subjects other than theology in his early Roman period. In the dedication to Philip II he began by saying: "Since I came to Rome from Spain, besides other most noble studies to which I applied myself several years, I have spent much time and effort in music."[54] Again in the third sentence he harps on the same string: "I worked most sedulously to perfect myself in that study to which as if by some hidden natural instinct I was drawn."

Beginning in January, 1569, Victoria was engaged as *cantor y sonador del órgano* at the Aragonese church of S. Maria di Monserrato in Rome, with a monthly salary of one scudo.[55] (This national church, built about 1495, houses the tombs of the two Spanish popes.) Victoria's duties doubtless included those of chapelmaster as well as "singer and organist." Just as it continued the Spanish custom at Rome to call Palestrina a mere *cantor* of St. Peter's as late as 1575—even though he had already succeeded Animuccia in the chapelmastership on March 1, 1571[56]—so also Victoria's post of *cantor y sonador del órgano* (like Bach's at Leipzig) probably meant not so much that of vocalist as of *director musices*.

Victoria's playing of the organ at S. Maria di Monserrato reminded Casimiri of Palestrina's similar first appointment. On October 28, 1544, Giovanni Pierluigi was named *organista* and *maestro di canto* in the cathedral of his home town. Later in Rome he stopped playing the organ. But Victoria not only made his professional debut as church organist: he also continued active on the organ bench—as will later be shown—until the very eve of his death. Indeed, during his last seven years at Madrid (1604-1611) he occupied no other musical post but that of convent organist.

But this is to anticipate. From January, 1569, until 1574 Victoria continued to draw his monthly salary of one scudo at S. Maria di Monserrato. In 1573 he began singing, at least occasionally, in the other Spanish church at Rome, S. Giacomo degli Spagnoli (= Santiago parish).[57] This church paid him six scudi in April [1573] for the printed partbooks of his maiden publication (the *Motecta* of 1572) and for certain undated services as singer. This same national Church of St. James engaged him every year from 1573 through 1580 (except 1578) to sing at the Corpus Christi celebration. Each year he brought with him additional singers. From 1573 through 1577 the Santiago authorities paid him four scudi, in 1579 six scudi and sixty baiocchi, in 1580 nine scudi and sixty baiocchi. Apparently, these sums were intended for his assisting singers as well as for himself. On November 18, 1582, the Santiago treasurer paid him and an unspecified number of choristers the lump sum of nine scudi for help at the services celebrating the victory gained on July 27 by the Spanish naval forces over those of the Portuguese pretender Antonio, Prior of Crato (battle of Terceira island in the Azores).[58] In addition to sums received from the two Spanish churches in Rome, Victoria also was hired occasionally by other churches in Rome. On May 24, 1573, for instance, he was paid five scudi for music on Trinity Sunday at the Church of SS. Trinità dei Pellegrini.[59]

A more regular source of additional income was tapped in 1571—this being the year when he was first hired at his alma mater, the Collegium Germanicum, as an instructor. Besides the provision of quarters and food, he was paid fifteen giulii (a scudo and a half) monthly for his teaching.[60] The rector at the moment was P. Sebastiano Romei. That consent of the Society general, Francisco de Borja, was sought (and obtained) is known from a letter dated October 24, 1571. On the preceding June 30, Borja had left for Madrid with a commission from Pius V. In Spain he was to cement a tripartite league—France, Spain, and Portugal—against the Turk. He was also to iron out difficulties between the papacy and the Spanish court. During his absence from Rome, P. Jerónimo Nadal was deputized to act as general in his stead. Borja entered Madrid on September 30, 1571. Nadal's letter to Borja, dated October 24, describes various intervening events at Rome. Nadal says: "The German seminary remains very tranquil; there are many students, and new arrivals every day. . . . Without my knowing it, good Sebastian [Romei, the Rector] has engaged the musician Victoria who was formerly in the seminary; for 15 giulii monthly he teaches the boys [seminarians], etc. Your Paternity will decide whether this arrangement is to be continued. In everything else Father Sebastian is very devoted to the work. . . . "

The next year has been called the most momentous in Victoria's life;

for it was in 1572 that he published his first book of motets. As will be shown below at pages 442-445, this collection contains nearly all the choicer motets published during his lifetime. Since his fame even now rests so largely on his motets, this one imprint may be described as the bedrock on which his reputation is founded. The preface, addressed to his "most illustrious patron, His Eminence Otto Cardinal von Truchsess," begins thus:[61]

Truly, most renowned Cardinal, since the time that You took me under Your protection I believe that I have so busied myself in creative work that there would be no cause to regret my accomplishment, did my talent but equal my industry. . . . As an earnest of my gratitude to Your Eminence I have dedicated to You certain pious songs, musically elaborated after the fashion commonly known as Motets, which I hope may be found useful by all the well-disposed, and especially by those skilled in musical science.

Next Victoria enumerates his reasons for publishing:

I   From the moment of Your taking me under your protection You have omitted absolutely nothing that would conduce to my development and enlargement. It now behooves me who am forever so closely bound to You by the claims of gratitude to acknowledge not only privately but publicly—and in some especially striking manner—my wholehearted appreciation and indebtedness for the favors You have already dispensed and are at present most liberally dispensing.

II   As for these compositions—at once works of art and of piety—to whom better might they be dedicated than to You who take such keen delight in pious song, and have throughout Your whole life so encouraged the divine cult? And to whom would it be more fitting that I should offer these first fruits of my labor than to You who have given me the means whereby to produce them and whose bounty has made possible the acquisition of the greater or lesser knowledge comprehended in them?

Victoria continues in like vein to the end. Although we need not accept too seriously his protestation that he had learned *all* he knew in music since Cardinal Truchsess became his patron, he seems to have wished the world at large to believe that he had acquired most of his musical technique after arriving in Rome. As for the specific terms of his association with Truchsess, both Pedrell and Casimiri agree that just possibly he may have succeeded Jacobus de Kerle as the cardinal's private chapelmaster—Kerle having entered Truchsess's service in 1562, and having accompanied him to Spain in early 1564 and to Dillingen in May of the same year.[62] On August 18, 1568, Kerle became organist of Augsburg Cathedral.[63] Truchsess reached Rome shortly before July 24, 1568.[64] Victoria may well have become private chapelmaster to the cardinal toward the close of 1568: remaining with him until 1572 or thereabouts. Cardinal Truchsess died on April 2, 1573.[65]

In 1573 Victoria occupied posts in both the German College and the Roman Seminary: for the one acting as instructor in plainsong; for the other, as chapelmaster. When initially employed at the Collegium Germanicum in the autumn of 1571 he "taught the boys." He certainly was not chapelmaster of the German College in that year. As yet, the college lacked any regularly constituted choir. Loyola's original constitutions of 1552 laid upon the students only the duty of hearing Mass and reciting the Office. But in 1573 new constitutions were drawn up. Students henceforth were to learn *chorale cantum* as well as *omnia quae ad Templum . . . pertinent.*[66] Therefore, when P. Girolamo Nappi (d. 1648) noted in his *Annali del Seminario Romano* [written 1640][67] that Victoria on June 25, 1573, "came to the German College as *cantore*," some such activity as that of drillmaster in Gregorian Chant is probably to be understood as having been his new office. Nappi also records that Victoria was *maestro di cappella* of the Roman Seminary in the same year. As for the exact date on which Victoria became Roman Seminary maestro, Casimiri thought he may have succeeded Palestrina as early as the autumn of 1571—Palestrina having stopped teaching on September 25, 1571 (at which time his two sons "graduated" from the seminary).[68] Whatever Victoria's beginning date, Nappi's annals at least prove that the twenty-five-year-old Spaniard was not accounted unworthy to fill the forty-eight-year-old Italian master's shoes in 1573.

Late in the same year, the Jesuit superiors (to whom, as has already been shown, control of both German College and Roman Seminary had been entrusted from the beginning) decided that the time had come to separate the German nationals from the Italian *convittori* in the Collegium Germanicum. This was obviously an hour when the Germans, far from home, needed every psychological support. To divert their youthful minds as the moment for their separation drew nigh—seven in the evening of October 17, 1573—the rector and his aides organized a gala farewell party. Nappi describes this gala occasion at great length.[69]

Because the impending separation had kept the students so downhearted the whole year, it was decided to bring it off as smoothly as possible, and with the least show of grief, by making a musical occasion of it. Tomás Luis de Victoria, unsurpassable composer, was instructed to write suitable music, so that the transfer might be made into a solemn and yet a joyous event. Moreover, the whole Papal Choir was invited for Mass in the morning and for a meal The meal over, the papal singers brightened the afternoon with much chaffing and laughter. At nightfall, as the hour for parting drew nigh, the guests became ever more genial. The separation from the Italian students took place at seven in the evening under the light of numerous torches. During the sounding of the *Ave Maria*, the Germans and Italians took fond farewell in the same large hall where until the hour of leavetaking they had sung (though often mixing lament with song).

Then everyone went downstairs to the gate. The Germans departed walking two by two. They made a long procession of over a hundred. P. Michele Lauretano, Rector, and other fathers from the Collegium Germanicum accompanied them. In the meantime music sounded all the way to the Palazzo della Valle. In the large hall of this palace was prepared an altar. Here Psalm 136 [= 137], *Super flumina Babylonis illic sedimus et flevimus* ("By the rivers of Babylon, there we sat down and wept"), was sung. After supper, a very lively party with much music was staged in the same hall to distract the students from the thought of their schoolmates left behind. But even so, the German students remembered the affection shown by the Italians, and for a long time there was imprinted in their thoughts the love that the Italians had shown their nation.

As Victoria's previous biographers have pointed out, this very psalm, set *a 8*, was printed in his *Liber Primus Qui Missas. Psalmos, Magnificat . . . Aliaque Complectitur* (Venice: Angelo Gardano, 1576).

In the jubilee year 1575, Gregory XIII (whose liberality to the Society of Jesus exceeded that of every previous pope) gave the Collegium Germanicum new quarters adjacent to the Church of S. Apollinare on condition that this become the college church. Therefore, as *moderator musicae* of the German college, Victoria in 1575 became, simultaneously, chapelmaster of S. Apollinare.[70] The obligation of maintaining the cult in this church made it necessary to train a true *cappella musicale*, which could sing polyphony as well as chant. No longer was it possible for Victoria to carry his teaching duties in the college simultaneously with a Sunday and feast-day schedule in the national church of S. Maria di Monserrato—where, indeed, his payments for chapelmastering came to an end in 1574. Fortunately for his success at S. Apollinare, the rector of the German College, P. Michele Lauretano, enthusiastically endorsed sacred musical studies. Himself a former choirboy at Loreto, he ordered students of the college not to wear the gown of an alumnus until they had progressed in music at least sufficiently to sing the psalm-tones from memory.[71] He convoked the entire student body at set intervals, and sat by while Victoria examined individual students. Because he himself reprimanded the slothful and commended the industrious, Victoria was able to develop an outstanding choir.

Not only did Victoria continue *Collegii Germanici in Vrbe Roma Musicae Moderator* throughout 1576 (in which year he published his second collection) but also throughout 1577. Then, on February 2, 1578, a new maestro appears in the roster of college officials—Francesco [Soriano?].[72] From July, 1579, to February, 1590, the Neapolitan composer Annibale Stabile serves as chapelmaster in the college and church.[73] Victoria is willing, however, to revisit his alma mater on special occasions. He returns, for instance, at Epiphany in 1585. According to a college manuscript diary, "A *Benedictus* [sung at Lauds] with organ accompaniment made an extraordinary effect, because Maestro Victoria, the composer of the *Benedictus*, was present."[74]

On March 6 and 13, 1575, Victoria was admitted to minor orders (lector and exorcist). On August 14, 1575, after examination by Roman diocesan authority to determine his fitness, and after provision with a benefice in León diocese, he was ordered subdeacon; on Thursday, August 25, deacon; on Sunday, August 28, priest. The ordaining bishop on each of these three occasions was Thomas Goldwell, exiled diocesan of St. Asaph.[75] Each of the ceremonies took place in the English church St. Thomas of Canterbury. This church still stands on the Via di Monserrato just across the street from the Aragonese church at which Victoria first began his career as chapelmaster—S. Maria di Monserrato. Bishop Goldwell (*ca.* 1510-1585), an Oxford graduate—B.A., 1528; M.A., 1531; B.D., 1534—lived to be the last surviving member of the pre-Reformation English hierarchy. After holding various responsible posts at Rome he became in 1574 "vicegerent for Cardinal Savelli, the cardinal vicar, an office which involved his acting for the pope as diocesan bishop of Rome."[76] Victoria was approximately twenty-seven when ordained. He was made priest sooner after being ordered deacon than was usually allowed.

After quitting the Collegium Germanicum, he next joined the newly founded community of secular priests presided over by St. Philip Neri—the Congregation of the Oratory. He was admitted to a chaplaincy at S. Girolamo della Carità on June 8, 1578—retaining it until May 7, 1585 (on which date he was succeeded by Paolo Cornetta).[77] Neri himself dwelt at St. Jerome's until 1583. Victoria therefore lived on terms of daily intimacy with this remarkable spiritual leader during half a decade. Neri's community (the rules for which were confirmed in a papal bull dated July 15, 1575) was organized along unique lines. Its members were not allowed to bind themselves with vows. Members might not be transferred from one house to another. The priests in the community did not relinquish their personal property and were indeed expected to maintain themselves.[78] Victoria's support came from various Spanish benefices, all of which seem to have been conferred by Pope Gregory XIII. On May 1, 1579, this famous reformer of the calendar issued a brief conceding Victoria a simple benefice worth 200 ducats annually in Zamora diocese (S. Miguel at Villalbarba).[79] This same brief mentions four other benefices already conceded— San Francisco at Béjar in Plasencia diocese (35 ducats), San Salvador at Béjar (24 ducats), San Andrés at Valdescapa in León diocese (24 ducats), and another rent in Osma diocese (24 ducats). Victoria's total income from these several benefices after 1579 would have been 307 ducats annually. Fortunately, he was to be awarded more lucrative benefices in the course of the next two decades. Indeed, no sixteenth-century Spanish composer can challenge his success in garnering lucrative benefices. Only because of his income from such benefices was he able to devote himself to unremunerated spiritual labors at S. Girolamo della Carità. Without such income he might have been tied to the exacting routine of music-mastering at the Jesuit collegium that was his alma mater.

While a resident priest at St. Jerome's, Victoria published four collections: two in 1581[80] and another two in 1583. In 1585 he published two further collections. All of these except the *Motecta* of 1583 (which was but an enlarged reprint of the *Motetca* of 1572) were issued in lavish folio. Such were the beauty and the luxury of these 23- by 16-inch folios (91, 94, 148, 87, and 100 leaves) that Palestrina seems to have grown envious. The five folios—*Cantica B. Virginis*, 1581; *Hymni totius anni*, 1581; *Missarum Libri Duo*, 1583; *Officium Hebdomadae Sanctae*, 1585; and *Motetca Festorum Totius anni*, 1585—were respectively dedicated to (1) Michele Bonelli, a cardinal who was a nephew of Pope Pius V and who had been Victoria's schoolmate *ca.* 1565 in the Collegium Germanicum, (2) Pope Gregory XIII, (3) Philip II, (4) the Blessed Trinity, and (5) the twenty-three-year-old Charles Emmanuel I of Savoy, who at Saragossa on March 11, 1585, wedded the Princess Catherine, daughter of Philip II by Anne of Austria.

The dedications to Cardinal Bonelli and Pope Gregory XIII bespeak gratitude for favors received; those to Philip II and his son-in-law Charles Emmanuel solicit future favors. In his dedication to Philip II, Victoria declares himself exhausted from continuous musical toil during many years. He proposes now to return home, but hopes not to be coming empty-handed after his lengthy absence in Italy. Henceforth his goal will be a quiet life spent in the discharge of his priestly duties.[81] He trusts that his masses will not prove unworthy of Philip's chapel. He craves a dignity conferred at Philip's hands. In his dedication to Charles Emmanuel he says that it was Giovenale Ancina, a fellow Oratorian and a Savoyard,[82] who urged him to send his collected motets to Turin; and that he was the more easily persuaded thereto because of the duke's impending union with the Spanish house. He avers that his previously published motets will be found to be printed more accurately in the present edition. Playing upon his own name, *Victoria*, he hopes that his dedication volume will prove an omen of victory in every enterprise the duke undertakes.

From Ancina's Latin *epigramma* that follows the dedication, some further biographical grain can be gleaned. Ancina asserts that Victoria—now famous throughout Italy, and beloved at Rome—has recently begun to be known even in the Indies.[83] If he is already the cynosure of all the young masters at Rome, what will he not be in times to come when he reaches maturity? asks Ancina rhetorically. (Victoria, precocious when he first published his motets at Venice in 1572, still qualified as a young man when at thirty-seven he republished them for a second time in 1585.) Ancina's twenty-two distichs, like preludial matter in most printed books of the time, laud Victoria to the skies. But, quite unusually, they do not pass the bounds of provable fact. Even if his assertion that Victoria's fame has spread to the Indies cannot be supported with a document dated 1585, it can be supported by one dated March 12, 1598.[84] On that date Victoria empowered two Sevillian deputies to collect 100 pesos (81.6 ducats) transmitted from Lima. Dr. [Alvaro Nuñez de] Solís, an attorney at the Peruvian capital, had sent this sum. As *alcalde* in the Peruvian Casa de la Moneda (an office to which Solís was appointed on August 21, 1589),[85] he perhaps forwarded payments due Victoria from the Lima Cathedral for music books sent out to the capital of the viceroyalty: or sums sent from Cuzco.

Only after ten years spent in annually renewed association with the infant Oratorian community did an associate become a voting member of Neri's group. Victoria did not continue long enough to become a decennial father and therefore a full-fledged Oratorian. Since his period of service lasted only seven years (June 8, 1578-May 7, 1585) it was quite right for Paolo Aringhi, the first historian of the Oratorian community, to say that Neri "intended to receive another musician and celebrated composer named Victoria."[86] Aringhi, whose manuscript history of the community, *Vitae, Sententiae, Gesta et Dicta Patrum Congr.is Oratorii de Urbe a S. Philippo Nerio fundatae hic a Paulo Aringhio Cong. eiusdem Presbit.⁰ diligenter collectae*, is preserved at the Biblioteca Vallicelliana at Rome, under signatures O 58.-60, mentions Victoria only in passing (MS O 58.1): his main business at the moment being a life history of Francisco Soto (who did become a full-fledged Oratorian). After alluding to Neri's unfulfilled intention, Aringhi goes on to say that the saint hoped that Victoria would "compose music for the daily exercises at the Oratory." Victoria, however, "went back to his native land in order to put his affairs in order, and did not return [to Rome]."

Resettlement in Spain   The likeliest year for Victoria's resettlement in Spain is 1587. From 1587 until her death in 1603 he was chaplain to the Dowager Empress María living in retirement at the Royal Convent of Barefoot Clarist Nuns (Madrid). During these seventeen years he also served as maestro of the priests' and boys' choir attached to the convent. From 1604 until his death in 1611 he was convent organist. Obviously, any understanding of his career from 1587 to 1611 predicates some knowledge of his surroundings.

This particular convent, the full title of which during Victoria's lifetime was *Monasterio de las Descalzas de Santa Clara de la Villa de Madrid*,[87] was founded in 1564. The first abbess, Sor Juana de la Cruz, enjoyed the highest connections. Her brother, Francisco de Borja, had been Duke of Gandía before becoming third general of the Society of Jesus. The principal patroness until 1573 was Joanna (b. 1535)—sister of Philip II—who married Prince John of Portugal and after his death (1554) gave birth to Sebastian, last of the house of Aviz. Fortunately for the convent that she endowed so liberally, she was an avid music lover.[88] According to her *escritura fundacional* (1571), the thirty-three rigidly cloistered nuns comprising the convent proper were to hear Mass in a small chapel attended by priests, all of whom (in addition to numerous other requirements) were to be accomplished singers of plainchant and polyphony.[89] Always separated from the nuns by a grille, they were to be over thirty years of age, Latin scholars, and of unexceptionable fame. They were to have no other offices nor duties, and were never to remain overnight outside the chaplains' residency. They were to take their meals separately and each to have his own servant. The *capellán mayor* was to have two servants. One month's vacation was allowed them each year. Their daily duties included the singing of two Masses—one to be votive with deacon and subdeacon. They were to sing vespers of major feasts, and Christmas matins. Instrumentalists were to be hired at Easter, Corpus, and throughout the octave of the latter.

Philip II, not quite content with every detail of his sister's *escritura fundacional* of 1571, issued a new *declaración* in 1577 which Gregory XIII approved in 1578. The number of chaplains was increased to twelve "so that three could sing each part." Their salaries were to be doubled—400 ducats being henceforth paid each chaplain and 800 to the *capellán mayor*. Polyphony was henceforward to be sung at every major festival. Passions on Palm Sunday and Good Friday as well as *Tenebrae* were to be sung polyphonically. The secretly elected chapelmaster was to hold office for life (article 37). His duties were to include instruction of four youths during an hour each day. For teaching the choirboys he was to receive an extra 10,000 maravedís annually. Henceforth the convent organist, not necessarily a chaplain, was to be paid 40,000 maravedís. These rules remained in force until 1601, in which year they were superseded by a new *reglamento* issued by Philip III. The new rules reduced the number of chaplains from twelve to nine, but added to the convent staff two clergy "with excellent voices" whose primary duty was to sing. They were to be chosen for their *buenas voces para que puedan servir y sirvan los días de música*. The "musical days" on which polyphony was to be sung were left to the discretion of the *convento y abadesa* (convent and abbess). The two extra singing clergy were each to receive 200 ducats annually. The new articles allowed for the importation of additional clergy on solemn festivals, and especially during Holy Week. The 1601 *reglamento* also increased the number of choirboys to six. These were to be taught plainsong, polyphony, and counterpoint by the chapelmaster;

and were to rehearse daily. The pay of each boy was set at fifty ducats. Last, the 1601 rules provided for the regular employment of a *bajón* [fagottist] "who shall serve in the said chapel every day music is performed and assist the choir with his instrument." His pay was to be 40,000 maravedís annually. Before appointment, the bassoonist was to be examined by both chapelmaster and *músicos*.

The Dowager Empress María (1528-1603), whose personal chaplain Victoria became during 1586-1603, enjoyed the triple distinction of being daughter of an emperor—Charles V—wife of an emperor—Maximilian II (d. October 12, 1576)—and the mother of two emperors—Rudolph II and Matthias. Choosing not to remain at Prague after her husband's death, but to return to her homeland, she and the most devout of her fifteen children— the Princess Margaret—set out from Prague on August 1, 1581; sojourned at Genoa from October 16 to November 8; and reached Madrid on March 6, 1582.[90] After a short visit with Philip II, who was in Portugal at the time, both mother and daughter took up residence at the Descalzas Reales convent in Madrid, which was to remain the home of both until death. On March 25, 1584, Margaret professed solemn vows; henceforth being protected by the laws of cloister.

When Victoria at thirty-eight became personal chaplain to the fifty-eight-year-old dowager empress, he took up residence adjacent to the premier convent in Spain. In vain he was sought in 1587 by such cathedrals as those at Saragossa and Seville. Doctor Pascual de Mandura, canon of the Seo at Saragossa and historian of events from 1579 to 1601 at the Seo— older of the two cathedrals at Saragossa—mentions the futile attempt in 1587 to lure Victoria to the Aragonese capital (see his *Libro de Memorias*, copy at the Biblioteca Nacional, Madrid, MS 14047). According to Doctor Pascual, the Saragossa chapter sat on December 23, 1587, with the intent of electing a chapelmaster to succeed José Gay. Melchor Robledo had died in the preceding spring. A successor had been found on June 26 in Gay, native of Valencia. Within three months of taking office, however, Gay died. To avoid the expense of another formal competition so soon after the election of Gay, the Seo canons at the chapter meeting of December 23 sought to agree upon a "name" personality. A sufficiently renowned individual could perhaps be elected by the chapter, simply on the strength of his former achievements. Victoria's name was mentioned immediately. "But they knew that he could not be obtained, and that when approached prior to the previous election [in June] he had written that he had been invited to Seville to share company with Guerrero; but did not want to go because he did not care for Andalusia and was accustomed to the manners of Castile; and wished to end his days in Castile."[91]

In addition to the advantages of: (1) personal association with the devout

and highly cultivated dowager empress, (2) luxurious and fastidious surroundings at the royal convent, (3) daily contact with his elder brother
Dr. Agustín (another of the empress's chaplains), (4) at least occasional
visits with his younger brother Juan Luis (who came to reside at Madrid
before 1591), and (5) living in the newly selected (1560) capital, Victoria
enjoyed many other advantages. Among these was greater freedom of
movement than could have been allowed at either Saragossa or Seville.
For instance, in 1591 he resided at Madrid—on March 4 becoming godfather of his infant niece Isabel de Victoria Figueroa in a baptismal ceremony at the parochial church of San Ginés. The next year (1592), however,
he was at Rome—on November 13 signing the dedication of his *Missae
quatuor, quinque, sex, et octo vocibus concinendae* to the Empress María's son,
Cardinal Albert (1559-1621), archbishop of Toledo (1584), and after 1599
ruler of the Spanish Netherlands. Then, before the end of the succeeding
year, 1593, he seemingly had resumed his regular duties of *maestro de capilla
de las Descalzas de Madrid*; for on December 3 of that year the chapter secretary of León Cathedral wrote him a letter asking that he suggest candidates
for the then vacant post of chapelmaster at León.[92] The very next year,
1593, may have found him again at Rome: or at least so Casimiri would
contend.[93] On July 7, 1593, news reached Rome that the Turks had been
decisively defeated beneath the walls of Sisak (near Zagreb). Eleven days
later, a service of thanksgiving was offered at the Church of S. Apollinare—
four cardinals of the Congregazione di Germania assisting.[94] According
to a manuscript seen by Casimiri, *Diario degli anni 1591-1593*, pages 62-63:
"outside singers were invited to sing at Mass, and very beautifully, etc.
After dinner, before commencing Vespers, a solemn Te Deum was chanted.
At Vespers (as at Mass in the morning) a new Victoria [or, victory] motet
was sung, with text from the Book of Judges [5:12], *Surge Debora et loquere
canticum*, which seemed to the cardinals present and all the rest who heard
it very a propos."

Casimiri reasons that Victoria must have been in Rome because the
motet was "new" and because it was "occasional." The victory that Deb-
orah's song celebrated was gained over *Sisara* (= Sisera, Judges 4). The
victory over the Turks was gained at *Sisak*. If Victoria's motet was composed specifically to celebrate the victory, then he must have been in Rome
at least from July 7 to 18, 1593. In all likelihood he still sojourned at Rome
on January 21, 1594. On that date a royal warrant was expedited to the
Spanish ambassador at Rome for 150 ducats payable to Victoria (fruits of
an absentee Cordovan benefice).[95]

Neither could such freedom of movement have been allowed Victoria
had he been a chaplain whose income derived from the original foundation
at Descalzas Reales. He seems not to have been one of the twelve chaplains

appointed on the 1577/1578 foundation; but, instead, the Empress María's private appointee. As such, he could have come and gone at her individual pleasure, rather than merely during the annual thirty-day vacation allowed the convent foundation chaplains. As clear-cut a reference as any to his personal circumstances from 1587 until the Empress María's death is perhaps to be found in his memorial, quoted in a royal cedula dated July 2, 1611.[96] Victoria, describing his career at Descalzas Reales, says in 1611 that "he had served 24 years as the empress's chaplain." These twenty-four years had been divided into two periods—the first lasting seventeen years (within her lifetime). During the seven since her death (February 26, 1603) he had "served in one of the three [endowed] chaplaincies that she left in the said convent." What is more, Victoria had "served 17 years as *maestro de capilla*, these 17 without any extra pay whatsoever." After her death he had resigned the chapelmastership "and for seven years henceforward had satisfactorily served as convent organist."

Among Victoria's other blessings while at the Descalzas Reales was an annual income from absentee benefices throughout the whole period, 1587-1611, which was considerably greater than the aggregate amount he could have realized from a mere cathedral chapelmastership anywhere in Spain —even at such opulent cathedrals as Toledo and Seville. The aggregate value of the position open at Seville Cathedral in 1587, for instance, was only 900 ducats annually. So testified Sebastián de Vivanco in a confidential report to the Ávila Cathedral chapter on October 30, 1587.[97] The value of the Ávila chapelmastership was even less: Vivanco made this fact plain when he said he would prefer to be in Ávila with less income than at Seville with more; simply because Ávila was his home town. Victoria—under consideration at both Saragossa and Seville in 1587—seems not even to have been thought of at Ávila when in the same year decision was taken to replace the ailing and corrupt Hernando de Issasi (who in 1573 and again in 1577 had contumeliously categorized Victoria's 1572 *Motecta* and 1576 Masses as unfit for use in Ávila Cathedral).[98] In 1579 Victoria already enjoyed benefices yielding 307 ducats annually. His list of rents grew steadily thereafter. During 1605 and 1606 he was enjoying an additional annual income of 920 ducats from the dioceses of Cordova, Segovia, Sigüenza, Toledo, and Zamora.[99] With a 1,227-ducat annual income simply from "pensions" collectable in these various dioceses, he was too affluent for any provincial chapelmastership to lure him away from Madrid.

It has hitherto been the custom to deplore the "poverty" that Victoria "endured" during his last years. Pedrell, for instance, closed his biographical summary with an indignant paragraph (quoted from ¡*Para música vamos!*) in which Victoria was said to have ended his days in a mean post, poorly paid, and ungratefully and despitefully used by the very nation that should have honored him.[100] Actually, the very documents that Pedrell collected should have stilled any such outcry against the Spanish nation. To take only the matter of his benefices: all were in Spain, and were therefore collated by Spanish bishops. All were simple (without cure of souls) and all were nonresidential. Don Francisco Reinoso (d. 1601), the bishop who collated him in the 150-ducat benefice at Cordova, visited Rome in 1581 or 1582.[101] He it was who while still canon at Palencia Cathedral (with the title of *abad de Husillos*) secured Soto de Langa for an editor of Juan Navarro's *Psalmi, Hymni ac Magnificat totius Anni*; and it was to him that Soto dedicated the collection when it was published at Rome in 1590. Reinoso was so ardent a music lover that it was at his own expense (*auctoritate, et sumptibus tuis*), testified Soto, that Navarro's music was published a decade after the composer's death.[102] Reinoso may quite well have met Victoria at Rome as early as 1581. Saint Theresa, writing to Reinoso's brother on May 20, 1582, alluded to Reinoso's visit in Rome and to his having there met the new general of the Society of Jesus, Claudio Aquaviva (elected 1581). In 1582 Victoria was no longer chapelmaster at either of the Jesuit colleges at Rome. But he can scarcely have missed meeting so distinguished a Spanish visitor at S. Giacomo degli Spagnoli—in which national church he still officiated as late as 1583—and more especially one who was so ardent a devotee of sacred music. Reinoso was, of course, but one of several bishops who honored him with a benefice. But if the biographies of the other Spanish bishops who collated him in ecclesiastical livings could be studied, each might be revealed a musically cultured diocesan, and one who knew his obligations to genius.

The Empress María paid him 120 ducats annually until her death in 1603. At her death she endowed three chaplaincies in Descalzas Reales convent. Victoria inherited one of these.[103] The pay continued at the rate of 120 ducats annually. On January 1, 1605, he needed a large sum of ready money—perhaps to pay the costs of printing his last work, the *Officium Defunctorum* dedicated to the empress's memory. He therefore sold his interest in the lifetime chaplaincy bequeathed him by the empress to a certain Doña Isabel Díaz y Poe for the sum of 720 ducats.[104] To guarantee her against loss should he die before the expiry of six years (120 ducats annually, times six), he mortgaged five benefices and his convent salary. Had he died the first year, she would have collected in the amount of her advance, 720 ducats. Each subsequent year she would have collected 120 ducats less. The five benefices whose incomes he pledged to Doña Isabel Díaz on January 1, 1605, did not include a 150-ducat benefice in Toledo archdiocese.[105]

During the empress's lifetime, Victoria, on his own word, received no extra pay for his services as convent chapelmaster.[106] After her death, he retired to the less strenuous duties of convent organist. For playing the organ, however, he did consent to draw a stipend over and above his chaplain's salary. During 1604-1605 he was each year paid 40,000 maravedís for playing the organ. Then in 1606, Philip III "as patron of the said convent" issued a cedula raising his annual salary to 75,000 maravedís.[107] In the same year the king raised the salary of Alonso del Cerro—the convent bassoonist—to the same amount.[108] It can by no means be doubted that Victoria was well treated at the convent and that it was of his own free will that he retired to the organ loft. On August 19, 1604, he witnessed the signing of a contract for a new convent organ, to be built by the Flemish organ builder in royal employ, Hans Brevos.[109] Added to the advantage of having a new instrument available during his last years was that of being able to call frequently upon a competent and eager substitute, Bernardo Pérez de Medrano. Because of the "great care and punctuality" with which Pérez de Medrano acted as substitute whenever called upon, and because he was "very competent and efficient," Victoria in 1611 used his influence with the king to have him named successor in the post when he should die. On July 2 (1611), Philip III formally confirmed Pérez de Medrano's right of succession.[110] On Saturday, August 27, only eight weeks later, Victoria (who perhaps foresaw his imminent decease) died; and was buried at Descalzas Reales.[111]

Thus, by far the largest source of Victoria's income during his last years in Spain came from benefices—some 1,200 ducats annually.[112] As personal chaplain to the empress, he enjoyed not only before her death, but afterward also, an added 120 ducats annually; together with the coveted right of residence until his death in the chaplains' house (Arenal Street) next to the convent. Furthermore, he collected 40,000 maravedís annually in 1604-1605 and 75,000 maravedís (200 ducats) each year from 1606 to 1611 for his services as convent organist. He enjoyed still another type of income during his last years. The amounts are somewhat more difficult to gauge accurately, since they came from the "sale" of his publications to various princes and cathedral foundations. But he is known to have empowered his agents to collect on March 12, 1598, the sum of 900 reales (approximately 82 ducats) due from Lima; on January 26, 1602, 50 ducats from Málaga Cathedral; on November 23, 1604, 100 ducats "given me by the most serene Archduke Albert of Flanders [dedicatee of his 1592 Masses] for some books of music"; on December 19, 1606, 150 reales (about 14 ducats) from Albarracín Cathedral.[113] These are the merest samplings. He undoubtedly received such "payments" by the score. In 1598, for instance, he placed an order for 200 sets of printed partbooks.[114] In 1600, when these were ready, he distributed them. A letter dated June 10, 1603, survives: Victoria writing from Madrid asks the Duke of Urbino (Francesco Maria II della Rovere) if a set of the 1600 books had been received at Urbino.[115]

The letter shows that Victoria had not only distributed sets of his 1600 publication far and wide, but that he had also kept tab of all those who had acknowledged receipt with a cash reward. The Duke of Urbino had not sent him a reward. Therefore he wrote as follows:

Most Serene Sir: Last year [1602] I sent Your Highness ten partbooks containing a musical miscellany. Among other things this collection contained a Battle Mass that gave my lord the king [Philip III] great pleasure. Since I have not been advised concerning their receipt, I have decided to send Your Highness another set of partbooks in their place, and to ask that they be accepted with my most distinguished compliments. And if it should please Your Highness to bestow a reward to help defray part of the printing expenses, You will deeply obligate me to Yourself all of my life; and I shall beseech Our Lord for Your Highness's health and prosperity.

Madrid, June 10, 1603.

The reward which Your Highness may be pleased to bestow can be given at Rome to Francisco de Soto, His Holiness's chaplain and singer.

Thome de Victoria
His Majesty's Chaplain

Victoria's total printing expenses for the 1600 partbooks reached 2,500 reales (227 ducats). Even if on average he received only 150 reales for each set—this being the amount sent from Albarracín, a poor cathedral[116]—and even if he collected from only half the princes and foundations to whom he remitted sets of partbooks, he still realized a clear profit of 12,500 reales (1,133 ducats) for his labors (or the equivalent of approximately one year's income from benefices). He probably realized still greater amounts from his 1592 Masses published at Rome, and from his 1605 *Officium Defunctorum* published at Madrid—both these having been printed in a luxury format and therefore commanding higher rewards. On the other hand, it must be remembered that after returning to Spain *ca.* 1587 he published only three times: in 1592, 1600, and 1605.

The dedications in each instance—*Missae quatuor, quinque, sex, et octo vocibus concinendae. . . . Liber secundus* (Rome: 1592), *Missae, Magnificat, Motecta, Psalmi* (Madrid: 1600), *Officium Defunctorum* (Madrid: 1605)—offer a certain number of biographical clues. In the 1592 dedication to Cardinal Albert, son of the Empress María, he lists his several reasons for having dedicated his "recently composed" masses: (1) the favors shown by the cardinal's mother, the dowager empress: especially her having named him one of her private chaplains; (2) the cardinal's known predilection for polyphony; (3) letters from the cardinal indicating his willingness to accept a dedication. Elaborating the last reason, Victoria says: "An important consideration [moving me to dedicate these masses to you] has been Your letters, in which You have signified to me that You would be pleased were this work to appear bearing Your name, thus taking its place alongside the other works published with Your patronage and now already for a long time circulating everywhere." Victoria does not say that he himself had dedicated any previous works to the cardinal-archduke. He merely refers to *caetera opera*. These "other works" must doubtless be understood to have been such publications as the *Avisos para soldados y gente de guerra*[117] and *Catechismus*,[118] already published at Madrid in 1590 and 1592, with dedications to the cardinal-archduke. Victoria, after listing his reasons for dedicating his masses to Cardinal Albert, adds that "many persons had urged him to finish composing the present group of masses." He had used what time remained amidst numerous other pressing duties. In his present collection would be found masses suitable for *omnes dies festos, qui per totum annum incidunt* ("all feasts throughout the entire year"). Moreover, he had included a Requiem Mass as well. Since the arrangement of masses in the 192-page volume follows the order of the church year, Victoria's scheme can be proved (from his explicit avowal in the dedication) to have been worked out deliberately; and not merely stumbled upon. The first is for Christmastide (*O magnum mysterium*), then (in order of appearance) one for use during pre-Lent and Lent (*Quarti toni*), one for Eastertide (*Trahe me post te*), one for Ascensiontide (*Ascendens Christus*), one for Assumption (*Vidi speciosam*), and, last, one for general use throughout the long stretch from Trinity until the end of the year (*Salve Regina*). As a postscript to these church-year masses, he adds a *Missa pro defunctis*. While carrying out this "chronological" plan, Victoria seems to have been aware of the fact that he was breaking new ground. Certainly none of Palestrina's collections of masses adheres to such a "chronological" scheme.

Victoria's 1600 dedication, late though it comes in his career, is his first to contain classical allusions. He cites Achilles and Alexander as lovers of music and praises Philip III, the dedicatee, for following in their footsteps. The resolution of diverse sounds in a polyphonic composition mirrors the harmony of that happy kingdom in which all wills are attuned to the will of the Almighty. He wishes no other reward than the satisfaction of having provided music suitable for those many occasions when the king assists at sacred functions in the convent founded by Joanna, his royal aunt.

The *Officium Defunctorum* published at Madrid in 1605 memorializes the Dowager Empress María who died two years earlier at the age of seventy-four. Her daughter Margaret remained at her side until the end on February 26, 1603.[119] On March 1, Philip III sent instructions for her burial from Valladolid. Attired in the habit of St. Clara, her body was laid to rest in the convent cloister (the bishop of Zamora, Fray Plácido de Todos los Santos, preaching the funerary sermon).[120] On March 19 a vigil in her behalf was sung at the convent: four extra singers being brought from Toledo Cathedral for the occasion.[121] Diego de Urbina, *regidor* of Madrid, published later in the year an account of the vigil, which he said lasted from half-past two until five in the afternoon. Although his account bears every mark of being painstakingly complete, he says nothing of Victoria's *Officium Defunctorum*: nor indeed does he so much as mention Victoria. Perhaps then we need not believe that Victoria composed so lengthy a work for performance only three weeks after her death. A much more imposing occasion for the first performance would have been the *solémnísimas y grandiosas honras* conducted on April 21-22 at SS. Peter and Paul,[122] the Jesuit church completed in 1567 on the present site of the Madrid Cathedral (of San Isidro). The *compañía*—magnificently endowed by the dowager empress[123]—determined beforehand to outdistance every previous attempt at honoring her memory, say the *Anales de Madrid* contemporaneously compiled by León Pinelo.[124] D. Tomás de Borja—newly elected archbishop of Saragossa (1603-1610), brother of the third Jesuit general, and uncle of the empress's major-domo[125]—sang the office. At the close of vespers, P. Luis de la Cerda delivered a Latin oration. Next day, the address after Mass was delivered by P. Jerónimo de Florencia, perhaps the most renowned preacher of the day. "From the moment that it was decided to conduct these ceremonies, the superiors of the society enjoined every father with talent to write poetry and compositions of all sorts in praise of Her Majesty."[126] Victoria, whose intimate associations with the society dated from 1565 if not earlier, cannot have been overlooked when the Jesuit superiors combed Madrid for the finest talent in the capital. Moreover, the supremely beautiful *Officium Defunctorum*, published at Madrid in 1605, and hitherto always considered the pearl of his works, would still have been hastily composed, even if it waited until so late as April 21-22 for its first performance.

In his lengthy dedication to the Princess Margaret (professed in religion at the age of seventeen [1584] under the name of Sor Margarita de la Cruz; died 1633), Victoria expressly states that he had composed his *Officium Defunctorum* "for the obsequies of your most serene mother." As in his 1600 dedication, he frequently intrudes classical allusions. Victoria lauds the whole house of Austria, beginning with Charles V who was the first to adopt *plus ultra* for his device. He praises the princess's choice of religion. He calls his present work a *Cygneam cantionem*—a "swan song." But doubtless he means "swan song" in an illative sense. The *Officium Defunctorum* would be a swan song for the empress, Victoria's benefactress. At the close, he voices the hope that he may in future, if Providence grants him length of days, present still better works to the princess. The dedication bears June 13, 1605, for its date.

Martín Pescenio, a fellow chaplain at Descalzas Reales (probably from Segovia diocese[127] and holder of one of the three convent chaplaincies endowed by the empress at her decease) contributes a Latin poem of thirty-three hexameters in postscript to the dedication. Pedrell, who was the first to translate the poem, decries its artificiality. Actually, the poem throws further light on such a phrase as *Cygneam cantionem* in the dedication. Pescenio closes thus: "Victoria, you lament our common benefactress in such exquisitely sad song as to bring to mind Orpheus lamenting Eurydice, or the cry of the expiring swan, or of Philomela grievously sobbing. Proceed then, for a long time adding artistic laurel to laurel. Become another Timotheus of Miletus. Mount up like a swan on wings supplied by Apollo until your appropriate name, Victoria, fulfills its happy augury."

The references to *cygnus* in lines 28 and 32 of the poem should forever silence those critics who, because of Victoria's own reference to *Cygneam cantionem*, would see him spelling out his intention to retire henceforth from artistic labors. Much has been made by Pedrell, and others, of Victoria's repeated "announcements" that he wished to retire from composing—first in the 1583,[128] and then again in the 1605 dedication. However, if read dispassionately, neither dedication gives one the right to picture Victoria as a Prospero ready to bury his art "certain fathoms in the earth" after having "required some heavenly music—which even now I do—to work mine end upon their senses." Victoria's artistic integrity is belied when his intent is reduced merely to that of an "airy charm" to be abjured, a "staff" to be broken, and a talent to be thenceforth buried "deeper than did ever plummet sound."

True, Victoria did not publish again before his death on August 27, 1611. But the time intervals between his 1585, 1592, and 1600 publications extended to seven and eight years, respectively. As J. Niles Saxton has observed, the number of his masses ought to have been rounded out with a *Regina coeli*. Who therefore can say that he would not have bequeathed a later volume containing such a mass (and perhaps still other works) had he lived beyond the age of sixty-three?

As the years closed in, Victoria drew ever closer to his own immediate family. His devotion to his elder sister, María de la Cruz, appears to have been especially tender and sympathetic. (See above, pp. 348-349.) It was doubtless this bond which inspired her to remember one of the composer's domestics in her will of September 1, 1610. Victoria's bestirring himself to assure his pupil and substitute, Bernardo Pérez de Medrano, the right of succession in the organ loft at Descalzas Reales (royal cedula dated July 2, 1611) speaks well for the composer's innate kindliness to subordinates as well as to personal servants.

Victoria died on Saturday, August 27, 1611, in the chaplain's house adjacent to the convent. He made his will before Juan de Trujillo, the notary, who had signed his sister's will on September 1, 1610.[129] Witnessing Victoria's will were his nephew Gerónimo de Mirueña (see above, p. 346) and Juan de Trimiño. The date of Victoria's death is attested in the parish register of San Ginés Church (the bounds of which parish included Descalzas Reales). Mitjana itemized the documentary source: *Parroquía de San Ginés, Libro segundo de Difuntos, folios 93ᵛ y 94*.[130] However, he copied the date of Victoria's death as August 7 and the name of the notary as Juan de Castillo: both of which errors were corrected by Pedrell.

Esthetic Philosophy   Not only do Victoria's Latin prefaces uniformly tend to be lengthier than Palestrina's, but also his dedications differ in containing phrases that, linked together, form something of a coherent esthetic philosophy. The following catena of phrases was forged by Dom David Pujol, *monje de Montserrat*, to whom must be given credit for having been the first to make such a list of phrases in his article "Ideas Estéticas de T. L. de Victoria" (*Ritmo*, Año XI, número 141 [extraordinario], December, 1940). Four dedications were drawn on: (1) *Hymni totius anni* (Rome: Domenico Basa, 1581); (2) *Cantica B. Virginis vulgo Magnificat quatuor vocibus . . . concinuntur* (Rome: Basa, 1581); (3) *Motecta* (Rome: Alessandro Gardano, 1583); (4) *Missarum Libri Duo* (Rome: Gardano, 1583). The hymns were dedicated to Pope Gregory XIII, the magnificats to Cardinal Bonelli (nephew of Pius V), the motets to Our Lady, and the masses to Philip II.

Of the thirteen excerpts below, the first six touch upon his own artistic development, and the remainder upon the origin and function of music.

Music is an art to which he was "instinctively" drawn (*ad quae naturali quodam feror instinctu* [1]).

Mastery, however, resulted from long years of hard work (*multos iam annos . . . versor, et elaboro* [1]).

Others with critical faculty gave support and encouragement (*ex aliorum iudicio mihi videor intelligere, non infeliciter* [1]).

Recognizing his talent as divinely bestowed, he felt the greater obligation to develop it, to bear fruit, and to return interest on his talent (*Id vero munus ac beneficium cum diuinum agnoscerem, dedi operam, ne penitus in eum, à quo bona cuncta proficiscuntur, ingratus essem, si inerti ac turpi otio languescerem, et creditum mihi talentum humi defodiens, iuxto expectatoque fructu dominum defraudarem* [1]).

He recognized, on the other hand, that despite his unremitting efforts all that he had accomplished had really been quite little indeed (*In quo etsi plus omnino conor quam possum, minus tamen praesto* [2]).

He hoped posterity would judge his efforts kindly (*vt longius progressus, quantum in me esset, praesentibus, posterisque prodessem* [4]).

Music, because instinct with rhythm and harmony, describes the very being of God (*Cui enim rei potius seruire Musicam decet, quàm sacris laudibus immortalis Dei à quo numerus et mensura manauit?* [4]).

Creation itself testifies to the divine harmony (*cuius opera vniuersa ita sunt admirabiliter suauiterque disposita vt incredibilem quandam harmoniam, concentumque prǣseferant et ostendant?* [4]).

Music is not man's invention, but his heritage from the blessed spirits (*ante quàm homines essent, in beatis illis mentibus esse inceperit* [2]).

Music of the right stamp serves not only to enhance the splendor of the cult but also to excite the faithful (*fidelisque Populi deuotionem Hymnis & canticis Spiritualibus dulcius excitandam* [3]).

That which of itself is inherently good can—and often does—deteriorate in man's hands (*Verùm, id quod ferme accidit rebus omnibus, vt à bono principio exortae, in deteriorem plerumque vsum torqueantur* [2]).

Nowadays, unfortunately, music does often serve depraved ends (*Quippe ea improbi quidam, ac prauis moribus imbuti homines abutuntur* [2]).

Music can affect for good or ill the body as well as the mind (*in animos influens, non animis solum prodesse videtur, sed etiam corporibus* [2]).

Victoria's Masses

Logically, any study of the twenty authenticated masses[131] ought to succeed examination of his motets—Victoria having based seven of the twenty masses on his own motets. He founded the following six masses on motets published in his maiden book of 1572: (1) *Ascendens Christus, a 5* [1592]; (2) *Dum complerentur, a 6* [1576]; (3) *O magnum mysterium, a 4* [1592]; (4) *O quam gloriosum, a 4* [1583]; (5) *Quam pulchri sunt, a 4* [1583]; (6) *Vidi speciosam, a 6* [1592]. One other mass—*Trahe me post te, a 5* [1592]—takes for its source the canonic motet of the same title published in his 1583 *Motecta.*

In five of these seven parodies, the same number of parts are used in the source motet and in the mass. By way of exception, the *Dum complerentur* Mass adds a voice and the *Trahe me post te* subtracts one.[132] Of the source motets, those with titles (1), (2), and (6) in the above list extend to two *partes*—material from both *partes* always appearing in the parody. The 1572 source motets belong to these feasts: (1) Ascension, (2)Pentecost, (3) Circumcision,[133] (4) All Saints, (5) Conception, and (6) Assumption of the Blessed Virgin. As for *Trahe me* in the 1576 motet collection, Victoria designates it as suitable for any feast of the Virgin. Thus, all seven source motets belong to feasts. In our own time Victoria's most frequently performed motets are his *O vos omnes* (with a text from Lamentations) and *Vere languores.* Never, though, did he parody any such languorous or grief-laden motet: only exultant ones. The joyous character of these source motets is etched in all the bolder relief by the climactic word with which each except *O quam gloriosum* and *Vidi speciosam* ends: Alleluia. Both *partes* of *Ascendens Christus* and *Dum complerentur* so conclude.

For a second group of three parody masses, each *a 8*—the *Salve Regina* [1592], *Alma Redemptoris* [1600], and *Ave Regina* [1600]—he chose as sources not the plainsong Marian antiphons (as one might in advance suspect), but his own polyphonic settings of these same antiphons published in 1572, 1576, and 1581. At one time or another, he published four different polyphonic settings of the *Salve Regina* (1572, *a 6*; 1576, *a 5*; 1576, *a 8*; 1583, *a 5*). It was the third of these (1576, *a 8*) which served as the basis for his parody mass of the same name. Although not so prodigal in providing published settings of the other Marian antiphons, he did leave two settings of each. The dates and number of voices in the paired settings of these other antiphons—*Alma Redemptoris, Ave Regina,* and *Regina coeli*—correspond so closely that some plan and forethought can be presumed. Of each, he left settings *a 5* and *a 8*. Those *a 5* were first published in his 1572 *Motecta,* and those *a 8* in his 1581 *Cantica B. Virginis.* Interestingly enough, his *Alma Redemptoris* and *Ave Regina* Masses (both of which were published for the first time in his last book of masses) levy material not from just one or the other of his polyphonic settings—the one *a 5,* the other *a 8*—but from both. Here, therefore, in his last book of masses (the only book published in Spain) he tries a new track so far as parody technique is concerned—one which Morales may just haltingly have forecast in his *Benedicta es coelorum* when he extracted material from two different motets (of the same name: one by Josquin, the other by Mouton), but which seems not to have been exploited by any other peninsular composer.[134]

In his last parody—his *Laetatus sum* Mass *a 12* [1600]—Victoria selected for a source the only one of his seven psalms conceived for the same large number of voices, Psalm 121 (= 122 A. V.). For three choirs of four voices each, this psalm was first published as the concluding item in his 1583 *Motecta.* Victoria again chose to parody not one of his psalms on some such plaintive text as "By the rivers of Babylon, there we sat down, yea, we wept" (Ps. 136 = 137 [A. V.]), nor on a didactic text such as "Unless the Lord build the house, they labor in vain that build it" (Ps. 126 = 127 [A. V.]). Rather, he chose to parody the one psalm that begins with the words "I rejoiced." As for his choice of original material to parody, this general rule may be adduced: he uses only material originally conceived in conjunction with joyous or hopeful texts. Even the *Salve Regina* Mass, *a 8,* scarcely violates this principle: for in the parody he echoes those phrases from his original setting which belonged to ameliorative or hopeful petitions; but not the music for such phrases as *gementes et flentes in hac lacrimarum valle* ("groaning and weeping in this vale of tears").

In each of the following four masses, Victoria adopted as his model a motet or chanson by some other composer: *Gaudeamus, a 6* [1576]; *Pro victoria, a 9* [1600]; *Simile est regnum, a 4* [1576]; *Surge propera, a 5* [1583]. For sources, he chose respectively: Morales's *Jubilate Deo omnis terra*, a festal motet *a 6* composed for the Nice peace parley of 1538; Clément Janequin's chanson *a 4, La bataille de Marignan*, celebrating the French victory over Swiss troops hired by the Milanese (during the battle fought on the northern outskirts of Melegnano—10 miles southeast of Milan—on September 13-14, 1515); Guerrero's Septuagesima motet *a 4* published in 1570; and Palestrina's Visitation motet *a 4* published in 1563.[135] Obviously, Victoria's penchant for parodying joyous sources carried through the whole body of his work: whether his source happened to be his own motet or was a piece by some other composer.

In order to complete a survey of Victoria's sources, his four paraphrase masses must also be mentioned, each elaborating plainsong: *Ave maris stella, a 4* [1576], *De beata Virgine, a 5* [1576], *Pro defunctis, a 4* [1583], *Officium defunctorum, a 6* [1605]. In the first of this group of paraphrases, he availed himself of the plainsong hymn of the same title; in the second, of Mass IX and Credo I; in the third and fourth, of the plainsong Office of the Dead and plainsong Requiem Mass. One mass, only, of the twenty published by Victoria seems to have been freely composed—in the sense that Palestrina's *Missa brevis* of 1570 or *Papae Marcelli* of 1567 is free— namely, the *Quarti toni* published in Victoria's third book (Rome: 1592).

Of his 20 authenticated masses it will thus be seen that 15 can be classified as parodies (11 of which are based on his own, and 4 on other composers' material), 4 as paraphrases, and 1 as a free mass. Palestrina, with whom Victoria is compared most frequently, left some 104 masses— of which 51 are classifiable as parodies, 35 as paraphrases, 7 as tenor, 6 as free, and 5 as canonic masses. Proportionately, parody looms as a much more important category in Victoria's few masses than in Palestrina's many. However, of Palestrina's 43 masses published during his lifetime (in the following years: 1554, 1567, 1570, 1582, 1585, 1590, 1591, 1592, 1593/4), twice as many must be called parodies (22) as paraphrases (11). In 5 of these 22 parodies, Palestrina used secular models—whereas only once did Victoria avail himself of a profane model. In 13 of the 22 parodies published during his lifetime, Palestrina turned to exterior models for source material, and in 5 to his own compositions. For a contrast, Victoria based only 4 on exterior sources but 11 on his own compositions.

As for number of parts, Victoria composed only 7 of his 20 authenticated masses *a 4* and 4 *a 5*. The others call for larger groups: he having composed 4 *a 6*, 3 *a 8*, 1 *a 9*, and 1 *a 12*. Guerrero, on the other hand, composed but one mass among his total of 18 for so many as six voices—all the rest having been written *a 4* or *a 5*. Of his 104 masses, Palestrina composed only 22 *a 6*, and 4 *a 8*: his other 78 utilizing a smaller number of parts. The fact that so many as 9 of Victoria's 20 masses call for six or more parts contrasts strikingly with both Guerrero's and Palestrina's proportions.

Although Victoria calls for a larger number of parts in his choral ensembles, and is the first important polyphonic composer who published added organ accompaniments, his masses—so far as length is concerned—run considerably behind Guerrero's and Palestrina's. *Dum complerentur, a 6* [1576], his longest mass, reaches a total of only 657 bars. The *Gaudeamus*, *a 6*, in the same book extends to 655 bars. Standing in third place among his masses, if length is the criterion, would be the *Surge propera, a 5*, from the 1583 book. Twelve of his masses fail to reach even 500 bars. On the other hand, only 10 among Palestrina's 48 masses published before 1595 fall below 500 bars. The *Ecce sacerdos* in Palestrina's first book even totals 844 bars, and is therefore 180 bars longer than Victoria's lengthiest mass; Palestrina's 45 masses published in 1554, 1567, 1570, 1582, 1590, 1593/4, and 1594, reach on average 612 bars; whereas Victoria's 18 (Requiems excluded) published in 1576, 1583, 1592, and 1600, extend to only 464. The following further breakdown may prove interesting. Palestrina's Kyrie eleison movements average 71 bars; Victoria's, on the other hand, average only 50 bars. Palestrina's Glorias average 120 bars, but Victoria's only 106. Palestrina's Credos average 192 bars, but Victoria's only 170. For the rest: the average length of their Sanctus movements runs 141 against 92; and of their Agnus movements, 88 against 46.

None of Victoria's masses includes so many as three Agnus movements and only seven masses include so many as two.[136] In his 1583 book, the *O quam gloriosum* Mass, *a 4*, concludes with but a single Agnus movement. In his 1592 book, not one mass among the half-dozen contains as many as two Agnus movements: the *Vidi speciosam* lacking any "miserere nobis" movement and all the others in the same 1592 set concluding without any "dona nobis pacem." Palestrina, on the other hand, only once (*Sicut lilium inter spinas, a 5* [1590]) failed to include at least two Agnus movements.

Such questions as those concerning the number of voices in Victoria's masses, and their over-all and individual-movement lengths, should not be asked merely for the purpose of tabulating general comparisons with Palestrina's usage. Rather, these and like questions should be asked to ascertain what trends, if any, Victoria followed during the quarter-century that elapsed between his first and last books of masses. In Palestrina's repertory, the same number of masses *a 6* are to be found in his 1570 book as in his 1590. If order of publication reflects chronology of composition, then we must assume that toward the end of his career Palestrina's tastes (so far as his preferred number of parts is concerned) still remained quite static. With Victoria, on the other hand, his demands—insofar as number of voices is concerned—mounted steadily toward the end of his career: the 1592 book being the first to contain a mass *a 8*, and the 1600 book being the first to contain masses both *a 9* and *a 12*. For another instance of Palestrina's conservatism: the over-all and individual-movement lengths drop only gradually from book to book. The average length of his seven masses in the 1567 is 606 bars; of the seven in the 1582, 559; of the eight in the 1590, 535. Compared with this gradual descent, Victoria's masses toboggan down a runway. The average length of the five masses in his 1576 book is 597 bars; but of the six in the 1592, 376; and of the four in the 1600, only 363. Moreover, it was Victoria who after compiling all five masses with two different Agnus movements in his 1576 book, and all but one with a pair of Agnus movements in his 1583, parsimoniously confined himself to a single Agnus in every one of his 1592 and 1600 masses.[137]

Seen in this kind of light, Victoria's personal procedures (and perhaps tastes) prove not to have remained static, but to have changed significantly during that comparatively short period of a quarter-century which separates his first from his last book of masses. In still other ways, the style of his masses can be seen to have changed just as sharply. Eight of the masses published before 1600 conclude with a canonic Agnus—two of these being such elaborate specimens as an eight-in-four and a three-in-one. None of the 1600 masses, on the other hand, concludes with a canonic Agnus. Furthermore, the 1576 book, and it alone, includes polytextual masses: the *Ave maris stella*, *a 4*, and the *Gaudeamus*, *a 6*.[138] Only in his masses published in 1576 and 1583 did he bow to the time-honored custom of beginning each principal movement in a parody mass with the initium of his source motet. After the *Surge propera*, *a 5*, of 1583 (parodied on the Palestrina motet *a 4* published twenty years earlier) he henceforth showed scant respect for the initium of any source motet. In the later parodies he also became more and more cavalier in his treatment of still other material extracted from his sources. Indeed, he used his sources after the 1583 book not as quarries that should be systematically worked from the top downward, but rather as open pits that he could enter at any level that suited his fancy. For another matter, the ratio of free to borrowed material shifts drastically in favor of "free" in his last masses. A comparison of such masses as *Surge propera* [1583] and *Laetatus sum* [1600] strikingly confirms this generalization.

Further proof that Victoria's technique of composing masses did not remain static but on the contrary steadily evolved is to be found in the amount of repetition that he allowed himself in different movements. In his youthful Guerrero parody—the *Simile est regnum coelorum* Mass, *a 4*—the first six bars of Kyrie I recur at the start of Agnus I.[139] But so long as he contented himself with only a single small patch carried over from one movement into another, he broke no new ground: even Morales in his *Quaeramus cum pastoribus* having carried over as much material. In his *Gaudeamus*, though not quite so abstemious, Victoria still repeated only the 14-bar passage with which Kyrie I ends during the corresponding final 14 bars of the Qui tollis;[140] and mm. 88-97 of the Credo (Et incarnatus) during the first 10 bars of Osanna II. In the *Dum complerentur* (with which his first book of masses concludes) two passages are repeated in different movements[141]—the last 20 bars of the Qui tollis equaling the last 20 of the Et in Spiritum; and the last 8 bars of Kyrie I equaling the last 8 of Agnus I. In the *Missa Quam pulchri sunt* with which his second book (1583) opens, the first 5 bars of Kyrie I are substantially repeated at the beginning of the Qui tollis.[142] In the *O quam gloriosum* which succeeds in this 1583 book, the last 8 bars of the Qui tollis equal the last 8 of the Et in spiritum;[143] and the last 8 bars of Kyrie II equal the last 9 of the single Agnus.[144]

Skipping over to the *Salve Regina* Mass, *a 8*, published in 1592, we find, however, that the number of repeated passages begins to rise. Measures 13-17 of Kyrie I equal, for instance, mm. 86-90 of the Gloria; mm. 1-7 of the Gloria equal 1-7 of the Agnus; mm. 34-42 of the Gloria equal 17-25 of the Sanctus; mm. 40-42 of the Gloria equal mm. 66-68 of the Credo.[145] A less exact kind of correspondence, but still an interesting similarity, will be found between the Domine Deus and the Benedictus.[146] Coming next to the masses published in his last book (1600), we discover that still larger blocs of repeated material are carried over from movement to movement. In the *Ave Regina*, *a 8*, mm. 39-49 of the Kyrie (II) equal mm. 15-24 of the Agnus Dei; and mm. 59-72 of the Gloria vividly recall mm. 26-36 of the Sanctus.[147] In the *Pro victoria*, *a 9*, mm. 1-8 of Kyrie I equal mm. 1-8 of the Agnus; mm. 36-42 of the Kyrie (II) equal mm. 16-22 of the Agnus; mm. 1-3 of the Gloria equal mm. 83-85 of the Credo; mm. 28-34 of the Gloria equal mm. 8_3-15_3 of the Agnus; mm. 59-76 of the Gloria equal mm. 133-150 of the Credo.[148] In his *Missa Laetatus*, mm. 87-106 of the Gloria equal mm. 160-179 of the Credo.[149]

No account has been taken in the preceding paragraph of repetitions within the same movement. In all his polychoral masses these also figure prominently. To cite repetitions of more than one bar in the *Ave Regina*: in the Kyrie, mm. 1-8_3 = 8_3-16_1; in the Gloria, mm. 59-63 = 63-67; in the Credo, mm. 34-37_3 = 37_3-41_1, mm. 91_4-93_1 = 93_2-94_3, mm. 94_4-96_2 = 96_4-98_2; in the Sanctus, mm. 26-29_1 = 29-32_1; in the Agnus, mm. 1-6_3 = 6_3-11_3. Or, to cite examples from the *Pro victoria*: in the Gloria, mm. 59-64_1 = 67-72_1; in the Credo, mm. 133-138_1 = 141-146_1; in the Sanctus, mm. 21-25_1 = 25-29_1 (= 47-51_1 = 51-55_1). Such repetitions as those just cited involve harmonic blocs. Always fond of repetitions and sequences in individual melodic lines, Victoria was to become ever more sequential and repetitious, so far as individual melodies are concerned, in his 1592 and especially in his 1600 masses.[150]

His modal preferences shifted strikingly between 1576 and 1600. All five principal movements in every 1576 mass but one end on chords built over G (masses with one flat in the signature: *Ave maris stella*, *Gaudeamus*, and *Dum complerentur*; or without flat: *Simile est regnum*): the exception being the *De beata Virgine*, which—like all other paraphrases of Mass IX—mixes modes. All five principal movements in every 1600 mass, on the other hand, end on F—one flat being always specified in the signature. In the 1583 book, the finals of the five parts of the Ordinary run thus: *Quam pulchri*, F with flat; *O quam gloriosum*, G without flat; *Surge propera*, D without flat. In the 1592 book, the finals run thus: *O magnum mysterium*, G with flat; *Quarti toni*, E; *Trahe me post te*, C; *Ascendens Christus*, G with flat; *Vidi speciosam*, G without flat; *Salve Regina*, G with flat. Or, to tally the totals: seven masses in the first three books belong to dorian or hypodorian, three to mixolydian or hypomixolydian, two to ionian or hypoionian, and one to hypophrygian. In the last book all four masses, on the other hand, are unmitigatedly in F Major. Because every mass in this last book is not only polychoral but remains exclusively in F Major throughout, we might almost suspect that it was not Victoria himself so much as it was the monarch to whom the collection was dedicated—Philip III—whose preference for bright major music determined the unanimous character of the book.

But, on the other hand, if his last masses are even more uniformly major than Mozart's symphonies, Victoria does shift meter (from duple to triple and vice versa) with considerable frequency in these last masses. Whereas, except for the Osanna, there is not a bar of triple-meter music to be found in such early masses as *Ave maris stella* and *Dum complerentur* (1576), there are 134 bars of triple-meter music among a total of 355 in his *Pro victoria* Mass (1600). These triple-meter shifts enliven every movement of the *Pro victoria* except the Agnus. The Christe eleison is in triple throughout; as is also the Osanna; and in the Gloria and Credo, a half-dozen triple-meter passages intrude *in medias res*: thereby creating exactly the mood of "alarums and excursions" which should have been captured in such a battle mass.

In sum: all these many stylistic changes to be seen in Victoria's masses set him apart from the conservative Palestrina, and ally him, rather, with the progressives of the late sixteenth century. Some critics have wished to compare him with El Greco. However overdrawn these comparisons may have been, there is still one unobserved likeness that must here be mentioned. Both artists altered their styles as they matured. The two paintings by El Greco, "Christ Driving the Money Changers from the Temple"—the early version (with soft lines and conventional figure dimensions) now hanging in the Minneapolis Institute of Art; the later (with agitated lines and elongated figure dimensions) belonging to the Frick Collection—illustrate the shifts that overtook El Greco's style.[151] Art critics now prefer the later El Greco to the earlier, whereas music critics seem to prefer the earlier Victoria to the later: only the *Officium defunctorum* of 1605—which is in part a reworking of the *Pro defunctis* of 1583—escaping the general neglect that has befallen Victoria's later masses.[152] But no matter which is preferred—his later or his earlier style—at least it will be conceded that certain fundamental differences separate his 1576 from his 1600 masses. The rapid tempo of his artistic evolution may be said to parallel El Greco's; whereas Palestrina's slower tempo parallels Titian's.

Because of their admitted importance as monuments of Spanish art, Victoria's masses ought to have provoked numerous individual analyses. The most renowned Spanish historian of this century does not mention them individually by name, however, in his "La Música en España" (1943, 1944, 1949). Just as Victoria's first patron was the German cardinal Otto von Truchsess von Waldburg; just as the first publication of his works outside Italy was the Dillingen 1589 edition of his *Cantiones sacrae*; and just as the first modern reprints were those published at Regensburg in Proske's *Musica divina* (1853-1869); so also the first analyses of these masses seem to have appeared in Peter Wagner's *Geschichte der Messe*, published at Leipzig in 1913.[153]

The first mass in 1576 invites comparison with Morales's like-named *Ave maris stella* Mass (1544).[154] Both masses break off into individual sections at exactly the same places in the wordy movements—Gloria and Credo; both reduce to three voices in the Et resurrexit and return to full choir at Et in spiritum; both again reduce to three voices in the Benedictus; both add an extra voice in Agnus II. Again, in such interior movements as the Christe, the Qui tollis, the Et incarnatus est, Et resurrexit, and the Benedictus, both composers choose to develop identical incises of the hymn.[155] Victoria's "original" counterpoint at the opening of his Agnus II resembles Morales's at the opening of his Sanctus and Agnus I. Although none of these clues taken individually seems wholly convincing, in the aggregate they do strengthen the likelihood that Victoria was well acquainted with Morales's mass.

If he was, he chose not to challenge the elder master on his own ground. Morales's mass—except for the solo movements—is canonic throughout. In other masses Victoria too includes formal canons; sometimes even three-in-one specimens: but not anywhere in this mass. Rather, he here elects to alternate paraphrase and cantus firmus treatments of the plainsong hymn, thus showing in this first mass his dislike of any too rigorous a scheme pursued throughout. The Christe eleison ends with eleven bars of treble breves, and Kyrie II closes with eight bars of tenor cantus firmus; the Gloria at "unigenite," the Credo at "Et in unum Dominum," and "Et vitam venturi saeculi," show treble instances; the Sanctus at mm. 5-8 and the Osanna, throughout, exhibit tenor instances; lastly, the *quinta pars* in Agnus II remains rather consistently a cantus firmus voice. For the rest, however, he paraphrases the hymn, oftenest in the top voice; or he constructs imitative points, using paraphrased incises of the hymn as head motives. No doubt the Victoria mass on this account loses the consistency of the Morales. Victoria—still in his twenties—shows none of the elder master's adroitness at inventing original motifs that can recur as counterpoints to the plainsong hymn in such different movements as the Patrem omnipotentem and the Et in Spiritum Sanctum—or, over a still larger arch: in Kyrie I, the Sanctus, and Agnus I. Morales's great architectural gifts, displayed in this mass and elsewhere, justly entitle him to comparison with Juan de Herrera; and it was just this talent that enabled him in his much longer mass to unify disparate age-groups of masonry into a convincing and harmonious whole. Victoria, who always chose to work on a smaller scale, did succeed, however, in leaving a much more genial and affable impression with his mass. The very transposition of the hymn up a fourth throws the vocal quartet into lighter and brighter registers. His unwillingness to commit himself to any single technique, paraphrase or cantus firmus, also prevents his manner from ever becoming tedious. A comparison of the number of printed accidentals is not so conclusive as it may seem— Victoria having been the first Spanish composer to specify all, or nearly all, his required accidentals. But for what it is worth, Victoria's Kyrie movements contain eight or nine more accidentals than are to be found in the whole of Morales's mass. Above all, his harmonies can always be analyzed in a modern G-minor sense, whatever the key signature; whereas Morales's harmonies, no matter how much ficta is applied, remain irretrievably modal in his *Ave maris stella*.

Just as in his first paraphrase Victoria bows to the hymn that was above all others popular in sixteenth-century Spain (Antonio de Cabezón alone contributed six versions of this one hymn to Venegas de Henestrosa's *Libro de cifra nueva* [Alcalá de Henares: 1557]);[156] so also in his first parody mass he pays tribute to the composer who above all other sixteenth-century peninsulars was honored in the reign of Philip II as the glory of Spain— Francisco Guerrero. *Simile est regnum coelorum*, in two *partes* (2 d *pars: Et egressus circa horam*), was first published in 1570. Since Victoria would have been still only twenty-two when the source was published, he probably composed his parody after the motet came out in print. Just as Morales honored Gombert, and Guerrero honored Morales, so Victoria pays tribute to his greatest Spanish contemporary when he places the Guerrero parody at the forefront of his first collection. Even if the position of this parody in the 1576 Masses was not a conscious gesture, Victoria pays Guerrero special honor by being the very first of a long line of Spanish composers to publish a parody of a Guerrero motet (see above, p. 136).

Victoria, always interested in mellifluous sound and harmonic perspicuity, does not here attempt the kind of closely knit parody that Morales and Guerrero usually produced. Only in the Sanctus of this particular mass does he so cling to motives from the source as not to loose hold on them for even a moment. The opening points of imitation in Kyrie I, Christe, Kyrie II, Et in terra pax, and Patrem omnipotentem share a common procedure. During each, he pairs the two lower and the two upper voices. One member of a pair starts with a quotation from the source motet followed by the other member answering with an original counterpoint. Abbreviated with capitals, the five points just alluded to may be thus schematized: GVGV. The first eight bars of Kyrie I are shown by way of example. As for the

specific source material used in the opening points, every principal movement in Victoria's mass, except the Credo, begins with the head motive of Guerrero's motet. Kyrie II, Qui tollis, and the Sanctus conclude with the final incise of Guerrero's *pars 2*. However, the order in which motives from the source are brought forward within movements is subject to wide variation. No individual movement of Victoria's mass fails at least somewhere to allude to the source. Even the Benedictus, *a 3*, which opens not with a point on a Guerrero motive, but with a point on the countersubject devised by Victoria at the beginning of Kyrie I, reverts halfway through to a Guerrero motive—the one associated with that part of the motet text at mm. 53-55 which reads "in vineam suam."

The text of Guerrero's Septuagesima motet (Matt. 20:1-2; 3-4) divides into nine incises for *pars 1*, and seven for *pars 2*. In conformity with the usual practice, Victoria made much more frequent use of the opening and closing incises of *partes 1* and *2* than he did of any of the other dozen incises. At least one of Guerrero's sixteen incises failed to stimulate his invention anywhere in the mass: the one in the motet at mm. 46-50. If he does refer to those incises found at mm. 73-76 and 90-96 in the source—as he may perhaps be said to have done respectively at *dona nobis pacem* (cantus) in his Agnus II, and at *suscipe* in his Qui tollis—these references are so glancing and remote as to be very uncertain echoes. Of some interest is the fact that he should at least twice in his mass have made much of the incise at mm. 82-85 setting *stantes fori* ("standing in the marketplace"). The last three measures of his Christe eleison and mm. 19-21 of the Credo (*unigenitum*) quote this particular phrase.

It was Peter Wagner who in 1913 first pointed to the link that unites the *Missa canonica* (Prague: 1580) of Jacobus Gallus [= Jakob Handl] with Victoria's *Simile est regnum coelorum*.[157] If the breve rests are omitted Gallus's ingenious *Missa canonica* can be performed throughout as a mass *a 8*—the second quartet following canonically, hard on the heels of the first quartet. Gallus, a protégé of the bishop of Olmütz, finished his masses during a two-year period in the latter's service, 1578-1580. The *Missa canonica*, the last of his masses *a 4* in the Prague imprint of 1580, was probably the last composed. If so, the example of Victoria's Agnus II in the 1576 *Liber Primus. Qui Missas, Psalmos, Magnificat . . . Complectitur* may well have fired his imagination to the exploit. At all events, their mutually intimate dealings with the same youthful Society of Jesus would have brought the 1576 publication of the *Collegii Germanici in Vrbe Roma Musicae Moderator* to Gallus's immediate attention.

Victoria concluded both his *Quam pulchri* (1583) and *Trahe me post te* (1592) with Agnuses containing a four-in-two canon; and his *Ascendens Christus* (1592) with an Agnus containing a three-in-one canon. He concluded the following five masses: *De beata Virgine* and *Gaudeamus* of 1576, *O magnum mysterium*, *Quarti toni*, and *Vidi speciosam* of 1592, with Agnuses containing a two-in-one canon. But only in his *Simile est regnum* did he conclude with an Agnus containing so elaborate a feat as an eight-in-four canon. His precedent for such extreme artifice is to be found at pages 61-62 in the same motet collection of 1570 from which he culled his source: the example being Guerrero's own *Pater noster, a 8* (first published, 1555; reprinted, 1566, 1570). The elder master having set the pace, the younger bravely climaxed his tribute to the "sage of Seville" with an eight-in-four canon—and moreover, one which is not thematically independent of the Guerrero *Simile est regnum* motet, but on the contrary constantly weaves fragments into the canonic lacework.

The third mass in Victoria's 1576 book recalls the first in Morales's *Liber primus* of 1544: if for no other reason than because both chose in their

De beata Virgine Masses to paraphrase plainsong Mass IX and Credo I. However, the similarities extend beyond those merely fortuitous likenesses to which a common source would give rise. Victoria has actually quoted Morales. His Osanna I, for instance, extensively quotes the Osanna II of Morales's *De beata Virgine, a 4.* Also, Victoria's Osanna II takes its cue from Morales's I, in that both draw out a canon based on the same plain-song incise. Significantly, Victoria includes a canon only in the Osanna II of his *De beata Virgine* Mass—no other Osanna containing one, nor for that matter any other movement in his twenty published masses except Agnuses and the Crucifixus of his *Alma Redemptoris* Mass (1600). Another echo resounds at Victoria's "Qui sedes." Here, both composers simultaneously break into triple meter. Both return to duple for the phrase "Quoniam tu solus." In his last Agnus, Victoria augments to seven parts. Tenor I follows cantus II in canon at the lower octave (not at the lower fifth, as Pedrell would have us believe).[158]

During the first four bars of "Qui sedes" the junior composer's cantus duplicates the elder's tenor: both masters notating "Who sittest at the right hand of God the Father" with voids. At *miserere nobis*, on the other hand, Victoria suddenly shifts from voids to blacks in all parts. Since such blacks are by no means a necessary, but merely an optional, method of notating the music that he conceived for "have mercy upon us," they serve in all likelihood as a means of contrasting the purity of Christ (who sits at the right hand) with the blackness of sinners (who implore mercy). Such an interpretation will by no means seem fanciful to a student who has exam-ined with care any of Victoria's personally superintended motet publica-tions. Among the many instances of eye-music to be seen in his motets, as telling an example as any will be found at the outset of his "De beata Virgine" motet *a 6* published for the first time in the same *Liber Primus. Qui Missas, Psalmos, Magnificat, . . . Aliaque Complectitur* (1576) that con-tains the *De beata Virgine* Mass now under discussion. Though headed by the duple signature, C, this motet, *Nigra sum sed formosa* ("I am black but beautiful"), begins with uniform blacks in all parts: only reverting to whites for the last syllable of "beautiful."

Another *De beata Virgine* Mass with which Victoria's Lady Mass *a 5* can usefully be compared stands at the head of Palestrina's 1567 book dedicated to Philip II. Victoria differs from the Roman master on at least one crucial issue: the amount of degree-inflection specified in print. By actual count, Victoria in his Kyries prescribes 24 accidentals; in his Gloria, 60; in his Credo, 91. But the parsimonious Palestrina specified only a meager 2, 8, and 15 in these same movements.

No ingenious application of ficta can turn Palestrina's melodic lines into a counterfeit of Victoria's. Throughout his *De beata Virgine* Mass, Victoria insists upon such stepwise progressions as f, g, f♯; or f♯, g, f[♮]; or b♭, c, b[♮]; or b, c, b♭—in other words, a semitonal ascent followed by a whole-step descent; or vice versa. Below will be seen some eighteen examples chosen at random from Kyrie and Gloria movements of his *De beata Virgine*.

Each illustrates the same type of melodic progression. Each has been checked against 1576 and 1583 imprints of this mass. These examples can be matched with similarly mannered melodic progressions taken from any early or late Victoria work whatsoever. For those who wish to see the surrounding polyphonic complex, the following eighteen melodic snatches can be conferred with Pedrell, *VicO*, II, 93-101 (Kyries: beginning at mm. 4, 9, 12, 20, 33, 50; Gloria: beginning at mm. 11, 18, 28, 32, 37, 48, 59, 77, 83, 103, 113, 114).

Victoria's *De beata Virgine* in both 1576 and 1583 imprints shows one or two niceties not to be surmised from Pedrell's edition. For instance, Et in terra pax, Domine Deus, and Qui tollis—that is, the movements of the Gloria—carry C instead of Victoria's customary ₵ for their mensuration sign. (Morales also employed C, by way of exception to his usual ₵, for the signature in certain movements of his *De beata Virgine* Mass, *a 5*; see above, page 48.) That Victoria did not choose C haphazardly may be inferred not only from the fact that all Gloria movements carry it, but also from its recurrence in all voices after the momentary shifts into Φ3 at "Qui sedes" (mm. 91-102) and "Cum Sancto Spiritu" (mm. 124-126). In contrast with the Φ3 proportional signature at both "Qui sedes" and "Cum Sancto Spiritu" of his *De beata* Gloria, he employs Φ3/2 for shifts to triple in such a Gloria as that of his *Surge propera* Mass (the basic meter of the *Surge propera* Gloria is ₵ instead of C). One other nicety in his *De beata*: the bassus in Kyrie, Gloria, and Sanctus carries the baritone clef; but in Credo and Agnuses, the bass clef.

Gaudeamus, the fourth mass in Victoria's 1576 set, no longer betrays a mere affinity with Morales but is actually parodied on the elder's 1538 peace motet. This mass and *Surge propera* (1583, Palestrina parody) share the distinction of being his two masses in which all the principal movements open with the head motive from the source. Although both the *Jubilate* motet and the *Gaudeamus* Mass call for six voices, Victoria specifies CCAATB: whereas Morales had called for CAATTB. Such a rearrangement naturally enhances the brilliance of the mass.[159] (Elsewhere, for that matter, Victoria consistently prefers light, high voices. In this 1576 book the "bass" of both *Ave maris stella* and *Simile est regnum* carries tenor clef; and in Kyrie, Gloria, and Sanctus of the *De beata Virgine*, baritone clef.) To afford as much variety as possible Victoria chooses a different vocal combination in each of the *Gaudeamus* solo movements. In the Christe, he calls for CCAT, in the Domine Deus for ATB, in the Crucifixus for CCAA, and in the Pleni for AATB. Only in the Pleni does he retain the Gaudeamus melodic ostinato that gives the mass its name. In the Benedictus (the fifth and final solo movement) he reverts to the same CCAA combination already used in the Crucifixus.

Not only does he so faithfully follow usual practice as to begin every principal movement in the *Gaudeamus* with the motet head motive, but also he hews to convention in this same mass when he closes both Kyrie I and Qui tollis peccata with the seven bars that end *pars 1* of the motet. In the last seven bars of Et in spiritum he quotes the concluding seven of *pars 2.* The intermediate material from the motet of which Victoria makes perhaps most telling use will be found at mm. 71-74 in the source. Both the Et incarnatus (Credo, mm. 88-97) and the first ten bars of the Osanna following the Benedictus quote this material (extended by repetiton). However, he changes Morales's layout of voices so that CCAATB (Pedrell edition) replaces Tenor-Sextus-Cantus-Quintus-Altus-Bassus in the source. This particular patch of quoted music sets the words *O felix Paule, O vos felices principes* (O happy Paul, O you happy monarchs) in the motet.

In Morales's *Jubilate,* the ostinato—a voice apart—is not imitated by any of the five other voices. In the mass, the ostinato, though still a voice apart, does occasionally provoke a melodic imitation in such movements as the Qui tollis ("Quoniam tu solus") and Et in Spiritum ("Qui cum Patre"). In Kyrie I, at the close of Qui tollis, and in Agnus II, the ostinato-bearing voices break out with the word *Gaudeamus.* At other times Victoria fits the liturgical words to the melodic ostinato. In Agnus II an added tenor swells the number of parts. Cantus II, followed by tenor I (in canon at the suboctave), sings the plainsong introit during this last climactic movement: both repeating not only the introit incipit (five times) but here also the catchword *Gaudeamus.* Never perhaps in sixteenth-century music has such a merely occasional work as Morales's motet been lifted to loftier heights that in this mass. If for no other reason then because it conjoins the two most celebrated names in Spanish Renaissance music it should be known. Better still, its intrinsic worth does both masters the highest honor.

In *Dum complerentur, a 6,* the mass with which the 1576 book closes, Victoria parodies his own Pentecost motet *a 5* published in 1572. In contrast with the Guerrero and Morales motets of two *partes* chosen for earlier parody in this book, Victoria's original 162-bar motet is in responsory form. The amount carried over from *pars 1* into *pars 2* occupies half the motet. *Pars 1* extends to 86 breves, the last 41 of which are repeated at the close of *pars 2.* As is Victoria's practice, he opens both *partes* of his motet with points of imitation combining two head motives. We have already seen at page 000 that in his *Simile est regnum* Mass he began by combining two head motives when he alternated motive G from the source with an original motive, V, in this order: GVGV. However, since both A and B were already present in the opening point of his *Dum complerentur* motet (*VicO,* I, 59):

his task at the outset in his mass of the same name (*VicO*, **IV**, 29) becomes more that of rearrangement, than the invention of any new "B"
motive:

The Et in terra pax opens exactly as does Kyrie I. Even when at Domine
Deus he reduces to four voices for a solo movement, he still busies himself
devising a new ABAB combination (*VicO*, **IV**, 35):

In the Benedictus, he ornaments his "A" motive; working both "A" and
"B" in double harness (*VicO*, **IV**, 51):

In Agnus I he embellishes both "A" and "B" motives[160]—driving even the
ornamented versions as a team, however (*VicO*, **IV**, 53):

Only at the beginning of the Sanctus does he devise truly free counterpoint to motive "A."

Four movements begin with conventionally monothematic points of imitation: Christe eleison (= bassus, mm. 19-21 in source), Kyrie II (= cantus, mm. 35-37 in source), Crucifixus (= motive "B," extended), Pleni sunt. Two movements start with motives from the source riding the waves of freely invented homophony: the Qui tollis (altus II = motive "A," extended), and Et incarnatus (cantus = cantus, mm. 70-74 in source). Both the Qui tollis and the Et in Spiritum Sanctum close with identical 20-bar passages, expanding the refrain of the source (mm. 70-86 = 146-162 in motet).

In the final Agnus he forgoes canon. But he does epitomize the motet. Motives "A" and "B" intertwine everywhere. Among the transformation of "A," the following are perhaps the more important:

During the sixteen-bar peroration, this last variant of motive "A" (first heard in the bassus) alternately bolsters the other six voices and floats on the crest of the polyphonic sea (in cantus I and II). The sharping of the second note in the last variant harks back to mm. 3-4 of the source motet. Victoria, the first peninsular composer to specify precisely the accidentals that he desires, makes it plain throughout both his motet and mass that for him C♮ and C♯, F♮ and F♯, are freely interchangeable notes in any point of imitation (mm. 4 [tenor II], 11 [bassus], 17 [tenor II], of Kyrie I; and *passim*).

Victoria's second book of masses (1583) bears the interesting title *Missarum Libri Duo* ("two books of masses")—the obvious reason being that it contains all five of the 1576 masses, plus four previously unpublished masses. The new additions comprise not just the *Pro defunctis* (which Pedrell wished to list as the only new mass in this 1583 book)[161] but also two parodies *a 4* of original motets—*Quam pulchri sunt* and *O quam gloriosum*; and a superb parody *a 5* of *Surge propera* from Palestrina's *Motecta festorum totius anni . . . quaternis vocibus . . . Liber primus* (1563).

The three parodies in his 1576 book were modeled on motets of two *partes*; but the three parodies added in his 1583 book are modeled on motets of one *pars*. In the *Quam pulchri* Mass he weaves new material into the opening points of Kyrie I, Et in terra pax, Patrem omnipotentem, Sanctus, and Agnus I. In the *O quam gloriosum*—departing from his custom—he quotes not just individual motives from the source but transfers intact whole blocks of polyphony from motet into mass. In the *Surge propera* he pays homage to Palestrina with a few consistently monothematic points of imitation: the head motives of which derive exclusively from the source without any admixture of freely invented material.

Palestrina, senior though he was to Victoria, awaited the example of Victoria's *Dum complerentur* Mass before embarking upon his first parody of an original motet. His *Missarum cum quatuor et quinque vocibus liber quartus* of 1582 is his first book to contain such a parody (the *Lauda Sion* Mass opening this book is based on his own motet published in 1563). Because of the closeness of publication dates, a comparison of Palestrina's parody procedures in the *Lauda Sion* Mass, *a 4*, with Victoria's procedures in masses similarly modeled on original motets should have value. In both the Christe and the Kyrie II of the *Lauda Sion* Mass, Palestrina, like Victoria, combines newly invented countersubjects with head motives from his source. But thereafter in his mass he dismisses these countersubjects, as if they are merely *ad hoc* matter unworthy of further consideration. Victoria, on the other hand, returns to his countersubjects time and again in later movements. For example, the countermelody (altus) at the outset of Kyrie I in the *Quam pulchri* Mass (*VicO*, II, 38): is not immediately thereafter dismissed from service with an "honorable discharge"; but is instead

pressed into duty in every one of the four voices during Kyrie I; and again combined with the same head motive at the outset of both the Qui tollis (*VicO*, II, 42) and (minus the first note) the Patrem omnipotentem. It is this exalting of his newly invented countersubject to equal dignity with the derived head motive which, for a first contrast, distinguishes Victoria's method from Palestrina's. Second: Palestrina throughout each major movement borrows material from the source in seriatim order. Victoria, while beginning every principal movement with the initial motive from the source motet in such a mass as *Quam pulchri* (f a b♭ a), thereafter does not bind himself to any rigorous plan. In the three sections comprising the Gloria, for instance, he cites successively material to be found in the motet at mm. 1-5 (= 1-5, Gloria), 9-15 (= 7-11), 70-75 (= 20-25), 58-64 (= 37-43), 78-85 (= 45-52); mm. 1-3 in combination with mm. 78-80 (= 53-55); mm. 1-5 (= 75-80), 29-34 (= 110-115), 72-77 (= 128-136).

In both Agnuses I (*a 5*) and II (*a 6*) of the *Quam pulchri*, Victoria constructs canons: the first at the unison between the two tenors, the second (of a four-in-two kind) between paired cantus and paired bassus voices. The two canonic Agnuses are thus cemented: the Agnus I canon, which opens with the derived head motive (tenor I *dux*, tenor II *comes*), is encased within a newly invented countersubject moving in tenths (*VicO*, II, 53):

This countersubject (plus-signs) then in turn becomes the initium of the paired canonic voices in Agnus II (*VicO*, II, 54):

During the four-in-two canon, cantus I and bassus I move almost exclusively in tenths. In consequence, cantus II and bassus II (following at the unison) travel usually in tenths. Although this parallel motion inevitably reduces the four-in-two canon to less of a pyrotechnic feat than Guerrero or Lobo might have carried off, such continuously mellifluous motion between pairs of outer voices undoubtedly vivifies the idea of *Quam pulchri sunt gressus tui* ("How beautiful are thy footsteps") better than would a more cerebral solution of the canonic problem. Some might even claim that Victoria never intended by a four-in-two canon to exhibit learning, but instead to illustrate in musical terms the pursuit of "beautiful footsteps."

The *O quam gloriosum*, *a 4*, modeled on the All Saints' motet *a 4* with which his 1572 *Motecta* began, has received as many accolades as any Victoria mass. Tovey chose the motet as "one of the most perfect examples existing," and printed it entire in his article on "Motet" for the fourteenth edition of the *Encyclopaedia Britannica* (XV, 851-852). In his article on "Mass" in the same encyclopedia, he inserted short excerpts from Kyrie I, Christe, Kyrie II, the Et in terra pax, and the Osanna (*ibid.*, XV, 24-25) to illustrate Victoria's application of the parody technique. Peter Wagner also attested the extraordinary popularity of this particular mass[162]—reprinting excerpts from both Kyrie I and the Patrem omnipotentem. Withal, the mass cannot be called Victoria's most typical. For example, he never once refers to the opening incise of the source anywhere in the mass. For another matter, he transfers the whole polyphonic complex from motet into mass in such movements as Kyrie I, Christe, and Kyrie II; but quotes only individual lines from his source in the other masses described previously. When not availing himself of the whole complex, he composes so independently of his source in *O quam gloriosum* as to give the impression that this is a free, instead of a parody, mass. It also seems less than typical for him to have concluded without a canonic Agnus, especially when the roll is called of those masses that do so conclude—*Simile est regnum*, *De beata Virgine*, *Gaudeamus*, *Quam pulchri sunt*, *O magnum mysterium*, *Quarti toni*, *Trahe me post te*, and *Ascendens Christus*.

In *Surge propera* (found to have been parodied on Palestrina's motet by Gustave Reese), all the principal movements commence with the head motive of the source; so do certain intermediate sections as well: the Crucifixus, Et in Spiritum, and Benedictus. At the outset of three sections (Kyrie I, Et in terra pax, and the Benedictus) Victoria bandies only Palestrina's head motive in the points. Since the parody calls for five voices, and the source for only four, his abstemiousness in these few opening points seems all the more remarkable: especially when it is remembered how unanimously the opening points of his Guerrero parody alternated borrowed with original themes. In the Palestrina parody, he returns to his more usual method in the opening points of Patrem omnipotentem, Crucifixus, Et in Spiritum, Sanctus, Agnus I and II, each of which incorporates original material. He betrays his artistic individuality when he throws a wimple around the Palestrina head motive at its every appearance (except Et in Spiritum Sanctum)—thus softening it:

He cites four or five other motives from the source with some frequency. The last of these also becomes more graceful in his transformation:

Other motives that find their way into the parody come in the motet at mm. 26-28, altus ("Jam enim hiems transiit" = Kyrie II [mm. 47-49], Patrem omnipotentem [mm. 64-67], Et in spiritum [mm. 180-183, 220-223], Agnus I [mm. 1-4]); mm. 29-35, cantus (= Kyrie II [mm. 50-55], Et in terra [mm. 23-27], Patrem omnipotentem [mm. 65-70], Crucifixus [mm. 109-112], Et in spiritum [mm. 221-226]); mm. 42-27 ("imber abiit" = Et in terra pax [mm. 40-44], Et in Spiritum Sanctum [mm. 198-202]); mm. 57-62 ("flores apparuerunt" = Christe [mm. 26-40], Patrem omnipotentem [mm. 31-34], Crucifixus [mm. 132-135], Sanctus [mm. 15-20, mm. 23-29]; Osanna II).

The countersubjects that he composes to match Palestrina's head motive in the opening points of the Patrem omnipotentem and the Et in Spiritum are sufficiently alike to justify the supposition that he intends a cross-reference. However, in only one point of imitation—that which opens Agnus II—does Victoria seem to have tried combining two motives from the source. Here the cantus sufficiently resembles the altus at mm. 26-28 of the motet:

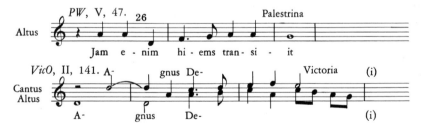

to suggest that Victoria deliberately intends working two different motives from his source in double harness. Even so, the allusion is not exact. Unlike Morales, whose skill at combining disparate motives from his sources can never be praised sufficiently, Victoria seems always to have placed sheer beauty of sound and an easy flow of tonic-dominant harmony ahead of all other goals.

Victoria's *Surge propera* Mass extends to 633 bars (Kyrie: 25, 21, 20; Gloria: 154; Credo: 238; Sanctus: 46, 56; Agnus: 35, 40). In the 1583 imprint of this mass he specifies a total of 362 accidentals (Kyrie: 12, 7, 12; Gloria: 91; Credo: 133; Sanctus: 25, 39; Agnus: 22, 21). Of these 362 accidentals, 227 are sharps. Thus, his accidentals here (as in *De beata Virgine*) reach a surprising total. On average, he requires more than one in every other bar of *Surge propera*, with sharps in every third bar. The Palestrina source motet, on the other hand, lacks so much as a single accidental anywhere (either in 1571 or 1590 reprints: no known copies of the original Roman edition of 1563 survive). The Palestrina mass *a 5* in dorian, published in 1582—*Eripe me de inimicis meis*—can also be compared fruitfully This mass, parodied on a Jean Maillard motet (1559), was originally published without any title other than *Missa prima*: it remaining for Haberl to christen it when he published Volume XIII of the complete works. The head motive closely resembles the "original" head motive conceived by Palestrina for his *Surge propera* motet. Indeed, the *Eripe me* head motive matches with the *Surge propera* in every respect save rhythm:

PW, XIII, 59.   Palestrina

Ky- ri- e,   Ky- ri- e e- le- i- son.

Palestrina's *Eripe me* Mass extends to 695 bars (24, 30, 25; 125; 204; 116, 76; 47, 48). However, a total of only 145 accidentals can be found in the original imprint (5, 7, 6; 28; 57; 25, 3; 5, 9). Of these 145 accidentals, some 65 are sharps. In Victoria's slightly shorter parody mass, published one year later, in the same number of movements and same mode, calling for the same number of voices and using an almost identical head motive; the junior master on the other hand calls for considerably more than twice as many accidentals, and—more amazingly—three and a half times as many sharps. This comparison between Palestrina's rate of degree-inflection and Victoria's can be made between almost any two masses of these masters, with analogous results. Whatever their unstated preferences, at least Victoria was vastly more concerned with printed degree-inflection than was Palestrina.

As every student of the period knows, the component elements of a sixteenth-century polyphonic Requiem were not standardized. Therefore, the first question when any *Missa pro defunctis* is under discussion must be: "what movements are included?" Morales's Requiem *a 5*, printed in 1544 (*Missarum liber secundus*), differs from Victoria's *Pro defunctis* in containing only such sections as belong to a Mass for the Dead. We must look to Mo-

rales's *Officium defunctorum* for the invitatory, psalms, lessons, and responsories sung, not at Mass, but (as the title implies) in the burial office. Palestrina's *Missa pro defunctis, a 5*—printed in his first book (1554)—resembles
Morales's in including only such elements as belong properly to a Mass.
Even those which he selects from the Mass, however, are so few in number
that his *Pro defunctis* extends to but half Morales's length. He omits even the
introit that gives the Requiem Mass its name, and begins instead with
Kyrie-Christe-Kyrie movements. He then skips over the gradual and sequence that Morales included—proceeding directly to the offertory, Domine Jesu Christe; adds a polyphonic setting of its versicle, Hostias et
preces; continues with Sanctus-Benedictus; and concludes with Agnuses.[163]
None of his movements opens with a plainsong incipit; none is a cantus
firmus movement. Guerrero's *Pro defunctis, a 4* (1566) resembles both the
Morales and the Palestrina in including only such elements as belonged
to a Mass for the Dead (but according to pre-Tridentine Braga usage).
Opening with a setting of the introit, the Guerrero 1566 Requiem proceeds
thence to the Kyries and to the gradual. Expecially fine are his polyphonic settings of John 11:25-26 and Psalm 41 [= 42]:2-3. Then comes
a setting of the offertory; next, Sanctus-Pleni-Osanna followed by Bene-
dictus-Osanna; then three Agnuses; and lastly a *communicanda* (= communio), *a 5* (Lux aeterna). As with Morales's 1544 exemplar, and in
contradistinction to Palestrina's 1554 Requiem, Guerrero's 1566 *Missa pro
defunctis* made a frequent feature of printed plainsong incipits.

Guerrero published a second Requiem in 1582. What distinguishes his
second from his first is the insertion not only of a six-voice motet, *Hei mihi
Domine*, before the Agnuses; but also his concluding the second Requiem
with a responsory and versicles that belong to the *Exsequiarum ordo* (burial
service). In the burial service, the Libera me responsory with its three versicles—Tremens factus, Quando coeli movendi, and Dies illa—comes immediately before the last prayers. Victoria, like Guerrero in 1582, closes his
Pro defunctis (1583) with these same burial service additions. When repub-
lishing his 1583 Requiem in 1592, Victoria appended still another two
responsories that belong not to the Mass, but to the Office for the Dead.
These 1592 additions are to be sung at Matins: Credo quod Redemptor in
the first nocturn, Peccantem me in the third. Thus, the 1583 and 1592
imprints both contain more than just music for the Mass of the Dead.
These imprints also include polyphony for parts of the burial service and
office for the dead.

Throughout his *Pro defunctis* Victoria always confides the borrowed plainchant to his top voice. Morales in 1544 artfully varied his sonorities by
giving the plainsong to altus II in the gradual and to supranus II in the
offertory. Victoria contents himself with assigning it to the one voice; he

also gives all the plainchant incipits and Responsorium interludes (as printed in 1583) to the cantus and to no other voice: whereas Morales on occasion gave the incipits to altus II and supranus II as well; and Guerrero in 1582 the incipit of the burial service versicle *Quando coeli movendi* to a baritone (F-clef on middle line). As for still other distinctions, Morales set the whole of the *In memoria aeterna* and *Hostias et preces* versicles polyphonic-ally; whereas Victoria left the incipit of the first and the whole of the second in plainsong. Morales set *In memoria* as a trio, except the last two words, "non timebit" (which he set as a separate movement, *a 5*); Victoria follows an opposite course, never atomizing the phrases of a versicle into separate polyphonic movements. Morales set the pre-Tridentine sequence *Pie Jesu*: neither Guerrero (1566 and 1582) nor Victoria, on the other hand, include any sequences whatsoever.

Just as Palestrina's 1554 version of the *Pro defunctis* has been generally considered to be a more hopeful document than Morales's of 1544 (see above, page 80), so likewise Victoria's of 1583 strikes a more happily ex-pectant note. To take only the matter of pitches: Morales required his su-pranus to sing A's below Middle C even when "lux perpetua" was being implored (*MME*, XV, 124, mm. 31-32). Only twice in his entire Requiem did he write so high a note as d^1 for his top voice (*MME*, XV, 121, meas. 52; 134, meas. 37). Throughout his offertory, although he specified both supranus I and II and gave the quoted plainsong to supranus II, he sub-merged the quoted plainchant a fourth below the pitch later to be chosen by Palestrina. In the gradual he submerged the quoted plainsong an octave below the pitch later to be chosen by Victoria. The latter's lighter and brighter registers cannot be construed merely as examples of the trend up-ward in later sixteenth-century vocal music. (Guerrero so late as 1582 still quotes the plainsong of the gradual and of its versicle a fifth below the level to be chosen by Victoria in 1583; the Agnus plainsong in Guerrero's 1582 Requiem similarly travels a fourth lower than Victoria's.) As if pitch were in itself no sufficient clue, Victoria's brighter colors are also manifest in the amount of sharping which he requires. After we exclude the numerous notes where Morales's intentions are left in doubt so far as sharping of the plainsong-bearing part is concerned, there still remain some other places where he unequivocally intended a natural instead of the sharp specified at the analogous moment in Victoria's Requiem. These may be found at the following places in the Morales and Victoria works, respectively: mm. 19_3, $49_3 = 17_{2-4}$, 42_4 in their graduals; 98_3 and $99_3 = 77_{2-3}$ in their *In memoria* versicles; 19_3, $44_3 = 23_3$, 46_4 in their offertories; $45 = 35_{2-4}$ in their Pleni's; 21_1, $44_1 = 17_3$, 37_3 in their communio's. Moreover, Victoria's harmonic progressions remain so suave and smooth at all times that a "Victorian" composer might have conceived them. So proleptic a harmonic sense as he revealed in the *Dies illa* versicle distinguishes him not only from Morales but also from Guerrero (whose setting of the same burial service versicle is to be seen above at page 203). The whole of the Victoria versicle will not be shown here. But for a preliminary test, his first seven bars can be compared with Guerrero's (*VicO*, VI, 119):

The next six Victoria masses, because they appeared together in his 192-page Roman imprint of 1592, *Missae quatuor, quinque, sex, et octo vocibus concinendae*, should be considered as a group. Five are parodies of original motets; whereas the other, entitled *Quarti toni*, appears to be a free mass. The first in the album is based on his own 1572 Circumcision motet of single *pars—O magnum mysterium.*[164] The distance that Victoria had traversed in the intervening two decades is admirably illustrated at the very openings of motet and mass. In the motet (*VicO*, I, 11), he was still content to suffer bare fifths and octaves between the two counterpointing voices. But in the mass (*VicO*, II, 69), he insists—even at the sacrifice of the imitation—upon outlining full-blooded triads.

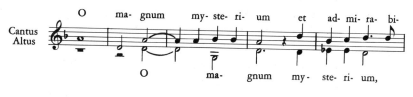

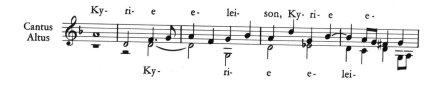

At the start of the Sanctus (*VicO*, II, 77) he again eschews any exact imitation for the sake of outlining triads.

Paradoxically, the one incise of the source which he ignores throughout is the most statically chordal (mm. 40-44: "O beata Virgo"). This passage, like the opening of the *O quam gloriosum* motet, may fail to appear in the corresponding mass because it could only be quoted—not developed.

In the wordy movements he journeys straight through without changing his vocal combination anywhere and without deferring to any motives from the source. True, the Qui tollis recalls "jacentem in praesepio," and Patrem omnipotentem recalls "ut animalia." But for the rest, he goes his own free way: a way carpeted with sweet-smelling flowers that lack learned thorns to prick one's feet. His sprightliness in such passages as "deprecationem nostram" (Qui tollis, meas. 49), "visibilium et invisibilium," "Genitum non factum, consubstantialem" (Patrem omnipotentem, mm. 7-10, 27-29), "Et iterum venturus est" (Et incarnatus, mm. 71-73), and "et vivificantem" (Et in Spiritum Sanctum, mm. 84-85) exceeds any shown hitherto in his 1576 or 1583 masses. Indeed, in such passages as these his "heart dances with delight," much as if he were writing a madrigal to be sung on a summer's day.

His *Missa Quarti toni*, second in the 1592 book, has usually been classed as a free mass because (1) apart from innocuous rising scale-passages such as occur at the openings of Kyrie II and Patrem omnipotentem, no carry-over of motives from movement to movement is discernible; and (2) with the exception of the *Missa pro victoria*, his ascertained parodies all bear titles that lead directly to their sources. Only the *Quarti toni* Mass cultivates the hypophrygian; that he was never at any time overly fond of the "fourth tone" can be confirmed from a study of the motets. Among forty-four motets, only three adhere to it. Those three—*Senex puerum portabat, Sancta Maria succurre miseris*, and *Domine non sum dignus*—set texts that deal respectively with the old man, Simeon; the miserable and weak who cry out for aid; and the unworthiness of the communicant (*VicO*, I, 17, 19, 39). Some critics have sought to compare the opening incise of *Senex puerum* with the Christe eleison; and mm. 18-26 with Kyrie II; but such remote likenesses, not to mention the slight resemblance between the opening incises of *Domine non sum dignus* and the Sanctus (bassus), are hard to take seriously. When his three "fourth tone" motets are studied, it is at once obvious that none of the three exults or leaps for joy. On the other hand, all the original motets that he can be proved to have parodied do so exult.

As in the *O magnum mysterium* Mass, the sole movement of the *Quarti toni*[165] for trio is the Benedictus; and the only movement augmenting to a quintet is the single (canonic) Agnus. Throughout the single Agnus of both masses, cantus II follows cantus I at the unison. These masses betray still other structural similarities. In the Glorias he bursts once, and once only, into triple meter; and at the same words—"Cum Sancto Spiritu." In both Credos he similarly interpolates two short passages in triple meter. During these interpolations he contents himself for the nonce with chordal writing.

Although Victoria does, of course, explicitly assign his *Quarti toni* to hypophrygian, it cannot be gainsaid that a perfectly tidy (if anachronistic) harmonic analysis of the whole mass in A minor can be given. Even the crucial cadences at the ends of Kyrie II, Qui tollis, Et in Spiritum, and the Osanna yield to such an analysis: if one grants that each ends on a dominant chord. The benefits to be gained from an analysis of this unique mass—the only one he assigned to a "tone"—soon become obvious. If even in this mass he so anticipates the harmonic procedures that a baroque composer writing in A minor would have followed, a fortiori his other masses prove even more amenable to major-minor analyses.

Several tests to prove that Victoria no longer felt himself bound by the old laws of modal usage, and gave allegiance instead to the newer laws of major and minor key, can be applied. First, the mass may be searched for any chordal nexus involving E minor-A minor. This will be a crucial test. If every time an E-chord happens to be followed by an A-chord, he must sharp the third of the E-chord (G♯), then obviously the E-chord has sacrificed what independence it once enjoyed in truly modal music to take on a new role of fetch-and-carry in "key music."

The A-minor chord follows triads, built over E a total of thirty-three times during the course of the *Quarti toni* (Kyrie: mm. 6, 24, 25, 40; Gloria: mm. 2, 19, 28, 30, 43, 44, 49, 57; Credo: mm. 6, 25, 35, 43, 50, 52, 80, 85, 86[2], 97; Sanctus: mm. 9, 18, 20, 22[2], 25, 36; Agnus: mm. 15, 16, 21). Four of these places, and four only, involve the progression E minor-

A minor (Kyrie: meas. 25; Sanctus: mm. 35-36; Agnus: mm. 15, 16). The others involve E Major-A minor. To vivify these figures, we should compare Victoria's *Quarti toni* with another "quarti toni" *a 4* extending as nearly as possible to the same length. Palestrina's *Sine nomine, a 4,* from his *Liber secundus* (1567) dedicated to Philip II, comes as close to fulfilling these conditions as any—it being his shortest hypophrygian mass. No less than twenty-five instances, not of E Major-A minor progressions, but of an A-minor chord preceded by an obligatory E minor—obligatory because of skips involving the notes G to C, or for other reasons—have been inventoried in this Palestrina "quarti toni" (Kyrie: mm. 7, 10, 20-21, 24-25, 26, 29; Gloria: mm. 19, 48-49, 59-60, 73-74; Credo: mm. 4, 7, 109, 117, 124; Sanctus: mm. 37-38, 40-41; Benedictus: meas. 48; Agnus I: mm. 11, 42, 42-43; Agnus II: mm. 3-4, 19-20, 22, 51). Palestrina's twenty-five E minor-A minor progressions would be doubled or tripled if Casimiri's extremely liberal application of ficta were not respected. Even so, the comparison between Victoria's four with Palestrina's twenty-five obligatory E minor-A minor progressions is most revealing. It demonstrates beyond cavil that as firmly together as they may have stood on other issues, Palestrina still knew how to write genuinely modal music; whereas Victoria with his eyes on the future came no nearer to classic hypophrygian than did Bach in his choral harmonization of *Befiehl du deine Wege.*[166]

The five-part mass *Trahe me post te* succeeds the *Quarti toni* in Victoria's 1592 book. Like Gombert's *Media vita* and *Beati omnes* Masses (and also like Palestrina's *O magnum mysterium*), the *Trahe me post te* Mass calls for one less voice part than the motet (1583) on which it is based. The model, a four-in-two canon, differs from all his other sources in having been a canonic motet. The mass differs from all others in being his only mass using the C chord for its finals. Because he needs no accidentals in order to convey the ubiquitous "major" feeling, this mass boasts only 62 flats and sharps. In *O quam gloriosum*, on the other hand, he needed 147 printed accidentals to achieve the same "major" feeling—merely because its finals happening to be G chords, the necessary sharped leading tones could not be indicated in his "key signature."

The *Trahe me* Mass quotes its source exactly in one movement—the Agnus (mm. 25-58 of the source equal mm. 5-38 of the parody). Except for the few slight rhythmic adjustments needed to accommodate different texts, the notes in all six parts are identical. Victoria in the Agnus, *a 6,* therefore violates his rule forbidding the transfer of the whole polyphonic complex from model to parody. His single previous violation of this rule came to view in the Kyries of his *O quam gloriosum* Mass. In both the *O quam gloriosum* motet and the *Trahe me* motet, he set supremely jubilant texts. It may at first strike us as odd that his aesthetic sense permitted him to add "Lord have mercy" and "Lamb of God who taketh away the sins of the world, have mercy on us" to music originally conceived for "O how glorious is that realm in which all the saints rejoice with Christ," and for "Draw me: we will run after thee to the odour of thy ointments." The fact that he could so unhesitatingly have transferred blocs from these two joyful motets—not into Gloria or Sanctus of his parodies, but into Kyrie and Agnus—allows us to infer that for him the whole of any Mass was a joyful experience. He never chose to parody any other than a jubilant motet; yet he above every other Renaissance composer was the supreme artist when such grief-laden texts as *Vere languores* and *O vos omnes* were at issue. His quotations in the Kyrie and Agnus of *O quam gloriosum* and of *Trahe me* therefore justify the assumption that these movements, in his esthetic, partook of the generally exultant character of the Mass as a whole. Whatever the explanation, it is at least certain that at the close of his *Trahe me* motet, ten Hallelujahs are shouted exultantly; and that the identical music— down to the last note in the sixth voice—returns to the hearer at the end of the *Trahe me* Mass setting the phrases "sins of the world" and "have mercy on us" (repeated six times).

Just as the *Quarti toni* is Victoria's last mass *a 4*, so the *Ascendens Christus* is his last *a 5*. For his source he returns to his favorite book—his 1572 *Motecta*. The *Ascendens Christus* motet, *a 5*, closely resembles the motet *Dum complerentur* (also *a 5*) so far as form is concerned. Both are in aBcB (responsory) form; in both, the length of "B" very nearly equals that of "a" or "c." In *Ascendens Christus* the "B" refrain extends through mm. 41-71 (*pars 1*); and through mm. 108-138 (*pars 2*). In *Dum complerentur* the "B" refrain extends through mm. 45-86; and through mm. 121-162. Both motets call for the same group of voices (CQATB). In both motets he reverses the roles of cantus and quintus during the "B" refrain at the close of *pars 2*. Both are ostensibly in transposed dorian (= G minor). Even the festivals for which each was written, Ascension and Pentecost, link them together in the church calendar.

The following similarities in the masses deserve mention: (1) Kyrie I, Christe, Patrem omnipotentem, Crucifixus, and Benedictus in both the *Dum complerentur* and *Ascendens Christus* masses open with head motives from the source; (2) endings of Qui tollis and Et in Spiritum in each hark to the "B" refrain; (3) Gloria and Credo break at exactly the same places in each and reduce voice parts in the same sections (Domine Deus and Crucifixus); (4) no triple-meter passages intrude anywhere in Kyrie, Gloria, or Credo movements of either mass; (5) the lively, spurting rhythms that were encountered frequently in wordy movements of both the *O magnum mysterium* and *Quarti toni* Masses are conspicuously absent from Gloria and Credo of either the *Ascendens* or *Dum complerentur*. Among the dissimilarities, on the other hand, are these: (1) The 1576 mass contains such archaic treatments of dissonance as the incomplete nota cambiata and the escaped note (Et in terra pax, mm. 31 and 62), but not the 1592;[167] (2) *Ascendens*, in conformity with the other 1592 masses, concludes with a single Agnus; (3) the *Ascendens* Agnus includes a *trinitas in unitate* canon: whereas neither of the *Dum complerentur* Agnuses exhibits any canon whatsoever; (4) in *Ascendens*, the head motive at the opening incises of both Et in terra pax and Sanctus suffers a "sea change" that makes it quite difficult of recognition; (5) in *Ascendens*, Victoria makes no formal attempt to work two motives in points of imitation, although this working in double harness distinguished many such points in *Dum complerentur*; (6) in the *Ascendens* Mass he never, recognizably, alludes to any important new motive from *pars 2* of the motet (such as the one at mm. 96-98); (7) the number of bars everywhere in both masses differs considerably (*Ascendens* movements are in every instance much shorter). To be specific, in *Dum complerentur* the number of bars is 24, 27, 24 in Kyries; 165 in Gloria; 216 in Credo; 70, 58 in Sanctus-Benedictus; and 34, 39 in Agnuses—as against 13, 11, 13; 85; 138; 48, 41; and 31 in the corresponding movements of the *Ascendens Christus* Mass (making a total of 657 measures in the 1576 mass as against only 380 in the 1592 mass).

At the outset of the dedicatory epistle to Cardinal Albert, Victoria avers that the 1592 *Missae* had been newly composed (*hoc opusculum, quod nunc denuo conscripsi*). Whether he means this assertion to cover the entire contents of the 1592 book need not here be argued. Presumptively he did. As has been shown in the preceeding paragraph, the *Ascendens* Mass shares numerous "middle-period" traits: of which more up-to-date treatment of dissonance, less rigorous reworking of source material, a single Agnus, and overall brevity are crucial. But, like Beethoven's *Symphony, No. 8*, this mass does lapse into some significant throwbacks. The deference to the head motive from *pars 1* of the motet, the lack of any madrigalian touches in the wordy movements, and the uniformity of the meter in Gloria and Credo, are each in their way as retrospective as the *Tempo di menuetto* of Beethoven's Opus 93.

The same voices sing the three-in-one canon in the *Ascendens* Agnus as in the last Agnus of Guerrero's *Missa Inter vestibulum* (1566): namely, cantus II = superius II, altus, and tenor I. In both the Victoria and the Guerrero masses, the same three outer parts surround the three canonic voices: cantus I = superius I, tenor II, and bassus = basis. The intervals of canonic imitation (but not the order of voice-entries) also match—an octave separating tenor I from cantus II, and a fourth separating the altus from tenor I. Both movements (indeed, both masses) are in transposed dorian. Guerrero, the more dexterous contrapuntist, poses himself more difficult problems: (1) he insists upon beginning his canon with the head motive from the source; (2) he does not introduce rests quite so frequently; (3) his canonic Agnus lasts 47 breves; but Victoria's, 31. Guerrero during 47 breves specifies a mere 10 accidentals—of which 7 are actual sharpings, and another 2 are precautionary sharps (= naturals) before the note E. Victoria in 31 breves specifies 29 accidentals—none being merely precautionary, and 23 raising the pitch by a semitone. The ratio is striking—almost five times as many obligatory accidentals per breve in the one as in the other composer. This phenomenon would not be so worthy of notice were it to be found only in isolated instances: it is of importance because the ratio will be found to differentiate Victoria's usage from Guerrero's in a general sense.

Victoria models his *Vidi speciosam* Mass *a 6* upon his Assumption motet of the same name *(a 6)*, first published in the 1572 collection. Like the two motets *Ascendens Christus* and *Dum complerentur* the *Vidi speciosam* (*2 partes*)[168] is in responsory-form—the length of "B" approximating that of "a" or "c" (aBcB = 47, 38: 37, 38). The *Vidi speciosam* motet abounds in archaic dissonance-treatment; and in tantalizing chromaticisms. At meas. 43 the sextus leaps up a fourth from a dissonant escaped note. At mm. 58 (tenor 1), 59 (quintus), 69 (bassus), 132 (quintus), 133 (tenor 1), and 144 (bassus) a series of ornamental resolutions involve dissonant under-notes approached by leap; of the kind signaled by asterisks in the following example (*VicO*, I, 113):

At mm. 73 and 148 the chromatic cantus cannot be cured by any ficta remedy (*VicO*, I, 114):

In the mass, on the other hand, Victoria uses no escaped notes. Neither does he ever skip to any dissonant under-note when ornamenting resolutions. The Crucifixus (*a 4*) repeats at mm. 80-83 ("Et iterum") the same chromatic ascent found at "et lilia" in the motet. Between the antepenultimate and penultimate bars of the Benedictus, the bassus outlines the first three notes of the nota cambiata figure: after which the bassus leaps up a fourth. The so-called consonant fourth occurs twice during the Credo in this form (*VicO*, IV, 61, 64):

Vidi speciosam brings the total of Victoria's masses parodied after *Canticum canticorum* motets to four; the other masses are *Quam pulchri sunt* (Song of Songs 7:1), *Surge propera* (2:10), and *Trahe me* (1:3). Morales wrote only one such mass—*Vulnerasti cor meum* (Song of Songs 4:9); Guerrero, also, composed only one—*Surge propera amica mea* (Song of Songs 2:10). Because of Victoria's disproportionate attention to texts from this epithalamium, he occupies a unique position among Spanish composers. His concern with Song of Songs texts allies him with the most celebrated of contemporary Spanish poets, Fray Luis de León (1527-1591): a major cause of whose imprisonment from March, 1572, until December, 1576, was his translation into the vernacular of the book that contains more perfumed language than any other in the canon. The ardor, the longing, and the ecstasy of this unique book invaded Victoria's motets; and in turn the masses parodied after Canticles motets.

Vidi speciosam, last of the Canticles masses and last of the six-part masses (excluding the 1605 Requiem), is also his last without an organ accompaniment. As in the opening incise of the motet, so also in the mass, he effectively contrasts the lower three voices with the upper three; such antiphony, quoting mm. 1-9 of the source, distinguishes the outset of both Kyrie I and the Sanctus. Although he makes more use of material drawn from *pars 1* than *pars 2* (Kyrie I = mm. 1-9; Christe = mm. 55-62_1; Kyrie II = mm. 62-70; "in gloria Dei Patris Amen" = mm. 76-85; Sanctus = mm. 1-9; Osanna II = mm. 50-52), he does in this parody—as in the *Dum complerentur* Mass—draw now and then on *pars 2* as well (Qui tollis = mm. 86-90; Patrem omnipotentem = mm. 113-115).

The *Salve Regina* Mass, the omega of the 1592 book, is at the same time the alpha of three based on his Marian antiphons. The fact that only a *Regina coeli* Mass is lacking to complete a cycle of masses based on his original settings of those four Marian antiphons that are to be sung at the close of each day after the office (Advent to Purification: *Alma Redemptoris*; February 2 to Wednesday of Holy Week: *Ave Regina coelorum*; Eastertide: *Regina coeli*; Trinity season: *Salve Regina*) has provoked the interesting speculation that Victoria did project, if not actually complete, such an additional, fourth Marian antiphon mass.[169] Of the three that do survive, *Salve Regina* is modeled on his setting *a 8* of the antiphon published in 1576 (*VicO*, VII, 120-130): each of the other two masses takes for its model both original settings of the corresponding antiphon. The two settings of *Alma Redemptoris*, *a 5* and *a 8*, had appeared in 1572 and 1581, respectively;[170] so had his settings *a 5* and *a 8* of the *Ave Regina coelorum* antiphon.[171] Because each of the Marian antiphon masses calls for eight voices, because these eight voices divide into antiphonal four-part choruses, because each mass has an added organ accompaniment, and because this organ accompaniment always duplicates the four parts of Chorus I; the *Salve Regina*, *Alma Redemptoris*, and *Ave Regina coelorum* Masses make a triptych—despite the eight years by which the publication of the *Salve Regina* Mass preceded that of the other two.

These several similarities are not the only reason for studying the three masses conjointly. In addition, they share certain structural likenesses. At the Christe of each, Victoria reduces to five or four parts. In the Glorias of both *Salve* and *Alma* Masses, he breaks at the same places—at the Domine Deus reducing to quartet or trio, and at the Qui tollis resuming eight parts. In the Credos of all three masses he divides at Et incarnatus (without reducing voices), at Crucifixus (reducing to four voices), and at Et in Spiritum (resuming eight parts). During the Benedictus of each mass he reduces to five or four parts. Canon, so frequently found in the final movements of other masses, does not enter the single Agnus concluding each of these three masses. Indeed, only one canon appears anywhere in these three masses; this unison canon involves cantus I and II in the Crucifixus, *a 4*, of the *Alma Redemptoris*.

In the wordy movements of all three masses Victoria charms the listener with darting, springy rhythms that suggest light *parlando*. He adds zest by changing frequently from duple to triple meter. Because, like Luca Marenzio in his madrigals, he forgoes any attempt at assigning individual voices the whole text, he is able to traverse wide valleys of Gloria and Credo with easy seven-league steps. His more "advanced" treatment of dissonance conforms with the other "modernistic" trends in these masses. He rarely resorts to such archaic dissonance usages as the escaped note,[172] and he eschews the "incomplete" nota cambiata. Nor does he use such dissonances as under-notes, approached by leap, in ornamental resolutions. He does use the consonant fourth and does increase the number of chord-progressions involving cross relations. Although not exceeding the accidentals applied in his earlier works (B♮ [♯], F♯, C♯, B♭, and E♭),[173] he contrives transitory "modulations, from G minor to all the nearly related keys except E♭ Major in the *Salve Regina* Mass; and from F Major to all except A minor in the *Alma Redemptoris* and *Ave Regina* Masses.

Among the many interesting snatches in the *Salve Regina* Mass which prove to have been borrowed directly from the 1576 antiphon *a 8*, the following involve the whole polyphonic complex and not just a single strand. Italicized measure numbers refer to the antiphon: (1) in the Kyries, mm. 1-8 = *37-43*, mm. 19-26 = *26-33*, mm. 33-41 = *153-163*; (2) in the Gloria, mm. 1-9 = *18-26*, mm. 24-31 = *87-92*, mm. 43-51 = *116-123*; (3) in the Credo, mm. 1-6 = *132-137*, mm. 54-62 = *78-88*, mm. 69-72 = *116-119*; mm. 160-168 = *194-201*; (4) in the Sanctus, mm. 1-4 = *54-56*, in the Benedictus, mm. 1-8 = *116-122*; (5) in the Agnus, mm. 1-10 = *18-26*, mm. 16-27 = *182-192*. Tabulations of the material transferred from 1572 and 1581 antiphons into the *Alma Redemptoris* and *Ave Regina* Masses have been undertaken by Saxton,[174] and have revealed similarly high incidences of borrowing. In none of his previous masses did Victoria borrow more freely or more extensively from his 1572, 1576, and 1581 publications than in his Marian antiphon masses.

The slight changes made during transfer from antiphon to mass served various purposes. One such purpose seems to have been the "modernization".of dissonance-treatment; another to have been the tightening of loose cadences. Both these ends were attained in the following transfer from *Salve Regina* antiphon (mm. 18-24) to mass (Gloria, mm. 1-6). In the mass he eliminates the escaped note in the tenor (fifth bar) and halves the penultimate chord in the cadence.[175] In his other changes, Victoria (1) adds muscle and sinew to thin harmonies when he increases the number of dissonant suspensions; or (2) he widens the harmonic spectrum when he injects cross relations. When he borrowed the *Et Jesum* section of the antiphon (mm. 116-123)[176] for use in the Domine Deus of the mass (Gloria, mm. 43-51)[177] he attained both these ends. For every three dissonant suspensions

in the model, he injects six into the parody. No cross relations enrich the 1576 antiphon; but these are numerous in the 1592 mass—the Domine Deus in three bars specifying one such cross relation (mm. 47-48) and implying another (meas. 46).

Such alterations confirm a thesis already proposed: namely, that Victoria's art by no means remained static; but on the contrary matured steadily. Although his polychoral masses have never received the praise

given *Quam pulchri* and *O quam gloriosum*, their polish and refinement can be denied by none who minutely compares them with their models. At the very least they are worthy compeers of Palestrina's eight-part *Confitebor tibi, Laudate Dominum, Hodie Christus natus est,* and *Fratres enim ego accepi.*

Palestrina's polychoral masses were published without organ accompaniment in 1585 *(Confitebor tibi)* and 1601. All Victoria's polychoral masses, on the other hand, were published with an organ part duplicating chorus I, except when the middle or lower voices move so swiftly as to make an exact version extremely difficult for two hands. For instance, Victoria simplifies the organ part of the *Salve* Mass at meas. 15 in Kyrie I, mm. 37-38 in Et in terra pax, during the last nine bars of Et in Spiritum, and at mm. 19-20 of the Sanctus. Although the *Salve* Mass contains no passages unplayable on manuals alone, the *Alma Redemptoris* and *Ave Regina* occasionally include chords that presuppose F_1, C_1, and $B_1\flat$ pedal notes—both hands not being able to grasp the four notes. Such chords appear exclusively in wordy, and presumably loud, movements.

The *tessiture* of all voices (CCCAATBB) lie extremely high, even for Victoria, in his *Salve* Mass. Interestingly enough, the organ part is prefaced by this legend: *Ad quartam inferiorem*("[sounding] at a fourth lower"). Since all eight voices when transposed down a fourth dwell in regions inhabited more customarily by other Spanish vocal music of the period, this legend in the organ part should perhaps be accepted at face value. In major Spanish ecclesiastical establishments two or more accompanying organs tuned at different pitches were usually available. For proof, the *Relacion delo que declaro Diego del Castillo se deuia remediar en los quatro organos de S. Lorenço el Real . . . 1587 años* may be consulted. Listed as MS 14025.194 at the Biblioteca Nacional in Madrid, this "account of those things that Diego del Castillo said ought to be remedied in the four organs of San Lorenzo [El Escorial] in the year 1587" reveals that the pitch of two organs *fuessen tres puntos mas baxos que los otros dos* ("was a third lower than the pitch of the other two"). Both Castillo, royal organist, and Melchor de Miranda, first organist in Toledo Cathedral, agreed that it would be preferable to tune the pairs of organs a fourth apart *(hauian destar vna quarta)* rather than a major third. Victoria may well have been alluding to this practice of tuning one organ in each pair a fourth apart when, only five years after Castillo's *Relación* (1587), he published his *Salve Regina* Mass (1592): heading the organ part with *Ad quartam inferiorem*. But whether or not it is agreed that the *Salve* organ part was intended for an instrument "sounding a fourth lower," it is interesting to observe that (1) the *Alma Redemptoris* and *Ave Regina* organ parts are not headed *Ad quartam inferiorem;* (2) the *Alma* and *Ave* masses call for voices of generally lower range; (3) their organ parts presuppose the availability of pedal notes in wordy movements (F_1, $B_1\flat$, C), whereas none such are implied in the *Salve.*

In his *Salve* Mass, Victoria calls for only four accidentals: B$\flat$, E$\flat$, F$\sharp$, C$\sharp$. These four again comprise his entire repertory in the 1600 masses: A$\flat$'s are never specified nor implied in Victoria's masses; and G$\sharp$'s occur in his masses only in the absence of E$\flat$'s. This last generalization may be confirmed from the *Surge propera* and *Quarti toni* which do include G$\sharp$'s.

However, the fact that none of the organ-accompanied masses contains any G♯ cannot be taken as proof that his organ keyboard lacked the note. Both the Marian Litanies and the polyphonic setting of St. Thomas Aquinas's Corpus Christi sequence (published in 1585) call for G♯'s in the organ-parts (mm. 44-45 in *Litaniae*; meas. 69 in *Lauda Sion Salvatorem*).[178]

Victoria's fondness for vocal movements that ascend semitonally and then descend immediately by whole-step—or vice versa—did not abate in his Marian antiphon masses. Cantus 1 of the *Salve* Mass shows examples at Kyrie I, mm. 14-16; Qui tollis, mm. 71-73, 87-89; Patrem omnipotentem, mm. 6-7, 51-53; Crucifixus, mm. 87-88; Et in Spiritum Sanctum, mm. 147-149, 154. Cantus 1 must sing also this unmistakable chromaticism in the Osanna (mm. 31-32):

VicO, IV, 95.

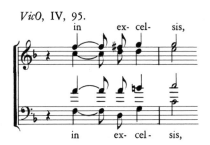

If the three Marian antiphon masses congregate together, the *Missa pro victoria*—which Victoria referred to as his "Battle" Mass—stands apart from all others in his repertory by reason of its secular model, Clément Janequin's *La bataille de Marignan*; and because of the extremely vivacious and picturesque style adopted in such movements as Kyrie II, Et in terra pax, Patrem omnipotentem, Et in Spritum Sanctum, and even the Agnus Dei.

Victoria's ebullient parody *a 9* (1600) could not contrast more strongly with Guerrero's *Missa della batalla escoutez, a 5* (1582). A past master of secular as well as of sacred style, Guerrero insisted upon obliterating every whiff of secular aroma from his parody of the chanson. He excluded, for instance, all the repeated note fanfares, the scurrying scales, and the myriad short-lived metrical shifts which vivify the Janequin chanson. For trumpet signals he substituted smoothly flowing lines. When veering to Φ_2^3 he did so not in the middle of a movement, but at its beginning. (Kyrie II and the Osanna carry such a triple-meter signature.) Only four of his movements failed to begin with Janequin's serious head motive: the Christe (= Phifres soufflez), Kyrie II (= Avanturiers), the Domine Deus, and the Osanna (= Avanturiers). His Domine Deus took for initium not a motive from the chanson but instead the opening incise of Kyrie II in Janequin's own properly cassocked parody (published at Lyons, 1532, in *Liber decem missarum a praeclaris musicis contextus*). For these reasons Guerrero's *Batalla* Mass is hard to distinguish stylistically from his 1566 and 1582 parodies based on motets. During Agnus I, for instance, he followed the same time-honored course that he took in the Sanctus of his *Sancta et immaculata*, the Osanna of *Beata Mater*, and Agnus I of *Simile est regnum* Masses; enormously lengthening the time values of the Janequin initium and making it serve as this kind of ostinato (in cantus II):

In Agnus II, he augmented to eight parts. But even while doing so, Guerrero did not for a moment abandon close imitative writing.

By contrast, Victoria in 1600 includes fewer imitative points than Janequin in his chanson. He fires off salvos of repeated notes in Kyrie II, even daring to use the same colorful music conceived by Janequin for the onomatopoeical *frerelelelan fan, frerelelelan fan* (chanson, *pars 2*). At "Filius Patris" in the Gloria he appropriates Janequin's music for *la la la, tarirarira la reyne (pars 2)*; at "Et resurrexit" in the Credo, *Bendez soudain, gentilz gascons (pars 1)*; at "Et iterum" in the Credo, *Et orrez, si bien escoutez, / Des coups ruez de tous costez (pars 1)*. In his single Agnus he quotes again Janequin's twenty-one-gun-salute music for *frerelelelan fan, frerelelelan fan*. When he fires off his shots during "dona nobis pacem," Victoria anticipates Beethoven. The latter's drum-and-trumpet instrumental prelude to "dona nobis pacem" in the *Missa solemnis* has attracted similar attention because of the military context within which the suppliant prays for peace.

Victoria—whose list of distinguished patrons exceeds that of any other sixteenth-century Spanish composer—dedicated his *Missae, Magnificat, Motecta, Psalmi, & alia* to Philip III. Because his *Pro victoria* beseeches victory, some commentators have surmised that he had in mind a specific battle or campaign. If so, he cannot have besought victory in any engagement during the reign of Philip III. Philip II did not die until September 13, 1598. The complete contents of Victoria's forthcoming volume were at that very moment in a Madrid printer's hands, awaiting a price estimate for the impression. On October 1, Victoria signed the printing contract with Julio Junti de Modesti.[179] Thus, the "Battle" Mass along with everything else in the forthcoming collection will have to be thought of as a work composed while Philip III was still a prince in his minority. That it did signally please the light-minded and pleasure-loving young Philip III can be proved. Victoria wrote from Madrid on June 10, 1603, to the Duke of Urbino. Sometime in the previous year he had sent this duke the several partbooks of his 1600 publication. As yet he had not received payment. In his letter he expressly names the "Battle" Mass as the one item that gave the youthful Philip III greatest pleasure.[180] His understandable eagerness to please the twenty-year-old prince may well account for the unique stamp of his *Missa pro victoria*.

Certainly the work bears all the marks of having been written to gratify the featherweight tastes of this well-intentioned but frivolous young prince. That Philip III lacked all the weightier virtues of both his father and his grandsire has long been accepted as a historical truism. His musical tastes were known, even before he ascended the throne, to tend exclusively toward light secular songs. So much is attested in Antonio de Obregón y Cerezada's *Discursos sobre la filosofia moral de Aristoteles* (Valladolid: Luis Sánchez, 1603), at pages 182-186. Obregón y Cerezada—a royal tutor—recounts how the young prince called upon Luis Honguero[181] to sing 39 five-line stanzas of the elegant trifle *En la noche serena*. After ascending the throne he wasted hundreds of thousands of ducats on idle show. His favorite composer Mateo Romero ("Maestro Capitán") catered to his taste for bright, major polychoral masses and motets; and never bothered with learned devices. Géry de Ghersem, Philippe Rogier's favorite pupil, should logically have succeeded as director of choral music in the royal chapel when Philip III mounted the throne. Romero, however, gained the post within a month of Philip II's death.[182] The much more erudite Ghersem, after hopefully remaining in Madrid for a short time, returned to Brussels in 1604 (died at Tournai, 1630).

The *Missa pro victoria* calls for CCCAATTBB; but none of the three cantus parts ascends above e¹♭. For the lowest note in bassus II, he touches D_1 (in the Patrem omnipotentem, meas. 27). Bassus I and II never move in truly independent parts when the two choruses sing together. Quite often, the upper voices do no more than interchange notes of static chords. In nine-part *tutti* passages (Kyrie II; "simul adoratur" and "Confiteor" of the Credo; Agnus Dei), the harmonic rhythm is especially slow. Just as this mass contains by far his greatest number of staccato repeated notes and of running quavers, so also it shows the highest incidence of short exclamatory V-I-V and I-IV-I chordal progressions ("Et vitam" in Credo).

For a model upon which to base his *Missa Laetatus, a 12*, Victoria chooses his own Psalm 121 (= 122), *a 12*, first published in 1583. Verses 4-5, 7-12 (*Liber usualis* numbering) are scored full; the others for four or three voices. In this, his only psalm *a 12*,[183] he alludes nowhere to a psalm-tone. All the more interesting in view of his failure to cite any psalm-tone in the source is the fact that cantus IV, temporarily the highest voice, does sing Tone I (to the mediation) at Et incarnatus in the mass. This plainsong quotation may be pure accident, however.

Again, as in the nine-part *Pro victoria*, tutti passages are rare in both

Laetatus psalm and mass. Essentially works for three four-part choruses, psalm and mass depend upon antiphony for their most striking effects. Though in the mass such solo movements as Christe, Domine Deus I and II, Crucifixus, and Benedictus open with imitative points, the other movements lack any. Again, as in the other 1600 masses, (1) his "key" is boldly F Major; (2) four accidentals are employed—B♮ (= ♯), F♯, C♯, and E♭; (3) the highest note in any of the four cantus parts is e^1♭; (4) the lowest note in either bass part is D_1; (5) in tutti passages, the three lowest voices move in octaves or unisons. In the organ parts, the notes D_1, F_1, and G_1 support chords not negotiable by two hands: and must be presumed to have been played on the pedal. These pedal notes appear exclusively in such wordy movements[184] as Et in terra pax (mm. 8-19), Qui tollis (mm. 96, 98), Patrem omnipotentem (mm. 7-10), and Et in Spiritum Sanctum (mm. 122, 125-126, 147, 161, 163, 165, 171). Since these pedal notes appear always in loud contexts, the organ was more than an optional "for practice only" part, and had the added virtue of lending weight at climaxes.

Victoria reverses the roles of choruses I and III throughout—chorus III in the 1600 mass singing what was allotted to chorus I in the 1583 psalm (cf. Kyrie II with "Fiat pax"; and Patrem omnipotentem with "Illuc enim");[185] and vice versa. In both 1583 psalm and 1600 mass the organist persists in duplicating chorus I. This switching of roles therefore means that the organ part differs also—even though the aggregate of the dozen voices remains identical in such sections as Kyrie II and the opening of Patrem omnipotentem.

Whatever the distinctive merits of Victoria's 1600 masses, his muse during his late forties would be deemed by the majority of critics to have drooped (like the muse of certain later-day Romanticists)—were these 1600 masses the only works from his final period in Spain whereupon to rest a judgment. Fortunately, he is spared this judgment by virtue of his "swan song," the *Officium defunctorum*, published at Madrid in 1605. At another place has been given an account of the circumstances that called forth this "crowning work of a great genius," as Karl Proske dubbed it.[186] Wholly apart from its more serious subject matter, the *Missa pro defunctis* in the 1605 imprint (folios 1-18) would win greater sympathy than the 1600 masses, (1) because the individual sections are not forever tediously in "F Major", and (2) because the bright bauble of antiphony does not distract him like an eternal plaything.

So far as the parts set polyphonically are concerned, Victoria's two *Pro defunctis* Masses—the first of 1583 and the second of 1605—resemble each other closely. In the 1583 offertory he requires *Quam olim* to be sung polyphonically after the versicle *Hostias et preces*; though not in the 1605 offertory.[187] The 1583 mass includes polyphony for three Agnuses; but the 1605 for only I and III. Otherwise, the succession of polyphonic numbers is the same throughout both masses. To turn now to the music added for the Office of the Dead and the Burial Service: both the 1583 and 1605 publications provide polyphonic settings of the *Libera me* responsory. The music for the versicle of this responsory—*Tremens factus sum ego, a 3*—is indeed identical in both publications. The 1605 publication continues with a motet, *Versa est in luctum* (the words taken from Job 30:31 and 7:16*b*), and a lesson, *Taedet animam meam* (Job 10:1-7), to be sung at the first nocturn of matins.

Just as Victoria becomes ever more concise in his 1592 and 1600 books of masses, so also the 1605 Requiem (as a whole and in most of its individual sections) is shorter than the 1583. Instead of 43 + 35 bars in the 1583 gradual, 109 in the offertory, and 19 + 17 in the Sanctus; 23 + 23 bars comprise the 1605 gradual, 78 the offertory, and 17 + 16 the Sanctus. The 1583 Requiem included polyphony for Agnuses I, II, and III; but in 1605 he sets only I and III.

Throughout the 1583 Requiem, the plainsong was confided uniformly to the highest of the four voices.[188] As a general rule, the paraphrased plainsong is to be found in cantus II of the 1605 version. In the offertory, he gives it to the altus. Victoria sharps several notes in the 1605 plainsong-bearing voices which were obligatorily natural in the 1583. For such natural versus sharp notes, compare graduals: mm. 9-11 vs. 8; offertories: mm. 5 vs. 2, 39 vs. 27, 98 vs. 70; Sanctuses: meas. 11 vs. mm. 11-12; Benedictuses: meas. 16 vs. meas. 12. Examples from the two Benedictuses are shown below. No one can doubt that in the 1583 version the f marked with an asterisk must be natural; nor that in the 1605 the f must be sharped: yet the identical plainchant is at stake. After he returned to Spain, did Victoria deliberately accede to local usage, which throughout the sixteenth century always called for far more sharping in plainsong than was elsewhere customary? Significantly enough, any change of accidental in the plainsong-bearing voice in 1605 involves sharping: no notes sharped in 1583 become naturals in the 1605 Requiem.

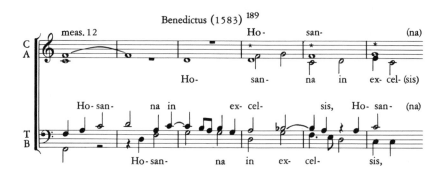

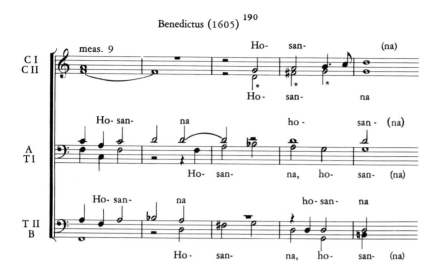

Benedictus (1605) [190]

In no one number of either the 1583 or 1605 Requiem does he call for more than four different accidentals. The introit and opening Kyries of both Requiems carry B♭ in their signatures: B♮, F♯, C♯, and E♭ are therefore the accidentals. In the 1583 gradual, his accidentals are F♯, C♯, G♯, and B♭; in the 1605, all these except B♭. Although the accidentals in the remaining pieces of each Requiem never exceed four, the fact that he uses a different set in the introits from the set in the graduals or offertories lends variety. To vary the cadences he chooses A for the finals of the graduals (each Requiem), D for the offertories, A for the Sanctuses, and G for the Benedictuses, the Agnuses, and the Communios. This change of final from number to number—and with it the orbit of cadences surrounding the final—gratifies the ear in a way that none of his other masses (except the *De beata Virgine*) is permitted to assuage the listener.

The 1605 Requiem calls for an abundance of low D_1's in the bass. These are buttressed, however, by D an octave above in tenor II; or if tenor II sings some other note, by two notes, D_1 and D, appearing conjointly in the bass part. The bass line, although not unvocal, abounds in fourths, fifths, and octaves. Cantus I reaches g^1 in the gradual. The disposition of voices, CCATTB, proves of itself that Victoria foresaw the dangers of too thick and muddled a conglomeration of low voices. The addition of a cantus I as a counterpointing voice *above* the plainsong-bearing voice (cantus II) is in itself a masterstroke. The vocal orchestration shows everywhere the most exquisite refinement.

As for dissonance-treatment, he excludes the time-honored nota cambiata, but does make considerable use of the consonant fourth in suspensions. On occasion, he even specifies the "consonant" seventh (see Introit, meas. 48):[191]

Were the chord marked by an asterisk in the next example to be met in a later composer's works it would be classed at once as a (secondary) dominant seventh chord (Benedictus, meas. 16):[192]

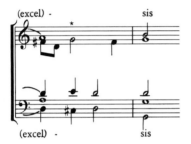

Throughout the 1605 Requiem he frequently uses for their *Affekt* other inverted "secondary seventh chords." Examples may be seen in the Graduale (meas. 28 [erit *justus*]), Offertorium (meas. 20$_2$), Sanctus (meas. 11$_4$), Communio (mm. 10$_2$, 40$_2$); in the motet *Versa est in luctum* (meas. 56$_2$), in the responsory *Libera me* (meas. 68$_2$ [Requiem ae*ter*nam]), and in the lesson *Taedet me* (mm. 25$_3$, 68$_3$). Two examples from *Taedet me* are reproduced here.[193] However frequent their use in the 1605 Requiem,

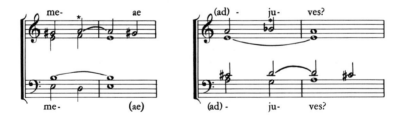

such chords do not figure in the 1583 Requiem. Victoria also makes interesting use of the augmented chord in *Versa est in luctum* (meas. 25) to reinforce in musical terms the idea of *flentium* ("weeping"):

VicO, VI, 142.

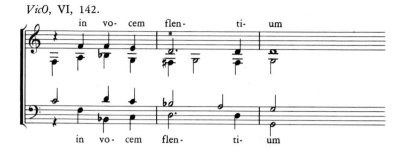

With six real parts at his disposal, the upper two of which cross freely, he contrives a number of passages that sound as if parallel block-chords were intended. As early as mm. 7-9 of the Introit, the ear is deceived—especially if cantus ɪ stands beside cantus ɪɪ during performance—into believing that he wrote such impressionistic parallelisms between cantus ɪ and bassus as the following:

VicO, VI, 124.

Similarly striking mock-parallelisms mark the outset of Kyrie II. These make their most telling effect when two octaves separate the outer voices; and when the mock-parallelism involves roots in stepwise relation.

In this Requiem, perhaps more than any of his other masses, Victoria writes "expressive" harmony. As especially telling proofs of his "expressive" powers may be cited the passages at *ne cadant in obscurum* ("nor let them fall into darkness") in the Offertorium;[194] after "let light eternal shine upon them" at *Quia pius es* ("because Thou art merciful") in the Communio;[195] and after "spare me, O God" at *nihil enim sunt dies mei* ("for my days are nothing") in *Versa est in luctum*.[196] At *obscurum*, he achieves an impressively dark and somber sound, with the first-inversion of G minor standing in phrygian relation to A Major. At *Quia*, a sudden shaft of tenderness overflows the listener when a quite unexpected A-Major chord succeeds a general pause in the six parts. At *nihil enim sunt*, he pushes his cantus ɪ up to e¹ in a shrill lament, juxtaposing the first-inversion D-minor chord with E Major.

The Lectio is a homophonic piece.[197] Imitative play is held to a minimum, for that matter, in all sections of the Requiem, including the Responsorium for the Absolution.[198] When voices do perchance move independently, he writes faster notes more freely in inner than outer voices. These rapid inner passages cast a haze around the chord changes, much as a painter's chiaroscuro suffuses a canvas with half-lights in place of sharp outlines.

Magnificats   In 1576 Victoria published his first six magnificats—a pair each for Tones I, IV, and VIII. Five years later he published, again at Rome, a complete set of sixteen. The 1581 book contains an odd- and even-verse setting for each of the eight tones. Ten of the 1581 settings (Tones II, III, V, VI, VII) were new. The remainder were reprinted from his 1576 *Liber Primus. Qui Missas, Psalmos, Magnificat, . . . Aliaque Complectitur*. Strange though it may seem when one considers their respective ages, Victoria's 1581 *Cantica B. Virginis*[199] did not follow, but preceded by a decade, the only such book that Palestrina published in his lifetime—*Magnificat octo tonorum. Liber primus* (Rome: Alessandro Gardano, 1591). Palestrina, whose first book of masses was published when Victoria was a six-year-old boy, delayed offering any of his magnificats to the public until the end of his career, after he had published music in all the other sacred and secular categories that he was to cultivate. That the elder master's 1591 magnificats were not gleaned from early notebooks, but had been "recently composed," can be learned from this phrase in the dedication of his magnificats to Gregory XIV: *liber hunc a me nuper lucubratum*.

Nowhere does Victoria show himself more *echt Spanier* than by the prompt publication of his magnificats. Both his great compatriots, Morales and Guerrero, had published magnificats early in their careers. Morales's magnificats began to be printed in 1542, only two years after his first masses; Guerrero's *Canticum B. M. quod Magnificat nuncupatur, per octo musicae modos variatum* (Louvain: 1563) appeared three years before any of his masses. Later in the century, other Spanish composers paid like-minded attention to the polyphonic magnificat. Juan Navarro's *Psalmi, Hymni ac Magnificat* (Rome: 1590), Sebastián de Vivanco's *Liber Magnificarum* (Salamanca: 1607), and Sebastián Aguilera de Heredia's *Canticum Beatissimae Virginis Deiparae Mariae* (Saragossa: 1618) prove the point. Among composers who were not successful in bringing their music into print, Hernando Franco (d. 1585) left no polyphonic masses whatsoever; but instead, magnificats in each of seven tones.

For Spanish composers, as for Palestrina, the eight tones meant, of course, eight melodic formulas. Each tone began with a recognized initium, rose to a reciting note that was the same as the *confinalis* of the correspondingly numbered mode, dropped at a *mediatio* halfway through each verse, and concluded with a *terminatio* which might, or might not, be the *finalis* of the correspondingly numbered mode. In Palestrinian and Victorian usage, Tones I and II (always transposed to one flat) ended over G; Tones III, V, and VII, over A; Tone IV, over E; Tone VI, over F (flat in signature); Tone VIII, over G. Both composers left magnificats of two general types: settings in which (1) alternate verses were sung polyphonically, or (2) all twelve verses were sung polyphonically. Of the second type, Palestrina left only one exemplar—a polychoral Magnificat *a 8* still in manuscript at his death (Cappella Sistina, Codex 29). In his *Missae, Magnificat, Motecta, Psalmi, & alia* (Madrid: 1600) Victoria, on the other hand, published two polychoral specimens setting all twelve verses of Mary's Canticle polyphonically. Interestingly enough, three of the twelve verses in the 1600 Magnificat Primi toni (vv. 1, 4, 5) and four in the 1600 Sexti toni (vv. 1, 2 [revised], 7, 9) had already been published in 1576 and 1581, respectively—as individual sections of his alternate-verse Magnificats in Tones I and VI.

Like Palestrina and like the majority of Spanish composers of magnificats, Victoria always "bows" to the Tone in which he happens to be composing a given magnificat: (1) by closing all six or all twelve verses in any given magnificat over G(♭), G(♭), A, E, A, F(♭), A, G, for Tones I through VIII, respectively. (2) He also pays tribute to the tone by treating its initium frequently as a head motive. (3) Toward the close of a verse, Victoria, like Palestrina (and any number of others), often makes the *terminatio* serve as the head motive in a concluding imitative point. (4) Both composers are wont to paraphrase the formula, to extend it by insertions, and to repeat or sequence both *mediatio* and *terminatio* in a given individual voice part. (5) Almost invariably both Victoria and Palestrina take the colon at the end of each half-verse as a signal for a cadence; after which a new imitative point emerges.

Sometimes Victoria even makes of the tone a slow-motion cantus firmus. Instances may be seen in his Tone I Fecit (altus); Tone II Quia respexit (tenor) and Suscepit (altus); Tone II Et exultavit (cantus) and Esurientes: first half (cantus); Tone III Deposuit (cantus); Tone V Deposuit: first half (cantus); Tone VI Quia respexit (cantus); Tone VII Fecit: first half (tenor); Tone VIII Sicut locutus (cantus). At other times, he pays homage to the formula by threading it in slow-motion notes through concluding movements in canon with itself. The Sicut erat movements at the close of his Tones I, II, III, V, VI, and VIII Magnificats so conclude. By virtue of these Sicut erat canons, each of which contains the Tone in breves and semibreves playing tag with itself, and each of which augments to six parts (except Tone VI which augments to five), Victoria joins the party of Morales, who similarly closed with canonic movements. Indeed, so closely does he follow in Morales's footsteps that he even omits the concluding canon in his Tone IV Sicut erat—Morales having similarly eschewed canon at the close of this particular Tone.

In his 1591 printed set Palestrina, on the other hand, never reverted to cantus firmus treatment of the formula. Even in his two even-verse sets left unpublished at his death Palestrina resorted to this archaic treatment of the formula so rarely that the occasions can be counted on the fingers of one hand (e.g., Lateran Magnificats: Tone I, a 5, Sicut erat; Tone III, a 6, Esurientes). Nor did he conclude any of his sixteen *Liber primus* magnificats with a canon. True, he thus concluded the Tones III, VI, and VII of his so-called *Liber secundus* (unpublished at his death; actually an early set) and the Tones IV, V, VI, and VII of his Lateran set (now referred to as *Liber tertius*, and like *Liber secundus* an early set). But even though his first-hand acquaintance with Morales's magnificats has been proved infallibly (see above, pp. 88-89), Palestrina asserted a freedom from Morales's canonic practice which Victoria never chooses to declare. For instance, Palestrina contrived his greatest number of canons in a *quarti toni* magnificat (Lateran set). Also, he exercised his ingenuity with specimens involving cancrizans (Sicut erat of Lateran Tone V) and contrary motion (Sicut erat of Lateran Tone VI): never using canon, after the Spanish manner, solely to apotheosize the plainsong formula.

Victoria continues to allude to the plainsong formula even in movements during which he reduces parts. In none of his solo movements does he reduce to a duo, as did Morales in the Fecit of his Tone III and Esurientes of his Tone VI. However, trios occur frequently enough: in the Et misericordia of Tones III, V, VI, VII; in the Fecit of Tones II, III, VI, VII; in the Deposuit of Tones II, V, VII; in Esurientes of Tone VIII; and in the Sicut locutus of Tone IV. Each of Victoria's Fecit trios calls for ATB or TTB. Palestrina preferentially suggested the idea "He hath showed strength" by massing his voices; only once in any *Liber primus* Fecit did he reduce to a trio (though four times in an Esurientes). Victoria, more of a colorist, suggests the "strength" idea by excluding the treble. His interest in vocal color as such is illustrated even in movements a 4 such as the Et misericordia's of his Tones I, II, IV, and VIII; each of which shifts from CATB to a higher combination: CCAT, CAAT, or CCAA. Palestrina made no corresponding gesture in his "And His mercy is on them" movements for four parts: each of which calls uniformly for CATB. Victoria requires CCAT, CCAA, and CAAT in the Esurientes movements of his Tones II, III, and V. But Palestrina, when continuing with quartet, neglected the subtlety of changed vocal color. His "The needy" movements for Tones II, III, IV, and VIII (*Liber primus*, 1591) call uniformly for CATB.

Victoria's colorism finds vent not only in his vocal registration but also in the vastly greater number of accidentals that he specifies. To cite figures: his odd-verse Tone III contains 45; his even-verse Tone III, 32 printed accidentals. Palestrina's 1591 imprint shows only 5 accidentals in the Tone III odd-verse, and 11 in the Tone III even-verse. Victoria's odd-verse Tone VII shows 69 accidentals; Palestrina's, only 16. Yet the Roman master's *Liber primus* was the later book by a decade, and contains "recently composed" (*nuper lucubratum*) magnificats. Frequently, Victoria's accidentals cause cross relations. Where the same cross relations recur at the close of successive movements, as for instance just before the last cadence in the Quia fecit and Esurientes movements of his even-verse *quinti toni*, he doubtless repeats for the sake of unity (*VicO*, III, 48-49).

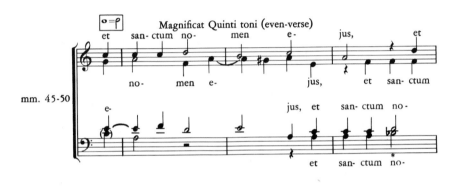

mm. 45-50

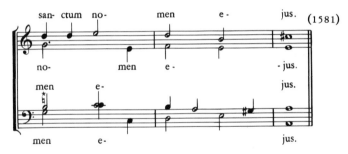

nm. 99-103

Victoria's cadences at the ends of movements often involve a lengthy pedal in an interior or upper voice. Meanwhile, the other parts wend their way to a close in "linkèd sweetness long drawn out." Such pedals come at the end of every movement but two in his Tone I even-verse, of all but one in his Tone III even-verse, of all but one in his Tone IV odd-verse, of three in his Tone V even-verse, of all but two in his Tone VI even-verse, and of three in his Tone VIII odd-verse—not to mention individual movements in the other magnificats. He also bolsters the Amen effect at numerous closes when he repeats or sequences the last incise. Such musical end-rhyme invariably accompanies text-repetition. For that matter, text-reiteration anywhere in a movement usually inspires melodic repetition or sequence. In the accompanying examples culled from his odd-verse *quinti toni*: (1) the Suscepit Israel excerpt illustrates end-rhyme; (2) the Et misericordia shows not just end-rhyme of the ABZZ type, but of the ABZZZZ type; this particular excerpt also illustrates a highly characteristic cadential tag—namely, the skip of an octave or a fifth in the highest voice (timentibus eum, *eum*, timentibus eum, *eum*); (3) the Deposuit *a 3*, shown in entirety, again exemplifies ABZZZZ form. In each of the illustrations "Z" paraphrases the *terminatio* of the Tone. It also is noteworthy that in both second and third examples Victoria specifies cross relations (at the points marked with asterisks).

Magnificat Quinti toni (odd-verse)

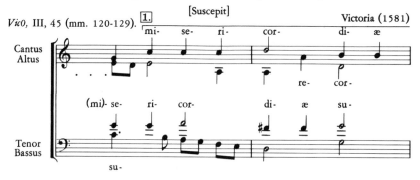

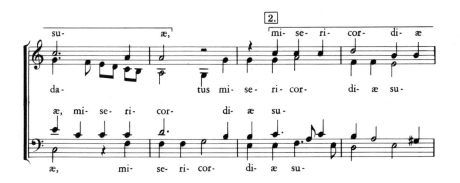

[Et misericordia]

Vic0, III, 43-44 (mm. 64-76).

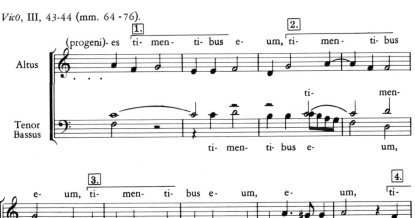

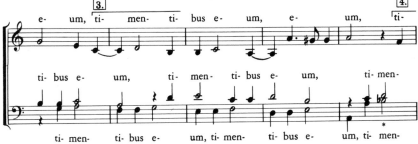

Deposuit

Vic0, III, 44 (mm. 77-105).

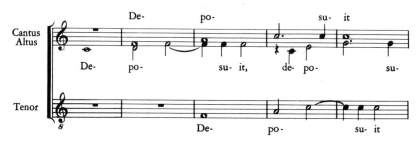

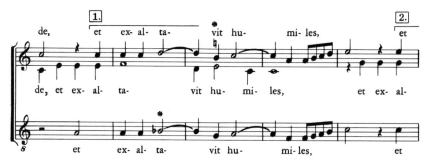

By way of contrast, Palestrina's endings in the *Liber primus* magnificats are all clipped—even abrupt. As a rule, he avoids concluding pedals; and only sporadically does he resort to musical end-rhyme.

Above at page 387 Victoria's weaving of two diverse head motives into an opening point of imitation was discovered to have been a characteristic feature of his youthful style. Since the magnificats belong also to his first period—the complete sixteen having been published when he was but thirty-three—it is not surprising to discover him again writing points that combine an original with a derived head motive. A good example of such a point can be found at the opening of the even-verse *quinti toni* (*VicO*, III, 47). In this point the altus starts with an original head motive. The cantus

enters at the second bar with the initium of Tone V. At meas. 4 the bassus imitates the altus at the suboctave. In the succeeding bar the tenor enters with the initium of the Tone. Or, using G for Gregorian (instead of Guerrero, as in the *Simile est regnum* points), the successive entries may be abbreviated thus: VGVG. Other examples of such points may be seen in the Tone I Anima mea (VGVG), Sicut locutus (GVGV); Tone III Et exultavit (GVGV), Quia respexit (GVGV), Esurientes (VGVG), Suscepit (GVGV); Tone IV Quia respexit (VGVG), Esurientes (VGVG); Tone V Esurientes (VGVG); Tone VII Anima mea (VGVG); Tone VIII Anima mea (GVGV), Sicut locutus (GVGV).

In his youth Victoria also favored escaped notes. From a dissonant weak crotchet (= quaver) at the bottom of a descending scale-line he would leap upward a fourth to a syncope. This type of escaped note recurs an appreciable number of times in the magnificats. Here is an example (*VicO*, III, 31):

This excerpt (fifth and sixth bars before the close of the even-verse Tone III) is matched by two others of identical type in the same Sicut erat. The escaped note makes an even stronger effect at the third bar of the Tone V Sicut erat (*VicO*, III, 50)—the dissonance now protruding in the lowest

sounding voice. For other examples of escaped notes see the Tone IV Esurientes (sixth bar); Tone VI Sicut erat (fifth); Tone VII Deposuit (fourth), Sicut erat (seventh); Tone VIII Quia respexit (sixth), Sicut erat (thirteenth).[200] What makes all these escaped notes doubly interesting is Victoria's partiality to them in his youthful magnificats and his avoidance of them in his 1600 magnificats—even though the 1600 magnificats contain individual movements reprinted from his 1581 *Cantica B. Virginis*. Palestrina, in contrast with Victoria, never used so much as a single escaped note leaping upward a fourth to a syncope in any magnificat:[201] whether in the *Liber primus* set printed as "recent" works in 1591, or in the two sets left unpublished at his death and now accepted on all sides as *opere giovanili*.[202]

By comparison with escaped notes of the type indicated, Victoria's other dissonances in the 1581 magnificats make a less Spenserian impression. *Note cambiate* occur, but always with scale ascent after the downward leap. Side by side with the archaic escaped notes he specifies an obligatory chromaticism (top voice at the beginning of the Tone VII Sicut locutus) that Palestrina would have carefully avoided.

VicO, III, 68.

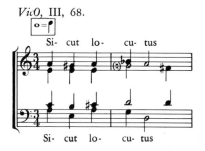

Among the many happy brush-strokes applied in individual magnificats, the following make an especially felicitous effect in performance. (1) A sequential scale figure suavely descends (tenths between outer voices) at *ecce enim ex hoc* (repeated) in the odd-verse Tone II.[203] (2) In the odd-verse Tone III, the altus darts upward a ninth, only to fall dramatically at *de sede* ("from their seat").[204] This graphic touch is but one of several that Palestrina was to apply at identical spots in his 1591 magnificats. He too scurries up the same distance on the same syllable in his magnificat of the same Tone (*Liber primus*).[205] (3) Victoria favors pedals at endings. He also makes effective use of *ein Ton* passages when the text dwells on such ideas as "For behold from henceforth" (odd-verse Tone IV)[206] and "to Abraham and to his seed forever" (even-verse Tone IV).[207] (4) When undergirding the topmost voice with moving harmonies in such *ein Ton* passages, he saves the most poignantly stabbing harmonies for the moment when the upper voice looses its iron grip on the reciting tone, as for instance on the last syllable of *Abraham et semini ejus* (even-verse Tone IV, meas. 108). (5) At *dispersit superbos, superbos* in the even-verse Tone V, he resorts to melodic sequence—tenths again separating outer voices. Much of the mellifluousness of Victoria's magnificats comes from the thirds and tenths in honeyed sequence-chains that he never tires of writing. The parallel tenths involve not only minims and semibreves, but also on occasion semiminims (= quavers) as well (*magna qui potens* of even-verse Tone VII). (6) He word-paints *mihi magna* ("hath done great things to me") with bold octave-leaps in both the even-verse Tones VII and VIII. (7) In the even-verse Tone VII he word-paints *mente cordis* ("conceit of their heart") with a perky run followed by a plunge. (8) Both *dispersit superbos* and *Esurientes* in the even-verse Tone VIII utilize the same melodic figure. Victoria often unifies by repeating some melodic or harmonic fillip in two successive verses.

In his two polychoral magnificats—the Tone I *a 8* and Tone VI *a 12*, published at Madrid in 1600—Victoria did not produce wholly independent works, but harked back to the Tone I of 1576 and Tone VI of 1581 for verses 1, 4, and 5; and 1 (shortened), 2 (revised), 7, and 9, respectively. The 1600 *Missae, Magnificat, Motecta, Psalmi, & alia* was, of course, the collection dedicated to the youthful and somewhat frivolous Philip III. Like his masses in this same collection, the two magnificats are in those tones that approximate most closely to modern minor and major. In nearly every new magnificat movement, the 1600 verse will be found to be considerably shorter than the corresponding 1576 or 1581 verse. The 1576 Quia respexit lasts 31 breves, and the 1600, only 19; the 1576 Fecit, 21 bars, and the 1600, only 15; the 1576 Deposuit, 24 bars, and the 1600, only 9. Quite evidently, he was as eager to abridge individual verses of the two polychoral magnificats as he was to shorten his 1600 masses. For other distinctions: only one movement of the 1576 Tone I, and none of the 1581 Tone VI, called for triple meter. On the other hand, the 1600 Tone I Fecit, Deposuit, Sicut locutus, and Gloria; and the 1600 Tone VI Quia fecit, Fecit, Sicut locutus, and Gloria; begin in triple meter: usually remaining in triple throughout. No movements of the 1576 Tone I or 1581 Tone VI changed meter at mid-verse. But four verses of the 1600 magnificats thus shift gear in mid-course. The 1576 and 1581 movements did not include such rigorously symmetrical phrases as do the 1600 Tone I Gloria and Tone VI Quia fecit. The 1600 Tone I Fecit and Esurientes; and the Tone VI Quia respexit, Fecit, Deposuit, and Gloria; contain the same light *parlando* rhythms that were found to be typical of wordy movements in his 1592 and 1600 masses (see above, pages 398, 411). When Victoria does venture to insert a canon in his 1600 Tone I, he apologetically entitles it *si placet*[208] —printing it as an optional alternate to a first-choice noncanonic Et misericordia. For the rest, he avoids canon as rigorously in the 1600 magnificats as in his 1600 masses.

The dissonance treatment in the 1600 magnificats also betrays Victoria's last period. Were no other clues from which to date these all-verse polychoral specimens available, their late origin could be guessed because of the purging of escaped notes from the newly composed movements. None of the verses transferred from the 1576 or 1581 Tone I or VI, for that matter, allows escaped notes. A melodic mannerism present in his early, middle, and late period works which finds abundant illustration in the 1600 magnificats is the f–e–f♯, f♯–g–f♮, b♮ (= ♯)–c¹–b♭, b♭–a–b♮ type of "delayed" chromaticism that was first noticed as a favorite turn in his *De beata Virgine* Mass of 1576 (see above, pages 384-386).

Motets In modern anthologies, Palestrina is represented with a section of some mass. Victoria, on the other hand, is invariably anthologized with some such motet as *Vere languores* or *O Domine Jesu Christe*. Evidently, Victoria continues to be more heartily admired—even by those who know him best—for his miniatures rather than for his large canvases.

This emphasis on Victoria's motets in modern anthologies is the more interesting because Palestrina's motets number approximately 265, but Victoria's only 44. True, the latter's total will grow if all the items that he published with a covering title of *Motecta* are included. He thus published the four Marian antiphons—*Alma Redemptoris, Ave Regina coelorum,* and *Regina coeli*, each *a 5,* and *Salve Regina, a 6,* in his 1572 book; together with the additional settings *a 8* of these antiphons in 1581. By stipulation, however, these will be excluded from his motet repertory; just as settings of these same antiphons are usually excluded from Palestrina's list of motets. However the count is taken, the Roman master's list will be found to contain more than five times as many motets as Victoria's. Palestrina also composed five times as many masses as the junior master.

Half of Victoria's motets call for vocal quartet. Considerably less than a third of Palestrina's are scored for so small a number of voices. Only 9 of Victoria's call for five voices; but 108 of Palestrina's. In his 18 (not 19) motets *a 6*, Victoria invariably calls for two tenors, and never for two basses. This fact in itself should have alerted dictionary-compilers,[209] not to mention Pedrell,[210] against accepting the six-part *Pastores loquebantur* as Victoria's; since it calls for two basses. Composed by Guerrero, this last-named work was included as a courteous gesture in Victoria's 1585 *Motecta Festorum Totius anni*.

Despite the great number of Palestrina's motets, only twenty (excluding duplicate settings of the same text) make use of texts also chosen by Victoria.[211] Even these twenty texts do not always correspond exactly—one or another version sometimes continuing with a *pars 2* or in some other way suffering alteration. In the following list will be given first the number of parts in the Palestrina version or versions, then the number in the Victoria. (1) *Ascendens Christus in altum* (*a 4: a 5*); (2) *Ave Maria* (*a 4, a 5,* and *a 8: a 8*); (3) *Benedicta sit Sancta Trinitas* (*a 4: a 6*); (4) *Congratulamini mihi* (*a 4* and *a 8: a 6*); (5) *Doctor bonus* (*a 4: a 4*); (6) *Dum complerentur dies* (*a 6: a 5*); (7) *Estote fortes* (*a 6: a 4*); (8) *Gaudent in coelis animae sanctorum* (*a 4: a 4*); (9) *Nigra sum* (*a 5: a 6*); (10) *O Domine Jesu Christe* (*a 6* and *a 8: a 6*); (11) *O lux et decus Hispaniae* (*a 5: a 5*); (12) *O magnum mysterium* (*a 6: a 4*); (13) *O quam metuendus* (*a 5: a 4*); (14) *O sacrum convivium* (*a 5: a 4* and *a 6*); (15) *Pueri Hebraeorum* (*a 4: a 4*); (16) *Quam pulchri sunt* (*a 4* and *a 5: a 4*); (17) *Senex puerum portabat* (*a 5: a 4*); (18) *Surrexit pastor bonus* (*a 4* and *a 8: a 6*); (19) *Trahe me post te* (*a 5: a 5*); (20) *Tu es Petrus* (*a 6* and *a 7: a 6*).

Because of the more personalized reaction to text expected in motets, analysis of the specimens in the above list ought to reveal some of the more important differences between the musical esthetic of these two composers who have so long been paired in the popular estimation.

1 To begin with *Ascendens Christus* (*PW*, VII, 55-57; *VicO*, I, 53-58): Baini claimed for Palestrina's setting "an elegance on a par with that of the handsomest and richest tapestries in the Vatican Museum."[212] Even so, Palestrina's setting (not published in his lifetime) cannot be considered to be one of his major efforts. Its stiff and unimaginative head motive, which consists merely of an ascending scale in semibreves throughout an octave from G to g, contrasts unfavorably with Victoria's lithe and soaring head motive.

2 In his *Ave Maria, a 8* (*PW*, VI, 121-124), Palestrina entrusts the first two incises of the familiar plainsong alternately to the lowest voice of each quartet. Thus submerged, the plainsong quotation cannot be comprehended readily. Victoria's *Ave Maria, a 8*, also opens with an allusion to the first incise of the thrice-familiar plainsong. On the other hand, Victoria confides it not to the bottom but to the top voice. Thus exposed, it cannot fail of recognition. Elsewhere in his motets he follows the same course, always giving any plainsong quotation to his highest voice. For other instances, reference may be made to the openings of *Ne timeas, Ecce sacerdos magnus*, and *Veni sponsa Christi (VicO,* I, 22, 46, 50). In *Estote fortes*, to be discussed later, Victoria makes a cantus firmus of the plainsong antiphon. Still conforming with his rule, he consigns it to the uppermost part.

3 Although Palestrina elsewhere in his *Liber primus* casts an entire motet (*Tollite jugum meum*) in so distinctive a meter as Φ, and although he calls for temporary shifts to triple meter in such other motets of his Book I as *Lauda Sion* and *O quantus luctus*, he makes no overt symbolical allusions in his "Blessed be the Holy Trinity" motet *a 4*, either in meter, number of parts, or phraseology, to the trinity concept. Victoria, none of whose motets is cast in triple throughout, differs from Palestrina when he pits three voices against another three as a structural device in his *Benedicta sit Sancta Trinitas, a 6 (VicO,* I, 118-121). His phrases divide so symmetrically into blocs comprising three breves each that some forethought must be presumed. The first 24 measures, for instance, parse thus: 3 + 3, 3 + 3, 3 + 3, 3 + 3. Admittedly the subsequent divisions are not so clear-cut. But the larger pulse in threes tends to persist even after he abandons antiphony between trios. That the antiphonal trios and the three-breve phrases were planned deliberately seems the likelier when it is remembered that amidst 76 breves of ¢ music in *Duo Seraphim*, he inserted 12 semibreves in triple (signature: 3) to set the phrase *et hi tres unum sunt* ("and these three are one").[213]

4 Of Palestrina's two motets entitled *Congratulamini mihi*—one *a 4* published in his *Liber primus*, and the other *a 8* left in manuscript and not published until the 1860's (*PW*, VII, 167-171)—the first, but not the second, can be compared with Victoria's motet *a 6 (VicO,* I, 129-132). The text of the Roman master's second motet (*a 8*) alludes to the incident recorded in John 20:11-18, and duplicates that of his motet *a 4* only so far as the first half-dozen words are concerned. That of his *a 4*, on the other hand, duplicates exactly the text of Victoria's *a 6*: the sole difference being that the Spaniard adds Alleluias at the end. Palestrina assigns his motet *a 4* to the Presentation, but Victoria his *a 6* to the Nativity, of the Virgin. Both composers probably refer to the initium of the same plainsong in their head motives: when they begin with repeated notes in dactylic rhythm, and then leap up a fourth. Palestrina chooses A Major for his final chord, and writes intermediate cadences on A-minor, G-Major, and E-minor chords. Victoria, whose only motet closing on A bears for its title *O quam metuendus est locus iste* ("O how fearful is this place"), chooses instead a tender mode: F, prefixed by one flat in the signature. Seven Victoria motets of single *pars* and four of two *partes* belong to the F mode, with B♭ in the signature. Each joins a happy, gracious, positive, or affirmative text (*Benedicta sit Sancta Trinitas, Congratulamini mihi, Duo Seraphim* [*Tres sunt*], *Ecce Dominus* [*Ecce apparebit*], *Gaudent in coelis, O decus apostolicum, O Regem coeli* [*Natus est nobis*], *O sacrum convivium* [*Mens impletur*] a 4, *O sacrum convivium* a 6, *Quam pulchri sunt, Surrexit pastor bonus*). In *Congratulamini mihi* the Virgin expresses her delight because of the unique favor promised from on high. Joy being the mood of the text, Victoria would have violated his own esthetic of mode had he chosen A instead of F (with flat) for his setting of this particular text. Brief transitory "modulations" occur, carrying the hearer toward C Major, D minor, and even G minor (mm. 26, 35, and 60). But the harmonic train can quite properly be said to travel on F-Major tracks throughout. As usual, the number of Victoria's accidentals vastly exceeds Palestrina's. The Roman master specified only one— C♯ for the third of the closing chord. Raffaele Casimiri, who went to fanciful extremes when suggesting ficta (because he wished to endow Palestrina's music with the wealth of harmonic color that properly belongs to Victoria's), could find only nine places where such ficta accidentals might possibly be intruded. Nineteen obligatory accidentals are to be seen in Victoria's 1572 imprint.

5 The example of the two *Doctor bonus amicus Dei Andreas* motets is a particularly apt one, because of the light that it throws on the subtler distinctions between Palestrina's and Victoria's motet styles. The elder master's four-part setting matches the younger's so far as number of parts and modality is concerned. Furthermore, a common indebtedness to a plainsong initium must be presupposed in this motet, as in *Congratulamini mihi*: since CAB in both *Doctor bonus* motets begin with identical intervals. Rhythmically, however, the Victoria head motive is more emphatic than the Palestrina. The elder master neutralizes as best he can the accent on "bo-". On the "-mi-" of *amicus* he also guards carefully against emphasis. Victoria, by contrast, sets the Latin as if it were his own native Castilian, governed by similar laws of rhythmic accent. The text of this motet

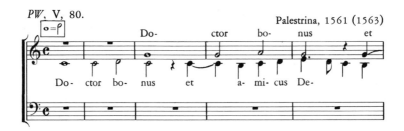

PW, V, 80.   Palestrina, 1561 (1563)

has been translated thus: "Andrew, worthy teacher and friend of God *was led to a cross*. From *afar he beheld the cross* and exclaimed, '*Hail Cross!* May my master Christ, receive unto Himself the disciple who hangs from thee'." The italicized words receive quite different treatments at Palestrina's and at Victoria's hands. Palestrina at "was led to a cross" constructs a point of imitation on the smoothest and most innocuous of motives. Victoria's cantus after a triadic descent leaps up an octave, rises still another degree, then settles downward in exhaustion a fifth. Palestrina seems intent on minimizing *crucem*; Victoria, on maximizing it. Or, to give still other illustrations of their use of musical symbolism: when Victoria reaches *longe* ("afar"), he responds with an appropriately lengthy cantus melisma

reaching sixteen notes; whereas Palestrina at the same word contents himself with one note to a syllable in all parts. At *vidit crucem* ("he beheld the cross"), Victoria suddenly expands into solemn homophony in semibreves and breves: whereas Palestrina keeps his previous even pace of minims and semiminims, as if nothing of importance were now transpiring. Upon reaching the end of the phrase (after *dixit*), Victoria interjects a general pause in all parts. This dramatic gesture, repeated by him at a similarly ecstatic moment in *Vere languores*, focuses attention on *Salve Crux* as nothing else could do.[214] Palestrina, on the other hand, allows no moment of expressive silence to intervene. In order to blunt the edge of *Salve* he even immerses it in a tide of running crotchets (= quavers). Great artist though he undoubtedly was, Palestrina seems everywhere content to have seen the crucifixion of Andrew "through a glass darkly"; whereas Victoria always seeks to view the scene "face to face," to see the cross as he sees *dulce lignum* in his famous motet *Vere languores*, and himself to participate in the blood, the sweat, and the tears. This burning desire to participate in the passion, and to suffer with the martyrs and above all with Christ, has, of course, been often referred to as a typical feature of Theresan mysticism.

6 Just as the Palestrina and Victoria settings of *Doctor bonus* share a number of significant external features, so also their settings of *Dum complerentur* (2d *pars: Dum ergo essent*) resemble each other in several

remarkable ways. To enumerate: (1) Their Pentecost motets are in two *partes*, each of which sets an identical amount of text. (2) Both are responsory-form motets—the "B" in Palestrina's aBcB reaching 32 breves; in Victoria's, 31. (In both, "B" is ushered in with the words *tamquam spiritus vehementis*.)[215] (3) Not only do the two composers choose the same amount of text for both *partes* and the two adopt the same aBcB form, but also they each use approximately the same amount of canvas over which to paint their two panels: 84 + 66 breves in Palestrina's motet; 86 + 76 in Victoria's. To look now at their diptychs in another light and to study the differences: (1) In Palestrina's setting *a 6* (Rome: 1569) ending on F Major (B♭ in signature), interior parts often cross each other; but cantus and bassus are never crossed by any inner voice. In Victoria's setting *a 5* (Venice: 1572) closing on G (B♭ in signature), cantus and quintus cross constantly. Moreover, they switch roles in the second "B" of aBcB. By virtue of their constant crossing they create a synthetic top vocal line that throughout both *partes* constantly hovers around one note, d^1. This hovering creates a mood of suspenseful expectancy that corresponds with the excited, on-edge, mood of the text (Acts 2:1-2). (2) Palestrina takes a black-and-white picture—specifying only 3 accidentals in 150 breves. Victoria shoots his in technicolor—specifying 135 accidentals in 162 breves. This number would no doubt have been even greater had he, like Palestrina, called for six instead of five voices.

7   In Victoria's *Estote fortes*, *a 4*, for the Feast of Apostles and Evangelists, the borrowed plainsong antiphon becomes a cantus firmus sung by the highest voice. Palestrina's setting *a 6*, since it survives in Cappella Sistina Codex 38, cannot postdate 1563.[216] He too reduces the speed of the plainsong antiphon below that of the other parts. But instead of a cantus firmus, Palestrina uses the plainsong as *dux* and *comes* of a canon at the fifth between tenor I and cantus II: thus obscuring the Gregorian melody in inner voices. To preserve the neutral character of the plainsong, Palestrina inderdicts ficta at the places where Victoria specifies accidentals. He does so by part-writing involving octaves and fifths, which makes it impossible for even the most enthusiastic modernizer to sharp, for instance, the third syllable of *accipietis* or the last of *aeternum* (*PW*, XXXI, 76, 78: mm. 44, 46; 83, 85 [in each case, tenor I followed by cantus II]). Victoria at these moments wears the *mantello ibèro*: which, indeed, he was never quite able to doff—despite any report to the contrary from Giovanni Maria Nanino.[217] Victoria also shows allegiance to peninsular plainsong tradition when he ignores the second note of the liquescent neum that belongs to the word *bello*. Palestrina transcribes the two elements of the cephalicus with notes related in the 3:1 ratio, so far as time values are concerned.

8   In their motets *a 4* entitled *Gaudent in coelis* (Palestrina, 96 bars; Vic-

toria, 57), both composers defer to the Common of Martyrs antiphon (second vespers) by choosing Mode VI and by beginning with the plainsong initium. Palestrina grounds his entire motet on the plainsong: assigning snatches first to cantus, then to bassus, then to tenor, then to altus. Both motets burst into triple meter at *exultant*. Since Victoria's duple "time signature" was ₵, he uses this signature at the shift to triple: ₵$\frac{3}{2}$; thence relapsing during the final eight bars into ₵. Because in *Estote fortes* his opening signature was also ₵, Victoria similarly chose ₵$\frac{3}{2}$ for his signature when in the coda he suddenly advanced from ₵ into triple meter. On the other hand, in his Christmas motet *a 6, Quem vidistis pastores*—a responsory-form motet, which in both "B" sections veers into triple for *collaudantes Dominum* and then back into duple for *Alleluia*—he uses not ₵$\frac{3}{2}$ but ₵3 for the triple-meter signature. The reason for this difference is not hard to find. Since the duple-meter sections in *Quem vidistis pastores* are all headed C, rather than his more usual ₵, a different proportional signature must be used for the triple-meter sections. (In Victoria's usage C corresponds with our modern $\frac{2}{2}$ or *alla breve* concept; his ₵ agrees with our $\frac{4}{4}$ [minim = crotchet]. For other of his motets using the C, rather than ₵ mensuration, see *Congratulamini mihi* and *Surrexit pastor bonus*.)

9 Victoria's exquisite Song of Songs motet *a 6, Nigra sum sed formosa* ("I am black but beautiful"), opens with arrant eye-music. The first half-dozen notes in all parts appear as blacks. His symbolic intent cannot be questioned. Notes that in any other context would be voids have been blackened at the outset. Published for the first time in 1576, this ₵ motet in the original editions presupposes that the singers will know the rules of coloration in vogue during Tinctoris's epoch. The first note in all parts, for example, appears as a black semibreve = dotted minim. Voids replace blacks at "beauti*ful*." At "Arise, make haste my love, and come" (Song of Songs 2:10-12*a*), Victoria word-paints *surge* with a running scale compassing a ninth (altus). At *flores apparuit* he resorts to light, springy rhythms, with chord-changes on every crotchet. Palestrina's Song of Songs motet of the same title (published in 1584) sets a continuous passage of scripture rather than the cento chosen by Victoria. The elder master now shows that he has learned from the younger, just as Haydn in his 1790 symphonies shows that he has learned from Mozart. Everywhere greater warmth is infused. In 68 breves, for instance, he specifies 43 accidentals; Victoria specified 65 accidentals in 69 breves of his *Nigra sum*. Both motets are cast in the same mode transposed: which makes the number of accidentals specified by each composer the more significant.

10 Victoria's *O Domine Jesu Christe, a 6*, first published in his 1576 *Liber Primus* and reprinted in his 1585 *Motecta Festorum Totius anni*, was also published in the latter year as an item in his *Officium Hebdomadae Sanctae*.

Pedrell, taking his cue from the Holy Week Office, printed it as item 3 in Volume V of the complete-works edition (pp. 119-121); rather than in Volume I, which was supposed to have contained the *Motecta*. In every respect save one, Victoria's text matches the *O Domine Jesu Christe, a 6*, published in Palestrina's *Liber primus motettorum quae partim quinis, partim senis, partim septenis vocibus concinuntur* (1569). The one phrase in which they differ is "I beseech thee." Palestrina begins with *te*. Victoria (in conformity with Guerrero's usage) ends with *te*. Not only do Palestrina and Victoria agree to use the same number of parts, but also they choose the same mode (G, mixolydian). Both insert a dramatic pause before "I beseech thee." Both set the first "O Lord Jesus Christ" *a 4*, the second *a 6*; the first "wounded on the cross" for one trio, the second for the opposing trio. Palestrina's setting, some eleven breves shorter than Victoria's, even includes a few turns of melody that the junior master echoed: his first *sit vita mea* resembling Victoria's last. But Victoria's setting, unlike Palestrina's, gives each individual voice the whole text (broken by suitable rests at punctuation). The ecstatic droop of a fifth in the highest voice, between the last two syllables of *potatum* ("drinking"), betrays Victoria as surely as glistening eyes reveal El Greco. He repeats the same droop, within the same harmonic context, at *videte* ("behold") in his *O vos omnes*.

11 Palestrina's motet *a 5, O lux et decus Hispaniae*, commemorates the patron of Spain, St. James. First published in his *Motettorum quae partim quinis, partim senis, partim octonis vocibus concinantur* of 1575, it may well have been written for one of the visits to the Spanish Church of St. James paid by members of the papal choir on almost every July 25, the national day. A second *pars, O singulare praesidium*, closes on the G-Major chord. At the end of *pars 1*, he cadences authentically to C. If we class as an intermediate cadence the close of *pars 1*, Palestrina's St. James motet belongs to mixolydian. Victoria's single-*pars* motet—first published in his *Motecta Que Partim, Quaternis, Partim, Quinis, Alia, Senis, Alia, Octonis, Alia, Duodenis, Vocibus, Concinuntur* of 1583—belongs to the same mode. In this motet Victoria spins a unison canon at a distance of three breves between cantus I and II. His other motets *a 5* including such a canon are rare—the only two being *Gaude Maria* and the Transfiguration motet, *Resplenduit facies ejus*. In neither of these others does he quote plainsong in the canonic voices. Probably he did not intend to do so in *O lux et decus Hispaniae* either; and it is therefore hazardous to pin any faith on the few melodic similarities between the plainsong antiphon copied into the Codex Calixtinus and Victoria's canonic cantus parts. Peter Wagner's transcription of the neums for this antiphon may be seen in his *Die Gesänge der Jakobusliturgie zu Santiago de Compostela* (*Collectanea Friburgensia*, 1931), at page 77. But the text if not the melody of the antiphon sung at the shrine *ca.* 1150 matches Palestrina's *pars 1* and Victoria's single *pars*. Victoria reserves his one transitory modulation away from G into A minor for the phrase "the first to be crowned with martyrdom." The mounting fervor of the melodic sequences on the repeated *sanctissime Jacobe* (mm. 12-20) add another typically Victorian tinge in this fine tribute to the national saint. Even the canon never quenches the inner fire that distinguishes Victoria's version from Palestrina's polished but not enthusiastic setting.

12 No two homonymous motets are more interesting to compare than Palestrina's and Victoria's parallel settings of *O magnum mysterium*. In only this instance did both composers choose the same motet text; and then later return to construct parody masses on their original motets. Palestrina's motet *a 6* (1569) continues with a second *pars*, *Quem vidistis pastores*, and is for Christmas. Victoria's *O magnum mysterium, a 4*, is of single *pars*, and is designated as a Circumcision motet. Still more interesting, the text as set by Victoria continues with *Beata Virgo cujus viscera meruerunt portare Dominum Christum*: words that in modern liturgical use form the "B" of the aBcB plainsong, *O magnum mysterium* (fourth responsory for Christmas Vespers). Palestrina, who considered *O magnum mysterium* a Christmas text, omitted the *Beata Virgo* phrase; although he did seem aware that the text is a responsory. It will repay us to disentangle the liturgical associations before beginning any detailed study. Circumcision, with its premonition of the shedding of blood on the cross, has always been recognized as a less joyous feast than Nativity. Because Circumcision foreshadows Crucifixion, it is entirely appropriate for Victoria's *O magnum mysterium* to link with his thrice-famous *Vere languores* (Maundy Thursday). Measures 40-44 of his *O magnum mysterium* duplicate at the lower fourth mm. 52-56 of *Vere languores*. In the Circumcision motet, the text at mm. 40-44 refers to the Blessed Virgin, who was by the Most High judged worthy to bear (*portare*) the Child Jesus within her own self. In the Maundy Thursday motet, the text at mm. 52-56 refers to the wondrous wood and nails adjudged worthy by the Most High to bear (*sustinere*) the King of Kings during his hours of agony. Had Victoria's *O magnum mysterium* been composed for Christmas, as was Palestrina's, there would have been something quite incongruous in his having carried over music from it into a motet for so solemn an occasion as the night of the Last Supper. But because he had not Christmas but Circumcision in mind, the carryover serves the highest artistic purposes. Such a prolepsis symbolizes in musical terms the intimate link that has always, according to traditional exegesis, united the one occasion with the other.

13 *O quam metuendus*, for the dedication of a church, was one of the seven motets *a 4* published for the first time in Victoria's *Motecta Festorum Totius anni* of 1585. Palestrina's motet *a 5*, first published a decade earlier in his *Liber tertius*, reaches 84 breves; Victoria's version extends to only 42. Both masters treat the last syllable of *aliud* as a halfway house, setting "-ud" with a long and a dotted long, respectively, in their cantus parts. As usual, Victoria's setting can be the more easily sectionalized of the two versions: his cadences being more decisively marked, more patiently prepared, and more extensively confirmed than the elder master's. Clear-cut divisions are hard to establish in Palestrina's setting because of the overlapping of entries and the lightness of the cadences; whereas Victoria's version divides unequivocally into $11 + 9 + 11 + 11$ breves.

14 By way of exception, Victoria composed not one but two settings of the Corpus Christi text, *O sacrum convivium*—the first *a 4* (equal voices), the second *a 6*. In both the *a 4* and *a 6* he sets exactly the same amount of text. The *a 4* divides into two *partes*; the *a 6* comprises a continuous single *pars*. Palestrina's setting *a 5*, published in 1572 (the same year in which both of Victoria's were published), comprises only the singe *pars*. While all three versions are (for every practical purpose) F-Major pieces, only the Palestrina makes any use of the sixth-tone Corpus Christi plainsong antiphon. After two introductory bars, Victoria's *a 4* so condescends to *Vierhebigkeit* as to divide with utmost regularity into $4 + 4 + 4 + 4 + 4 + 4$ bars. For added regularity, he even writes the same kind of 7–6 suspension over d in bars 3, 7, 11; also, he begins each four-bar group (mm. 5, 9, 13) with the same resolving tonic chord of F Major. In Victoria's *a 6*, he induces a different kind of regularity—but still a balanced phrase structure in contrast with Palestrina's asymmetry. Beginning with the first full chord, Victoria writes a phrase 9 minims long. Immediately he answers with a repetition in lower voices, also 9 minims long. The four bars at mm. $30\text{-}34_1$ become mm. $34\text{-}38_1$ at the suboctave; the three at mm. $49\text{-}52_1$, after serving at the suboctave in mm. $52\text{-}55_1$, are repeated at pitch in mm. $55\text{-}58_1$. With these doublets and tercets he carves on the face of his setting *a 6* a less regular profile than is to be seen at the beginning of his motet *a 4*. Even so, the symmetry is such that any casual listener can feel the poise versus counterpoise.

15 *Pueri Hebraeorum*, omitted from such a standard list of Victoria's motets as that given in *Grove's Dictionary* (1954), ought to be accounted one on Victoria's own authority: he having included it in his *Motecta* of 1572 (where it is assigned to Palm Sunday). Because he also included it in his *Officium Hebdomadae Sanctae* of 1585, Pedrell (*VicO*, V, 111-112) separated it from the *Motecta*. But inconsistently Pedrell printed *Vere languores*, also included in Victoria's Holy Week Office, among the *Motecta* in Volume I of the *Opera omnia* (1902). We cannot have it both ways. *Pueri Hebraeorum* has as much right to be called a motet as *Vere languores*. Both Victoria's setting and Palestrina's (*Liber secundus*, 1584) presuppose a quartet of high voices. The words of the Palestrina belong to the first antiphon sung during distribution of palms on Palm Sunday; those of the Victoria, to the second antiphon. Victoria's head motive lacks the first note in the plainsong antiphon; but otherwise shows a sufficient likeness for derivation to be supposed. At "vestimenta prosternebant" he bends low in descending sequential chord-progressions that aptly suggest the idea of "stooping to lay their garments in the way."

16   *Quam pulchri sunt gressus tui* serves as title of both the *secunda pars* of Palestrina's *Sicut lilium, a 5* (1569), and of two single-*pars* motets. He designates the first *a 4* (1563) *In festo Conceptionis Beatae Mariae*; the second *a 5* belongs to his Song of Songs set (1584). Only the first two of these three versions should be compared with Victoria's motet *a 4*. The Song of Songs version continues with different words. Palestrina's 1563 version belongs to mixolydian, but his 1569 to aeolian mode. If either mode had enjoyed strong emotional connotations in his mind, he could not have set the same text indifferently in two such basically antithetical modes. Victoria, for whom each mode seems to have enjoyed strong affective associations, set *Quam pulchri* in neither of these modes; but instead in lydian with signature of one flat (= F Major). At the outset of his *Quam pulchri* an interesting Victorian mannerism comes to the fore: a running-crotchet figuration in which the "strong" note of each pair outlines a static chord held through several minims. Measures 5-6 illustrate the point exactly. The strong affective connotation, not only of modes but of chords remote from the tonic of any given mode, is illustrated effectively at meas. 52. For the word "divine" he introduces at this bar his one A-Major chord followed by his one D-Major chord in the entire 87 measures. Victoria's motet, the suave gracefulness of which matches that of a Marenzio madrigal, owes much of its charm to the contrasts in texture between rhythmic homophony and unaccented polyphonous lacework. At *filia* ("daughter") and *oculi* ("eyes") all voices dance together in a perky rhythm. But for the second syllable of *eburnea* ("ivory") he spins out a 19-note melisma in the tenor, and only slightly shorter melismas in the other voices.

17   Because both are *quarti toni* motets, Palestrina's *Senex puerum portabat, a 5* (1569) and Victoria's *a 4* (1572) admirably illustrate their differing concepts of Mode IV. In 82 breves the Roman master specifies eight G♯'s and one F♯. In 63 breves (while scoring for one less voice part) Victoria calls for 29 G♯'s, 6 F♯'s, and 5 C♯'s. Or, to state the case more succinctly: for every ten breves *a 5* Palestrina specifies one accidental; for every three breves *a 4* Victoria demands two accidentals. Nor is Palestrina's quota of accidentals measurably to be increased by the addition of ficta. Victoria twice specifies augmented chords on principal beats (mm. 22_4 and 51_2). His shifts to C and A (mm. 20-21, 31, 40) highlight the drama of the text.

18   Palestrina's two settings of the Easter text *Surrexit pastor bonus* again

confirm a generalization offered previously. For the one, *a 4* (1584), he chose lydian with flat (F Major). For the other, *a 8*, he chose transposed dorian. Thus, neither mode seems to have enjoyed the more joyous connotation in his mind. Victoria's setting *a 6* conforms with Palestrina's *a 4* so far as choice of mode is concerned; but, because of his reliance on antiphony as a structural device, more nearly approaches Palestrina's *a 8* insofar as formal outline goes. All three motets open with an upward leap of a fifth. Palestrina in his *a 4* answers the head motive with an inversion. Victoria never busies himself with inversions in any motet. In his *Surrexit* he instead busies himself with drama: witness the contrast that he makes between the prevailing sunshine and the dark cloud passing briefly over the sky at "worthy to die." Unlike Palestrina, he repeats this phrase three times. At the first *mori* he calls for his first E♭ in the motet (meas. 47). At *dignatus* (meas. 55) he specifies his only f♯. By suddenly switching from minim-motion to breves in all voices he dramatizes *mori* each time the dread word "die" is mentioned. By suddenly veering off into such foreign chords as E♭ Major and D Major (followed by G Major), he emphasizes the same phrase. None of these dramatic touches distinguish Palestrina's 1584 motet of the same mode.

19 Victoria's *Trahe me post te*, *a 6* (1583), contains a four-in-two canon and is therefore unique: no such venture is to be found elsewhere in his motets. The sense of the words obviously suggested the double canon: "Draw me: we will run after thee." Two feet running after two feet find an apt musical symbol in such a four-in-two canon. This and *Ne timeas, Maria* are his only two motets in unmitigated ionian. *Trahe me* is also unique because throughout its 58 breves only one accidental is to be seen. His text is a bright paean from beginning to end; therefore he can continue with the same stops throughout. Palestrina's *Trahe me post te* (1584) continues beyond the first half of Song of Songs 1:3—only the "a" part of which verse was set by Victoria. Since in his longer motet (transposed dorian) Palestrina contended with a volte-face in mood between the first and second halves of the verse, he had no incentive to write either "running after thee" canons, or to maintain a frenetically joyful mood throughout. Indeed, his over-all mood tends more toward languor rather than enterprise.

20 Palestrina's two settings of *Tu es Petrus*—the first in single *pars*, *a 7* (1569); the other, *a 6* (1572), in two *partes*—prove again that for him mode and *Affekt* were not linked inseparably. His *a 7* is in ionian (C); his *a 6* in mixolydian (G). His *a 6* more nearly matches Victoria's motet of the same name (1572) than does his *a 7*. Both Palestrina's *a 6* and Victoria's: (1) continue with a second *pars* (Matt. 16:19*b*) entitled *Quodcumque ligaveris*; (2) are in responsory-form, aBcB; (3) are in mixolydian. For Palestrina the aBcB proportions run 50 + 34; 45 + 34. For Victoria they run 37 + 28; 37 + 28.

Victoria, as elsewhere in his aBcB motets scored with two trebles, reverses the roles of cantus I and II during the second "B." He begins his "B" on the fourth beat of meas. 37 in *pars 1*, but on the second of meas. 103 in *pars 2*. Victoria's motet is shorter not because he uses less melisma but because Palestrina repeats several incises of the text as many as four times. Both commence *pars 1* with high trio, and *pars 2* with low trio. Both string out long melismas on *pe*tram, ec*cle*siam, coe*lo*rum. Both close their "a" and "c" sections on C-Major chords. Despite these likenesses, Victoria manages to assert his individuality. For Palestrina's 7 accidentals in 163 breves—all F♯'s—Victoria in only 130 breves specifies 32 F♯'s and 4 C♯'s. This plethora of sharps enables Victoria to treat all excursions into C Major as merely transitory modulations, quickly effaced by cadences back to G.

I   A question hitherto deferred calls now for an answer: What of the accidentals that Victoria "changed" in successive editions of his printed motets? This problem has been dealt with at length in P. Samuel Rubio's article, "Historia de las reediciones de los Motetes de T. L. de Victoria y significado de las variantes introducidas en ellas" (*La Ciudad de Dios: Revista cuatrimestral de cultura e investigación*, Año 66, vol. 162, no. 2 [May-Aug., 1950], pp. 313-352). The following is a précis of this article.

Victoria published his first book of motets at the age of twenty-four (1572). Enlarged and revised, this collection was reissued in 1583, 1585, 1589 (twice), and 1603. These reëditions came from his hands enriched in some instances with additional motets; and in other instances with certain motets lightly retooled. No attempt has thus far been made to give any exact account of these reëditions. True, Pedrell promised in the introduction to Volume I of the *Opera omnia* published at Leipzig by Breitkopf und Härtel to list all the variants that had crept into these reëditions. But he failed signally to redeem his promise. What he did do was to muddy the waters by giving only a few variants from the "reëdition of 1585." Even these were first introduced not in the 1585 reëdition but in that of 1583. Moreover, Pedrell paid absolutely no heed to any other reëdition— even though the title of the 1589 included such a phrase as *quae quidem nunc melius excussa* and the title of the 1603 such a phrase as *noviter recognita*. As a result, Pedrell's sporadic footnotes calling attention to the variants in the "1585" edition have done more harm than good: they have lulled other scholars asleep in the false belief that these retouchings, and these only, are to be seen in any edition published after 1572.

As a foundation upon which to erect any sturdy superstructure, it now becomes necessary to begin with an exact bibliography of the successive editions. The *editio princeps*, issued at Venice by the firm of Antonio Gardano, comprises six partbooks, CATBQS. The CATB partbooks contain 52 pages each. In order to make the page numbers of the motets in Quintus and Sextus partbooks conform with those in the CATB books, Q begins at page 17 and S at page 35. The 33 motets (divided into groups of 14 *a 4*, 9 *a 5*, 9 *a 6*, and 1 *a 8*) are within each group arranged chronologically (in church calendar order). Apart from five faults of punctuation in the title and occasional slips in the capitalization of titles of individual motets, Pedrell's bibliographical details can in this particular instance be trusted. He did fail to signalize the whereabouts of the three surviving sets, not all of them complete: Valladolid Cathedral, the Archivo del Corpus Christi (Patriarcal) in Valencia, and the library of Münster University. Anglés in *AM*, III (1948), p. 95, gave a faulty transcription of the 1572 title, though he did correct some of Pedrell's faults in punctuation.

The first reëdition (copies of which are preserved at Regensburg and in the British Museum) was issued in eight quarto partbooks at Rome in 1583 by Alessandro Gardano. This imprint contains 53 items: 16 *a 4*, 12 *a 5*, 13 *a 6*, 11 *a 8*, 1 *a 12*. Of the 20 additional pieces in this edition, 7 were herein published for the first time—the other 13 having first appeared in either his 1576 composite book of masses, his 1581 magnificats, or his 1581 hymns. Roman publishers on other evidence are known to have been more parsimonious with printed accidentals than Venetian. The mere fact that certain sharps in the Venetian imprint of 1572 do not appear in the Roman imprints dated either 1576, 1583, or 1585 cannot be taken as proof that Victoria during the intervening years had so changed as no longer to approve of the abundant diminished fourths ($f\sharp$–$b\flat$)found in the earlier imprint. Rather, the omitted accidentals deserve study in their over-all context. The very sharps omitted in 1583 and 1585 reappear in the Venetian edition of 1603. Guaranteed in the title to be *noviter recognita*—newly overlooked— this last imprint codifies his mature judgment.

As for the bibliographical details of the 1583 *Motecta*, Pedrell made so many mistakes in transcribing even the material on the title page and its verso as to place in doubt his having ever personally examined the edition. For instance, he gave *duodecim* for *duodenis*, omitted the *cum* between *Coelo* and *Christo*, and the *ergo* between *pietatis* and *à se factos*: not to mention punctuation errors. He was also in error when he averred that *O lux et decus Hispaniae* had been published previously.

As a footnote to his bibliography of the 1585 *Motecta Festorum Totius anni*, Pedrell criticized Haberl for the "nonsensical suggestion not worthy of being refuted— put forward no doubt, merely for the love of talking and of making idle suggestions" that Guerrero may have instructed the youthful Victoria. But unfortunately on the very page containing this denunciation of Haberl, Pedrell himself fell into the error of attributing one of the elder master's motets to Victoria. His bibliography of the 1585 was so incomplete as to omit the papal privilege on the verso of the title page, a fact that suggests he never saw the title page in question. The papal privilege lists by name all Victoria's previous publications. By checking this list we are now able to affirm positively that none of his publications prior to 1585 has been lost. The purported changes of accidentals in the 1585 had actually all been made in the 1583 edition—

another reason for believing that Pedrell never saw the 1583 partbooks.

The Milan imprint of 1589 consists of eight partbooks. The contents duplicate the 1583 set. In the title appears this phrase: *quae quidem nunc vero melius excussa.* Eight of the motets were retouched in this edition. The most important of these revisions is to be seen in the *secunda pars* of *Cum beatus Ignatius.* A dozen breves are compressed within five at the words *diaboli in me veniant* ("devils approached me"). The sudden approach of the demons is perhaps better realized in the revision; but Ignatius's stolidity is better suggested in the original version.

A second imprint of 1589 bearing *Cantiones Sacrae* for its title-heading[218] was issued at Dillingen in eight partbooks. In the printer's dedication of the set to the Dean of Augsburg Cathedral, mention was made of the fact that Victoria's honeyed music, most apt for inciting devotion, had not been published previously in Germany. This particular edition possesses no assured value for textual students— there being no indication that Victoria oversaw the printing.

The fifth and last reëdition of the motets was printed at Venice in 1603 by Angelo Gardano.[219] Since the title page of this last reëdition contains the phrase *noviter recognita,* its text deserves careful collation with those of 1572 and 1589 (Milan). The reappearance of the various sharps in this 1603 edition which had been first inserted in the *editio princeps,* but were for some reason left out of the 1583 and 1585 Roman imprints, can mean only one thing: whatever his reviser's intentions at the age of thirty-five or forty-one, he at the age of fifty-five preferred his pristine versions. Apart from the 1572, 1583, 1585, 1589 (two), and 1603 editions, two others of his motets—now lost—may possibly turn up at some future date: those of 1590 (Dillingen) and 1602 (Frankfurt). But since these German editions—the former existence of which is certified by book catalogues published at Frankfurt in 1592 and 1611—would not have reflected Victoria's own personal judgment, their loss does not bear on the problem of textual variants.

The kind of diminished fourth that Victoria frequently required in 1572, but purportedly came later to dislike, may be illustrated from the cantus of *Vere languores* (mm. 20-28):

VicO, I, 25.

cu- jus li- vo- re sa- na- ti su- mus, cu-

jus li- vo- re sa- na- ti su- mus

Although the c^1♯'s are to be seen in the editions of 1572, 1583, 1589 (both), and 1603, they do not appear in the *Officium Hebdomadae Sanctae* published at Rome in 1585. Or, for another example, tenor I at meas. 60 of his *Ave Maria, a 8*, and tenor II at meas. 64 exhibit the following diminished fourth:

VicO, I, 150.

o- ra pro no- bis pec- ca- to- ri- bus

Diminished because of the f♯'s in all editions except the composite *Liber Primus* of masses, psalms, magnificats, et cetera, published at Rome in 1576, this interval would seem to be a perfect fourth in this latter imprint—the sharp before the f failing to appear.

Specific examples of the same kind of apparent vacillation can be multiplied at great length. See *Pueri Hebraeorum*, mm. 15₄, and 44₄, and *Quam pulchri sunt*, meas. 55₄, for leading tones sharped in Venetian and Milanese editions but naturals or flats in Roman. The final chords in *pars 1* of *Ascendens Christus in altum*, *Dum complerentur*, and *Quem vidistis pastores* appear to be G minor in Roman editions but major in Venetian.

Raffaele Casimiri, relying upon Pedrell's edition and not on the originals, contended that Victoria in 1585 deliberately doffed the Iberian mantle and adopted Roman dress instead.[220] Casimiri assumed it to be self-evident that the accidentals "suppressed" in the 1585 imprint were struck out by Victoria himself. He failed to take account of the fact that Roman printers were at best chary with accidentals, and that Victoria in the 1589 Milanese and 1603 Venetian editions restored the very ones supposedly struck out in the 1585 Roman imprint. In his haste to make his point Casimiri claimed that in "the 1585 revision" Victoria changed as many as 20 breves in *Super flumina Babylonis*; whereas actually the only change consisted in the addition of four new measures (= breves). The shortening of the coda at the end of *Doctor bonus* from six to three breves in the 1583 edition (= 1585) would provide more conclusive proof that Victoria succumbed to outside musical influences (1) were it not an isolated instance, and (2) were it not for the fact that he himself returned to the longer coda in the "newly overlooked" edition of 1603.

II   As a second addendum, a summary must here be given of an article by the same Victoria authority, P. Samuel Rubio, entitled "Una obra inédita y desconocida de Tomás Luis de Victoria" (*La Ciudad de Dios*, Año 65, vol. 161, no. 3 [Sept.-Dec., 1949], pp. 525-559).

Pedrell's *Opera omnia*, volume VIII, contains a *Missa Dominicalis* copied from a personally owned codex that was originally the possession of the Cathedral at Tortosa (Catalonia) where he was born. Casimiri alleged this mass to be, on internal evidence, a spurious work. (See R. Casimiri, "Una 'Missa Dominicalis' falsamente attribuita a Tommaso Ludovico de Victoria," *Note d'archivio*, Anno X, no. 3 [July-Sept., 1933], pp. 185-188.) Aside from this "spuriosity," Pedrell made no attempt to use manuscript sources—even passing by those which were obviously known to him, such as MS 682 at the Biblioteca Central in Barcelona. This particular source, which enters his *Catàlech de la Biblioteca Musical de la Diputació de Barcelona* as item 385 (Vol. I, pp. 244-246), contains two motets *a 4* that bear Victoria's name. The one, *Quam pulchri sunt*, concords with his motet of the same name in his printed collections, and contains only a few variant readings. the other, *O doctor optime . . . beate Augustine*, is not to be found in any of Victoria's printed collections, and was therefore not published in the Pedrell edition.

The Barcelona manuscript can on external grounds be dated before 1597. In 1623 it belonged to Narciso Puig, who had received it *ca.* 1597 as a gift from Jerónimo Romague. Both donor and receiver were beneficed Catalonian clergy. Consisting of 127 leaves written in a single hand throughout, with no principle evident in the arrangement of its contents, the manuscript in all likelihood was copied by the donor, Romague, while he was still serving as chapelmaster in a St. Augustine's Church or a *convento* of the Augustinian Order. Six motets, among a total of sixty-six items in the manuscript, laud the bishop of Hippo. None honor any other nonscriptural saint except St. Cecilia. Only one each honors the four scriptural saints. The composer whose name appears most frequently is Maillart, with thirty pieces—among them two masses (one a Requiem), two magnificats, a Salve, and motets honoring SS. Augustine and Cecilia. After Maillart, Palestrina comes next with six motets; then Victoria with two and Robledo with one item. Twenty-five items lack attributions.

Victoria's *Motecta Festorum Totius anni* (Rome: 1585) contains several motets for commons of saints (Apostles and Evangelists, One Martyr, Several Martyrs, Confessors who were Bishops, Confessors not Bishops, Virgins, Dedication of a Church). Notably lacking, however, from the *Commune Sanctorum* section is any motet for the Common of Doctors. The motet preserved in MS 682 at the Biblioteca Central in Barcelona (folios 58ᵛ-60) remedies such an omission, and may have been added in some subsequent edition now lost. *O doctor optime* can be sung in honor of any of the twenty-five doctors of the church merely by substituting a different name at mm. 32-34. Such motets with blank spaces in the text, where any of several saints' names can be intruded at will, are of frequent occurrence in the Spanish repertory. In the Santiago Codex at Valladolid, Morales's *Hoc est praeceptum meum* and Francisco Guerrero's *Gloriose confessor Domini* contain such blank spaces. In Guerrero's printed motets, 1570, this last is headed

De sancto Dominico, and Dominic's name inserted at the blank space. But any other confessor's name would be equally appropriate: just as any other doctor's name would be appropriate in *O doctor optime*.

If these circumstances argue sufficiently in favor of *O doctor optime* to warrant giving it serious consideration, what of the other external evidences for Victorian authorship? (1) Each of his Common of Saints motets adopts as text a first or second vespers antiphon associated with the magnificat (except *Ecce sacerdos magnus*). *O doctor optime* conforms with the general rule. (2) The modality of each Common of Saints motet—except that of *Hic vir* and *O quam metuendus*—matches that of the plainsong antiphon. Similarly, the modality of *O doctor optime* corresponds with that of the plainsong antiphon. (3) *Quam pulchri* at folios 62ᵛ-64 in the manuscript under consideration departs sufficiently from the notes of all known printed editions to suggest that it was copied from an edition of Victoria's motets now lost (that is, one printed after 1585). This same hypothetical lost edition may also have served as the source of *O doctor optime*.

As for internal marks, the following seem sufficiently important to itemize:

(1) Victoria characteristically divides his single-*pars* motets, so far as the texts will allow, into two parts of approximately equal length separated by a general pause in all voice parts. This caesura comes immediately before an epithet of adoration such as *O beata Virgo, Salve Crux, Dulce lignum*; or an intercessory plea such as *intercede, deprecor, gregem tuam protege*; or the name of a saint such as *Joannes Baptista*. It is for the purpose of emphasizing these ejaculations that he precedes them with silence in all voices. To see the principle in operation, we can examine *Doctor bonus, O decus apostolicum, O magnum mysterium, Sancta Maria succurre miseris, Ne timeas Maria, Vere languores, Cum beatus Ignatius (pars 1), Descendit angelus Domini* (both *partes*), and *O Domine Jesu Christe*. The Barcelona motet, *O doctor optime*, conforms with the same principle.

(2) The turns of melody in the upper voice part at "divinae legis amator" and "deprecare pro nobis" (*O doctor optime*, mm. 37-40, 49-52) are commonplaces in Victorian motets; as are also the cadences at mm. 14-15 and 27-29. In general, Victoria confirms his final cadences (V-I or VII⁶-I) with a short coda of some few breves' duration. During this, a part or two sustain the "tonic" as pedal, while the other voices move to IV (also VI) and thence return to I. Exactly this type of coda is to be found at mm. 58₃-60 of *O doctor optime*.

(3) A specific trait that distinguishes Victoria from other members of the Roman school, such as Palestrina, the elder Nanino, Francesco Soriano, Felice Anerio, and also from Luca Marenzio (considered both as a madrigalist and as a sacred composer), is his articulation of phrases by means of unequivocal cadences. His zeal for the clear-cut phrase is indeed one of his most characteristically Spanish traits. *O doctor optime*, if actually his, illustrates the same jointed phraseology found everywhere in his attested work.

(4) In a point involving four or more parts, Victoria never starts with one outer voice and then chooses for the second entering part the opposite outer voice. In 123 out of 251 points he brings in the lowest voice last. Usually the time lag between successive entries does not exceed a breve or three semibreves. In motets—though not in hymns or magnificats—Victoria always begins his answer on a note belonging to the final chord of the motet. These general rules are confirmed in *O doctor optime*, and therefore strengthen the attribution.

III   That Victoria's motets were sufficiently popular in Germany to win reprints at Dillingen in 1589, and perhaps also at Frankfurt in 1592 and 1611, was made known so long ago as 1844 in Fétis's *Biographie universelle des musiciens* (VIII, 453). Further reprints of individual motets other than those listed in standard bibliographies can now be mentioned. The first of these will prove of exceptional interest to those who can conceive of his motets as having been performed in no other way except *a cappella* during his lifetime. On the contrary, they were at least occasionally made vehicles for the display of Italian solo singers' virtuosity. In Giovanni Battista Bovicelli's *Regole, Passaggi di Musica, Madrigali, e Motetti Passeggiati*[221] (Venice: Giacomo Vincenti, 1594), the editor—who describes himself as a cathedral musician at Milan—reprints at pages 53-63 Victoria's *Vadam et circuibo* (a Song of Songs motet *a 6* first published in Victoria's maiden book, 1572). But Bovicelli, whose purpose is to adapt this motet by "Tomaso Ludouico de Vittoria" for performance *da Concerto*, rather than to reprint it merely for performance *da Cappella*, introduces the most exaggerated ornamentation. At page 14 he says: "When singing not *da Cappella* but *da Concerto*, the beat must be extremely slow, so that scales in semiquavers (and the like) filling in leaps may be executed as precisely as an exercise." Shown below is the ornamentation that Bovicelli prescribes for the soloist (*Regole*, pp. 53-54).

The irregular barring is Bovicelli's. For purposes of comparison, Victoria's
original top part is shown above Bovicelli's revamp. Bovicelli, of course,
makes it clear that only a single soloist shall execute ornaments. The other
parts shall serve merely as Gibeonites, enacting accompanists' roles.
Still further light can be thrown on the uses to which Victoria's motets were
put so early as a decade after his death. Johannes Donfried (1588-1654),
in his *Promptuarium Musicum*, I (published at Strasbourg in 1622), adds a
figured bass to Victoria's *O magnum mysterium*. Amazingly, he does not
specify so much as one accidental absent from the original 1572 imprint. In
contrast with the other late Renaissance composers anthologized by Donfried, and whose motets he was forced to supply liberally with additional
sharps and flats (because without them too much depended on the intelli-

gence of singers), Victoria's motet in this miscellany proves to have been decked out so completely with accidentals in its original edition that Donfried needed add not a single posthumous sharp or flat.

Hymns   Diego Ortiz, chapelmaster at the viceregal court in Naples, published a set of hymns in his *Musices Liber primus* (Venice: Antonio Gardano, 1565). But obviously neither he nor Victoria was the first Spaniard to write them. Both Anchieta and Peñalosa, even before the turn of the century, had composed scattered hymns. Rudolf Gerber offered a penetrating study of these earlier settings in his article "Spanische Hymnensätze um 1500" (*Archiv für Musikwissenschaft*, X, 3 [1953]).

Several distinguishing traits set the hymns of all Victoria's Spanish predecessors apart as a definite genre, and prevent confusion of their hymns with their motets. (1) A motet—even when the text is to be classified liturgically as a *hymnus* (as in Sepúlveda's *Exultet coelum laudibus*)—will consist of a series of imitative points, in each of which points any allusion to a Gregorian melody will be wholly at the discretion of the composer. As a general rule, plainsong allusions do not occur anywhere in a motet. But in a hymn, on the other hand, the composer will not only choose for his text a *hymnus* properly classifiable as such in liturgical books, but also without fail will quote the Gregorian hymn-melody to be found in some service-book. (2) What is more, the entire Gregorian melody in any given stanza of a polyphonic hymn will be quoted, or paraphrased, in some one individual voice. Where several stanzas are set polyphonically, then the voice part that quotes or paraphrases the Gregorian hymn-melody may migrate. Most often, however, the plainsong-bearing voice will be found to be the cantus. Four parts being the norm, the other three almost invariably supply "accompaniment" for the plainsong-bearing part. The other parts, either by *Vorimitation* between incises of the source melody or in other ways, may show plainsong "influence." (3) Not only are hymns always set stanza by stanza, but (like magnificats and psalms) they also call for the alternation of polyphony with plainsong. The earliest composers, such as Anchieta and Peñalosa, seem to have contented themselves with setting only a single strophe polyphonically. Bernardino de Ribera in his St. James's hymn *Huic caeli ab altis sedibus* repeated identical music during alternate strophes (see above, page 325). Since the metrical identity throughout a hymn makes possible such repetition, we may even surmise that Anchieta and Peñalosa intended their polyphonic settings of stanza 1 to serve for stanzas 3, 5, and so forth, in a given hymn. Juan Navarro seems to have been the first Spaniard to provide different polyphonic settings for successive odd or even strophes of a given hymn. (4) When even stanzas of a given hymn receive polyphonic treatment, as in Navarro's, Victoria's, and Guerrero's hymns, the net effect equals: theme (plainsong)—variation I (polyphony)—theme—variation II —theme—variation III—theme—variation IV; when odd stanzas, then: variation I (polyphony)—theme (plainsong)—variation II—theme— variation III—theme, and so forth.

Throughout his *Hymni totius anni secundum Sanctae Romanae Ecclesiae consuetudinem, qui quattuor concinuntur vocibus* (Rome: Domenico Basa, 1581),[222] Victoria chooses the same core of texts and adheres to the same chronological order found both in Guerrero's hymns (*Liber vesperarum* [Rome: Domenico Basa, 1584] and in Palestrina's (*Hymni totius anni . . . nec non hymni religionum* [Rome: 1589]). Palestrina, of course, adds ten *hymni religionum* (nos. 36-45). These include hymns for the feasts of such saints as James the Greater, Augustine of Hippo, Francis of Assisi, Albert (d. 1192, bishop of Liège), Anthony of Padua; and in honor of the "Carmelite" prophets Elijah and Elisha. Victoria contents himself with thirty-two hymns that match Palestrina's nos. 1-35; except that: (1) Palestrina adds the Christmas alphabetical hymn (Lauds) *A solis ortus cardine*; (2) Palestrina sets *Vexilla regis prodeunt*, *Deus tuorum militum*, and *Jesu corona virginum*, twice each; (3) Victoria sets twice the Corpus Christi hymn by St. Thomas Aquinas, *Pange lingua gloriosi*. Victoria's alternate setting (his no. 32) bears the superscription *more hispano* ("Spanish manner")—and is based on the peninsular melody rather than the Roman. The fact that in 1581 Victoria provided alternate settings of only one hymn—a Corpus Christi hymn—may be connected with his services each Corpus Christi from 1573 through 1580 (except 1578) at the Spanish Church of Santiago in Rome: for which he received handsome sums ranging anywhere from four to nine scudi. (Where, by way of exception, he provided alternate settings for a motet text, *O sacrum convivium*, the occasion was again Corpus Christi.)

Guerrero's 1584 set (with a total of only twenty-four) lacks eight hymns included in Victoria's 1581 set. From Guerrero's *Liber vesperarum* are omitted the Holy Innocents and Quadragesima hymns found at nos. 3 and 6 in Victoria's set; the St. Peter's Chair, Conversion of St. Paul, and St. Peter's Chains at nos. 13 (January 18), 14 (January 25), and 19 (August 1); and the Common of Many Martyrs (Eastertide) and Common of Saint not a Virgin and not a Martyr at nos. 27 and 30. Guerrero, like Victoria, composes even verses polyphonically, leaving odd verses to be plainchanted. Palestrina, in opposition to both, composes odd verses polyphonically. At the outset of each strophe 1, Palestrina requires his tenor to plainchant the hymn incipit (three or four words, not a complete line of poetry). But since, except for this incipit, he always composes the rest of the first stanza, as well as the whole of strophes 3, 5, and 7, polyphonically (granting that the hymn extends to so many strophes), his forty-five hymns are correctly classified as "odd verse."

Victoria prints *in toto* the plainchant for every first strophe. His having done so permits us not only to observe his treatment of the plainsong without having to hunt for his source, but also to compare the plainsong hymn-melodies of which he availed himself (at least so far as incipits are concerned) with the plainsong versions used by Palestrina (1589). Apart from transpositions down a fourth or fifth in Victoria (nos. 7, 9, 16, 19, 29 in 1581 set = nos. 9, 11, 18, 21, 32 in 1589 set), the plainsongs themselves occasionally differ materially, or even drastically. In the 1581, the plainchants of the nos. 11, 12, and 18 differ materially from those of the nos. 7, 13, and 20 in the 1589. Victoria's plainsong melody in his Transfiguration hymn (no. 20) *Quicumque Christum quaeritis* contrasts so sharply with Palestrina's (no. 22) as to deserve being called an entirely different melody. On the other hand, the apparent distinctions found at Victoria's nos. 9 and 17 must be ascribed to Pedrell's careless editing. The plainsong clefs in both nos. 9 and 17 should have read baritone, not bass clef. When a count is taken, Victoria is discovered to have assigned the plainsong verses some dozen times to the bass, and otherwise to the tenor.

Throughout the *Christe Redemptor omnium* hymns for Christmas and for All Saints' (Victoria's nos. 2 and 22) the plainsong is identical, except for clef and voice part to which it is assigned (no. 2 in tenor clef to the tenor, no. 22 in baritone clef to the bassus).[223] A rather delicate problem is therefore posed. So great an artist as Victoria must deliberately have intended that in the Christmas hymn the plainsong verses should sound easy and unstrained, but in the All Saints dramatically stentorian. The November 1 hymn also contrasts with the December 25 by reason of its mensuration sign. Every polyphonic verse in the November 1 carries C instead of the ₵ universally found elsewhere in Victoria's hymns.

In the *Ut queant laxis* (no. 16) he even allows the plainsong to close each odd verse on D (untransposed dorian), whereas each polyphonic closes over G (transposed dorian: B♭ in signature). By such an expedient, the bassus can intone the plainchant verses: even though odd and even verses must oscillate between untransposed and transposed Mode. I. Palestrina in his hymn of the same name transposed both plainsong and polyphony. Surely Victoria had his reasons for following an opposite course. His hypersensitive ear may have preferred the low, relaxed sound of basses on such phrases as *laxis resonare fibris* and *promissi dubius* in strophes 1 and 3 of Paul the Deacon's celebrated hymn for St. John Baptist's Nativity.

Victoria always contents himself with the modality of his plainsong source—transposed or untransposed. He often reduces to three voice parts in strophe 4 when the hymn extends to so many as six or seven stanzas. Even when he reduces the number of parts, each polyphonic stanza still closes over an identical final. Both Guerrero and Palestrina differ from Victoria in often augmenting to five parts during a concluding stanza. Victoria never goes beyond four. Guerrero augments during the concluding stanzas of eleven hymns; Palestrina, during the last of twenty-nine.

Almost invariably, both Guerrero and Palestrina introduce a canon during the last stanza. Guerrero even resorts on occasion to such intricacies as a canon by inversion (in the last polyphonic strophe of *Ut queant laxis*) and in cancrizans (during the final of *Urbs beata Jerusalem*). Guerrero each time indulges in such pyrotechnics not for mere display but for expressive purposes. Still another Spanish hymn-composer frequently ends with a canonic strophe—Juan Navarro. At least ten of the twenty-seven Vespers hymns in his *Psalmi, Hymni ac Magnificat* (Rome: 1590) so terminate. Navarro's *Ut queant laxis* even includes a three-in-one enigma canon. For Victoria to have eschewed canons in his hymns separates him not only from Palestrina, his Roman senior, but also from Guerrero and Navarro. Another difference: Palestrina switches frequently from duple to triple meter during last polyphonic strophes. At such times, $\oint_2^3$ is the new signature in the last strophe. Victoria veers to such a signature during the concluding strophes of only his nos. 8, 12, 21, 24, 27, and 32.

Victoria also differs from Palestrina when he repeats himself from hymn to hymn. Although Pedrell seems not to have noticed the duplicate music provided for the *Gloria tibi* at the end of nos. 8, 24, and 27, each is identical. At the end of *Rex gloriose*, Pedrell even trifles with the reader by inserting, without explanation, *Gloria tibi Domine . . . ut supra folio 66*—a rubric devoid of sense in his edition. Only a student working with the 1581 original possesses the key. (Pedrell did not correlate his transcriptions with folio numbers in the 1581 edition.) Neither did he note the duplication at nos. 14 and 17; Victoria's one polyphonic stanza for *Doctor egregie Paule* equals the last for his *Aurea luce*. Further, his one polyphonic strophe at no. 13 proves identical with his no. 19: not only musically but even textually. Yet Pedrell did not notice the identity. For the last four bars of no. 13 (St. Peter's Chair) he offered the transcription marked "a" in the accompanying example. For the last four of no. 19 (St. Peter's Chains) he supplied the version marked "b". Evidently, he missed the error marked with an asterisk below in "a". The different accidentals at mm. 9 (bassus: F♯ vs. F♮) and 41 (cantus: g♯ vs. g♮) seem also to have escaped him.

(a) *Vic0*, V, 44.

(b) *VicO*, V, 61.

Holy Week Music   Apart from the 1583 *Motecta* (which was an enlarged reprint of the 1572 collection bearing the same title), Victoria's *Officium Hebdomadae Sanctae* (Rome: Domenico Basa, 1585) enjoys the distinction of having been his only publication not dedicated to some prelate, prince, or king. The dedication reads instead to the Triune Deity. As if the unique character of the 1585 *Officium* were not sufficiently presaged by so unusual a dedication, there is still one other external circumstance that stamps it as a work by which he set great store. At the Vatican Library, a handwritten copy (*Cappella Sistina MS 186*) survives of the nine lamentations belonging to the *Officium* (three each for Maundy Thursday, Good Friday, and Holy Saturday). The Cappella Sistina MS 186 version—manifestly earlier than the printed—bears the usual elegant stamp of Victoria's art. But refined though this earlier version be, the nine lamentations have been again distilled in an alembic and their salt tears purified still further before reaching print in 1585. We today lack such preliminary drafts of any other major printed works by Victoria. Only these handwritten lamentations survive to reveal what exquisite tooling he gave his compositions before publishing them.

The printed lamentations differ from those in Cappella Sistina MS 186 by virtue of such changes as the following. (1) The nine in print have always been shortened—sometimes slightly, sometimes drastically. In manuscript, the number of breves in the nine lamentations runs thus: 118, 126, 120; 111, 112, 132; 122, 128, 136. But the lengths of the nine printed lamentations run thus: 112, 93, 111; 72, 97, 81; 87, 88, 123 [or 118]. Artfully, Victoria has shortened by snipping out a minim here, omitting a semibreve or breve there. This telescoping often forces alien chords into closer juxtaposition, thereby sharpening the poignancy of the progressions. Only in the printed version, for instance, does the train of harmonies in Jeremy's prayer (Holy Saturday, third lesson [*VicO*, V, 181]) throb with these chords— a, G, F, C, G, d, A, g, A, D. The stabbing sorrow of this opening passage parallels the opening of Palestrina's *Stabat Mater* (*PW*, VI, 96-108). Even the chord spellings are remarkably similar.

(2) When composing the version extant in Cappella Sistina MS 186, Victoria had recourse to a corrupt text for the second lesson of Maundy Thursday. His defective text coupled the Hebrew letter *Zain* with a verse that ought properly to follow the letter *Heth* instead. When revising for the press, he omitted the music for both the letter *Zain* and the verse that follows improperly. At one stroke he thus shortened and corrected himself. He also revised for the press by dropping the third *Aleph* and its verse from the third lesson for Feria VI and the first *Teth* with its verse from the first lesson for Holy Saturday.

(3) In the printed version he softened square melodic contours with graceful passing notes.[224] At the same time, he reduced the number of melodic curls in ornamental resolutions, especially those of the type involving a lower neighbor.[225] He also heightened interest by devising several light imitations. The 1585 printed lamentations are therefore less continuously chordal, the outer parts less jumpy, and the cadences less stereotyped.

(4) The printed version contains many more accidentals, especially sharps. Whether these were to have been supplied by singers using the manuscript version need not be argued here. However, when the manuscript version does specify so unusual a melodic interval as a diminished fourth, the printed version, by voice-crossing, attains the same sound of g$\sharp$ followed by c^1 without his forcing any one voice to sing so un-Palestrinian an interval. Comparison of the passages (*VicO*, VIII, 25, meas. 62; V, 132, meas. 57) gives grounds for supposing that the copyist of Cappella Sistina MS 186 specified at least the more unusual accidentals that were required by the composer.

It was perhaps such "offensively Spanish" twists as the diminished fourth, the rigid adherence throughout each lamentation to the same mode, the greater emphasis on the *Jerusalem convertere* ending each lamentation, and even perhaps the increased length of individual verses in a given lamentation, which caused Giuseppe Baini as long ago as 1828 to protest against Victoria's jeremiads in his *Memorie storico-critiche* (Vol. II, p. 190, n. 573). "If they do not suffer from being too Flemish in style, they are on the other hand too Spanish," he asserted. He even spoke of their having been *generate da sangue moro* (begotten of Moorish blood). Victoria's ancestry can have contained no such blood—his *expediente de limpieza de sangre* presented at the time he was appointed the Empress María's chaplain precluding such a possibility. (Baini was the first to suggest that *sangue moro* flowed in Victoria's veins: a legend that still persists among those who confuse the *more* of *more hispano* with *moro*.)

Baini was also mistaken when he categorized Victoria's lamentations as unfit for use in the papal chapel. Haberl exposed this error when he came to edit Palestrina's four books of lamentations in 1888 (*PW*, XXV, i): "He [Baini] maintained also that these [lamentations] had never been used by the papal choir; yet they are to be found, beautifully copied in Cod. 186 at the Sistine archive. Scored in the customary way they bear telltale signs of use!" (See *Bausteine für Musikgeschichte*, 2. Heft, p. 172.) Not only was Cappella Sistina MS 186—the 28-leaf manuscript to which Haberl referred—well known by Baini, but also Baini knew such other contents of Victoria's *Officium Hebdomadae Sanctae* as the two passions. He even lauded these two dramatic-type passions—the first according to St. Matthew (for Palm Sunday), and the second according to St. John (for Good Friday)— or at least he praised them highly when writing the first volume of his biography (*Memorie*, Vol. I, p. 361, n. 433). But upon reaching his second volume he reversed his favorable opinion of Victoria's Holy Week music. In an excess of devotion to his hero, he perhaps read too much between the lines of the Latin dedication prefacing Palestrina's *Lamentationum Hieremiae Prophetae* (Rome: Alessandro Gardano, 1588). In this dedication to Pope Sixtus V, Palestrina complained of the poverty that prevented him from issuing his lamentations in folio—constraining him to publish them, instead, in small partbooks: *Multa composui, edidique, multo plura apud me sunt: a quibus edendis retardor ea, quam dixi angustia* ("I have composed many things, some of which I have published, but more of which remain yet unpublished, delayed as I am by the narrow circumstances of which I spoke"). Possibly, Palestrina's publication disappointments did mount into envy of the sumptuous Holy Week folio that his junior, Victoria, was able to issue in 1585. Or at least this pique is what Baini thought he read between the lines of the 1588 dedication.

After bewailing Palestrina's poverty, Baini criticized Victoria's lamentations for being baldly chordal, disfigured by useless repetitions of text, tiresomely constructed, and "bastardized" art (*op. cit.*, Vol. II, p. 190, n. 573). As for their being baldly chordal, it is indeed true that even in the revised printed edition the lamentations show relatively few points of imitation. So, for that matter, do the lamentations of such earlier composers as Carpentras, Morales, and Arcadelt. Only Crecquillon among the more prominent mid-sixteenth-century composers had sought rigorously independent contrapuntal lines when writing lamentations. Precisely because lamentations were customarily slow and chordal, Ghiselin Danckerts (papal singer, 1538-1565) had railed against them in his "Sopra una differentia musicale" (Rome: Biblioteca Casanatense, *MS 2880*).[226] He had censured the tiresome plodding along in the "note-against-note" style and the lack of beautiful runs in semiminims or quavers, which was the rule in lamentations. Foreigners might continue to write such dull stuff if they liked, contended Danckerts. But members of the new Roman school were purposely avoiding lamentations, simply because they disliked the manner in which such dirges were customarily written, he said. The late date at which Palestrina turned to the writing of those lamentations published in 1588 as his *liber primus*, and the fact that he was prompted to compose even these by Pope Sixtus V (1585-1590), who felt that Carpentras's out-of-date lamentations should be superseded, tends to bear out Danckerts's thesis.

However, because the idiom itself demanded chords, Victoria deserves the greater praise for having found ways to overcome monotony. His Maundy Thursday and Good Friday lamentations contain enough semi-minim scale-passages to soften the chordal outlines. He constantly changes the angle of the light pouring through his stained-glass windows by shifting back and forth from lower to higher voice groupings. When thus shifting, he mercifully abstains from reiterating text. Despite Baini's charge of repetitiousness, Victoria rarely takes any occasion to repeat text. Indeed, when he shifts vocal combinations, he is as a rule quite content for any one voice to sing mere snatches of the liturgical text. When veering from CCA to ATB to CCA, or from CAT to ATB and back, he does not ask the bass to sing words already sung by the cantus, or vice versa. Only in his Jerusalem movements does he repeat text. As a matter of fact, Baini's accusation just here borders on the ironical because Palestrina, and not Victoria, was the composer who insisted upon entrusting any one voice in a given lamentation with the entire text. Palestrina was again the composer who insisted upon repeating the words *De lamentatione Jeremiae Prophetae* at the beginning of each set of three. He was also the composer who set the most verses in each lamentation. No Palestrina lectio ever fails to contain at least two Hebrew letters, with their corresponding verses. Victoria, on the other hand, never sets more than two Hebrew letters, and often merely one, with their corresponding verses. In the 1585 imprint he omits the Zain of Lectio II and Lamed of Lectio III for Maundy Thursday; the Teth of Lectio I, a phrase of the Mem of Lectio II, the third Aleph and the Beth of Lectio III for Good Friday; the second Heth of Lectio I, and the Ghimel of Lectio II for Holy Saturday. Only in the Lectio I for Maundy Thursday and Lectio III for Holy Saturday do both composers set the same quantity of text: Palestrina elsewhere always setting the greater amount. In Victoria's Maundy Thursday Lectio I and Good Friday Lectio III the measure count runs 112 and 123 [118], respectively; in Palestrina's 1588 imprint the count for these same *lectiones* runs 116 and 126, respectively. Obviously, Victoria was not more prolix—even when setting the same amount of text. In the other *lectiones* his lengths trail whole laps behind Palestrina's, because of the textual differences.

Baini next protested against the tedious construction of Victoria's lamentations. Each does, it is true, end with a *Jerusalem convertere* during which he increases the number of parts. Palestrina, attaching less importance to the Jerusalem movements, sometimes fails to augment. The greater store that Victoria set by these movements can also be told by counting the number of *aliud* Jerusalem movements in the 1585 imprint. The second lectio for Maundy Thursday and the last two for Holy Saturday conclude with such alternate Jerusalem movements. The Jerusalem closing the Good Friday Lectio III is identical with the *aliud* Jerusalem at the end of the Holy Saturday Lectio III.

Some critics have reprehended Victoria for cadencing over the same final at the close of each verse in a given lamentation. Thus, the finals throughout the three lamentations for Maundy Thursday read F (♭ in signature), G (♭), and E, respectively; for Good Friday, G, F (♭), and D; for Holy Saturday, F (♭), E, and D. But if such repetition of finals is deemed tedious, then Palestrina was even more wearisome. His finals in all three of his lamentations for Maundy Thursday (1588) read F (♭ in signature); what is more, every half-verse as well as verse ends over F.[227] Victoria cadenced at will to chords over the fifth or fourth degrees when concluding half-verses in his various lamentations.

After each set of three lamentations in the 1585 imprint come six transposed-dorian (G[♭]) *responsoria*; three for the second nocturn, and the other three for the third nocturn. As in Marc' Antonio Ingegneri's familiar set of twenty-seven Responses for Holy Week (1588)—formerly ascribed to Palestrina—the form in each of Victoria's eighteen is also *aBcB*: with *c* standing for the versicle. Just as all but one of Ingegneri's twenty-seven Responses reduce from four voices to three in the versicle, so also all but one of Victoria's eighteen so reduce in the versicle. Throughout, both composers call for the same number of parts; however, Ingegneri differs by always requiring CATB; whereas Victoria in the especially plangent second and fifth of each six Responses calls instead for CCAT. Much more frequently than Victoria, Ingegneri begins full. Starting with all voices, he also tends to continue in block-chord fashion through the whole of a response. Victoria's voices converse with each other constantly, whereas Ingegneri's declaim in unison.

To carry the comparison further, Victoria specifies twice as many accidentals. In the six for Maundy Thursday, for instance, he inserts 162. In the same six for Maundy Thursday, Ingegneri decrees only 63. The searching intensity of Victoria's settings can often be ascribed to chord changes that involve conflicting accidentals at close quarters over the same root. For another distinction, Victoria word-paints whenever possible. Such phrases as "Judas, that worst traitor," "Led as a lamb to the slaughter," and "Darkness spread over the face of the earth," find inexpressibly vivid musical counterparts in Victoria's 1585 responses.

Of the two dramatic passions in Victoria's *Officium Hebdomadae Sanctae*, Gustave Reese presciently observed: "Performed in the Sistine Chapel during Holy Week for well over three hundred years, these Passions have probably achieved greater distinction than any other polyphonic settings of the Latin words."[228] That for St. Matthew is the longer by 68 breves. In this passion—for Palm Sunday, a festal day—Victoria quite properly resorts to such artifices as *si placet* canons *a 2*,[229] opening points of imitations in sections *a 4* and *a 3*,[230] and even a certain amount of vocal *fioriture* in the longest continuous section.[231] But in the St. John Passion—for Good Friday, the day of the crucifixion—he seems deliberately to have stripped his continuously four-part music as bare as the disrobed Christ stretched on a cross. In the last set of three lamentations, Victoria similarly contented himself with a stark minimum of musical devices.

He rounds out his Holy Week music with three exquisite motets, *Pueri Hebraeorum* (CATB) and *O Domine Jesu Christe* (CAATTB), both for Palm Sunday, and *Vere languores* (CATB) for Good Friday. Each had made its debut in a previous publication—the first and third in 1572, the second in 1576.[232] He rightly brings these over from earlier collections. Nothing more perfect than each can be imagined. They are as quintessentially Victoria as the bitter-sweet Nocturnes Op. 27, no. 1, and Op. 72 are typically Chopin. True, both composers knew their moments of strength and grandeur. But whereas other contemporaries equaled their expressions of pride and passion, none surpassed and few approached their articulations of pathos. Both achieved their expressive ends by manipulating harmonic congeries in ways so individual as to leave an indelibly personal imprint on even the smallest pieces that they wrote.

Besides the three motets, Victoria also includes an even-verse setting of Zachary's canticle (Luke 1:68-79);[233] a *fabordón* for Psalm 50 [= 51] (*Miserere mei Deus*); a five-part setting of the hymn stanza by St. Thomas Aquinas—*Tantum ergo* (fifth strophe of *Pange lingua gloriosi*); four-part settings of the Improperia (Reproaches) for Good Friday; and an even-strophe setting, for use on Holy Saturday, of the hymn *Vexilla Regis*. Appropriately enough, his setting of Venantius Fortunatus's famous processional hymn (written in 569 for the reception at Poitiers of a Splinter from the True Cross) comes at the close of the Holy Saturday music.

Both the *Tantum ergo* and the *Vexilla Regis* incorporate plainchants of local Spanish provenience. Although Victoria does not specify the Spanish origin of the cantus firmus in the *Tantum ergo* (second soprano), it duplicates the plainsong at item 32 of his 1581 *Hymni totius anni*, which is headed *more hispano*. Quite interestingly, Victoria shapes the cantus firmus into a succession of breves, semibreves, and lesser-value notes that often parse in rhythmic groups of five semibreves. Navarro, when he assigned the same Spanish plainsong to the superius in his *Psalmi, Hymni ac Magnificat* (item 21), reduced the melody to a regular succession of trochees (breve + semibreve). Such external signs as these two Spanish-plainsong hymns, the typically Spanish emphasis on the *Jerusalem convertere* in the lamentations, the *fabordón* Miserere, and perhaps such touches as the uniform modality of the *responsoria*, stamp the *Officium* with a national label. In all likelihood the music throughout was first conceived for the Church of S. Maria di Monserrato or of S. Giacomo degli Spagnoli in Rome—these being the two Spanish parishes that he served professionally from 1569 to 1582. Even the idea of collecting such an *Officium Hebdomadae Sanctae* must be thought of as peculiarly Spanish—no similar *officium* having been issued by any important contemporary in Italy, France, Germany, or England.

Psalms, Antiphons, Sequences, and Litany

Of the seven psalms published in the *Opera omnia*, Volume VII, pages 1-67, the first five (culled from 1576, 1581, and 1583 Roman imprints) were composed for use at vespers, and the seventh and last (extracted from the 1600 Madrid imprint) for use at compline. Unlike Navarro's vesper psalms, Victoria's are all (1) polychoral, (2) organ-accompanied, (3) *durchkomponiert*; and (4) only occasionally (and then casually) allude to the Gregorian psalm-tones. Throughout Psalms 109, 116, and 135, he shifts back and forth at will between the two four-part groups. In these psalms he does not reduce to a small group during one verse and then expand during another. However, in the other four psalms (112, 121 [*a 12*], 126, and 136) he shifts to smaller vocal groups during middle verses. In *Laudate pueri* (Ps. 112), for instance, he scores verses 1-3 and 6-10 full, but verse 4 for CCA and verse 5 for CATB. Only in Psalm 121 does he employ so many as three four-part choruses. All the rest call for two. Since Psalm 121 begins in triple meter, it enjoys the distinction of being his only psalm with triple meter used anywhere else than in the concluding ascription *Gloria Patri et Filio et Spiritui Sancto*. Also, Psalm 121 is his only psalm on which he composed a parody mass (*a 12*, 1600).

The occasion for which *Super flumina Babylonis* was composed happens to be well known (see above, page 358). Unlike Victoria's other six psalms, it does not end with the obligatory triune ascription. This fact alone would suggest that it was not intended for vespers. In addition, only a small portion of the psalm has been set. First performed on the evening of October 17, 1573, *Super flumina* reached print as the concluding item in his 1576 *Liber Primus. Qui Missas, Psalmos, Magnificat . . . Complectitur* (no. 27). The scene of the première was the large hall of the Palazzo della Valle. Members of the papal choir were engaged specially for the event. When he later republished this same psalm as the concluding item in his *Motecta Festorum Totius anni* (no. 37) he retooled it with his usual fastidious care. Instead of dividing verse 3 into separated halves—the first sung as a snippet by chorus I, the second by chorus II—he telescoped the halves. Meanwhile, he rewrote the second half and tightened the cadence by omitting three semibreves. He also altered the last chord from a lethargic tonic to a suspenseful dominant. As revised for the 1585 *Motecta*, this particular psalm became in reality a Lenten motet in two *partes*, each of which is a continuous piece of music.

Just as *Super flumina* can with propriety be called a motet, so also the ten Marian antiphons at pages 68-130 of the *Opera omnia*, Volume VII, may as cogently be classed with his motets. Four of the ten are settings of the *Salve Regina*; two each are settings of the antiphons sung after compline in Advent, Lent, and Eastertide—*Alma Redemptoris Mater*, *Ave Regina coelorum*, and *Regina coeli*. Allusion has already been made above at pages 405-410 and 371, to Victoria's parody masses constructed on his Marian antiphons; and attention drawn to the absence from the extant repertory of a *Regina coeli* Mass that by rights should have been composed to complete his scheme. His maiden motet collection of 1572 already contains all his five-voice settings of each antiphon but the *Salve*; to compensate, it includes his six-voice of the *Salve*. In 1576 he adds a *Salve*, a 5, a *Salve*, a 8, and a *Regina coeli*, a 8. In 1581 he publishes eight-voice settings of the *Alma Redemptoris* and *Ave Regina*, and in 1583 another five-voice of the *Salve*. In general it can be said of the 1572 antiphons that he quotes the plainchant in the middle voices; and of the later antiphons that he quotes the chant in the top voice.

The four transposed-dorian Salves—1572 *a 6*, 1576 *a 5*, 1576 *a 8*, 1583 *a 5* —are by no means of uniform hue. Each may be sharply differentiated from its companions. In cantus II of the 1572 *a 6*, for instance, he introduces an ostinato after Morales's best manner. During *partes 1* and *2* the one word *Salve* is repeated incessantly. In notes of breve value, cantus II reiterates the plainsong initium fourteen times. Rests intervene between each quotation. In the 1576 Salve *a 8*, by way of exception he so respects the verse divisions of the chant as to compose each verse as an independent piece of music. In the 1576 *a 5* he writes his only alternating-verse Salve. Here, odd verses are to be plainchanted, and even verses sung polyphonically. In his 1583 *a 5* he compresses the whole antiphon into two continuous *partes* totaling only 79 bars (44 + 35)—the 1576 in four *partes* having reached 181 bars! Only in the 1583 does he veer momentarily into triple meter. On every count, these four Salves can be shown to serve quite different musical purposes. Their individual physiognomies are the more remarkable when one considers their identical modality, plainchant foundation, and the liturgical context within which each was to have been sung.

Nothing more delightful can be imagined than the Easter, Whitsun, and

Corpus Christi sequences which Pedrell reprinted at pages 147-150, 141-146, and 135-140 of the *Opera omnia*, Volume VII. The Corpus sequence, *Lauda Sion Salvatorem*, was the first to have been published (1585). The other two were printed for the first time in his 1600 Madrid omnibus collection. In none of the three does Victoria set every strophe of the sequence. On the contrary, he culls five from the *Lauda Sion* (strophes 1, 2, 5, 12, 23), six from the *Veni Sancte Spiritus* (1, 3, 5, 7, 9, 10), and five from the *Victimae paschali laudes* (4-8). Throughout each sequence he joins them in a continuous whole, leaving no opportunity for the plainchanting of the intervening strophes once the polyphony starts.

Each is composed *a 8*—the organ accompaniment duplicating Chorus I. In the Easter sequence (which must be acknowledged one of the most charming pieces that Victoria ever wrote) he composes for CCCAATTT, and in the others for two antiphonal choruses of CATB. Throughout each he adheres to the mode of the plainsong: dorian (transposed) for the Easter and Whitsun sequences, and mixolydian for the Corpus. In the Easter he emphasizes the drama of the question "Tell us what you saw, Mary" by repeating it after her first answer. The Easter sequence comes closer than any other Victoria short piece to capturing the flavor of the popular Spanish villancico. With Spanish instead of Latin words it would find itself completely at home, for instance, among Guerrero's villancicos (*Canciones y villanescas espirituales*, 1589). The shifts from triple to duple meter are handled in the most captivating way, and the exuberance of the last Alleluias cannot be overpraised. Altogether, this is a piece that needs discovery.

In the Corpus sequence, Victoria engages in a play of syncopated homophony at mm. 36-46 which some enthusiast for the African element in music will one day tell us echoes the Negro strains heard throughout Spain and Mexico during the sixteenth century. The words *sit jucunda, sit decora mentis jubilatio* inspire him to this outburst of jazzy revelry.

The Litany of Our Lady, with which Volume VII of the *Opera omnia* concludes, invites comparison with the several by Palestrina published in Volume XXVI of the Haberl edition: particularly the one that starts with identical text at pages 67-70. As in the case of Palestrina's litanies, Victoria's can best be described as "animated antiphonal homophony." Both Victoria's choirs comprise the conventional CATB. At *Causa nostrae letitiae* ("cause of our joy") he breaks abruptly into triple meter. Instances of such a break for similar praises of the Virgin occur in *PW*, Volume XXVI, at pages 69, 75, and 84.

Since the text is so repetitive, Victoria shows remarkable restraint when he echoes musical phrases only at the opening (Kyrie and Christe), end (first and second miserere's), and, momentarily, for three *ora pro nobis* in the triple-meter section. The subdued character of the prayers finds a counterpart in his prevailingly low-pitched lines. The highest of the eight voices in this *Litaniae de Beata Virgine* never rises above d^1. The second bass descends so low as D$_1$. No lower note is to be found in Victoria's entire vocal repertory.

Victorian Spuriosities Charles L. Cudworth in "Ye Olde Spuriosity Shoppe: or, Put it in the *Anhang*" (*Notes of the Music Library Association*, 2d ser., XII, 1 and 4 [Dec., 1954, and Sept., 1955], 25-40, 533-553), drew up a long list of popular works foisted on famous composers. Although he did not mention the "hymn" *a 4*, *Jesu dulcis memoria*, nor the *Missa Dominicalis*, printed at pages 1-2 and 5-14 of the *Opera omnia*, Volume VIII, these two works can be added to Cudworth's already extensive list.

Jesu dulcis memoria was palmed off as Victoria's by the same Joseph Napoléon Ney (1803-1857, eldest son of Marshal Ney) who was also the first to fob off Marc' Antonio Ingegneri's twenty-seven *Responsoria* as Palestrina's.[234] Haberl—who did his own editing and was therefore alive to Palestrina's stylistic traits—sensed at once the improbability that these Responses were really Palestrina's: and in 1892 published them with the remark that they could quite well have been written by any respectable composer of the Roman school as late as 1600. In 1898 he announced discovery of the original Ingegneri imprint of 1588, thus setting at rest any further doubts. But meanwhile, *Jesu dulcis memoria* still goes the rounds as Victoria's. Even in *Grove's Dictionary* (5th ed.; 1954), Volume VIII, page 772, it passes unchallenged as Victoria's. As long ago as 1943 Hans von May argued persuasively that it cannot be Victoria's. None of the authenticated works contains a D♯ (*Jesu dulcis memoria*, meas. 19) nor an upper dissonant neighbor on the first of two quavers (mm. 8 [tenor], 10 [altus]). Also out of style are the unprepared inverted dominant-seventh chord (meas. 5) and the downward leap of a fourth from a dissonant minim (mm. 8-9). When Victoria introduces diminished fourths in his melodic lines they almost invariably proceed upward, not downward as at mm. 20 and 22 of *Jesu dulcis memoria*. Also, since the text forms the first strophe of a hymn, we should remember that in his published hymns Victoria sets even, not odd, stanzas.

The *Missa Dominicalis* was "discovered" by Pedrell, who when he came to publish it committed himself so finally as to declare that *la obra es, indudablemente, de Victoria* (*VicO*, Vol. VIII, p. xcvii). But Casimiri proved irrefragably in his "Una *Missa Dominicalis* falsamente attribuita a Tommaso Ludovico de Victoria" (*Note d'archivio*, X, 3 [July-Sept., 1933], 185-188) that this alternation mass *non possa essere di Tommaso Ludovico da Vittoria*. In this article he adduced nineteen examples of untypical procedures: among them, the upward leap of a major sixth, unprepared sevenths,

sevenths and diminished fifths quitted by leap (other than those in changing-note figures), and "booby" consecutives.

These tokens suggest that Pedrell's edition has served its day,[235] and that a critical reëdition of Victoria's works is now overdue. His 350th anniversary in 1961 may well be the year in which the Spanish Institute of Musicology issues the first volume.[236] The composer who according to Gilbert Chase is matched only by Palestrina as the supreme master of religious polyphonic music; whom Gustave Reese classes as one of the great masters of the Late Renaissance; who, according to Paul Henry Lang, spoke with a "dramatic expressiveness that is without parallel in purely choral literature";[237] and whom encyclopedists from Tovey to Slonimsky have unanimously called the "crown" of the Spanish school and voted the "greatest of Spanish composers"; deserves such a tribute.

NOTES TO SECTION III

1 All biographical disclosures in this opening section not otherwise acknowledged were first announced in D. Ferreol Hernández's article, "La cuna y la escuela de Tomás L. de Victoria," *Ritmo*, año XI, núm. 141 (extraordinario) (Dec., 1940), pp. 27-34.

2 *Ibid.*, p. 27: Iten mando y digo que por quanto yo soy en mucho cargo y obligacion a Francisco Luis, mi hijo legitimo y primogenito, ansi por razon de los muchos e leales seruicios que de el he rescebido y espero de rescebir como por otras muchas causas e razones, que a ello me mueuen, he tenido y tengo intencion de le mejorar por la presente e le mejoro al dicho Francisco Luis mi hijo legitimo e mayor de otros mis hijos e hijas en el tercio de todos mis bienes ansi muebles como raices, aciones e derechos, auidos e por auer.

Y ansi mismo aya la dicha mejora del dicho tercio de mis bienes que ansi hago al dicho Francisco Luis mi hijo en unas casas que yo oue e compre de Alonso de Cogollos, vecino que fue desta cibdad, que son en las que al presente biuo, situadas en la calle de los caualleros y de el horno.

3 Felipe Pedrell, *Tomás Luis de Victoria Abulense: Biografía, Bibliografía* (Valencia: Manuel Villar, 1918), pp. 191-192 (Apéndice 38).

4 *Ibid.*, p. 175 (Apéndice 36). Pedrell mistook "Negra" for "Neira."

5 Raffaele Casimiri, "Il Vittoria: Nuovi documenti per una biografia sincera di Tommaso Ludovico de Victoria," *Note d'archivio*, XI, 2 (April-June, 1934), 118-121. On page 119 (line 36) Casimiri surmised that the licenciado died shortly before 1620. With more likelihood he died before 1600.

6 Pedrell, *op. cit.*, page 158, complained that no archivist in Ávila would take the necessary time to track down notices concerning the composer. But in view of Pedrell's own unwillingness to search at Ávila, his obviously contemptuous attitude toward the citizens of the town (*op. cit.*, pp. 153-157), and the use to which he put documents collected by "anonymous friends," the ill success that attended his demands for new notices from Ávila *anticuarios* can well be understood. The cathedral *Actas capitulares*, as well as the municipal records consulted by D. Ferreol Hernández, have in recent years yielded a respectable lode of such notices. Below are reproduced in chronological order seven such notices, all extracted from Ávila capitular acts, and all mentioning the composer or his publications.

A.C., 1572-3-4-5, fol. 29ᵛ: *Miercoles 15 de abril 1573. / Thome de Victoria residente en Roma hizo presente a sus mercedes por mano de Juan Luis de Victoria su tio de seis cuerpos de libros de musica enquadernados que parece quel dicho Tome a compuesto. Recibieronlos y mandaron quel maestro de capilla* [Hernando de Yssasi] *y musicos los prueven y hagan relaçion en cabildo de su pareçer.* (Wednesday, April 15, 1573. Tomás de Victoria, living in Rome, has made their worships [i.e., the cathedral chapter] a present which was delivered by his uncle, Juan Luis de Victoria, of six bound music partbooks [*Motecta* (Venice: Antonio Gardano, 1572)], which the said Tomás seems to have composed. They were received, and order taken that the chapelmaster [Hernando de Yssasi] and musicians try them out and report their opinion to the chapter.)

Fol. 31ᵛ: *Martes 5 de mayo 1573. / A la petiçion que se dio de parte de tome de victoria para que le grateficasen los seis libros que dio de musica para la yglesia respondieron que por el presente no auia lugar de poderse haçer.* (Tuesday, May 5, 1573. In reply to the petition presented in Tomás de Victoria's behalf requesting some gratification for the six music books that he gave for cathedral use, the chapter rules that at present no such acknowledgment can be made.)

A.C., 1576-1577, fol. 108ᵛ: *Miercoles 9 de enero*

1577. / Juan Luis de Bictoria dio una peticion ofreciendo un libro de canto de organo que tambien dio con ella para que si fuere al proposito para la dicha iglesia le tome dando por el la gratificacion que a sus mercedes pareçiere. Que le auia compuesto un maestro de capilla sobrino suyo criado en esta santa iglesia. Sus mercedes que le vea el maestro de capilla y refiera su pareçer y si la iglesia tiene necessidad del. (Wednesday, January 9, 1577. Juan Luis de Victoria offered a petition and with it a book of polyphony [*Liber Primus. Qui Missas, Psalmos, Magnificat . . . Aliaque Complectitur* (Venice: Angelo Gardano, 1576)] asking that if it proved suitable for use in this cathedral it be accepted and the gratification given for it which seemed just to their worships. He said that it was composed by a chapelmaster who is his nephew and who was reared in this cathedral [i.e., as a boy chorister]. Their worships decided to have the chapelmaster [Yssasi] look it over and tell whether in his opinion the cathedral needed it.)

Fol. 114ᵛ: *Viernes 25 de enero de 1577. / Que se llame para el miercoles para determinarlo que se a de hazer del libro de Canto de organo que traxo Juan Luis.* (Friday, January 25, 1577. A meeting was called for Wednesday to decide what should be done about the book of polyphony [1576 *Liber Primus*] brought by Juan Luis [de Victoria].)

Fol. 115: *Miercoles 30 de enero. / Auiendo sido para ello llamados se resoluieron en que el libro de canto de organo que traxo a la iglesia Juan luis de victoria se le buelva por que la fabrica esta muy alcançada y no tiene de presente con que le poder pagar.* (Wednesday, January 30 [1577]. A meeting having been called to decide the matter, it was resolved that the book of polyphony [1576 *Liber Primus*] brought to the cathedral by Juan Luis de Victoria should be returned to him, since the treasury is quite depleted and funds are not presently at hand to pay for it.)

Fol. 167: *Viernes 6 de setiembre 1577. / Juan Luis de Bictoria por una petiçion ofreçio para el seruicio desta santa iglesia un libro de canto de organo del maestro Victoria su sobrino. Sus mercedes le mandaron reçibir y poner en el inventario delos libros de la musica.* (Friday, September 6, 1577. Juan Luis de Victoria petitioned the chapter to accept for use in the cathedral a polyphonic book [1576 *Liber Primus*] by his nephew, the [chapel]master Victoria. Their worships ordered that it be received and entered in the catalogue of the [cathedral] music books.)

A.C., 1587-1588-1589, fol. 13ᵛ: *Jueves diez y nueve de febrero 1587. / El maestro Victoria embio dos libros de canto de organo en papel para esta iglesia. Mandaron los Reçebir y que se le den por ellos cien Reales y que los pague el Receptor dela fabrica.* (Thursday, February 19, 1587. The chapelmaster Victoria sent for use in this cathedral two polyphonic books [printed] on paper. It was ordered that they should be accepted and 100 reales given for them: this sum to be disbursed by the cathedral treasurer.)

Concerning Hernando de Yssasi, chapelmaster at Ávila Cathedral from January 7, 1567, until July 31, 1587, see below, note 34. The number of times that Yssasi was reprimanded, Yssasi's futile attempts to publish, and his professional incompetence, doubtless goaded his envy and spite. The chilly reception of Victoria's first two publications in his natal town should not be held against the chapter, but against the chapelmaster upon whom the canons perforce depended for an opinion. In Victoria's lifetime such gratifications as chapters disbursed were usually recommended by incumbent chapelmasters. Only after Victoria became famous abroad could he triumph over Yssasi's petty criticisms.

At Seville and Toledo Cathedrals the tale was different. Guerrero warmheartedly recommended the youthful Victoria's publications to the Sevillian chapter (September 3, 1578; September 18, 1587). See above, pages 161 and 169. See also note 80 below. Ginés de Boluda, chapelmaster at Toledo, was another who championed Victoria's publications. See Pedrell, *op. cit.*, pp. 190-192 (Apéndice 37). On September 9, 1585, Boluda recommended paying 200 reales for Victoria's *Missarum Libri Duo* (Rome: Alessandro Gardano, 1583).

7 Pedrell, *op. cit.*, p. 197: *y me perdone que yo quisiera tener dos mil ducados que la dejar* ("and [God] pardon me for wishing that I had 2,000 ducats to leave her").

8 *Ibid.*, p. 192 (Apéndice 39).

9 *Ibid.*, p. 193 (Apéndice 40).

10 *Ibid.*, pp. 196-197.

11 Casimiri, *op. cit.*, pp. 164-165.

12 Pedrell, *op. cit.*, p. 199 (lines 19-20).

13 *Ibid.*, p. 169 (lines 13-14).

14 *Ibid.*, p. 170-171 (Apéndice 19).

15 *Ibid.*, p. 198 (line 33).

16 *Ibid.*, p. 172 (Apéndice 26).

17 *Ibid.*, p. 169 (Apéndice 10).

18 Dr. Agustín did not succeed in one of the three convent chaplaincies endowed at her death in 1603 by the Empress María. His brother the composer did so succeed. See Pedrell, *op. cit.*, p. 172 (Apéndice 27).

19 *Ibid.*, p. 192 (Apéndice 39).

20 *Ibid.*, p. 167 (Apéndices 3, 4, 5).

21 *Ibid.*, p. 168 (Apéndice 9).

22 *Ibid.*, p. 198 (lines 14-15).

23 See V. Fernández Asís, *Epistolario de Felipe II* (Madrid: Ed. Nacional, 1943), p. 435 (line 10).

24 See above, note 6.

25 *A.C., 1550-1551,* fol. 25ᵛ: *Iten quel maestro de capilla de cada dia que tuuiere seruicio su hora de lection de canto de organo y que procure que aprouechan en el contrapunto.* Among the rules to be found in the *Statutos Capitulares de Avila (ca.* 1546) is one requiring that the *maestro* teach from noon until two every day except Fridays and feast days (fol. 28ᵛ). The number of choirboys was set at twelve, of whom four served regularly at the altar, and the remainder in the *coro* (fol. 148).

26 *A.C., 1550-1551,* fol. 28ᵛ: *Que se libren al maestro de capilla tres ducados para vn libro de musica de xvi magnificas de Morales.*

27 *Ibid.*, fol. 44: *Que los señores dean y maestrescuela vean el orden que se puede y debe tener en el mostrar los moços de coro canto de organo y contrapunto y lo traten con el maestro de capilla y den dello relaçion en cabildo.*

28 *A.C., 1551-1552-1553,* fol. 97: *Quel maestro de capilla antes que muestre canto de organo a ningun moço de coro si primero no diere fianças de seruir el tiempo que es obligado.*

29 *A.C., 1554-1555-1556,* fol. 46: *Mandaron que de aqui adelante no se reçiban moços de choro sino traxeren competentes sobrepelizes y ropillas.*

30 *A.C., 1556-1557-1558-1559,* fol. 50: *Yten mandaron que de aqui adelante no se pague el ducado que a cada moço de coro llamado seise se daua en cada terçio si no que acabado este cesse ya este salario.*

31 *Ibid.*, fol. 74ᵛ: *Viernes 4 de nouiembre 1558. / Resoluieron que Peñalosa* (Ávila Cathedral contralto, 1551-1565) *vaya por Chacon el maestro de capilla questa en Syguença y se libraron ocho ducados y que se le dara la media raçion que vaco por Spinar y mas lo que se apreçiare que valiere.*

32 *Ibid.*, fol. 84: *Proveyeron y mandaron se pongan editos para la racion del maestro de capilla publicando bale cien mill maravedis y se provehera para quinze de abril verna.*

33 *Ibid.*, fol. 93: *Y luego de boto de la mayor parte proveyeron al dicho Ribera de la racion entera, media questa baca por Espinar y media que se le ha de dar*

de la fabrica sacados los diez myll maravedis segund esta dicho.

34 According to Collet, *Le mysticisme musical espagnol*, page 289, a certain "Hernando Isassi" served as chapelmaster at Valencia Cathedral from 1564 to 1568, and again from 1576 to 1578. However, since Collet merely copied a list of Valencian chapelmasters already drawn up by José Sanchis y Sivera (*La catedral de Valencia* [Valencia: Imp. de Fr. Vives Mora, 1909]), he could not personally vouch for its accuracy. The data supplied below were gathered during first-hand examination of the cathedral acts at Ávila. Entries are summarized in English, rather than translated.

A.C., 1565-1566-1567-1568, fol. 78: *Martes 7 de henero 1567. / Auiendo sido llamados para ello trataron y resoluieron de reçebir por maestro de capilla a Hernando de Yssasi y resoluieron se le de la raçion que esta baca que tubo nabarro. / Yten se le de de salario de fabrica treinta mill maravedis al año y para ayuda de costa veinte ducados al año diez por nabidad y diez al corpus christi por el trabaxo a de tener en hazer lo que conbiene para soleniçar las dichas fiestas como esta iglesia acostunbra.* (Yssasi's salary shall be the same amount formerly paid Navarro: 30,000 maravedís annually, plus 20 ducats for extra services at Christmas and Corpus Christi.)

A.C., 1569-1570-1571, fol. 26: *Jueves 3 de março 1569. / Mandaron quel maestro de capilla Hernando de Yssasi haga de su parte lo que esta ordenado y deue hazer el maestro de capilla de esta santa yglesia y que de no mas de las dos liciones mañana y tarde en lo que es de su profession de canto y musica.* (Yssasi must stick to his duties and teach only what he is supposed to teach, morning and afternoon.)

Fol. 95: *Viernes 15 de junio de 1571. / Reprehendieron al maestro de capilla Hernando de Yssassi* [sic] *que no aprovechan en su poder los moços de coro en el contrapunto ni en el canto de organo y no auer tenido para la fiesta del corpus cosas de lustre si no baxas y comunes.* (Yssasi is to be reprimanded because the choirboys make no gains either in counterpoint or in polyphony. The music performed at the Corpus festival was trivial and commonplace.)

A.C., 1572-1573-1574-1575, fol. 13: *Lunes 1 de diziembre 1572. / Mandaron que yo diga al maestro de capilla tenga quenta con mostrar los moços de manera que aprovechen y se parezca y que los musicos y ellos se exerçiten en su profission. Yten que se canten sin amor ni odio las obras buenas sean de quien se fueren y que salgan de cosas ordinarias y que los señores hernando diaz y francisco sanchez vean lo que se deve cantar a la nabidad y aquello se cante.* (Yssasi must improve his teaching, and the choirboys must show results. The musicians must practice much more assiduously. Excellent music by renowned masters is being sung so listlessly that it sounds completely ordinary. Hernando Díaz and Francisco Sánchez [cathedral bass since 1551] shall decide what is to be sung at Christmas.)

Fol. 25ᵛ: *Jueves 5 de Março 1573. / Auiendo sido para ello llamados attento quel señor raçionero yssasi maestro de capilla a sido amonestado se recoja en hazer su ofiçio de sus lectiones a los moços de coro por que no luzen ni dan muestra que saben nada y se quexan algunas personas de su tracto y que no ay razon ni quenta en los libros de canto de organo si no que se rompen cantando en ellos los muchachos avyendose de guardar y que canta cosas muy ordinarias y façiles y que no admitte a cantarse obras de otros auctores y que no reside en la yglesia como deve y que anda en platica y tracto de minas siendo como es burla y perdiçion todo y el tiempo y dineros que gasta por lo qual siendo como es benefiçiado en esta sancta yglesia pierde de su oppinion y honor / que las fiestas que tiene obligacion de hazer como nabidad y corpus las compone tarde y escasas y a tiempo que ya no ay lugar de consejo ni remedio para escoger lo que mas conviene / que a tenido poca quenta y tiene en lo que le a sido encargado en lo tocante a su offiçio / mandaronle quitar ocho mill maravedis de su prebenda y salario por el tiempo que fuera la voluntad del cabildo / lo qual yo le intime en su persona y respondio palabras de toda obediençia y comedimiento y que el se esforçara de servyr a la yglesia y a sus mercedes con todas sus fuerças.* (Yssasi has already been admonished. The choirboys continue ignoramuses. The choirbooks are in utter confusion and are constantly maltreated by the very boys who are supposed to guard them. Extremely commonplace and easy things are sung. Works by good composers are excluded. He does not spend the time at church which his office requires. Instead he goes about chattering of mines and indulging in other tomfoolery. He spends lavishly. He does not respect the dignity of his office. Whatever he composes to discharge his duties at such festivals as Christmas and Corpus is always late and little. He never leaves time for choice of anything better. His salary shall therefore be reduced by 8,000 maravedís. He must promise to obey and to improve.)

Fol. 111ᵛ: *Viernes 29 de octubre 1574. / Leyose una carta de su señoria Illma. del señor obispo en repuesta de otra que se le auia escripto acerca del offiçio dela semana santa que a compuesto en canto el maestro de capilla hernando de ysasi. Su señoria encargase de liçençia al dicho maestro para que vaya a Madrid a procurar liçençia para imprimir el dicho offiçio. / Sus mercedes se la dieron sin que oviese termino limitado y que se baya passada la fiesta de todos sanctos y dia de los difunctos.* (A reply from His Excellency, Álvaro de Mendoza [bishop of Ávila, 1565-1577], concerning the Holy Week Office composed by the chapelmaster Hernando de Yssasi was read. The bishop recommends that Yssasi be given leave of absence to go to Madrid for the printing license. The chapter allows Yssasi such leave after November 2.)

A.C., 1576-1577, fol. 34: *27 de abril 1576. / Que los señores chantre y canonigo angulo supliquen a su señoria por el maestro de capilla y sochantre, que los*

tiene presos, tenga por bien de removerles la carçeleria. / Quel señor maestro maldonado protector del clero pida y suplique a su señoria mande que la carçel eclesiastica se adereçe y repare porque esta muy maltratada. (The precentor and Canon Ángulo shall request His Excellency the bishop to order the release of the chapelmaster and succentor, both of whom are at present imprisoned. Canon Maldonado, guardian of clergy, will ask His Excellency to approve repairs of the ecclesiastical jail, which is at present in miserable shape.)

A.C., 1578-1579, fol. 64: *Viernes 18 de julio 1578. / Ordenaron y mandaron quel maestro de capilla haga cantar a los musicos cosas diferentes assi en las misas de canto de organo como en las bisperas so pena de seis reales por cada bez que faltare en esto lo qual pena executen los contadores del coro sin ninguna remision. / Yten y porque los musicos no se escusen con dezir que por falta de exerçiçio no las pueden cantar mandaron quel maestro de capilla representandose en el coro a la prima y pidiendo liçençia para que le cuenten assista en la cantoria para que los musicos acudan a hazer exerçiçio y aprovar lo que han de cantar los quales assimesmo presentandose en el coro a la prima se la cuenten acudiendo al dicho exerçiçio y assimesmo ordenaron que se les cuente la nona si acudieren a la cantoria a exercitarse. / Fol. 64ᵛ: / Yten ordenaron y mandaron que de aqui adelante qualquiera musico que cantando al facistol o echando contrapunto herare haziendo falta notable los contadores del coro por cada bez le echen media real de falta. / Yten encargaron y mandaron al maestro de capilla que de aqui adelante haga que en las fiestas prinçipales aya todas las diferençias de musica que pudiere haziendo cantar a los niños por que se exerçiten. / Yten ordenaron y mandaron que pidiendo el maestro liçençia a los contadores del coro para componer entre semana alguna obra que se aya de cantar la fiesta siguiente los contadores le cuenten y si no la compusiere le tornen a descontar lo que le ouieran contado y le echen de falta dos reales la qual liçençia se entiende no haziendo falta en lo arriba dicho.* (Yssasi must vary his repertory of polyphonic masses and vespers, on pain of six reales each time that he repeats stale items. The singers are at present declining to perform new works because they claim they are not allowed sufficient time to rehearse novelties. He shall therefore be permitted, after having registered his presence at prime, to withdraw with them to a practice parlor. They shall also be permitted to rehearse during none. From now on, any singer who makes a serious blunder during the singing of a polyphonic composition, or when improvising counterpoint, shall be fined half a real each time. From now on, Yssasi's choirboys must shine at all principal festivals. To prove that they have practiced they must sing all the known kinds of variation on a given melody. Whenever Yssasi applies for special leave to compose something during the week before an approaching festival, he shall be granted such leave. But if he fails to produce the promised new work, then he shall be charged for all the time lost during the said week and fined two reales.)

A.C., 1587-1588-1589, fol. 46ᵛ: 8 de Julio 1587. / El chantre propuso y dixo quel officio y ministerio del maestro de capilla desta santa iglesia tiene gran neçessidad de remedio porque Hernando de Ysasi que al presente le haze esta ya viejo y cansado y no atiende a lo que es neçessario y conviene para el uso y exerçiçio de su offiçio y que al presente esta en esta cibdad Sebastian de Bibanco maestro de capilla que ha sido de la santa iglesia de Segovia . . . (The precentor declared the great need for a new chapelmaster. Yssasi is old and tired. He does not attend even to the most vital details. At present Sebastián de Vivanco, former chapelmaster at Segovia, is here in Ávila . . .)

Fol. 57: *Viernes 31 de julio 1587. / Quel maestro de capilla Hernando Yssassi no se entremeta en hazer cosa que toque al oficio de maestro de capilla sino que atienda a su descanso y quietud y quel arcediano de Olmedo de parte del cabildo se lo diga ante mi el secretario.* (Yssasi, retired chapelmaster, is not to meddle in anything touching the office that he formerly held. He is to rest, and to keep quiet. The archdeacon of Olmedo shall tell him the chapter's will. I, the secretary, am to be present as witness.)

35 Bolea occupied the organ prebend as early as September 17, 1551. In 1553 and again in 1555 he was reproved by the chapter for various bits of negligence. He was always acknowledged to be a fine player, however. On April 5, 1553, the chapter ordered that he arise in time to play the organ at matins, on pain of a salary deduction amounting to twelve ducats. On June 7, 1555, the chapter requested that he *use las diferencias de organo que se tañe porque no se dañen* (change the stops on the organ he was playing so that they would not be damaged). On October 22, 1556, the chapter ruled *que racionero que fue Damian de Bolea sea descontado desde cinco de septiembre que partio pues se quedo en Çaragoza* (that the salary of Damián de Bolea, former prebendary, cease as of the previous September 5, his date of departure from Ávila for Saragossa, it being now apparent that he intended to remain there).

36 Águila continued as organ prebendary until at least January 4, 1574. Alonso Gómez, aged twenty-one, succeeded to the organ prebend on October 21, 1587. The organ was by no means the only instrument heard in Ávila Cathedral during Victoria's youth. At Ávila, as in other large Spanish cathedrals, a corps of some half-dozen woodwind players constituted a part of the regularly employed music staff. Their instruments included *chirimías*, *sacabuches*, and probably *flautas*. Victoria cannot have been exposed to much *a cappella* singing at Ávila—if, indeed, any. For notices concerning instrumentalists at Ávila, see capitular acts for January 8, 1557 (salary schedule); July 5, 1559 (pay increases); July 9,

1568 (cathedral instrumentalists must give free lessons to all those desirous of learning how to play); May 4, 1573 (penalties for not performing on San Segundo's Day); August 2, 1574 (while playing at the canonical hours, the instrumentalists must remove their hats; this act of respect to the *officio divino* has sometimes been omitted). When describing the musical environment in which Victoria was reared, one ought also to mention the sacred dances that were the rule at Corpus and Assumption in Ávila, just as at Toledo, Seville, and elsewhere. A typical notice occurs in the Ávila *Actas capitulares, 1578-1579*, at fol. 34: *Miercoles 23 de abril de 1578. / Que para el dia de corpus se hagan dose danças.*

37 *A.C., 1551-1552-1553*, fol. 43: *Miercoles Segundo dia de nouiembre 1552. / Primeramente que se llame para el viernes para hazer vn regalo a antᵒ de Cabeçon. / Viernes quatro de Nouiembre MDLij. / Auiendo oydo para ello llamados mandaron quel señor dean haga a antᵒ de cabeçon vn Regalo como le Pareçiere y sele libre.*

38 *A.C., 1554-1555-1556*, fol. 89: *Viernes çinco de junio 1556. / Que se haga a antᵒ de cabeçon vn Regalo como le Pareçera al señor dean.*

39 Santiago Kastner, "Antonio de Cabezón," *Grove's Dictionary of Music and Musicians* (5th ed.), II, 3-4.

40 Pedrell, *op. cit.*, p. 21.

41 *Ibid.*, p. 158. The salvos that he fired at all previous and contemporary Victoria scholars effectively diverted attention from his own thin line. His appendices do not represent his own research. Even the date of Victoria's death was ascertained not by Pedrell, but by Mitjana.

42 Sta. Teresa de Jesús, *Obras*, ed. by P. Silverio de Santa Teresa (Burgos: Tip. de "El Monte Carmelo," 1915-1924), I, 176 (n. 1).

43 *Ibid.*: "God has given these fathers a singular gift: that is, of treating each student as an all-important indivudual but without the slightest show of favoritism. As a result unity and truth prevail, in conformity with Christ's true teachings."

44 Antonio Astraín, *Historia de la Compañia de Jesús en la asistencia de España* (Madrid: Sucs. de Rivadeneyra, 1902-1925), III, 202.

45 *Obras*, VII, 53 (letter dated January 17, 1570).

46 Andreas Cardinal Steinhuber, *Geschichte des Collegium Germanicum Hungaricum in Rom* (2d ed.; Freiburg im Breisgau: Herder, 1906), I, 130, said that Victoria remained in the college twelve years —whence Haberl deduced that he entered in 1566. See Casimiri, *op. cit.*, p. 113.

47 Casimiri, *op. cit.*, p. 114.

48 *Dictionary of National Biography* (New York: Macmillan Company, 1908), IV, 1214.

49 See R. Stevenson, "Shakespeare's Interest in Harsnet's *Declaration*," *PMLA*, Sept., 1952, pp. 898-902.

50 Ignacio Iparraguirre, *Historia de los ejercicios de San Ignacio* (Rome: Institutum Historicum S. I., 1955), pp. 7-8.

51 Steinhuber, *op. cit.*, p. 8.

52 Otto Ursprung, *Jacobus de Kerle (1531/32–1591): Sein Leben und seine Werke* (Munich: Hans Beck, 1913), pp. 36-38.

53 Casimiri, *op. cit.*, pp. 122, 130.

54 *Ibid.*, p. 185.

55 *Ibid.*, p. 170.

56 *Ibid.*, pp. 124-125.

57 *Ibid.*, pp. 171, 173-174.

58 *Ibid.*, p. 174 (item 7, n. 4).

59 *Ibid.*, p. 171 (item 5).

60 *Ibid.*, pp. 125, 171-172 (Doc. IV).

61 Pedrell, *op. cit.*, pp. 52-53.

62 Ursprung, *op. cit.*, pp. 36-38, 39.

63 *Ibid.*, p. 76.

64 *Ibid.*, p. 50, n. 14.

65 *Allgemeine Deutsche Biographie* (Leipzig: Duncker & Humblot, 1887), XXIV, 640.

66 Casimiri, *op. cit.*, p. 172 (Doc. V, 2).

67 *Ibid.*, p. 136. Concerning Nappi and his manuscript, see Casimiri, "Disciplina musicae," *Note d'archivio*, XII, i (Jan.-Feb., 1935), 2 (n. 3).

68 Casimiri, "Il Vittoria," p. 137.

69 *Ibid.*, pp. 139-140.

70 *Ibid.*, p. 140. This particular appointment,

because of Pope Gregory XIII's donation in 1575, gave rise to the common report in Spain that Victoria was "the pope's chapelmaster." On June 15, 1580, an inventory of the music books was ordered in Toledo Cathedral, and this was completed on August 13. Item 8 in this inventory reads: *otro libro grande de canto de organo, enquadernado en tablas con cubiertas de bezerro, con diez bollones y ocho cantoneras y manos de alaton escripto en papel de marca mayor en que ay missas y magnificas. con una Illuminacion al principio. con las armas de don Joan nauarra, capiscol y canonigo desta Sta. Iglesia a la qual lo dio el dicho don Joan. que le truxo de Roma. y le hizo Victoria. Maestro de capilla del Papa.* (another large polyphonic book, bound in leather-covered boards, embossed with ten brass clamps, and brass-tipped at the corners and on the clasps, copied on highest-quality water-marked paper, containing masses and magnificats and with an illumination for a frontispiece. With the arms of Don Juan Navarra, precentor and canon of this cathedral. Given the cathedral by Canon Navarra, who brought it from Rome. Composed by Victoria, chapelmaster to the pope.)

71 Casimiri, "Il Vittoria," p. 140, n. 3.

72 *Ibid.*, p. 146.

73 According to Giuseppe Baini, *Memorie storico-critiche* (Rome: Soc. Tipografica, 1828), I, 70 (n. 109), Stabile served as *maestro di cappella* at St. John Lateran from September, 1575, through May, 1576. In January, 1592, he became chapel-master at St. Mary Major. The chronology in *Grove's Dictionary* (5th ed.), VIII, 29, requires revision.

74 Casimiri, "Il Vittoria," p. 153. Perhaps the Benedictus in question was the same as that *a 4* published during the same year in the *Officium Hebdomadae Sanctae* as item 13 (reprinted in the Pedrell edition of Victoria's complete works, Vol. V, pp. 143-146). In the latter he alternates odd plainsong verses with even polyphonic verses. For the chant, he avails himself of the *Canticum Zachariae* (Luke 1:68-79) as sung on Maundy Thursday (*Liber usualis* [1947], p. 538). In verses 2 and 4 the paraphrased chant floats above in cantus. In verse 8 it is submerged in the tenor. Victoria's splendidly virile setting concludes with a triple-meter *Sicut erat* marked "suo tempore." As sung on Maundy Thursday, the Benedictus concludes without any *Gloria Patri . . . Sicut erat*. His having printed such an optional concluding *Sicut erat* suggests that he meant his *Officium* Benedictus to be sung on other occasions as well.

75 *Dictionary of National Biography* [1908], VIII, 97.

76 *Ibid.*, VIII, 99.

77 Casimiri, "Il Vittoria," p. 151.

78 *The Catholic Encyclopedia*, XI, 272.

79 Casimiri, *op. cit.*, p. 154.

80 Victoria, in a letter to the Sevillian Cathedral chapter dated January 14, 1582 (printed as an appendix in Juan B. de Elústiza's *Estudios musicales*, Tomo I [Seville: Imp. de la "Guía Oficial," 1917]), speaks of the 1581 *Cantica B. Virginis* and the 1581 *Hymni totius anni* as constituting not two volumes but rather a single book of vespers music. He also speaks of this single volume as having been published at his own expense. His letter, even though printed in 1917, has not thus far caught the eye of Victoria specialists. Pedrell knew nothing of it. Elústiza discovered the original in the Sevillian Cathedral archive (at the time of finding it, he was cathedral organist at Seville). He rightly pointed out that Guerrero had already interceded for Victoria with the Sevillian chapter in September, 1578. Moreover, Victoria alludes to this intervention in his first sentence. Guerrero was in Rome at the very moment that Victoria dispatched the letter —as can be known from letters that Guerrero wrote to his chapter on November 13, 1581, and April 20, 1582. See above, pages 163-164. Because *Estudios musicales* seems not to be widely accessible, the letter is reprinted below with an English paraphrase.

Creo a dos años que enbie al Mº Guerrero un libro de misas para que en mi nombre le presentase a V.S. para servicio de su sancta Iglesia. supe que hiço lo que yo le pedi por md. y que V.S. me hiço favor de rescibirle, y aunque desto tuve gran contento e tenido alguna pena por no me aver hecho V.S. merced corresponderme si se avia servido de mi pequeño ingenio. envio al presente a V.S. un libro de bisperas, que yo a mi costa e hecho imprimir aqui en Roma. creo agradara a V.S. la impresion, porque aunque haya muchos cantores en esa sancta iglesia, es bastante punto para todos. contiene salmos, hymnos de todas las festividades del año y deciseis Magnificas de todos los tonos y quatro salves a cinco y a ocho. suplico a V.S. resciba mi buena voluntad, que esta terne pronta para todo lo que tocare al servicio de V.S. en esta corte. Guarde ntro. Sr. las muy illustres personas de V.S. muchos años. de Roma 14 de Henero de 1582. besa las muy illustres manos de V.S. su capellan

*Thome Luis
de Victoria*

Some two years ago I forwarded your worships through Maestro Guerrero a book of masses for use in your cathedral. Your kind acknowledgment of its receipt fulfilled my best expectations. But although I was delighted with your generous

response I have been rather ashamed that I did not in reply inquire whether you had found my modest settings useful. I am now sending a book of vespers, which I have had published at my own expense here in Rome. I believe that you will like the printing, because although there is a large force of singers in your cathedral the print is large enough for all to read. It contains psalms, hymns for all the feasts of the year, sixteen magnificats in every tone, and four Salves, *a 5* and *a 8*. I beg you to accept my compliments, and assure you that I shall gladly perform any service here in Rome that you may require. May Our Lord preserve you throughout many years. Rome, January 14, 1582. Your servant in Christ to command,

Tomás Luis de Victoria

81 Casimiri, "Il Vittoria," p. 186: . . . *volui vt defessus, commentandi finem iam facerem, et aliquando perfunctus laboribus honesto in otio conquiescerem, animumque ad diuinàm, vt sacerdotem decet, contemplationem traducerem.* . . Interpreted literally, these phrases would, of course, mean that at the early age of thirty-seven Victoria already wished to retire from composing in order to devote himself wholly to contemplation.

82 Concerning Giovenale Ancina (1545-1604), native of Fossano, see *Enciclopedia Cattolica*, I (1948), 1170a.

83 Pedrell, *op. cit.*, p. 88.

84 *Ibid.*, pp. 167-168 (item 7).

85 *Libros de Cabildos de Lima*, XI (1588-1593), transcribed and annotated by John Bromley (Lima: Torres Aguirre, 1942), p. 153.

86 Casimiri, "Il Vittoria," p. 148 (*prima redazione*).

87 Fr. Juan Carrillo, *Relacion historica de la Real Fundacion del Monasterio de las Descalças de Santa Clara de la villa de Madrid, con . . . las Vidas de la Princesa de Portugal doña Iuana de Austria su fundadora y de la M. C. de la Emperatriz Maria, su hermana* (Madrid: Luis Sánchez, 1616).

88 For a list of her music books, see "Inventarios de la Infanta D.ª Juana," in Cristóbal Pérez Pastor, *Noticias y documentos relativos a la historia y literatura españolas*, II (Madrid: Imp de los sucs. de Hernando, 1914), pp. 335-337, 344-348. Her library included volumes devoted wholly to works by Carpentras (item 35), Pierre Colin [fl. 1532] (item 51), Francisco Guerrero (item 188) Josquin des Prez (items 34, 41), Morales (items 52, 178), and Bartolomé de Quebedo (item 168). Her collection also contained several volumes of secular song (items 41, 174, 175, 180, 181, 182(?), 186, 190, 196, 197); in these were copied chansons in French; madrigals and villanescas in Italian; and canciones, ensaladas, and villancicos in Spanish. For further information on her musical ability, see José M. March, *Niñez y juventud de Felipe II: Documentos inéditos* (Madrid: Ministerio de Asuntos Exteriores, 1942), II, 447.

89 José M. Fernández, "Tomás Luis de Victoria," *Tesoro sacro-musical*, XIX, 8 (Aug., 1935), 70. Fernández's monograph forms an invaluable supplement to Casimiri's "Il Vittoria."

90 March, *op. cit.*, II, 440-441.

91 Pascual de Mandura, "Libro de Memorias": *En 23 de Deziembre miercoles* [1587] *se trato de elegir maestro de capilla por la muerte de Josepe Gay y se representaron algunos y fueron Garro maestro de capilla de Siguença Monente natural de la villa de Erla que estaua en la capilla de Su Magd Vitoria aunque se sabia no podia venir como el escriuio en la election passada* [26 de junio] *que hauia sido llamado para Sebilla y para en compañia de Guerrero y no quiso yr por no agradarle la tierra y estar acostrumbrado a los ayres de la suya y que queria acabar en ella.*
Interestingly enough, both Victoria and St. Theresa of Ávila were of one mind, so far as Seville was concerned. She considered that "the injustices rampant in these parts [Seville] are amazing, and also the untruthfulness and double-dealing; this place certainly deserves its bad reputation" (Letter 93 dated April 29, 1576, from Seville [*Obras de Sta. Teresa de Jesús*, ed. by P. Silverio de Santa Teresa, VII, 227]); "not much sincerity is encountered in those parts [Seville]" (Letter 108, dated September 9, 1576 [*Obras*, VII, 282]); "here [Seville] one sees nowadays the deplorable condition of spiritually minded people" (Letter 140, dated November, 1576 [*Obras*, VII, 374]). The fact that Victoria should have inveighed against Seville gives one the right to believe that on some journey to or from Italy he had visited the New York of sixteenth-century Spain.
Since Canon Pascual de Mandura's "Libro de Memorias de las cosas que . . . se han offrecido . . . desde el Agosto del año 1579 hasta el año 1601 inclusive" has not thus far been exploited by Spanish historians, the section beginning at folio 184 in Biblioteca Nacional MS 14047 has been summarized in the following seven paragraphs.
After the death of Melchor Robledo, whose fame covered all Spain and Italy, the chapter anxiously began searching for a worthy successor. At first, some other already famous chapelmaster was sought. The choice fell on Juan Arnal of Tarazona. But he very courteously declined. Then the chapter decided to stage an open competition for the post. Announcement of the im-

pending competition was distributed on April 15, 1587, with a three-month time limit for entering candidacies. The three who entered their names were José Gay, native of Valencia and chapelmaster at Gandía; Martín Pérez, chapelmaster of Badajoz; and Cristóbal Téllez, chapelmaster at Berlanga. Upon arrival Téllez declared, however, that the other candidates were so inferior it would demean him to compete against them. He also offered certain other captious objections.
Juan Arnal of Tarazona (who had been invited to succeed Robledo, but had declined) was requested to judge the examination. While in Saragossa, he stayed with Mosén Pedro Ojo, interim chapelmaster since Robledo's death. The battery of tests began on Monday, June 15, with counterpoint above a given Alleluia. On Tuesday, Pérez and Gay were each invited to add a third voice to a duo from a Josquin mass or a fifth voice to a movement *a 4.* Pérez demurred, claiming that his opponent had seen the duo in advance. Another duo was then selected at random to which he sang a third part. Afterward he returned to the first duo (the one to which he had objected) and sang a third part. He refused to write a third or fifth part, however; because, he said, ability to write such an added part was not a necessary accomplishment for a chapelmaster.
Arnal then assigned each a plainsong upon which to compose a motet for Wednesday afternoon, and a villancico for Thursday afternoon. On Wednesday morning Pérez conducted a Josquin mass. In the afternoon Gay first solfaed his motet with other singers and then sang it through with text. Pérez followed suit, doing exactly the same. For this particular event the choir enclosure was so crowded with musicians (and others) from far and near that guards had to be posted at the entrances.
On Thursday, June 17, during vespers, Pedro Ojo (interim chapelmaster since Robledo's death) asked that Pérez be allowed to sing his villáncico first. This request was denied. Both villancicos were well received. Just as on Wednesday afternoon, an immense crowd was again on hand to hear both contestants' music. On Friday afternoon each was asked to add a third voice to a duo composed especially for the occasion by Arnal himself; and also a third part to a duo from another Josquin mass. Neither candidate, however, succeeded with the Josquin duo, and the session ended with much argument over purely musical questions.
On Saturday, Arnal attended a chapel meeting at which he said that neither candidate exceeded the other: and that indeed both were too poor to endorse for so distinguished a chapelmastership as that of the Seo. The chapter therefore told each candidate to return to his home and there await further word. The chapter allowed Gay and

Pérez twenty ducats each for travel expenses. But Téllez from Berlanga was dismissed with nothing—since he had refused to compete and had impugned the good faith of the chapter. At last on Friday, June 26, almost a week later, a chapter vote was taken. Gay was named by a 4-3 decision. He died, however, on September 10, thus throwing the post open a second time within the same year. To avoid the delay and expense of still another competition, names of possible candidates were discussed in a chapter meeting held on December 23 [1587]. Garro, chapelmaster of Sigüenza, Monente, a member of the royal chapel, and Victoria were mentioned at that meeting. [Here follows the passage that is quoted at the head of this note in Spanish, and paraphrased in English at page 363].

In the meantime, good reports had been received concerning the same Téllez who had so haughtily refused to compete against Gay and Pérez the previous June. He was invited (almost in desperation), and took office on January 31, 1588. Five years later he accepted a call to Sigüenza. Announcement of a new competition to name his successor was released to the public on October 26, 1593. Francisco de Silos, who had recently succeeded Arnal at Tarazona, won the post in a contest conducted early in December. He was elected by an overwhelming majority on December 10.

However, Silos soon proved somewhat negligent in giving the public instruction at the cathedral which Robledo and others before him had given every day, not only to choirboys but to any others interested in learning music. On June 16, 1595, the chapter therefore voted that he be rigidly instructed: (1) to give such a lesson in person every ordinary day of the year at the cathedral; (2) never, except with express chapter approval, to accept outside engagements for his choristers; (3) to guard both the old and new choirbooks with utmost vigilance. In particular, he was not to lend the choirbooks to anyone, to see that they never traveled outside the cathedral, and were never used for merely casual instruction of the choirboys.

92 Elústiza-Castrillo, *Antología musical*, p. LXXXIII.

93 Casimiri, "Il Vittoria," p. 157

94 Allen, Borromeo, Paravicini, Piatti. The favorable impression made by Victoria on the segment of the hierarchy most influential in German church affairs contributed largely to his early fame throughout Catholic Germany. As concrete proofs of the approval that he won, such reprints of his *opera* as the Dillingen of 1589, the Dillingen of 1590, and the Frankfurt on Main of 1602 can be mentioned. See P. Samuel Rubio, "Historia de las reediciones de los Motetes de T. L. de Victoria y significado de las variantes introducidas en ellas," *La Ciudad de Dios*, CLXII, 2 (May-Aug., 1950), 332-333.

95 Pedrell, *op. cit.*, p. 166 (II, 2).

96 Rafael Mitjana, *Estudios sobre algunos músicos españoles* (Madrid: Sucs. de Hernando, 1918), pp. 234-236.

97 Ávila, A. C., *1587-1588-1589*, fol. 60 [second foliation]: *Viernes 30 de otubre 1587. / Que la iglesia de sevilla llamava ofreçiendole media Raçion y doçientos ducados y cinquenta fanegas de trigo de salario cada año que todo llegaria a noveçientos ducados. . .*

98 See above, notes 6, 34.

99 Pedrell, *op. cit.*, pp. 172-173 (items 27, 29-30).

100 *Ibid.*, p. 164.

101 Teresa de Jesús, *Obras*, IX (1924), 185 (n. 2).

102 Introduction reprinted in Manuel Joaquim, *Vinte livros de música polifónica* (Lisbon: Ramos, Afonso & Moita, 1953), pp. 2-3.

103 Pedrell, *op. cit.*, p. 172 (lines 26-27). Also, Mitjana, *op. cit.*, p. 235 (lines 3-6).

104 Pedrell, *op. cit.*, p. 172 (item 27). Also, Cristóbal Pérez Pastor, *Bibliografía madrileña: parte tercera* (Madrid: Tip. de "Rev. de Archivos, Bibliotecas y Museos," 1907), p. 520 (item 27). Every word at pages 166-175 in Pedrell's *Tomás Luis de Victoria* (Valencia: Manuel Villar, 1918) —as well, of course, as the same material at pages LXXXIV-XC in Volume VIII of his *Opera omnia* edition—was copied from Pérez Pastor, *Bibliografía madrileña*, III, 518-521. In his *Opera omnia*, Volume VIII, he even allowed Pérez Pastor's text to be translated into French and German.

105 Pedrell, *op. cit.*, p. 173 (item 30); Pérez Pastor, *op. cit.*, III, 521 (item 30).

106 Mitjana, *op. cit.*, p. 235, lines 6-8 (. . . *siruio en la Capilla del diez y siete años, de Mro. de Capilla, sin ynteres ninguno . . .*).

107 *Ibid.*, p. 232, line 26.

108 *Ibid.*, p. 233.

109 Pedrell, *op. cit.*, pp. 171-172 (item 24); Pérez Pastor, *op. cit.*, III, 520 (item 24). The empress bequeathed the funds for the new organ and remodeled choir enclosure. See León Pinelo, *Anales de Madrid: Reinado de Felipe III*, ed. by R. M. Téllez-Girón (Madrid: Estanislao Maestre, 1931), p. 213 (item 80). She left 4,000 ducats *para hacer el coro del Monasterio de las Descalzas*.

110 Mitjana, *op. cit.*, pp. 235-236.

111 *Ibid.*, p. 239; Pedrell, *op. cit.*, pp. 201-202.

112 However, even an annual income of 1,200 ducats would not have sufficed to allow him any luxuries. For a *descansada vida* (comfortable life), 3,000 ducats was considered a minimum. Second-rate bishops such as those of Coria and Lugo received 30,000 and 25,000 ducats. See León Pinelo, *op. cit.*, pp. 214-215.

113 Pedrell, *op. cit.*, pp. 167-168 (item 7), 169 (item 12), 172 (item 26), 174 (item 33); also, Pérez Pastor, *op. cit.*, III, 518-521 (items 7, 12, 26, 33).

114 Pedrell, *op. cit.*, p. 168 (item 8).

115 *Ibid.*, p. 179.

116 The poverty of Albarracín Cathedral can be documented. See P. B. Gams, *Series episcoporum* (Regensburg: G. J. Manz, 1873), p. 4, col. 2: "el obispado era muy pobre, y la Diocesis."

117 Pérez Pastor, *Bibliografía madrileña*, I (1891), 162.

118 *Ibid.*, I, 192.

119 León Pinelo, *op. cit.*, pp. 60-61.

120 *Ibid.*, p. 61.

121 Pedrell, *op. cit.*, p. 142. He quotes from Diego de Urbina's *Las honras y obsequias Reales . . . martez diez y ocho y miercoles diecinueve de Marzo, año de 1603*.

122 León Pinelo, pp. 62, 222. Concerning the Jesuit church, see Elías Tormo, *Las iglesias del antiguo Madrid* (Madrid: A. Marzo, 1927), p. 150.

123 Tormo, *op. cit.*, p. 151.

124 León Pinelo, p. 62. Within eight weeks of her death 35,000 Masses were offered in her behalf by members of the *compañia* in Spain and in Germany.

125 *Ibid.* Flecha the Younger dedicated his 1581 ensaladas to Don Juan de Borja, the em-

press's major-domo. Cerone (p. 151) praised Borja for being the only one in Madrid to organize musical academies along Italian lines.

126 León Pinelo, *op. cit.*, p. 222.

127 Pedrell, *op. cit.*, p. 171 (item 22); also, Pérez Pastor, *op. cit.*, III, 520 (item 22). As transcribed by the latter, *Pescenio* was made to read *Perserio*. Pescenio's third name, according to the 1605 imprint, was Hasdale—a most unusual metronymic.

128 See above, note 81.

129 Pedrell, *op. cit.*, p. 200.

130 Mitjana, *op. cit.*, p. 239.

131 J. Niles Saxton's unpublished Master's thesis, "The Masses of Victoria" (Westminster Choir College, Princeton, N. J., 1951), was found to be one of the most penetrating studies thus far attempted. I take pleasure in acknowledging the further aid graciously given by Mr. Saxton during private conversations. His adviser at the time of writing his essay at the Westminster Choir College was Professor Joseph Kerman.

132 Gombert's *Beati omnes* (*a 4*) and *Media vita* (*a 5*) Masses each are parodied on his own motets and each reduce the number of voices in the source by one. Reduction, however, occurs only rarely in Spanish parodies.

133 In the present-day breviary, *O magnum mysterium* serves as the fourth responsory at Christmas matins (versicle added). It has been deleted from the Circumcision office to which it formerly belonged.

134 Gombert in his *Missa Forseulement* used two models. See Reese, *Music in the Renaissance*, p. 347.

135 For this date, see *Le opere complete di Giovanni Pierluigi da Palestrina*, ed. by R. Casimiri (Rome: Fratelli Scalera, (1939), Vol. III, p. ix.

136 Requiems not counted.

137 Note also that the Osannas of both the *Pro victoria* and *Laetatus* Masses of 1600 (*VicO*, VI, 52, 54; 95, 97) are identical.

138 In Osanna I of the *Ave maris stella* Mass the tenor sings the hymn text, first strophe (*VicO*, II, 15-16). Throughout Kyrie I, at the end of the Gloria, and throughout the last Agnus of the *Gaudeamus* Mass, either altus I (= altus II of 1583 edition) or cantus II intones the first word of the plainsong incipit (*VicO*, IV, 1-2, 10, 27-28).

139 *VicO*, II, 21, 34.

140 *VicO*, IV, 2, 10.

141 *Ibid.*, pp. 38-39, 46-47; 30, 54.

142 *VicO*, II, 38, 42.

143 *Ibid.*, pp. 60, 64.

144 *Ibid.*, pp. 57, 68.

145 *VicO*, IV, 73, 80; 75, 97; 77, 94; 77, 86.

146 *Ibid.*, pp. 78, 96.

147 *VicO*, VI, 4, 25; 9, 21.

148 *Ibid.*, pp. 26, 55; 29, 56-57; 30, 44; 33, 55-56; 36-37, 48-49.

149 *Ibid.*, pp. 72-74, 90-92.

150 On sequences in Palestrina's masses, see Peter Wagner, *Geschichte der Messe* (Leipzig: Breitkopf und Härtel, 1913), p. 435.

151 José Camón Aznar, *Dominico Greco* (Madrid: Espasa-Calpe, 1950), I, 114; II, 842.

152 Collet in *Le mysticisme musical espagnol*, pages 446-447, voiced an opinion that is still current.

153 Wagner, *op. cit.*, pp. 421-429.

154 The *Ave maris stella* should be of particular interest to students of music in the Americas. It was copied into the celebrated *Códice del Convento del Carmen* (Osanna II and Agnus II movements excepted) and has been reprinted recently from that Mexican source in Jesús Bal y Gay's edition, *Tesoro de la Música Polifónica en México*, I, at pages 49-83.

155 Collet's analysis of Victoria's *curieuse correspondance thématique* at pages 431-433 of *Le mysticisme musical espagnol* somewhat loses force by virtue of this discovery.

156 *MME*, II, 121-131.

157 Wagner, *op. cit.*, pp. 424, 336-337.

158 *VicO*, II, 116-118.

159 Concerning Morales's motet, see above, pages 18-19 and 97-102.

160 Embellished "b" = motive in bass at mm. 19-20 (source).

161 *VicO*, Vol. VIII, p. XXXIII, n. 1; also, *Tomás Luis de Victoria* (1918), p. 74, n. 1.

162 Wagner, *op. cit.*, pp. 424-426.

163 *PW*, X, 138-152.

164 See above, note 133. Palestrina's motet text (*Opere*, V, 184-188) veers off with other words at mm. 38-62.

165 All attempts to find a source for the *Quarti toni* Mass have met with failure. Because it "lays no great stress on imitation, symmetry, or contrast, though it is not without them," because "external means of giving shape are secondary," because "the centre of gravity lies throughout in music-making itself," *Quarti toni* might even remind us of another *Quarti toni*—the *Mi-mi* by Ockeghem.

166 *Bach Gesellschaft*, XXXIX, 185 (nos. 18, 19). This same melody is, of course, better known as an associate of the *O Haupt voll Blut und Wunden* chorale text.

167 The 1572 source motet *Ascendens Christus* (*VicO*, I, 53-58) showed at meas. 105 a "Landini" cadence. Significantly, no such cadence intrudes in the 1592 parody. On the rhythmic side, the persistent use of this figure (found only five times in the source [mm. 74, 78, 80, 84, 86]):

makes a rather interesting feature of the parody. Victoria liked this figure throughout his entire career.

168 *Secunda pars* (*VicO*, I, 114-118) should preferably have been transcribed with beats 1 and 3 of the 4 in a bar interchanged.

169 Saxton, *op. cit.*, pp. 22, 39a.

170 *VicO*, VII, 68-72, 73-80.

171 *Ibid.*, pp. 81-84, 85-90.

172 Escaped-notes at *VicO*, IV, 86 (meas. 66 of Credo), 98 (meas. 16 of Agnus), 102 (meas. 35 of Kyrie).

173 G♯ is not used in the polychoral masses,

although it is used frequently in the *Quarti toni*.

174 Saxton, *op. cit.*, pp. 37a-40a.

175 That he deliberately revised the fifth bar of the antiphon in order to eliminate the escaped-note can be further confirmed by examining meas. 5 of the Agnus.

176 *VicO*, VII, 126.

177 *VicO*, IV, 78.

178 *VicO*, VII, 154, 140.

179 *VicO*, VIII, p. LXXXV.

180 *Ibid.*, p. XCII. See above, page 368, for further details.

181 Obregón y Cerezada eulogizes Luis Honguero [= Onguero] as a paragon who sang with "completely relaxed countenance, unparalleled accuracy, unmatched suavity and sweetness, absolute equality of head and chest registers." This same Honguero enters Victoria's biography at least three times. On August 17, 1604, Victoria authorized him to collect 150 ducats due on his pension from Cordova diocese; and again, on January 16, 1606, to collect his Cordova pension for 1605. Honguero may have come from Cordova, but his income included an annual 150-ducat income from Toledo archdiocese. Sometime before 1605 he ceded Victoria his rights to this Toledo pension. See Pérez Pastor, *Bibliografía madrileña*, III, 520 (item 23), 521 (items 31, 34).

If Obregón y Cerezada's praise was justified and if Victoria and Honguero enjoyed such intimate association as the documentation suggests, Victoria's friendships during his later years were musically more congenial than has hitherto been imagined.

182 Pedrell, *Tomás Luis de Victoria* (1918), p. 105. Mathieu Romarin [= Mathias Rosmarin = Mateo Romero] was born *ca.* 1575 at Liège. His father may have been the Julián Romero de Ibarrola (native of Torrejoncillo, d. 1575) who captained three companies under the Duke of Alva in the Low Countries. In company with a dozen other new choirboys recruited from the Low Countries, he was enrolled on June 28, 1586, in the royally endowed *Colegio de Cantorcillos* at Madrid. This choir school was, of course, a feeder for the *capilla flamenca* of Philip II. Boys aged eight to twelve of good voice and deportment were received for education in the Colegio de Cantorcillos at royal expense. In return they served at secular as well as at religious festivals. When he entered, George de La Hèle was still *maestro* and Philippe Rogier *teniente*, or second

master. La Hèle died, however, only two months later (August 27, 1586), and was succeeded by Rogier (b. Arras *ca.* 1562). Romero spent seven years under Rogier in the Colegio de Cantorcillos—"graduating" on December 1, 1593: at which time his name appears in the choir school list spelled, not "Mathieu Romarin" as heretofore, but "Mateo Romero." This change may in itself be taken as proof of his decision henceforth to adapt himself as fully as possible to Spanish manners and usage.

Upon leaving the colegio he entered the adult *capilla flamenca*. At the untimely age of thirty-four Rogier died (February 29, 1596). Two years later Philip II died (September 13, 1598). On October 19, 1598, as one of the first official acts in his new reign, Philip III appointed Romero *maestro* of the royal chapel and Géry de Ghersem as *teniente*. The cedula mentioned the fact that both had served previously as royal singers.

During the interim since Rogier's death, discipline in the Colegio de Cantorcillos had deteriorated. The *capellán mayor* believed the remedy should include a new set of disciplinary rules. On December 16, 1598, he therefore presented for the young king's approval a much more rigid set of constitutions. Romero, the new head of the colegio as well as maestro of the chapel, objected strenuously to certain provisions. But after being threatened with excommunication and loss of six months' pay he signed on January 17, 1599. The rules in the new *Constituciones del m* ^{e} *y niños cantorcicos dela Real cap* ^{a}, can be summarized as follows: (1) the boys must be taught to read and write, (2) to know their catechism and (3) the elements of Christian doctrine; (4) they must sing a *Salve Regina* every night before Our Lady's *imagen*; (5) the maestro can keep no more than three servants, or two if a relative visits him; (6) the teniente [Ghersem] must always accompany the cantorçillos to the palace, or in his stead the maestro, should the teniente be sick; (7) the teniente must teach, but the maestro sets up the schedule; (8) the maestro is responsible for their cleanliness and their feeding; (9) the maestro must give them new clothes when needed; (10) an inventory of everything in the house must be taken, and signed by the maestro; (11) no women, except a nurse over forty, are allowed; (12) the door must be bolted every night, at eight (winter), or nine (summer).

On January 21, 1599, the court left Madrid, spending several months first in Valencia, then Barcelona, then Saragossa. In 1600 the court visited Segovia, Ávila, Salamanca, and Valladolid, to which last-named city Philip III transferred his court in 1601. In 1601 Claudio de la Sablonara copied a Mass *a 19*, sixteen Christmas and Epiphany villancicos *a 5, 7, 8, 9, 10,* and *unas completas para los menestriles* (compline for voices and instruments), all by Romero. In 1604 Sablonara copied various masses and motets for

2, 3, and 4 choruses, and sixteen more villancicos *a 7, 8, 9, 12, 14, 15* and *23*: all by Romero. In 1605 he copied a motet *a 10, Deus meus respice in me* (Ps. 21), and a parody mass *a 8* based on Lassus's chanson (1570) for the same number of voices, *Un jour l'amant*. This mass was written to celebrate the birth of the future Philip IV on April 8, 1605. Sablonara also copied in 1605 at least sixteen villancicos by Romero—one *a 12* with eight instruments.

Beginning in 1605, Romero was appointed to a succession of lucrative benefices. At the time of his ordination to the priesthood, April 9, 1605, he was named Capellán de la Casa de Borgoña. On the third anniversary of his ordination he was appointed capellán de banco. On November 18, 1623, he was named Capellán de los Reyes Nuevos at Toledo—an appointment entitling him to an annual income in cash and kind of 3,000 reales. In 1641 João IV named him to a lucrative nonresidential chaplaincy in the Portuguese royal chapel. Small wonder, then, that he was able to lend large sums to such subordinates in the *capilla flamenca* as, for instance, Philippe Dubois, who when he died on February 9, 1611, left a will mentioning a 500-real debt to Romero.

Romero taught the future Philip IV not only the musical rudiments but also how to compose, conduct, and play the bass viol. On March 4, 1620, as an example, he signed a receipt for a *contrabaxo bihuela de Arco, que de un xuego de ocho bihuelas . . . y dicho contrabaxo con su arquillo se entrego al dicho Mateo rromero por Mandado de Su Mg^d para enseñar a tañerle al Principe nuestro señor* ("bassviol belonging to a chest of eight viols, and the said bass with bow was delivered to Mateo Romero by order of His Majesty so that he might teach Prince Philip how to play it").

Musical enthusiasm at court knew no bounds during the 1620's and 1630's; and Romero, or Maestro Capitán as he had long familiarly been known (perhaps because his father had been so famous a Spanish captain in the Netherlands), dominated every festivity. The duke of Neuburg, Wolfgang Wilhelm (1578-1653), arrived at court in October 1624, and at his departure on March 13, 1625, carried back to Munich the song collection in future to be known as the *Cancionero de Sablonara* (copied by Claudio de la Sablonara, royal chapel scribe from 1599 to

After thirty-five years as maestro of the *capilla flamenca*, Romero retired on February 22, 1634. He continued to draw full pay, however. His successor was Carlos Patiño. Henceforth during the century only native-born Spaniards were to conduct the royal chapel. But even though he was retired, Philip IV, his erstwhile pupil, still found ways to use Romero. Early in 1638, for instance, the king dispatched him to Portugal. There he was instructed to visit the Duke of Braganza (who two years later was to ascend the throne as João IV). The latter's intentions were

already feared. Romero, it was hoped in Madrid, would sound out the duke. The two had first met at Lisbon in 1619 in the course of a state visit of Philip III (Philip II of Portugal). In the meantime the duke had become known everywhere as one of the foremost musical enthusiasts of the epoch. But Romero, who had no taste for mixing music with politics, and who was too old to relish traveling, *iba muy contra su voluntad* ("went very unwillingly" [*Noticias de Madrid*, January 5, 1638]). Whatever his instructions, he conducted himself while in Portugal with the utmost discretion. Proofs of the favor he won with his host are found in the lucrative chaplaincy that João IV conferred upon Romero as soon as he was crowned king, and in the enormous quantity of Romero's music which he collected for his private library. No less than seventy of Romero's compositions were inventoried in the *Primeira parte do Index da Livraria de Musica do . . . Rey Dom Ioão IV* (Lisbon: 1649).

The repertory that Romero conducted while royal chapelmaster can be known from a five-page *Conocimiento y cargo de los Libros de canto que se le entregan para seruir en la dicha capilla* of November 22, 1612. In this year the active choral library reached thirty-eight books. The printed Mass collections included Morales's Book II of 1544, La Hèle's *Octo Missae* of 1578, Guerrero's Book II of 1582, Rogier's *Missae sex* of 1598, and Alonso Lobo's *Liber primus* of 1602; and in addition various volumes of Palestrina's and Lassus's masses. The other composers whose works were represented in quantity included Cornelius Canis, Rodrigo Ceballos, Clemens non papa, Crecquillon, Claudin de Sermisy, and Victoria.

Romero died at Madrid on May 10, 1647, aged approximately seventy-two. As heir he named Doña Antonia de Ayala. Contemporary tributes of an extremely fulsome nature can be read in Juan Ruiz de Robledo's *Laura de música eclesiástica* (1644), the original of which survives in El Escorial library and a copy of which is preserved in MS 1287 at the Madrid Biblioteca Nacional; in João IV's *Difensa de la musica* (Lisbon: 1649); and in a manuscript account of uncertain provenience by Lázaro Díaz del Valle y de la Puerta first published in the February 24, 1868, issue of the *Revista y Gaceta Musical de Madrid*.

Barbieri collected a dossier of information from which the details in this note have been extracted. See "Papeles del Fondo Barbieri," *MSS 14069* (Biblioteca Nacional). Jesús Aroca, when publishing his edition of the *Cancionero musical y poético del siglo XVII recogido por Claudio de la Sablonara* (Madrid: Tip. de la "Rev. de Arch., Bibl. y Museos," 1916 [1918]), gathered a limited amount of biographical data at pages 327-330. This edition contains the twenty-two secular songs of Romero which Sablonara chose to include among the "pearls and gold" of the songbook presented to the Duke of Neuburg,

Wolfgang Wilhelm, at his departure from Madrid on March 13, 1625. Rafael Mitjana, at pages 241-248 of his lengthy "review" of Aroca's edition (*Revista de Filología Española*, VI, 3 [July-Sept., 1919], offered a few additional details concerning Romero. A somewhat misleading condensation of Mitjana's notes on Romero appeared in the *Enciclopedia universal ilustrada*, Volume IX, Apéndice (1933), at page 388. J. B. Trend, because he translated the Espasa-Calpe article without confirming the dates, contributed a rather unsatisfactory biography to *Grove's Dictionary of Music and Musicians* (5th ed.), VII, 221.

183 Only one other Victoria work *a 12* (three 4-part choruses) reached print during his lifetime —the *Magnificat Sexti toni* (1600). See *VicO*, III, 95-106. Psalm 104, *Confitemini Domino* (*a 12*), sung on Trinity Sunday, 1573 (see *VicO*, Vol. VIII, p. XIX) does not descend to us.

184 The Sanctus shows such chords at mm. 9 and 13.

185 *VicO*, VII, 35 (= VI, 62); VII, 29 (= VI, 75).

186 *VicO*, Vol. VIII, p. LXIX.

187 *VicO*, VI, 110-111 (1583); 133-134 (1605). Note also that the text of the 1583 offertory differs from that of the 1605. In the 1583 he set *libera animas fidelium defunctorum* (*VicO*, VI, 108), whereas in the 1605 he inserted "omnium" as an added word—*libera animas* omnium *fidelium defunctorum* (*VicO*, VI, 131). The 1605 text corresponds with present-day usage. Concerning the significance of this change, see Saxton, *op. cit.*, page 50a.

188 The plainsong incipits at the beginnings of the versicle In memoria (*VicO*, VI, 106, 130) and the offertory Domine Jesu Christe (VI, 108, 131) differ materially.

189 *VicO*, VI, 113.

190 *Ibid.*, p. 136.

191 *Ibid.*, p. 126.

192 *Ibid.*, p. 136. See also Graduale, meas. 15² (p. 129). However, this latter instance may involve a misprinted f¹ in cantus I for d¹.

193 *Ibid.*, pp. 148, 150.

194 *Ibid.*, p. 132.

195 *Ibid.*, pp. 139, 140.

196 *Ibid.*, p. 142.

197 *Ibid.*, pp. 148-151.

198 *Ibid.*, pp. 143-147.

199 Pedrell omitted ten words when he attempted to transcribe the full title (*VicO*, Vol. VIII, p. XXIX; and *Tomás Luis de Victoria* [1918], p. 60). See Casimiri, *op. cit.*, p. 183, n. 2. Casimiri found no less than forty-five other serious errors in Pedrell's transcriptions of titles and dedications.

200 *VicO*, III, 39, 60, 63, 69, 71, 79.

201 Knud Jeppesen, *The Style of Palestrina and the Dissonance* (Copenhagen: Levin & Munksgaard, 1927), p. 185.

202 *Opere complete*, Vol. XVI (Rome: Fratelli Scalera, 1943), p. xiv.

203 *VicO*, III, 11-12.

204 *Ibid.*, p. 24.

205 *Opere complete*, XVI, 16.

206 *VicO*, III, 32-33.

207 *Ibid.*, p. 40.

208 *Ibid.*, p. 87.

209 *Grove's Dictionary* (5th ed.; 1954), VIII, 774.

210 *VicO*, I, 142-146.

211 Sequences (e.g., *Lauda Sion*) and Marian antiphons excluded.

212 Baini, *op. cit.*, II, 330. In Palestrina's *Ascendens Christus* the lines are almost as stiff as in the *XI exercisi sopra la scala* (*PW*, XXXI, 99-111).

213 *VicO*, I, 38.

214 The altus at the word "Salve" (mm. 41-44 [*VicO*, I, 4]) sings the initium of the Salve Regina plainsong, in semibreves. This interesting touch recalls the identical treatment of interjected Salves in such previous Spanish motets as Guerrero's *Ave Virgo sanctissima*; but is not matched by any similar touch in Palestrina's *Doctor bonus*.

215 At *VicO*, Vol. I, pp. 64-65, note Victoria's insertion of extra Alleluias before "tamquam." As a result his *pars 2* exceeds the length of Palestrina's.

216 F. X. Haberl, *Bibliographischer und thematischer Musikkatalog des päpstlichen Kapellarchives* (Leipzig: Breitkopf und Härtel, 1888), p. 18.

217 Baini, *op. cit.*, I, 362 (n. 433).

218 Casimiri, *op. cit.*, p. 190.

219 Exemplar at Uppsala. See R. Mitjana, *Catalogue critique et descriptif des imprimés de musique des XVIᵉ et XVIIᵉ siècles conservés a la Bibliothèque de l'Université Royale d'Upsala* (1911), Vol. I, no. 486.

220 Casimiri, *op. cit.*, pp. 133-134.

221 Cf. F. X. Haberl's introduction to *PW*, Vol. XXX. At pages iv-vi he prints Bovicelli's "revamp" of the cantus from Palestrina's madrigal *Io son ferito*. Bovicelli's barring of the *Vadam et circuibo* motet has the merit of exposing the phrase structure. Pedrell always straightjacketed everything he edited behind bar lines that force the first note to start sounding on "1"—even when the harmonic rhythm of a *pars* is thereby thrown askew (as in *pars 1* of this motet [see *VicO*, I, 97-100]).

222 When reprinted at Venice in 1600 by Giacomo Vincenti, the title of this collection was changed to read *Hymni totius anni iuxta ritum Sanctae Romanae Ecclesiae.*

223 An additional e♭ is to be found prefixing the twenty-seventh note in the plainsong at no. 22. Cf. *VicO*, V, 4, 67.

224 Cf. bassus at "plena" in Feria V, Lectio I (*VicO*, VIII, 15, mm. 33-39 = V, 123, mm. 33-38); cantus I and bassus at "convertere" in Lectio II (*VicO*, VIII, 22, mm. 109-126 = V, 129, mm. 80-93); upper three voices at "nostrum" in Sabbato Sancto, Lectio III (*VicO*, VIII, 51, mm. 30-31 = V, 182, mm. 27-28); cantus I at "extraneos" in Lectio III (*VicO*, VIII, 52, mm. 43-45 = V, 182, mm. 40-43). In the altus at "Jod" of Feria V, Lectio III (*VicO*, VIII, 23, meas. 5 = V, 130, meas. 5), he at one and the same moment eliminates the leap of a fourth upward to a syncope from a dissonant crotchet and softens the melodic contour with an innocuous passing-note. Attention was called above to the similar "progress" in treating such escaped notes which marks the style of his later masses and magnificats. Cf. pp. 406, 427.

225 Cf. *VicO*, VIII, 25, meas. 50, and V, 131, meas. 45; VIII, 26, mm. 85, 89, and V, 133, mm. 79, 83; VIII, 27, meas. 101, and V, 134, meas. 92; VIII, 28, meas. 120, and V, 134, meas. 111.

226 See Claude V. Palisca, "The Beginnings of Baroque Music: Its Roots in Sixteenth-Century Theory and Polemics," (Ph.D. dissertation, Harvard University, 1953), pp. 105-106.

227 Palestrina varied his finals in his other published *lectiones* (Good Friday and Holy Saturday).

228 Reese, *Music in the Renaissance*, p. 604.

229 *VicO*, V, 114.

230 *Ibid.*, pp. 117 ("Alios"), 118 ("Sine").

231 *Ibid.*, p. 117 ("salvum" [bassus]).

232 See pages 439 and 436 for comparisons of Victoria's *Pueri Hebraeorum* and *O Domine Jesu Christe* with Palestrina's motets of similar titles.

233 Cf. Casimiri, *op. cit.*, p. 153 (section 26). See above, pp. 358-359, 470 (note 74).

234 *PW*, Vol. XXXII, page v, note 1.

235 Hans von May in his doctoral dissertation, *Die Kompositionstechnik T. L. de Victorias* (Bern: Paul Haupt, 1943), offered at pages 151-152 a list of thirty-three errors that he had discovered in the Pedrell edition of Victoria's complete works; twenty-one of which were wrong notes, six of which were wrong time values. Even so, the tale was far from complete. Walter Hirschl in his hitherto neglected, because unpublished, study, "The Styles of Victoria and Palestrina: A Comparative Study, with Special Reference to Dissonance Treatment" (Master's thesis, University of California [Berkeley], 1933), not only anticipated many of May's conclusions by a decade, but also offered an even fuller list of Pedrell's editorial errors. These included the leap of a seventh (*VicO*, V, 114, mm. 43-44; VII, 10 meas. 141); unprepared sevenths on "strong" beats (*VicO*, V, 91, meas. 34₃; 193, meas. 29₃ [Responsorium 8], VI, 144, meas. 16₃ [Responsorium]; VIII, 54, meas. 91₁ [Lectio 3]); dissonant upper auxiliary [minim] quitted by leap (*VicO*, IV, 18, meas. 192₄); upward resolutions of dissonant suspensions (*VicO*, II, 80, meas. 212; VIII, 32, meas. 6₄ [Lectio 2]); use of wrong clefs (*VicO*, IV, 86, meas. 64; VI, 124, meas. 7; 125, meas. 17; VII, 126, mm. 122, 124; VIII, 52, meas. 59); and other miscellaneous impossibilities (*VicO*, II, 74, mm. 42, 50₂; III, 78, meas. 76₄; IV, 55, meas. 71₃; 106, meas. 58₃; V, 115, meas. 75₄; 116, meas. 89; 118, meas. 165; 149, meas. 9; 154, meas. 26; VI, 42, meas. 52₄; VII, 126, meas. 123₄; 154, meas. 47). Hirschl also took issue with Pedrell's careless and usually incorrect transcription of Victoria's triple-meter signatures (p. 105). With equal justification he might have impugned

Pedrell's carelessness in distinguishing between Victoria's C and ₵ signatures.

Working with no other data than that supplied by Pedrell, Hirschl concluded that Victoria "acquired or developed a much more modern and appreciative attitude towards the effect of minor triads, both as initial and final chords of compositions than had his contemporary, Palestrina" (p. 8). Victoria, for instance, began no less than twenty-six times with a full minor triad. Considering the fact that Palestrina scarcely ever began full, Victoria's having begun full so many times with a minor triad seemed especially significant to Hirschl. He also found instances of minor triads before a double-bar in several of Victoria's masses. Hirschl next pointed to the fact that whereas Jeppesen was able to explain all Palestrina's apparent chromaticisms either as misprints or as dead intervals, Victoria occasionally used chromaticisms that cannot be explained away on either ground (p. 9). Hirschl also pointed to Victoria's now well-known predilection for the diminished upward fourth as a melodic interval (p. 13): Palestrina having never, seemingly, used such an interval.

Palestrina not infrequently wrote an accented dotted minim followed by an upward leap to a crotchet (Jeppesen [1927], pp. 59-60). Victoria used such a figure only four times (*VicO*, I, 16, meas. 72; III, 33, meas. 53; 48, meas. 35; IV, 34, meas. 46). Palestrina preferred, if at all possible, that the third voice part should fill out a triad at its moment of entry. Victoria "does not seem to attach as much importance to having the third voice fill out the triad as does Palestrina" (Hirschl, p. 26). Instead, Victoria seems often content to bring in the third voice "against a suspended-note, allowing the resolution of the suspension" to fill out the triad; or to assign it merely the role of duplicating a note in the two other voice parts. Victoria "probably felt [in such instances] that the imitation was of too much importance to be broken for the sole purpose of filling out a triad" (p. 32).

Palestrina and Victoria also differ in their attitude toward dissonance on the third crotchet of a descending four-note series (beginning on a strong beat). In Palestrina, "after a descending progression of four tones, the voice [frequently] moves up the degree of a second" (Jeppesen [1927], p. 112). This particular descending figure of four crotchets followed by a stepwise turn upward to a minim or semibreve, with the third of

the four crotchets a dissonance, hardly ever occurs in Victoria—frequently though it appears in the works of Palestrina. For Victoria's isolated uses see *VicO*, I, 74, meas. 40; 94, mm. 91_2, 95_4; II, 33, meas. 26_2.

Victoria, even when writing chordally, occasionally introduces dissonances of minim value. "The most striking thing about most [of such minim dissonances] is that they form either dissonant triads or seventh chords which are then properly resolved. This would indicate that Victoria might have had a more intimate knowledge of what could be termed 'later harmonic technique' than is ordinarily supposed" (Hirschl, pp. 55-56). Victoria seems even to have known how to use the so-called Italian augmented-sixth chord according to rules of part writing which baroque composers were later to observe.

If the study of Victoria's works, based on no more than the Pedrell edition, has yielded such interesting stylistic discoveries as the above, it is not to be doubted that at some future date even more acute style distinctions can begin to be made. Although Victoria may never be shown to have called for D♯'s, or for such rhythms as ♩ ♪ and ♬ with minims as tactus, or to have indulged in melodies founded on triads, or in plentiful sequences and repetitions, both melodic and harmonic, or to have used chromaticisms for expressive purposes—all of which features distinguish, for instance, Lassus's motet style—he can already, on the basis of present knowledge, be shown to have developed a detail technique that, properly understood, contrasts with Palestrinian mannerism.

Among the advantages to be gained from such a surer understanding of Victoria's special traits will be a canon not only purified of the spurious *Missa dominicalis*, but also a canon at the same time enriched with such hitherto unknown motets as the three published by P. Samuel Rubio in his *Antología polifónica sacra*, Volumes I (1954) and II (1956)—*Ego sum panis vivus* (I, 287-293), *Beata es Virgo* (II, 61-70), and *Beati immaculati* (II, 328-332).

236 P. Samuel Rubio—an Augustinian—has announced his intention of publishing a new critical edition, though not necessarily under the auspices of the Barcelona Institute.

237 *Music in Western Civilization* (New York: Norton, 1941), p. 268.

BIBLIOGRAPHY

The following short-title bibliography includes only such printed works and unpublished dissertations or theses as are cited in this volume. It does not include standard dictionaries, encyclopedias, and liturgical books. Only those modern musical editions that contain literary matter quoted in the foregoing text enter the bibliography. Sixteenth- and seventeenth-century works belonging to the ML and MT categories in the Library of Congress classification system have been listed; but not those belonging to the M category.

Académie royale des sciences, des lettres et des beaux-art de Belgique. *Biographie nationale*, XXIV. Brussels: Émile Bruylant, 1928-1929.

Adami da Bolsena, Andrea. *Osservazioni per ben regolare il Coro de i Cantori della Cappella Pontificia.* Rome: Antonio de' Rossi, 1711.

Alaleona, Domenico. "Le laudi spirituali italiane nei secoli XVI e XVII e il loro rapporto coi canti profani," *Rivista musicale italiana*, XVI, 1 (1909).

———. *Studi su la Storia dell' Oratorio musicale in Italia.* Turin: Fratelli Bocca, 1908.

Alemán, Mateo. *Ortografía castellana.* Mexico City: Jerónimo Balli, 1609.

Ambros, A. W. *Geschichte der Musik*, Vols. III - IV. Breslau: F. E. C. Leuckart, 1868-1878; Vol. V [Otto Kade]. 1882.

Andrés, Alfonso. "Libros de canto de la Capilla de Felipe II," *Música sacrohispana*, X, 6, 7, 8-9, 10-11, 12 (June, July, Aug.–Sept., Oct.–Nov., Dec., 1917).

Anglés, Higinio. "Dades desconegudes sobre Miguel de Fuenllana, vihuelista," *Revista Musical Catalana*, XXXIII, 388 (April, 1936).

———. "El Archivo Musical de la Catedral de Valladolid," *Anuario musical*, III (1948).

———. "El 'Pange lingua' de Johannes Urreda, maestro de capilla del Rey Fernando el Católico," *Anuario musical*, VII (1952).

———. "Historia de la música española," in Johannes Wolf, *Historia de la música* [Spanish trans.]. Barcelona: Ed. Labor, 1934.

———. "La música conservada en la Biblioteca Colombina y en la Catedral de Sevilla," *Anuario musical*, II (1947).

———. *La música española desde la edad media.* Barcelona: Biblioteca Central, 1941.

———. "La obra musical de Morales," *Anuario musical*, VIII (1953).

———. "Palestrina y los 'Magnificat' de Morales," *Anuario musical*, VIII (1953).

Anglés, Higinio and José Subirá. *Catálogo Musical de la Biblioteca Nacional de Madrid.* Barcelona: Instituto Español de Musicología, 1946-1951. 3 vols.

Antonio, Nicolás. *Biblioteca hispana nova.* 2d ed.; Madrid: Joachim de Ibarra, 1783-88. 2 vols.

Apel, Willi. "Early Spanish Music for Lute and Keyboard Instruments," *Musical Quarterly*, XX, 3 (July, 1934).

―――. *The Notation of Polyphonic Music, 900-1600.* 4th ed.; Cambridge, Mass.: The Mediaeval Academy of America, 1949.

Aráiz Martínez, A. *Historia de la música religiosa en España.* Barcelona: Ed. Labor, 1942.

Ariño, Francisco. *Sucesos de Sevilla de 1592 á 1604.* Seville: Imp. de Rafael Tarascó y Lassa, 1873.

Aroca, Jesús, ed. *Cancionero musical y poético del siglo XVII recogido por Claudio de la Sablonara.* Madrid: Impr. de la "Rev. de Arch., Bibl. y Museos," 1916.

Arteaga, Esteban. *Le rivoluzioni del teatro musicale italiano.* Bologna: Stamperia di C. Trenti, 1783-1788. 3 vols.

Artusi, Giovanni Maria. *L'arte del contraponto.* Venice: Giacomo Vincenti, 1598.

Asenjo Barbieri, Francisco. *Cancionero musical de los siglos XV y XVI.* Madrid: Real Academia de Bellas Artes de San Fernando, 1890.

Astraín, Antonio. *Historia de la Compañía de Jesús, en la asistencia de España.* Madrid: Sucs. de Rivadeneyra, 1902-1925. 7 vols.

Atienza, Julio de. *Nobiliario español.* Madrid: M. Águilar, 1948.

Baini, Giuseppe. *Memorie storico-critiche della vita e delle opere di Giovanni Pierluigi da Palestrina.* Rome: Società Tipografica, 1828. 2 vols.

Bal y Gay, Jesús. "Fuenllana y la transcripción de la música de los vihuelistas," *Nuestra Música*, IV, 15 (July, 1949).

―――. "Nota a una canción de Lope de Vega, puesta en música por Guerrero," *Revista de Filología Española*, XXII, 4 (1935).

―――, ed. *Cancionero de Upsala.* Mexico City: El Colegio de México, 1944.

―――. *Romances y Villancicos Españoles del Siglo XVI.* Mexico City: La Casa de España, 1939.

―――. *Tesoro de la música polifónica en México: El Códice del Convento del Carmen.* Mexico City: Instituto Nacional de Bellas Artes, 1952.

―――. *Treinta canciones de Lope de Vega puestas en música.* Madrid: Residencia de estudiantes, 1935.

Barbosa Machado, Diogo. *Bibliotheca Lusitana.* Lisbon: Ignacio Rodrigues and others, 1741-1759. 4 vols.

Barbour, J. Murray. *Tuning and Temperament.* East Lansing: Michigan State College Press, 1951.

Barwick, Steven. "Sacred Vocal Polyphony in Early Colonial Mexico." Ph. D. dissertation, Harvard University, 1949.

Bermúdez de Pedraza, Francisco. *Antiguedad y excelencias de Granada.* Madrid: Luis Sánchez, 1608.

―――. *Historia eclesiastica, principios y progressos de la ciudad, y religion catolica de Granada.* Granada: Andrés de Santiago, 1638.

Bermudo, Juan. *Comiença el arte Tripharia*. Osuna: Juan de León, 1550.

————. *Comiença el libro llamado declaracion de instrumentos*. Osuna: Juan de León, 1555.

————. *Comiença el libro primero de la declaracion de instrumentos*. Osuna: Juan de León, 1549.

Boethius. *Opera*. Venice: Johannes et Gregorius de Gregoriis, 1491/1492.

Boscán, Juan. *Las obras de Boscan y algunas de Garcilaso de la Vega repartidas en quatro libros*. Barcelona: Garles Amoros, 1543.

Bordes, Charles. "Étude Palestrinienne," *La Tribune de Saint-Gervais*, VI, 1 (Jan., 1900).

Brandão, Mario, ed. *Documentos de D. João III*. Coimbra: Universidade, 1938. 2 vols.

Brenet, Michel. "Jean Mouton," *La Tribune de Saint-Gervais*, V, 12 (Dec., 1899).

————. *Musique et musiciens de la vielle France*. Paris: Lib. Félix Alcan, 1911.

————. "Notes sur l'introduction des instruments dans l'églises de France," *Riemann-Festschrift*. Leipzig: Max Hesses Verlag, 1909.

Bromley, John, ed. *Libros de Cabildos de Lima*, XI (1588-1593). Lima: Torres Aguirre, 1942.

Bukofzer, M. *Studies in Medieval and Renaissance Music*. New York: Norton, 1950.

Burgos, City of. *Relacion verdadera, del recebimiento, que la muy noble y muy mas leal ciudad de Burgos . . . hizo a la Magestad Real de la Reyna nuestra señora doña Anna de Austria*. Burgos: Philippe de Iunta, 1571.

Burney, Charles. *A General History of Music*. London: 1776-1789. 4 vols.

Calvete de Estrella, Juan. *El felicissimo viaie d'el muy alto y muy poderoso principe Don Phelippe*. Antwerp: Martin Nucio, 1552.

Camón Aznar, José. *Dominico Greco*. Madrid: Espasa-Calpe, 1950. 2 vols.

Carrillo, Juan. *Relacion historica de la Real Fundacion del Monasterio de las Descalças de Santa Clara de la villa de Madrid*. Madrid: Luis Sánchez, 1616.

Casimiri, Raffaele. "Disciplina musicae," *Note d'archivio*, XII, 1 (Jan.-Feb., 1935).

————. "I Diarii Sistini," *Note d'archivio*, I (1924), III (1926), IV (1927), IX (1932), X (1933), XI (1934), XII (1935), XIII (1936).

————. "Il Vittoria: Nuovi documenti per una biografia sincera di Tommaso Ludovico de Victoria," *Note d'archivio*, XI, 2 (April-June, 1934).

————. "Melchior Robledo, maestro a Saragozza: Juan Navarro, maestro ad Avila nel 1574," *Note d'archivio*, XI, 3-4 (July-Dec., 1934).

————. "Sebastiano Raval: musicista spagnolo del sec. XVI," *Note d'archivio*, VIII, 1 (Jan., 1931).

————. "Una 'Missa Dominicalis' falsamente attribuita a Tommaso Ludovico de Victoria," *Note d'archivio*, X, 3 (July-Sept., 1933).

Castro, Adolfo de, ed. *Poetas líricos de los siglos XVI y XVII*. Madrid: M. Rivadeneyra, 1872.

Celani, Enrico. "I Cantori della Cappella Pontificia nei secoli XVI-XVIII," *Rivista musicale italiana*, XIV (1907).

Cerone, Pedro. *El Melopeo y Maestro*. Naples: J. B. Gargano and L. Nucci, 1613.

Cervantes, Miguel. *Segunda parte del ingenioso cavallero Don Quixote de la Mancha*. Madrid: Francisco de Robles, 1615.

Cervantes de Salazar, Francisco. *Tumulo Imperial*. Mexico City: Antonio de Espinosa, 1560.

Chacón, Alonso. *Vitae, et res gestae pontificum Romanorum et S.R.E. Cardinalium*. Rome: P. et A. de Rubeis, 1677. 4 vols.

Chase, Gilbert. "Juan Navarro *Hispalensis* and Juan Navarro *Gaditanus*," *Musical Quarterly*, XXXI, 2 (April, 1945).

———. "Origins of the Lyric Theater in Spain," *Musical Quarterly*, XXV, 3 (July, 1939).

———. *The Music of Spain*. New York: Norton, 1941.

Ciruelo, Pedro. *Cursus quattuor mathematicarum artium liberalium*. Alcalá de Henares: Arnau Guillén de Brocar, 1516.

Collet, Henri. "Contribution à l'étude des théoriciens espagnols de la musique au XVIᵉ siècle," *L'Année musicale*, II (1912).

———. *Le mysticisme musical espagnol*. Paris: Lib. Félix Alcan, 1913.

———, ed. *Un Tratado de Canto de Organo (Siglo XVI): Manuscrito en la Biblioteca Nacional de Paris*. Madrid: Ruiz Hnos. Sucs., 1913.

Coradini, F. "Francesco Corteccia (1504-1571)," *Note d'archivio*, XI, 3-4 (July-Dec., 1934).

Corbin, Solange. "Le *Cantus Sibyllae*: Origines et premiers textes," *Revue de musicologie*, XXXI (July, 1952).

Coussemaker, Edmond de. *Scriptorum de musica medii aevi*. Paris: A. Durand, 1864-1876. 4 vols.

Covarrubias Orozco, Sebastián de. *Tesoro de la lengua castellana, o española*. Madrid: Luis Sánchez, 1611.

Cózar Martínez, Fernando de. *Noticias y documentos para la historia de Baeza*. Jaén: Est. tip. de los Sres. Rubio, 1884.

Díaz Rengifo, Juan. *Arte poetica española*. Salamanca: Miguel Serrano de Vargas, 1592.

Domínguez Ortiz, Antonio. "Un informe sobre el estado de la Sede hispalense en 1581," *Hispania Sacra*, VI, 11 (1953).

Doni, Anton Francesco. *La Libraria*. Venice: Gabriel Giolito, 1550.

Doorslaer, Georges van. "Georges de la Hèle, maître de chapelle-compositeur, 1547-1587," *Bulletin de l'Académie royale d'archéologie de Belgique* (1924).

Dorez, Léon. *La Cour du Pape Paul III, d'après les registres de la trésorerie secrète*. Paris: Ernest Leroux, 1932. 2 vols.

Einstein, Alfred. "Cristobal de Morales: *Missa Queramus cum pastoribus,*" *La Rassegna musicale*, X (Nov., 1937).

_____. *The Italian Madrigal.* Princeton: Princeton University Press, 1949. 3 vols.

Eitner, R. *Bibliographie der Musik-Sammelwerke.* Berlin: Leo Liepmannssohn, 1877.

Elústiza, Juan B. de. *Estudios musicales,* Tomo I. Seville: Imp. de la "Guía Oficial," 1917.

Elústiza, J. B. de and G. Castrillo Hernández. *Antología musical: Siglo de oro de la música litúrgica de España.* Barcelona: Rafael Casulleras, 1933.

Enríquez de Ribera, Fadrique. *Viage de Jerusalem.* Madrid: Francisco Martínez Abad, 1733.

Esperabé Arteaga, Enrique. *Historia [pragmática é interna] de la Universidad de Salamanca.* Salamanca: Imp. y. Lib. de F. Nuñez Izquierdo, 1914-1917. 2 vols.

Espinel, Vicente. *Diversas rimas.* Madrid: Luis Sánchez, 1591.

_____. *Relaciones de la vida del escudero Marcos de Obregon.* Madrid: Juan de la Cuesta, 1618.

Eximeno y Pujades, Antonio. *Don Lazarillo Vizcardi.* Madrid: M. Rivadeneyra, 1872-1873. 2 vols.

_____. *Dubbio di d. Antonio Eximeno sopra il saggio fondamentale pratico di contrappunto.* Rome: Michelangelo Barbiellini, 1775.

Fernández, Alonso. *Historia y anales de la ciudad y obispado de Plasencia.* Madrid: Juan González, 1627.

Fernandez, Antonio. *Arte de musica.* Lisbon: Pedro Craesbeeck, 1626.

Fernández, Benigno. *Impresos de Alcalá en la Biblioteca del Escorial.* Madrid: Imp. Helénica, 1916.

Fernández, José M. "Tomás Luis de Victoria," *Tesoro Sacro-Musical,* XIX, 8 (Aug., 1935).

Fernández Asís, V. *Epistolario de Felipe II.* Madrid: Ed. Nacional, 1943.

Florimo, Francesco. *La scuola musicale di Napoli.* Naples: Stab. tip. di Vinc. Morano, 1881-1883, 3 vols.

Fogliano, Ludovico. *Musica theorica.* Venice: Io. Antonius & Fratres de Sabio, 1529.

Foronda y Aguilera, Manuel de. *Estancias y viajes del Emperador Carlos V.* Madrid: R. Acad. de la Historia, 1914.

Fox, Charles W. "Accidentals in vihuela tablatures," *Bulletin of the American Musicological Society,* no. 4 (General report, 1938).

_____. "Cristóbal de Morales: Opera Omnia. Vol. II," *Notes of the Music Library Association* (Dec., 1954).

Frotscher, Gotthold. *Geschichte des Orgelspiels und der Orgelkomposition.* Berlin: Max Hesse, 1935-1936. 2 vols.

Frouvo, João Alvares. *Discursos sobre a perfeiçam do Diathesaron*. Lisbon: Antonio Craesbeeck de Mello, 1662.

Galilei, Vincenzo. *Dialogo. . . . della musica antica, et della moderna*. Florence: Giorgio Marescotti, 1581.

――――. *Fronimo dialogo. . . . nel quale si contengono le vere et necessarie regole del intavolare la musica nel liuto*. Venice: Girolamo Scotto, 1568-1569.

――――. *Fronimo, dialogo. . . .* Venice: G. Scotto, 1584.

Gallardo, Bartolomé José. *Ensayo de una Biblioteca Española de libros raros y curiosos*. Madrid: M. Rivadeneyra and M. Tello, 1863-1889. 4 vols.

Gams, P. B. *Series episcoporum*. Regensburg: G. J. Manz, 1873.

Gante, Pedro de. *Relaciones . . . 1520-1544*. Madrid: Imp. de M. Rivadeneyra, 1873.

García Icazbalceta, J. *Bibliografía Mexicana del Siglo XVI*. México: Lib. de Andrade y Morales, 1886.

Gaspari, Gaetano. *Catalogo della Biblioteca del Liceo Musicale di Bologna*. Bologna: Lib. Romagnoli dall'Acqua, 1890-1905. 4 vols.

Geiger, Albert. "Bausteine zur Geschichte des iberischen Vulgär-Villancico," *Zeitschrift für Musikwissenschaft*, IV (Nov., 1921).

――――. "Juan Esquivel: Ein unbekannter spanische Meister des 16. Jahrhunderts," *Festschrift . . . Adolf Sandberger*. Munich: Ferdinand Zierfuss, 1918.

Gellius, Aulus. *Noctes Atticae*. Lyons: Seb. Gryphius, 1555.

Gerber, Rudolf. "Spanische Hymnensätze um 1500," *Archiv für Musikwissenschaft*, X, 3 (1953).

Gerbert, Martin. *Scriptores ecclesiastici de musica sacra*. St. Blaise: Typis San-Blasianis, 1784. 3 vols.

Gesner, Conrad. *Bibliotheca instituta et collecta*. Zürich: C. Froschower, 1583.

Gestoso y Pérez, José. *Ensayo de un diccionario de los artífices que florecieron en Sevilla desde el siglo XIII al XVIII inclusive*. Seville: Of. tip. de la Andalucía Moderna, 1899-1909. 3 vols.

Gombosi, O. "Zur Frühgeschichte der Folia," *Acta Musicologica*, VIII, 3-4 (1936).

Goovaerts, Alphonse. *Histoire et bibliographie de la typographie musicale dans les Pays-Bas*. Antwerp: Pierre Kockx, 1880.

Gudiel, Gerónimo. *Compendio de algunas historias de España*. Alcalá de Henares: I. Iñiguez de Lequerica, 1577.

Guerrero, Francisco. *Viage de Hierusalem*. Valencia: Juan Navarro, 1590.

Guerrini, P. "Per la storia della musica a Brescia: Frammenti e documenti," *Note d'archivio*, XI, 1 (Jan.-March, 1934).

Gutiérrez, C. *Españoles en Trento*. Valladolid: Inst. "Jerónimo Zurita," 1951.

Haberl, F. X. *Bibliographischer und thematischer Musikkatalog des päpstlichen Kapellarchives im Vatikan zu Rom*. Leipzig: Breitkopf und Härtel, 1888.

_____. *Die römische "schola cantorum" und die päpstlichen Kapellsänger*. Leipzig: Breitkopf und Härtel, 1888.

Hawkins, John, Sir. *A General History of the Science and Practice of Music*. London: T. Payne, 1776. 5 vols.

Hernández, D. Ferreol. "La cuna y la escuela de Tomás L. de Victoria," *Ritmo*, año XI, núm. 141, extraordinario (Dec., 1940).

Hewitt, Helen, and Isabel Pope, eds. *Harmonice Musices Odhecaton*. Cambridge, Mass.: Mediaeval Academy, 1942.

Hiff, Aloys. *Catalogue of Printed Music published prior to 1801 now in the Library of Christ Church, Oxford*. Oxford University Press, 1919.

Hirschl, Walter. "The Style of Victoria and Palestrina: A Comparative Study, with Special Reference to Dissonance Treatment." Master's thesis, University of California, 1933.

Hispanic Society. *A History of The Hispanic Society of America: Museum and Library*. New York: Hispanic Society, 1954.

Horsley, Imogene. "Improvised Embellishment in the Performance of Renaissance Polyphonic Music," *Journal of the American Musicological Society*, IV, 1 (Spring, 1951).

Illing, Carl-Heinz. *Zur Technik der Magnificat-Komposition des 16. Jahrhunderts*. Wolfenbüttel: Georg Kallmeyer, 1936.

Iparraguirre, Ignacio. *Historia de los ejercicios de San Ignacio*. Rome: Institutum Historicum S. I., 1955.

Jeppesen, Knud. *The Style of Palestrina and the Dissonance*. Copenhagen: Levin & Munksgaard, 1927.

João IV. *Difensa de la musica moderna contra la errada opinion del Obispo Cirillo Franco*. Lisbon: n. p., 1649.

_____. *Difesa della musica moderna contro la falsa opinione del vescovo Cirillo Franco* (Venice: n. p., *ca.* 1666). Italian trans. of preceding.

_____. *Primeira parte do index da livraria de musica* [Lisbon: Paulo Craesbeeck, 1649]. Repr.; Oporto: Imp. Portugueza, 1874.

Joaquim, Manuel. *Vinte livros de música polifónica do Paço Ducal de Vila Viçosa*. Lisbon: Afonso & Moita, 1953.

_____, ed. *O Cancioneiro musical e poetico da Biblioteca Públia Hortênisa*. Coimbra: Instituto para a alta cultura, 1940.

Kade, Otto. *Die ältere Passionskomposition bis zum Jahre 1631*. Gütersloh: C. Bertelsmann, 1893.

Kastner, Santiago. *Contribución al estudio de la música española y portuguesa*. Lisbon: Ed. Ática, 1941.

_____. "La música en la Catedral de Badajoz," *Anuario musical*, XII (1957).

_____. "Los manuscritos musicales nº 48 y 242 de la Biblioteca General de la Universidad de Coimbra," *Anuario musical*, V (1950).

————. *Música Hispânica*. Lisbon: Ed. Ática, 1936.

Killing, Joseph. *Kirchenmusikalische Schätze der Bibliothek des Abbate Fortunato Santini*. Munster i/W: Aschendorffsche Buchdr., 1908.

Kinkeldey, Otto. *Orgel und Klavier in der Musik des 16. Jahrhunderts*. Leipzig: Breitkopf und Härtel, 1910.

Kircher, Athanasius. *Musurgia universalis*. Rome: F. Corbelletti, 1650.

Koczirz, Adolf. "Die Gitarrekompositionen in Miguel de Fuenllana's Orphénica lyra (1554)," *Archiv für Musikwissenschaft*, IV (1922).

Körte, Oswald. *Laute und Lautenmusik bis zur Mitte des 16. Jahrhunderts*. Leipzig: Breitkopf und Härtel, 1901.

Kroyer, Theodor. *Der vollkommene Partiturspieler*. Leipzig: Breitkopf und Härtel, 1930.

La Fage, Adrien de. *Essais de Diphthérographie musicale*. Paris: O. Legouix, 1864.

Latassa y Ortín, Félix de. *Bibliotheca antigua de los escritores aragoneses*. Saragossa: Medardo Heras, 1796. 2 vols.

————. *Bibliotecas antigua y nueva . . . aum. y refund*. Saragossa: C. Ariño, 1884-1886. 3 vols.

————. *Biblioteca nueva de los escritores aragoneses que florecieron desde el año de 1500*. Pamplona: J. de Domingo, 1798-1802. 6 vols.

Leitão Ferreira, Francisco. *Noticias chronologicas da Universidade de Coimbra, segunda parte: 1548-1551*. Coimbra: Universidade, 1944. 3 vols.

León Pinelo, Antonio Rodríguez de. *Anales de Madrid: Reinado de Felipe III*. Ed. by R. M. Téllez-Girón. Madrid: Estanislao Maestre, 1931.

Lesure, François, and G. Thibault. "Bibliographie des éditions musicales publiées par Nicolas du Chemin," *Annales Musicologiques*, I (1953).

Liberati, Antimo. *Lettera scritta . . . in risposta ad una del Sig. Ovidio Persapegi*. Rome: Mascardi, 1685.

Livermore, A. "The Spanish Dramatists and their Use of Music," *Music & Letters*, XXV, 3 (July, 1944).

Llorens, José M. "Cristóbal de Morales, cantor en la Capilla Pontificia," *Anuario musical*, VIII (1953).

————. *Cappella Sixtinae Codices musicis notis instructi*. Vatican City: Biblioteca Apostolica Vaticana, 1960.

López Calo, José, "Músicos españoles del pasado. Escuela granadina," parts 1-4, *Tesoro Sacro-Musical*, 1959/2, 4-5; 1960/2.

López de Gómara, Francisco. *La conquista de Mexico*. Saragossa: Agustín Millán, 1552.

López de Haro, Alonso. *Nobiliario genealógico de los reyes y titulos de España*, Vol. I. Madrid: Luis Sánchez, 1622; Vol. II. Madrid: Vda. de F. Correa de Montenegro, 1622.

López Ferreiro, Antonio. *Historia de la santa a. m. iglesia de Santiago de Compostela.* Santiago: Imp. y. enc. del Sem. Conciliar Central, 1898-1909. 11 vols.

Lorente, Andrés. *El porque de la musica.* Alcalá de Henares: Nicolás de Xamares, 1672.

Lozano González, Antonio. *La música popular, religiosa y dramática en Zaragoza.* Saragossa: Julián Sanz y Navarro, 1895.

Lueger, Wilhelm. "Die Messen des Thomas Crecquillon." Ph.D. dissertation, Bonn University, 1948.

Maggs Bros. *Books Printed in Spain and Spanish Books Printed in Other Countries.* London: Maggs Bros., 1927.

Mal-lara, Juan de. *Recebimiento que hizo la muy noble y muy leal Ciudad de Seuilla.* Seville: Alonso Escrivano, 1570.

Manuel II. *Livros antigos portuguezes, 1489-1600.* London: Maggs Bros., 1929. 2 vols.

Manuzio, Aldo, ed. *Lettere volgari di diversi nobilissimi huomini . . . terzo libro.* Venice: Manuzio, 1567.

March, José M. *Niñez y juventud de Felipe II: Documentos inéditos.* Madrid: Ministerio de Asuntos Exteriores, 1942. 2 vols.

Marcos Durán, Domingo. *Sumula de canto de organo.* Salamanca, n. p., *ca.* 1507.

Marineo Siculo, Lucio. *De rebus Hispaniae memorabilibus.* Alcalá de Henares: Miguel de Eguía, 1533.

Martínez de Bizcargui, Gonzalo. *Arte de canto llano y contrapunto y canto de organo.* Saragossa: George Coci, 1508. Also Saragossa, 1512, 1517, 1538 [*añadida y glosada*], 1541, 1549, 1550; Burgos: Juan de Junta, 1511, 1528 [*añadida y glosada*], 1535.

Matute y Gaviria, Justino. *Hijos de Sevilla.* Seville: Of. de El Orden, 1886-1887. 2 vols.

May, Hans von. *Die Kompositionstechnik T. L. de Victorias.* Bern: Paul Haupt, 1943.

Menéndez [y] Pelayo, Marcelino. *Historia de las ideas estéticas en España.* 2. ed. corr. y aum. Madrid: Imp. de A. Pérez Dubrull, 1890-1903. 5 vols.

———. *San Isidoro, Cervantes y otros estudios.* Buenos Aires: Espasa-Calpe, 1942.

Mexia, Pedro. *Historia del Emperador Carlos V.* Ed. by J. de M. Carriazo [Col. de Crónicas Españolas, VII]. Madrid: Espasa-Calpe, 1945.

Milán, Luys. *Libro intitulado El Cortesano* [Colección de libros españoles raros ó curiosos, VII]. Madrid: Sucs. de Rivadeneyra, 1874.

Minsheu, John. *A Dictionarie in Spanish and English.* London: Edm. Bollifant, 1599.

———. *A most copious Spanish dictionarie.* London: n. p., 1617.

Mitjana y Gordón, Rafael. "Cancionero poético y musical del siglo XVII," *Revista de Filología Española*, VI, i (Jan., 1919).

———. *Catalogue critique et descriptif des imprimés de musique des XVIe et XVIIe siècles conservés à la Bibliothèque de l'Université Royale d'Upsala*, I. Uppsala: Almquist & Wiksell, 1911.

———. "Comentarios y apostillas al *Cancionero poético y musical del siglo XVII*, recogido por Claudio de la Sablonara," *Revista de Filología Española*, VI (1919).

———. *Don Fernando de Las Infantas.* Madrid: Centro de estudios históricos, 1918.

———. "El Padre Francisco Soto de Langa," *Musica Sacro-Hispana*, Vol. IV, nos. 8-10; Vol. V, nos. 1, 3, 8-9 (Aug.-Oct., 1911; Jan., March, Aug.-Sept., 1912).

———. *Estudios sobre algunos músicos españoles del siglo XVI.* Madrid: Sucs. de Hernando, 1918.

———. *Francisco Guerrero (1528-1599): Estudio crítico-biográfico.* Madrid: Talleres poligráficos, 1922.

———. "La Musique en Espagne," *Encyclopédie de la musique et dictionnaire du conservatoire.* Ed. by A. Lavignac, *Partie 1*, IV. Paris: C. Delagrave, 1914.

———. "Nuevas notas al 'Cancionero musical de los siglos XV y XVI' publicado por el Maestro Barbieri," *Revista de Filología Española*, V, ii (April-June, 1918).

———. "Nuevas noticias referentes a la vida y las obras de Cristóbal de Morales," *Música sacro-hispana*, XII, 2 (Feb., 1919).

———. *Para música vamos.* Valencia: F. Sempere, 1909.

Moll Roqueta, Jaime: "Cristóbal de Morales en España," *Anuario musical*, VIII (1953).

———. "Músicos de la Corte del Cardenal Juan Tavera (1523-1545): Luis Venegas de Henestrosa," *Anuario musical*, VI (1951).

Monserrate, Andrés de. *Arte breve, y compendiosa.* Valencia: Pedro Patricio Mey, 1614.

Montanos, Francisco de. *Arte de canto llano.* Ed. by Joseph de Torres. Madrid: Diego Lucas Ximénez, 1705; Miguel de Rézola, 1728.

———. *Arte de canto llano.* Ed. by Sebastián López de Velasco. Madrid: Imprenta Real, 1648.

———. *Arte de cantollano con entonaciones comunes de Coro y Altar y otras cosas diversas.* Salamanca: Francisco de Cea Tesa, 1610.

———. *Arte de musica theorica y pratica.* Valladolid: Diego Fernández de Córdova y Oviedo, 1592.

Monumentos de la Música Española, II. *La música en la Corte de Carlos V.* Ed. by H. Anglés, 1944.

———, III. *Luys de Narváez: Los seys libros del Delphin de música.* Ed. by E. Pujol, 1945.

———, IV. *Juan Vásquez: Recopilación de Sonetos y Villancicos.* Ed. by H. Anglés, 1946.

————, VI, XII. *Francisco Correa de Arauxo: Libro de tientos y discursos de música*. Ed. by S. Kastner. 1948, 1952.

————, VII. *Alonso Mudarra: Tres libros de música en cifra*, Ed. by E. Pujol, 1949.

————, VIII, IX. *Cancionero musical de la Casa de Medinaceli (Siglo XVI)*. Ed. by M. Querol Gavaldá. 1949, 1950.

————, XI, XIII, XV, XVII. *Cristóbal de Morales, Opera Omnia*. Ed. by H. Anglés. 1952-1955. Vols. 1-4.

————, XVI. *Francisco Guerrero, Opera Omnia*. Ed. by M. Querol Gavaldá. 1955. Vol. 1.

Morgado, Alonso. *Historia de Sevilla*. Seville: Andrea Pescioni and Juan de León, 1587.

Morley, Thomas. *A Plaine and Easie Introduction to Practicall Musicke*. London: Peter Short, 1597.

Morphy, G., ed. *Les Luthistes espagnols du XVIᵉ siècle*. Leipzig: Breitkopf und Härtel, 1902. 2 vols.

Moser, H. J. *Paul Hofhaimer*. Stuttgart: J. G. Cottasche Buchhandlung, 1929.

Muñoz, Andrés. *Viaje de Felipe Segundo á Inglaterra . . . (impreso en Zaragoza en 1554)*. Madrid: M. Aribau, 1877.

Obregón y Cerezeda, Antonio. *Discursos sobre la filosofía moral de Aristoteles*. Valladolid: Luis Sánchez, 1603.

Ornithoparc[h]us, Andreas. *Micrologus, or Introduction*. Trans. by John Dowland. London: T. Adams, 1609.

————. *Musice actiue micrologus*. 2d ed.; Leipzig: Valentin Schumann, 1519.

Ortiz, Diego. *Trattado de glosas sobre clausulas y otros generos de puntos en la musica de violones* [Rome: V. and L. Dorico, 1553]. Ed. by Max Schneider. Cassel: Bärenreiter, 1936.

Ortiz de Zuñiga, Diego. *Annales eclesiasticos y seculares de la muy noble y muy leal ciudad de Sevilla*. Madrid: Juan García Infançon, 1677.

Otaño, N. "Un nuevo dato sobre Tomás Luis de Victoria," *Musica sacro-hispana*, VI, 7 (July, 1913).

Oudin, César. *Tesoro de las dos lenguas francesa y española*. Paris: Marc Orry, 1607.

Pacheco, Francisco. *Libro de descripcion de verdaderos Retratos de Illustres y Memorables varones. . . . En Sevilla 1599*. Facsim. ed. Seville: Rafael Tarascó, 1881-1885.

Pacifici, Vincenzo. *Ippolito II d'Este: cardinale di Ferrara*. Tivoli: Soc. de storia e d'arte, 1920.

Palau y Dulcet, Antonio. *Manual del librero hispanoamericano*. 2d ed.; Barcelona: Librería Palau, 1948-1957. 10 vols.

Palisca, Claude V. "The Beginnings of Baroque Music." Ph.D. dissertation, Harvard University, 1953.

Palliser, Fanny ["Mrs. Bury"]. *Historic Devices, Badges, and War-Cries*. London: Sampson Low, 1870.

Pastor, Ludwig von. *The History of the Popes*, vols. 6-26. Ed. by R. F. Kerr and Ernest Graf. St. Louis: B. Herder, 1923-1937.

Pedrell, Felipe. *Antología de organistas clásicos españoles*. Madrid: Ildefonso Alier, 1908.

———. *Cancionero musical popular español*. Valls: Eduardo Castells, 1918-1922. 4 vols.

———. *Catàlech de la Biblioteca Musical de la Diputació de Barcelona*. Barcelona: Diputació Provincial, 1908-1909. 2 vols.

———. *Diccionario biográfico y bibliográfico de músicos y escritores de música españoles*. Barcelona: Tip. de V. Berdós y Feliu, [1897].

———. *Emporio científico é histórico de organografía musical antigua española*. Barcelona: J. Gili, 1901.

———. "Folk-lore musical castillan du XVIe siècle," *Sammelbände der Internationalen Musikgesellschaft*, I (1899-1900).

———. *Hispaniae schola musica sacra*, Barcelona: J. Pujol, 1894-1898. 8 vols.

———. "Libros de musica españoles raros ó desconocidos," *Revista crítica de historia y literatura españolas, portuguesas é hispano-americanas*, Vol. IV, nos. 7-8, 9-10 (July-Aug., Sept.-Oct., 1899).

———. *Tomás Luis de Victoria*. Valencia: Manuel Villar, 1918.

Pena, Joaquín, and H. Angles. *Diccionario de la Música Labor*. Barcelona: Editorial Labor, 1954. 2 vols.

Penney, Clara L. *List of books printed 1601-1700 in the Library of The Hispanic Society of America*. New York: The Hispanic Society, 1938.

Perceval, Richard. *Bibliotheca hispanica*. London: John Jackson, 1591.

Pérez Pastor, Cristóbal. *Bibliografía madrileña*. Madrid: Tip. de la "Rev. de Arch., Bibl. y Museos," 1891-1907. 3 vols.

———. "Escrituras de concierto para imprimir libros," *Revista de Archivos, Bibliotecas y Museos*, tercera época, I, 8-9 (Aug.-Sept., 1897).

———. *Noticias y documentos relativos á la historia y literatura españolas*, II. Madrid: Sucs. de Hernando, 1914.

Petitot, Claude B., ed. *Collection complète des mémoires relatifs à l'histoire de France*, t. 37. Paris: Foucault, 1823.

Pirro, André. *Histoire de la musique de la fin du XIVe siècle à la fin du XVIe*. Paris: Lib. Renouard, 1940.

Poblet, Joan. *Diccionario muy copiosa de la lengua española y francesca*. Paris: Matthieu Guillemot, 1604.

Pope, Isabel. "El Villancico polifónico," *in* J. Bal y Gay, ed., *Cancionero de Upsala*. Mexico City: El Colegio de México, 1944.

_____. "Musical and Metrical Form of the Villancico," *Annales Musicologiques*, II (1954).

_____. "The 'Spanish Chapel' of Philip II," *Renaissance News*, V, 1-2 (Spring-Summer, 1952).

Pujol, Juan. *Opera Omnia*. Ed. by H. Anglés. Barcelona: Biblioteca de Cataluña, 1926-1932. 2 vols.

Querol Roso, Leopoldo. *La poesía del Cancionero de Uppsala*. Valencia: Imp. Hijo F. Vives Mora, 1932.

Quevedo Villegas, Francisco de. *Obras Completas* (prose works). 2d ed., edited by Luis Astrana Marín. Madrid: M. Águilar, 1941.

Rabelais, François. *Les OEuvres . . . contenans la vie, faicts & dicts heroiques de Gargantua & de son filz Panurge, avec la Prognostication Pantagrueline*. Lyons: n. p., 1553.

Radiciotti, Guiseppe. "Due musicisti spagnoli del sec. XVI in relazione con la corte di Urbino," *Sammelbände der Internationalen Musikgesellschaft*, XIV (1912/1913).

_____. *L'Arte musicale in Tivoli nei secoli XVI, XVII, e XVIII*. Tivoli: Stab. tip. Maiella di Aldo Chicca, 1921.

Ramos de Pareja, Bartolomé. *Musica practica* [Bologna: Baldassare da Rubiera, 1482]. Ed. by Johannes Wolf. Leipzig: Breitkopf und Härtel, 1901.

Reese, Gustave. *Fourscore Classics of Music Literature*. New York: The Liberal Arts Press, 1957.

_____. "Maldeghem and his Buried Treasure: A Bibliographical Study," *Notes of the Music Library Association*. VI (1948).

_____. *Music in the Middle Ages*. New York: Norton, 1940.

_____. *Music in the Renaissance*. New York: Norton, 1954.

Riaño, Juan Facundo. *Critical and Bibliographical Notes on Early Spanish Music*. London: B. Quaritch, 1887.

Riemann, Hugo. *Geschichte der Musiktheorie im IX-XIX. Jahrhundert*. Leipzig: M. Hesse, 1898.

Rojas, Agustín de. *El Viage entretenido*. Lérida: Luys Monescal, 1611.

Rojo, Casiano. "The Gregorian Antiphonary of Silos and the Spanish Melody of the Lamentations," *Speculum*, V, iii (July, 1930).

Rojo, Casiano, and Germán Prado. *El Canto Mozárabe*. Barcelona: Diputación Provincial, 1929.

Rokseth, Yvonne. *La musique d'orgue au XVᵉ siècle*. Paris: E. Droz, 1930.

Román, Hierónimo. *Republicas del mundo*. Salamanca: Juan Fernández, 1594-1595. 3 vols.

Rosa y López, Simón de la. *Los Seises de la Catedral de Sevilla*. Seville: Imp. de F. de P. Díaz, 1904.

Rubio, Samuel. "El archivo de música de la Catedral de Plasencia," *Anuario musical*, V (1950).

———. "Historia de las reediciones de los Motetes de T. L. de Victoria," *La Ciudad de Dios*, CLXII, 2 (May-Aug., 1950).

———. "La Capilla de Música del Monasterio de El Escorial," *La Ciudad de Dios*, CLXIII, nos. 1-3 (Jan.-Dec., 1951).

———. "Una obra inédita y desconocida de Tomás Luis de Victoria," *La Cuidad de Dios*, CLXI, 3 (Sept.-Dec., 1949).

Rubio Piqueras, Felipe. *Códices Polifónicos Toledanos*. Toledo: n.p., 1925.

———. *Música y Músicos Toledanos*. Toledo: Est. tip. de suc. de J. Peláez, 1923.

Ruiz de Lihory, José. *La música en Valencia: Diccionario Biográfico y Crítico*. Valencia: Est. tip. Domenech, 1903.

Sachs, Curt. *Rhythm and Tempo: A Study in music history*. New York: Norton, 1953.

Sáenz de Aguirre, Joseph. *Collectio maxima conciliorum omnium Hispaniae et Novi Orbis*, II-III. Rome: J. J. Komarek, 1693-1694.

Sáenz de Baranda, Pedro. "Noticia de los españoles que asistieron al Concilio de Trento," *Colección de documentos inéditos para la historia de España*, IX. Madrid: Vda. de Calero, 1846.

St. Amour, Sister M. P. *A Study of the Villancico up to Lope de Vega*. Washington: Catholic University of America Press, 1940.

Sáinz de Robles, F. C. *El teatro español: Historia y antología*. Madrid: M. Aguilar, 1942. 2 vols.

Salazar, Adolfo. *La música de España*. Buenos Aires: Espasa-Calpe, 1953.

Salinas, Francisco. *De Musica libri Septem*. Salamanca: Mathias Gastius, 1577.

Salvá y Mallen, Pedro. *Catálogo de la Biblioteca de Salvá*. Valencia: Imp. de Ferrer de Orga, 1872. 2 vols.

Sampayo Ribeiro, Mario de. *Os Manuscritos Musicais nos. 6 e 12 da Biblioteca Geral da Universidade de Coimbra*. Coimbra: Atlântida, 1941.

Sánchez, Tomás, ed. *Poetas Castellanos anteriores al siglo XV* [*Bibl. de Autores Españoles*, LVII]. Madrid: Suc. de Hernando, 1921.

Sanchis y Sivera, José. *La Catedral de Valencia*. Valencia: Imp. de F. Vives Mora, 1909.

Sandoval, Prudencio de. *Historia de la vida y hechos del emperador Carlos V*. Pamplona: Bartolomé Paris, 1614-1618. 2 vols.

Sanpere y Miquel, Salvador. *De la Introducción y Establecimiento de la Imprenta en las Coronas de Aragón y Castilla*. Barcelona: Tip. "L'Avenç," 1909.

Saxton, J. Niles. "The Masses of Victoria." Master's thesis, Westminster Choir College, Princeton, N.J., 1951.

Schering, Arnold. *Geschichte der Musik in Beispielen*. Leipzig: Breitkopf und Härtel, 1931.

————. "Musikalischer Organismus oder Deklamationsrhythmik?" *Zeitschrift für Musikwissenschaft*, XI (1928-29).

————. "Takt und Sinnliederung in der Musik des 16. Jahrhunderts," *Archiv für Musikwissenschaft*, II (1920).

Schmidt-Görg, Joseph. "Die acht Magnifikat des Nikolaus Gombert," *Spanische Forschungen der Görresgesellschaft*, Erste Reihe, 5. Band (1935).

Segovia, City of. *Relacion verdadera del recibimiento que hizo la ciudad de Segouia a la magestad de la reyna nuestra señora doña Anna de Austria.* Alcalá de Henares: Juan Gracián, 1572.

Serrano y Sanz, Manuel. *Autobiografías y memorias.* Madrid: Lib. ed. de Bailly-Bailliére é Hijos, 1905.

Siebmacher, Johann. *Grosses und allgemeines Wappenbuch (Wappen der deutschen Souveraine und Lande).* Ed. by G. A. Seyler. Nuremberg: Bauer und Raspe, 1909.

Sigüenza, Fray José de. *Historia de la Orden de San Geronimo*, tercera parte. Madrid: Imp. Real, 1605.

Silva, Innocencio Francisco da. *Diccionario Bibliographico Portuguez.* Lisbon: Imp. Nacional, 1858-1862. 6 vols.

Solar-Quintes, Nicolás A. "Morales en Sevilla y Marchena," *Anuario musical*, VIII (1953).

Soler, Antonio. *Llave de la modulacion, y antiguedades de la musica.* Madrid: Joachin Ibarra, 1762.

————. *Satisfacción a los reparos precisos.* Madrid: Antonio Marín, 1765.

Sousa Viterbo, Francisco Marques de. *A litteratura hespanhola em Portugal.* Lisbon: Imp. nacional, 1915.

————. *Os Mestres da Capella Real nos Reinados de D. João III e D. Sebastião.* Lisbon: Calçada do Cabra, 1907.

Spell, Lota M. "Music in the Cathedral of Mexico in the Sixteenth Century," *Hispanic American Historical Review*, XXVI, 3 (Aug., 1946).

Steinhuber, Andreas Cardinal. *Geschichte des Collegium Germanicum Hungaricum in Rom.* Freiburg i/B: Herder, 1906.

Stevenson, Robert. *Cathedral Music in Colonial Peru.* Lima: Pacific Press, 1959.

————. "Cristóbal de Morales: A Fourth-Centenary Biography," *Journal of the American Musicological Society*, VI/1 (Spring, 1953).

————. *Juan Bermudo.* The Hague: Martinus Nijhoff, 1960.

———— *Music in Mexico: A Historical Survey.* New York: Crowell, 1952.

————. "Music research in Spanish libraries," *Notes of the Music Library Association*, 2d ser., X, 1 (Dec., 1952).

————. "Sixteenth- and Seventeenth-Century Resources in Mexico," *Fontes artis musicae* (1954/2; 1955/1).

———— *Spanish Music in the Age of Columbus.* The Hague: Martinus Nijhoff, 1960.

_____ *The Music of Peru: Aboriginal and Viceroyal Epochs*. Washington: Pan American Union, 1960.

_____, ed. *Cantilenas Vulgares puestas en música por varios españoles* (Colombina Cancionero [ca. 1490], literary texts). Lima: Pacific Press, 1959.

_____. *La música en la Catedral de Sevilla (1478-1606): Documentos para su estudio*. Los Angeles: Raul Espinosa, 1954.

Straeten, Edmond Van der. *La musique aux Pays-Bas avant le XIXe siècle*. Brussels: G.-A. van Trigt, 1867-1888. 8 vols.

Strunk, Oliver. "Guglielmo Gonzaga and Palestrina's *Missa Dominicalis*," *Musical Quarterly*, XXXIII, 2 (April, 1947).

_____ · *Source Readings in Music History*. New York: Norton, 1950.

Subirá, José. *Historia de la música española e hispanoamericana*. Barcelona: Salvat, 1953.

_____. *La Música en la Casa de Alba: Estudios históricos y biográficos*. Madrid: n.p., 1927.

Tapia, Martín de. *Vergel de Musica*. Burgo de Osma: Diego Fernández de Córdova, 1570.

Teresa de Jésus, Sta. *Obras*. Ed. by P. Silverio de Santa Teresa. Burgos: Tip. de "El Monte Carmelo," 1915-1924. 9 vols.

Thalesio, Pedro. *Arte de canto chão com huma breve instrucção*. Coimbra: Diego Gomez de Loureyro, 1618.

Tiby, Ottavio. "La musica nella Real Cappella Palatina di Palermo," *Anuario musical*, VII (1952).

_____. "Sebastian Raval: A 16th century Spanish musician in Italy," *Musica Disciplina*, II, 3 and 4 (1948).

Tormo, Elías. *Las iglesias del antiguo Madrid*. Madrid: A. Marzo, 1927.

Torres, Melchior de. *Arte ingeniosa de Musica, con nueua manera de auisos breues y compendiosos sobre toda la facultad della*. Alcalá de Henares: Pedro de Robles and Juan de Villanueva, 1566.

Tovar, Francisco. *Libro de musica pratica*. Barcelona: Johan Rosenbach, 1510.

Trend, J. B. "Catalogue of the music in the Biblioteca Medinaceli, Madrid," *Revue hispanique*, LXXI, 160 (Dec., 1927).

_____. "Cristóbal Morales," *Music & Letters*, VI, i (Jan., 1925).

_____. *Luis Milan and the Spanish Vihuelistas*. London: Oxford University Press, 1925.

_____. "Salinas: A Sixteenth Century Collector of Folk Songs," *Music & Letters*, VIII (1927).

_____ · *The Music of Spanish History to 1600*. London: Oxford University Press, 1926.

_____. "The Mystery of Elche," *Music & Letters*, I (1920).

_____. "The Mystery of Sybil Cassandra," *Music & Letters*, X (1929).

Trumpff, G. A. "Die Messen des Cristobal de Morales," *Anuario musical*, VIII (1953).

Ursprung, Otto. *Jacobus de Kerle (1531/32-1591): Sein Leben und seine Werke*. Munich: Hans Beck, 1913.

_____. "Neuere Literatur zur spanischen Musikgeschichte," *Zeitschrift für Musikwissenschaft*, XII (Oct., 1929).

Vasconcellos, Joaquim de. *Os musicos portuguezes*. Oporto: Imp. Portugueza, 1870. 2 vols.

Vega Carpio, Lope de. *El Peregrino en su patria*. Seville: Clemente Hidalgo, 1604.

Vergara y Martín, *Estudio histórico de Ávila y su territorio*. Madrid: Hernando, 1896.

Vicente, Gil. *Copilaçam de todalas obras*. Lisbon: Joam Alvarez, 1562.

Villafranca, Luys de. *Breue Instrucion de Canto llano*. Seville: Sebastián Trugillo, 1565.

Villalón, Cristóbal de. *Ingeniosa comparacion entre el antiguo y lo presente* [Valladolid: N. Tyerri, 1539]. Repr.; Madrid: Sociedad de bibliófilos españoles, 1898.

Vitali, Pietro. *Le pitture di Busseto*. Parma: Stamperia ducal, 1819.

Vogel, Emil. *Bibliothek der gedruckten weltlichen Vocalmusik Italiens*. Berlin: A. Haack, 1892. 2 vols.

Wagner, Peter. *Geschichte der Messe*. Leipzig: Breitkopf und Härtel, 1913.

Ward, John. "The Editorial Methods of Venegas de Henestrosa," *Musica Disciplina*, VI (1952).

_____. "The *Vihuela de mano* and its Music (1536-1576)." Ph.D. dissertation, New York University, 1953.

Watkins, Glenn E. "Three Books of Polyphonic Lamentations." Ph.D. dissertation, University of Rochester, 1953.

Westrup, J. A. "Song," *Oxford History of Music*. 2d ed., vol. 2, pt. 2. London: Oxford University Press, 1932.

Wolf, Johannes. *Geschichte der Mensural-Notation*. Leipzig: Breitkopf und Härtel, 1904. 2 vols.

Young, Edward. "The Contrapuntal Practices of Victoria." Ph.D. dissertation, University of Rochester, 1942.

Zacconi, Lodovico. *Prattica di musica*. Venice: Girolamo Polo, 1592.

Zapata, Luis. *Miscelánea* [*Memorial histórico español*, *XI*]. Madrid: Imp. Nacional, 1859.

Zarco Cuevas, Julián. *Catálogo de los manuscritos castellanos de la Real Biblioteca de El Escorial*. Madrid: Imp. Helénica, 1924-1929. 3 vols.

Zarlino, Gioseffo. *Le istitutioni harmoniche*. Venice: n.p., 1558.

_____. *Istitutioni harmoniche*. Venice: Francesco de i Franceschi Senese, 1573.

INDEX

Alphabetizing carries through to the first punctuation, regardless of the number of words. Foreign titles beginning with articles are alphabetized under *Il, El, Le, Der*, and so forth. Names in the Notes of merely bibliographical consequence are excluded from the Index. Academic and ecclesiastical titles are forgone, except when essential to identification. Homonymous individuals are separately indexed, but members of the same family (e.g., Juan Peraza *senior* and *junior*) are grouped under one heading. Place names of unusually frequent occurrence, such as Rome and Seville, are not indexed exhaustively. Italics designate the more important page references. Throughout this Index—as in the foregoing text—the printers have not been restrained from syllabifying Spanish words according to English norms.